OXFORD ISLAMIC LEGAL STUDIES

Series Editors:
Anver M. Emon, Clark Lombardi, and Lynn Welchman

RELIGIOUS PLURALISM AND ISLAMIC LAW

Dhimmīs and Others in the Empire of Law

OXFORD ISLAMIC LEGAL STUDIES

Series Editors:
Anver M. Emon, Clark Lombardi, and Lynn Welchman

Satisfying the growing interest in Islam and Islamic law, the Oxford Islamic Legal Studies series speaks to both specialists and those interested in the study of a legal tradition that shapes lives and societies across the globe. Islamic law operates at several levels. It shapes private decision making, binds communities, and it is also imposed by states as domestic positive law. The series features innovative and interdisciplinary studies that explore Islamic law as it operates at each of these levels. The series also sheds new light on the history and jurisprudence of Islamic law and provides for a richer understanding of the state of Islamic law in the contemporary Muslim world, including parts of the world where Muslims are minorities.

ALSO AVAILABLE IN THE SERIES

Narratives of Islamic Legal Theory
Rumee Ahmed

Religious Pluralism and Islamic Law

Dhimmīs and Others in the Empire of Law

ANVER M. EMON

OXFORD
UNIVERSITY PRESS

OXFORD
UNIVERSITY PRESS

Great Clarendon Street, Oxford, OX2 6DP
United Kingdom

Oxford University Press is a department of the University of Oxford.
It furthers the University's objective of excellence in research, scholarship,
and education by publishing worldwide. Oxford is a registered trade mark of
Oxford University Press in the UK and in certain other countries

First Edition published 2012
Impression: 2

British Library Cataloguing in Publication Data
Data available

Library of Congress Cataloging in Publication Data
Library of Congress Control Number: 2012938697

ISBN 978–0–19–966163–3

Printed in Great Britain by
CPI Group (UK) Ltd, Croydon, CR0 4YY

For
Allyssa and Hafez Atticus

Series Editor's Preface

The Oxford Islamic Legal Studies series was created to promote studies informed by close engagement with Islamic legal texts and with important issues in contemporary legal theory and policy. In this second volume in the series, co-editor Anver M. Emon theorizes the legal regime governing minority religious communities living permanently in Muslim-ruled lands, the *dhimmīs*. In doing so, Emon juxtaposes the pre-modern legal regime with more contemporary ones, and he provocatively challenges widely held views about the regulation of minority religious communities in both Islamic and Western liberal democratic constitutional regimes.

In pre-modern Islamic law, *dhimmī* rules established rights, obligations and responsibilities for the members of *dhimmī* communities. Examining Islamic legal doctrines governing the *dhimmī* across different legal schools (*madhāhib*), Emon points out that the jurists who developed the *dhimmī* rules shared a number of common assumptions. These include ones about the universal scope of the Islamic message, about the preferability of an imperial model of governance, and, finally, about the nature of the legal and administrative institutions that would keep order in a Muslim empire. These premises informed the juristic expectations about the effects of *dhimmī* rules on the *dhimmī* communities and on society at large. From this insight, Emon draws several conclusions. First, he argues that if we accept the assumptions that underlay the *dhimmī* rules, those rules would seem intelligible, appropriate, legitimate, and just. On the other hand, a person who does *not* share the jurists' views about morality and society may view the pre-modern *dhimmī* rules as unintelligible, inappropriate, illegitimate, or unjust. Many Muslims and non-Muslims around the world no longer accept the basic assumptions that informed the pre-modern *dhimmī* rules. Emon explores how the embrace of modern assumptions has informed modern views of the *dhimmī* rules. He explains why many people in the contemporary world find the pre-modern rules problematic. Finally, in a section that is sure to be controversial, Emon turns his attention to liberal democratic states and to the legal regimes that they have developed to regulate minority faith communities. He points out that liberal democratic regimes make their own assumptions about ethics, about society and about the effects that particular rules will have in society. Emon then compares the pre-modern Islamic regimes with modern liberal democratic ones. Provocatively, he concludes that if one looks at the social effects each system was supposed to produce, their regulatory dynamics prove to be quite similar.

Clark B. Lombardi
Lynn Welchman

Acknowledgments

This book represents nearly eight years of research, conversation, and dialogue with friends, colleagues, and mentors from various parts of the globe. It is a better study because of them, and to them all I owe a deep sense of gratitude. I alone am responsible for any failings that remain. When I was a PhD student at UCLA writing my dissertation on Islamic Natural Law Theories, I had the good fortune of completing an LLM at Yale Law School, where I met Owen Fiss. A generous scholar committed to expansive learning, he took an interest in my work on Islamic law. With his support and the encouragement of the late Father Robert Burns, I decided to undertake a second doctorate at Yale Law School. This book is the result of that second research endeavor—an endeavor enriched and deepened by my conversations with Owen Fiss, Paul Kahn, and Anthony Kronman, all of whom oversaw my research at Yale and have continued to support me throughout my career ever since. Furthermore, through the support of both Owen Fiss and Anthony Kronman, I had the good fortune of presenting aspects of this work to international audiences at Yale Law School's Middle East Legal Studies Seminar, first in Athens, Greece (2009) and later in Amman, Jordan (2011). I wish to thank the members of the MELSS community for their discussion of my work at those meetings and for their camaraderie over the years. I want to specifically mention Asli Bali, Leora Bilsky, Bernard Haykel, Chibli Mallat, Andrew March, Robert Post, George Priest, Aziz Rana, and Muhammad Qasim Zaman. I specifically want to acknowledge Adel Omar Sherif for his friendship and generous spirit—and for the long talks we have whenever we meet, which are all too infrequent. I also want to acknowledge Wael Hallaq for his early advice on this project and for his memorable intervention at the Athens meeting.

The University of Toronto Faculty of Law has been my intellectual home since 2005, and I am indebted to the support the institution and my colleagues have given me over the years. My Dean, Mayo Moran, has supported and encouraged my research and the different directions it has taken me. My colleagues have been tremendously generous with their time and advice as I sought to weave different threads of my research together into this study. In particular, I would like to thank Lisa Austin, Alan Brudner, Jutta Brunee, Yasmin Dawood, David Dyzenhaus, Mohammad Fadel, Darlene Johnston (now at the University of British Columbia), Karen Knop, Ian Lee, Sophia Moreau, Marianna Mota Prado,

Jennifer Nedelsky, Denise Reaume, Carol Rogerson, David Schneiderman, Martha Shaffer, Simon Stern, and Michael Trebilcock. I want to single out Audrey Macklin for her friendship, and for always making herself available to me as I besieged her with numerous inquiries about matters related to this study and other things entirely. Across the University, I have benefitted greatly from colleagues in different departments, and want to thank Amira Mitermaier, Karen Ruffle, and Laury Silvers for their infectious enthusiasm. Other colleagues have helped me more deeply appreciate the implication of research in law for fertile interdisciplinary possibilities. In this regard, special thanks go to Sandra Bucerius, Joseph Carens, Paul Gooch, Pamela Klassen, Anna Korteweg, David Novak, Mark Toulouse, and Melissa Williams.

At the University of Toronto, I have had the good fortune of working with tremendous students. I have learned so much from them, and have benefitted from our discussions on issues of Islamic law and legal theory. In this vein, I want to specifically recognize Shari Golberg, Paul Nahme, Ahmed Saleh and Youcef Soufi. I also want to express my deepest gratitude for the tireless efforts of two research assistants who worked on this project and others: Kate Southwell and Jenna Preston. It was a joy to discuss with them the finer points of law, governance, and accommodation in pluralist societies; I benefitted tremendously from those discussions. They have since moved on to pursue important endeavors in the legal profession—the profession will be enriched because of them.

I am indebted to the editors and delegates of Oxford University Press for their support of my work. Working with Alex Flach and Natasha Flemming is an author's dream. I am fortunate to have the chance to work with such committed and visionary editors. Portions of this book have appeared elsewhere in earlier versions. I appreciate and thank the editors and publishers of those venues for giving me an opportunity to develop my ideas. Selections from those publications appear herein in modified and more developed formats. In particular, I draw upon the following previously published articles in Chapters 5 and 6: "The Limits of Constitutionalism in the Muslim World: History and Identity in Islamic Law," in *Constitutional Design for Divided Societies*, ed. Sujit Choudhry (Oxford: Oxford University Press, 2008); "To Most Likely Know the Law: Objectivity, Authority, and Interpretation in Islamic Law," *Hebraic Political Studies* 4, no. 4 (2009): 415–40; and "Islamic Law and the Canadian Mosaic: Politics, Jurisprudence, and Multicultural Accommodation," *Canadian Bar Review* 87, no. 2 (February 2009): 391–425. Also, my deep appreciation to Canada's SSHRC for its support of this research.

I owe a deep debt of gratitude to friends who have been my creative interlocutors for years, and without whose constant pressing and engagement, this work and indeed my life, would be far less rich. Rumee Ahmed read a full draft of an early version of this book, offering comments and insights that have made it a better book. He and Ayesha Chaudhry remind me of how community—intellectual and otherwise—knows no bounds. Benjamin Berger and Oonagh Breen have been my most keen interlocutors about what the law can be since we were graduate students at Yale Law School. Though we have lived in different parts of the world since our days in New Haven, I am blessed to count them as friends and partners in our venture to explore the possible in law. Mark Ellis, a friend and co-collaborator on another project, has pushed me in important ways to appreciate the importance of relating theory to practice and to expand the scope of how I imagine my work to relate to the world around us. Robert Gibbs has been my co-collaborator on far too many projects to list here. His friendship and intellectual depth have been and remain integral sources of inspiration for me. Andrea L. Hill not only read an early version of this book, but various modified chapters thereafter. A mezzo-soprano in Paris, she brings to all she does the heart of an artist and the precision of a logician. Since 1989, William C. Kwong has been one of my toughest readers and greatest friends. For this book, he offered critical insights on Chapter 7. More importantly, he has been my window into the thought worlds of peoples and communities who frequently do not find expression in the all-too-often rarified halls of the academy. Ziba Mir-Hosseini brings her vast amount of energy to all she does, including encouraging me in my research endeavors. I want to thank her and her colleagues at Musawah and CEWLA for bringing me to Cairo, Egypt to present the basic framework of this study. Adam Seligman not only read an early draft of this book, but also put me to work in Bulgaria so that I could see first hand how ideas can translate into attitudes on the ground, sometimes for better and sometimes for worse. His commitment to thinking through ideas in the world of the mundane, the particular, and the embedded is a constant reminder to me of how truly inspiring scholarship often requires us to descend from the ivory tower and roll up our sleeves. My friend and long-time mentor Denise Spellberg reviewed an early version of this book, which enabled me to make important changes that vastly improved the study. But more importantly, she has supported me and my work since my early days in graduate school. She has read everything I have written, and has believed in me at times when I did not.

My deep thanks and endless gratitude go to my parents, Akhtar and Rashida Emon, whose generosity and support know no bounds. They have seen me through all the various stages of my life (academic and otherwise), and remain steadfast in their love and support of me. My heartfelt thanks go to the members of the Case family, who have shown nothing but respect, support, and enthusiasm for the time I've spent on this project, including when I had to excuse myself from family events from time to time. In fact, Elaine and Andrea brought their musical gifts to my research as I struggled with the fugal nature of this project. Last but not least, there is my spouse, Allyssa. I've saved her for last in part because it is not easy to put into words the gratitude I have for her love and support. Words are inadequate to express my profound appreciation for her unwavering support of my research, and most of all her patience with me as I often lost track of time and space when working away at this project. On top of all of that, as I was putting the final touches to this book, she gave birth to our son Hafez. To the two of them I dedicate this book.

Contents

Introduction

Well before the onset of the twenty-first century, academic and popular debates have either implicitly or explicitly positioned Muslims, Islam, and Islamic law as the paradigmatic "Other" to be managed and regulated through policies of multiculturalism and human rights.[1] This is especially the case in societies identified by such labels as *western*, *liberal*, *democratic*, or some combination thereof. That paradigm is mirrored in Muslim majority countries that both acknowledge an Islamic contribution to their core values, and participate in a global network in which that Islamic content is at times suspiciously viewed from the perspective of liberal democratic approaches to good governance and individual autonomy, which have become standard benchmarks of governance, or at least are perceived to be so.[2] The suspicions about Islam and Muslims tend to beg one important question that animates considerable debate in popular venues and the public sphere, i.e., whether or not Muslims, in light of their faith commitments, can live in peace and harmony with others, and treat all people, regardless of their faith traditions, with equal dignity and respect.[3] To use the more common terms of reference,

[1] See, for example, Natasha Bakht, "Family Arbitration Using Sharīʿa Law: Examining Ontario's Arbitration Act and its Impact on Women," *Muslim World Journal of Human Rights* 1, no. 1 (2004): Article 7. On religion in liberal constitutional legal systems more generally, see Caryn Litt Wolfe, "Faith-Based Arbitration: Friend or Foe? An Evaluation of Religious Arbitration Systems and Their Interaction with Secular Courts," *Fordham Law Review* 75 (2006): 427–69. For research centers and academic initiatives devoted to the study of religion in the public sphere, see the University of Toronto's "Religion in the Public Sphere Initiative"; Columbia University's "Institute for Religion, Culture and Public Life." For a center devoted to the study of Islam and Muslims in particular, see the University of Exeter's "European Muslim Research Centre."

[2] For policy-oriented studies that negotiate the tensions this dynamic creates, see United States Agency for International Development (USAID), *Afghanistan Rule of Law Project: Field Study of Informal and Customary Justice in Afghanistan* (Washington D.C.: USAID, 2005); Noah Feldman, *What We Owe Iraq: War and the Ethics of Nation Building* (Princeton: Princeton University Press, 2006). For an analysis of how a Muslim majority country (i.e., Egypt) negotiates its commitments to its Islamic values alongside its commitments to constitutional commitments to citizenship and equality for both its Muslim majority and non-Muslim minority (i.e., Coptic Christians), see Rachel M. Scott, *The Challenge of Political Islam: Non-Muslims and the Egyptian State* (Palo Alto: Stanford University Press, 2010).

[3] Such debates occur in both scholarly and public arenas. One highly public endeavor has been the work of those behind the letter "A Common Word Between Us and You," which consists of a letter from Muslim clerics to Christians about their shared values. See

the question can be restated as follows: "Do Muslims and their religious tradition (in particular Islamic law) have the capacity to *tolerate* those who hold different views, such as religious minorities?"

The question about tolerance and Islam is not a new one. Polemicists are certain that Islam is not a tolerant religion.[4] As evidence they point to the rules governing the treatment of non-Muslim permanent residents in Muslim lands, namely the *dhimmī* rules that are at the center of this study. These rules, when read in isolation, are certainly discriminatory in nature. They legitimate discriminatory treatment on grounds of what us moderns would call religious faith and religious difference.[5] The *dhimmī* rules are invoked as proof-positive of the inherent intolerance of the Islamic faith (and thereby of any believing Muslim) toward the non-Muslim. Some Muslims and others, on the other hand, seek to portray Islam as a welcoming and respectful tradition.[6] They do not give much weight to the *dhimmī* rules as indicative of an Islamic ethos regarding the non-Muslim living in Muslim lands. Further, historians of Islam have shown that its historical and legal traditions contain examples that vindicate both perspectives of tolerance and intolerance toward the non-Muslim, thereby suggesting that the question about whether Islam is tolerant or not is one that cannot be answered definitively one way or another.[7]

This study problematizes *tolerance* as a conceptually helpful or coherent concept for understanding the significance of the *dhimmī* rules that governed and regulated non-Muslim permanent residents in

<http://www.acommonword.com/> (accessed July 14, 2010). For scholarly approaches to this debate, see Andrew March, *Islam and Liberal Citizenship: The Search for an Overlapping Consensus* (Oxford: Oxford University Press, 2009); Mohammad Fadel, "The True, the Good, and the Reasonable," The Theological and Ethical Roots of Public Reason in Islamic Law," *Canadian Journal of Law and Jurisprudence* 21, no. 1 (2008): 5–69. Louise Marlow addresses the tensions between egalitarianism and social differentiation in early Islamic thought, though does not address the *dhimmī* in any great detail. Consequently, while that study offers an important set of insights into philosophies of political community, identity and difference, the difference posed by the *dhimmī* raises a host of questions not addressed in Marlow's study: Louise Marlow, *Hierarchy and Egalitarianism in Islamic Thought* (Cambridge: Cambridge University Press, 1997).

[4] Indeed, this view is foregrounded in the titles of certain books. See, for example, Robert Spencer, *The Truth About Muhammad: Founder of the World's Most Intolerant Religion* (Washington D.C.: Regnery Publishing, 2006); idem, *Religion of Peace? Why Christianity Is and Islam Isn't* (Washington D.C.: Regnery Press, 2007).

[5] For an important study on the concept of "religion" and its role in demarcating the non-secular, see Talal Asad, *Formations of the Secular: Christianity, Islam, Modernity* (Palo Alto: Stanford University Press, 2003).

[6] This was one of the main topics of the letter "A Common Word," which opined on Islamic teachings of love of God and one's neighbor as principles that are shared by both Muslims and Christians. For the text of the letter and supporting documents, visit The Official Website of *A Common Word*: <http://www.acommonword.com/> (accessed July 14, 2010).

[7] For more on these distinct approaches, see Chapter 1.

Islamic lands. In doing so, it suggests that the Islamic legal treatment of non-Muslims is symptomatic of the more general challenge of governing a diverse polity. Far from being constitutive of an Islamic ethos, the *dhimmī* rules are symptomatic of the messy business of ordering and regulating a diverse society. This understanding of the *dhimmī* rules allows us to view the *dhimmī* rules in the larger context of law and pluralism. Further, it makes possible new perspectives from which to analyze Sharīʿa as one among many legal systems; and that far from being unique, it suffers similar challenges as other legal systems that also contend with the difficulty of governing amidst diversity. A comparison to recent cases from the United States, United Kingdom, France and the European Court of Human Rights shows that however different and distant premodern Islamic and modern democratic societies may be in terms of time, space, and tradition, legal systems face similar challenges when governing a populace that holds diverse views on a wide range of values.

This study is organized around four major themes, all of which are interrelated. One might even find the work fugal, in the sense that the basic focus on the *dhimmī* rules makes possible these thematic departures, all of which are distinct and can stand alone from each other, and yet together reverberate with a harmony that offers something richer and more robust. The *dhimmī* rules raise important thematic questions about tolerance; rule of law and governance; and the way in which the aspiration for pluralism through the institutions of law and and governance is a messy business. A bottom line in the pursuit of pluralism is that it can result in impositions and limitations on freedoms that we might otherwise consider fundamental to an individual's well-being, but which must be limited for some people in some circumstances for reasons extending well beyond the claims of a given individual. This introduction will outline the four basic themes that animate this study, showcasing their distinct contributions to the study of the *dhimmī* rules, and illuminating how, in the aggregate, they raise important questions about the scope of freedom possible through the law in a context of diversity and difference.

THEME A: THE LIMITS OF "TOLERANCE"

The first theme focuses on the premodern Sharīʿa-based rules governing non-Muslim permanent residents in Islamic lands. The technical term of art for this group is *dhimmīs*, and the rules governing them are thereby called the *dhimmī* rules. According to Islamic legal doctrines, the *dhimmīs* would enter the *ʿaqd al-dhimma*, or contract of protection (whether express or implied) with the ruling Muslim authorities. That contract permitted them to maintain their distinct faith traditions and to live in peace under Muslim rule. Under the terms of this contract, *dhimmīs* agreed to live by certain conditions in return for peaceful residence in Muslim lands. The *dhimmī* rules were those conditions. Hence, the *dhimmī* rules cannot be viewed today in isolation as mere legal artifacts. They were part of the political compromise made between the ruling authorities and the minority groups that became subjected to the Muslim sovereign. The *dhimmī* rules, in other words, were a legal expression of the way in which the Muslim polity contended with the fact of diversity and governed pluralistically.

As previously indicated, the *dhimmī* rules often lie at the centre of contemporary debates about whether the Islamic faith is tolerant or intolerant of non-Muslims.[8] Some suggest that these rules had, at one time, only limited real-world application and thereby are not significant for appreciating the tolerant nature of the Islamic tradition and history today. Others suggest that these rules were possible because of the inherent intolerance of the Islamic tradition of other faith traditions.[9] Both arguments are not without their justifications. The former view finds support in historical records that illustrate the important role non-Muslims played in Muslim-ruled lands, whether economically, politically, or otherwise. The second view is bolstered by historical incidents of persecution, premodern rules that discriminated on religious grounds, and reports of human rights watch groups that detail incidents of persecution (both official and unofficial) against non-Muslim citizens of Muslim states today. These two perspectives are pitted against one another in both the scholarly and popular arenas of debate and dialogue. Furthermore, a mere cursory review of popular books written on the subject reveals how "tolerance" provides the analytic frame for the debate. For those inclined to the view of Islam as tolerant and peace-loving, the following are noteworthy:

- Khaled Abou El Fadl, *The Place of Tolerance in Islam* (Beacon Press, 2002).
- M. Fethullah Gülen, *Toward a Global Civilization of Love and Tolerance* (The Light, Inc., 2004).

[8] For a discussion of the historiography on the *dhimmī* rules, see Chapter 1.

[9] Mark R. Cohen writes about these two positions as they pertain to the history of Jews living in premodern Christian and Arab/Islamic milieus. His labels for these positions are "the myth of an interfaith utopia" and the counter-myth of the "neo-lachrymose conception of Jewish-Arab History," Mark R. Cohen, *Under Crescent & Cross: The Jews in the Middle Ages* (1995; reissue, Princeton: Princeton University Press, 2008), 6–9. Cohen's use of "myth" to describe these two positions informs the historiographic approach of this study, though his particular labels are not utilized herein.

For those who consider Islam an intolerant faith, Robert Spencer has two contributions of special note:

- *Religion of Peace? Why Christianity Is and Islam Isn't* (Regnery Press, 2007).
- *The Truth about Muhammad: Founder of the World's Most Intolerant Religion* (Regnery Press, 2006).

This study suggests that the frame of "tolerance" does little to explain the intelligibility of the *dhimmī* rules. The weakness of the "tolerance" frame is revealed once we consider how "tolerance" often hides the underlying regulatory features of governance that spark the need to discuss tolerance in the first place.

Definitions of tolerance vary, and this is not the place for a sustained analysis of the vast literature on the issue. However, Leslie Green's account offers us a useful starting point for our analysis: "As a distinctive moral and political ideal, tolerance has a particular structure: it involves the notion that an activity is wrong or to be disapproved, together with the idea that one has moral reasons for not acting on that disapproval in certain ways."[10] Tolerance is neither acceptance nor merely indifference. It implies not simply allowing people to live peacefully with their differences, but instead a disapproval by some of the differences of others.

Importantly, tolerance is meaningful in a context of power relations, such that being tolerant is at once to be disdainful of difference while also having the power and authority to grant the freedom to others to be different. Bernard Williams, for instance, remarks that we may "think of toleration as an attitude that a more powerful group, or a majority, may have (or may fail to have) toward a less powerful group or a minority."[11] Likewise D. Raphael states: "Toleration is the practice of deliberately allowing or permitting a thing of which one disapproves. One can intelligibly speak of tolerating, i.e., of allowing or permitting only if one is in a position to disallow. You must have the power to forbid or prevent, if you are to be in a position to permit."[12]

Tolerance is employed at levels formal and informal, private and public. On the small, private scale, tolerance may be witnessed in the context of a

[10] Leslie Green, "Pluralism, Social Conflict, and Tolerance," in *Pluralism and Law*, ed. A. Soetman (The Hague: Kluwer Academic Publishers, 2001), 85–105, 99.

[11] Bernard Williams, "Tolerating the Intolerable," in *The Politics of Toleration: Tolerance and Intolerance in Modern Life*, ed. Susan Mendus (Edinburgh: Edinburgh University Press, 1999), 65–76, 65–6.

[12] D.D. Raphael, "The intolerable," in *Justifying Toleration: Conceptual and Historical Perspectives* (Cambridge: Cambridge University Press, 1988), 137–54, 139.

religious family contending with the wayward son who has left the family's faith tradition yet nonetheless welcoming him to family gatherings.[13] On a large, public scale (which is the main focus of this study), tolerance is evident in the way public authorities use their legally proscribed powers to contend with the extent and scope to which minority cultural and religious practices can be accommodated.[14] The law is not the only way in which public authorities manifest tolerance, but it is a common one, as suggested by various studies on tolerance that are concerned with what sorts of laws should or should not exist to regulate difference in society. As Williams remarks, "discussions of tolerance have often been discussions of what laws should exist—in particular, laws permitting or forbidding various kinds of religious practice—and the laws have been determined by the attitudes of the more powerful group."[15] When tolerance is understood as a mask for governing diverse societies, we find that minority perspectives are not necessarily condemned, banned, or otherwise excluded. Room may be made for minority group members to act in accordance with their traditions. The scope of that room, however, will be defined (and restricted) in terms of the law in accordance with majoritarian attitudes about the public sphere, the public good, and the polity as a whole.

When the law is viewed in this fashion—as an instrument that can be deployed by some over and against others—we cannot fail to recognize that the language of "tolerance," when used concomitantly with legal doctrines associated with governance and regulation, operates as a cover that hides the operation of power on the bodies of minorities. For Wendy Brown, who critiques tolerance discourses in the liberal state, the language of tolerance "masks the role of the state in reproducing the dominance of certain groups and norms."[16] This is not to deny that tolerance is an important value; it certainly has a place in contemporary political discourse.[17] But that should not allow us to forgo critiquing the assumptions that underlie how polities draw the line between the tolerable and the intolerable. Rainer Forst perspicaciously points out that "we must be suspicious of the way the limits of toleration have been and are drawn between the tolerant and the intolerant/intolerable. One

[13] Wendy Brown, *Regulating Aversion: Tolerance in the Age of Identity and Empire* (Princeton: Princeton University Press, 2008), 4.

[14] See Chapter 7 for recent examples of court decisions, legislation, and constitutional enactments.

[15] Williams, "Tolerating the Intolerable," 66.

[16] Brown, *Regulating Aversion*, 84.

[17] For both a critique of liberal individualist conceptions of tolerance, and a persuasive argument for a group-based approach to tolerance, see Adam B. Seligman, "Tolerance, Tradition, and Modernity," *Cardozo Law Review* 24, no. 4 (2003): 1645–56.

always needs to ask who draws those limits, against whom, on the basis of what reasons, and what motives are in play."[18] To dress the *dhimmī* rules with the vocabulary of tolerance or intolerance masks their contribution to a discourse of Sharīʿa as a mode of regulating a polity. Consequently, this study draws upon the critiques of tolerance to offer an initial point of departure in the study of the *dhimmī* rules, namely to show how and why the *dhimmī* rules are best understood as symptomatic of the challenge that arises when governing diverse societies.

THEME B: "SHARĪʿA" AS "RULE OF LAW"

To describe Sharīʿa as a mode of regulating a polity is to imagine a legal culture in which the law and the institutions of governance are distinguishable and yet aligned in an ongoing enterprise of regulation and management. Sharīʿa is more than legal doctrines (*fiqh*) or interpretive activity (*ijtihād*), for instance; it is more than the work of jurists operating outside the realm of governance and politics. Rather, as posited herein, Sharīʿa offers a discursive site about the requirements of justice as understood by premodern jurists within a legal, historical, and political context, whether real or imagined. To capture this relationship between law and governance, this study proposes that Sharīʿa is better appreciated if understood as Rule of Law. To advance the view of Sharīʿa as Rule of Law requires building upon and, to some extent, departing from other approaches to the characterization of Sharīʿa. It also requires explaining how "Rule of Law" is being used in this study and why it offers an important contribution to the study of Sharīʿa generally, and to an understanding of the *dhimmī* rules in particular. This section will introduce how Sharīʿa as Rule of Law offers an important vantage point for conceptual and theoretical inquiries into Sharīʿa, and will address how and why Rule of Law is being used in this study to characterize Sharīʿa. A more developed and extensive analysis of these two issues is provided in Chapter 5.

Sharīʿa as Rule of Law

When describing Sharīʿa, some choose to start with a literal definition of the term, which refers to a place from which to drink and draw water, or a path toward water. From that literal definition, though, the word is quickly infused with legal import, bearing the meaning "[t]he religious

[18] Rainer Forst, "The Limits of Toleration," *Constellations* 11, no. 3 (2004): 312–25, 314.

law of God."[19] Beyond these initial starting points, debate arises over how to give further specification to the term. To introduce Sharīʿa as Rule of Law, an analysis of two distinct but related approaches to Sharīʿa will suffice. The first approach focuses on the distinction between Sharīʿa and *fiqh,* and the second approach focuses on the juristic class (as opposed to the ruling regime) and their legal literature as the primary, if not sole, source of material concerning and defining the Sharīʿa.

The first approach is reflected in the work of contemporary scholars of Islamic law who define Sharīʿa in part by distinguishing it from *fiqh,* which are the doctrinal traditions developed by jurists over centuries. They hold that

> God's law as an abstraction is called the *Sharīʿah* (literally, the way), while the concrete understanding and implementation of this Will is called *fiqh* (literally, the understanding) ... The conceptual distinction between *Sharīʿah* and *fiqh* was the product of a recognition of the inevitable failures of human efforts at understanding the purposes or intentions of God. Human beings, the jurists insisted, simply do not possess the ability to encompass the wisdom of God. Consequently, every understanding or implementation of God's Will is necessarily imperfect because ... perfection belongs only to God.[20]

This approach, definition-by-distinction, is a significant development in the field of Islamic legal studies and offers a first and important starting point to explain the conceptual purchase of defining Sharīʿa as Rule of Law.

Those seeking to distinguish Sharīʿa from *fiqh* often do so with a particular purpose, namely to make space for new interpretations of Islamic law (i.e., for new *ijtihād*).[21] Whatever might be the animating purpose, the distinction they make draws upon premodern Islamic legal theories of authority and legitimacy, and in doing so, begs an important set of legal philosophical questions about the implication of that distinction on the meaning of Sharīʿa itself as a term of art. As I have written elsewhere, the distinction between *fiqh* and Sharīʿa draws

[19] E.W. Lane, *Arabic–English Lexicon* (1863; reprint, Cambridge: Islamic Texts Society, 1984), 2: 1535. To appreciate the ongoing salience of definitional debates about the term, see Edward Omar Moad, "A Path to the Oasis: *Sharīʿah* and reason in Islamic moral epistemology," *International Journal for Philosophy and Religion* 62, no. 3 (2007): 135–48.

[20] Khaled Abou El Fadl, *Speaking in God's Name: Islamic Law, Authority, and Women* (Oxford; Oneworld Publications, 2001), 32. See also, Ziba Mir-Hosseini, "The Construction of Gender in Islamic Legal Thought and Strategies for Reform," *Hawwa* 1, no. 1 (2003): 1–28. For another approach to qualify the authority of *fiqh*, see Michael Mumisa, *Islamic Law: Theory & Interpretation* (Beltsville, Maryland: Amana Publications, 2002).

[21] See, for example, Mir-Hosseini, "Construction of Gender."

upon a philosophical debate about epistemology and authority.[22] That distinction found expression in premodern legal theory treatises (*uṣūl al-fiqh*) in the difference between what jurists called the *uṣūl* and the *furūʿ*. For Muslim jurists, the *uṣūl* are core values that are unchanging, and not subject to interpretation (i.e., *ijtihād*). The *furūʿ*, on the other hand, are all other claims of value, which may change and are subject to interpretation. These latter claims of value have only limited authority, where such limitation is a function of the epistemic limits of the jurist who interprets limited legal sources to arrive at a claim of value. The *furūʿ*, in other words, represent legal claims of value that are both authoritative pronouncements of the law, but also epistemically vulnerable to reinterpretation and change. Importantly, the premodern debate on *uṣūl* and *furūʿ* contributes either directly or indirectly to the contemporary argument of those who distinguish between Sharīʿa and *fiqh*. To claim that Sharīʿa and *fiqh* are different and distinct is in large part to emphasize the limited authority of the *fiqh* based on human epistemic limitations, and thereby create space for others to contribute legitimately to the ongoing development of *fiqh* norms in a changing world.

The distinction between Sharīʿa and *fiqh*, justified and supported by reference to the premodern debates on *uṣūl* and *furūʿ*, is meant to undercut the scope of authority that can be claimed for a particular doctrine of *fiqh*. It does not, however, offer any conceptually thick definition of Sharīʿa, except in negative terms: Sharīʿa is not *fiqh*. But this begs the question, "What is Sharīʿa?" To say it is the law in the "mind of God" may speak to the pious humility of the juristic interpreter who claims only a limited authority for his or her pronouncement of a *fiqh* norm. But that avoids the definitional issue entirely. This turn to the epistemic limitations on *fiqh* does little to help us understand what Sharīʿa is or can mean. Rather, it leaves Sharīʿa in a veritable conceptual "no-man's land" since it is beyond the reach of human epistemic capacities, at least in any deterministic fashion.

The second, though related, approach to the study of Sharīʿa focuses less on how to define Sharīʿa in legally philosophical terms, and more on the study of the sources that are understood to constitute the corpus of Sharīʿa. For instance, much scholarship on Sharīʿa tends to focus on the work of premodern jurists and the literature that they produced. Indeed, the work of premodern jurists has become so central to the modern study of Islamic law that the twentieth-century scholar of Islamic law, Joseph Schacht, famously wrote that Islamic law is an "extreme case of

[22] Anver M. Emon, "To Most Likely Know the Law: Objectivity, Authority, and Interpretation in Islamic Law," *Hebraic Political Studies* 4, no. 4 (2009): 415–40.

jurists' law."[23] Likewise, although Khaled Abou El Fadl recognizes that in Islamic history there were many voices of authority and legitimacy,[24] he nevertheless holds that Muslim jurists "had become the repositories of a literary, text-based legitimacy. Their legitimacy based itself on the ability to read, understand, and interpret the Divine Will as expressed in texts that purported to embody the Divine Will."[25] So while the Muslim jurist (and, by extension, his written legacy) embodied only one type of authority in Islamic history, that particular form of authority carried considerable weight for those keen to understand what God wants or demands of them.

The focus on premodern jurists and their writings is not entirely surprising, given the availability of extant sources of Islamic law, which more often than not are the sources written by jurists (e.g., *fiqh, uṣūl al-fiqh*). Sources of Islamic law as administered in courts or other tribunals did not often survive given the limits of preservation and record keeping, as well as the function such documents served, namely to account for dispute resolution rather than doctrinal development and justification. In instances where they have survived, they are often piecemeal or in a clerical shorthand that requires considerable historical circumspection to decipher and appreciate.[26]

One analytic consequence of viewing Sharīʿa through the eyes of premodern jurists is that it dangerously elides the jurist's authority with the sum total of what Sharīʿa has to offer. This danger is evident in a discussion Abou El Fadl has about a hypothetical posed by the premodern Shāfiʿi jurist Abū al-Maʿālā al-Juwaynī (d. 1098). Al-Juwaynī posited a Ḥanafī husband and a Shāfiʿī wife, both of whom are *mujtahids,* or, in other words, jurists who are equally capable of arriving at authoritative legal conclusions. Suppose the husband declares to his wife in a fit of anger that he divorces her. According to al-Juwaynī, the Ḥanafīs held that such a pronouncement is invalid and ineffective, whereas the Shāfiʿīs considered it to be valid. Are the husband and wife still married? To put it differently, and perhaps more cheekily, where should they sleep at night? According to the Ḥanafī husband they are married, but according to the Shāfiʿī wife they are divorced. Which view should prevail? Certainly the two parties can

[23] Joseph Schacht, *An Introduction to Islamic Law* (1964 reprint, Oxford: Oxford University Press, 1993), 5.
[24] Abou El Fadl, *Speaking in God's Name,* 12.
[25] Abou El Fadl, *Speaking in God's Name,* 12.
[26] Ghislaine Lydon, *On Trans-Saharan Trails: Islamic Law, Trade Networks, and Cross-Cultural Exchange in Nineteenth-Century Western Africa* (Cambridge: Cambridge University Press, 2009); Leslie Peirce, *Morality Tales: Law and Gender in the Ottoman Court of Aintab* (Berkeley: University of California Press, 2003).

insist on their respective views and claim to be justified in doing so; but to resolve the dispute, the parties must resort to a legal process, namely adjudication. According to al-Juwaynī, if they submit their case to a judge or *qāḍī,* the judge's decision, based on his own analysis, is binding on both parties. The *qāḍī*'s decision is authoritative not because it accords with one specific legal rule or another; rather, it is authoritative because of the imperium tied to his institutional position.[27] Abou El Fadl, however, disagrees with al-Juwaynī and suggests that in the hypothetical above, if the judge decides in favor of the husband, the wife can and should resist as a form of conscientious objection and thereby enjoy the protections afforded to her by the law of rebellion in Islam (*aḥkām al-bughāt*).[28]

Where he writes about this hypothetical, Abou El Fadl is principally interested in distinguishing the law of God from human determinations of that law, and thereby preserving the moral standing of the individual to assert his or her convictions before God without the imposition of external agents. However, his argument about rebellion betrays a tendency to view Islamic law as a jurist's law that speaks to the authority of the individual against all others.[29] A Rule of Law perspective on Abou El Fadl's criticism of al-Juwaynī and support for the wife as conscientious objector might raise the following observations and questions.

- For instance, the fact that the husband and wife would go to a court at all presumes that the parties live in an organized society where the court holds some degree of jurisdiction and dominion and is answerable to the governing authorities under which it operates. By submitting their case to the judge, do the parties expressly or impliedly consent to the court's jurisdiction?
- By agreeing to be members of a political society governed by the Sharīʿa, do the husband and wife enter into a social contract with each other (and

[27] Abū al-Maʿālā al-Juwaynī, *Kitāb al-Ijtihād min Kitāb al-Talkhīṣ* (Damascus: Dār al-Qalam, 1987), 36–8.

[28] Khaled Abou El Fadl, *The Authoritative and Authoritarian in Islamic Discourses: A Contemporary Case Study*, 3rd ed. (Alexandria, Virginia: al-Saadawi Publications, 2002), 60 n. 11. He holds a similar position concerning a second hypothetical al-Juwaynī posed. See Abou El Fadl, *Speaking in God's Name*, 161–2.

[29] The force of Abou El Fadl's argument is severely undercut if one considers a slight variation on the same hypothetical. Suppose the judge decided in favor of the wife. Abou El Fadl's logic would suggest that the husband could also ignore the judicial outcome and claim the protections of the law as a conscientious objector. Abou El Fadl's logic would effectively give some, though perhaps not full, legal protection to the husband if subsequently charged with rape. The odiousness of this particular outcome, which in fairness Abou El Fadl does not address, offers an important incentive to explore why the Rule of Law perspective offers an important lens through which to view doctrinal treatises such as the one by al-Juwaynī.

others in the polity) to forgo certain freedoms (like rebellion in the event of an unfavorable court decision) so that they may maximize their enjoyment of other freedoms?
- If the husband and wife undertake certain obligations and responsibilities to participate in organized political society, does it make sense to suggest (without further consideration) that the wife in the above hypothetical can and should rebel?

Sharīʿa as Rule of Law suggests that to allow the wife to rebel in this case implicates more than just simply whether the wife-jurist holds that a divorce pronounced in anger is valid or not. The substantive doctrine is certainly part of the calculus, but so too are the role and authority of institutions and the political commitments individuals make (or are presumed to make) to live in society organized pursuant to a law that is enforced by officials holding certain offices. Sharīʿa as Rule of Law reminds us that substantive doctrine is only one part of the calculus, and perhaps not always the most important part. Furthermore and perhaps most importantly, Sharīʿa as Rule of Law asks us to consider the possibility that, when offering this hypothetical, al-Juwaynī resolved the conflict in light of the above considerations.

These questions and considerations illustrate that behind the articulation of a legal doctrine lies a host of background assumptions that link the Sharīʿa's doctrines to the institutional and political framework within which those rules were intelligible. To view Sharīʿa as Rule of Law forces a reconsideration of the near-monopoly of authority granted to premodern jurists and their literary corpus in defining the content and intelligibility of Sharīʿa. Sharīʿa as Rule of Law is a reminder to remain ever cognizant of the absences in the evidentiary record, and the implication those absences may have on our ability to reflect and represent Sharīʿa in a robust fashion. In particular, Sharīʿa as Rule of Law requires that we acknowledge the multiple sites of authority that animated and influenced juristic writings about Islamic legal doctrines, and which thereby constituted Sharīʿa as a whole, such as the governing and institutional setting that animated the jurists' legal culture (whether real or imagined). Together, these constitutive features contributed to the conceptual heft of Sharīʿa as a discursive site for contestations about justice, amid competing authorities, not all of which would necessarily lead to the same result. Sharīʿa as Rule of Law is offered herein as a technical term of art that captures the complex ways that law, society, and politics may have interacted to discipline the way Muslim jurists interpreted and espoused the law in light of a more general purpose of organizing life under an Islamic system of governance.

The rhetoric of Rule of Law: Sharīʿa as a claim space

If Sharīʿa as Rule of Law offers a framework that gives heft to Sharīʿa as a conceptual term, a two-fold question remains to be addressed: "What is meant by Rule of Law and in what more specific analytic sense does viewing Sharīʿa as Rule of Law offer new and greater theoretical purchase on Sharīʿa discourses of both the past and the present?"

Definitions of Rule of Law abound.[30] Among more general definitions, Thomas Carothers offers a typical example. He states that to have Rule of Law is to have

> a system in which the laws are public knowledge, are clear in meaning, and apply equally to everyone. They enshrine and uphold the political and civil liberties that have gained status as universal human rights over the last half-century...The central institutions of the legal system, including courts, prosecutors, and police, are reasonably fair, competent and efficient. Judges are impartial and independent, not subject to political influence or manipulation. Perhaps most important, the government is embedded in a comprehensive legal framework, its officials accept that the law will be applied to their own conduct, and the government seeks to be law-abiding.[31]

Among political and legal philosophers, any definition of Rule of Law will often differ depending on the scholar and his or her particular approach to law. For instance, legal philosopher Joseph Raz, reflecting on its broadest meaning, writes that Rule of Law "means that people should obey the law and be ruled by it."[32] Yet from the perspective of political and legal theory, Raz reads Rule of Law in a narrower sense, "that the government shall be ruled by the law and subjected to it. The idea of the [R]ule of [L]aw in this sense is often expressed by the phrase 'government by law and not by men.'"[33] Focusing on the systemic features of law and governing in accordance with it, Lon Fuller suggests that the Rule of Law is the "enterprise of subjecting human conduct to

[30] Brian Z. Tamanaha, *On the Rule of Law: History, Politics, Theory* (Cambridge: Cambridge University Press, 2004), 3 (quoting International Commission of Jurists, *The Rule of Law in a Free Society* (Geneva, 1959), p. VII).

[31] Thomas Carothers, "The Rule of Law Revival," *Foreign Affairs* 77, no. 2 (Mar–Apr. 1998): 95–106, 96.

[32] Joseph Raz, "The Rule of Law and Its Virtues," *The Law Quarterly Review* 93 (1977): 195–211, 196.

[33] Raz, "The Rule of Law," 196. See also, James Tully, *Public Philosophy in a New Key*, 2 vols (Cambridge: Cambridge University Press, 2008), 2: 92. While Tully approaches Rule of Law in relation to his more particular interest in constitutional democracy, he shares with Raz a similar understanding of Rule of Law and its role in defining the scope and limits of government power and authority.

the governance of rules."[34] This enterprise of law, he writes, requires the law to be developed, promulgated, and enforced in a fashion that upholds a commitment to the "inner morality of the law." In this context, inner morality demands the fulfillment of various principles of legality, violation of which, Fuller argues, "does not simply result in a bad system of law; it results in something that is not properly called a legal system at all. . . ."[35] James Tully approaches Rule of Law from the perspective of democratic legitimacy, and argues that "the exercise of political power in the whole and in every part of any *constitutionally* legitimate system of political, social and economic cooperation should be exercised in accordance with and through a general system of principles, rules and procedures, including procedures for amending any principle, rule or procedure."[36] He continues by requiring that those "who constitute the political association...or their entrusted representatives, must also impose the general system on themselves in order to be sovereign and free, and thus for the association to be *democratically* legitimate."[37]

The above authors offer broad definitions of Rule of Law, focusing on different aspects that are important for this study. Raz emphasizes the role Rule of Law plays in limiting government. Fuller links Rule of Law to governance by reminding us that government is not simply an object to be understood, but rather reflects a process of ruling in ever-changing contexts. Tully refers to Rule of Law to emphasize the importance of the law conferring legitimacy on political action by reference to general principles and processes that transcend the specifics of a given context or situation.

The varying definitions of Rule of Law offered above reflect both core ideas that animate discussions of Rule of Law, and the difficulty in offering a cohesive and determinate definition of the phrase. Indeed, there is increasing research to show that the phrase defies any systemic definition.[38] Furthermore, Rule of Law has assumed a panacea-like (if not trendy) quality in recent decades, being offered as the principal solution to the development of effective, efficient, and just government

[34] Lon Fuller, *The Morality of Law*, rev. ed. (New Haven: Yale University Press, 1969), 106.

[35] Fuller, *Morality of Law*, 39–81. Fuller lists eight principles that define the enterprise of law: (1) generality of the rules; (2) promulgation of the rules; (3) general nonretroactivity of the law; (4) clarity of the rules; (5) noncontradiction of rules; (6) rules must not require the impossible; (7) constancy of the law through time; and (8) congruence between official action and declared rule.

[36] Tully, *Public Philosophy*, 2:93 (emphasis in original).

[37] Tully, *Public Philosophy*, 2:93 (emphasis in original).

[38] Jørgen Møller and Svend-Erik Skaaning, "On the Limited Interchangeability of Rule of Law Measures," *European Political Science Review* 3, no. 3 (2011): 371–94.

in transitional states.[39] The trendiness of the phrase, coupled with the absence of an agreed upon definition, are certainly reasons enough to be skeptical of its usage, whether in this study or elsewhere.

Far from trying to define Rule of Law, or from using it in any prescriptive sense, though, this study recognizes that a significant characteristic of Rule of Law is its *rhetorical* power at the site of contestations about justice. Writing about the rhetorical feature of Rule of Law, John Ohnesorge states: "Rule of Law rhetoric is more typically invoked when a commentator wishes to criticize a particular legal rule or judicial decision."[40] The indeterminacy about the definition of Rule of Law makes possible a view of it as a conceptual site in which contestations between competing and compelling interests are resolved using a disciplined mode of inquiry that is nonetheless framed by and embedded within the given political context in which individuals, officials, and institutions of government make demands on each other. Ironically, therefore, the ambiguity of the phrase "Rule of Law" and the political purposes for which it is deployed, gives credence to the thesis that Rule of Law creates what this study calls a *claim space* within which arguments about the demands and requirements of justice are made.

Throughout this study, "Rule of Law" refers to the "claim space" for legitimate legal argument and, by implication, raises important questions about the constitutive features that define and delimit that space. In other words, to view Rule of Law as a claim space immediately begs a question about the borders and boundaries that give shape to that space. Appreciating the shape of that space is important because of its implications on what counts as a legal argument, as opposed to some other sort of argument or claim (e.g., historical, philosophical, anthropological, poetic, etc.). Indeed, the border to the claim space is what renders arguments made within that space *intelligible* as a species of legitimate legal argument. The border can be constituted by a pre-commitment to the kinds of arguments, sources, and institutions that are authoritative and those that are not. It may also be constituted by the legal education that is deemed a prerequisite to participating in the claim space within which legal arguments are made. The border of that claim space will also, as argued throughout this book, take into account the species of political

[39] See, for example, Fareed Zakaria, "The Rise of Illiberal Democracy," *Foreign Affairs* 76 (1997): 22–43; Charles E. Tucker, Jr, "Cabbages and Kings: Bridging the Gap for More Effective Capacity-Building," *University of Pennsylvania Journal of International Law* 32 (2011): 101–25.

[40] John K.M. Ohnesorge, "The Rule of Law," *Annual Review of Law and Social Science* 3 (2007): 99–114, 102.

organization within which a legal system operates.[41] In short, the claim space is defined and bordered by reference to doctrinal, institutional, and systemic features of a given polity.

To approach Rule of Law in this rhetorical fashion is meant to draw attention to the conditions that legitimate and render intelligible particular claims made in the pursuit of justice. By denoting a "claim space," Sharīʿa as Rule of Law implicitly recognizes the rhetorical power by which claims of justice are proffered and espoused. That power can draw upon a vast repository of concepts and ideas, none of which uniquely or singularly defines what Sharīʿa is, but all of which contribute to what it can and does signify about what counts as law, justice, and legitimacy. To describe Sharīʿa as Rule of Law, therefore, is to appreciate Sharīʿa discourses as emanating from within a claim space, and thereby to prompt important questions about the constitutive features that both delimit that space and contribute to the intelligibility of claims of justice made therein.

As a term of art that focuses on how claims of justice are justified and legitimized, Sharīʿa as Rule of Law offers a conceptual framework for analyzing the operation and imposition of the force of law. This is not to say that Sharīʿa as Rule of Law merely appreciates the law as being principally an exertion of power. The fact that the law exerts power (whether persuasively, institutionally, or otherwise) is hardly novel or interesting. Certainly this study will address the hegemonic character of the law, and in particular, the ways in which it operates upon the bodies of minority members within a polity. More importantly though, by analyzing the *dhimmī* rules from the perspective of Sharīʿa as Rule of Law, this study reflects upon the conditions that gave *intelligibility,* purpose, and legitimacy to the *dhimmī* rules and the extent to which those conditions reflected presumptions of a complex legal and political context. Intelligibility is not simply about desconstructing the *dhimmī* rules to reveal the power dynamic underlying them, though that is an important part of the analytic process. Intelligibility reflects the deliberately affirmative, constructive agenda of the law that Sharīʿa as Rule of Law seeks to reveal.[42] Consequently, while this study aims to disrupt and destabilize inherited presumptions about Islamic law in

[41] On the place of institutions within the framework of legal interpretation, see Cass R. Sunstein and Adrian Vermeule, "Interpretation and Institutions," *Michigan Law Review* 101, no. 4 (2003): 885–951.

[42] The emphasis on intelligibility takes inspiration from the work of Boaventura De Sousa Santos, who advocates a type of legal scholarship that moves beyond postmodern modes of analysis that adopt deconstruction as an end in itself. Boaventura De Sousa Santos, *Toward a New Legal Common Sense: Law, Globalization, and Emancipation*, 2nd ed. (London: Butterworths, 2002). For an illuminating review and critique of De Sousa

general and the *dhimmī* rules in particular, it does so fully cognizant of the fact that legal systems, whether Sharīʿa or otherwise, by their nature play a constitutive, affirmative, prescriptive role in the development and design of a just society.

THEME C: RULE OF LAW, HISTORY, AND THE ENTERPRISE OF GOVERNANCE

The analytic heft of Sharīʿa as Rule of Law also lies in the historical lens it trains on the conditions of intelligibility and their constitutive contribution to the claim space of Sharīʿa. Specifically, by analyzing and tracking the *dhimmī* rules across time and across legal systems, this study explores and identifies the degree to which the intelligibility of the premodern *dhimmī* rules shifts as the prevailing conditions and presumptions that give shape to a claim space also shift. In doing so, it vests in Sharīʿa as Rule of Law a historical perspective on the study of Sharīʿa as a legal tradition of both historical import and contemporary relevance.

For premodern Muslim jurists, the conditions that bounded the claim space of Sharīʿa may have included competing epistemic techniques of legal interpretation, theological first principles, or inherited frameworks of governance inherited from the near or distant past. For the modern Muslim jurist, those conditions have changed as political communities have shifted from imperial models to state-based ones, and to complex modes of domestic and international regulation. Without adopting a historical perspective on the constitutive features of a Rule of Law claim space, such features may remain so implicit in the minds of jurists of a particular legal tradition as to be nearly hidden from critical analysis (whether their own or others'). Particularly troubling, though, is that the more hidden they are, the more they may persist in informing later legal arguments, even when other countervailing conditions arise over time and across space. To identify and name what may be so unarticulated as to be hidden from view—but which nonetheless conditions how and why the law regulates those subjected to the law—both disturbs and disrupts by no longer taking it for granted. Once disturbed and disrupted—once identified and named—a particular vision of the good life or the public good, for instance, can be scrutinized and its contribution to the law managed and regulated, especially in those cases where the particular

Santos' study, see Heidi Libesman, "Between Modernity and Postmodernity," *Yale Journal of Law and the Humanities* 16 (2004): 413–23.

vision (and the rules it informs) loses its intelligibility as shifts across time challenge earlier presumptions of what once constituted the good life or the best means to achieve it.

One presumption or condition underlying the premodern *dhimmī* rules that will be identified, named, and foregrounded is the relationship between legal doctrine and argument on the one hand, and the underlying governing enterprise that set a political backdrop to the premodern juristic imagination on the other hand. Disrupting this presumption is the key task of the third theme concerning the *dhimmī* rules. The shape and form that the claim space of Sharīʿa can take is in part determined by the political and institutional order of which it is a part. In fact, in some cases, the intelligibility of a particular legal doctrine may be deeply dependent upon the assumed institutional and political environment in which that rule was or will be applied or otherwise made manifest. Drawing upon what some have called the "institutional turn" in legal philosophy,[43] this study will show that the intelligibility of legal doctrines such as the *dhimmī* rules is intimately linked to the enterprise of governance in a mutually supportive and constitutive fashion.

That the conceptual contribution of Rule of Law generally, and Sharīʿa as Rule of Law specifically, should suggest a substantive, mutually constitutive relationship between law and governance should not be surprising. For instance, in his report to the Security Council, then-UN Secretary-General, Kofi Annan, stated that Rule of Law:

> refers to a *principle of governance* in which all persons, institutions and entities, public and private, including the State itself, are accountable to laws that are publicly promulgated, equally enforced and independently adjudicated, and which are consistent with international human rights norms and standards. It requires, as well, measures to ensure adherence to the principles of supremacy of law, equality before the law, accountability to the law, fairness in the application of the law, separation of powers,

[43] See, for instance, Sunstein and Vermeule, "Interpretation and Institutions," 885–951. See also Scott Shapiro, *Legality* (Cambridge: Belknap Press, 2011), 6, who proffers an "organizational turn" in legal philosophy. In the field of international law, Jacob Katz Cogan writes about the "regulatory turn," which includes "both doctrinal and structural elements, instituting duties and establishing enforcement mechanisms" between states and international organizations. Jacob Katz Cogan, "The Regulatory Turn in International Law," *Harvard International Law Journal* 52 (2011): 322–72, 325. In the field of Islamic legal studies, various scholars have already begun this important work. See David S. Powers, *Law, Society and Culture in the Maghreb, 1300–1500* (Cambridge: Cambridge University Press, 2002); Kristen Stilt, *Islamic Law in Action: Authority, Discretion and Everyday Experiences in Mamluk Egypt* (Oxford: Oxford University Press, 2012); Muhammad Khalid Masud, Brinkley Messick and David S. Powers, *Islamic Legal Interpretation: Muftis and their Fatwas* (Cambridge: Harvard University Press, 1996).

> participation in decision-making, legal certainty, avoidance of arbitrariness and procedural and legal transparency.[44]

Drawing upon the Secretary-General's language, the United States Agency for International Development (USAID) links Rule of Law to the implementation of democracy as a particular political model of organization and governance: "[T]he term [Rule of Law] usually refers to a state in which citizens, corporations, and the state itself obey the law, and the laws are derived from a *democratic consensus*."[45] In the move from one document to another are two important factors. First, Rule of Law is very much connected to the mechanisms of governance, ordering and regulation of a society, or to what will be called herein the "enterprise of governance"—an enterprise that consists of the various rules, institutions, and protections that contribute to the well-being of a polity, both at the individual and collective levels. Second, the enterprise of governance is very much a juridified object in which the law plays a pivotal role in giving shape and aim to the enterprise; conversely, the prevailing conditions of the enterprise delimit the scope and extent of the law. Drawing upon the work of James Tully, "enterprise of governance" captures the official institutional features of legitimate governance and those who legitimately exert the authority to govern in the name of the polity. Given this study's focus on law and the exercise of government authority, the "enterprise of governance" is narrower than Tully's "relationship of governance," which applies broadly to "any relationship of knowledge, power and subjection that governs the conduct of those subject to it, from the local to the global."[46]

To further illustrate how Rule of Law illuminates the mutually constitutive relationship between law and the enterprise of governance, a brief example from US constitutional jurisprudence will suffice. When the US Supreme Court decided *Brown v Board of Education* in 1954 and thereby reversed the prevailing doctrine of separate-but-equal enshrined by the 1896 *Plessy v Ferguson* decision, the Court instigated an important jurisprudential debate about the authority and legitimacy of

[44] United Nations Security Council, *The Rule of Law and Transitional Justice in Conflict and Post-conflict Societies: Report of the Secretary-General*, S/2004/616 (New York: August 23, 2004), para. 6 (emphasis added).

[45] US Agency for International Development (USAID), *Guide to Rule of Law Analysis: The Rule of Law Strategic Framework; A Guide for USAID Democracy and Governance Officers* (Washington D.C.: USAID, 2010), 6 (emphasis added). The report can be accessed at: <http://www.usaid.gov/our_work/democracy_and_governance/publications/pdfs/ROL_Strategic_Framework_Jan-2010_FINAL.pdf> (accessed May 25, 2010).

[46] Tully, *Public Philosophy*, 1:3.

judicial review.[47] Judicial review, it has been argued, poses an important challenge to the democratic principles of the country. To what extent can and should unelected, appointed judicial officers effect legal outcomes that impact society at large, or—in more provocative terms—legislate from the bench? This question about the authority and legitimacy of judicial review is often captured by the phrase "the counter-majoritarian difficulty,"

John Hart Ely, in his justification of judicial review, reveals that the difficulty of "counter-majoritarianism" in judicial review is intelligible because of an assumed political commitment to democratic governance. Writing about American legal and political culture, he remarks that "[w]e have as a society from the beginning, and now almost instinctively, accepted the notion that a representative democracy must be our form of government."[48] In other words, democratic political commitments underlie the American polity's conception of governance and its laws. In light of this political presumption and commitment, the counter-majoritarian difficulty of judicial review becomes an *intelligible* problem:

> When a court invalidates an act of the political branches on constitutional grounds . . . it is overruling their judgment, and normally doing so in a way that is not subject to "correction" by the ordinary lawmaking process. Thus the central function, and it is at the same time the central problem of judicial review: a body that is not elected or otherwise politically responsible in any significant way is telling the people's elected representatives that they cannot govern as they'd like.[49]

The intelligibility of the problem of judicial review depends in part on a presumption that democracy is a constitutive feature of political organization and governance. Without that democratic pre-commitment, judicial review arguably does not pose the same problem. If the pre-commitment were to a different political form, such as a dictatorship, it is unlikely that the counter-majoritarian authority of the judiciary would lead to concerns about majoritarian representation.

Attentiveness to the mutually constitutive relationship between law and the enterprise of governance is significant for a consideration of the *dhimmī* rules. Without an appropriate understanding of the political assumptions or pre-commitments premodern jurists made when construing the *dhimmī* rules, the intelligibility of the *dhimmī* rules is

[47] Philip Bobbitt, *Constitutional Fate: Theory of the Constitution* (New York: Oxford University Press, 1982), 3.

[48] John Hart Ely, *Democracy and Distrust: A Theory of Judicial Review* (Cambridge: Harvard University Press, 1980), 5.

[49] Ely, *Democracy and Distrust*, 4–5.

vulnerable to anachronistic assessments. In fact, as Chapter 1 illustrates, the *dhimmī* rules have been subjected to anachronistic assessments in large part because of insufficient attention to the political order that jurists imagined when arguing for and justifying the *dhimmī* rules, and conversely the contribution of the *dhimmī* rules to the fulfillment and perfection of that presumed political order.

The reference to the jurists imagination of an enterprise being constitutive of Sharīʿa discourses draws upon Benedict Anderson's study of the nation and of nationalism as invoking an imagined community. For Anderson, a nation is "*imagined* because the members of even the smallest nation will never know most of their fellow-members, meet them, or even hear of them, yet in the minds of each lives the image of their communion."[50] Premodern jurists may not have known or fully experienced life in an imperial enterprise of governance; nonetheless their development of legal doctrines such as the *dhimmī* rules was premised in part upon their recognition that within a Muslim empire, different people can and will belong differently. That Islamic legal doctrines had the effect of defining and delineating community is not limited to legal debates on the *dhimmī*. David Friedenreich also draws on Benedict Anderson in his study of food regulations in Christianity, Judaism, and Islam. He shows that because "foreign food regulations express particular systems of classifying insiders and outsiders, they reveal the ways in which their participants imagine their own communities, other religious communities in their midst, and *the broader social order in which these communities are embedded*."[51]

By framing Sharīʿa as Rule of Law to reveal the mutually constitutive influence of law and the enterprise of governance, this study suggests that the intelligibility of the *dhimmī* rules is premised on the premodern jurists' pre-commitment to an imperial mode of governance, whether real or imagined. In her important study on the Ottoman Empire, Karen Barkey provides a useful characterization of Empire that offers a baseline reference for what premodern Muslim jurists may have imagined the enterprise of governance to be. She writes:

> An empire is a large composite and differentiated polity linked to a central power by a variety of direct and indirect relations, where the center exercises political control through hierarchical and quasi-monopolistic relations over groups ethnically different from itself. These relations are,

[50] Benedict Anderson, *Imagined Communities: Reflections on the Origin and Spread of Nationalism*, rev. ed. (London: Verso, 1991), 6.

[51] David M. Freidenreich, *Foreigners and Their Food: Constructing Otherness in Jewish, Christian, and Islamic Law* (Berkeley: University of California Press, 2011), 8 (emphasis added).

> however, regularly subject to negotiations over the degree of autonomy of intermediaries in return for military and fiscal compliance.[52]

Notably, Barkey's definition above specifies ethnic difference, though that need not be the only form of difference. As this study suggests, for Muslim jurists developing the *dhimmī* rules with an imperial backdrop in mind, the relevant difference was principally religious identity.

Paying attention to the boundaries that define and delimit the claim space of Sharīʿa, the Rule of Law analytic frame reveals how with the demise of that imagined imperial mode, the intelligibility of the *dhimmī* rules suffers considerable dissonance when invoked in contemporary contexts where the boundaries of contemporary Rule of Law claim spaces are considerably different than what premodern jurists may have imagined. This does not mean that the *dhimmī* rules cannot assume a *new* intelligibility. Any new intelligibility, however, must itself be analyzed in terms of the modern claim space within which today's Muslim jurists or government officers invoke the *dhimmī* rules.

For instance, as Muslim states have embarked on Islamization policies, they have come under scrutiny concerning their treatment of religious minorities.[53] The fact that such states persecute religious minorities in the name of, and by reference to, Islamic legal rules concerning the *dhimmī* is in part the impetus for the vast literature on the *dhimmī*, including this study. By invoking Sharīʿa broadly, these regimes often seek to legimate their sovereign authority. But when they invoke the *dhimmī* rules in public discourse, they often pay little attention to the historical and legal contexts in which those rules arose, and which once gave the rules intelligibility. Nor do they account for how the contemporary conditions of the enterprise of governance beg important questions about the ongoing authority, legitimacy, and relevance of the *dhimmī* rules. The Rule of Law frame discloses that while the *dhimmī* rules that are invoked are the premodern ones, what they *signify* depends on how they are utilized within the prevailing enterprise of governance. Resort to the premodern rules in a modern political context forces us to consider whether, how, and to what end *premodern answers* are offered in response to *modern questions* of governance. Indeed, the more interesting question, arguably, is what the modern questions are, and whether, to what extent, and under what conditions of intelligibility the premodern answers still have something to say.

[52] Karen Barkey, *Empire of Difference: The Ottomans in Comparative Perspective* (Cambridge: Cambridge University Press, 2008), 9.

[53] See, for example, Human Rights Watch, *World Report: 2009* (New York: Human Rights Watch, 2009).

THEME D: MINORITIES AND THE HEGEMONY OF LAW

One important question of governance—one that arguably transcends the premodern and modern periods—concerns the fact that where diversity exists, governing enterprises will often attempt some form of regulation and accommodation of minorities. This question does not concern *whether* a state will accommodate, but rather *how* it will do so and in light of what circumstances. The *how* of such regulation is often achieved by use of legal rules that manage the scope and extent to which a minority claimant's particularity will be given room for expression in a polity. The use of law to regulate this scope of activity immediately begs questions about the mutually constitutive relationship between law and the enterprise of governance, thereby invoking Rule of Law as an organizing conceptual framework of analysis. The *how* of regulation and accommodation thereby offers a significant site for examining and naming the underlying values that legitimate any particular ruling regime.

Importantly, a critical thrust of this study is to illuminate how Rule of Law not only reveals the mutually constitutive relationship between law and the enterprise of governance, but also, and most poignantly, the hegemonic potential of that relationship in a context of diversity where minority groups make claims upon the ruling regime. Whether the focus is on Islamic law or modern nation-states contending with constitutional claims of religious freedom, the fact of diversity creates the conditions for the hegemony of the enterprise governance through the law, regardless of region, time period, and legal system. In particular, as this study suggests, the hegemony that a Rule of Law analysis discloses is most evident when minority groups present a challenge to the extent and scope of the ruling regime authority. In contests involving minority claimants, the mutually constitutive relationship between law and the ruling regime has the potential of supporting, enhancing, and legitimating majoritarian interests,[54] often by limiting the burden on the governing enterprise to justify its denial of recognition or accommodation of minority interests. This is certainly the case with the *dhimmī* rules, but is not unique to Islamic law. Chapter 7 will illustrate this shared quality by examining how courts in liberal democratic societies such as in Western

[54] To uphold social, often majoritarian, interests, by itself, is not the problem. Legal scholars have shown that legal rules in developing areas of law often have socio-cultural foundations. See, for example, Robert Post, "The Social Foundations of Privacy: Community and Self in the Common Law Tort," *California Law Review* 77, no. 5 (1989): 957–1010. The problem identified here, though, is when upholding majoritarian interests comes at the cost of minority claimants, whose claims might be viewed as challenges or threats to the common good, social well-being, and so on.

Europe and the United States justify limits on when, where, and how the covered Muslim woman can cover or veil. Certainly the political systems assumed by and underlying Sharīʿa as Rule of Law and contemporary liberal constitutional states are vastly different. Ironically, though, despite the difference between their specific doctrines, legal systems, and governing enterprises, the dynamics of governing amidst diversity unite both systems in their respective hegemonic potential.

AN OVERVIEW

The *dhimmī* rules provide the vehicle for both exploring the analytic purchase of considering Sharīʿa as Rule of Law, and uncovering the hegemonic potential that lies at the intersection of the law and the enterprise of governance when minorities make claims for accommodation and inclusion. Rule of Law is offered as an alternative to the all-too-common reliance on "tolerance" to study and characterize the *dhimmī* rules. As will be shown in Part I of this study, the *dhimmī* rules represent a premodern juristic vision of an imperial Islamic polity in which governance through conquest and empire necessarily implied the existence of non-Muslims who came under Muslim rule. Whether or not jurists operated outside of and separate from the realm of government, they nonetheless imagined and developed a jurisprudence that was itself influenced and informed by the demands of an enterprise of governance that faced the challenge of governing amidst diversity.

Furthermore, the *dhimmī* rules offer a departure point for appreciating the historical dimension to the intelligibility of norms arising from within a Rule of Law claim space. As the backdrop of governance has changed—shifting from an imperial model to a modern state model—the intelligibility of the *dhimmī* rules has shifted as well. With the shifts in underlying modes of governance, the *dhimmī* rules no longer bear the same intelligibility they once had. Although they often remain today part of an informal discourse about identity, and in very limited cases, part of formal legal regimes, the *dhimmī* rules have since lost their original intelligibility. The challenge today is to understand the implications on the intelligibility of the *dhimmī* rules when the imperial assumptions underlying them give way to the realities of contemporary modes of governance.

Perhaps one of the more provocative theses of this study is that the *dhimmī* rules are hardly unique in the hegemonic dynamic that they reveal about the law, especially in cases where minorities make claims upon and against the enterprise of governance. As will be explored in Part II of this study, and in particular in Chapter 7, the hegemonic potential of the law is endemic to the very endeavor of governing amidst diversity. Consequently, whether the legal system under consideration is religious or secular, premodern or modern, this study argues that minorities present a poignant discursive site that reveals the hegemonic tendencies of the mutually constitutive relationship between the law and the enterprise of governance.

This book proceeds in seven chapters organized in two parts. Part I focuses entirely on the history, doctrines, and legal reasoning of the *dhimmī* rules. Chapter 1 provides an historical context to the source texts and historical narratives that informed jurists as they debated and developed the *dhimmī* doctrines. As suggested, jurists seemed to hold various political assumptions that thereby contributed to their understanding of the law and its content. In fact, the original intelligibility of the *dhimmī* rules depended upon a pre-commitment to a polity that was defined in imperial, expansionist terms and deemed legitimate because of its commitment to the spread of the universal message of Islam.

Additionally, Chapter 1 positions this study in light of the existing historiographic literature on the *dhimmī*. That historiography reveals two dominant myths that underlie earlier studies of the field, namely the myths of persecution and harmony. These myths adopt the view either that Islam persecutes non-Muslims or that Islam is a faith that is open and warm to non-Muslims. A third innovative development in historical scholarship problematizes these myths by examining cases and periods in which non-Muslims were treated fairly, despite being subjected to doctrinal rules that operated against them because of their religious commitments. This historical scholarship is an important contribution to the field that takes us considerably farther than the writings associated with both myths. However, while this scholarship finds comfort in the inconsistency between practice and doctrine, it nonetheless takes for granted the inevitability of the discriminatory doctrinal rules. This study builds upon the existing historical scholarship; but rather than taking the doctrinal rules for granted, it traces their development and the grounds (both legal and extra-legal) for their legitimacy.

Chapters 2, 3, and 4 address the *dhimmī* rules themselves and the Rule of Law dynamics they reveal. The three chapters show, in the aggregate, how the *dhimmī* rules were developed in relation to an Islamic universalist ethos made manifest in the world by the aspiration for imperial conquest in which the non-Muslim was permitted to retain his faith while living in the Muslim polity. The ethics of univeralism, imperialism, and accommodation conflicted at times, thus rendering the *dhimmī* rules an important site to examine how jurists developed legal doctrines in light of ethical values that were not always easily reconcilable. Chapter 2 reviews the ways in which Muslim jurists reconciled the *dhimmī*'s exceptionalism with an Islamic universalist ethos through different and competing theories of contract and obligation. Chapters 3 and 4 analyze the *dhimmī* rules as sites of contestation between competing imperatives, namely of the *dhimmī*'s private interest and an often vague reference to the broader public good. These two chapters offer different analytic perspectives on how jurists drew upon and reconciled a range of ethical arguments such as Islamic universalism, its corollary of subordination, and an accommodative spirit represented by the theme of contract.

For instance, as discussed later in this study, jurists debated why *dhimmīs* had to pay a poll tax (*jizya*). Some held that they paid it to manifest their commitment to a social contract they made with the Muslim polity, whereby they were to abide by Muslim rule in return for security and religious freedom.[55] Others argued that the *jizya* was part of a larger program of domination and humiliation exerted upon *dhimmīs* to turn them away from their faith and toward the Islamic message. These alternatives were the endpoints of a spectrum of norms within which different rules of law were possible.

The fact that some options became doctrinal and others did not is not taken for granted in this study. Certainly, jurists used the theme of Islamic universalism, and its corollary of subordination, to limit the scope of legal possibilities in order to ensure the dominance and superiority of Islam and Muslims over the non-Muslim. However, the jurisprudence of contract offered Muslim jurists a mode of legal argument designed to respect and protect *dhimmī* interests as participants in the Muslim polity. Using these themes and legal arguments, Muslim jurists generated rules that permitted some degree of accommodation and ensured the continuity of an Islamic imperial enterprise of governance that could not escape the fact of demographic diversity.

How they decided on a particular doctrine from a range of possibilities depended in part upon how jurists addressed a host of questions about the implication of diversity on the enterprise of governance and its ethics of empire and Islamic universalism, such as:

[55] Mahmoud Ayoub, "Dhimmah in Qur'ān and Hadīth," *Arab Studies Quarterly* 5, no. 2 (1983): 172–82; idem, "The Islamic Context of Muslim–Christian Relations," in *Conversion and Continuity: Indigenous Christian Communities in Islamic Lands, Eighth to Eighteenth Centuries*, eds Michael Gervers and Ramzi Jibran Bikhazi (Toronto: Pontifical Institute of Mediaeval Studies, 1990), 461–77, 470.

How could Islam claim to be a universal faith for all of humanity if, under the Sharīʿa, non-Muslims were permitted to practice their own faith traditions?

Were non-Muslims given a grant of autonomy that put them outside the Islamic framework, despite living under Muslim sovereign rule?

If so, how much autonomy should be granted to them before the sovereign authority of the ruling regime would be threatened?

If non-Muslims could have their own laws applied to them, would those laws be applied through the general courts that applied Sharīʿa-based norms?

If so, did that mean other religious traditions were equally as authoritative as Sharīʿa-based norms?

If so, how could that be reconciled with an underlying universalist Islamic ethos that framed and otherwise legitimated various modes of government action by reference to the application of Sharīʿa?

These are just some of the questions that animated premodern Muslim jurists and which this study tracks for the purpose of illuminating the conditions that made such questions intelligible in the first place.

Part II transitions from the premodern period to the modern one by addressing whether and to what extent the minority claimant in both Muslim-majority states and liberal democratic ones eerily and ironically suffers the hegemony of the law for reasons that echo the rationale of the *dhimmī* rules of the premodern era. To facilitate the transition, Chapter 5 offers an extended inquiry into the conditions of intelligibility of the premodern claim space of Sharīʿa, and examines the implication of changes in those conditions on the ongoing intelligibility of premodern Sharīʿa-based norms in the Rule of Law claim space of modern states.[56] By inductively drawing upon key doctrinal, education, and institutional features of premodern Islamic legal history, Chapter 5 gives content to the idea of Sharīʿa as Rule of Law and thereby outlines its analytic purchase when used to frame the *dhimmī* rule in the premodern and modern periods. Specifically, Chapter 5 explores premodern notions of authority, epistemology, and institutional design to give content to a concept of

[56] Chapter 5 proceeds with the caveat that what we mean by Rule of Law, what Sharīʿa as Rule of Law signifies, and what premodern Muslim jurists had in mind when developing legal doctrines are distinct but related questions. For a recent contribution to the ongoing debates about the ambiguity of "Rule of Law" as a phrase and field of inquiry, as well as the need to think about "Rule of Law" in comparative perspective (with special reference to the Islamic legal perspective), see Randy Peerenboom, "The Future of Rule of Law: Challenges and Prospects for the Field," *Hague Journal of the Rule of Law* 1 (2009): 1–10. For a general overview of the meaning of "Rule of Law" and the implications of different approaches to defining this concept, see Tamanaha, *On the Rule of Law*.

Sharīʿa as Rule of Law that, as suggested herein, identifies the mutually constitutive relationship between the law and enterprise of governance. The features examined are meant to be illustrative and not exclusive. In the aggregate, they help paint a picture of the boundaries that delimited the premodern claim space of Sharīʿa, and thereby conditioned the intelligibility of legal doctrines, such as the *dhimmī* rules.

Chapter 6 explores whether and to what extent the development of the modern state in Muslim lands has altered the boundaries of the state's claim space of Rule of Law, and the implications of those changes on the intelligibility of premodern Islamic legal rules, such as the *dhimmī* rules, in modern contexts. Muslim-majority countries have been criticized on various grounds for invoking the *dhimmī* rules or contributing to a culture of religious intolerance that in some fashion draws upon the premodern Islamic tradition. Human rights advocacy groups launch and justify their critiques by relying on international human rights treaties and declarations that uphold religious freedom and the right to be free from religious discrimination. Wealthy nations impose sanctions or financial constraints on countries that violate such human rights norms. Yet, such strategies have not been entirely successful. Leaders of Muslim states and Islamist groups accuse human rights activists of a type of hegemony and colonialism that has less to do with the merit of human rights than with the power of certain groups to enforce their own particular moral vision. Indeed, some of the most poignant examples that fuel the cultural relativists come from the Muslim world and the doctrines so often associated with Sharīʿa.[57]

To contend with the *dhimmī* rules as they are invoked in contemporary contexts suggests that any Rule of Law analysis will necessarily have a historical component. Using the *dhimmī* rules as a mechanism for comparing premodern and modern conditions of intelligibility, Chapter 6 explores whether and how historical shifts in underlying sovereign models—namely the shift from the imperial model, to the colonial model, to the modern state in an international system of equally sovereign states—calls for deliberation not only about the intelligibility of the premodern *dhimmī* rules, but also about Sharīʿa as Rule of Law across historical periods. A review of two case studies from the countries of Saudi Arabia and Malaysia will reveal that what made Islamic legal doctrines intelligible in the premodern world, arguably, inhibits them

[57] Elisabeth Reichert, "Human Rights: An Examination of Universalism and Cultural Relativism," *Journal of Comparative Social Welfare* 22, no. 1 (2006): 23–36; Catherine E. Polisi, "Universal Rights and Cultural Relativism: Hinduism and Islam Deconstructed," *World Affairs* 167, no. 1 (2004): 41–7; Abdullahi Ahmed An-Na'im, "Religious Minorities under Islamic Law and the Limits of Cultural Relativism," *Human Rights Quarterly* 9, no. 1 (1987): 1–18.

from retaining that same intelligibility in the modern world. This does not mean that premodern doctrines are *wrong* in some abstract, metaphysical sense. Indeed the question of right and wrong runs the risk of anachronism when considering a legal tradition as old as Islamic law. Rather, premodern rules such as the *dhimmī* rules might be viewed as *inappropriate* answers to modern questions of governance amidst diversity, non-responsive if not entirely irrelevant. One cannot assume that premodern doctrines such as the *dhimmī* rules retain some original intelligibility when the conditions that gave them such intelligibility have fundamentally altered. If the *dhimmī* rules anticipated an imperial model of governance, that model has yielded to the modern nation-state model. The era of globalization has also ushered in transnational networks of knowledge transfer, particularly via the internet, that lack political authority but offer persuasive authority for those living in vastly different parts of the globe. Chapter 6 shows how any Rule of Law analysis of the *dhimmī* rules today cannot appreciate their intelligibility without also taking account of fundamental historical shifts in the way law relates to and constitutes the prevailing political order.

This study concludes with Chapter 7, which shifts gears entirely to illustrate how the Rule of Law dynamics revealed by the premodern *dhimmī* rules are not unique to the Islamic legal tradition, but plague any enterprise of governance that must contend with diversity. As such, this study contributes to the growing literature on Rule of Law, governance, and pluralism[58] and argues that democratic liberal states and their legal systems also suffer from a hegemonic potential when confronted by a minority claimant. Chapter 7 addresses recent controversies in law and governance in Europe and North America, where various governments have had to contend with the scope and limits of their multicultural and accommodationist policies.[59] Specifically, it analyzes in detail recent

[58] Sujit Choudhry, ed., *Constitutional Design for Divided Societies: Integration or Accommodation* (Oxford: Oxford University Press, 2007); Ayelet Shachar, *Multicultural Jurisdictions: Cultural Differences and Women's Rights* (Cambridge: Cambridge University Press, 2001); Suzanne Last Stone, "The Intervention of American Law in Jewish Divorce: A Pluralist Analysis," *Israel Law Review* 34 (Summer 2000): 170–210, 190.

[59] For studies on this issue in different contexts and from different disciplines, see Anver M. Emon, "Conceiving Islamic Law in a Pluralist Society: History, Politics, and Multicultural Jurisprudence," *Singapore Journal of Legal Studies* (December 2006): 331–55; Ayelet Shachar, *Multicultural Jurisdictions*. For recent court decisions involving questions of accommodation, see *Multani v. Commission scolaire Marguerite-Bourgeoys*, [2006] 1 SCR 256, 2006 SCC 6; *Bruker v. Marcovitz*, [2007] 3 SCR 607, 2007 SCC 54. The Quebec provincial government, after various public outcries about the scope of religious accommodation, created a special "reasonable accommodation" commission led by the philosopher Charles Taylor and the historian Gerard Bouchard, to investigate and delineate policies of accommodation: Charles Taylor and Gérard Bouchard, *Building the Future, a Time for Reconciliaton: Report* (Quebec City: Commission

court decisions and legislation concerning the covered Muslim woman. In the United States, Canada, the United Kingdom, and continental Europe, the covered Muslim woman provides an important trope for debates about the values of a nation. The covered Muslim woman who seeks an accommodation from the state offers a focal point for examining the mutually constitutive relationship between the law and the democratic constitutional enterprise of governance. As will be shown in Chapter 7, that mutually constitutive relationship makes hegemony against the minority claimant both possible and likely inescapable.

Returning to the themes of this study, the *dhimmī* rules reflect an important discursive site about how the minority claimant all too often becomes a vehicle for defining the limits of tolerance and the nature of and mutual relationship between law and governance. There is much that this study hopes to accomplish, though by the end of the book, the reader will likely be left wanting. The study begins with a discussion of the *dhimmī* rules, and ends by situating the *dhimmī* in a larger dynamic that is, at the very least, sobering. The end is not a happy one; there is no "solution" proffered, but only a reminder to remain vigilant. Whether the "problem" concerns the *dhimmī* rules, or the plight of minorities more generally (religious or otherwise), this study asks the reader to contend with and be ever mindful of the hegemony that arises from the mutually constitutive relationship of the law and the enterprise of governance, particularly in cases where minorities make claims upon the state.

de consultation sur le pratiques d'accomodement reliées aux differences culturelles, 2008).

Part I

After Tolerance: The *Dhimmī* Rules and The Rule of Law

1

Dhimmīs, Sharīʿa, and Empire

This chapter provides an overview of competing approaches to the study of the *dhimmī* rules. Along the way, it will show why "tolerance" does not fully explain the complex legal regime governing the *dhimmīs.* It will conclude by suggesting that the *dhimmī* rules, in the aggregate, reflect the kinds of tensions that plague any legal system contending with the fact of diversity. Building on much of the literature about the *dhimmī*, this chapter interweaves historiographical review and historical analysis to set the backdrop for appreciating how Sharīʿa as Rule of Law offers a better framework for appreciating the intelligibility of the *dhimmī* rules.

This chapter will illuminate how the *dhimmī* rules and the messy business of which they are symptomatic are particularly intelligible when viewed as juristic responses to the governance model of empire and expansion. The early history of Islamic conquest proffers multiple models of governing amidst diversity, namely the models of cleansing, lease/rent, and treaty/tax. Those models were employed in different circumstances and to competing ends. Importantly, as will be shown, the application of each model is premised on a justificatory logic that draws upon arguments of law and legality. The discussion of each model will illustrate through the analysis of legal argument how the image of the Muslim polity transformed from being an enterprise of governance defined by reference to a small and at times fledgling city, to an enterprise of governance defined in terms of an imperial model. That imperial model sets the historical backdrop for the rest of Part I, which will examine the *dhimmī* rules in greater detail.

1.1 AFTER "TOLERANCE" IN *DHIMMĪ* STUDIES: FROM MYTH TO RULE OF LAW[1]

The *dhimmī* refers to the non-Muslim permanent resident in Islamic lands. The rules governing the *dhimmīs* are called the *dhimmī* rules and have been subject to considerable scrutiny. The academic interest in the *dhimmī* rules has much to do with the fact that they are facially discriminatory in ways that offend contemporary sensibilities. There is no denying the fact that such rules discriminated because the *dhimmī* was not a Muslim. Examples of such rules include: limitations on whether *dhimmīs* could build or renovate their places of worship; clothing requirements that distinguished the *dhimmīs* from Muslims; special tax liability known as the *jizya*; and their incapacity to serve in the military. These rules and others like them constituted the regime of *dhimmī* rules and offer a focal point for this study's approach to Sharīʿa as Rule of Law.

One critique animating this study concerns how contemporary scholars often approach the *dhimmī* rules using the frame of "tolerance," which, as noted above, is fraught with limitations. "Tolerance" more often than not conceals the relationships of power and governance that give intelligibility to debates about the degree to which minority groups and practices are given space and autonomy within a polity. In the case of *dhimmī* studies, tolerance has offered entry points for scholars to address the *dhimmī* rules, both as a matter of historical practice, and as a point of reference for characterizing Islam and Muslims more broadly.

Using "tolerance" as a starting point, those writing about the *dhimmī* rules sometimes indulge certain myths about Islam that are principally interpretations of history that do not contend with the tensions operating in the legal system and its contributions to governance amidst diversity.[2] As Mark Cohen has ably shown, the two predominant myths hovering over the *dhimmī* rules are those of harmony and persecution.[3] Adherents of the myth of harmony generally argue that the different religious groups coexisted in peace and harmony, with each non-Muslim group enjoying a degree of autonomy over its internal affairs. This image

[1] Notably, some authors provide excellent overviews of the field of *dhimmī* laws and will be referenced throughout this study. See, for example, Yohanan Friedmann, *Tolerance and Coercion in Islam* (Cambridge: Cambridge University Press, 2003); ʿAbd al-Karīm Zaydān, *Aḥkām al-Dhimmiyīn wa al-Mustaʾminīn fī Dār al-Islām* (Beirut: Muʾassasat al-Risāla, 1988).

[2] For a concise overview of the myths and counter-myths, see Mark Cohen, "Islam and the Jews: Myth, Counter-Myth, History," in *Jews among Muslims: Communities in the Precolonial Middle East*, ed. Shlomo Deshen and Walter Zenner (New York: New York University Press, 1996), 50–63.

[3] See for instance, Cohen, *Under Crescent & Cross*.

is constructed by reference to periods of Islamic history where the different religious groups seem to have coexisted without substantial turmoil or persecution. Those adopting the myth of harmony might privilege historical practice over legal doctrine, or argue that the rules were more academic than reflective of a lived reality. For instance, while some rules prohibited non-Muslims from holding high governmental office, historical records show that non-Muslims held esteemed positions within ruling regimes, often to the chagrin of Muslim elites.[4]

Related to the historical argument is the reference to certain periods of Islamic history as emblematic of the virtues of tolerance and even a robust pluralism. In particular, reference is often made to the period of Islamic rule in the Iberian Peninsula or al-Andalus. This was a period that is often described as one of harmonious interaction between Muslims, Jews, and Christians. It is often posited in contrast to a soon-to-come Reconquista and Inquisition led by a Catholic Spain. For instance, Maria Rosa Menocal writes:

> In principle, all Islamic polities were (and are) required by Quranic injunction not to harm the dhimmi, to tolerate the Christians and Jews living in their midst. But beyond that fundamental prescribed posture, al-Andalus was . . . the site of memorable and distinctive interfaith relations. Here the Jewish community rose from the ashes of an abysmal existence under the Visigoths . . . Fruitful intermarriage among the various cultures and the quality of cultural relations with the dhimmi were vital aspects of Andalusian identity . . .[5]

Menocal does not ignore the fact that tensions existed in the Andalusian period. But those tensions were not always between religious groups. Rather, as she notes, political friction existed among the Muslim ruling elites, thereby rendering minority groups important political allies to different elite factions among the Muslim populace.

Notably, Menocal's work contributes to an ongoing debate within Andalusian studies, namely whether the climate of "tolerance" existed, or whether describing that period in terms of tolerance adopts a too-presentist perspective on any reading of the past. As Anna Akasoy reminds, "[p]opular attitudes still reveal a simplistic general picture, but

[4] Mark Cohen, "Medieval Jewry in the World of Islam," in *The Oxford Handbook of Jewish Studies*, ed. Martin Goodman (Oxford: Oxford University Press, 2002), 193–218; Roger M. Savory, "Relations between the Safavid State and its Non-Muslim Minorities," *Islam and Christian–Muslim Relations* 14, no. 4 (October 2003): 435–58.

[5] Maria Rosa Menocal, *The Ornament of the World! How Muslim, Jews, and Christians Created a Culture of Tolerance in Medieval Spain* (Boston: Little, Brown and Company, 2002), 30.

debates among historians are now much more nuanced."[6] That nuanced historical reading reveals serious concerns about the available sources, and the kinds of historical data that can be gleaned from them, keeping in mind the historical Andalusian context, as opposed to any present context or set of values. For Akasoy, an important lesson to be gained from the recent ink spilled on Islamic Spain is how that history is instrumentalized for contemporary, ideological purposes. She concludes: "one lesson to be learned not so much from history... but from the way it is presented is just how much negotiating the past is part of negotiating the present."[7]

The view that al-Andalus offers today a model for peace and harmony ignores the fact that Muslim jurists writing in that period preserved the *dhimmī* rules. For example, even the famous philosopher Ibn Rushd (Averroes), who was also a famous jurist, wrote about the *dhimmī* rules in his well-known treatise *Bidāyat al-Mujtahid wa Nihāyat al-Muqtaṣid.*[8] In other words, the historical argument concerning periods of peace and harmony does little to address why and to what effect the *dhimmī* legal doctrines were developed, taught, and perpetuated in premodern legal sources during historical periods in which peace and tolerance arguably prevailed.

Those adopting the myth of harmony do not ignore the *dhimmī* rules. They too are concerned about the facially discriminatory implications of such rules. One approach they adopt regarding the rules is to deny that the facially discriminatory legal treatment was historically significant or was meant to disparage those of different religious traditions. For example, some argue that the *jizya* tax was merely an administrative matter used to organize society. *Jizya* was a non-Muslim tax, they argue, whereas the *zakāt* was the Muslim tax. Both groups paid taxes and, as such, the *jizya* should not be considered a discriminatory tax that speaks to an underlying Muslim intolerance of the religious Other.[9]

[6] Anna Akasoy, "*Convivencia* and its Discontents: Interfaith Life in al-Andalus," *International Journal of Middle East Studies* 42 (2010): 489–99, 491.

[7] Akasoy, "*Convivencia* and its Discontents," 498.

[8] Ibn Rushd al-Ḥafīd, *Bidāyat al-Mujtahid wa Nihāyat al-Muqtaṣid*, eds ʿAlī Muʿawwaḍ and ʿĀdil ʿAbd al-Mawjūd (Beirut: Dār al-Kutub al-ʿIlmiyya, 1997).

[9] Abdelwahab Boudhiba, "The Protection of Minorities," in *The Different Aspects of Islamic Culture: The Individual and Society in Islam*, eds A. Boudhiba and M. Maʿrūf al-Dawālibī (Paris: UNESCO, 1998), 331–46, 340–1. See also, Ghazi Salahuddin Atabani, "Islamic *Sharīʿah* and the Status of Non-Muslims," in *Religion, Law and Society: A Christian–Muslim Dialogue* (Geneva: WCC Publications, 1995), 63–9, who writes that religious classifications in Islam are for making distinctions in the hereafter, but not in worldly terms. He writes that the *dhimmī* concept is not one of disparagement, but rather allowed historical minority communities to maintain the distinctiveness they needed to survive. In other words, it was a means of preserving religious pluralism, not squashing it. Likewise, see also Fazlur Rahman, "Non-Muslim Minorities in an Islamic State," *Journal Institute of Muslim Minority Affairs* 7 (1986): 13–24, 20, who writes that the *jizya* was a tax in lieu of

This position, however, is contradicted by early historical sources that characterize the Qur'ānic verse stipulating the *jizya* tax as animated by the ethic of subordination and humiliation—a topic that will be addressed extensively in Chapters 3 and 4.

Others adopting a harmonious reading of Islam and Islamic law suggest that while the rules were very much part of the Islamic tradition, they do not reflect the essential character or aspirations of the Islamic value system.[10] For instance, Isma'il Faruqi writes that the discriminatory rules reflect the "personal understanding" of specific jurists, but are not inherent to the religion as such.[11] He does not explain what this means, though. Likewise, Murad Hoffman acknowledges that non-Muslims were discriminated against under the law, but limits the discriminatory impact to three modes: exclusion from military service; liability for paying the *jizya* to receive military protection (a service charge, as he calls it); and preclusion from being head of state.[12] He further argues that the juristic tradition, which developed other discriminatory measures, only illustrates how Muslims did not live up to the true precepts of Islam.[13] In other words, the *dhimmī* rules are a deviation from the true Islamic vision, whatever that may be.

Another tactic is simply to suggest that times have changed and hence so too have the laws of society. This approach often waves away the premodern doctrines without attempting to understand the underlying logic and context that made them intelligible in the first place. Archie deSouza, for example, argues that the term *ahl al-dhimma* need not be used anymore to designate the non-Muslim population of a modern Muslim state. He argues that if we take seriously the precept that changed circumstances require a change in the law, we will recognize that society has changed and so the medieval law has little relevance today. For deSouza, non-Muslims have become "authentic partners" with Muslims in their respective nations. Because of their partner status in

military service. Furthermore, not all non-Muslims paid the *jizya*. He refers to 'Umar's receipt of the *zakāt* from a Christian tribe as an example. This is likely a reference to the Banū Taghlib. Notably, Rahman does not mention that Banū Taghlib was required to pay a higher rate of *zakāt* tax than Muslims, which some have suggested equaled the amount they would have paid under a *jizya* scheme.

[10] See, for example, Sheikh Showkat Hussain, "Status of Non-Muslims in Islamic State." *Hamdard Islamicus* 16, no. 1 (1993): 67–79, 76; 76; Rahman, "Non-Muslim Minorities in an Islamic State," 20.

[11] Ismail R. Faruqi, "The Rights of non-Muslims under Islam: Social and Cultural Aspects," in *Muslim Communities in non-Muslim States* (London: Islamic Council of Europe, 1980), 43–66, 49.

[12] Murad Wilfried Hoffman, "The Protection of Religious Minorities in Islam," *Encounters* 4, no. 2 (1998): 137–48, 143.

[13] Hoffman, "The Protection of Religious Minorities in Islam," 145.

these countries, there is no need to provide special protection pacts, or to employ special laws to designate and distinguish them from the Muslim populace.[14] While deSouza's policy conclusions are commendable, his treatment of the *dhimmī* rules provides little insight into why these laws were developed in the first place, and no real guidance for contending with the fact that these laws are part of a historical record that arguably continues to have normative weight for Muslims the world over.

For the above authors, historicizing and contextualizing the legal tradition is crucial to their enterprise, as is utilizing indefinite claims about the real "spirit" of Islam. Despite the different tactics employed, most of the authors above share a similar approach to the *dhimmī* doctrines themselves: they avoid engaging the legal tradition in terms of its own internal jurisprudential, institutional, or political context. Their arguments may address some rules, but only in piecemeal fashion. Their conclusions have little to offer those interested in understanding the underlying jurisprudence and background values that rendered these rules intelligible, legitimate, and authoritative.[15]

The myth of harmony stands in stark contrast to the myth of persecution. The myth of persecution suggests that endemic to the Muslim mindset is a notion of the non-Muslim as not only the Other, but also as the subservient, submissive, and the politically disempowered. Those adopting the myth of persecution often rely upon the *dhimmī* rules as evidence for their position. They also emphasize historical accounts of Muslim rulers oppressing non-Muslims. In fact, rulers often referred to Sharīʿa-based doctrines to justify their persecution; but often they did so as a pretext in order to satisfy the political demands of special interest groups among the Muslims and to preserve their legitimacy as Muslim rulers over a sometimes fractious polity.[16] Consequently, while

[14] Archie deSouza, "Minorities in the Historical Context of Islam," *al-Mushīr* 40, no. 2 (1998): 72–81.

[15] See also, Kasim Abdo Kasim, "Religion and Citizenship in Europe and the Arab World," in *The Dhimmis and Political Authority*, ed. Jorgen S. Nielsen (London: Grey Seal, 1992), 31–8, who writes that there are obligatory duties and recommended duties that fall upon the *dhimmīs*. The former are part of the Pact of ʿUmar, but the latter contradict the spirit of the Qur'ān. But again, he neither indicates what that Qur'ānic spirit is, nor develops a theory of pluralism and tolerance by which he judges the inherited *dhimmī* doctrine. Likewise, A.D. Muztar, "Dhimmis in an Islamic State," *Islamic Studies* 18, no. 1 (1979): 65–75, 72–3, writes that the medieval tradition of discrimination runs contrary to the spirit of Islamic law and "can never be accepted as religiously justified." Again, there is no argument or legal theory by which he substantiates this statement. Like the others noted above, his position is for the most part conclusory, and is clearly embedded within a political agenda to espouse Islam as a tolerant religion and Muslims as a tolerant people.

[16] See, for example, John O. Hunwick, "The Rights of Dhimmis to Maintain a Place of Worship: A 15th Century Fatwa from Tlemcen," *al-Qantara* 12, no. 1 (1991): 133–56; C.E. Bosworth, "The Concept of Dhimma in Early Islam," in *Christians and Jews in the Ottoman*

the myth of harmony often represents the law as mere technicality in academic books, the myth of persecution relies on the law to illustrate Islam's inherently intolerant nature. Importantly, contemporary beliefs and attitudes about tolerance and pluralism are often anachronistically projected backward as standards by which to judge the past.[17]

The myth of persecution is no less problematic for its emphasis on the historical to the detriment of a meaningful engagement with the jurisprudential. Perhaps the most alarmist works on this topic are the studies by Bat Ye'or, the pseudonym of an independent scholar of Egyptian-Jewish origins. Some might find this focus on her work here inapposite for a scholarly monograph,[18] since her work on the *dhimmī* has been criticized as less than scholarly.[19] That does not alter the fact, though, that her arguments contribute to this field of inquiry, where scholarly and polemical arguments do battle.[20] For instance, David Frum, a former Fellow at the American Enterprise Institute, takes issue with American-Muslim leaders who complain about a climate of intolerance against Islam and Muslims in the United States. Espousing the virtues of American tolerance toward Muslims, he turns the table on American Muslims by pointing out their own intolerance for critique. To do so, he

Empire: The Functioning of a Plural Society, ed. Benjamine Braude and Bernard Lewis, 2 vols (New York: Holmes & Meier Publishers, 1982), 41; Bernard Lewis, *Semites and Anti-Semites: An Inquiry into Conflict and Prejudice* (New York: W.W. Norton & Co., 1986), 123; Jacques Waardenburg, "Muslim Studies of Other Religions: The Medieval Period," in *The Middle East and Europe: Encounters and Exchanges*, eds Geert Jan van Gelder and Ed de Moor (Amsterdam: Rodopi, 1992), 10–38, 13; idem, *Muslim Perceptions of Other Religions: A Historical Survey* (Oxford: Oxford University Press, 1999), 23; Richard Gottheil, "An Answer to the Dhimmis," *Journal of the American Oriental Society* 41 (1921): 383–457, who translates an essay in which the *dhimmī* is abused.

[17] Haggai Ben-Shammai, "Jew Hatred in the Islamic Tradition and the Koranic Exegesis," in *Antisemitism Through the Ages*, ed. Shmuel Almog (Oxford: Pergamon Press, 1988), 161–9.

[18] The same could be said about the analysis of the works above, which contribute to the myth of harmony. But like Ye'or's work, the works of those above also contribute a particular strain of argument within the field of *dhimmī* studies that cannot be ignored, and indeed offer a significant historiographic contribution to the *dhimmī* studies field.

[19] Robert Irwin, "Book Reviews: Islam and Dhimmitude: Where Civilizations Collide," *Middle Eastern Studies* 38, no. 4 (2002): 213–15; Paul Fenton, "Book Review: Islam and Dhimmitude," *Midstream* 49, no. 2 (2003): 40–1; Johann Hari, "Amid all this panic, we must remember one simple fact—Muslims are not all the same," *The Independent*, August 21, 2006, 25.

[20] Scholarly and not-so-scholarly sources on both sides of the tolerance debate are many. See for instance, Robert Spencer, ed., *The Myth of Islamic Tolerance: How Islamic Law Treats Non-Muslims* (New York: Prometheus Books, 2005); idem, *The Truth about Muhammad: Founder of the World's Most Intolerant Religion* (Washington D.C.: Regnery Publishing, Inc., 2006); idem, *Islam Unveiled: Disturbing Questions about the World's Fastest-Growing Faith* (San Francisco: Encounter Books, 2002), 143–64; Aaron Tyler, *Islam, the West and Tolerance: Conceiving Coexistence* (New York: Palgrave MacMillan, 2008); Khaled Abou El Fadl, *The Place of Tolerance in Islam* (Boston: Beacon Press, 2002); Yohanan Friedmann, *Tolerance and Coercion in Islam* (Cambridge: Cambridge University Press, 2003).

refers to the work of Bat Ye'or on the *dhimmī* under Islamic law, and the way she and her work on the *dhimmī* are marginalized and demonized. He writes:

> From Pakistan to Britain, from Nigeria to France, writers who express skepticism about the teachings or record of Islam risk violent death. Bat Ye'or is a very great scholar: original, authoritative, lucid...Her native language is French, but her French publisher timidly let her book go out of print, despite scholarly accolades and strong sales. When she spoke at Georgetown, irate Muslim students shouted her down, unreprimanded by their university, and the same thing happened to her at the University of London and at Brown.[21]

Frum is less interested in the contents of Ye'or's actual scholarship. Yet she and her scholarship are made to represent a value of truth and freedom, in opposition to an Islamic intolerance and distortion. He concludes: "under the rules of Western civilization, fair and truthful criticism is not only permissible: It is a duty."[22] Ye'or's work informs not only debates about Islam and tolerance, but also domestic US debates about truth on the one hand, and the presumed inability of Muslims to be honest dealers on the other hand. Even more, in 2010, the Center for Security Policy issued a report, *Sharī'ah: The Threat to America,* which relied in part upon Ye'or's work to characterize Sharī'a as the "pre-eminent totalitarian threat of our time."[23] Members of the team that authored the report were thereafter involved in a nationwide campaign to promote state legislation to outright ban Sharī'a.[24] Furthermore, in his nearly 1,500-page treatise, Oslo terrorist bomber Anders Breivik justifies his anger at European multiculturalism policies and his antagonism against Islam in part by citing extensively the work of Bat Ye'or, prompting some to question whether Ye'or (and others who contribute to the polemics on Islam and intolerance) bear some (moral) responsibility for Breivik's actions.[25] So while some might avoid referring to Ye'or's work, the themes she writes about nonetheless contribute to an ongoing debate about Islam, human rights, tolerance, and religious freedom. For that reason, her analysis

[21] David Frum, "What's Right," *National Review* 54, no. 24 (December 23, 2002): 60.

[22] Frum, "What's Right," 60.

[23] *Shariah: The Threat to America, an Exercise in Competitive Analysis, report of Team BII* (Washington D.C.: Center for Security Policy, 2010) <http://shariahthethreat.org/wp-content/uploads/2011/04/Shariah-The-Threat-to-America-Team-B-Report-Web-09292010.pdf> (accessed October 28, 2010).

[24] For a review of the legislative bans and the security context that informed them, see Anver Emon, "Banning Sharī'a," *The Immanent Frame* <http://blogs.ssrc.org/tif/2011/09/06/banning-shari'a/> (accessed October 28, 2011).

[25] Colby Cosh, "The Making of a Monster," *Macleans* 124, no. 31 (August 15, 2011): 26; Jim Lobe, "Terror in Oslo," *Washington Report on Middle East Affairs* (September–October 2011): 18.

of *dhimmī* rules is reviewed here to help illustrate the extreme mythic poles that undeniably exist in *dhimmī* historiography so as to facilitate a better understanding of where this study situates itself within the received historiographical tradition.

Adherents of the myth of persecution often rely on legal doctrine to prove their point. They too invoke the law only in a piecemeal fashion, without due attention to the details embedded in complex legal argument. Additionally, they reproduce premodern legal texts in translation as if their meaning and significance are transparent and obvious to the modern lay reader.[26] For example, Ye'or writes of how non-Muslim communities could not build new places of worship and were limited in the extent to which they could restore pre-existing ones.[27] But she neither reveals how this restriction was contested nor examines why it was contested at all. For some jurists, whether a religious community could build a new place of worship depended on the demographics of the relevant township. If the township included both *dhimmīs* and Muslims, then Ye'or is correct in asserting her position. But if the township was a presumably predominant *dhimmī* village then she is incorrect, as will be discussed below concerning Ḥanafī jurisprudence. She certainly has sources at her disposal to support her conclusions; but her inattentiveness to how the sources are themselves framed within the discipline of the law renders her conclusions partial at best. Through her selective use of evidence, she paints a picture of persecution without engaging the nuances of the legal tradition. Attentiveness to the nuance of legal argument, though, will show how viewing Sharīʿa as Rule of Law allows us to appreciate how the law represents a sometimes tricky management and balance between the interests of individuals and of the ruling authorities who aspire to govern an imperial order that is demographically diverse.

The two myths of harmony and persecution offer extreme positions, between which other approaches fall.[28] Fundamentally, though,

[26] See for instance, Walter Short, "The Jizya Tax: Equality and Dignity under Islamic Law?" in *The Myth of Islamic Tolerance: How Islamic Law Treats Non-Muslims*, ed. Robert Spencer (Amherst, New York: Prometheus Books, 2005), 73–90, whose footnotes exceed the length of his main text in the article, and who quotes large sections from premodern *fiqh* manuals with little analysis or explanation.

[27] Bat Ye'or, *The Dhimmi: Jews and Christians Under Islam* (Associated University Press, 1985), 57; idem, *Islam and Dhimmitude: Where Civilizations Collide* (Cranbury, NJ: Associated University Presses, 2002), 83–5, where her references for the "unanimous opinion" of Muslim jurists are to the texts by two Shāfiʿī jurists (al-Māwardī and al-Nawawī).

[28] See, for instance M.L. Roy Choudhury Sastri, "The Status of *Dhimmis* in Muslim States, with Special Reference to Mughal India," *The Journal of the Greater India Society* 12, no. 1 (1945): 18–48, 20, who follows Tritton in suggesting that the caliph did not always observe the letter of the law, and that the treatment of *dhimmīs* often depended on the attitude of the ruler in power.

proponents of both myths seem to take the historical legal doctrines as givens, and present them with an eye on present political ramifications. Those presentist concerns are certainly important. Many who write in this area want to know answers to compelling political questions, such as: "What will Muslims do today when they live as neighbors with non-Muslims in a pluralist/global setting?[29] Do the conceptions of the religious Other that once animated the *dhimmī* rules remain in the modern mindset of Muslims in a way that will create a culture of discrimination, if not outright persecution, against religious minorities in Muslim majority states?"[30] These questions arguably make the history and doctrine of the *dhimmī* laws poignant and contentious. But to analyze the historical Islamic doctrine on *dhimmīs* in such a fashion is not only anachronistic, but also hides important questions about the nature of law generally and Islamic law specifically. In particular this approach misses questions about the relationship between law and the modes of governance in Islamic history, where diversity was an inescapable fact.[31]

More recently, historians have developed critical scholarship in social history that illustrates the weaknesses of both myths as explanatory vehicles of Islam and Islamic law. This development is effectively seen in an important article on *dhimmīs* in the Ottoman court system by the historian Najwa al-Qattan.[32] By focusing on records (*sijill*) of local Ottoman courts of general jurisdiction (*Mahkama*), al-Qattan weaves a fascinating account of how *dhimmīs* utilized the Ottoman legal system, brought suits against Muslims, and seem to have preferred the Sharīʿa-based Ottoman courts over the tribunals of their own religious

[29] For scholarly, public policy, and popular literature on this issue, see Andrew March, *Islam and Liberal Citizenship: The Search for an Overlapping Consensus* (Oxford: Oxford University Press, 2009); Mohammad Fadel, "The True, the Good, and the Reasonable: The Theological and Ethical Roots of Public Reason in Islamic Law" *Canadian Journal of Law and Jurisprudence* 21, no. 1 (2008): 5; Cheryl Benard, *Civil Democratic Islam: Partners, Resources, and Strategies* (Santa Monica: RAND, 2003); Tariq Ramadan, *Western Muslims and the Future of Islam* (Oxford: Oxford University Press, 2004); Abou El Fadl, *The Place of Tolerance in Islam.*

[30] Wadi Zaidan Haddad, "*Ahl al-Dhimma* in an Islamic State: The Teaching of Abu al-Hasan al-Mawardi's *al-Ahkam al-Sultaniyya*," *Islam and Christian–Muslim Relations* 7, no. 2 (1996): 169; Kate Zebri, "Relations Between Muslims and Non-Muslims in the Thought of Western-Educated Muslim Intellectuals," *Islam and Christian–Muslim Relations* 6, no. 2 (1995): 255–77, 258.

[31] A similar critique can be made of the contemporary debates and polemics about *jihād* as an essential feature of Islamic belief. For a historical critique that situates *jihād* in a larger context of sanctified violence across space, time, and traditions, see Thomas Sizgorich, "Sanctified Violence: Monotheist Militancy as the Tie that Bound Christian Rome and Islam," *Journal of the American Academy of Religion* 77, no. 4 (December 2009): 895–921.

[32] Najwa al-Qattan, "*Dhimmis* in the Muslim Court: Legal Automony and Religious. Discrimination," *International Journal of Middle East Studies* 31 (1999): 429–44.

community. While she takes issue with prior historical scholarship on the degree to which minority communities enjoyed formal autonomy,[33] she nonetheless recognizes that non-Muslim communities possessed a certain degree of judicial autonomy. *Dhimmīs* had the right to litigate most of their legal affairs in their own communal tribunals as long as their cases did not cross religious boundaries, involve capital crimes, or threaten public order and security.[34] But, as al-Qattan adeptly shows, Christians and Jews regularly made appearances in the Ottoman courts.[35] *Dhimmī* resort to the Ottoman court is not entirely surprising, since the general court was the principal organ for maintaining and recording public documents such as land grants.[36] Furthermore, the Ottoman court was the only court with enforcement power, unlike the *dhimmīs*' confessional tribunals.[37] Significantly, aside from cases where use of the Ottoman court was necessary, there are instances where *intra*-communal disputes were voluntarily brought to the Ottoman court when they could have been litigated in confessional tribunals.[38] Al-Qattan shows that among *dhimmīs*, there was a preference for the

[33] Al-Qattan positions her article in part against a historiography that held that in the Ottoman regime, different non-Muslim religious groups were organized into autonomous communities (*millet*) with their own judges to handle private matters governed by their religious laws. Recent scholarship has suggested, though, that a centralized *millet* system did not in fact materialize until the late Ottoman period. Rather, in the empire's efforts to deal with European powers and assure them of fair treatment of religious minorities in the empire, the foreign office often employed the term "*millet*" to assure its European neighbors that the minorities were respected and enjoyed autonomy over their own affairs. Benjamin Braude, "Foundation Myths of the *Millet* System," in *Christians and Jews in the Ottoman Empire: The Functioning of a Plural Society*, eds Benjamin Braude and Bernard Lewis, 2 vols (New York: Holmes & Meier Publishers, 1982), 1:69–88, 69–72; idem, "The Strange History of the Millet System," in *The Great Ottoman–Turkish Civilization*, ed. Kemal Cicek, 2 vols (Ankara: Yeni Turkiye, 2000), 2:409–8.

[34] Al-Qattan, "*Dhimmis* in the Muslim Court," 429.

[35] Although the absence of *dhimmī* court records leaves a gap in understanding what the communal courts were doing, existing records reveal rabbinical directives forbidding Jews from using the Mahkama, thus implicitly suggesting that Jews may have been using the Ottoman courts. Al-Qattan, "*Dhimmis* in the Muslim Court," 429. See also, Bert F. Breiner, "*Sharīʿa* and Religious Pluralism," in *Religion, Law and Society: A Christian–Muslim Discussion*, ed. Tarek Mitri (Geneva: WCC Publications, 1995), 51–62; Joseph R. Hacker, "Jewish Autonomy in the Ottoman Empire: Its Scope and Limits. Jewish Courts from the Sixteenth to the Eighteenth Centuries," in *The Jews of the Ottoman Empire*, ed. Avigdor Levy (Princeton: Darwin Press, 1994), 153–202, 157; Avigdor Levy, "Introduction," in *The Jews of the Ottoman Empire*, ed. Avigdor Levy (Princeton: Darwin Press, 1994), 1–150, 18.

[36] Al-Qattan, "*Dhimmis* in the Muslim Court," 429.

[37] Al-Qattan, "*Dhimmis* in the Muslim Court," 429.

[38] Al-Qattan, "*Dhimmis* in the Muslim Court," 430. See also, Ronald C. Jennings, "Zimmis (Non-Muslims) in Early 17th Century Ottoman Judicial Records: The Sharīʿa Court of Anatolian Kayseri," in *Studies in Ottoman Social History in the Sixteenth and Seventeenth Centuries: Women, Zimmis, and Sharīʿa Courts in Kayseri, Cyprus and Trabzon* (Istanbul: The Isis Press, 1999), 369.

Sharīʿa's rules of inheritance and the use of the court as a marriage and property registry.[39]

Al-Qattan's research reveals two important points. First, when non-Muslims utilized the Ottoman court, they knowingly invoked the jurisdiction and application of Islamic law in their case. In other words, the Ottoman court did not rule by the *dhimmīs*' communal law. Second, far from discriminating, the Ottoman court offered a leveling mechanism that disregarded social status, place of residence, or religious background. The court, according to the *sijill* records, was not the arena of extra-legal or illegal discrimination.[40] The Ottoman court and its legal order provided a default legal system, and litigants were treated with equal fairness. According to al-Qattan, *dhimmīs* presumably opted for Ottoman courts instead of communal tribunals for various reasons, including the fact that they could get a fair hearing and prevail in an action, even against a Muslim party. Al-Qattan's research shows that such outcomes were possible, and thus poses an important historical challenge to those adopting the myth of persecution.

Importantly, al-Qattan's conception of discrimination and fair treatment has more to do with judicial discretion and administration, as opposed to the substantive doctrine of the law. Her research does not challenge the fact that Islamic legal doctrines discriminated against non-Muslims. Rather, she acknowledges that, as a matter of law, non-Muslims were not allowed to testify as witnesses against Muslim parties on behalf of another party, as will be discussed in Chapter 3.[41] Al-Qattan's point is that despite this legal disability, non-Muslims were not subjected to discrimination whereby Muslim parties would capitalize on their Muslim identity when bringing cases to the Ottoman courts.[42] Even more, she argues that while *dhimmīs* could not, as a matter of law, testify on behalf of plaintiff co-religionists, the latter did not necessarily lose their cases. Either *dhimmī* petitioners would have other sorts of evidence or they would have Muslim witnesses testify on their behalf. In such cases, the *dhimmī* had a fair chance of prevailing.[43] While legal doctrines handicapped non-Muslims in some ways (i.e., witness

[39] Al-Qattan, "*Dhimmis* in the Muslim Court," 433.

[40] Al-Qattan, "*Dhimmis* in the Muslim Court," 436.

[41] Al-Qattan, "*Dhimmis* in the Muslim Court," 436–7.

[42] Al-Qattan, "*Dhimmis* in the Muslim Court," 437.

[43] Ronald C. Jennings, *Christians and Muslims in Ottoman Cyprus and the Mediterranean World, 1571–1640* (New York: New York University Press), 132–3; idem, "Zimmis (Non-Muslims) in Early 17th Century Ottoman Judicial Records," 347–412; Kemal Cicek, "A Quest for Justice in a Mixed Society: The Turks and the Greek Cypriots Before the Sharīʿa Courts of Nicosia," in *The Great Ottoman–Turkish Civilization*, ed. Kemal Cicek, 2 vols (Ankara: Yeni Turkiye, 2000), 2:472–91.

testimony against Muslims), the actual treatment of non-Muslims in the Ottoman court seems to suggest that the court was an arena of fairness and justice, regardless of the petitioner's religious identity. The religious commitments of the parties to an action does not seem to have affected the outcome of cases.

This highly important development in *dhimmī* studies is framed as a study of social history, and thereby takes for granted the legitimacy of the *dhimmī* rules without investigating the underlying legal logic that animated the rules themselves. This is not a criticism of al-Qattan's article; she makes an undeniably important contribution to the literature on *dhimmīs* in Islamic history. It is meant only to suggest that the historical study of *dhimmīs* can lead to different conclusions depending in part on how the historical inquiry is framed. Al-Qattan's work offers a social-historical analysis. As such, it is not designed to present a jurisprudential perspective from which we can understand the underlying logic that normalized the *dhimmī* rules.[44] Al-Qattan's article shows that despite such normalization, non-Muslims could strategize ways to seek their desired ends, and they were in part successful because of a climate of judicial impartiality that existed independent of the law and its jurisprudence.[45]

To offer a different but complementary approach to the study of *dhimmī* rules, this study will focus on the legal reasoning that justified the *dhimmī* rules themselves, and what that reasoning reveals about the jurists' assumptions about justice and its enforcement in a Muslim polity. Adopting a critical legal-historicist approach through the "Rule of Law" frame adopted herein, this study examines the mutually constitutive relationship between law and the enterprise of governance, while avoiding "tolerance" as an organizing conceptual framework, given the all-too-presentist attitudes "tolerance" tends to anachronistically import into analyses of the *dhimmī* rules.[46]

[44] For instance, Joseph Sadan, "The 'Latrines Decree' in the Yemen Versus the Dhimma Principle," in *Pluralism and Identity: Studies in Ritual Behavior*, eds Jan Platvoet and Karel Van Der Toorn (Leiden: Brill, 1995), 167–85, 169, writes how the treaties establishing one's *dhimma* status could be seen as part of a program of liberal toleration or as a means of maintaining a negative attitude toward non-Muslims and keeping them subservient to the Muslim population. Perhaps given the sovereignty of Sharīʿa and the competing interests to be balanced, both values coexisted for reasons that will be discussed below.

[45] For a similar inquiry into the possibilities of non-Muslims participating in various capacities in Ottoman governance, see Christine M. Philliou, *Biography of an Empire: Governing Ottomans in an Age of Revolution* (Berkeley: University of California Press, 2011).

[46] There are other methodological approaches one could adopt when researching the treatment of non-Muslims under an Islamic imperium. For instance, Youssef Courbage and Philippe Fargues adopt a demographic approach to studying the lives of Jews and

The remainder of this chapter will be devoted to revisiting certain periods in Islamic history to understand the relationship between Islamic legal developments and the enterprise of governance. This task will be undertaken in two complementary ways:

- first by examining the way in which different modes of governance amidst diversity in early Islamic history were justified by arguments of legality; and
- second, by exploring how certain legal doctrines and arguments are intelligible when viewed in the context of an imperial enterprise of governance.

In its early history, the Muslim polity progressed from being a nascent polity within the confines of Medina to an expansive empire adding territories through conquest and diplomatic negotiation. This imperial model contributed a normative backdrop to the juristic imagination of what the law should be, how it should work, and upon whom it should operate.

1.2 IN THE BEGINNING . . .

Islamic imperial expansion did not occur from the very outset of Muḥammad's mission as a Prophet. Nor did it begin immediately upon his migration to Medina, when he assumed a political role. Rather, the imperial ethic that animated the early Muslim polity developed over a period of years. Along the way, different approaches and tactics were used to manage the existence of non-Muslims in the nascent Muslim polity located in Medina, and thereafter to manage the lands lying far from Medina but falling under the political authority of the Prophet and his successors in Medina. The transition from securing the stability of Medina to expanding throughout the Arabian Peninsula led to different models of governing amidst diversity. Such models are noted herein using the following descriptive labels: cleansing, lease/rent, and treaty/tax. Cleansing was perhaps the most violent form of conquest, namely the forced removal of non-Muslims, whether by expulsion or execution. Lease/rent and treaty/tax offered the newly expanding empire an opportunity to utilize the expertise of local populations while maintaining ultimate control of new lands or deriving economic benefits in the form of taxes. Lease/rent cases involved peoples who were conquered by Muslim

Christians in the Islamic world: Youssef Courbage and Philippe Fargues, *Christians and Jews under Islam*, trans. Judy Mabro (London: I.B. Tauris Publishers, 1997).

forces who nonetheless negotiated an agreement to maintain possession (but not sovereign control) of the territory while offering rents (sometimes quite substantial) derived from their cultivation of the land. Treaties and taxes provided the possibility of expanding the influence of the Medinan polity without the cost of military battle and conquest. In such cases, diplomats from neighboring tribes may have wanted to secure positive relations with the Muslim polity as a deterrent to military engagement and possible conquest. The treaty/tax model allowed for political alliances to flower while management of the land did not necessarily shift to the Muslim polity. As the Muslim polity expanded and began conquering more and more regions, the model of governance amidst diversity often involved a combination of lease/rent and treaty/tax.

To expand and manage newly acquired lands, Muslim leaders often incorporated local institutions and their personnel into the administration of regional affairs, which would cut against the cost and scope of violence and military oversight required.[47] The local populace was often the most knowledgeable about its affairs and could provide efficient management, while ensuring payment of taxes or rents to the Muslim political regime. Importantly for this study, though, the incorporation of a local populace (many of whom were not Muslim) contributed to the need to consider the ramification of diversity as a constitutive feature of Islamic models of governance and, thereby, of the boundaries of the claim space of Sharīʿa.

1.2.1 Securing Medina, ensuring existence: The battles with Quraysh and the Jewish tribes

Soon after Muḥammad's installment in Medina as a leader and ruling figure, he had to contend with threats to the very existence of the nascent Muslim polity. Within Medina were groups of individuals who were less than enthusiastic about his arrival. Furthermore, he had to respond to the existential threat posed by the forces of Mecca, who would not tolerate the rise of Medina in competition with Meccan dominance in the region. Muḥammad's early efforts, military and otherwise, involved managing these two fronts of political instability. His early years in Medina were punctuated by three significant battles with the forces of Mecca. After these three battles, Muḥammad was able to maintain the stability of

[47] H.A.R. Gibb, *Studies on the Civilization of Islam*, eds Stanford Shaw and William Polk (Princeton: Princeton University Press, 1962), 47–61; Ira Lapidus, *A History of Islamic Societies* (1988; repr., Cambridge: Cambridge University Press, 1991), 60–3.

Medina and began looking beyond its borders to expand the influence of the Muslim polity. Ultimately, he took control of Mecca itself in 630 CE, and thereafter expanded his and the Muslim polity's influence across the Arabian Peninsula.

The early history of Medina offers three examples of the cleansing model, which Muḥammad used to govern amidst diversity. The three examples concern the three Jewish tribes in Medina. These three Jewish tribes—the *Banū Naḍīr, Bānū Qurayẓa,* and *Bānū Qaynuqāʾ*—were deemed in an original founding document, the *wathīqat al-Madīna,* to be part of the new polity founded by Muḥammad in Medina. That document, often called the "Constitution of Medina," set out the relations between the various tribes in Medina and posited the Prophet as the leader of the community with the authority to resolve and arbitrate conflicts. Whether the "Constitution of Medina" was a single document or a collection of documents is debated by historians and is not central to the analysis herein. Nonetheless, it seems from historical records that Muḥammad and the Jewish tribes had treaties that delineated the latter's membership in the Medinan polity. Debate rages whether the Jewish tribes were considered part of the new *umma* (nation) or an *umma* of their own living alongside the new Muslim one.[48]

At the conclusion of each battle with the Meccan troops, Muḥammad had to contend with a Jewish tribe that was claimed to have violated its treaty with Muḥammad. Each crisis with the Jewish tribes occurred amidst existential concerns about the future of the Muslim polity in Medina. In other words, the harsh treatment of the Jewish tribes occurred in the context of pressing concerns about security and military threats from external forces. Muḥammad had to govern a Medinan polity marked by considerable diversity at a time of grave concerns about security and war.

In these instances of cleansing, Muḥammad exercised what contemporary political theorists along the lines of Carl Schmitt might call the "sovereign exception." In his recent development of Schmitt's theory,

[48] On the reliability of historical sources on the existence of Muḥammad's treaties with the Jews, see Michael Lecker, "Did Muḥammad Conclude Treaties with the Jewish Tribes Naḍīr, Qurayẓa, and Qaynuqāʾ?" in *Dhimmis and Others: Jews and Christians and the World of Classical Islam*, eds Uri Rubin and David Wasserstein (Tel Aviv: Eisenbrauns, 1997), 29–36. Notably, Lecker disputes whether the Jewish tribes were part of the Umma treaty, in contrast to what is noted above. For the purpose of this analysis, the specific point about the Jewish tribes' inclusion in the *wathīqa* is not at issue. For an overview of disputes about the document, its authenticity, and how different versions of the document contribute to considerable debates about the inclusion of the Jewish tribes in the Muslim polity, see Anver M. Emon, "Reflections on the 'Constitution of Medina': An Essay on Methodology and Ideology in Islamic Legal History," *UCLA Journal of Islamic and Near Eastern Law* 1, no. 1 (Fall/Winter 2001–02): 103–33.

Paul Kahn recalls that the sovereign exception presumes a rule or norm that operates and prevails under ordinary circumstances. The exception is only meaningful as an exception when circumstances dictate, such as the circumstances of emergency. "The norm, Schmitt often says, requires ordinary circumstances for its operation; the exception occupies those circumstances that are less—or more—than ordinary. The quality of the exception is always one of self-limitation: the exception cannot become normal."[49] The angst arising from Schmitt's "sovereign exception" is that such exceptional behavior will be rendered as normal and even normative. Indeed, Kahn notes: "the nature of norms is such that the exception is always subject to normalization: law will seek to extend to the exceptional decision."[50] Viewing Muḥammad's actions against the Jewish tribes as a type of sovereign exception raises concerns about the implication of this early history on the development of an Islamic ethos toward the religious Other. It is therefore important, from a Rule of Law perspective, to juxtapose this early historical record with later historical developments and the later-developed *dhimmī* doctrines to examine the relationship between the evolving conditions of the enterprise of governance and what ultimately became the legal norms governing religious minorities under premodern Islamic law.

In the case of the Jewish tribes, the threat they posed to the project of the new polity was managed and regulated using the model of cleansing, which can hardly be called pluralistic. Indeed it is the complete opposite of pluralism. The application of that model was made effective and legitimate in retrospect by the forceful logic of legality and legal processes. For instance, after the Medinan victory against the Meccans at the first battle, the Battle of Badr (2/624), the Prophet gathered the Jewish tribe of Qaynuqā' and proclaimed to them: "Oh Jewish people, be wary that God may descend [upon you] something akin to the vengeance that has befallen the Quraysh. Submit, for you know that I am a dispatched prophet, who you shall find in your books and who God has assigned to you."[51] The people of Qaynuqā' did not submit to the Prophet's request, but nonetheless assured him of their support: "Oh Muḥammad, you see that we are your people (*qawmuka*)."[52] Yet they also warned him that his easy victory at Badr would not mean an easy victory against the Banū Qaynuqā': "By God, if we were to wage war against you, you would learn

[49] Paul Kahn, *Political Theology: Four New Chapters on the Concept of Sovereignty* (New York: Columbia University Press, 2011), 34. [50] Kahn, *Political Theology*, 34.

[51] Ibn Hishām, *al-Sīra al-Nabawiyya*, eds Muṣṭafā al-Saqā, Ibrāhīm al-Abyārī and ʿAbd al-Ḥafīẓ Shalbī (Beirut: Dār al-Maʿrifa, n.d.), 2:47.

[52] Ibn Hishām, *al-Sīra al-Nabawiyya*, 2:47.

that we are the people" to be feared.[53] They at once proclaimed their loyalty as well as their capacity to defend and ward off any aggressive measures by the Prophet and his followers.

The opportunity to strike at the Banū Qaynuqāʾ arose due to a fight in the marketplace that left a Muslim and a Jew dead. A Muslim woman had come to the market place in the quarter of the Banū Qaynuqāʾ to sell her wares, but she was insulted by a Jewish businessman. A Muslim man who witnessed the event came to her aid and in the ensuing fight, the Jewish businessman was killed. Out of revenge, the Jews gathered and killed the Muslim man. As a result, hostility between the Muslims and Jews arose, prompting the Prophet to exercise his power of arbitration, as provided for in the *wathīqat al-Madīna.* But the Banū Qaynuqāʾ would not yield to the prophet's authority to resolve the dispute. The Prophet laid siege to their quarter until they agreed to yield to his authority and rule (*ḥattā nazalū ʿalā ḥukmihi*), and were subsequently expelled from the town.[54]

Importantly, this episode invokes certain images of legality. First, the Banū Qaynuqāʾ had an agreement with the Prophet, and that agreement provided Muḥammad would resolve all disputes in Medina. Second, the Banū Qaynuqāʾ breached that agreement by refusing to yield to the Prophet's authority. As such, they were in violation of a treaty and were considered enemies to the polity. As noted by the early biographer of the Prophet, Ibn Hishām (d. 213/828), on the authority of Ibn Isḥāq, "the Banū Qaynuqāʾ were the first Jews to breach (*naqaḍū*) what was between them and the Messenger of God, God's peace and blessing upon him, and wage war in the period between [the battles] of Badr and Uḥud."[55] Here, the existence of a contract or treaty, the breach of that contract, and the assertion of the Prophet's authority as arbiter of disputes, in the aggregate provided arguments of legality to justify the outcome to the conflict, namely the ultimate expulsion of this Jewish tribe, a physical cleansing by deportation.

Arguments of legality were also used to justify retrospectively the Prophet's expulsion of the Banū Naḍīr, the second Jewish tribe in the city. After the battle of Uḥud, which was not an outright victory for either the Medinans or the Meccans, the Prophet visited the Banū Naḍīr to seek their financial assistance. The Banū Naḍīr were not only part of the Medinan polity, but they were also known to be a wealthy tribe. The Prophet was accompanied by his companions Abū Bakr and ʿUmar b. al-Khaṭṭāb. During the course of the discussions, and after agreeing

[53] Ibn Hishām, *al-Sīra al-Nabawiyya*, 2: 47. See also Martin Lings, *Muhammad: His Life Based on the Earliest Sources* (Rochester, VT: Inner Traditions International, 1983), 161.

[54] Ibn Hishām, *al-Sīra al-Nabawiyya*, 2:48.

[55] Ibn Hishām, *al-Sīra al-Nabawiyya*, 47.

to assist the Prophet, the elders of the tribe departed momentarily. While awaiting their return, the Prophet received a vision (*al-khabar min al-samā'*) showing that the elders were actually plotting his death.[56] He abruptly left; his companions remained seated, thinking the Prophet would return shortly. When he did not, the two companions departed and followed the Prophet, who had returned to the center of Medina. When Abū Bakr and 'Umar ultimately found the Prophet, Muḥammad revealed what he saw and prepared to take action against the Banū Naḍīr on the ground that they breached their pact with Muḥammad. The Prophet then dispatched Muḥammad b. Maslama to the Banū Naḍīr to tell them that the Prophet knew of their plans and of the Prophet's demand that they leave the town. After some negotiations back and forth, the Banū Naḍir were given limited time to abandon Medina with only what they could carry on the backs of their camels.[57]

Certainly, there is a complex relationship between the Prophet, the Muslims and the Banū Naḍīr. The equivocal results of Uḥud did not bode well for the internal security and well-being of Medina or for the stability of the Prophet's rule. Those Muslims who had come from Mecca arrived with little to call their own, while other groups in Medina, such as the Banū Naḍīr, lived in considerable economic comfort. From the Banū Naḍīr's perspective, the lack of a clear victory at Uḥud suggested that the future of Muḥammad's leadership might be coming to an end, so the Banū Naḍīr might have been wary of putting their political support behind someone who might not lead Medina for much longer. These circumstances illuminate a complex political, economic, and social situation in Medina after the Battle of Uḥud. Despite these complex circumstances, the relations between the Banū Naḍīr and the Prophet were represented by later historians and commentators as fully defined by the pact that was made between them upon the Prophet's arrival in Medina. In other words, an otherwise fraught political, social, and economic set of relationships was represented by premodern historians by reference to a treaty that, in juridical fashion, reduced this complex relationship to either compliance or breach.

A similar approach characterized the treatment of the Banū Qurayẓa, the third and final Jewish tribe in Medina. In a third attempt to quell Muḥammad and his followers, the leaders of Mecca raised a large army and marched on Medina. To their surprise, they found surrounding Medina a trench. An unusual technique of warfare, the trench forced

56 Ibn Hishām, *al-Sira al-Nabawiyya*, 2:190.
57 Muḥammad b. Jarīr al-Ṭabarī, *Ta'rīkh al-Ṭabarī: Ta'rīkh al-Umam wa al-Mulūk* (Beirut: Dār al-Kutub al-'Ilmiyya, 1995), 2:84; Lings, *Muhammad*, 203.

the Meccans to revise their planned attack on the city. The one area where the city's fortifications were weak was near the quarter controlled by the Banū Qurayẓa. But as that tribe had a treaty with the Prophet that they were reluctant to breach, they had to be strongly induced to forgo that treaty and help the Meccans defeat Muḥammad. Ḥuyay b. Akhṭab, the leader of the Banū Naḍīr—which was banished after Uḥud—was with the Meccans and undertook the challenge of convincing the Banū Qurayẓa to abandon Muḥammad and his people. At first the leader of the Banū Qurayẓa, Kaʿb b. Asad, refused to change his tribe's allegiance: "I have made a covenant (*ʿāhadtu*) with Muḥammad and I am not one to repudiate what is between me and him."[58] After much heated discussion, Kaʿb agreed to abandon the treaty-based relationship with Muḥammad. When the Prophet heard about the Banū Qurayẓa's defection, he sent representatives to confirm the rumor. When these representatives made their inquiries to members of the Banū Qurayẓa, they were met with defiance: "Who is the messenger of God? There is no covenant or contract between us and Muḥammad."[59] Consequently when the Battle of the Trench was concluded and Muḥammad and his followers were victorious, their attention turned to the Banū Qurayẓa. Muḥammad ordered his army to lay siege to the area of the city inhabited by the Banū Qurayẓa. After many weeks of suffering the siege, the Banū Qurayẓa opened the gates to the quarter and submitted themselves to Muḥammad's judgment. Members of one of the Arab tribes that had converted to Islam, the Banū Aws, asked the Prophet to show leniency to the Banū Qurayẓa. In response, the Prophet asked whether they would prefer that a leader of the Banū Aws decide the fate of the Banū Qurayẓa. In particular he asked: "Would you be satisfied, oh people of Aws, if someone from among yourselves decided (*an yaḥkuma*) [their fate]?"[60] Here, the term used to refer to decision and resolution is derived from the trilateral root *ḥ-k-m,* which was used above to refer to the Prophet's authority to settle the conflict between the Muslims and the Jews of Banū Qaynuqāʿ. That root forms the origin of words that deal with adjudication, arbitration, and rulings.[61]

Saʿd b. Muʿādh, chief of the Banū Aws, was in Medina recovering from a wound he received in battle, and was convinced that he would succumb to it in a matter of time. Saʿd was vested with the authority to decide the fate of the Banū Qurayẓa. His decision: the men would be executed, the women and children would become captives, and their property apportioned to

[58] Ibn Hishām, *al-Sīra al-Nabawiyya*, 2:220.
[59] Ibn Hishām, *al-Sīra al-Nabawiyya*, 2:222.
[60] Ibn Hishām, *al-Sīra al-Nabawiyya*, 2:239.
[61] Ibn Manẓūr, *Lisān al-ʿArab*, 3rd ed. (Beirut: Dār Ṣādir, 1994), 12:140.

the conquering forces. The men were indeed executed, and the captives and property were divided among all those who participated in the siege of the Banū Qurayẓa.[62] In the case of the Banū Qurayẓa, the trappings of legality exist in terms of a contract governing a particular relationship, and an arbitral process meant to control for various interests.

The three cases above illustrate a particular model of governing amidst diversity, namely the model of cleansing. In each case, though, the highly exceptional acts taken against the Jewish tribes were considered justified (and even normalized) in premodern Islamic literature because highly complex and politically fraught relationships were regulated (and even reduced) by reference to documents and processes that reflected the language and authority of the law. The legal elements included references to arbitral authority (*ḥukm*), treaties (*ʿahd*), and a juridification of complex relationships to a matter of either compliance or breach. What these terms imply about the early history of Muḥammad's prophecy is not transparent if one were merely to read the relevant texts in their original Arabic or in translation. Indeed, while some might be inclined to ask about the historical details of the Prophet's arbitral office, the facticity of that office is less relevant for this study than the way in which the language describing the Prophet's role draws upon the images of legality that later become significant for Muslim jurists seeking to develop a legal order. The Jewish tribes are said to have conspired with the Quraysh against the Muslims; in doing so, they were held to have violated a treaty struck with Muḥammad. The punishment they received, though harsh, was retrospectively justified by reference to legal arguments arising from contract-based principles.

Significant for the purpose of this study is how each of the three cases above intermingle legality with a vision of a nascent polity under threat. The cleansing model can certainly contribute to the homogeneity of a polity. Homogeneity may be an important feature in the early stages of a polity's formation, especially when it also faces an uncertain political future. In this case, the exceptionality of the cleansing model is normalized and rendered intelligible by reference to the law, despite (or perhaps because of) the otherwise highly fractious and at times volatile Medinan polity struggling simply to survive. As Fred Donner indicates, Muḥammad pursued a policy of consolidation that required him to establish his authority in Medina and quell the threat posed by the Quraysh. The three battles noted above gave him the chance to do just that. "Thus the success against the Meccans at Badr appears to have strengthened Muḥammad's hand enough to allow him to exile the

[62] Lings, *Muhammad*, 229–33.

B. Qaynuqāʾ, and the collapse of the Meccan siege of Medina at the battle of the Trench led to a swift and ghastly reckoning for the B. Qurayẓā, who had tried to help the Meccans during the siege."[63] These three incidents offered the necessary conditions for Muḥammad to bolster his authority and to ensure the sheer existence of a nascent Medinan polity whose future was at best uncertain and plagued by insecurity. That existential boost no doubt came at a serious cost to the minorities who once lived in that polity. Those costs, though, were retrospectively deemed justified by reference to legal arguments of contract. Premodern Muslim historians and jurists put the law and legal arguments in service of the nascent enterprise of governing the Medinan polity. Consequently, while historians often view this early history as a narrative of political maneuvering and consolidation, this analysis reveals a legal dimension to that story. The pursuit of a stable polity through cleansing was later justified and even normalized in part by reference to instruments and arguments of legality that reduced highly complex and existentially fraught situations into a binary legal calculation.[64]

1.2.2 Moving beyond Medina: From survival to empire

The existential crisis that faced Medina in its early years subsided after each battle with Meccan forces. Following the Medinan victory at the Battle of the Trench, the Meccans realized that Muḥammad and his followers were not to be defeated militarily. The victory over the Meccan forces at that third battle spelled the beginning of the end of Quraysh opposition. The Prophet, however, was ever mindful that outlying tribes continued to threaten the security and stability of the nascent but now growing Muslim polity at a crucial time in its existence. Furthermore, Muḥammad was not content to limit the scope of the prophetic message to the Medinan oasis. The outcome of the Battle of the Trench signaled a new political vision for the more firmly established Muslim polity in Medina. That political vision involved conquest and expansion; the era of Islamic imperialism had arrived. As Donner indicates,

> At the outset [Muḥammad] had little if any effective support from nomadic groups . . . but by the time of the conquest of Mecca he was backed by contingents from several nomadic tribes of the Ḥijāz. As he entered the last years of his career, nomadic groups increasingly found that they had to come to

[63] Fred McGraw Donner, *The Early Islamic Conquests* (Princeton: Princeton University Press, 1981), 63.

[64] For a useful overview of some of these events, see Hugh Goddard, "Christian–Muslim Relations: A Look Backward and a Look Forwards," *Islam and Christian–Muslim Relations* 11, no. 2 (2000): 195–212, 197.

terms with the Islamic state, in part because it controlled the main agricultural and market centers in the Ḥijāz, upon which the nomads depended.[65]

The development of an imperial vision of the Muslim polity entailed new and evolving models for governing amidst diversity. The early history of a polity struggling for its very existence provided the political backdrop to legal arguments justifying cleansing. In the era of imperialism, new political realities arose that demanded increased commitment to diversity as a constitutive feature of the imagined enterprise of governance (i.e., a commitment to an imperial model of pluralism). Giving juridical form to the new political reality, the Prophet employed two devices to foster an expansionist and pluralist vision, the legal regimes of lease/rent and treaty/tax.[66]

The model of lease/rent is evident in how Muḥammad dealt with the predominantly Jewish town of Khaybar. The Prophet turned his attention to Khaybar after the victory at the battle of the Trench. Khaybar had grown in previous years ever since the Banū Naḍīr took up residence in Khaybar after being banished from Medina. The reason for the Prophet's concern with Khaybar, according to early sources, is that its leaders had supported the Quraysh in their campaign against the Muslims in Medina and used their contacts with other tribes to create a groundswell of support for the Quraysh against the Muslims of Medina. Although their active campaign against the Prophet had failed, the people of Khaybar presented a security threat to what was still a young but growing Muslim polity.

The Prophet organized an army to march on Khaybar. After days of laying siege, the Prophet's army was able to break through, one by one, the various fortifications protecting Khaybar from external invaders. When defeat was imminent, the inhabitants of Khaybar negotiated a settlement with the Prophet whereby they would abandon their homes without their belongings or riches. Nearby, the inhabitants of Fadak learned what happened to the people of Khaybar and negotiated a settlement with the Prophet along the same terms. In other words, the Prophet was able to gain control and possession over the land and riches of Fadak without waging a battle. This prompted the Khaybarites, however, to return to the Prophet with a suggestion and possible modification of their settlement. They suggested that the Prophet allow them to work the fields of Khaybar, and in return the Prophet would receive half of all

[65] Donner, *Early Islamic Conquests*, 63.

[66] Importantly, in some cases, the Prophet exercised his discretion to pay out gifts to various tribes to reconcile them to the increasing power and authority of the Muslim polity. This form of relationship-building reflects the discretionary authority of the Prophet as leader. Donner, *Early Islamic Conquests*, 65.

proceeds from the township. Since the inhabitants of Khaybar knew the lands and had experience cultivating them, they were in a better, more experienced position than the Prophet and his followers to maximize the land's productivity. The Prophet agreed to the arrangement on condition that if he wanted them to abandon the lands, they had to do so. The people of Khaybar agreed to the condition; thus they retained possession of the land and could cultivate it, but the land itself became spoils of war to be divided among the Muslims (*kānat khaybar fayʾ bayna al-muslimīn*).[67] The example of Khaybar illustrates how property regimes involving leasing and rent can provide a legal device to manage diversity in an era of imperial expansion. The people of Khaybar retained possession of their property, and were able to work the land as long as they contributed to the ongoing financial needs of an expanding empire by paying rents into the imperial coffer. The lease was terminable at will, thereby asserting the new sovereign's ultimate control over the underlying land. The lease, combined with the rent, represented the expanding authority of an imperial sovereign as financial support for the empire's expansion policies.

The treaty/tax model was an alternative to the lease/rent model. Used in the context of diplomatic relation-building, the treaty/tax model established diplomatic relationships of peace and security between the Prophet's polity and outlying tribes who required assurance of their own security from assault or conquest. For example, after the Prophet's conquest of Mecca, it became clear to neighboring tribes that he and the Muslim polity had assured themselves considerable authority and longevity in the Arabian Peninsula. Tribes that were worried about their autonomy sent diplomatic delegations (*wufūd*) to negotiate terms of mutual recognition and acknowledgement with the Medinan polity. As Hugh Kennedy writes, these diplomatic missions were more often initiated by the other tribes, which were "anxious to enter into friendly relations with so powerful an organization as the new *umma*. In the year 9/630 numerous tribes sent delegations (*wufūd*) to make terms with the Prophet. They came to acknowledge Muḥammad as the Prophet of Allah and in many, but by no means all, cases agreed to pay the *ṣadaqa* or alms to Medina."[68] In these cases, treaties and taxes such as the *ṣadaqa* ensured the mutual recognition of Muḥammad's polity and the outlying tribes, while granting to the anxious tribes a measure of security amidst the expanding empire Muḥammad and his followers were otherwise cementing through conquest. The treaty/tax model, like the lease/rent model,

[67] Ibn Hishām, *al-Sīra al-Nabawiyya*, 2:337.

[68] Hugh Kennedy, *The Prophet and the Age of the Caliphates: The Islamic Near East from the Sixth to the Eleventh Century* (London: Longman, 1986), 44.

offered a legal device that upheld and perpetuated the imperial design of a newly expanding polity, in part by ensuring peaceful relations without military conquest, and economic growth through taxes and tributes.

The treaty/tax model became particularly important in animating if not justifying the later military expeditions led by Abū Bakr upon the Prophet's death. Muḥammad's death in 11/632 ushered a crisis of legitimacy for the young polity. The most immediate crisis was how to transfer leadership of the polity. In a series of dramatic political events, which might have resulted in the break-up of the Medinan polity into various factions, the Prophet's companion Abū Bakr was selected as the first person to occupy the position of political leadership over the Muslim polity: he assumed the office of caliph.[69]

Abū Bakr's accession to this office did not necessarily mean that the tribes that had made pacts with Muḥammad would honour Abū Bakr's leadership. Many tribes that had made peace agreements with Muḥammad and paid monetary tribute argued that they were no longer obligated to pay tribute; the legitimacy of Medinan leadership died with the Prophet, they held. Others, however, were of the view that Muḥammad's mission was not limited to matters of personal faith; that the tribes could not forgo their obligation to pay their tribute tax to Medina; and that they had to continue to honor their treaty obligations, which were due to Abū Bakr in his capacity as caliph and leader of the new Medina-based empire. Abū Bakr, convinced that the treaties must hold and that the tribes could not rebuke them, waged war against the recalcitrant tribes. These battles are called in Islamic sources the *Ridda* Wars or Wars of Apostasy.

Whether the recalcitrant tribes can truly be considered apostates is a matter of some debate.[70] Some tribes may have reverted to their old tradition and repudiated Islam. In some cases, certain individuals declared themselves prophets for their people following Muḥammad's death, thus earning for themselves (in premodern chronicles) the title of apostate or grand liar (*al-kadhdhāb*).[71] Importantly, other groups seemed to consider their commitment to Islam to be separate and distinct from

[69] For more on the history of succession after the Prophet's death and the debates that early history spawned, see Patricia Crone, *God's Rule—Government and Islam: Six Centuries of Medieval Islamic Political Thought* (New York: Columbia University Press, 2005).

[70] M. Lecker, "al-Ridda (a.)," *Encyclopaedia of Islam, Second Edition*, eds P. Bearman; Th. Bianquis, C.E. Bosworth, E. van Donzel and W.E. Heinrichs (Leiden: Brill, 2009; Brill Online, University of Toronto, at <http: www.brillonline.nl/subscriber/entry?entry=Islam_SIM> accessed February 6, 2009).

[71] W. Montgomery Watt, "Musaylima b. Ḥabīb, Abū Thumāma," *Encyclopaedia of Islam*, eds P. Bearman, Th. Bianquis, C.E. Bosworth, E. van Donzel and W.P. Heinrichs (Leiden: Brill, 2008; Brill Online, University of Toronto, accessed September 4, 2008).

their political submission to the leadership of Abū Bakr and the Medina-based polity; as such they did not necessarily repudiate Islam, but they refused to pay the tribute tax to Medina.

If taxes and treaties were legal devices that helped constitute the vision and aspiration of the enterprise of governance, then any repudiation of the tax and the treaty would be considered a direct attack against an enterprise of governance that had been defined in an expanding, imperial fashion. Consequently, it matters little whether a tribe abandoned the Muslim polity by renouncing its faith or merely by refusing to pay taxes. Donner writes:

> [E]very *ridda* movement represented at heart an attempt to oppose the hegemony of the Islamic state based in Medina. This was as true of those movements whose members declared themselves loyal to Islam but refused to pay the tax to Medina as it was of those movements that rejected as well Muḥammad's claim to prophecy, and it applied as much to movements arising in areas once under direct Islamic rule . . . as to those arising in areas never under Islamic rule . . . that wanted to remain free thereof.[72]

The *Ridda* Wars represented a challenge not only to the cohesion of the Muslim polity but also to its outward expansion. An imperial vision provided a backdrop that gave intelligibility to the legalistic arguments about treaties, taxes, and military engagements such as the *Ridda* Wars.

Abū Bakr's regime was principally spent maintaining the polity and its integrity. His successor's regime witnessed, on the other hand, massive imperial expansion. The second caliph, ʿUmar b. al-Khaṭṭāb (r. 13–23/634–644 CE), is credited with ushering in a remarkable period of expansion during his tenure in office. Under his leadership, Muslim forces penetrated into what is now known as Iran, Iraq, Syria, and Egypt. This expansion brought Muslim forces into contact with a multitude of diverse peoples, while the Muslim forces themselves were often small and directed to ongoing expansionist military campaigns. Furthermore, the aim of the empire was not to settle in newly acquired lands, but rather to spread the Muslim polity's political authority. Consequently, as armies moved further afield, the organization of newly acquired lands fell to those who were already there, namely the local populace. For instance, writing about the conquest and settlement of Iraq, Donner states:

> [T]he primary objective of the Islamic regime in its expansion into Iraq was not the dispossession of the indigenous peasant populace and the settlement of Iraq by Arabs, but rather the seizure of political control over the country in order to draw off the tax revenues for the benefit of the

[72] Donner, *Early Islamic Conquests*, 86.

> Islamic state . . . In order to ensure the continued inflow of taxes, the regime attempted to secure the general stability of the countryside and clearly realized that the productivity of the area depended upon the retention of most of the lands by the native peasantry.[73]

Importantly, the continued existence of the local population in an Islamic polity contributed to the background assumptions underlying the Islamic imperial vision. This imperial vision continued well into the Umayyad dynasty's regime (r. 661–750) and arguably became part of the normative vision for later jurists contending with the challenge of governing amidst diversity. An expanding imperial polity will by its very nature come into contact with new lands and people. The early model of cleansing, if applied in an imperial context, would not have worked, and instead would have been counter-productive to an expanding polity. Indeed, cleansing in the years of expansion would have undercut the utilization and productivity of the new lands that came under imperial control. It is therefore not surprising that as political aspirations shifted from merely securing existence to expanding influence, a pluralist ethic became an increasingly important component of the vision of the formal enterprise of governance. But it was a pluralist ethic bounded and delimited by the aspirations of empire. That ethic, embedded in an imperial framework, became a more significant constitutive feature not only of the imperial enterprise of governance, but also of the legal arguments and models used to regulate relationships with the Other. The lease/rent and treaty/tax models offer two examples of how to govern amidst an expanding enterprise of governance in which diversity was a constitutive feature of the enterprise itself.

The above analysis of the models of cleansing, lease/rent, and treaty/tax suggests a close relationship between legal argument and the enterprise of governance. Additionally, this inquiry into the early imperial history of the Islamic polity has revealed the imperial background that arguably animated Muslim jurists as they developed legal doctrines concerned with the regulation of diverse populations within the Muslim polity. As suggested below, the *dhimmī* rules assume a particular legal intelligibility when viewed in light of the early period of Muslim conquest and expansion of the Arabian Peninsula, the Levant, Iraq, Iran, and Egypt. In the process of conquest, Muslims encountered Christians in both Egypt and Syria, Zoroastrians in Persia, and smaller groups of Jews in various locations. The process of incorporating these groups within an expanding Muslim empire contributed to the ways in which Qur'ānic verses and *ḥadīth* traditions were brought to bear upon the development

[73] Donner, *Early Islamic Conquests*, 240.

of a legal regime for an imperial enterprise of governance that was forced to contend with diversity.

1.3 ISLAMIC UNIVERSALISM, EMPIRE, AND GOVERNANCE

This section further expands on the background values Muslim jurists managed when deciding how to regulate non-Muslims living in Islamic lands. Those values drew not only upon the history of imperial expansion, but also on the ideal of universalism. This rendered empire and expansion normative for jurists who contended with the existence of *dhimmīs* as part of their legal vision of an imperial model of Islamic government. In other words, the background value of Islamic universalism and the historical model of imperial expansion provided the normative framework and conceptual content (sometimes in tension with each other) that informed how jurists developed rules on the *dhimmī*. These background factors were thereby constitutive components of the intelligibility of the *dhimmī* rules.

An ethic of universalism is not unique to Islam. It is an ethic common to most traditions that are deemed to benefit all of humanity. Such traditions can be religious, as evidenced by Christians seeking to create a world that correlates with values and ideals that emanate from their tradition. For instance, James D. Hunter recognizes that for a Christian, engaging and changing the world to reflect the values of Christianity is an important feature of being a committed Christian: "To be Christian is to be obliged to engage the world, pursuing God's restorative purposes over all of life, individual and corporate, public and private."[74] How that engagement with the world manifests itself, though, is a different matter. For instance, eliding Christian ideals with legal theory, Hugo Grotius expounded a natural law theory in a manner that effectively justified Dutch colonialism.[75] As Barbara Arneil indicates, many have viewed Grotius' natural law theory as linked directly to his views on imperialism, in particular Dutch imperial aspirations.

The imperative to engage the world in terms of Christian values also explains the extent of Christian-inspired missionary activity around the world. In Africa, for instance, the increase of US-based Christian missionary activity has prompted one scholar to suggest that the

[74] James Davison Hunter, *To Change the World* (Oxford: Oxford University Press, 2010), 4.

[75] Barbara Arneil, "John Locke, Natural Law and Colonialism," *History of Political Thought* 13, no. 4 (1992): 587–603, 590–1.

new millennium is the "greatest missionary era."[76] Christian Non-Governmental Organisations (NGOs) in Africa have been able to gain a significant foothold in light of international changes in development policy, which emphasize a reduced role for the state and an increased role for non-state actors, such as voluntary organizations and NGOs.[77] The role of missionary NGOs in the new development context raises important questions about how their missionary activities are folded into the foreign policy agendas of different developed states, such as the United States, which utilizes such organizations as part of its own foreign policy. Julie Hearn writes that in Africa, the United States Government

> has played a leading role in promoting NGOs, and distributes some forty per cent of its global development assistance to them. This can be very clearly seen in Kenya, where some ninety per cent of its aid programme, administered by the United States Agency for International Development (USAID), is channeled through NGOs and the private sector. Of the NGOs with which USAID works, US evangelical missions are a significant constituency, both as direct grantees and, more generally, in furthering the US government's broad policy goals.[78]

Other universalist claims might resonate in more political than religious terms, and yet nonetheless share with other universalist value systems an imperial potential. For instance, with the fall of the Berlin Wall in 1989 and the end of the Cold War, many heralded the end of the twentieth century as a victory for democracy. Some, such as Francis Fukuyama, went so far as to proclaim unabashedly, if not hubristically, the end of history. He meant the triumph of liberal democracy for the purpose of creating political order and stability while ensuring the well-being of individuals living in a polity together.[79] Relying on a teleological notion of history—"a directional evolution of human societies"—he offered an empirical analysis that supported his normative claim about the adequacy of liberal democratic institutions.[80] Addressing his critics five years later, he characterized his normative claim as follows:

> [L]iberal democracy and free markets constitute the best regime, or more precisely the best of the available alternative ways of organizing human societies . . . It most fully (though not completely) satisfies the most basic human longings, and thereby can be expected to be more universal

[76] Julie Hearn, "The 'Invisible' NGO: US Evangelical Missions in Kenya," *Journal of Religion in Africa* 32, no. 1 (2002): 32–60, 32.
[77] Hearn, "The 'Invisible' NGO," 33.
[78] Hearn, "The 'Invisible' NGO," 34.
[79] Francis Fukuyama, *The End of History and the Last Man* (New York: Free Press, 1992).
[80] Francis Fukuyama, "Reflections on *The End of History*: Five Years Later," *History & Theory* 34, no. 2 (1995): 27–43, 27.

> and more durable than other regimes or other principles of political organization.[81]

His normative claim incorporates a view of liberal democracy as having a universal appeal.

Yet in light of political events since the publication of his book, Fukuyama revealed the ways in which his normative claims about liberal democracy and free markets can offer ideological cover to the imperatives of empire. For instance, after the US-led invasions of Afghanistan and Iraq and the electoral victory of Hamas, Fukuyama was asked about the then-prevailing US foreign policy of spreading democracy. Fukuyama critiqued it, but principally because it might work to America's foreign-policy disadvantage. He wrote at that time:

> It is a flawed strategy because democracy is going to make problems worse, as in the case of Hamas, in the short run. That does not mean democracy is not some ultimate part of an effective policy. One of the ways you deal with the underlying problem of terrorism is by letting the Islamists grow up and get used to the realities of power. This certainly can be dangerous, because, in the end, the way they exercise that power may well be against the interests of the West.[82]

In other words, his commitment to democracy remains tied to a particular set of distinctively American or Western interests that are exported abroad.[83] Moreover, democracy promotion can have the effect of perpetuating the hegemonic authority of the status quo. Political scientists who study the Middle East have suggested that attempts to promote democracy in the region have more often than not preserved the authoritarian status quo. For instance, 2005 and 2006 were considered by many leading officials in the Bush administration to be an "Arab democratic spring," though they certainly pale in comparison to what has transpired in the region since January 2011. Yet the implication of increased democratization in countries such as Egypt and Jordan is suspect to say the least. Asli Bali, writing about the Egyptian elections in 2005, raises questions about the meaningfulness of democracy when authoritarian regimes "accommodate elections without relinquishing their grip on power."[84] Ellen Lust, writing about Jordanian elections, concludes that far from destabilizing authoritarian regimes, elections

[81] Fukuyama, "Reflections on *The End of History*," 29.

[82] Francis Fukuyama, "There are No Short Cuts to '*The End of History*'," *New Perspectives Quarterly* 23, no. 2 (2006): 35–8, 36.

[83] Fukuyama, "There are No Short Cuts," 37.

[84] Asli Bali, "From Subjects to Citizens? The Shifting Paradigm of Electoral Authoritarianism in Egypt," *Middle East Law and Governance* 1, no. 1 (2009): 38–89, 39.

have the effect of stabilizing them by casting the election itself as a mode of patronage distribution. If authoritarian elections are principally about the distribution of patronage, Lust concludes, international efforts to promote democracy "provide yet more resources to become the basis of electoral competition over patronage."[85] Democracy promotion, therefore, has the potential to serve and maintain a hegemonic imperative. In the cases of Egypt and Jordan, the hegemonic imperative was to maintain authoritarian control through the promotion of indices of democracy, such as elections.

The Islamic tradition has no shortage of materials professing that the Qur'ān and prophetic message were not just for the Arabs of Medina, but rather for all of humanity. Qur'ānic verses can be read as characterizing the Qur'ān and the prophetic mission of Muḥammad as having universal appeal and aspirations. In one verse in which the Qur'ān addresses Muḥammad's mission, the verse describes his mission in terms of the aspiration of the Qur'ānic message: "Say. . . This Qur'ān has been revealed to me so that by it I can warn you and whoever it may reach (*wa man balagha*)."[86] Later exegetes interpreted this verse to give an expansive import to Muḥammad's prophecy and the aspiration of the Qur'ānic message. For instance, al-Ṭabarī (d. 310/923) held that the warning the Prophet was to issue concerned God's punishment of all those who disbelieve. That warning extended beyond the confines of the Arabian Peninsula, where Muḥammad was met with opposition; it applied to all people, without limitation (*sā'ir al-nās*) since there is no end to effectuating the Qur'ānic aspirations (*in lam yantahin ilā al-ʿamal bi mā fīhi*).[87] The later exegete al-Qurṭubī (d. 671/1273) explained the normative implications of the universal aspiration of the Qur'ānic message. To have the Qur'ān and the Prophet's tradition reach others was to make a normative claim upon their obedience and allegiance. In other words, once faced with the message of the Qur'ān, people could not deny its existence or claim ignorance of it. Rather, according to al-Qurṭubī, for the Qur'ān and the Prophet's tradition (*sunna*) to reach people was immediately to imply that those people are commanded by God to accede to the values and requirements elaborated therein (*tablīgh al-Qur'ān wa al-sunna ma'mūr bihimā*).[88]

85 Ellen Lust-Okar, "Reinforcing Informal Institutions through Authoritarian Elections: Insights from Jordan," *Middle East Law and Governance* 1, no. 1 (2009): 3–37, 36–7.

86 Qur'ān 6:19.

87 Muḥammad b. Jarīr al-Ṭabarī, *Tafsīr al-Ṭabarī min kitābihi Jāmiʿ al-Bayān ʿan Ta'wil Āy al-Qurʿān*, eds Bashshār ʿAwād Maʿrūf and ʿIṣām Fāris al-Ḥarastānī (Beirut: Mu'assasat al-Risāla, 1994), 3:231.

88 Muḥammad b. Aḥmad al-Qurṭubī, *al-Jāmiʿ li Aḥkām al-Qur'ān* (Beirut: Dār al-Kutub al-ʿIlmiyya, 1993), 6:257.

The universalist ethos of Islam offered jurists and rulers a normative vision or telos to be manifested in the world through an imperial model of formal governance. The historical record suggests that such imperial ambitions were more often aspirations than real; indeed, some have argued that universalist ambitions were often limited by the highly contingent contexts in which they were invoked.[89] If this study were a political history, the disjunction between aspiration and reality would be an important feature of this analysis. Given the focus on the jurists and their jurisprudence, however, the aim here is to understand the imagined political norms that animated the way jurists developed their legal doctrines.

For instance, Khalid Blankinship, writing about early Islamic expansion under the Umayyad Dynasty, argues that the Umayyad Dynasty (r. 41–132/661–750) based its legitimacy in large part on its effort to manifest a universalist Islamic faith through conquest and expansion, or through what he calls the "Jihad State." From a purely pragmatic perspective, conquest provided the Umayyads sufficient spoils of war with which to pay their soldiers and feed the imperial coffers. As the Muslims conquered more land and taxed non-Muslims, the revenues provided financial support to uphold and expand the empire.[90] By linking conquest to the universalist Islamic ethos using the *jihād* ethic, the Umayyads converted what might have been viewed as an opportunist use of force into an imperial mission legitimated and justified by reference to Islam and the fulfillment of God's will on earth.

The non-Muslim living under the authority of a Muslim polity presented to Muslim jurists the fact of diversity to which the law had to respond. On the one hand, the *Ridda* Wars emphasized the importance of maintaining the coherence and spread of the Islamic message (its universal ethos) by preserving and extending the Islamic imperium. On the other hand, the importance of cultivating lands for the empire's economic well-being forced jurists to contend with the implication on an Islamic universalism of permitting non-Muslims to reside in Muslim lands and retain their faith commitments. As Muslim forces continued to expand the Islamic empire, they soon found themselves to be a minority ruling over regions populated by a majority of non-Muslims. Conversion to Islam may certainly have reduced the disparity, but as Richard Bulliet

[89] Ira M. Lapidus, "Between Universalism and Particularism: The Historical Bases of Muslim Communal, National, and Global Identities," *Global Networks* 1, no. 1 (2001): 37–55.

[90] Although the *jizya* offered an important source of tax revenue for the Muslim polity, it was not always applied in fact. Khalid Yahya Blankinship, *The End of the Jihad State: The Reign of Hisham Ibn ʿAbd al-Malik and the Collapse of the Umayyads* (Albany: State University of New York Press, 1994), 23, 27.

and others have suggested, conversion to Islam seems to have occurred gradually over generations.[91] As a minority ruling over a majority of non-Muslims, Muslim forces required the cooperation of local populations to cultivate lands and collect taxes, as noted above. In other words, imperial expansion had to be envisioned and framed in light of both the fact of diversity and an Islamic universalist ethos.

The result was a pluralist approach to governance of which the *dhimmī* rules were symptoms. Indeed, helping to negotiate the tension between empire and universalism was one of the fundamental tasks the *dhimmī* rules fulfilled.[92] *Dhimmīs* were, on the one hand, excluded from the *Muslim community* because of their difference in faith. On the other hand, *dhimmīs* were included in the *Muslim-ruled polity* because of their physical residence and payment of the *jizya* for the benefit of the governing enterprise. Legal doctrines regarding the *dhimmī* reflected this insider–outsider duality. For instance, the *dhimmīs' jizya* liability provided a significant tax base for supporting the Muslims who fought the *jihād* to expand the empire. At the same time, as noted below, the *jizya* presented an opportunity to hierarchize society along confessional lines to uphold the superiority of the Islamic message and its adherents over and against all Others. Premodern historians noted that under the Umayyad regime, *dhimmīs* began to convert to Islam. With their conversion, Islamic law rendered them immune from any *jizya* tax burden, thereby diminishing the empire's tax revenue. However, historical records indicate that the Umayyads nonetheless continued to impose the *jizya* on newly converted Muslims, a position that aroused considerable controversy given its departure from the prevailing legal requirements about the cessation of *jizya* liability upon conversion.[93] Before their conversion, these new Muslims were mere residents in the Muslim polity. After their conversion they became more than residents; they were insiders to the Muslim community. The *dhimmī* as insider is entitled to the same protections as Muslims, but the *dhimmī* as outsider is a reminder of the ongoing universalizing mission of the Islamic faith. Conversion becomes the mark of the mission's success. To continue taxing newly converted Muslims with the *jizya*, therefore, prioritized empire over universalism—a

[91] Richard Bulliet, *Conversion to Islam in the Medieval Period: An Essay in Quantitative History* (Cambridge: Harvard University Press, 1979); Michael G. Morony, "The Age of Conversions: A Reassessment," in *Conversion and Continuity: Indigenous Christian Communities in Islamic Lands, Eighth to Eighteenth Centuries*, eds Michael Gervers and Ramzi J. Bikhazi (Toronto: Pontifical Institute of Medieval Studies, 1990), 135–50. For demographic accounts of the experience of non-Muslims under Islamic rule, see Courbage and Fargues, *Christians and Jews Under Islam*.

[92] Blankinship, *The End of the Jihad State*, 3–13.

[93] Blankinship, *The End of the Jihad State*, 87–9, 114.

prioritization that jurists criticized. Consequently, the *dhimmī* offers an important site for us to consider the scope to which the law generally, and Islamic law specifically, can and must include, accommodate, and marginalize minorities, where the prevailing enterprise of governance is characterized by a universalizing ethos made manifest through forms of domination, whether conquest, empire, or otherwise.

1.4 EMPIRE, UNIVERSALISM, AND SHARĪʿA AS RULE OF LAW

The brief example above illustrates that, as the ruling authority's legitimacy was tied to its adherence to Sharīʿa,[94] the development of Sharīʿa-based doctrines such as the *dhimmī* rules were informed by jurists' vision of empire as the telos of Islamic government. Political legitimacy may have been dependent upon the ruler's adherence to the law, but the content of the law was also in many cases influenced by the prevailing enterprise of governance. A universalist, imperial, theo-political agenda informed and influenced how jurists structured and justified the entitlements and protections *dhimmīs* could expect as members of an Islamic polity. Sharīʿa as Rule of Law reminds us that not only did Sharīʿa-based doctrines constitute the legitimacy of the sovereign enterprise of governance, but also a political theory of empire contributed to the content and intelligibility of the *dhimmī* rules. Sharīʿa as Rule of Law recognizes that *fiqh* doctrines such as the *dhimmī* rules were constituted in the context of a ruling power governing over a diverse region, whose legitimacy was deeply tied to an Islamic universalist and imperial ethos. As the empire spread to include considerable numbers of other religious groups, questions arose about their place within an Islamically defined polity. Those questions could not be and were not separable from the underlying political theory of a universalist empire.

For example, in a reported tradition, the Prophet rejected the possibility that there could be two faiths in the Arabian Peninsula. This particular tradition raised for jurists important questions about who can live in the Arabian Peninsula. According to Yohanan Friedmann, Muslim forces fought Arab *polytheists* without offering any truce options, but whether Muslims could offer truce options to Arab *Jews* or Arab *Christians* was a matter of dispute. Generally, the People of the Book (i.e., Jews and

[94] Wael B. Hallaq, *Sharīʿa: Theory, Practice, and Transformations* (Cambridge: Cambridge University Press, 2009), 131–2; Knut S. Vikør, *Between God and the Sultan: A History of Islamic Law* (Oxford: Oxford University Press, 2005), 185.

Christians) were entitled to maintain their religion while paying the *jizya*, and thereby receive the protection of the Muslim empire. But not all Jews and Christians were necessarily afforded this treatment. Muslim jurists debated whether Arab Jews and Christians could remain non-Muslim and reside in Arab lands by paying the *jizya*.

Some jurists argued that the *jizya* option only applied to those who could trace their genealogy to the tribe of Israel—the Banū Isrāʾīl. Among the Jews and Christians were those who were descendents of the original tribe of Israel; these were the people who received the message of God through Moses and Jesus and passed it along to their subsequent generations. Only those descended from the Banū Isrāʾīl, according to premodern Muslim jurists, were granted the option of claiming *dhimmī* status.[95] A second group of Jews and Christians, they held, were ethnically unrelated to Banū Isrāʾīl, such as Christians and Jews of Arab descent.[96] This latter group was generally denied any option to claim *dhimmī* status and pay the *jizya*.

The ethnic limit existed alongside a time limit. Muslim theologians and jurists held that at an unspecified, but nonetheless very real, point in time the adherents of Judaism and Christianity corrupted (*taḥrīf/tabdīl*) the divine messages given to Moses and Jesus. According to Friedmann, "[c]ertain jurists maintain[ed] that after this corruption took place, it was not legitimate anymore to embrace Judaism or Christianity. Those who converted to these two religions at this late stage are therefore ineligible for *dhimmī* status."[97]

Jurists who gave legal effect to the issues of time and ethnicity based their position on the historical treatment of Arab Christians in the Arabian Peninsula. For instance, historical records indicate that the second caliph ʿUmar b. al-Khattāb (r. 13–23/634–644) held that Arab Christians were not People of the Book, and he was not prepared to tolerate their existence until they embraced Islam. Indeed, he ushered in a policy of expelling non-Muslim Arabs from the Arabian Peninsula, leading the Banū Najrān tribe of Arab Christians to leave the region.[98] This policy reflected the universalizing ethos of Islam (given the issue of textual corruption and the elision of ethnicity and religious identity) and

[95] Yohanan Friedmann, "Classification of Unbelievers in Sunni Muslim Law and Tradition," *Jerusalem Studies in Arabic & Islam* 22 (1998): 163–95.

[96] Friedmann, "Classification of Unbelievers in Sunni Muslim Law and Tradition," 167; idem, *Tolerance and Coercion in Islam*, 65–9, who associates this restrictive view principally with al-Shāfiʿī.

[97] Friedmann, *Tolerance and Coercion in Islam*, 60.

[98] Goddard, "Christian–Muslim Relations," 196.

the use of expulsion in furtherance of an imperial agenda that manifested a universalist ethos.

Yet, the universalist ethos had its limits, especially when the imperative of empire was jeopardized. For instance, despite ʿUmar's attitude against non-Muslim Arabs, he could not sacrifice empire at all costs. Even ʿUmar had to recognize that a hostile attitude toward the non-Muslim Arabs might prove harmful to the efficacy of Islamic imperial rule and expansion. So while the Banū Najrān may have left, ʿUmar allowed another Arab tribe, the Banū Taghlib, to retain their Christian faith without expulsion from the Arab Peninsula. Notably, the Banū Taghlib was a strong tribe, and threatened to join the ranks of the Byzantine Empire if they were not given favorable treatment under the Islamic regime. There is some suggestion that ʿUmar "tolerated" Banū Taghlib because of this tactical concern. So, while he was dissatisfied with allowing Arab Christians to maintain their faith in the Arabian Peninsula, he nonetheless incorporated Banū Taghlib into the Muslim polity for reasons having to do with preserving the imperial enterprise of governance.[99] ʿUmar remained fully aware of the challenge the Banū Taghlib posed to the coherence of a universalist faith tradition, though. Consequently, while he "tolerated" their presence in the empire, he also placed certain limits on them, arguably in furtherance of an Islamic universalism. For instance, he decreed that they could not baptize their children.[100] Furthermore, the fourth caliph, ʿAlī b. Abī Ṭālib (r. 35–40/656–661), prohibited Muslim men from marrying the women of Banū Taghlib because he did not know whether the tribe embraced Christianity before or after the corruption of their tradition.[101]

The conflicting examples of Banū Najrān and Banū Taghlib illustrate how both the universalizing ethos of Islam (e.g., the expulsion of Banū Najrān) and the imperative of empire (e.g., the concession to Banū Tahglib) provided the circumstances of intelligibility to the *dhimmī* rules. The legal rules regarding ethnicity, time, and religious identity demarcated when rulers had to fight non-Muslims and when they could countenance possibilities of co-existence, on condition of paying the *jizya*.[102] The

[99] Interestingly, the Banū Taghlib did not want to pay the *jizya*, as they considered it humiliating for an Arab tribe to pay that particular tax. Consequently, ʿUmar conceded to their demands and allowed them to pay the Muslim tax, but at double the rate. Some studies suggest that the doubled rate of the Muslim tax might have approximated the *jizya* rate, but was applied under a different name to save the Banū Taghlib any sense of embarrassment or humiliation. Friedmann, "Classification of Unbelievers," 171–2.

[100] Friedmann, "Classification of Unbelievers," 170–1.

[101] Friedmann, "Classification of Unbelievers," 172.

[102] The juristic discussion surrounding the Prophetic tradition about the Arab Peninsula contributed to a vast debate about who can and cannot be non-Muslim, in terms of an Islamic universalistic ethos that was made manifest in the Arab world and

notable example was the Banū Taghlib; the demands of empire required modification of the general rules. However, while the Banū Taghlib could remain in the Muslim polity, they were subjected to specific regulations that indirectly had the effect of upholding a universalist Islamic message, while maintaining the efficacy of an imperial enterprise of governance that could not ignore the pragmatics of expansion.

As the empire expanded, the changing contexts presented new challenges to the development of legal doctrines regulating the scope of any pluralist commitment. For instance, as Muslims conquered parts of Iraq and Persia, they came into contact with Magians, which generally connotes Zoroastrians. Although the Qur'ānic verse on *jizya* technically applies only to those who have received scriptural revelation, the contingencies of conquest led Muslim conquerors to apply the rules of *jizya* and the contract of *dhimma* to those outside the Abrahamic traditions. The practice of taking *jizya* from Zoroastrians may be explained by simple pragmatics, but was legally justified by reference to traditions of the Prophet in which he was reported to have done so. However, this is not to suggest that the Zoroastrians were treated similarly to Christians and Jews. According to some jurists, since Zoroastrians were deemed equivalent to polytheists, Muslims could take the *jizya* from them, but could not marry their women or eat their meat.[103] The fact of diversity and the imperative of imperial management may have led to an increase in the scope of inclusion. The limiting content of that inclusion, though, reflects a marginalization that vindicates the universalism of the Islamic message while providing for efficient imperial management.

1.5 THE CONTRACT OF PROTECTION: A LEGAL INSTRUMENT OF POLITICAL INCLUSION AND MARGINALIZATION

The tension between the universal ethos and the fact of diversity brought on by an imperial agenda was jurisprudentially negotiated

expanded thereafter. Some would suggest that the Prophetic tradition need not connote a principle of discrimination at all. Muhammad Hamidullah argues that this Prophetic tradition reflects the Prophet's political aim to secure a region of safety, security, and homogeneity for Muslims struggling to survive. Muhammad Hamidullah, "Status of Non-Muslims in Islam," *Majallat al-Azhar* 45, no. 8 (1973): 6–13, 10. While this perspective is important for its interpretive contribution to the corpus of the Islamic tradition, it does not undermine the more general argument here about how the tradition reflects the challenge of governing in a pluralist setting.

[103] Michael G. Morony, *Iraq after the Muslim Conquest* (Princeton: Princeton University Press, 1984), 301. See also Freidenreich, *Foreigners and Their Food.*

by jurists using the contract of protection, called in Arabic the *ʿaqd al-dhimma*. They used the contract of protection to move from the fact of diversity to a commitment to a pluralistic ethic of imperial governance. The *dhimmī*, as non-Muslim permanent resident, paid the *jizya* and thereby entered the contract of protection. This contract governed the relations between the Muslim polity and the *dhimmīs*. This is not to suggest, as a historical matter, that each and every *dhimmī* signed or otherwise consented to the terms of a specific contract. Rather, the contract provided a paradigm within which jurists developed legal expectations in the form of regulations for the *dhimmīs*, Muslims, and officials who oversaw the enterprise of governance. The *dhimmīs*' rights and entitlements in the Muslim polity, we will learn, did not inhere in the *dhimmī* as an individual, but rather were derived from a contract whose terms and content were the subject of considerable legal debate over the centuries. The contract of protection, in Islamic legal theory, served both political and legal functions. It was political in that it was the conceptual device jurists used to reconcile an Islamic universalist ethos with the fact of diversity arising from a commitment to empire. It represented the political agreement between the Muslim sovereign and the non-Muslim community in the interest of the latter's relative freedom and the sovereign's efficient management of the empire. Legally, the contract was the site of debates about the scope of the *dhimmī*'s freedom in the empire. In other words, the contract represented a juridified political site for the legal debates about the content of what we are calling the *dhimmī* rules.

The idea of the contract of protection had its historical provenance in the oft-discussed "Pact of ʿUmar." This pact is said to have been the product of negotiations between the second caliph ʿUmar and Christians in Syria. In this pact, the Christian leaders wrote to ʿUmar outlining the conditions they would fulfill in order to receive protection under the new Muslim imperium. This pact was invoked at various points in Islamic history as a means of regulating society and appeasing more conservative Muslim forces that demanded strict application of the law. This pact included conditions such as:

- Non-Muslims will not build new places of worship;
- Non-Muslims will not replace dilapidated places of worship in the areas where Muslims live;
- Muslims can take refuge in non-Muslim places of worship and should be treated hospitably for three days;
- Non-Muslims will not teach their children the Qur'ān;

- Non-Muslims will not prevent relatives from converting to Islam;
- Non-Muslims will not ride upon saddles or carry weapons.[104]

There is intense discussion in the secondary literature about the Pact of 'Umar's historical authenticity. Did it originate during the reign of 'Umar b. al-Khaṭṭāb or was it a later invention retroactively associated with 'Umar—the caliph who famously led the initial imperial expansion—to endow the contract of *dhimma* with greater normative weight? A.S. Tritton has suggested that the Pact is a fabrication. He writes that if the Pact were authentic, then Muslim conquerors would have known about it and applied its terms to their agreements with their non-Muslim subjects. Yet later treaties from different regions suggest that the provisions of the Pact of 'Umar were not applied uniformly.[105] Dennet, on the other hand, believes that the Pact of 'Umar was no different from any other treaty negotiated in that period, and that it is well within reason that the Pact we have today, as preserved in al-Ṭabarī's chronicle, is an authentic version of that early treaty.[106] Milka Levy-Rubin, in her superb study of early Islamic surrender agreements, including the Pact of 'Umar, suggests that the terms found therein have pre-Islamic origins. With such comparative corroboration of the terms of such agreements, Levy-Rubin argues that early surrender agreements such as the Pact of

[104] For a list of such conditions reportedly in the original Pact of 'Umar and recorded in later agreements with the non-Muslim community, see Hunwick, "The Rights of *Dhimmis* to Maintain a Place of Worship," 152–4; Bosworth, "The Concept of *Dhimma* in Early Islam," 46; Richard J.H. Gottheil, "Dhimmis and Moslems in Egypt," in *Old Testament and Semitic Studies*, eds Robert Francis Harber, Francis Brown and George Foot Moore, 2 vols (Chicago: University of Chicago Press, 1908), 1:353–414, 382–4.

[105] Despite 'Umar's ban on employing non-Muslims in government posts, non-Muslims held significant government offices throughout Islamic history. The ban on building new churches arose consistently after 150/767, but not before, thereby suggesting that imputing such bans to 'Umar is likely a later development. Early historical sources such as those written by al-Ṭabarī (d. 310/923) and al-Balādhurī (d. 278–9/892) do not mention restrictions on dress, again suggesting that such provisions were later creations that were projected backward to the time of 'Umar to give the provisions greater normative force. A.S. Tritton, *The Caliphs and their Non-Muslim Subjects: A Critical Study of the Covenant of 'Umar* (London: Frank Cass and Co., Ltd, 1970). For those following Tritton's analysis, see, Ben-Shammai, "Jew Hatred in the Islamic Tradition and the Koranic Exegesis," 161–9; Hunwick, "The Rights of *Dhimmis* to Maintain a Place of Worship," 134; Gudrun Kramer, "Dhimmi ou Citoyen: Réflexions reformists sur le statut de non-musulmans en société Islamique," in *Entre Reforme Sociale et Mouvement National*, ed. Alain Roussilon (Cairo: CEDEJ, 1995), 577–90. Gottheil, "Dhimmis and Moslems in Egypt," 357, who predates Tritton, also indicated as early as 1908 that the Pact of 'Umar was possibly fabricated.

[106] Daniel C. Dennett, *Conversion and the Poll Tax in Early Islam* (Cambridge: Harvard University Press, 1950), 63–4. For early versions of the document, see Muḥammad b. Jarīr al-Ṭabarī, *Ta'rīkh al-Ṭabarī*, 2:448–9; Ibn 'Asākir, *Ta'rīkh Madīnat Damashq*, ed. 'Umar b. Gharāma al-'Amrawī (Beirut: Dār al-Fikr, 1995), 2:178–79.

ʿUmar are historically authentic.[107] This study is not concerned with the authenticity of the Pact as such. Rather, of significant interest is how the Pact, as part of the imagined conquest history, contributed to the way in which later legal developments were concretized and legitimated.

For instance, the Pact of ʿUmar was often reissued by subsequent rulers as a means to contain the upward mobility of non-Muslims, and thereby uphold the legitimacy of the ruler in the eyes of the Muslim elite.[108] The Pact also offered a point of reference for ongoing debates about the scope of *dhimmī* duties and the degree to which *dhimmīs* could be constrained in new and different ways. For instance, under the Latrines Decree in nineteenth-century Yemen, *dhimmīs* were required to clean the latrines in the city. Muslims were considered above such labor, and so the task was delegated to non-Muslims. But to impose this duty on *dhimmīs* went beyond the express terms of the Pact of ʿUmar. Some jurists held that the Pact set for all time the rights and duties of the *dhimmīs,* and so the *dhimmīs* could not be burdened with such tasks. Yet others, such as al-Shawkānī (d. 1255/1839), said the Pact represents a historical example that did not preclude the development of new rights and duties of *dhimmīs* as circumstances changed. This debate, and al-Shawkānī's point in particular, shows how the contract of protection offered a site of legal debate where Muslim jurists reflected on the ongoing challenge of governing a Muslim polity amidst the fact of diversity.[109]

1.6 A GENEALOGY OF THE *DHIMMĪ* RULES: *DHIMMĪS* IN THE QURʾĀN AND SUNNA

As noted above, *dhimmīs* were non-Muslims who lived permanently in regions under Muslim rule. The term *dhimmī* is related to the term *dhimma,* which refers to a pledge of security.[110] In this context it connotes both the pledge that non-Muslims made (either expressly or impliedly) with the Muslim ruling establishment, and the latter's commitment to ensure the *dhimmīs*' protection. Pursuant to the doctrine on the contract of protection, or the *ʿaqd al-dhimma*, the *dhimmīs* agreed to abide by certain conditions, in return, they were allowed to live peacefully in the Islamic empire. The basis and authority for the contract of *dhimma* and its conditions (implicit or otherwise) were found in scriptural and legal sources dating from the early Islamic centuries.

[107] Milka Levy-Rubin, *Non-Muslims in the Early Islamic Empire: From Surrender to Coexistence* (Cambridge: Cambridge University Press, 2011).

[108] Haddad, "*Ahl al-Dhimma*," 174.

[109] Sadan, "The 'Latrines Decree.'"

[110] Ibn Manẓūr, *Lisān al-ʿArab*, 12:221.

For instance, the Qur'ān invokes a special status for certain non-Muslims living under Muslim rule in Qur'ān 9:29:

> Fight those who do not believe in God or the final day, do not prohibit what God and His prophet have prohibited, do not believe in the religion of truth, from among those who are given revelatory books, until they pay the *jizya* from their hands in a state of submission.[111]

This verse raises various issues such as: who are those given revelatory books, what is the *jizya,* and what does it mean to be in a state of submission?

First, who are the people given revealed books? The interpretive tradition suggests that the people intended by this verse were the Jews and Christians, as they were (and still are) understood within Islamic theology to have received divine revelation.[112] Identifying which Christians and Jews could take advantage of the *jizya,* for premodern jurists, required inquiring into both the history and genealogy of those claiming special status, as already discussed.

Second, what was the *jizya*? This was a special poll tax non-Muslim permanent residents paid to maintain their faith and live peacefully within the Muslim empire.[113] Notably, premodern jurists debated whether only Jews and Christians, as the People of the Book (*ahl al-kitāb*), were entitled to this option of peaceful coexistence within the Muslim empire upon payment of the *jizya*. As the historical tradition suggests, this entitlement was (not surprisingly) expanded to others as the Muslim empire grew. Consequently, when Muslims conquered Persia and encountered Zoroastrians, commanders allowed the local religious population there to reside peacefully in the empire and maintain their faith, as long as they paid the *jizya*. Likewise in India, when Muslims conquered that region, polytheists were allowed to pay the *jizya* and live a "tolerated" existence under Muslim rule.[114] This is not to suggest that the People of the Book and others were treated alike. Although all these groups were able to live peacefully within the Muslim empire on condition of payment of the *jizya,* the People of the Book were held in higher esteem than others. That higher esteem was reflected in legal doctrines. For

[111] Qur'ān, 9:29.

[112] In later periods of Islamic history, this term was extended to include others as well. For a general overview of the phrase and its Qur'ānic roots, see G. Vajda, "Ahl al- Kitāb," *Encyclopaedia of Islam*, eds P. Bearman et al.

[113] Studies have shown that the poll tax was not a Muslim invention. The Byzantine and Sassanian Empires both imposed a poll tax on Jews residing within their respective territory. See, Morony, *Iraq after the Muslim Conquest*, 306, 317–20.

[114] *Al-Fatāwā al-Alāmgirīyya = Al-Fatāwā al-Hindiyya fī Madhhab al-Imām al-Aʿẓam Abī Ḥanīfa al-Nuʿmān* (Beirut: Dār al-Maʿrifa, 1973), 2:244–5.

instance, Muslim men could marry the women of the People of the Book, but not the polytheists. Muslims could eat the meat slaughtered by People of the Book, but not by polytheists or Zoroastrians.[115] Those without revelation posed a tension in the law—they were "tolerated" but could not be embraced by Muslims in matters of kinship and trade.

The third issue is how premodern jurists understood what it meant for those paying the *jizya* to be in a "state of submission." Some held that it referred to being in a state of subordination, thereby characterizing the payment of *jizya* as a mechanism of subordination.[116] Indeed, the theme of subordination existed throughout the Islamic legal tradition. For instance, in his 1921 article, Richard Gottheil translated an essay written by a Muslim who recounted how the Prophet allegedly cautioned Muslims against trusting the non-Muslim.[117] For instance, al-Miqdād b. al-Aswad al-Kindī, a friend of the Prophet, was traveling one day with a Jewish man. When morning broke during their journey, al-Miqdād suddenly remembered something the Prophet said: "No Jew is on good terms with a Moslem unless he has up his sleeve some scheme to trap him." Al-Miqdād confronted his Jewish companion with his suspicion that the latter was planning some scheme. The Jewish man, taken by surprise, agreed to admit his scheme on the condition that al-Miqdād not harm him. When al-Miqdād promised, the Jewish traveler said "Since I have been traveling with you, I have been planning for you to lose [sic] your head, so that I might trample it under my foot."[118] Contrary to traditions of harmony, this one depicted the Prophet counseling cautious suspicion when encountering non-Muslims. Whether this tradition is authentic or not, it nonetheless reveals how Muslims writing after the early period of Islam considered the religious Other as posing a threat to the security and well-being of Muslims.

[115] Friedmann, "Classification of Unbelievers in Sunni Muslim Law and Tradition," 167; Gudrun Kramer, "Dhimmi or Citizen? Muslim–Christian Relations in Egypt," in *The Christian–Muslim Frontier: Chaos, Clash or Dialogue?* ed. Jorgen S. Nielsen (London: I.B. Tauris, 1998), 35–6; Morony, *Iraq After the Muslim Conquest*, 301; Freidenreich, *Foreigners and Their Food*, 146–50.

[116] Mahmoud M. Ayoub, "The Islamic Context of Muslim–Christian Relations," in *Conversion and Continuity: Indigenous Christian Communities in Islamic Lands, Eight to Eighteenth Centuries*, eds Michael Gervers and Ramzi Jibran Bikhazi (Toronto: Pontifical Institute of Mediaeval Studies, 1990), 461–77; Ziauddin Ahmed, "The Concept of Jizya in Early Islam," *Islamic Studies* 14, no. 4 (1975): 293–305; Bosworth, "The Concept of *Dhimma* in Early Islam," 1:37–54; M. Izzi Dien, *The Theory and the Practice of Market Law in Medieval Islam: A Study of* Kitāb Nisāb al-Iḥtisāb (Cambridge: E.J.W. Gibb Memorial Trust, 1997), 51–2; Haddad, *"Ahl al-Dhimma* ," 169–80. For an early exegetical commentary reflecting this attitude, see Abū Bakr al-Jaṣṣāṣ, *Aḥkām al-Qurʾān*, ed. ʿAbd al-Salām Muḥammad ʿAlī Shāhīn (Beirut: Dār al-Kutub al-ʿIlmiyya, 1994), 3:127–8.

[117] Gottheil, "An Answer to the Dhimmis," 417–18.

[118] Gottheil, "An Answer to the Dhimmis," 429–30.

Other jurists wrote that the reference to submission refers to how payment of the *jizya* was a symbolic act of acknowledging the legitimacy and imperium of the Sharīʿa under which the non-Muslim lived.[119] The Qur'ānic phrase was read, therefore, to ensure law, order, and authority, but not humiliation.[120] For instance, the premodern Ḥanbalī jurist Ibn Qudāma wrote that the permanent contract of protection for *dhimmīs* must meet two conditions: first, the payment of the *jizya* must be made on a regular basis; second, and most significantly, the contract must provide for the application of the laws of Islam (*iltizām aḥkām al-islām*), namely the *dhimmīs* acceptance of any rulings against them in terms of the enforcement of various claims, and their commitment to abstain from prohibited conduct.[121] An incident involving the Christian Arab tribe of the Banū Najrān offers a historical example that supports the law-and-order reading of the *jizya* verse. These Christians came to visit Muḥammad in order to establish a political relationship with him and his newfound polity. Although the Muslims and the Christians differed in their understanding of the nature of Christ, they agreed to disagree. On political matters, though, the Christians agreed to recognize the legitimacy of Muhammad's political authority and to pay taxes to him.[122] This historical example offered jurists a reconciliation of the claims of universal truth, sovereign authority, and effective governance amidst diversity using the legal model of treaty/tax.

A third position, held by jurists such as Fakhr al-Dīn al-Rāzī (d. 606/1209), was that the *jizya* requirement and other rules imposed on *dhimmīs* were intended to provide an incentive for the non-Muslims to convert. The purpose behind such provisions was not to humiliate or subjugate, but to incentivize conversion to Islam.[123] Humiliation or subordination may be unavoidable, but they were not the principal aim or purpose of the rules; rather, they were instrumental to the central objective of conversion to Islam.

In the aggregate, these different readings of the Qur'ānic verse suggest that as jurists debated how to govern amidst diversity, they contended

[119] Ahmad Dallal, "Yemeni Debates on the Status of Non-Muslims in Islamic Law," *Islam and Christian-Muslim Relations* 7, no. 2 (1996), 181–92, 189; Haddad, *"Ahl al-Dhimma"* 172–3.

[120] Haddad, *"Ahl al-Dhimma,"* 173, who refers to al-Māwardī in support of this position.

[121] 'Abd Allāh b. Aḥmad Ibn Qudāma, *al-Mughnī* (Beirut: Dār Iḥyā' al-Turāth al-ʿArabī, n.d.), 8:500.

[122] Goddard, "Christian-Muslim Relations," 196.

[123] Jane Dammen McAuliffe, "Fakhr al-Dīn al-Rāzī on Ayat al-Jizya and Ayat al-Sayf," in *Conversion and Continuity: Indigenous Christian Communities in Islamic Lands, Eight to Eighteenth Centuries*, eds Michael Gervers and Ramzi Jibran Bikhazi (Toronto: Pontifical Institute of Mediaeval Studies, 1990), 103–19.

with multiple and at times conflicting trends. Some trends dominated the debates on one legal dispute, while other trends informed a different legal issue. Each trend carried weight, but influenced legal outcomes differently depending on various circumstances associated with a particular issue.

1.7 CONCLUSION

This chapter set out to undermine the usefulness of "tolerance" as an organizing principle or concept for an analysis of the *dhimmī* rules. As various critics have argued, tolerance hides more than it reveals. In particular, it hides the relationships of power and governance that underlie most, if not all, debates about tolerance. Tolerance hides not only asymmetries of power between majority and minority populations, but it also pays too little attention to how those asymmetries are managed and even normalized at the intersection of law and the enterprise of governance. This study, therefore, acknowledges the significant limitations of "tolerance" as an organizing concept and instead delves into the details of legal debates about the *dhimmīs* to reveal how and to what extent the intelligibility of the *dhimmī* rules depends on viewing them as indices of the challenge of governing pluralistically through an imperial enterprise of governance that is legitimated by a universalist attitude toward humanity.

The *dhimmī* presents a site of contest between the aspirations of universalism and the logistical realities of empire. As discussed above, the feasibility of empire sometimes required that non-Muslims be permitted to live peacefully in the empire. To suggest otherwise would require cleansing the empire of diversity, which would actually work contrary to the management requirements of an empire. Yet, to permit the non-Muslim to remain non-Muslim in an Islamic polity might be seen as contrary to the ethic of an Islamic universalism. The contract of protection and the *dhimmī* rules offered important mechanisms by which to resolve this conflict. Consequently, the legal attempt to resolve this conflict of ethical imperatives cannot be reduced to a single theme, whether of persecution or harmony. Rather, as will be shown throughout this study, the intelligibility of the *dhimmī* rules for premodern Muslim jurists was based on the image of an imperial enterprise of governance that made manifest in a diverse world the universal message implicit in the Qur'ān and Muḥammad's prophetic mission.

2

Reason, Contract, and the Obligation to Obey: The *Dhimmī* as Legal Subject

As discussed in the introduction, Sharīʿa as Rule of Law is used in this study to connote a claim space about the demands of justice, where the intelligibility of any legal argument made from within that claim space is in part determined by the boundaries that help define and delimit that claim space. As will be discussed in Part 2 in greater detail, the claim space takes shape in light of a variety of factors, such as a curriculum of training, institutions of learning, and institutional bodies devoted to the settlement of disputes. Additionally, intelligibility is informed by the authoritative doctrines jurists developed and recorded in numerous volumes of *fiqh* books. The *dhimmī,* as a member of the Muslim polity, existed in a society in which these boundary-features of the Sharīʿa claim space were social facts, as was the *dhimmī*'s presence in the polity. The *dhimmī* was not only the object of legal debate, therefore, but in his or her very presence, constituted a certain factual reality that contributed to delimiting the claim space of Sharīʿa.

If Sharīʿa is understood to be a "religious" law, one might reasonably ask why the *dhimmī* should be subjected to a legal tradition that was not his own. In other words, to consider Sharīʿa as purely "religious" begs a fundamental (though very modern) question about the *dhimmī* and the Rule of Law*: why not hold the* dhimmīs, *whether Jew or Christian, to their own religious legal orders?* The question is intelligible if the "religious" is distinguished from the non-religious, or secular, and if the "religious" and the "secular" are considered to affect and govern different and separable aspects of life and social well-being. But the intelligibility of the question above is significantly diminished once Sharīʿa is understood as Rule of Law. If we appreciate the extent to which law is in a mutually constitutive relationship with the enterprise of governance, then Sharīʿa is not a "religious" tradition that merely regulates the private relationship between the believer and his or her God. Rather, Sharīʿa as a claim space about the demands of justice confounds the modern dichotomy between the secular and religious, and claims jurisdiction over the whole set of human affairs, whether private or public, "religious" or "secular."[1]

However, just because Sharīʿa as Rule of Law confounds entrenched conceptual dichotomies in contemporary traditions of law and politics does not mean that premodern jurists thought the entirety of Sharīʿa-based doctrines applied to *dhimmīs.* They created their own dichotomy between rules of ritual practice (*ʿibādāt*) and rules of general welfare (*muʿāmalāt*). Premodern jurists recognized that certain types of doctrines might be specific to Muslim ritual practice (*ʿibādāt*), while others regulated the kinds of affairs that can be the appropriate subject for general rules of obligations (*muʿāmalāt*). This dichotomy had various implications, including establishing a basis by which to limit the scope and extent to which the *dhimmī* was liable to Sharīʿa-based doctrines. This dichotomy allowed Muslim jurists

- to define the scope and extent to which the *dhimmī* was liable under Sharīʿa-based norms; and
- to justify the imposition of certain Sharīʿa-based obligations upon the *dhimmī.*

Examining how jurists theorized obligation to the law is crucial if we are to appreciate how and in what ways the *dhimmī* was construed as a legal subject under a Sharīʿa-based legal system. As will be outlined below, jurists developed competing theories to ascertain and explain how and to what extent *dhimmīs* were obligated to abide by Sharīʿa-based norms. To develop their theories, jurists reflected upon:

- the nature and capacity of human reason to know Sharīʿa-based values;
- whether or not human reason was shared across communities of faith; and
- whether or not the shared capacity of human reason was sufficient to justify imposing Sharīʿa-based obligations on the *dhimmī.*

Fundamentally at issue for the premodern jurists was whether or not there was a universal reason across humanity, and if so whether it was sufficient to justify obligations to Sharīʿa-based norms. As will be illustrated below, jurists agreed that Muslims and non-Muslims could equally reason to Sharīʿa-based values, but they disagreed about whether

[1] For a critique of the 'secular' as it relates to the 'religious', see Asad, *Formations of the Secular.*

that was sufficient to justify imposing Sharīʿa-based obligations on the *dhimmī*. Those who did not consider the shared capacity to reason as sufficient to justify imposing *fiqh* doctrines on the *dhimmī* required that *dhimmīs* also *acquiesce* to be subjected to Sharīʿa-based obligations.

To acquiesce to the full scope of Sharīʿa-based norms, though, left two options for the *dhimmī*. The first was conversion to Islam. In this case, the *dhimmī* no longer remained a *dhimmī* and instead shifted his status once he became Muslim. In the absence of conversion, the other model was based on contract. Under this model, the *dhimmī* did not convert to Islam, and instead undertook to live in an Islamically based enterprise of governance. Whether or not premodern jurists considered reason to be sufficient justification for holding *dhimmīs* to Sharīʿa-based obligations, jurists generally agreed that the *dhimmīs*' obligations and entitlements under the law were best characterized in terms of contract, namely the contract of protection (*ʿaqd al-dhimma*). For premodern Muslim jurists, the contract of protection was a mechanism that allowed the enterprise of governance to account for the fact of diversity, as it also ensured order and peace in an Islamic society. Consequently, the contract of protection was not merely a legal concept, but also functioned politically as a constitutive element of a pluralist enterprise of governance.

2.1 REASON AND THE OBLIGATION TO OBEY

The fundamental question jurists addressed when considering the imposition of Sharīʿa-based obligations upon the *dhimmī* had to do with whether and to what extent the *dhimmī* could be subjected to such norms. Since Sharīʿa-based norms concern both religious ritual (*ʿibādāt*) and matters of social ordering (*muʿāmalāt*), Muslim jurists often debated the extent to which the *dhimmī* should be subjected to the full scope of Sharīʿa-based doctrine. A corollary of this debate focused on how to determine which specific rules applied to the *dhimmīs*. Reviewing these debates is important because the scope of the *dhimmī*'s obligations and entitlements under the law will reveal how jurists understood the legal position, and thereby the social standing, of the *dhimmī* in the Muslim polity. In other words, to the extent Sharīʿa-based doctrines constituted the enterprise of governance, they did so in part by situating the *dhimmī* as both insider and outsider in terms of rules and regulations to be enforced by the ruling regime. Consequently, by explicating the scope to which the *dhimmī* was held to Sharīʿa-based norms, the jurists constituted the social, political, and legal standing of the *dhimmī* in an Islamic polity, and thereby gave content to the vision of an Islamic enterprise of governance that governs amidst diversity.

The debate about the extent to which non-Muslims were obligated (*taklīf*) to abide by Sharīʿa can be found in legal theory treatises (*uṣūl al-fiqh*) in which jurists addressed the general conditions under which one becomes obligated (*mukallaf*) to abide by the Sharīʿa. Certainly if our starting point is that Sharīʿa connotes a legal system, we might find this discussion about obligation somewhat redundant—law obviously would imply obligation. Nevertheless, the debates on obligation are important because they give content to the idea of being a legal subject; reveal the difference in the scope of obligation between Muslims and *dhimmīs* and lay bare key implications for understanding the conditions for being a full or partial participant in political society.

Sayf al-Dīn al-Āmidī (d. 631/1233) wrote that before one can be obligated under the law, he must have rational capacity (*ʿāqil*) and understand what it means to be obligated (*fāhim li'l-taklīf*).[2] These conditions are necessary in order for one to know and appreciate the nature of God, the obligations stemming from the divine discourse (*khiṭāb*), and the requirement to obey the divine will. In short, anyone who has the ability to know God and to know the requirement to obey the divine can be legitimately subjected to the Sharīʿa.[3]

Knowledge of both God and the requirement to obey the divine will, though, may differ in content and scope, depending on the way one defines his or her relationship to God and the divine message. For al-Āmidī, one's duties and entitlements may vary depending on whether he is Muslim or non-Muslim, since the two relate to God differently. Others argued, to the contrary, that all human beings have the same capacity to know what obligation means and to morally reason to the good and the bad (*ḥusn, qubḥ*). For the latter group, no distinction should be made between Muslims and non-Muslims for the purpose of determining whether someone is obligated to abide by the Sharīʿa. Rather, for this latter group, the universality of reason justified subjecting the *dhimmī* to Sharīʿa-based norms to the same degree and extent as Muslims.[4]

[2] Sayf al-Dīn al-Āmidī, *al-Iḥkām fī Uṣūl al-Aḥkām* (Beirut: Dār al-Fikr, 1997), 1:106–7.

[3] Al-Āmidī, *al-Iḥkām*, 1:107.

[4] On the debates about *ḥusn* and *qubḥ*, see Kevin Reinhart, *Before Revelation: The Boundaries of Muslim Moral Thought* (Albany: SUNY Press, 1995); Anver Emon, "Natural Law and Natural Rights in Islamic Law," *Journal of Law and Religion* 20, no. 2 (2004–2005): 351–95; idem, *Islamic Natural Law Theories* (Oxford: Oxford University Press, 2010). Others opposing this view on *ḥusn/qubḥ* and the determination of the law where there is no scripture (*min qabla wurūd al-sharʿ*), also believed it implicated the nature and definition of obligation (*taklīf*). See ʿAlī b. ʿAbd al-Kāfī al-Subkī and Tāj al-Dīn al-Subkī, *al-Ibhāj fī Sharḥ al-Minhāj* (Beirut: Dār al-Kutub al-ʿIlmiyya, n.d.), 1:155.

These two theories of obligation recognized the equal capacity of Muslims and *dhimmīs* to reason to Sharīʿa-based norms. Such norms, jurists argued, are apparent to all who can reason. But, as will be shown below, both groups recognized that despite the shared reason of both Muslims and *dhimmīs,* the *dhimmīs* nonetheless have historically enjoyed certain immunities from Sharīʿa-based obligations—immunities that have been transmitted over generations and constitute authoritative precedent. For jurists espousing the sufficiency of universal reason to justify imposing Sharīʿa-based norms on the *dhimmī,* inherited authoritative precedents limited the scope of the *dhimmī*'s liability under Sharīʿa. If reason is universal, what explains these limits on the *dhimmī*'s scope of obligation? The difficulty of harmonizing a commitment to universal reason with inherited precedent—which circumscribed the scope of the *dhimmī*'s obligations—suggested to other jurists that something more than mere reason was required to establish and define one's obligation to abide by Sharīʿa-based norms. Those who denied the sufficiency of reason alone to justify imposing Sharīʿa on the *dhimmī* required some form of acquiescence.

Since a universal reason could not provide a sufficient basis for establishing a *dhimmī*'s delimited obligation, the prevailing model jurists relied upon was based on contract. The contract of protection became for them the political and legal site of deliberation about the scope, extent, and limits of the *dhimmīs*' liability to adhere to Sharīʿa-based norms. *Dhimmīs* were rendered liable to some Sharīʿa-based obligations because they deterred conduct that both Muslims and non-Muslims could avoid and from which both mutually benefitted. *Dhimmīs* were liable to these rules, what some jurists called the *muʿāmalāt,* because the rules were defined as pertaining to certain matters that are of general, day-to-day concern (*maʿnā dunyawī*), and thereby worked to the benefit of both Muslims and *dhimmis.*[5] Of course, determining what constitutes a general concern and a desired benefit was something that jurists fiercely debated when considering which rules did or did not apply to the *dhimmī.* Once having determined that distinction, the *dhimmī* was theoretically obligated to abide by the relevant category of rules, all of which were legally deemed to be implicit in the contract of protection. The contract of protection delineated the scope of the *dhimmī*'s liability, and thereby the *dhimmī*'s inclusion in the Muslim polity. But in defining the scope of liability, the contract was also a reminder of how the *dhimmī* was not an insider to the Muslim community, not one of "us." As shown

[5] Abū Bakr al-Sarakhsī, *al-Muḥarrar fī Uṣūl al-Fiqh,* ed. Abū ʿAbd al-Raḥmān ʿAwīḍa (Beirut: Dār al-Kutub al-ʿIlmiyya, 1996), 1:52.

below, contractarian paradigms offered the conceptual space where jurists considered whether and to what extent the *dhimmīs*' difference rendered them insiders and outsiders in the Muslim polity.

2.1.1 A universal law for the rational being

The Muʿtazilite al-Qāḍī ʿAbd al-Jabbār (d. 415/1025) considered all of humanity to have the same capacity to know and follow God's obligations. The only relevant difference for him was whether we actually uphold the obligations through our acts and deeds.[6] He wrote,

> The goodness of obligating the believer is well established. But there is no sense to its goodness unless [God] most high has empowered him [to do] what is obligated of him...All of this is [the same] for the unbeliever...There is no difference between them [the believer and unbeliever] except that the believer makes good choices for himself, uses his reason, and believes. The unbeliever does not choose well for himself because of his misfortune (*shiqāwa*) and does not believe. That does not deny that God is gracious on both of them together.[7]

For ʿAbd al-Jabbār, there was no fundamental difference between Muslims and non-Muslims that should justify limiting the application of Sharīʿa-based norms to either of them. Both shared the same rational capacities to know God and the divine will. In fact, the Ḥanafī jurist al-Jaṣṣāṣ argued that the Qur'ān unambiguously holds that non-Muslims will be punished for not abiding by the laws of Islam. He cited Qur'ān 42:7, which narrates a conversation between those in Paradise asking those in Hell the following:

> What has brought you to hell? They say: We were not among those who prayed nor did we feed the poor. We indulged in sinning together and considered the final day a lie, until certainty [now] comes to us.

This verse suggested to al-Jaṣṣāṣ that non-Muslims who failed to abide by the tenets of the Islamic faith would be punished in hell. For al-Jaṣṣāṣ, if their punishment was to be just and legitimate, then they could only be punished in hell if they were also obligated *while alive* to uphold such requirements.[8] Since the Qur'ān suggests that they will be punished for

[6] Al-Qāḍī ʿAbd al-Jabbār, *Sharḥ al-Uṣūl al-Khamsa* (Beirut: Dār Iḥyā' al-Turāth al-ʿArabī, 2001), 344–5, 348, 349. Abū Bakr al-Jaṣṣāṣ (d. 370/981) also held that unbelievers are obligated not only to adhere to Islamic principles and rules (*mukallafūna bi sharā'iʿ al-Islām wa aḥkāmihi*). Abū Bakr al-Jaṣṣāṣ, *al-Fuṣūl fī al-Uṣūl*, ed. Muḥammad Muḥammad Tāmir (Beirut: Dār al-Kutub al-ʿIlmiyya, 2000), 1:329.

[7] ʿAbd al-Jabbār, *Sharḥ al-Uṣūl*, 346.

[8] Al-Jaṣṣāṣ, *al-Fuṣūl*, 1:329. See also Abū Isḥāq al-Shīrāzī, *al-Tabṣira fī Uṣūl al-Fiqh*, ed. Muḥammad Ḥasan Haytū (1980; reprint, Beirut: Dār al-Fikr, 1983), 81. Al-Sarakhsī,

violating God's law, then they must have been obligated to abide by it. To view reason as universally shared allows everyone equal access to the same shared values, and thereby means that nothing fundamentally prevents the *dhimmī* from being legitimately subjected to Sharīʿa-based obligations.

Nonetheless, jurists such as al-Jaṣṣāṣ allowed for some exceptions, given the fact of diversity. To impose the full scope of Sharīʿa-based norms on *dhimmīs* would fundamentally disrespect the *dhimmīs*' differences in beliefs, thereby violating the Muslim regime's obligations toward the *dhimmīs* under the contract of protection, as will be further discussed in Chapter 3. But if all humans equally share a universal reason that gives them access to public values of the good and the bad, how can *dhimmīs* nevertheless be exempted from some parts of the Sharīʿa but not others? Furthermore, which parts of the Sharīʿa can be suspended for them, which parts cannot be waived away, and how does one tell the difference? Al-Jaṣṣāṣ recognized the conceptual dilemmas underlying this issue. He knew that to believe in a universal reason can lead to the conclusion that the full scope of Sharīʿa-based norms should be obligatory on all, without limitation. However, he also recognized that the law granted *dhimmīs* exceptions. Indeed, he could not ignore the inherited precedent limiting the scope of the *dhimmīs*' obligations. Consequently and perhaps unsurprisingly, al-Jaṣṣāṣ stated: "Like all [people, the *dhimmīs*] receive the discourse about having faith. But they are able to avoid it and its laws by [paying] the *jizya*."[9] The reference to "*jizya*" here arguably operated as al-Jaṣṣāṣ' shorthand reference to the contract of protection and its terms (i.e., the *aḥkām al-dhimma*). For al-Jaṣṣāṣ, the *dhimmī* was obligated to abide by the Islamic message. Nonetheless, the reality of diversity and prior precedent reflected a commitment to a pluralist enterprise of governance, which informed how jurists such as al-Jaṣṣāṣ theorized about the *dhimmīs*' subject-hood and scope of liability under a Sharīʿa-based legal system.

This commitment and its contribution to the content of the law is reflected in how al-Jaṣṣāṣ harmonized an Islamic universalist ethos with support for pluralism. He could not ignore addressing how Muslims could allow non-Muslims to enter a contract of protection that ultimately perpetuates disbelief in Islamic lands, especially if universal reason allows for the potential to know and appreciate the divine discourse. Al-Jaṣṣāṣ held that implicit in the duty to obey the Sharīʿa is a certain

al-Muḥarrar, 1:52, argues that this verse does not imply any obligation on the non-Muslim in the mundane world, but does imply punishment in the hereafter.

[9] Al-Jaṣṣāṣ, *al-Fuṣūl*, 1:330.

precondition. Arguing by analogy, al-Jaṣṣāṣ said that although a Muslim is commanded to pray, his prayer is not accepted if he is in a state of impurity; but being in a state of impurity does not vitiate the general obligation to pray. In the same way, the non-Muslim has been commanded to abide by the Sharīʿa. His disbelief, though, renders invalid any of his ritualistic acts that conform with Sharīʿa-norms; only if he were to convert would his devotional acts be accepted. In other words, the existence of obligation assumes certain preconditions that the *dhimmī* does not meet. And yet, for al-Jaṣṣāṣ, this was not to suggest that the original obligation to adhere to the Sharīʿa never existed. The obligation to adhere to the Sharīʿa existed, despite introducing a precondition that limited the scope to which the obligation could legitimately be imposed on someone.[10] Jurists such as al-Jaṣṣāṣ may have adhered to the sufficiency of reason to justify obligation, but they recognized that reason alone was not enough to justify imposing Sharīʿa-based obligations on the *dhimmī*. Something more was required. As will be noted below, that "something" was expressed through the law by reference to contract.

2.1.2 Difference in community, difference in law

In opposition to the views of al-Jaṣṣāṣ and ʿAbd al-Jabbār was one that recognized the universality of reason, but considered it insufficient to justify the imposition of the full scope of Sharīʿa-based obligations on the *dhimmī*. This second group accepted the universality of reason, but argued that reason could only lead one to knowledge of God, but not to being liable to Sharīʿa-based obligations. Consequently, they distinguished between having the capacity to know that a divine discourse exists, and being obligated to adhere to its tenets with the threat of sanction.

The Ashʿarite Abū Bakr al-Bāqillānī (d. 403/1013) held that jurists generally agreed that God's message included non-Muslims as part of its audience. Like the Muslims, non-Muslims are commanded to acknowledge God and the veracity of God's messengers, which ultimately upholds the universalist ethos of the Islamic message.[11] He argued that when God commands people to pray and to avoid things that are prohibited (*al-maḥẓūrāt*), God addresses all of humanity and not just Muslims.[12] In

[10] Al-Jaṣṣāṣ, *al-Fuṣūl*, 1:329. This is a common example in this debate, and will be evident in the discussion of other authors below. See also Abū al-Muẓaffar al-Samʿānī, *Qawāṭiʿ al-Adilla fī al-Uṣūl*, ed Muḥammad Ḥasan Ismāʿīl al-Shāfiʿī (Beirut: Dār al-Kutub al-ʿIlmiyya, 1997), 1:107.

[11] Abū Bakr al-Bāqillānī, *al-Taqrīb wa al-Irshād al-Ṣaghīr*, ed. ʿAbd al-Ḥamīd b. ʿAlī Abī Zunayd (Beirut: Muʾassasat al-Risāla, 1998), 2:184.

[12] Al-Bāqillānī, *al-Taqrīb wa al-Irshād*, 2:186.

this sense, God's message must be understood as universally accessible and thereby knowable by all.

A shared capacity to know God and His will, though, does not mean that all people are equally subjected to Sharīʿa-based obligations. Al-Bāqillānī distinguished between Muslims who are obligated to abide by Sharīʿa-based obligations, and non-Muslims who are not equally obligated. He justified the difference in their legal status on the ground that Muslims acknowledge that they are part of God's audience in the Qurʾān, but non-Muslims do not. Having the same capacity to reason and to know God, therefore, is not the same as *acquiescing* to a set of values, ideals, or rules of obligation.[13] To be obligated to abide by God's commands also requires certain conditions (i.e., *sharṭ*) indicating that one acquiesces.[14]

To emphasize his point, al-Bāqillānī noted that not all Muslims are obligated to abide by God's commands in the same way. Jurists developed dispensations for slaves, travelers, and women. In other words, some may be obligated to the full extent of the law, while others enjoy certain exemptions due to their circumstances, however defined. In the same fashion, he argued, non-Muslims are not required to adhere to the full scope of Sharīʿa-based requirements.[15] For instance, non-Muslims performing Islamic rituals of worship cannot expect to achieve salvation, since their disbelief precludes any resulting reward. That does not mean they have no capacity to know and acknowledge God and His prophets. Mere capacity, though, is not tantamount to acquiescence; and without acquiescence there is no meaningful way to hold the *dhimmī* legitimately obligated to Sharīʿa-based norms. A non-Muslim's performance of Islamic rituals means nothing until he participates as a Muslim and fulfills the necessary precondition of belief.[16]

The distinction between the capacity to know the divine discourse and the condition of belief (and thus acquiescence) is directly related to upholding the universality of the Islamic message, while creating space for a pluralist imperial enterprise of governance. By acknowledging the universal capacity to know the divine discourse, al-Bāqillānī upheld the universalist ethos of Islam. But by requiring the precondition of faith as a form of acquiescence, he legitimated the accommodation of the *dhimmīs*' differences in the form of exemptions from Sharīʿa-based obligations. Hence, the *dhimmī* could live in the Muslim polity and disbelieve in the Islamic message without at the same time undermining the universal

[13] Al-Bāqillānī, *al-Taqrīb wa al-Irshād*, 2:185–6.
[14] Al-Bāqillānī, *al-Taqrīb wa al-Irshād*, 2:186.
[15] Al-Bāqillānī, *al-Taqrīb wa al-Irshād*, 2:187.
[16] Al-Bāqillānī, *al-Taqrīb wa al-Irshād*, 2:192.

ethos of Islam—an ethos that served as a legitimating foundation for an imperial enterprise of governance.[17]

The question that remained, however, concerned the extent to which *dhimmīs* were exempted from Sharīʿa-based obligations. In other words, on what basis can we distinguish between those obligations from which *dhimmīs* are exempted, and the others from which they are not? For al-Bāqillānī, the scope of exemptions will be reflected in authoritative source-texts (*samʿ*) and notions of propriety (*tawqīf*), as opposed to logical argument.[18] Much like al-Jaṣṣāṣ, he argued that the consensus of the *umma* (*ijmāʿ al-umma*) certified that while non-Muslims are part of God's audience, certain of God's laws are not imposed on non-Muslims, given prior precedent on the matter.[19] Certainly, non-Muslims may be punished in some eschatological afterlife for their lack of faith, but as a matter of law they are exempted from some requirements in the here-and-now.[20]

Despite differing views on the sufficiency of reason as a basis for obligation, the legal implications were similar for both theoretical camps. Both camps recognized that while Muslims and non-Muslims both have the capacity to know the divine discourse and God's will, certain preconditions had to be met before the divine discourse could be legitimately applied to and enforced against the *dhimmī*. For the group who held universal reason to be sufficient, all people were liable to Sharīʿa-based norms; the only difference for them was that prior precedent nonetheless created certain exemptions for *dhimmīs*. For the second group, reason may allow both Muslims and non-Muslims to know and appreciate God's will, but there can be no obligation at all without first acquiescing to God's will. Despite their different departure points on the notion of reason and obligation, both groups recognized that the *dhimmī* is not subjected to all Sharīʿa-based norms and that, instead, the

[17] Al-Bāqillānī, *al-Taqrīb wa al-Irshād*, 2:193.

[18] Al-Bāqillānī *al-Taqrīb wa al-Irshād*, 2:187.

[19] The resort to *ijmāʿ* is significant and will be addressed in later discussions. For others who use *ijmāʿ* as a basis for determining when a non-Muslim is subject to Sharīʿa obligations or not, see al-Samʿānī, *Qawāṭiʿ al-Adilla*, 1:110.

[20] Al-Bāqillānī *al-Taqrīb wa al-Irshād*, 2:195. To offer a different example, the jurist al-Shīrāzī explained why a non-Muslim who converts to Islam is not required to make up ritual prayers and fasts that he or she missed while in a state of disbelief. Arguably, if non-Muslims have the capacity to know the divine discourse, why should they not be liable to make up prior prayers once they "acquiesce" to the requirements of Sharīʿa? For al-Shīrāzī, the fact that the non-Muslim later converts to Islam does not change the fact that he did not acquiesce to the Sharīʿa when he was a non-Muslim. Failure to fulfill this condition limits the scope of Sharīʿa liability, while preserving the meta-claim about the ontology of obligation. Al-Shīrāzī, *al-Tabṣira*, 83.

scope of the *dhimmī*'s obligation must be outlined and demarcated in some other fashion.

Enter the contract of protection.

2.2 CONTRACT IN THE LAW AND POLITICS OF PLURALISM

As jurists debated different theories of obligation, they were well aware of the institution of the contract of protection and its role in determining the *dhimmīs*' scope of exemption from Sharīʿa-based obligations. When al-Jaṣṣāṣ wrote that paying the *jizya* allowed the non-Muslim to avoid being subjected to all Sharīʿa-based obligations, he was not ignorant of how the *jizya* implied the existence of the contract of protection. In fact, when addressing the nature of the *jizya* and the conditions under which it was paid, al-Jaṣṣāṣ made specific reference to the contract of protection (*ʿaqd al-dhimma*).[21] Likewise, when al-Bāqillānī wrote that the scope to which non-Muslims were subjected to Sharīʿa-based obligations depended on received traditions, he could not have been unaware of the contract of protection as one of those received traditions.[22] Arguably, even as jurists offered competing theories of reason and obligation, the contract of protection lurked in the backdrop, providing a conceptual device that made possible both the obligation of *dhimmīs* to Sharīʿa-based norms, given a universal reason, and the limitations on their scope of liability when living in an Islamic polity, given authoritative precedents.

This section describes different modes by which a non-Muslim could enter the Muslim polity under premodern Islamic legal doctrines. The *dhimmī*, as a matter of legal doctrine, lived under a contract of *permanent* residency, while other non-Muslims could enter the Muslim polity only on a temporary basis. As will be shown below, of all the different Muslim/non-Muslim relationships under Sharīʿa-based doctrines, the *dhimmī* provides us a focal point to critically analyze how and to what end premodern Muslim jurists contended with how to govern pluralistically. More than any other non-Muslim in the Muslim polity whom jurists

[21] In fact, when addressing the nature of the *jizya* and the conditions under which it is paid in his Qurʾānic commentary, al-Jaṣṣāṣ made specific reference to the contract of protection (*ʿaqd al-dhimma*). Al-Jaṣṣāṣ, *Aḥkām al-Qurʾān*, 3:129.

[22] Al-Bāqillānī's awareness of the contract of protection can be inferred from his common reference to the consensus (*ijmāʿ*) among the jurists (*fuqahāʾ*), which limits the scope of the *dhimmī's* obligation to adhere to the full scope of the Sharīʿa. Al-Bāqillānī, *al-Taqrīb wa al-Irshād*, 2:184–97.

wrote about, the *dhimmī* was both insider and outsider; *dhimmīs* may have lived within the Muslim polity but they retained their differences. *Dhimmīs* thereby offer us an important discursive site to understand the challenges that face an enterprise of governance imagined in terms of an Islamic universalism, an ethic of empire, and the fact of diversity. Indeed, the *dhimmī*, the contract of protection, and the *dhimmī* rules constitute an important focal point for appreciating Sharīʿa as a claim space and its relationship to the enterprise of governance.

According to the Shāfiʿite jurist al-Māwardī (d. 450/1058),[23] a non-Muslim could enter different types of contracts with the Muslim polity, each of which had varying implications for the relationship between the non-Muslim and the Muslim polity. The first type of contract, *hudna*, was an agreement made by the political ruler or *imām* with non-Muslim enemies of the state (*ahl al-ḥarb*) to negotiate ceasefires. According to al-Māwardī, the *hudna* was a negotiated peace treaty lasting for a maximum of ten years and could even involve the Muslim polity paying the non-Muslims a tribute to stave off fighting. Only the ruler had the discretion to enter a *hudna;* he could do so if it was needed and was indisputably in the public interest (*ẓuhūr al-maṣlaḥa*).[24] The *hudna,* or peace treaty, however, had less to do with the way non-Muslims were included within the Muslim polity, and more to do with the relationship of peace between two otherwise warring polities.

The second contract, *ʿahd,* was a temporary agreement that allowed non-Muslims to enter Muslim lands for a period not exceeding four months, although some held that the maximum was one year. Like the *hudna,* the *ʿahd* could only be issued by the ruling authority and was granted only when it would provide some benefit (*maṣlaḥa*) for Muslim society. But unlike the *hudna,* the non-Muslim could pay for the entitlement to enter, although payment was not a condition for issuing the *ʿahd.*[25]

Like the *ʿahd,* the *amān,* or pledge of security, was a temporary permit of residency of limited duration.[26] Notably, the *amān* could be given by

[23] While this analysis will refer to al-Māwardī's commentary on the different forms of contract, other sources offer similar accounts. See for instance, Ibn Nujaym, *al-Sharḥ al-Baḥr al-Rāʾiq* (Beirut: Dār al-Kutub al-ʿIlmiyya, 1997), 5:167–85; Ibn Qudāma, *al-Mughnī*, 8:340–538.

[24] Abū al-Ḥasan al-Māwardī, *al-Ḥāwī al-Kabīr*, eds ʿAlī Muḥammad Muʿawwaḍ and ʿĀdil Aḥmad ʿAbd al-Mawjūd (Beirut: Dār al-Kutub al-ʿIlmiyya, 1994), 14:296. The limit of ten years is based on the peace treaty Muḥammad negotiated with the Quraysh, known as the Treaty of Ḥudaybiyya, which had a ten-year time limit.

[25] Al-Māwardī, *al-Ḥāwī*, 14:296–7.

[26] The time limits for an *amān* vary; for some it is for four months; for others it is for one year. J. Schacht, *EI*², s.v., "Amān." On the pre-Islamic analogues of *amān* that may have influenced its development in Islamic legal thought, see Levy-Rubin, *Non-Muslims in the Early Islamic Empire*, 32–4.

any Muslim to a non-Muslim. In other words, while the *hudna* and *ʿahd* were given at the discretion of the ruling authority, private individuals could issue pledges of safe conduct to non-Muslims, thereby rendering them temporarily secure in Muslim lands. The term of art referring to one who enjoyed the security of an *amān* was *mustaʾmin*.[27]

The *ʿahd* and *amān* were both temporary visitation permits that allowed non-Muslims to enter the Muslim polity. The fact that they were temporary emphasizes that their holder was an outsider to the Muslim polity—someone who fundamentally did not reside among Muslims with any permanency. Consequently, while these legal contracts certainly provided ways for non-Muslims to enter Muslim society, they offer us limited insight into how and why non-Muslims, who were part of Muslim society, presented a flashpoint for debate at the intersection of law and the enterprise of governance.

Literally translated as "contract of protection," the *ʿaqd al-dhimma* was the legal mechanism by which a non-Muslim was deemed either actually or fictively to contract into protected and permanent residency status in Islamic lands. Whether the contract was actual or fictional depended on whether the non-Muslims agreed to pay the *jizya* when offered the option of peaceful surrender (i.e., *ṣulḥiyya*) by conquering Muslim forces, or whether they refused and had terms of settlement imposed upon them through conquest (*ʿanwiyya*).[28] Additionally, a contract may have been applied to later generations, despite the lack of any actual consent from those subjected to its terms. In other words, the invocation of a contract of protection did not necessarily imply an actual written document with the terms and conditions of residence noted therein. Rather, the contract of protection was a legal concept that operated as a place-holder for the political agreement of *dhimmīs* to abide by Sharīʿa-based norms, but not to the same extent as Muslims who had, by virtue of their faith commitments, fully acquiesced to the full scope of Sharīʿa-based obligations.

According to al-Māwardī, the contract of protection posed the most significant type of contractual relationship (*awkad al-ʿuqūd*) between non-Muslims and Muslim society because:

- it provided security of residence;
- it was conditional on the *dhimmīs* paying a poll tax or *jizya*;

[27] Al-Māwardī, *al-Ḥāwī*, 14:297.

[28] Ibn Rushd al-Jadd, *al-Muqaddimāt al-Mumahhidāt*, ed. Muḥammad Ḥajjī (Beirut: Dār al-Gharb al-Islāmī, 1988), 1:368–9. For more on the significance of the distinction between conquest and peaceful surrender (*ʿanwiyya* and *ṣulḥiyya*), see Levy-Rubin, *Non-Muslims in the Early Islamic Empire*, 36–8.

- unlike the other contracts, it had no time limits; it was perpetual (*mu'abbad*); and
- it imposed a duty on the Muslim polity to protect (*dhabb*) the *dhimmīs* from aggressors, whether Muslim or not.[29]

Upon entering the contract of protection, the non-Muslim was characterized as a *dhimmī*, was entitled to certain protections, and was required to adhere to Sharīʿa-based norms to the extent the contract provided. The contract of protection was the legal mechanism that effectuated the legal (and thereby political, social, and economic) inclusion and accommodation of the *dhimmī* within the larger Muslim polity. The significance of the contract of protection for the pluralist commitment of an Islamic enterprise of governance is captured by a tradition from ʿAlī b. Abī Ṭālib (d. 40/661) in which he stated: "They [non-Muslims] pay the *jizya* so that their lives are [protected] like our lives, and their property is [protected] like our property."[30] ʿAlī's tradition has been interpreted to suggest that once the non-Muslim paid the *jizya*, entered the contract of protection, and thereby became a *dhimmī*, his life and property were as inviolable (*maʿṣūm*) as a Muslim's life and property, and had to be protected by the rulers who managed the Islamic enterprise of governance.[31]

However, as will be expounded upon in Chapters 3 and 4, the degree to which the *dhimmī* was considered an insider was offset by rules that were read into the contract and were designed to subordinate *dhimmīs* by reference to their difference. For instance, as discussed above about Qur'ān 9:29, the requirement to pay the *jizya* in a state of submission was construed by some jurists to convey a sentiment of subordination. The import of ʿAlī's statement, if read alongside Qur'ān 9:29, illustrates how source-texts can contribute to contrary imperatives of inclusion and marginalization that jurists had to resolve. In other words, premodern jurists considered the *dhimmīs* to be both insiders and outsiders, which is why the *dhimmī* rules provide us an important focal point for revealing the mutually constitutive relationship between law and the enterprise of governance. The contract of protection offered a premodern model by which to justify the sovereign demand for the *dhimmī*'s compliance with Sharīʿa norms, and by which to deliberate about the scope to which the Muslim polity can and should accommodate the *dhimmī*'s difference.

[29] Al-Māwardī, *al-Ḥāwī*, 14:297–8. See also Abū Ḥāmid al-Ghazālī, *al-Wasīṭ fī al-Madhhab*, ed. Abū ʿAmrū al-Ḥusaynī (Beirut: Dār al-Kutub al-ʿIlmiyya, 2001), 4:196; al-Nawawī, *Rawḍat al-Ṭālibīn wa ʿUmdat al-Muftīn*, 3rd ed. (Beirut: al-Maktab al-Islāmī, 1991), 10:321.

[30] Ibn Nujaym, *al-Baḥr al-Rā'iq*, 5:127 (*innamā badhalū al-jizya li-takūna dimā'uhum ka dimā'anā wa amwāluhum ka-amwālanā*). See also Zaydān, *Aḥkām al-Dhimmiyyīn*, 76.

[31] Ibn Nujaym, *al-Baḥr al-Rā'iq*, 9:20.

In other words, the contract was a site for a politico-legal discourse on the *dhimmī*'s obedience to the Muslim polity, as well as his inclusion, accommodation, and at times marginalization—all of that contributed to and constituted a complex image of the enterprise of governance and its qualified commitment to pluralism. The contrary imperatives of inclusion and exclusion should not be viewed as a sign of incoherence or inconsistency in the law. Rather, the conflicting imperatives reveal how the contract of protection and the *dhimmī* rules provided the site for diverse and at times contrary legal argument about the contours of a pluralistic enterprise of governance, which was not always easy to define or articulate, let alone achieve.

The complex and at times contradictory interests that fueled debates about the *dhimmī* rules suggest that any analysis of *dhimmīs* and the *dhimmī* rules cannot be reduced to a static interpretation of either harmony or persecution. Viewing them, instead, through the framework of Sharīʿa as Rule of Law reveals how jurists used the negotiative nature of contract to accommodate competing interests and to arrive at complex and, at times, conflicting conclusions. Indeed, the very nature of accommodation is a messy business. In the interest of accommodation, factual differences will justify legal rules that treat differently situated people differently. The legitimacy of such legal differentiation is fundamental to philosophical accounts of justice.[32] The pursuit of justice cannot ignore that, at times, factual difference between two people may require different legal treatment of the two; this feature of justice countenances a certain paradox of equality. Legal systems often legitimate certain forms of differentiation because of factual differences that are deemed legally significant (e.g., affirmative action). The fact of legal differentiation, therefore, is not by itself interesting. Rather, this study is interested in the aim and purpose of the legal differentiations, namely in what they reveal about the law and the image of the enterprise of governance.

2.3 CONCLUSION

By examining competing theories of obligation, this chapter has argued that the contract of protection offered the conceptual link between law

[32] Aristotle, *Nichomachean Ethics*, trans. Harris Rackham (Hertfordshire: Wordsworth Editions Limited, 1996), 118; Aḥmad b. Muḥammad Miskawayh, *The Refinement of Character*, trans. Constantine K. Zurayk (Beirut: American University of Beirut, 1968), 100–1. For the original Arabic, see Ibn Miskawayh, *Tahdhīb al-Akhlāq wa Taẓhīr al-Aʿrāf*, ed. Ibn al-Khaṭīb (n.p.: Maktabat al-Thaqāfa al-Dīniyya, n.d.), 123; Abū Naṣr al-Fārābī, *Fuṣūl Muntazaʿa*, ed. Fawzī Najjār (Beirut: Dār al-Mashraq, 1971), 71.

and the enterprise of governance in matters concerning the non-Muslim living under an Islamic imperium. Viewing the contract of protection from the perspective of Rule of Law, this chapter shows that the contract operated at both a legal and political level, allowing jurists to delineate the scope of the *dhimmī*'s obligations, all the while ensuring the integrity and coherence of an Islamic imperial enterprise of governance.

As shown above, two theories of obligation focused on the shared capacity of all human beings to reason. One theory held that this shared capacity to reason was sufficient to justify obligating the *dhimmī* to abide by Sharīʿa-based norms. Those adopting this theory, however, recognized certain limitations on the scope of the *dhimmī*'s obligation given the existence of prior precedents that exempted *dhimmis* from certain types of legal liability. The second theory held that while all humans have a shared capacity to reason, differences in community and value nonetheless require that we delimit the scope of obligation, given the importance of acquiescence to the notion of obligation. Both theories recognized a shared capacity to reason but also that reason alone was not sufficient to justify that *dhimmīs* were obligated to abide by Sharīʿa-based norms in the same fashion and to the same extent as Muslims. Instead, jurists developed the contract of protection to justify subjecting the *dhimmī* to the Sharīʿa, while allowing for exemptions from Sharīʿa-based liability. The contract of protection offered a mechanism that allowed the *dhimmī* to reside within the Muslim empire while preserving his or her traditions and value commitments amidst the universalist claims underlying an aspiration to an Islamic empire. The contract, thereby, offered a compromise position between the universalism of the Islamic message and the demands of imperial expansion, the latter of which made the encounter with the Other inevitable. Furthermore, by relying on the *dhimmī* as different, the contract model rendered the *dhimmī* as both insider and outsider, part of the Muslim polity but outside the Muslim community.

By viewing Sharīʿa as Rule of Law, we are better able to appreciate how the contract of protection operated at a political *and* legal level. *Politically*, it reflected an early contractarian argument that included the non-Muslim as a subject of the Muslim enterprise of governance. *Legally*, the contract offered the site of legal debate about the scope of Sharīʿa-based obligations on the *dhimmī* and the exemptions that *dhimmīs* could enjoy under the law in light of the sometimes competing ethics of universalism, empire, and pluralism. The legal doctrines read into the contract contributed to the integrity, coherence, and vision of an Islamic imperial enterprise of governance. Conversely, although the enterprise of governance required the law to be lifted or inapplicable for some people (such as *dhimmīs*), the authority of the law was nevertheless reinforced. In other words, even though legal exemptions meant that the *dhimmī* was not subjected to certain Sharīʿa-based norms, the zone of non-liability was still defined and delimited pursuant to the requirements of Sharīʿa-based doctrines of contract. Consequently, although the exemptions for *dhimmīs* may be interpreted as fostering toleration or respect, they also reinforced the authority and legitimating force of Sharīʿa-based norms. As much as certain laws did not apply to the *dhimmī*, the *dhimmī* still remained a legal subject of an Islamic enterprise of governance, and as such was legally and politically understood, defined, and situated in Sharīʿa-based terms—terms that situated the *dhimmī* as insider and outsider, a civic participant on the periphery, as "tolerated" but marginalized. For example, the Ḥanafī jurist al-Sarakhsī (d. 483/1090) wrote:

> The purpose of the contract of protection is to make the rules of Muslims obligatory with regard to those things contributing to the *muʿāmalāt*. The authority of the divine discourse (*ḥukm al-khiṭāb*) imposes [the rules] on them [*dhimmīs*], as it does on Muslims because of the obligation that exists, except where it is known by affirmative evidence that they are not obligated. [But] there is no disagreement that the discourse of law incorporates the [*dhimmīs*] by rebuking them in the hereafter (*ḥukm al-muʾākhidha fī al-ākhira*).[33]

While the *dhimmīs* were permitted to reside in the Muslim polity and were exempted from certain Sharīʿa-based obligations, as the quote from al-Sarakhsī suggests, nothing precluded the fact that *dhimmīs* were still worthy of divine condemnation.

As will be shown in the next chapter, legal debates about the *dhimmī* rules contributed to political debates about the nature of the enterprise of governance, and about the degree to which accommodation, subordination, and marginalization of difference contributed to the legitimacy of the enterprise of governance. Even when they were making exceptions for the *dhimmī* so as to accommodate difference, jurists nonetheless justified the characterization and legal treatment of the *dhimmī* in terms whose intelligibility is best appreciated by viewing the rules as stemming from a Sharīʿa claim space that was bounded, in part, by an imperial vision of the enterprise of governance. By granting freedom to the *dhimmīs* to live peacefully in the Muslim polity, the rules that exempted *dhimmīs* from Sharīʿa-based liability also defined them as being different. Furthermore, the scope of their

[33] Al-Sarakhsī, *al-Muḥarrar*, 1:52.

freedom from Sharīʿa-based obligations depended on the scope to which such freedom undermined the values and interests that animated and legitimated the enterprise of governance. Consequently, a critical irony in the accommodative spirit of the contract of protection is that while the *dhimmīs*' difference was sufficient grounds for creating legal exemptions, those exemptions preserved the *dhimmī* as both factually different and legally differentiable, thereby situating the *dhimmī* as an important focal point for illustrating the mutually constitutive relationship between the law and the enterprise of governance as it pertained to the scope and content of a ruling regime's commitment to pluralism.

3

Pluralism, *Dhimmī* Rules, and the Regulation of Difference

Chapter 2 showed that whether or not jurists agreed if universal reason could render *dhimmīs* obligated to abide by the Sharīʿa, they agreed that the *dhimmīs*' obligation to Sharīʿa-norms was dependent upon the terms of a contract of protection. As suggested earlier, though, the terms of the contract of protection were not entirely clear. To appreciate the terms of the contract of protection is less a matter of finding historical records, and more a matter of recognizing that the contract of protection was a juridified site for debate about the scope and limits of the *dhimmī*'s inclusion and accommodation in the Muslim polity. The contract of protection, in other words, was a conceptual device that reflected the dynamics of Sharīʿa as Rule of Law, namely the negotiative and mutually constitutive relationship between the law and the enterprise of governance. Consequently, far from being indicative of the tolerance or intolerance of Islam, the contract of protection and its associated provisions (i.e., the *dhimmī* rules) were symptomatic of the more general challenge of governing amidst diversity.

This chapter introduces legal debates on various *dhimmī*-related topics to showcase how the legal arguments reflected a broader, more general concern about the scope and extent to which the *dhimmī* was included and accommodated in the Muslim polity. Upon reviewing a series of debates on different legal issues (e.g., the *jizya,* charitable endowments, public displays of religious ritual, and so on), the chapter concludes by suggesting that the *dhimmī* rules were juridified attempts to imagine, construe, and define the public sphere and the enterprise of governance in light of the fact of diversity. In some cases, the contract of protection figured prominently as a device that required *dhimmī* interests to be accommodated. At other times, principles about the superiority of Islam over all other traditions were invoked to demarcate the limits of inclusion and accommodation. In the aggregate, the analysis shows that the *dhimmī* rules organized and stratified a diverse society for the purpose of ensuring the primacy of an Islamically defined public sphere in light of at times conflicting imperatives of empire and universalism. To read the *dhimmī* rules in this fashion contributes to the more general aim of this study, namely to understand how the intelligibility of legal doctrines is best appreciated by recognizing them as made within a claim space of justice that lies at the intersection of both law and governance.

Sharīʿa is not unique, as legal systems go, in rendering the minority (religious or otherwise) a site of politico-legal debate about the core values of society, the character of the public sphere, and the aspirations of the enterprise of governance. For instance, the Quebec government in Canada established a commission to study attitudes about religious accommodation and how to define and demarcate the limits of accommodation without sacrificing the core values that characterize the Quebec polity, however defined.[1] Additionally, recent years have witnessed a backlash in European and North American societies against the public presence of religious manifestations, as will be further discussed in Chapter 7. This backlash has taken on a particular attitude against Islam and Muslims since the tragic attack on the World Trade Center on September 11, 2001. The Swiss constitutional referendum against the construction of minarets arguably expressed a popular sentiment about the perceived inconsistency of a highly public Islamic symbol such as the minaret with the character and identity of Switzerland as a polity. Likewise, legislative enactments to ban the *niqāb* in many European countries reflect a concern that a particular spirit or value in these countries may be lost if *niqāb*-clad women walk the streets of European cities.[2] What the core values and public spirit are, however, is not always clear or even articulated. Nevertheless, advocates of such bans seem confident that by legally regulating the presence of minarets and *niqābs*, the core values at stake will survive intact.

These relatively recent constitutional and legislative enactments and proposals share an important characteristic with the *dhimmī* rules. All are concerned about the preservation of a particular way of life, political vision, or set of core values that are apparently threatened by the visible presence of religious symbols of the group identified as Other. In Islamic legal terms, the Other is the *dhimmī*. In Europe and North America, the Other has, in the years since September 11, 2001,

[1] See, the Report of the Reasonable Accommodation Commission of Quebec: Taylor and Bouchard, *Building the Future*.

[2] For more discussion on the Swiss constitutional referendum and the treatment of the covered Muslim woman, see Chapter 7.

become Muslims. Although this chapter and the study focus specifically on the *dhimmī* rules, more generally this study suggests that however the Other is defined, the public presence of the Other will constitute an important site for the mutually constitutive relationship between law and the enterprise of governance. Consequently, the Other's inclusion in the polity is vulnerable to the changing vicissitudes of history and politics that affect the policies of enterprises of governance, and thereby affect the intelligibility of arguments made within the claim space of the law.

3.1 CONTRACT AND POLL-TAX *(JIZYA)*: IMAGINING THE PLURALIST POLITY

The legal requirement of the *jizya* was a prerequisite for the *dhimmī* to enter a contract to be part of the Muslim society. But what was the function of the *jizya* itself given that the contract of protection had both legal and political implications? For instance, if *dhimmīs* consented to be part of the Muslim polity, why require the additional *jizya* payment at all? Wasn't their consent sufficient? The requirement to pay the *jizya* is stipulated in the Qur'ānic verse 9:29 and so could not simply be ignored given the significance of the Qur'ān as a source of law for Muslim jurists. Additionally, the historical practice of instituting and imposing the *jizya* during the era of early imperial expansion created a precedent for collecting this tax. Some modern reformers might be tempted to read out the *jizya,* and instead adopt consent-based social contract theories to theorize about inclusion of the Other in the Muslim polity. That may very well prove tempting, and certainly intelligible in light of modern legal regimes of immigration and citizenship that help define political community and identity in the modern state. For the purposes of this study, though, the analysis of the *jizya* proceeds with due attention to historical context and jurisprudential argument in order to tease out the intelligibility of the *jizya* to the premodern Muslim jurist.

The *jizya* provided the *dhimmīs,* quite literally, a "buy-in" option to enter a Muslim-ruled social polity. The *jizya* was a payment of money that permitted the *dhimmī* to enter and be part of an Islamically defined political society; the *jizya* therefore represented a condition precedent for the non-Muslim's inclusion into an Islamic polity. However, to posit the *jizya* as a way to ensure belonging in society begs a further question, namely, what was the society to which the *jizya* permitted entry? Or, to put it more bluntly, by paying the *jizya,* what was the *dhimmī* buying into? As this chapter will show, the *dhimmī* rules were often rationalized and justified by reference to the imagined Islamic polity into which the *dhimmī* sought entrance—a society that was committed to a pluralism defined and delimited in light of an imperial Islamic universalism.

3.1.1 *Jizya* history

The *jizya* seems to have provided a sizable tax base for the nascent Islamic empire, as Muslims conquered vast lands in Iraq, Persia, and Egypt, thereby bringing within their control large populations of non-Muslims.[3] Imposing poll-taxes and other regulatory measures on minority religious communities was not unique to the Islamic tradition. Rather, discriminatory regulations were utilized by many polities throughout antiquity, late antiquity, and the medieval period.[4] As Muslim forces expanded and conquered new lands, Muslims formed a minority. According to Wadi Haddad, the *jizya* made perfect sense in the early conquest period when the majority of those living under Muslim dominion were non-Muslim.[5] By taxing the non-Muslims, a revenue flow was generated that financed ongoing military operations, the construction of garrison towns, and various social support programs.[6] But, as non-Muslims began converting to Islam, and the Muslim minority turned into a Muslim majority, the potential return on the *jizya* tax began to diminish and adversely affected the abundance in imperial

[3] Some studies question the nearly synonymous use of the terms *kharāj* and *jizya* in the historical sources. The general view suggests that while the terms *kharāj* and *jizya* seem to have been used interchangeably in early historical sources, what they referred to in any given case depended on the linguistic context. If one finds reference to "a *kharāj* on their heads," the reference was to a poll tax, despite the use of the term *kharāj*, which later became the term of art for land tax. Likewise, if one finds the phrase "*jizya* on their land," this referred to a land tax, despite the use of *jizya* which later came to refer to the poll tax. Early history therefore shows that although each term did not have a determinate technical meaning at first, the concepts of poll tax and land tax existed early in Islamic history. Dennet, *Conversion and the Poll Tax*, 3–10; Aijaz Hassan Qureshi, "The Terms Kharaj and Jizya and Their Implications," *Journal of the Punjab University Historical Society* 12 (1961): 27–38; Hossein Modarressi Tabātabā'i, *Kharāj in Islamic Law* (London: Anchor Press Ltd, 1983).

[4] Michael Goodich, ed., *Other Middle Ages: Witnesses at the Margins of Medieval Society* (Philadelphia: University of Pennsylvania Press, 1998), 8–12; Alan Watson, *Roman Law & Comparative Law* (Athens, Georgia: University of Georgia Press, 1991), 29.

[5] Haddad, "*Ahl al-Dhimma* in an Islamic State," 170.

[6] State support of Muslims is connected with the payment registry called the *diwān*. However, there is some research to suggest that even non-Muslims were at times included on the *diwān* registry. Richard Gottheil, "A Fetwa on the Appointment of Dhimmis to Office," in *Zeitschrift fur Aṣyriologie und Verwandte Gebiete*, ed. Carol Bezold (Strassburg: Verlag von Karl J. Trubner, 1912), 203–14, 207.

coffers. This is not to suggest that the *jizya* institution died out; even regimes as late as the Ottomans imposed the *jizya* on non-Muslims.[7]

Beyond providing tax revenue for the empire, the *jizya* was also a tool of both inclusion and humiliation, thereby ensuring and vindicating Islamic universalist claims, and supporting the enterprise of empire. Authors debate whether the *jizya* was meant to subjugate and humiliate non-Muslims, or whether it was only intended as a service fee for military protection. Muhammad Hamidullah argues that the *jizya* was solely for protection. Without citing economic studies, he states, "So, the non-Muslims paid a little supplementary tax, the jizyah . . . which was neither heavy nor unjust."[8] Mahmoud Ayoub and Haddad argue instead that it served both functions: it was both a mode of subservience and a method of inclusion.[9] Hamidullah's account reflects the imperatives of the myth of harmony, while Haddad and Ayoub offer a historical account of the *jizya*'s complex social function in early Islamic history. To adopt the view that the *jizya* was either inclusive or an instrument of subservience ignores the possibility, indeed likelihood, that the *jizya* was neither one nor the other, but rather was both in purpose and effect. In this sense, the *jizya* cannot easily be characterized exclusively as an instrument of either harmony or persecution. Rather, the studies on the *jizya,* in the aggregate, suggest that the *jizya* was a complex symbol which can be viewed as a tool of marginalization or a mechanism of inclusion, but more fruitfully is understood as both.

3.1.2 Why the *jizya?*

As described above, the *jizya* can be understood as a legal instrument that facilitates the inclusion of the *dhimmī* in the Muslim polity, as well as a political tool of social stratification and revenue generation. The dual political/legal role of the *jizya* is evident in the way in which the early Companions of the Prophet and later Muslim jurists justified its imposition, while also making exceptions to its enforcement in order to take into account the shifting demands of the enterprise of governance.

[7] But as Oded Peri indicates, in places such as Jerusalem, the Ottomans were only collecting up to 45 per cent of the actual *jizya* owed to the state. Oded Peri, "The Muslim waqf and the collection of jizya in late eighteenth-century Jerusalem," in *Ottoman Palestine, 1800–1914: Studies in Economic and Social History,* ed. Gad G. Gilbar (Leiden: E.J. Brill, 1990), 287–97, 291. So even where the *jizya* was imposed, it is not clear whether there was an effective mechanism for collection.

[8] Muhammad Hamidullah, "Status of Non-Muslims in Islam," *Majallat al-Azhar* 45, no. 8 (1973): 6–13, 9.

[9] Ayoub, "The Islamic Context of Muslim-Christian Relations," 469; Haddad, "*Ahl al-Dhimma* in an Islamic State," 172.

Fakhr al-Dīn al-Rāzī (d. 606/1209) for instance, wrote how payment of the *jizya* was not intended to support or preserve disbelief in God. Instead, it had a dual purpose. First, it imposed on Muslims the duty to protect the lives and property of *dhimmīs* living in the Muslim polity.[10] Second, it constituted an incentive for *dhimmīs* to convert upon witnessing the virtues of Islam (*maḥāsin al-Islām*) as a way of life.[11] The incentive quality, though, was premised on the *jizya* also being a symbol of subordination in furtherance of conversion, thereby indirectly upholding the universalist ethic underlying the Islamic imperial enterprise of governance. For instance, al-Rāzī argued that payment of the *jizya* could achieve conversion because it inherently involved humiliation and subordination (*al-dhill wa al-ṣighār*):

> The nature of the rational person is to avoid bearing humiliation and subordination. If the unbeliever is given time and he witnesses the greatness of Islam and hears the proofs of its validity while observing the humiliation and subordination associated with disbelief, then it is clear (*ẓāhir*) that he will consider [all of] that to convert to Islam. This is the purpose of legally requiring the *jizya*.[12]

Notably, the financial support the *jizya* provided the empire was absent from al-Rāzī's list of rationales. This silence was common among many jurists who articulated the rationale for the *jizya*. They viewed the *jizya* as a legal rule directed at the Other, but remained silent on how the *jizya* requirement financially supported the enterprise of governance. Identifying this silence is one thing; trying to interpret its significance is another. It might mean that they viewed the legal rules of *fiqh* as separable from the enterprise of governance. It could reflect the fact that jurists assumed the existence of the enterprise of governance to the point of nearly taking it for granted. It could also signify that they were unwilling to incorporate as part of the rationale of the *jizya* rule the importance of providing financial resources to the governing institutions. All of these interpretations point to a similar conclusion: the fact that the *jizya* provided financial resources to the enterprise of governance was an undeniable consequence of the *jizya*, but not its juridically stated

[10] See also al-Ghazālī, *al-Wasīṭ*, 4:196; Ibn Rushd al-Jadd, *al-Muqaddimāt al-Mumahhidāt*, 1:368, who said the *jizya* paid to provide security (*ta'mīn*) and protection for non-Muslims who maintain their state of disbelief (*kufr*); Shihāb al-Dīn al-Qarāfī, *al-Dhakhīra*, ed. Sa'īd A'rāb (Beirut: Dār al-Gharb al-Islāmī, 1994), 3:457.

[11] Fakhr al-Dīn al-Rāzī, *al-Tafsīr al-Kabīr* (Beirut: Dār Iḥyā' al-Turāth al-'Arabī, 1999), 6:27.

[12] Al-Rāzī, *al-Tafsīr al-Kabīr*, 6:27. See also the Mālikī al-Ḥaṭṭāb, who related a similar rationale for imposing the *jizya* on non-Muslims. Al-Ḥaṭṭāb, *Mawāhib al-Jalīl*, ed. Zakariyyā 'Amīrāt (Beirut: Dār al-Kutub al-'Ilmiyya, 1995), 4:593.

purpose. The express purpose of the law was one thing, while the externalities it created were another. In this case, the jurists' silence regarding the *jizya*'s financial support of the enterprise of governance, at the very least, suggests how they understood and represented the purpose, aim, and function of the *jizya* in an Islamic polity.

However, a Rule of Law framework suggests that their understanding and representation can at best be regarded as only part of the significance of the *jizya.* Their silence on the *jizya*'s financial implications for the empire does not deny in any way that the *jizya* operated within a Rule of Law claim space constituted in part by the enterprise of governance. The intelligibility of the *jizya* draws upon the elision of the universalist ethos of Islam and its concretization through conquest and imperialism. In the process of conquest, Muslims encountered Christians in both Egypt and Syria, Zoroastrians in Persia, and smaller groups of Jews in various locations. Although the Qur'ān 9:29 only identifies the People of the Book as candidates for the *jizya* option, Chapter 1 shows how other groups were permitted to pay the *jizya* as the empire expanded pursuant to the imperative of *jihād.* As noted earlier, Blankinship writes that *jihād* legitimated the imperative of empire in the name of a universal message for all of humanity. *Jihād* thereby offered the language of legitimacy to an ethic of expansion for the purpose of spreading a message that was deemed to be sent for the benefit of the whole world. Economically, the *jihād* ethic also made possible the potential for vast spoils of war with which the Umayyads could pay their soldiers. With conquest came the spoils of war and taxes on newly acquired lands. In addition, the fact of religious diversity presented the Muslim polity with an additional mechanism for ensuring the financial viability of the imperial programme. By having non-Muslims pay the *jizya* to retain their faith but live in the Muslim polity, the *jizya* helped to constitute and perpetuate the empire and its expansion. The significance of the political and economic backdrop to the *jizya*'s intelligibility is further illustrated by examining the economic consequences of an empire that ceased to expand, such as toward the end of the Umayyad period. The spoils of war may have decreased, but the beneficiaries of the empire's coffers still needed to be paid. In this context, the *jizya* might be viewed as an important device for ongoing Muslim rule, if not expansion.[13] Fundamentally, therefore, the *jizya* linked the *dhimmī*'s legal status to the enterprise of governance, at

[13] Khalid Yahya Blankinship, *The End of the Jihad State: The Reign of Hisham Ibn 'Abd al-Malik and the Collapse of the Umayyads* (Albany: State University of New York Press, 1994), 3–13.

least as a matter of the economic reality of empire and conquest, if not by explicit jurisprudential design.[14]

The intelligibility of the *jizya* is best appreciated by viewing it as lying at the intersection of both legal theory and political theory. To put it differently, the claim space from which it arose was bounded by factors ranging from authoritative source-texts to the world of empire and expansion. For instance, when vast numbers of local non-Muslims began to convert to Islam, the Umayyad dynasty began to worry about the public treasury. The Umayyads continued to impose the *jizya* on newly converted Muslims, which led to great criticism of the legitimacy of their actions.[15] The limits on who must pay the *jizya* both restricted the power of the enterprise of governance and differentiated members of the Muslim imperial polity.

3.1.3 Who paid the *jizya*?

Generally, most jurists agreed that the People of the Book, the Magians, and even non-Arab polytheists were permitted to reside in Muslim lands by paying the *jizya*.[16] The tax liability could be imposed individually, thus making each *dhimmī* liable for payment, or it could be imposed collectively on the community as a whole.[17] Significantly, there were some debates about whether Arab non-Muslims were permitted to reside in Muslim lands, and thus be required to pay the *jizya*. Generally, Muslims fought Arab polytheists without giving them the option of establishing a truce. Ḥanafī jurists argued that since non-Arab polytheists could be enslaved, they could also be required to pay the *jizya*. Both slavery and the *jizya*, they argued, involve a diminution of standing and integrity (*salb al-nafs*).[18] On the other hand, Arab polytheists must either convert or be fought.[19] According to Ibn Nujaym, the Prophet was raised among

[14] This is not to suggest that the *jizya* was always applied in fact. As noted earlier, Muslim rulers recognized that imperial longevity could be achieved by paying off potential enemies. Blankinship indicates that in one case, the Muslim government actually paid a large sum to the Byzantine Empire to ensure a peaceful border and stem any ongoing warfare between the parties. Blankinship, *The End of the Jihad State*, 23, 27.

[15] Blankinship, *The End of the Jihad State*, 87–9, 114.

[16] Ibn Qudāma, *al-Mughnī*, 8:362; Al-Ghazālī, *al-Wasīṭ*, 4:198; al-Muḥaqqiq al-Ḥillī, *Sharāʾiʿ al-Islām fī Masāʾil al-Ḥalāl wa al-Ḥarām*, ed. Ṣādiq al-Shīrāzī, 10th ed. (Beirut: Markaz al-Rasūl al-Aʿẓam, 1998), 1:258.

[17] The significance of imposing the liability individually or collectively will be relevant in the discussion below on charitable bequests.

[18] Ibn Nujaym, *al-Baḥr al-Rāʾiq*, 5:187. See also al-Marghīnānī, *al-Hidāya: Sharḥ Bidāyat al-Mubtadiʾ*, ed. Muḥammad Darwīsh (Beirut: Dār al-Arqam, n.d.), 1:452.

[19] The Shiʿa jurist al-Ḥurr al-ʿĀmilī held that polytheists must convert or be killed, whether Arab or not. Al-Ḥurr al-ʿĀmilī, *Wasāʾil al-Shīʿa* (Beirut: Dār Iḥyāʾ al-Turāth al-ʿArabī, n.d.), 11:17.

the Arabs, and the Qur'ān was revealed in the Arabic language; hence the miracle of Islam should have been so evident to them that they had no excuse to remain non-Muslim.[20] If they did not convert to the faith given their ethnicity, their cultural affinities to the Prophet and his followers, or their appreciation of the Arabic of the Qur'ān, no tax could be presumed to incentivize their conversion. Since a principal aim of the *jizya* was to facilitate conversion, imposing the tax on Arab polytheists did not serve this key purpose.[21]

The Mālikī Ibn Rushd al-Jadd offered an alternative argument that was premised on the superiority of the Arab members of the Quraysh, thus introducing an ethnic and tribal element to the stratifying effect of the *jizya*. He held that the *jizya* could not be imposed on polytheist Arabs among the Quraysh since it was not permitted to make them suffer any humiliation or subordination given their genealogical lineage to the Prophet.[22] However, al-Ḥattāb disagreed. He held that since the members of Quraysh had already converted, any non-Muslim among them was actually an apostate from Islam. Consequently, he used the law on apostasy to address the existence of Qurayshī non-Muslims, while avoiding any adverse implications on the social status of Arab members of Quraysh.[23]

The example of 'Umar b. al-Khaṭṭāb's treatment of the Arab Christian tribes of the Banū Najrān and the Banū Taghlib illustrates how a limited commitment to pluralism was a necessary consequence of both ascribing to an Islamic universalist ethos, and pursuing imperial expansion in the face of a hostile enemy. For instance, as noted above, the Prophet allowed the Arab Christian tribe of the Banū Najrān to reside in the Muslim polity while paying a tribute under a treaty of protection or, in other words, a contract of *dhimma*.[24] But when 'Umar was caliph, he felt this privilege was no longer warranted. He ordered the Banū Najrān to evacuate their city, which they did, finding a new home in Iraq.[25] In this case, 'Umar sought to remove the Banū Najrān from the Arabian Peninsula in the interest of securing a firm grasp on the territory in the Peninsula.

'Umar could not, however, adopt a policy of expulsion in all cases unless he was willing to undermine the enterprise of imperial governance entirely. Like the Banū Najrān, the Banū Taghlib was an Arab Christian

[20] Ibn Nujaym, *al-Baḥr al-Rā'iq*, 5:187.
[21] For similar reasoning on this limitation, see al-Marghīnānī, *al-Hidāya*, 1:453.
[22] Ibn Rushd al-Jadd, *al-Muqaddimāt al-Mumahhidāt*, 1:376.
[23] Al-Ḥaṭṭāb, *Mawāhib al-Jalīl*, 4:594.
[24] Al-Balādhurī, *Kitāb Futūḥ al-Buldān*, ed. M.J. de Goeje (Leiden: Brill, 1866), 63–5.
[25] Al-Balādhurī, *Futūḥ al-Buldān*, 67. Irfan Shahîd, "Nadjrān." *Encyclopaedia of Islam, Second Edition*. Eds P. Bearman et al.

tribe that challenged the universalist ethos of Islam, since the tribe shared the Prophet's ethnicity, culture, and language, yet remained non-Muslim. Nonetheless, 'Umar permitted the Banū Taghlib to pay a tribute and thereby remain Christian in the Arab Peninsula. Even more, the Banū Taghlib did not agree to pay the *jizya.* For them, the *jizya* was a demeaning tax that they did not want to pay. 'Umar was advised to call their tribute by another name and permitted them to stay. 'Umar's surprising "tolerance" of Banū Taghlib's Christian commitments was in large part a response to their potential alliance with the Byzantine empire, which could pose a considerable challenge to 'Umar's imperial program. The examples of the Banū Najrān and Banū Taghlib reveal that the content of 'Umar's limited commitment to pluralism arose from a negotiation between the demands of imperial dominion and a commitment to an Islamic universalism. The story of the Banū Taghlib illustrates how their religious otherness presented a difficult dilemma for 'Umar, if viewed through the lenses of both an Islamic universalism and an imperial agenda.[26]

One might consider these two examples from 'Umar's reign as merely pragmatic and having little to do with Sharī'a as Rule of Law. 'Umar wanted to expand the empire and could expel the Banū Najrān at no political cost, while he could not do so with the Banū Taghlib given the Byzantine threat. His contrasting treatment of the two tribes, therefore, could be reduced to mere political pragmatism. While that is an entirely reasonable way to read 'Umar's actions, the problem with that reading arises when considering the implication of 'Umar's actions on the development of an Islamic legal tradition in which 'Umar was viewed as more than merely a political figure. 'Umar was both a Companion of the Prophet and the second caliph of the nascent Islamic polity. As caliph he was a political leader, but as a Companion he embodied in his words and actions a normative content that was relevant for later jurists as they studied and developed the law in subsequent centuries. For instance, writing centuries later, the Ḥanbalī jurist Ibn Qudāma (d. 620/1223) wrote about whether non-Muslims could reside in the Arabian Peninsula. In recounting the legal debates among the various schools, 'Umar's actions during his reign as Caliph-Companion, along with the Prophet's

[26] The Banū Taghlib presented various challenges to the image of Islamic rule and the competing notions of the Muslim polity and Muslim community. 'Alī b. Abī Ṭālib (r. 35–41/656–661), the fourth caliph, prohibited Muslim men from marrying the women of Taghlib. Generally, Muslim men are permitted to marry Christian or Jewish women, but 'Alī prohibited marriage with the women of Taghlib because he was not sure whether the tribe embraced Christianity before or after the corruption of the tradition. Friedmann, "Classification of Unbelievers," 172.

actions, contributed to the debate about whether, where, and for what purposes non-Muslims can enter or reside in the Arabian Peninsula.[27] Consequently, the implications of ʿUmar's actions as Caliph-Companion cannot be reduced to mere political pragmatism if we consider the long-term development of Sharīʿa discourses. His actions carried a normative weight that helped constitute the boundaries of the claim space of Sharīʿa, given the constitutive role a premodern legal education played in determining the sources of authority for legal argument. Juristic debates such as the ones addressed by Ibn Qudāma illustrate that ʿUmar's treatment of both the Banū Najrān and the Banū Taghlib, as incidents of governance, affected how later legal doctrine developed.

The examples of the Banū Najrān and the Banū Taghlib show that the *jizya,* as a legal rule, cannot be viewed in isolation from the larger political enterprise of imperial expansion. As al-Māwardī indicated, the *jizya* served a complex set of purposes: (1) the *jizya* permitted the inclusion of non-Muslims in the polity and the retention of their faith; (2) the *jizya* reminded the *dhimmīs* of their humiliated status as a conquered people (*adhillāʾ maqhūrīn*) and their subjection to Islamic law; and (3) the *jizya* offered non-Muslims an incentive to convert to Islam.[28] The *jizya* was a mechanism of *qualified* inclusion, because the *dhimmī* did not actively participate or contribute to the universalist, expansionist mission of Islam. *Jizya* payments were intended to provide for security and military protection (as well as to foster imperial expansion), but the *dhimmī* did not actually fight in imperial campaigns. In fact, *dhimmīs* could not forgo paying the *jizya* by serving in the military; they were not trusted to fight in good faith, according to premodern jurists. [29] Additionally, Muslim jurists considered the *jizya* to be a mark of subservience, humiliation, and even punishment (*ʿuqūba*).[30] Notably, the logic underlying the *jizya* requirement was not open to the possibility that the non-Muslim considered himself an integral part of the Muslim polity, a loyal subject, and genuinely interested in its ongoing prosperity. For these reasons, the *jizya* permitted the *dhimmī* a qualified inclusion in the Muslim polity. Although included in the Muslim polity, the *dhimmī* nonetheless represented a possible threat to the enterprise of governance, as defined in terms of Islamic universalism, military conquest, and imperial rule.

[27] Ibn Qudāma, *al-Mughnī*, 8:529–34. [28] Al-Māwardī, *al-Ḥāwī*, 14:283–4.

[29] Badr al-Dīn al-ʿAynī, *al-Bināya Sharḥ al-Hidāya*, ed. Ayman Ṣāliḥ Shaʿbān (Beirut: Dār al-Kutub al-ʿIlmiyya, 2000), 7:242.

[30] Al-Marghīnānī held that the term *jizya* is derived from the term *jazāʾ*, indicating a sufficient form of punishment (*ʿuqūba*). Al-Marghīnānī, *al-Hidāya*, 1:454.

3.2 INCLUSION AND ITS LIMITS: CONTRACT THEORY AND LIABILITY FOR THEFT

The *dhimmī* rules contributed to the ordering and stratification of an Islamic polity even when the rules sought to include and accommodate the *dhimmīs*' interests through the use of exceptions to general rules of application. The exceptions to liability and obligation were no less legal than the general rules; together, however, the general rules and exceptions functioned both to include and accommodate on the one hand, and to stratify on the other. An example of this dual nature of the general rule and legal exception is the general rule prohibiting theft and the scope of protection granted to the kinds of property that *dhimmīs* might own. The Qur'ān renders theft a crime with the stiff penalty of hand amputation. Also, according to premodern jurists, the thief had to return the property he stole if it was still in his possession. In the event the property was destroyed or otherwise converted, jurists debated whether the thief must compensate the victim in addition to suffering amputation.[31] These were the general rules applicable to a thief that, in the aggregate, preserved the individual's proprietary interests while also providing sufficient deterrence to limit the occurrence of socially destructive behaviors.

The punishment for theft is stipulated in the Qur'ān, a book that Muslims believe is the word of God revealed to the Prophet Muḥammad, but to which non-Muslims have no faith-based reason to adhere. Premodern Muslim jurists understood that *dhimmīs* did not consider the Qur'ān an authoritative source of law for themselves on faith-based grounds. Consequently they resorted to the contract of protection as the mechanism by which to legitimately impose Qur'ānically based obligations upon the *dhimmī*. As noted above, the contract of protection was in part a political agreement by which *dhimmīs* abided by the Sharīʿa. Which parts of the Sharīʿa they had to abide by, though, was not always easy to determine. In the case of theft, premodern jurists held that the *dhimmīs* were liable to the Qur'ānic prohibition against stealing someone else's property.[32] Because *dhimmīs* benefitted from the general protection and social order that arose from the deterrent effect of criminal penalities, Muslim jurists argued that *dhimmīs* also had to bear the burden of being liable to the same punishment in the event they committed theft.

[31] For a discussion of the debates on theft liability, see Anver M. Emon, "*Ḥuqūq Allāh* and *Ḥuqūq al-ʿIbād*: A Legal Heuristic for a Natural Rights Regime," *Islamic Law and Society* 13, no. 3 (2006): 325–91, 358–72.

[32] Qur'ān, 5:38.

Jurists argued that the contract of protection was the mechanism by which the *dhimmī* was included within the ambit of the Muslim polity. But how they understood the inclusive effect of the contract differed. For example, al-Ghazālī relied on a contract-based argument to hold that a *dhimmī* should suffer the same liability as a Muslim for theft because of "his obligation to our laws" (*li ilzāmihi aḥkāminā*).[33] By entering into the contract of protection, he suggested that *dhimmīs* agreed to abide by the Sharīʿa. In doing so, they derived a certain benefit from the security of expectation interests that the law provided. Effectively, al-Ghazālī recognized the *dhimmī* as a participant in Muslim society who benefitted from the protections afforded by the law. As a participant, the *dhimmī* was not only entitled to the benefits of living in a political society ruled by an enterprise of governance, but also had to endure the burdens. By using a contract-based argument, al-Ghazālī justified imposing the Sharīʿa on *dhimmīs*; in doing so, he used the contract to include them as part of the polity. Here, the *dhimmī* was as equally entitled and burdened as his Muslim neighbor, which implicitly reflected an attitude of inclusion.

For other jurists, the contract approach above permitted too much inclusion without sufficient demarcation and distinction between the Muslim "Us" and the *dhimmī* "Other." For instance, al-Shīrāzī argued that the legitimacy of applying the penalty for theft against the *dhimmīs* was that their own law and tradition forbade theft.[34] Consequently, even if they wished to assert their immunity on the grounds of their distinct faith commitments, they could not avoid liability for theft. The fact that their own tradition banned theft indicated their acceptance of the underlying values that arose from the ban. As such, holding them liable to the Sharīʿa ban did not violate their rights to autonomy and respect under the contract of protection. Like al-Ghazālī, al-Shīrāzī suggested that *dhimmīs* should bear the same burdens as Muslims. But al-Shīrāzī's argument was not premised on consent to Sharīʿa-based obligations via entry into the contract of protection. Rather, by allowing the *dhimmīs* to enter into a contract of protection, the law required the Islamic enterprise of governance to respect the *dhimmīs*' distinct tradition, which just happened to coincide with the demands of Sharīʿa-based doctrines on theft. It is as if al-Shīrāzī said: "The contract of protection requires Muslims to respect the *dhimmīs* and their adherence to their own traditions. Since the *dhimmīs*' tradition also bans theft, they can be

[33] Al-Ghazālī, *al-Wasīṭ*, 4:141.

[34] Abū Isḥāq al-Shīrāzī, *al-Muhadhdhab fī Fiqh al-Imām al-Shāfiʿī*, ed. Zakariyā ʿAmīrāt (Beirut: Dār al-Kutub al-ʿIlmiyya, 1995), 3:317.

held liable to our Sharīʿa bans on theft without any breach of contract." Al-Shīrāzī may have relied on the contract of protection to begin his analysis, but ultimately his emphasis was on the *dhimmīs'* otherness. In the interest of respecting their diversity, al-Shīrāzī implicitly "othered" them to a degree not present in al-Ghazālī's argument of inclusion. Admittedly, some might view the difference between these two approaches as one of degree rather than kind. Nonetheless, the contrast between al-Ghazālī and al-Shīrāzī illustrates that even when seeking to include the *dhimmī* as a legal subject of the Islamic enterprise of governance, the legal arguments used to justify their inclusion can have different implications on their standing and status within the polity. For al-Ghazālī, the argument of contract emphasized the shared experience of those living in organized society together. For al-Shīrāzī, the argument from contract emphasized the otherness of the *dhimmīs* living in a Muslim polity. In both cases, the *dhimmī* was subjected to the Sharīʿa-based bans on theft, but the rationales employed showcase different attitudes about the extent to which the *dhimmī* was included in the Muslim polity and also remained "othered."

3.3 ACCOMMODATION AND ITS LIMITS: CONTRABAND OR CONSUMER GOODS?

Jurists utilized legal arguments that limited not only the scope of the *dhimmī*'s inclusion in the Muslim polity, but also the degree to which an Islamic enterprise of governance could accommodate the distinct interests of *dhimmīs*. As noted earlier, the contract of protection required the enterprise of governance to protect the *dhimmīs'* property interests, just as it protected the Muslims' property interests. The scope of that protection, though, was called into question when the *dhimmīs'* property interests were viewed either as incompatible with other Sharīʿa-based norms or the values of an Islamic imperial enterprise of governance. Consequently, the contract became a site of legal debate and negotiation about the degree to which the *dhimmīs'* difference could be accommodated without impinging on other values that contributed to the legitimacy and functioning of the enterprise of governance. To demonstrate how the contract offered a negotiative site for deliberating on the scope of the *dhimmīs'* accommodation, this section addresses whether or not the *dhimmī* can consume alcohol and pork in an Islamic polity, and the limits on the capacity of the Sharīʿa legal system to redress wrongs to the *dhimmīs'* property interests in these items.

Certainly the *dhimmī*'s contract of protection upheld his interest in his private property. But this begs an important legal question—what counted as legally protected property? Not all property was equally protected under Islamic law. Only certain types of property were legally recognized as conveying rights of exclusive use and enjoyment. As the Ḥanafī al-Kāsānī said, the property that conveys such rights is considered *mutaqawwam*, or inviolable under the law.[35] Defining what counts as inviolable property could have an adverse impact on the *dhimmī*'s expectation interests under the law. Specifically, in the case of wine and pork, could *dhimmīs* consume such items in a Muslim polity? If they could consume such items, on what legal basis could they do so? And if they could legally own and consume wine and pork when living in a Muslim polity, then could *dhimmīs* also petition the enterprise of governance to punish anyone who stole the wine and pork products from them? These are important questions because of how they highlight the mutually constitutive relationship of the law and the enterprise of governance concerning the claims of minority members of a polity. For instance, Sharīʿa-based doctrines do not recognize wine and pork as *mutaqawwam*. Consequently, if the enterprise of governance were to punish someone for stealing the *dhimmī*'s wine or pork, it would employ the police force of an Islamic enterprise of governance to uphold the *dhimmī*'s property interests in items that have no legally recognized value in a Sharīʿa legal system. The irony of this possible outcome was not lost on premodern Muslim jurists. An analysis of their legal arguments on this issue will show that while Muslim jurists used the law to accommodate the *dhimmīs*' interests, the *dhimmīs* did not enjoy the same expectation interests that they would in the case of other types of property. The jurists' arguments about consumer goods such as wine or pork show how a commitment to pluralism and accommodation is nonetheless limited by commitments to certain public values whose content and weight arose out of the mutually constitutive relationship between the law and an Islamically defined enterprise of governance.

Consuming alcohol (*shurb al-khamr*) is a crime under Islamic law, with a penalty of forty or eighty lashes, depending on which school of law is referenced.[36] Additionally, the consumption of pork is prohibited to

[35] Abū Bakr b. Masʿūd al-Kāsānī, *Badāʾiʿ al-Ṣanāʾiʿ fī Tartīb al-Sharāʾiʿ*, eds ʿAlī Muḥammad Muʿawwaḍ and ʿĀdil Aḥmad ʿAbd al-Mawjūd (Beirut: Dār al-Kutub al-ʿIlmiyya, 1997), 9:292.

[36] The punishment for consuming alcohol is generally held to be forty lashes, although some schools such as the Mālikīs required eighty. For a discussion of this debate, see Ḥusayn Ḥāmid Ḥassān, *Naẓariyyat al-Maṣlaḥa fī al-Fiqh al-Islāmī* (Cairo: Dār al-Nahḍa al-ʿArabiyya, 1971), 73.

Muslims under their dietary laws. However, premodern Muslim jurists did not apply these prohibitions to *dhimmīs*; jurists allowed *dhimmīs* to consume both items. This begs the questions of why, on what basis, and with what limits? For jurists such as al-Ghazālī and al-Kāsānī, the *dhimmīs* were entitled under the contract of protection to have their own traditions respected. If their traditions prohibited something that Sharīʿa-based rules prohibit, then there was little room for the *dhimmī* to argue on contract grounds that he or she should be immune from Sharīʿa-based liability. But where the *dhimmīs*' tradition permitted one thing, and Sharīʿa-based doctrines prohibited it, jurists had to decide which tradition should prevail and why.

For al-Ghazālī, when *dhimmīs* entered the contract of protection, the contract's terms did not include liability for consumption of alcohol or pork because their own tradition permitted consumption of both.[37] Likewise, al-Kāsānī argued in similar fashion that *dhimmīs* could consume alcohol and pork because their tradition allowed them to do so. [38] For both jurists, the contract of protection accommodated the *dhimmī*'s difference and distinctiveness. Despite this grant of permission to *dhimmīs,* though, jurists limited the implications of this permission on other corollary issues of law and legal order. For instance, while jurists agreed that *dhimmīs* could consume alcohol, they nonetheless were concerned that unrestricted alcohol consumption by *dhimmīs* might endanger the social good. Consequently, while they permitted the *dhimmī* to consume alcohol, they developed legal rules banning public drunkenness or public displays of alcohol.[39] In other words, the jurists allowed the *dhimmīs* to consume alcohol, despite the Qur'ānic prohibition. But they were mindful to limit the scope of the *dhimmīs*' license in the interest of a public good whose content was informed by the general ban on alcohol consumption. In this case, then, while the *dhimmī* enjoyed an exception to a rule of general application, that rule of general application (i.e., prohibition on consuming alcohol) nonetheless gave content to a conception of the public good that found expression in corollary legal rules banning public drunkenness, for instance.

The dynamic of general rules informing a notion of the public good that was used to limit the scope of accommodation is further apparent in

[37] Al-Ghazālī, *al-Wasīṭ*, 4:152.

[38] Al-Kāsānī, *Badāʾiʿ al-Ṣanāʾiʿ*, 9:292. See also, Saḥnūn b. Saʿīd al-Tanūkhī (d. 240/854), *al-Mudawwana al-Kubrā* (Beirut: Dār Ṣādir, n.d.), 6:270, who did not apply the punishment for consumption of alcohol to the *dhimmī.*

[39] Al-Māwardī, *al-Ḥāwī*, 13:328; al-Shīrāzī, *al-Muhadhdhab*, 3:317; al-Muzanī, *Mukhtaṣar al-Muzanī*, in vol. 5 of Muḥammad b. Idrīs al-Shāfiʿī, *Kitāb al-Umm* (Beirut: Dār al-Fikr, 1990), 5:385; al-Kāsānī, *Badāʾiʿ al-Ṣanāʾiʿ*, 9:214. For a general discussion on the exception to the punishment for alcohol consumption, see Zaydān, *Aḥkām al-Dhimmiyyīn*, 179–80.

the legal debate about whether a *dhimmī* could petition the enterprise of governance to amputate the hand of a thief who stole the *dhimmī*'s pork or wine, on the basis of the Qur'ānic punishment for theft. Suppose a *dhimmī* stole wine or pigs from another *dhimmī*. This is an interesting case to consider because for both parties the items are presumably lawful for them to consume. Indeed, the Ḥanafī al-Kāsānī recognized that under the *dhimmīs*' law, the property was deemed as rights-conferring. But under Sharīʿa-based doctrine, such property was not rights-conferring since it was not *mutaqawwam*. Or as al-Māwardī noted, its destruction connoted no value (*lā qīma ʿalā mutlafihi*).[40] If the wronged *dhimmī* sought redress under Sharīʿa-based doctrines against the thieving *dhimmī*, should the Muslim judge punish the thieving *dhimmī* with the Qur'ānic punishment? If the judge did so, wouldn't that effectively be using the doctrine and institutions of a Sharīʿa legal system to enforce a right to a kind of property that is not regarded as value-conferring under Sharīʿa-based norms, but that is value-conferring under the *dhimmīs*' tradition? In other words, wouldn't the judge be applying the *dhimmīs*' tradition on property to effectuate a Qur'ānically based punishment? This question not only presented a certain irony to Muslim jurists. It also raised an important question about the priority of Sharīʿa doctrines over and against any other tradition of value. This was more than a mere conflicts of law issue. If viewed through the framework of Rule of Law, this problem posed a challenge to the sovereign integrity of the enterprise of governance.[41] To apply the *dhimmī*'s tradition would have involved channeling it through an adjudicating institution that was constituted in part by Sharīʿa-based norms as a source of its legal and political legitimacy. Put differently, the challenge for jurists was whether and to what extent the *dhimmī*'s tradition should or should not constitute, in part, the boundaries of the claim space of Sharīʿa as Rule of Law, which was defined in terms of an Islamic enterprise of governance and Sharīʿa-based norms and values. Certainly the *dhimmī* should be able to have certain expectation interests and legal protection under the contract of protection, but at what cost to the integrity of a Sharīʿa legal system embedded in an Islamic imperial enterprise of governance?

These systemic questions seemed to underlie what might seem a relatively straightforward question of whether the *dhimmī* can demand that the enterprise of governance punish the thief for stealing his wine

40 Al-Māwardī, *al-Ḥāwī*, 13:350.

41 A contemporary example that raises similar legal reservations is the current debate in the United States about whether or not it is appropriate to invoke international law in constitutional law disputes. See for instance, Kahn, *Political Theology*, 10. This particular issue will be addressed at greater length in Chapter 7.

or pork. Al-Kāsānī resolved the immediate question by emphasizing that wine and pork were not *mutaqawwam,* or had no legal value. Consequently, if a *dhimmī* stole wine from another *dhimmī,* he would not suffer the Qur'ānic punishment for theft, despite having stolen something that did not belong to him.[42] If such property had no value, then no theft technically occurred. To elevate the analysis to the systemic level, though, one can appreciate that for al-Kāsānī, to use the coercive power of an Islamic enterprise of governance to redress the theft of a type of property that is condemned by Sharī'a-based rules might appear to "over-accommodate" the *dhimmī* at the expense of either legal consistency, the public good sought through Sharī'a-based regulations, or both.

This is not to say, however, that a *dhimmī* whose pork or wine were stolen by another was without recourse. Even though the *dhimmī* was not able to pursue a criminal action against the thief on Qur'ānic grounds, some (but not all) jurists permitted the *dhimmī* to be compensated for the value of his lost property, such as wine or pork. The Mālikī Ṣaḥnūn held that where pork or wine were stolen from a *dhimmī,* the thief was not subjected to the Qur'ānic punishment, but was required to pay damages in the form of financial compensation (*aghrama thamnahu*).[43] Ibn Ḥazm noted various opinions that held the thief liable to both the Qur'ānic punishment and financial compensation, given that the property in question had value for the *dhimmīs* under their tradition. However, he also noted that others held that the thief only owed financial compensation, but was not subjected to the Qur'ānic punishment. And yet others held that the thief had no liability whatsoever. Importantly, in the interest of legal consistency and coherence, Ibn Ḥazm was critical of those who would deny the corporal sanction but allow financial contribution; if the property had no value for one sanction, how could it have value for another?[44] Ibn Ḥazm's critique is important if only to showcase that the legal inconsistency is intelligible if we appreciate how this particular issue sits at the intersection of both law and an enterprise of governance premised upon an Islamic universalism and imperial ethic. When these ethics come into conflict, we can see and appreciate the outcome in terms of the law.

The general bans on the consumption of alcohol and pork provide important insights into the way the law was used to accommodate *dhimmīs* and to limit the scope of that accommodation in the interest of a complex conception of the social good. The debates on these legal

[42] Al-Kāsānī, *Badā'i' al-Ṣanā'i',* 9:292.
[43] Ṣaḥnūn, *al-Mudawwana al-Kubra,* 6:278.
[44] Ibn Ḥazm, *al-Muḥallā bi'l-Athār,* ed. 'Abd al-Ghaffār Sulaymān al-Bandārī (Beirut: Dār al-Kutub al-'Ilmiyya, n.d.), 12:321–2.

doctrines, whether general rules or corollary issues, illustrate that Muslim jurists acknowledged, respected, and accommodated the *dhimmīs*' traditions by exempting them from certain Sharīʿa-based liabilities, as well as giving them qualified protections under the law. The scope of that accommodation was limited, though, where it posed a threat to the social good of the Islamic polity, which was defined in various ways (doctrinal, institutional, political, etc.) that could, at times, come into conflict with one another.

3.4 PROPERTY, PIETY, AND SECURING THE POLITY: THE CASE OF *DHIMMĪS* AND CHARITABLE ENDOWMENTS

If jurists limited the scope of accommodation out of concern for certain public values, it is reasonable to ask what those public values were. In the case of a *dhimmī* who consumed alcohol, the general rule prohibiting alcohol consumption did not apply; instead, an exception was created for the *dhimmī*, given a contractarian theory that paid respect to the *dhimmī*'s tradition. Yet the very rule that prohibited consumption of alcohol and was suspended in the case of the *dhimmī* nonetheless operated at a different level—the level of public policy or public weal—to inform a conception of the public good that thereby justified a different legal rule that prohibited any public drunkenness by the *dhimmī*. In this sense, the general legal prohibition helped to constitute the ethos of the Islamic polity and gave "Islamic" content to the enterprise of governance. To view Sharīʿa as Rule of Law allows us to recognize how the law and the enterprise of governance operate in relation to one another in this particular example. While the jurists themselves focused on general rules and exceptions, their debates operated at multiple levels, both as an articulation of the *dhimmī*'s scope of legal liability and as a mechanism for constituting political society, political order, and the guiding principles of governance amidst diversity. Alcohol consumption is but one example that illuminates how Sharīʿa as Rule of Law captures the mutually constitutive relationship of law and governance in a context of difference and diversity. Another example is the legal debate among jurists about whether *dhimmīs* could endow charitable trusts, or *awqāf* (sing. *waqf*), for the purpose of teaching the Bible or Torah.

To endow property in a trust was a right that accrued to a property owner as a private individual. To use one's property to create charitable endowments, though, was often intended to influence the public weal, whether in some small or large part. Private rights of ownership and bequest raised concerns for jurists when property was donated for public purposes that could contravene the public good. In other words, while private property rights might be protected, the scope of protection was limited in light of competing interests of a more general, public nature. Consequently, the juristic debate about whether and to what extent a *dhimmī* could endow a charitable trust had to account for the need to respect both the *dhimmī*'s private property interests and the imperative to protect the public good. Examining how jurists resolved this balance will reveal the often implicit factors that contributed to their notion of the public good and those that diminished it.

Two ways to create a charitable endowment were (1) a bequest that will take effect upon the testator's death (i.e., *waṣiyya*), and (2) an *inter vivos* transfer of property directly into a trust (*waqf*). Shāfiʿī and Ḥanbalī jurists generally agreed that *dhimmīs* could create trusts and issue bequests to any specified individual (*shakhṣ muʿayyan*), regardless of religious background, although some jurists limited the beneficiaries to one's kin group.[45] This permissive attitude was based on the legal respect for private ownership (*tamlīk*) and the rights the property owner held because of his claim on his property.[46] Shāfiʿī and Ḥanbalī jurists held that the *dhimmī*'s private property interest was sufficiently important to warrant the right to bequeath property to other individuals.

However, if the *dhimmī*'s bequest was to establish something that might adversely affect the public interest (understood in terms of an Islamic universalism), then the bequest was a sin against God and could not be valid under the Sharīʿa.[47] To hold otherwise would be to use the institutions of an Islamic enterprise of governance to legitimate practices that contravene an Islamically defined public good. Consequently, if a *dhimmī* created a charitable trust to support building a church or a school for Torah or Bible studies, Shāfiʿī jurists would invalidate the

[45] Al-Ghazālī, *al-Wasīṭ*, 2:397–8. Al-Māwardī, *al-Ḥāwī*, 8:328–30, wrote that there is a dispute about whether a non-Muslim can make a bequest to anyone other than a free Muslim of legal majority; al-Nawawī, *Rawḍa*, 5:317, held that a *waqf* could be for the benefit of a *dhimmī*, but not for an enemy of the state (*ḥarbī*) or apostate; al-Shīrāzī, *al-Muhadhdhab*, 2:323–4, allowed *waqfs* for specified *dhimmīs* but noted the debate about *waqfs* for the benefit of apostates or enemies of the state.

[46] Al-Ghazālī, *al-Wasīṭ*, 2:397–8. Abū ʿAbd Allāh b. Mufliḥ, *al-Furūʿ*, ed. Abū al-Zahrāʾ Ḥāzim al-Qāḍī (Beirut: Dār al-Kutub al-ʿIlmiyya, 1997), 4:513; Ibn Qudāma, *al-Mughnī*, 5:646.

[47] Al-Ghazālī, *al-Wasīṭ*, 3:41–2; al-Nawawī, *Rawḍa*, 6:107, allowed a *waṣiyya* to be for the benefit of *dhimmīs*, *ḥarbīs*, and apostates; Ibn Qudāma, *al-Mughnī*, 6:103, analogized a *waṣiyya* to a gift, and said that both could be given to *dhimmīs* and *ḥarbīs* in the *dār al-ḥarb;* Abu ʿAbd Allāh b. Mufliḥ, *al-Furūʿ*, 4:513l; al-Bahūtī, *Kashshāf al-Qināʿ ʿan Matn al-Iqnāʿ* (Beirut: Dār al-Kutub al-ʿIlmiyya, 1997), 4:442; al-Muḥaqqiq al-Ḥillī, *Sharāʾiʿ al-Islām*, 1:482.

waqf because it constituted a sin (*maʿṣiyya*), and thereby fell outside the scope of activity the law could uphold and protect.[48]

A precise, nearly syllogistic analysis was provided by the Shāfiʿī jurist al-Shīrāzī. First, he held that a charitable *waqf*, in its essence, is a pious endowment that brings one close to God (*qurba*). Second, he held that anyone who creates a charitable endowment through a bequest or *waṣiyya* will create an institution that bestows bounties (*hasanāt*) on others. Lastly, he concluded that any charitable endowment that facilitates sin (*iʿāna ʿalā maʿṣīya*) is not lawful.[49] Al-Shīrāzī held that charitable endowments that support a church or Torah reading school perpetuated disbelief in the land of Islam, and thereby were tantamount to sin; he argued that because the bounties from such charitable endowments were sinful, any such endowment was void (*bāṭila*) as a matter of law.[50] Al-Shīrāzī went so far as to liken such bequests to a bequest that armed the Muslim polity's enemies, thereby equating both in terms of their potential to inflict harm on the Muslim polity.[51] In other words, for al-Shīrāzī, a charitable endowment that supported the perpetuation of value systems that were contrary to the Islamic universalist ethos was not simply sinful and thereby legally invalid; it was a security threat that had to be contained for the benefit and perpetuation of the Islamic enterprise of governance. To validate and legally permit such charitable endowments as a matter of law would be to use the claim space of Sharīʿa, both in terms of its doctrines and institutions of enforcement, in a manner adverse to the interests of an Islamic enterprise of governance envisioned in both imperial and Islamic universalist terms.[52]

Contrary to this approach, Ḥanafī jurists addressed the power to bequeath using a hypothetical about a *dhimmī* who bequeathed his home to be a church, as opposed to leaving it to a specifically named person. Abū Ḥanīfa held this bequest lawful on the ground that this act constituted a pious, devotional act for the *dhimmī* (i.e., *qurba*), and must

[48] Al-Ghazālī, *al-Wasīṭ*, 2:397; Shihāb al-Dīn al-Ramlī, *Nihāyat al-Muḥtāj ilā Sharḥ al-Minhāj*, 3rd ed. (Beirut: Dār Iḥyāʾ al-Turāth al-ʿArabī, 1992), 5:366. The Jaʿfarī al-Muḥaqqiq al-Ḥillī interestingly held that a *Muslim* could not create a *waqf* to support a church, synagogue, or schools for studying the Torah or Bible. However, he allowed a non-Muslim to do so, thus introducing yet another complicated piece into the debate. Al-Muḥaqqiq al-Ḥillī, *Sharāʾiʿ al-Islām*, 1:459.

[49] Al-Shīrāzī, *al-Muhadhdhab*, 2:323–4.

[50] Al-Shīrāzī, *al-Muhadhdhab*, 2:341–2.

[51] For another argument, the Ḥanbalī Ibn Qudāma argued that a bequest could not be made to support schools for teaching the Torah or the Bible because both had been abrogated by the Qurʾān and contain corruptions. Ibn Qudāma, *al-Mughnī*, 6:105. See also al-Bahūtī, *Kashshāf al-Qināʿ*, 4:442.

[52] The nature of al-Shīrāzī's argument should be familiar to those concerned about efforts to block the building of mosques in countries such as the United States. Indeed, the polemics around Park 51 in New York City and the mosque project in Murfreesboro, Tennessee reflect analogous arguments about threat and security.

be respected just as Muslims respect the *dhimmī*'s faith in other regards. In other words, while both al-Shīrāzī and Abū Ḥanīfa viewed charitable endowments as bringing one closer to God, Abū Ḥanīfa differed in that he appreciated that bringing someone closer to God cannot be defined only in Islamic terms; closeness to God takes different forms depending on the tradition to which one belongs. Abū Ḥanīfa's students, Muḥammad al-Shaybānī and Abū Yūsuf, however, disagreed. They invalidated such a bequest because they (like al-Shīrāzī) deemed its subject matter sinful (*maʿṣiyya ḥaqīqa*) despite the *dhimmī*'s belief that it was a pious act.[53]

This dispute within the Ḥanafī school raised a fundamental question for jurists operating at the intersection of law and the enterprise of governance: by what terms of reference should one determine and evaluate the *dhimmī*'s act of charity?[54] To resolve this question, the Ḥanafī al-ʿAynī offered four possible outcomes:

- If a bequest involved a pious act in the *dhimmī*'s tradition but not in the Islamic tradition, many Ḥanafīs held that it should be allowed, although other schools (as well as other Ḥanafīs) disagreed.
- If the *dhimmī* made a bequest that would be a pious act for Muslims, like donating to support the Muslim pilgrimage to Mecca (i.e., *ḥajj*) or for building a mosque, the bequest was invalid, as it went against the *dhimmī*'s faith. However, if the bequest benefitted specifically named individuals, it was valid, since the *dhimmī*'s private interest as property owner was to be respected under the law.
- If the bequest concerned a subject matter that was lawful under the *dhimmī*'s beliefs and Islamic beliefs, it was valid.
- If the bequest involved a subject matter that was unlawful in both the *dhimmī*'s faith and the Muslim faith, it was invalid. The underlying subject matter would be a sin for both Muslims and *dhimmīs* to allow.[55]

By offering these alternatives, al-ʿAynī illustrated the underlying issues at stake, namely the *dhimmī*'s private property interests, the limits on the *dhimmī* in light of his tradition's requirements, and finally a juridically defined public good that limited the *dhimmī*'s scope to create charitable bequests. In the interest of upholding the *dhimmīs*' private property interests, al-ʿAynī granted them the authority to create pious endowments that

[53] Al-ʿAynī, *al-Bināya*, 13:495; Ibn Nujaym, *al-Baḥr al-Rāʾiq*, 9:302; al-Kāsānī, *Badāʾiʿ al-Ṣanāʾiʿ*, 10:500–1.

[54] Indeed, this was the dilemma in the jurisprudence noted by al-ʿAynī. Al-ʿAynī, *al-Bināya*, 13:495.

[55] Al-ʿAynī, *al-Bināya*, 13:496; Ibn Nujaym, *al-Baḥr al-Rāʾiq*, 9:302; al-Kāsānī, *Badāʾiʿ al-Ṣanāʾiʿ*, 10:500–1.

did not violate any precept in the *dhimmīs'* traditions or the Islamic one. In other words, if the charitable endowment was lawful under both the *dhimmīs'* and the Islamic tradition, there was no real conflict; to allow such bequests would uphold the Islamic values underlying the enterprise of governance, and respect the *dhimmīs'* tradition pursuant to the contract of protection. In such a case, the claim space of Sharīʿa would not countenance something that would run contrary to Sharīʿa-based doctrines, the public good, or an Islamic enterprise of governance.

Notably, the *dhimmī* could not bequeath a charitable endowment for something that was lawful under Islam but unlawful or of no legal significance under the *dhimmīs'* tradition, such as for instance the *ḥajj*. Respect for the *dhimmīs'* tradition, as required under the contract of protection, arguably animated this legal outcome. Interestingly, though, one cannot ignore the fact that the *dhimmī's* private rights of property disposition are limited by his own tradition, regardless of how a particular *dhimmī*-grantor might feel about the matter.

The most difficult issue had to do with whether the *dhimmī* could create a charitable endowment that upheld a value in his own tradition, but was contrary to Islamic values. This is the case on which jurists disagreed, as noted above. For some, to give legal effect to such endowments would be tantamount to giving legal effect to sin. Moreover, some jurists went so far as to consider such endowments security threats to the well-being of the polity. Others, such as some Ḥanafī jurists, allowed for such endowments. They recognized that the *dhimmī's* tradition considered such endowments valuable, and Muslim rulers were required to respect the *dhimmī's* traditions under the contract of protection.

To further complicate matters, the Mālikīs had their own approach, which carved out a middle ground between the two positions noted above. Mālikīs addressed the issue of charitable endowments by reference to the religious association of the testator, the framework of Islamic inheritance law, and the prevailing tax regime. Under Islamic inheritance law, two-thirds of a decedent's property was distributed pursuant to a rule of inheritance that designated percentage shares for specifically identified heirs. The decedent could bequeath the remaining one-third to non-heirs.[56] Mālikīs asked, though, whether a Christian *dhimmī* with no heirs could bequeath all of his property to the head of the Church. Generally, the Christian could give one-third of his estate to the Patriarch, but the remaining two-thirds escheated to the Muslim polity,

[56] On the rules of inheritance in the Qur'ān and Islamic law, see Qur'ān 4: 11–12; David Powers, *Studies in Qur'an and Hadith: The Formation of the Islamic Law of Inheritance* (Berkeley: University of California Press, 1986).

which was considered his lawful heir in this case.[57] Even if the testator left a testamentary instrument that transferred his whole estate to the Patriarchate, the above arrangement was to be carried out.[58]

The application of this general rule, however, depended on whether the *dhimmī*-decedent was personally liable to the governing regime for the *jizya* or whether the *dhimmī*'s community was collectively liable for the tax payment. If the *dhimmī* was personally liable for paying the *jizya* directly to the government, the above ruling on escheat to the government applied. The rationale for this rule was as follows: with the death of the *dhimmī*, the enterprise of governance lost its annual tax revenue from him. Consequently, the escheat of his estate was designed to account for the regime's lost revenue.[59]

But suppose the leaders of the *dhimmī*'s community collected the *jizya* from the community's members and delivered the payment to the ruling regime on behalf of the community. Furthermore, suppose the community collectively paid a pre-established collective *jizya*, and that the total sum did not decrease with deaths of community members. Under such circumstances, many Mālikīs allowed individual *dhimmīs* (presumably without heirs) to bequeath their entire estate to whomever they wished.[60] This particular ruling worked to the financial benefit of the enterprise of governance. The enterprise of governance still received the same *jizya* tax revenues. Any financial loss was distributed to the *dhimmī* community, since its tax liability did not diminish with the death of its community members. To offset that financial loss, the Mālikīs permitted *dhimmīs* to bequeath their entire estate to the community when they lacked any heirs.

In conclusion, when a *dhimmī* sought to donate money to endow a religious institution, Muslim jurists were concerned about giving such charitable institutions legal recognition. To use Sharīʿa-based legal categories and institutions to uphold non-Muslim religious institutions would seem awkward and ironic at best, illegitimate at worst, given a public good defined in terms of a universalizing Islamic ethos. The legal debate about the scope of the *dhimmī*'s power to bequeath property for

[57] Ibn Rushd al-Jadd, *al-Bayān wa al-Taḥṣīl* (Beirut: Dār al-Gharb al-Islāmī, 1988), 13:326–7.

[58] Ibn Rushd al-Jadd, *al-Bayān*, 13:326–7. See also al-Ḥattāb, *Mawāhib al-Jalīl*, 8:515, who relates this view, and critiques another that upholds the validity of any *waṣiyya* by a *kāfir*; al-Qarāfī, *al-Dhakhīra*, 7:12.

[59] Ibn Rushd al-Jadd, *al-Bayān*, 13:326–7. See also al-Qarāfī, *al-Dhakhīra*, 7:35.

[60] Ibn Rushd al-Jadd, *al-Bayān*, 13:326–7. However, Ibn Rushd did note others who disagreed with him, and held that the estate escheats to the state when there is no heir. Al-Qarāfī, *al-Dhakhīra*, 7:12, held the same view as Ibn Rushd al-Jadd, but also noted the disagreement on this issue.

religious purposes shows how Muslim jurists grappled with the effects of diversity on the social fabric of the Muslim polity. The disagreements and alternative outcomes can be appreciated as juridical attempts to account for and respect the *dhimmī*'s conception of piety and property interests, the public good, and the integrity of the enterprise of governance. The rules limiting the scope of the *dhimmī*'s bequeathing capacity were manifestations of a universalist ethos in the content and institutions of law. Regardless of the analytic route any particular jurist adopted, the legal debate in the aggregate illustrates that the intelligibility of the legal doctrines depended on circumstances such as source-texts and legal doctrine, as well as institutions (e.g., adjudication and taxation) of an enterprise of governance legitimated by an Islamic universalism.

3.5 THE SITES AND SOUNDS OF THE RELIGIOUS OTHER: *DHIMMĪS'* RELIGION IN THE PUBLIC SPHERE

If the contract of protection was designed in part to allow the *dhimmī* to retain his or her faith, did that also permit the *dhimmī* to ensure the continuity of his or her faith by passing it on to future generations? If so, then the discussion above on charitable endowments should raise some concerns. If charitable endowments for the support and development of schools for reading Torah or the Bible were restricted, if not void, under the law, how could *dhimmīs* nonetheless build or maintain their communities and faith practices? It is one thing to retain one's faith; it is another to preserve it and pass it on to future generations. If the preservation of a religious tradition other than Islam through a charitable endowment was considered a sin among some jurists, could Sharīʿa-based legal doctrines and institutions countenance the *dhimmīs*' effort to preserve their religious spaces, such as churches or synagogues, while living in a Muslim polity? The discussion above about charitable endowments suggests that not all jurists agreed on the answer to these questions. This was no different with respect to issues of whether *dhimmīs* could build and maintain their sites of worship, or perform various rituals that had a public impact, whether in terms of building or repairing religious sites, ringing church bells, or reading aloud from scripture in public.

3.5.1 Religious sites

The first issue to address is whether *dhimmīs* could build new sites of religious worship while living in an Islamic enterprise of governance.

Hunwick writes that whether non-Muslims could build new religious places of worship depended in large part on whether the town was purely *dhimmī*, newly conquered, or a brand new Muslim-built town.[61] Drawing upon Hunwick's analysis, this discussion will show that the ability of *dhimmīs* to build and repair places of worship depended on the type of land they occupied, their land tax liability, and whether the Islamic enterprise of governance took control of the land by conquest or treaty. Implicitly invoking the pragmatics of empire, an Islamic universalizing ethos, and the contract paradigm, Muslim jurists used demographic, historical, and financial arguments to determine the degree to which the *dhimmīs* could develop and enjoy places of worship for their respective communities.

In regions where the land was cultivated by Muslims (e.g., *amṣār al-islām*), such as Baṣra and Kūfā, *dhimmīs* were not allowed to build new places of worship. These were lands that Muslims occupied and claimed suzerainty over, as if the land were *terra nullius*, but in which the *dhimmīs* lived and had earlier erected places of worship. In such cases, places of worship that existed prior to the Muslim arrival could remain intact according to some jurists, although others counseled their destruction.[62]

If the land came under Muslim suzerainty by military conquest against the *dhimmīs*, the *dhimmīs* could not erect new religious buildings, and jurists debated whether old ones could remain or be refurbished.[63] Mālik, al-Shāfiʿī, and Aḥmad b. Ḥanbal required old religious buildings that remained after conquest to be destroyed.[64] A dominant Ḥanafī position was to require the *dhimmīs* to convert such buildings into residences rather than destroy them.[65] The Ḥanafī al-ʿAynī argued differently, suggesting that in such cases, if the *dhimmīs'* religious buildings became dilapidated, they could refurbish them and retain them as religious buildings. Dilapidated religious buildings, however, could not be abandoned so as to erect others in their place at different sites, since that

[61] Hunwick, "The Rights of the Dhimmis to Maintain a Place of Worship," 140, 145.

[62] Al-Ghazālī, *al-Wasīṭ*, 4:207; al-Māwardī, *al-Ḥāwī*, 14:320–1; al-Muzanī, *Mukhtaṣar al-Muzanī*, in al-Shāfiʿī, *Kitāb al-Umm*, 5:385; al-Nawawī, *Rawḍa*, 10:323; al-ʿAynī, *al-Bināya*, 7:255–6; Ibn Nujaym, *al-Baḥr al-Rāʾiq*, 5:190; al-Qārāfī, *al-Dhakhīra*, 3:458; Ibn Qudāma, *al-Mughnī*, 8:526–7; al-Bahūtī, *Kashshāf al-Qināʿ*, 3:151; al-Muḥaqqiq al-Ḥillī, *Sharāʾiʿ al-Islām*, 1:262.

[63] Ibn Nujaym, *al-Baḥr al-Rāʾiq*, 5:190. See also al-Māwardī, *al-Ḥāwī*, 14:320–1; Ibn Nujaym, *al-Baḥr al-Rāʾiq*, 5:191 held that existing buildings can be repaired, but cannot be expanded or transferred; Ibn Qudāma, *al-Mughnī*, 8:527–8.

[64] For example, see the Mālikī al-Qarāfī, *al-Dhakhīra*, 3:458; Ibn Qudāma, *al-Mughnī*, 8:526–7; al-Nawawī, *Rawḍa*, 10:323. See also the discussion by the Mālikī al-Ḥaṭṭāb, who surveyed the juristic disagreement about whether to allow old religious buildings to remain intact in areas conquered by Muslim forces. Al-Ḥaṭṭāb, *Mawāhib al-Jalīl*, 4:599.

[65] Al-ʿAynī, *al-Bināya*, 7:255–6.

would be akin to building anew. Further, such religious buildings could not be rebuilt or renovated to be bigger than they were before.[66]

If the land at issue fell under Muslim rule by means of a treaty between the *dhimmīs* and the Muslim forces, authority over the land (*mulk*) and land tax liability (*kharāj*) became decisive factors in determining whether *dhimmīs* could build or repair religious buildings. There were three possible outcomes that jurists contemplated:

- If the Muslim enterprise of governance assumed both authority over the land (*mulk al-dār lanā dūnahum*)[67] and responsibility for land tax liability (*kharāj*), the *dhimmīs* could keep religious buildings already present but could not build new ones.[68]
- If the Muslim enterprise of governance assumed authority over the land but the *dhimmīs* were collectively liable for the land tax, the existing religious buildings could remain and whether *dhimmīs* could build new religious buildings depended on the terms of the contract of protection that they negotiated with the Muslim conquerors.[69]
- If the *dhimmīs* retained authority over the land (*mulk al-dār lahum dūnanā*)[70] and were also responsible for the land tax (*kharāj*) they had the right both to keep the old religious buildings and to build new ones.[71]

In these examples, the determining factors were authority over the land and tax liability. If the *dhimmīs* enjoyed the benefits that accrued from holding authority over the land and bearing the burden of tax liability

[66] Al-ʿAynī, *al-Bināya*, 7:256.

[67] This particular Arabic phrase is used by al-Māwardī. *al-Ḥāwī*, 14:322.

[68] Al-Māwardī, *al-Ḥāwī*, 14:320–2; al-ʿAynī, *al-Bināya*, 7:255–6. The Ḥanbalī Ibn Qudāma held that in cases where Muslims retain sovereignty of the land and the *dhimmīs* only pay the *jizya*, one must look to the terms of the treaty to determine whether the *dhimmīs* have the liberty to erect new religious buildings: Ibn Qudāma, *al-Mughnī*, 8:526–7. For this Ḥanbalī opinion see also al-Bahūtī, *Kashshāf al-Qināʿ*, 3:151.

[69] Al-Nawawī, *Rawḍa*, 10:323; Ibn Nujaym, *al-Baḥr al-Rāʾiq*, 5:190. The Mālikī al-Qarāfī held that if the *dhimmīs* are responsible for the land tax, then they can keep their churches. But if they include in the treaty a condition allowing them to build new religious buildings, the condition is void except in land where no Muslims reside. However, in such regions, *dhimmīs* can erect new religious buildings without having to specify their right to do so in any treaty: Al-Qarāfī, *al-Dhakhīra*, 3:458.

[70] For this Arabic language, see al-Māwardī, *al-Ḥāwī*, 14:322.

[71] Al-Māwardī, *al-Ḥāwī*, 14:320–2; al-Ghazālī, *al-Wasīṭ*, 4:207; al-Nawawī, *Rawḍa*, 10:323; Ibn Qudāma, *al-Mughnī*, 8:526–7; al-Bahūtī, *Kashshāf al-Qināʿ*, 3:151. Fred Donner, *The Early Islamic Conquests* (Princeton: Princeton University Press, 1981), 240, indicates that early Muslim conquests were not focused on dispossessing the indigenous peoples of their lands. Rather, the focus was upon seizing political control over lands and drawing off tax revenues to support the Islamic governing regime.

to the Muslim enterprise of governance, they were permitted to enjoy certain privileges. If the Muslim authorities held the land and bore the tax burden, they could deny those privileges to the *dhimmīs.* Where the Muslims enjoyed the benefit of authority, but the *dhimmīs* bore the burden of tax liability, then the jurists allowed for some negotiation given the distribution of benefits and burdens. Notably absent was a possible fourth option, where the *dhimmīs* enjoyed authority over the land, but Muslims bore the tax burden payable to the Muslim enterprise of governance. If underlying the *dhimmī* rules was an ethic of an imperial enterprise of governance, this fourth option would actually work to the disadvantage of an expanding enterprise of governance, where regional Muslim elites paid the land tax but did not enjoy the benefits of authority and control over the land. Indeed, given the imperial assumptions that made the *dhimmī* rules intelligible, such a fourth option would be *un*intelligible. It is therefore not surprising that no such fourth option was mentioned by jurists.

Ḥanafī jurists such as al-ʿAynī approached the issue differently. He relied on population demographics to arrive at an appropriate accommodation. He held that *dhimmīs* could not build new religious buildings in the towns that Muslims had built and cultivated (*amṣār*). However, his general ban did not apply to the villages in which non-Muslims predominantly resided.[72] The Ḥanafī Ibn Nujaym qualified al-ʿAynī's exception by upholding the ban in both Muslim towns and *dhimmī* villages that were *in the Arabian Peninsula,* since the Prophet indicated that there could not be two faiths in the Arabian Peninsula.[73] Notably, al-ʿAynī considered this prophetic tradition to be weak in its authenticity, yet he recognized that it conveyed a general attitude against erecting religious buildings in the region, and so might be read as providing an exception to his exception.[74] Other Ḥanafīs rejected al-ʿAynī's initial demographically based exception to the general ban. Instead, they banned non-Muslims from erecting new religious buildings in both Muslim towns and *dhimmī* villages. They argued that

[72] Al-ʿAynī, *al-Bināya,* 7:257. See also al-Marghīnānī, *al-Hidāya,* 1:455. See also the Mālikī al-Ḥaṭṭāb, *Mawāhib al-Jalīl,* 4:600.

[73] Ibn Nujaym, *al-Baḥr al-Rā'iq,* 5:190. See also al-Marghīnānī, *al-Hidāya,* 1:455. The conquest of the Arabian Peninsula witnessed an expulsion of non-Muslims from the region. Relying on a tradition from the Prophet in which he rejects the possibility that there could be two faiths in the Arabian Peninsula, the second caliph ʿUmar b. al-Khaṭṭāb (r. 13–23/634–644) ushered a policy of expulsion, leading the Banū Najrān tribe of Arab Christians to leave the region. Goddard, "Christian-Muslim Relations," 196. This tradition was read by jurists as one of the bases for prohibiting *dhimmīs* from constructing religious buildings in Arab lands. Hamidullah, however, argues that this prophetic tradition was not premised on an agenda of minority religious persecution or intolerance. Rather, it reflects the Prophet's political aim to secure a region of safety, security, and homogeneity for Muslims. Muhammad Hamidullah, "Status of Non-Muslims in Islam," *Majallat al-Azhar* 45, no. 8 (1973): 6–13, 10.

[74] Al-ʿAynī, *al-Bināya,* 7:255.

Muslims resided in both areas. Their argument implicitly made it possible for the universalizing Islamic ethos of the public good to prevail, despite a limited Muslim population in predominantly *dhimmī* villages.[75]

For many jurists, the rationale for limiting the extent to which *dhimmīs* could build new religious buildings or preserve old ones had to do with ensuring the Islamic character of lands falling under the imperium of the Islamic enterprise of governance. For instance, the Shāfiʿī al-Māwardī held that churches and synagogues could not be erected in lands under Muslim rule (*amṣār al-Islām*) since they would undermine the dominance of Islam. In fact, he argued that allowing such construction would be a sin (*maʿṣiyya*) since non-Muslims congregated within them to preserve disbelief (*kufr*). In Islamic lands, he said, no faith other than Islam should be prominent (*ẓāhir*).[76] Even al-ʿAynī, who permitted exceptions to the general ban, knew that to allow Jews and Christians to construct religious buildings would impede the universalist imperative of Islam.[77] He wrote that such religious buildings in the land of Islam (*dār al-Islām*) enfeebled the presence and strength of Islam in the land (*tūrithu al-ḍaʿf fī al-Islām*).[78] The question for him and others, though, concerned the extent to which the Islamic empire could sustain its character while accommodating the religious Other. The justifications for these building restrictions and their exceptions show how Muslim jurists believed that *dhimmīs* counted as members of society and yet should be regulated such that the public presence of their contrary religious values would not run contrary to the integrity of an enterprise of governance premised upon a universalist Islamic ethos. There was no single approach that dominated the legal tradition; nonetheless the differences among jurists reveal the mutually constitutive relationship between the law and the enterprise of governance. The presumptions about the enterprise of governance contributed to legal decisions about the scope to which the *dhimmīs*' claims and interests could be accommodated. While jurists sought to accommodate *dhimmī* interests, the scope of that accommodation could not be so large as to threaten the well-being of an Islamic enterprise of governance, defined in light of a universalizing Islamic ethos made manifest through both empire and legal doctrine.

3.5.2 Religious sounds

A second issue, related to the one above, concerned the extent to which *dhimmīs* were allowed to engage in public displays of religious practice.

[75] Al-Marghīnānī, *al-Hidāya*, 1:455.
[76] Al-Māwardī, *al-Ḥāwī*, 14:321.
[77] Al-ʿAynī, *al-Bināya*, 7:255.
[78] Al-ʿAynī, *al-Bināya*, 7:255.

Jurists of both Sunnī and Shīʿa schools generally agreed that while *dhimmīs* could practice their faith in Muslim lands, they could not proselytize their faith, recite publicly from the Torah or Bible, or engage in public rituals of religious significance, such as carrying a cross or ringing church bells (*nāqūs*).[79] If they did so, jurists would not necessarily consider the contract of protection breached, but they would allow the ruling authority to subject the *dhimmī* to discretionary punishment (*taʿzīr*).[80] If through proselytization, *dhimmīs* directly or indirectly caused dissension in the faith of Muslims, Shāfiʿī jurists would consider the contract breached, thereby revoking the *dhimmī*'s protected status under the Islamic imperium and transforming him into an "enemy of the state." The legal effect of such revocation and redesignation was that if the *dhimmī* were killed while residing in the Muslim empire, there would be no legal consequences on his killer, akin to what Giorgio Agamben calls the *homo sacer*.[81] These examples illustrate how the *dhimmī*'s otherness constituted not just an alternative set of values, but was viewed as a potential threat. Recalling al-Shīrāzī's concerns about charitable endowments, *dhimmīs* who engaged in public displays of religious ritual, and indeed went so far as to challenge Muslims in their faith commitments, at the very least had to be punished and at most were security threats against the polity.

Importantly, for some jurists the threat was not in the fact that the *dhimmīs* performed their religious rituals, but rather that they performed the rituals *in public view*. For example, the Ḥanafī al-Kāsānī did not permit *dhimmīs* to display the cross in public because the cross was a sign of disbelief; but he did permit *dhimmīs* to display the cross and ring their bells privately in their churches. In other words, *dhimmīs* could practice their faith freely among themselves. Allowing them to practice their faith in public, though, was an entirely different matter. Such accommodation might be construed as granting their faith tradition equal or equivalent standing with the Islamic values and traditions that gave content to the public good of the Muslim polity, and which the Islamic enterprise of governance upheld and protected.

[79] Zaydān, *Aḥkām al-Dhimmiyyīn*, 84. For Shāfiʿī authors see al-Māwardī, *al-Ḥāwī*, 14:316; al-Muzanī, *Mukhtaṣar al-Muzanī*, in vol. 5 of al-Shāfiʿī, *al-Umm*, 5:385; al-Shīrāzī, *al-Muhadhdhab*, 3:314. See also the Shīʿa Muḥaqqiq al-Ḥillī, *Sharāʾiʿ al-Islām*, 1:260–1.

[80] Notably, whether breach of such conditions voided the contract or preserved the contract while allowing discretionary punishment was a subject of debate. See al-Nawawī, *Rawḍa*, 10:328–9, 333; al-ʿAynī, *al-Bināya*, 7:260.

[81] Al-Māwardī, *al-Ḥāwī*, 14:316; al-Muzanī, *Mukhtaṣar al-Muzanī*, 5:385. For a similar conception of the "enemy of the state," see Giorgio Agamben, *Homo Sacer: Sovereign Power and Bare Life*, trans. Daniel Heller-Roazen (Palo Alto: Stanford University Press, 1998).

Of course, whether such a threat was serious or not depended on the public sphere in question. In some cases, the public sphere was comprised of both Muslims and *dhimmīs.* In other cases, the public sphere was comprised predominantly, if not entirely, by *dhimmīs.* Given these demographic differences, the Ḥanafī jurist al-Kāsānī made exceptions to the general prohibition if the *dhimmīs* were the predominant, majority population in the village, even if there were some Muslims that lived there.[82] However, the Ḥanafī al-Marghīnānī rejected this exception, noting that those who transmitted the teachings of the Hanafī school's leading jurist, Abū Ḥanīfa, generally lived in villages where *dhimmīs* were majorities. He argued that Abū Ḥanīfa's students would have been sufficiently familiar with such demographic contexts and would have offered such exceptions if they were warranted. Since his students did not provide such an exception, al-Marghīnānī held that even where *dhimmīs* were the predominant group in a region, they were still restricted from public displays of religious ritual.[83]

Ḥanbalī jurists analyzed the legality of *dhimmī* public displays of religious ritual by reference to the kind of land at issue. For instance, Ibn Qudāma would not permit *dhimmīs* to engage in public religious displays—for example, ringing church bells—in towns that Muslims built, such as Baṣra or Kūfa.[84] In these cases, the land was regarded as *terra nullius,* thereby granting the Islamic enterprise of governance an uncontested imperium. Likewise, if *dhimmīs* lived in townships that came under the Islamic enterprise of governance through conquest, the Ḥanbalī Abū ʿAbd Allāh b. Mufliḥ prohibited the *dhimmīs* from public displays of their faith tradition, presumably because of the imperium that accrued to the enterprise of governance as a consequence of conquest. But, if *dhimmīs* lived in lands subjected to a negotiated treaty, the *dhimmīs'* legal capacity to publicly express their faith depended on the negotiated terms of the contract of protection agreed upon between them and the ruling regime.[85] In this case, Ḥanbalī jurists used the contract paradigm to introduce a negotiative, accommodative spirit.

To conclude, this discussion shows that Muslim jurists did not *universally* prohibit *dhimmīs* from practicing or exhibiting their faith publicly or from building new religious places of worship or maintaining old ones. They did, however, limit the scope of the religious Other's public presence in order to preserve the dominance of the Islamic character of the public sphere. Their legal arguments had an intelligibility that drew

[82] Al-Kāsānī, *Badāʾiʿ al-Ṣanāʾiʿ*, 9:449; see also the Mālikī al-Qarāfī, *al-Dhakhīra*, 3:458–9.

[83] Al-Marghīnānī, *al-Hidāya*, 1:455.

[84] Ibn Qudāma, *al-Mughnī*, 8:526–7.

[85] Abū ʿAbd Allāh b. Mufliḥ, *al-Furūʿ*, 6:250.

upon different types of arguments, such as demographics, conquest, and treaty-relationships. The conditions of intelligibility reveal that Muslim jurists relied on an Islamic universalist ethos and the politics of empire to determine whether, as a matter of law, *dhimmīs* could publicly perform religious rituals, build new places of worship, and maintain older ones. The different arguments across legal schools disclose the mutually constitutive relationship between law and the enterprise of governance. While some legal doctrines accommodated the *dhimmī,* the limit of any accommodation depended upon the extent to which it could undermine the security or integrity of the enterprise of governance, or the Islamically defined values that gave content to the public good.

3.6 FROM PRINCIPLE OF SUPERIORITY TO HOME CONSTRUCTION REGULATION

Whether the *jizya* was imposed on *dhimmīs* through conquest or negotiation, it was a precondition to forming the contract of protection. The contract provided a legal framework for what was a political debate about the core values of the Muslim polity and their implications on an enterprise of governance that could not avoid ignore diversity. The contract of protection was a juridified discursive site for a broader debate about the political status and standing of *dhimmīs.* The debates about the "terms" of the contract became the doctrinal corpus that has been referred to as the *dhimmī* rules addressed throughout this study.

Much of the legal debate canvassed in this chapter thus far has involved issues about Islamic values and the public sphere, whatever those may be. Often jurists simply made reference to the importance of upholding the Islamic value system. Indeed, their reference to this core value was expressed less in terms of any particular core value, and more in terms of the importance of ensuring the primacy, if not superiority, of Islamic values over all others. Their arguments of primacy and superiority drew upon the universalist ethos that operated in the background of many of the rules discussed herein. This section addresses a particular rule where the universalist ethos and its corollary proposition about the priority and superiority of Islam operate at a more immediate and apparent level in legal analysis. The specific rule is a regulation that limits the height to which a *dhimmī* may build his home if he has a Muslim neighbor. An examination of this rule will reveal in fairly stark terms that the contract of protection, as a negotiative site about the *dhimmīs'* scope of inclusion, was framed by an ethic of Islamic universalism and superiority that contributed to the boundaries of the claim space of Sharīʿa.

The textual genealogy of this building regulation had its origins in a statement that is often attributed to the Prophet Muḥammad, though mistakenly so. In a legal commentary on the purpose of the *jizya*, al-Māwardī not only referred to this statement, but also drew from it the corollary of superiority that can be inferred from a universalist Islamic ethos. Al-Māwardī wrote:

> The purpose of the contract of *jizya* is to strengthen Islam and its greatness, while diminishing disbelief and debasing it so that Islam can be dominant and disbelief muffled, just as the Prophet said . . . "Islam is superior and not superseded" (*al-islām yaʿlā wa lā yuʿlā*). The *imām* is commanded to establish whatever conditions upon them [*dhimmīs*] that lead to this.[86]

In this passage, al-Māwardī justified the purpose not only of the *jizya*, but also of the *dhimmī* rules more generally, by reference to a *ḥadīth* from the Prophet in which the latter espoused the superiority of Islam over all other faith traditions. For al-Māwardī, the import of the Prophet's statement suggested that the *imām* or ruler had to manifest that superiority through the enterprise of governance and its legal regime.

Before turning to the building regulation, a brief analysis of the supposedly prophetic statement is in order. There are two source-texts that speak to both the wording and sentiment of the statement quoted by al-Māwardī. In the first one, a Jew came to Muʿādh b. Jabal (d. 18/639) to seek testamentary advice concerning his heir, who was a Muslim. The Jew was concerned that their difference in religious belief might interfere with his heir's inheritance rights. According to Muʿādh, the Prophet stated that Islam increases one's opportunities, rather than diminishes them (*al-islām yuzīdu wa lā yunqiṣu*).[87] Muʿādh interpreted this tradition to mean that the difference in religion would not undermine the Muslim heir's inheritance from his Jewish kin.[88]

The second source-text is the one cited by al-Māwardī and is the more commonly cited of the two. It reads: Islam is superior and not superseded (*al-Islām yaʿlā wa lā yuʿlā*). The tradition can be found in the collections

[86] Al-Māwardī, *al-Ḥāwī*, 14:316.
[87] Aḥmad b. Ḥanbal, *Musnad al-Imām Aḥmad b. Ḥanbal*, ed. Samīr Ṭaha al-Majzūb et al. (Beirut: al-Maktab al-Islāmī, 1993), 5:299 ('72/22052). Friedmann, *Tolerance and Coercion*, 35, who also indicates variant traditions on the same theme.
[88] In his commentary, al-Bayhaqī explained that the underlying situation concerned a child who was Muslim, but had at least one parent who was not. For al-Bayhaqī, nothing about one's Islamic belief should interfere with his inheritance. Islam, in other words, increases and does not diminish one's opportunities: Abū Bakr al-Bayhaqī, *al-Sunan al-Kubrā*, ed. Muḥammad ʿAbd al-Qādir ʿAṭā (Beirut: Dār al-Kutub al-ʿIlmiyya, 1999), 6:338.

of both al-Dār Quṭnī[89] and al-Bukhārī. According to al-Bukhārī, the tradition concerned the funerary rites over a child who was Muslim but who had one or more parents who were not.[90] Interestingly, al-Bukhārī attributed this tradition to Ibn 'Abbās and not the Prophet, hence raising a question about the provenance of the tradition and thereby the extent of its normative authority.[91] Ibn 'Abbās stated that he and his mother had both converted to Islam, but his father did not. If Ibn 'Abbās had predeceased his father, would he have been entitled to a Muslim burial? Ibn 'Abbās responded that Islam is superior and not superseded, suggesting that he would be so entitled.

The later Ḥanafī jurist Badr al-Dīn al-'Aynī read the Ibn 'Abbās tradition as decisive on a range of possible answers to Ibn 'Abbās' original question, which are as follows:

- The child's religious status followed that of the parent who converted to Islam;
- The child's religious status followed his father's, regardless of whether his mother converted to Islam; or
- The child's faith followed his mother's, regardless of whether the father converted to Islam.

Interestingly, he did not seem to give weight to the fact that Ibn 'Abbās had converted to Islam. In other words, why should it matter if his father or mother or both had not converted, as long as Ibn 'Abbās converted to Islam and his identity could be proven for purposes of burial rites. This question may need to remain unanswered, given that it is not clear from the tradition how old Ibn 'Abbās was when he

[89] Al-Dār Quṭnī's version has the Prophet making this statement upon meeting two Meccan nobles on the day the Prophet conquered Mecca. Al-Dār Quṭnī, *Sunan al-Dār Quṭnī*, ed. Magdī al-Shūrā (Beirut: Dār al-Kutub al-'Ilmiyya, 1996), 3:176 (no. 3578). See also al-Bayhaqī, *al-Sunan al-Kubrā*, 6:338 (no. 12155). In his commentary on al-Dār Qutnī's version, al-Bayhaqī noted how two Meccan leaders, 'Ā'idh and Abū Sufyān, met the Prophet on the day the Muslims conquered Mecca. When introduced to both of them, the Prophet said: "This is 'Ā'idh b. 'Umrū and Abū Sufyān, [but] Islam is greater than [their greatness]; Islam is superior and not superseded." Al-Bayhaqī, *al-Sunan al-Kubrā*, 6:338.

[90] Ibn Ḥajr al-'Asqalānī, *Fatḥ al-Bārī: Sharḥ Ṣaḥīḥ al-Bukhārī*, eds Muḥammad 'Abd al-Bāqī and Muḥibb al-Dīn al-Khaṭīb (Beirut: Dār al-Ma'rifa, n.d.), 3:218. Al-Dār Quṭnī discussed the tradition in the chapter on marriage (*nikāḥ*). Badr al-Dīn al-'Aynī argued that the discussion of funerary rites speaks directly to the issue of Islam's superiority over others. He said: "Doesn't one realize that when the youth converts and dies, one prays over him? That is the blessing of Islam (*baraka al-islām*) and the grandeur of its worth." Badr al-Dīn al-'Aynī, *'Umdat al-Qārī Sharḥ Ṣaḥīḥ al-Bukhārī*, ed. 'Abd Allāh Maḥmūd Muḥammad 'Umar (Beirut: Dār al-Kutub al-'Ilmiyya, 2001), 8:244.

[91] Al-'Aynī criticized al-Bukhārī for not attributing the tradition to the Prophet. Al-'Aynī, *'Umdat al-Qārī*, 8:244.

converted, or whether he attained an age of legal majority to permit his choice to be legally meaningful. Nonetheless, al-ʿAynī understood (and thereby limited) the Ibn ʿAbbās tradition to pertain to young converts, funerary rights, and the respective roles of faith and kinship in defining identity in death.[92]

Importantly, the context that the two source-texts addressed, depending on which version is cited, involved either inheritance rights between kin of different faiths or the funerary rights of a child whose father may not have been Muslim. One might suggest that this narrow context should have limited the scope of application that this tradition could or should have had. Nonetheless al-Māwardī utilized the Ibn ʿAbbās tradition to substantiate the argument of Islam's superiority over all other traditions. Indeed, the context that seems to have animated Ibn ʿAbbās did not govern the scope to which his statement was used to justify subsidiary rules that had nothing to do with funerary rights or inheritance between kin of different faiths. Read as statement of principle, the Ibn ʿAbbās tradition contributed a certain content of superiority that allowed jurists to read into the law an ethos of superiority, and thereby develop specific rules of law that subordinated the non-Muslim. The rule of interest here is the one restricting the height to which *dhimmīs* could build their homes.

A close analysis of the legal debates on this building regulation permits a greater appreciation of the mutually constitutive relationship between the law and the enterprise of governance in a context of difference and minority groups.[93] According to various jurists, *dhimmīs* who lived next door to Muslims could not build their residences higher than the homes of their Muslim neighbors.[94] They justified this general rule of prohibition by reference to the tradition in which they claimed the Prophet (and not Ibn ʿAbbās) said that Islam is superior and not superseded (*al-Islām yaʿlā wa lā yuʿlā*).[95] Two important exceptions to this rule concerned *dhimmīs* who purchased a pre-existing home that was taller than his Muslim neighbor's home, and those who resided in

[92] Al-ʿAynī, *ʿUmdat al-Qārī*, 8:243.

[93] Yohanan Friedmann also recognizes the significance of this tradition in fostering an Islamic ethos of superiority. Friedmann, *Tolerance and Coercion*, vi, 35.

[94] Al-Ghazālī, *al-Wasīṭ*, 4:207–8, prohibited *dhimmīs* from building higher than Muslims, but acknowledged a debate about whether *dhimmīs* can erect buildings reaching the same height of Muslim buildings; al-Māwardī, *al-Ḥāwī*, 14:323; al-Nawawī, *Rawḍa*, 10:324 said that this prohibition applies even if the Muslim neighbor consents to the *dhimmī's* taller construction; al-Shīrāzī, *al-Muhadhdhab*, 3:314; Ibn Qudāma, *al-Mughnī*, 8:528; al-Bahūtī, *Kashshāf al-Qināʿ*, 3:150.

[95] Al-Māwardī, *al-Ḥāwī*, 14:323; al-Shīrāzī, *al-Muhadhdhab*, 3:314.

a neighborhood without Muslims nearby.[96] In both cases the *dhimmī* suffered no legal liability, regardless of the height of his home. The *dhimmī* was not liable for living in a tall home that he did not build. Indeed, to impose a fine on him for purchasing a taller home than his Muslim neighbor's would have been to hold him liable for something that was not his fault. Nor should the *dhimmī* limit the height of his home when living in a region in which Muslims were uncommon or not part of the *dhimmīs*' neighborhood.

Whether *dhimmīs* could construct buildings *equaling* (*musāwāt*) the height of their Muslim neighbor's building depended on whether the equal height undermined the presumption of Islam's superiority over other faiths. Those who denied *dhimmīs* the right to build to an equal height inferred from other rules concerning the dress and mounts of *dhimmīs* that the *dhimmī* was not equal in status to the Muslim. Consequently, the *dhimmī* could not presume to be equal by building a residence of equal height as his Muslim neighbor's.[97]

Jurists explained that this building regulation upheld the superiority of Islam and Muslims over other faiths and religious communities living in the Muslim polity. For instance, the Ḥanbalī Ibn Qudāma argued that if a *dhimmī* built a residence taller than his Muslim neighbor's, the Muslim neighbor would certainly suffer a harm (*ḍarar*) unlike others. What this harm involved, though, Ibn Qudāma did not explain. But he did not have to explain. Indeed, the core value of an Islamic superiority, which was always and already present—given a commitment to an Islamic universalism—was sufficient to extend the application of the Ibn 'Abbās tradition from the narrow issue of a young convert's religious status to a building code governing *dhimmī* home construction. The ethos of Islamic universalism, and its corollary of Islamic superiority, gave content to a conception of the public good, which in turn contributed content to legal rules that ordered and stratified society. The content of the public good, as a check on the *dhimmī*'s liberty to build, was derived from a source-text that was read to espouse the superiority of Islam, and thereby of the Muslim neighbors who must be protected from having to live in the *dhimmī*'s shadow.

Nonetheless, the exceptions to the general ban reveal an accommodative spirit that permitted the *dhimmīs* to develop their lands with a certain degree of liberty. Indeed, when reading the exceptions through the lens of Rule of Law, we can gain greater insight into the

[96] Al-Nawawī, *Rawḍa*, 10:325; Ibn Qudāma, *al-Mughnī*, 8:528–9; al-Bahūtī, *Kashshāf al-Qināʿ*, 3:150.

[97] Ibn Qudāma, *al-Mughnī*, 8:528.

mutually constitutive relationship between the law and the enterprise of governance. On the one hand, the exceptions to the building regulation were accommodative: the *dhimmī* was able to be a market participant and was not held liable for the actions of others (as in the case of buying a pre-existing home that was taller than his neighbor's). Likewise, the exception concerning *dhimmī* neighborhoods further enhanced the *dhimmī*'s freedom to develop his or her land without having to first undertake what could have been a costly and time-intensive survey of the heights of Muslim homes across a large swathe of land. These exceptions, therefore, granted the *dhimmī* a certain degree of freedom to purchase and develop his land and home. However, the exception concerning the *dhimmī* neighborhood drew upon a demographic analysis that should remind us of the way an imperial enterprise of governance operates in a context of diversity. Accommodation in this case does not necessarily run contrary to an Islamic universalism or an imperial ethos given certain assumptions about the *dhimmīs*' insularity and autonomy from the general Muslim populace, or in other words, their otherness.

3.7 *DHIMMĪS* IN PUBLIC: ON ATTIRE AND TRANSPORT

This study has shown that jurists struggled with the extent to which the *dhimmī* was both insider and outsider while residing within the Muslim polity. This struggle has been evident in the different *fiqh* debates, and it discloses to us how the premodern rules reflected contests over core values associated with an ethos of Islamic universalism (and its corollary of superiority) on the one hand, and the need to ensure the perpetuation of an enterprise of governance that contended with diversity across the lands over which it exercised dominion. The above analysis of the legal doctrines also indicates that even when jurists delineated rules and exceptions that included and accommodated the Other, the doctrines either made plain the otherness of the *dhimmī* or contributed to subsidiary doctrines that distinguished them and/or delimited the extent to which their difference could be part of the public sphere. Whereas the above analysis, therefore, illuminated the extent to which the *dhimmī* rules offered a site of ongoing and complex deliberation about inclusion and exclusion, the rules on clothing requirements and modes of transport, discussed below, do not admit of such complexity. These rules are notorious in the scholarly literature as examples that do not cut both ways. Rather, premodern jurists designed these rules to emphasize the *dhimmīs*' difference for the purpose of ensuring their subordination.

Dress restrictions are particularly disturbing—whether in an Islamic, Christian, or any other context—because of the role they can play in subordinating and marginalizing a targeted group.[98] In her analysis of *dhimmī* dress restrictions, Levy-Rubin shows that they had their origin in earlier modes of differentiation that existed in Sasanian society and culture.[99] Lichtenstadter suggests that the development of dress restrictions in Islamic law started gradually.[100] At first, the main imperative was to make sure that Muslims and non-Muslims did not assume the appearance of the other. The point of those rules, she argues, was both to distinguish between the conquering and conquered populace and to prevent intermarriage. But the specific forms such regulations took are not well known from this early period. Rather, the first substantial regulation that distinguished the two groups was one

[98] See for instance Canon 68 of the Fourth Lateran Council of 1215, which states:

> In some provinces a difference in dress distinguishes the Jews or Saracens from the Christians, but in certain others such a confusion has grown up that they cannot be distinguished by any difference. Thus it happens at times that through error Christians have relations with the women of Jews or Saracens, and Jews and Saracens with Christian women. Therefore, that they may not, under pretext of error of this sort, excuse themselves in the future for the excesses of such prohibited intercourse, we decree that such Jews and Saracens of both sexes in every Christian province and at all times shall be marked off in the eyes of the public from other peoples through the character of their dress. Particularly, since it may be read in the writings of Moses [Numbers 15:37–41], that this very law has been enjoined upon them.
>
> Moreover, during the last three days before Easter and especially on Good Friday, they shall not go forth in public at all, for the reason that some of them on these very days, as we hear, do not blush to go forth better dressed and are not afraid to mock the Christians who maintain the memory of the most holy Passion by wearing signs of mourning.
>
> This, however, we forbid most severely, that any one should presume at all to break forth in insult to the Redeemer. And since we ought not to ignore any insult to Him who blotted out our disgraceful deeds, we command that such impudent fellows be checked by the secular princes by imposing them proper punishment so that they shall not at all presume to blaspheme Him who was crucified for us.

H.J. Shroeder, "The Fourth Lateran Council of 1215: Canon 68," in *Disciplinary Decrees of the General Councils: Text, Translation, and Commentary* (St Louis: B. Herder, 1937), <http://www.fordham.edu/halsall/basis/lateran4.html> (accessed September 6, 2008).

[99] Levy-Rubin, *Non-Muslims in the Early Islamic Empire*, 96, 130–7.

[100] Lichtenstadter argues that the clothing restrictions may have been retrospectively put into ʿUmar's mouth given his reputation as a pious companion, leader of conquest, and an expert in law. Consequently, she suggests that the reports by later authors of what ʿUmar did only indicates that the clothing requirements arose later in history and were given the veil of authority by associating them with ʿUmar. Ilse Lichtenstadter, "The Distinctive Dress of Non-Muslims in Islamic Countries," *Historia Judaica* 5, no. 1 (1943): 35–52, 38. Bosworth, "The Concept of *Dhimma* in Early Islam," 48, argues that the Ḥanafī jurist Abū Yūsuf traces the dress requirements to the Umayyad caliph ʿUmar b. ʿAbd al-ʿAzīz (r. 99–101/717–720).

that denied *dhimmīs* the legal capacity to use horses for transport. The horse denoted honor, wealth, and power, all of which jurists denied to *dhimmīs*,[101] with certain exceptions,[102] to ensure the latter's sense of subordination.[103] The clothing restrictions appeared after the ban on horses.[104] Importantly, the clothing regulations did more than simply distinguish the *dhimmī* from the Muslim; they also served as a warning of potential danger and risk. For instance, if *dhimmīs* attended the communal bath, they had to distinguish themselves with particular forms of dress.[105] One jurist justified this requirement on the grounds that the *dhimmīs*' nakedness may pollute the water unbeknownst to the Muslims therein.[106] The *dhimmī* was therefore not only marginalized but was also deemed a threat to the health and purity of Muslims.

As was often the case with the *dhimmī* laws, whether they were actually enforced depended on the discretion of the ruler. Examples of when they were enforced include the reign of the 'Abbāsid caliph al-Mutawakkil (r. 232–247/847–861), who required the slaves of *dhimmīs* to wear a yellow badge.[107] Likewise, the Fātimid caliph al-Ḥākim (r. 386–411/996–1021), thought to have been insane, made the lives of *dhimmīs* miserable by requiring them to wear distinctive badges around their necks—such as crosses—and forbidding them to ride any animal.[108]

Jurists justified clothing requirements by reference to the need to distinguish, and ultimately to exclude.[109] For instance, al-Ghazālī argued

[101] Al-Ghazālī, *al-Wasīṭ*, 4:207; al-Māwardī, *al-Ḥāwī*, 14:327, who allowed *dhimmīs* to ride mules but not horses; al-Nawawī, *Rawḍa*, 10:325; al-'Aynī, *al-Bināya*, 7:257; Ibn Nujaym, *al-Baḥr al-Rā'iq*, 5:192; al-Marghīnānī, *al-Hidāya*, 1:455; Khalīl b. Isḥāq, *Mukhtaṣar Khalīl*, ed. Aḥmad 'Alī Ḥarakāt (Beirut: Dār al-Fikr, 1995), 106; al-Ḥaṭṭāb, *Mawāhib al-Jalīl*, 4:601; al-Qarāfī, *al-Dhakhīra*, 3:459; Ibn Qudāma, *al-Mughnī*, 8:533; al-Bahūtī, *Kashshāf al-Qinā'*, 3:145.

[102] Al-'Aynī, *al-Bināya*, 7:260; Ibn Nujaym, *al-Baḥr al-Rā'iq*, 5:192, who allows *dhimmīs* to ride horses in cases of necessity, but required them to dismount when Muslims pass them. See also al-Marghīnānī, *al-Hidāya*, 1:455.

[103] Al-Nawawī, *Rawḍa*, 10:325; al-Qarāfī, *al-Dhakhīra*, 3:459; Ibn Qudāma, *al-Mughnī*, 8:533; al-Bahūtī, *Kashshāf al-Qinā'*, 3:145.

[104] Lichtenstadter, "The Distinctive Dress," 45–6.

[105] Al-Nawawī required *dhimmīs* entering the baths to wear a *ghīyār* or shawl around the shoulders which is sewn in an uncustomary spot; Jews should wear yellow, Christians wear blue, and the Magians wear black or red: Al-Nawawī, *Rawḍa*, 10:326. See also al-Shīrāzī, *al-Muhadhdhab*, 3:312; Ibn Qudāma, *al-Mughnī*, 8:533.

[106] Al-Ghazālī, *al-Wasīṭ*, 4:208.

[107] Lichtenstadter, "The Distinctive Dress," 47–8.

[108] Lichtenstadter, "The Distinctive Dress," 49. For an overview of al-Ḥākim's life and rule, see M. Canard, "al- Ḥākim Bi-amr Allāh," *Encyclopaedia of Islam*. Eds P. Bearman et al.

[109] Many writers argue that the dress requirements for non-Muslims were intended to humiliate and degrade the non-Muslim population, and to impose on them social and political disabilities: Lewis, "Semites and Anti-Semites," 131; Ben-Shammai, "Jew

that the special clothing requirements were designed to distinguish *dhimmīs* from Muslims so that "we do not offer them [the traditional Muslim greeting of peace]" (*ḥattā lā nusallimu ʿalayhim*).[110] This nexus between dress and greeting arose during the reign of the Umayyad caliph ʿUmar b. ʿAbd al-ʿAzīz (r. 99–101/717–720). He once greeted a group of Arabs with the traditional Muslim greeting, only to find out subsequently that they were from the Christian Arab tribe of Banū Taghlib. To ensure against any future confusion between Muslims and Christians, the caliph ordered the Christians to cut their forelocks.[111] Commenting on ʿUmar's decision, al-Kāsānī explained that the Muslim greeting of peace was a sign of one's inclusion within the Muslim community.[112] As *dhimmīs* were not part of the Muslim community, yet lived as protected members of the Muslim polity, they had to be distinguished somehow to signify their exclusion from the former.[113] Whether the requirement was to cut forelocks or wear distinctive clothing, the fundamental purpose was to distinguish and demarcate the *dhimmīs*, and thereby to uphold their otherness in a Muslim polity.

The way in which jurists justified legal doctrines on clothing and mounts not only rendered *dhimmīs* as Other, but also as marginal and subordinated to Muslims. For instance, when walking in the streets, some jurists held that *dhimmīs* had to walk along the edges so as to allow

Hatred in the Islamic Tradition and Koranic Exegesis," 162. Others argue that the clothing requirements were intended to prevent assimilation of the non-Muslims into the Muslim population. In other words, the clothing requirement was a protective mechanism to ensure the continued life and longevity of the non-Muslim populace. Muhammad Hamidullah, "Status of Non-Muslims in Islam—II," *Majallat al-Azhar* 45, no. 9 (1973): 12–16, 12. This latter argument seems historically anachronistic. It assumes that the non-Muslim population was a minority community whose identity would be dissolved by the dominant Muslim population. But if we assume, as some have argued, that the restrictive requirements arose in the ninth century during the reign of al-Mutawakkil, the question that arises is whether the Muslims had become such a majority in these newly conquered areas as to pose a real threat to the cultural identity of non-Muslim minorities. As has been noted above, in the early conquest period, Muslims were in fact a minority population amidst a majority of non-Muslims. Studies on conversion suggest that shifts in demographics in favor of Muslim majorities occurred between the 8th and 11th centuries, CE, but may vary from region to region. Bulliet, *Conversion to Islam*; Morony, "The Age of Conversions: A Reassessment." A more likely rationale is that the rules on dress requirements and mount restrictions were designed to ensure that the conquering (but minority) Muslims remained distinct from the non-Muslim and thereby preserved their Muslim identity.

[110] Al-Ghazālī, *al-Wasīṭ*, 4:208. He held that Jews should wear yellow clothing, while Christians wear red and Magians wear black. See also al-Māwardī, *al-Ḥāwī*, 14:325, who said that Christians must wear black and Jews wear yellow; al-Bahūtī, *Kashshāf al-Qināʿ*, 3:145.

[111] Al-Kāsānī, *Badāʾiʿ al-Ṣanāʾiʿ*, 9:448. On the distinctive hairstyles, see also Ibn Qudāma, *al-Mughnī*, 8:533; al-Bahūtī, *Kashshāf al-Qināʿ*, 3:144.

[112] Al-Kāsānī, *Badāʾiʿ al-Ṣanāʾiʿ*, 9:448 (*min shaʿāʾir al-islām*).

[113] Al-Kāsānī, *Badāʾiʿ al-Ṣanāʾiʿ*, 9:448.

Muslims to walk through the centre.[114] This rule both physically and symbolically marginalizes the *dhimmī*. While the contract of protection permitted *dhimmīs* to reside in the Muslim polity, the dress and transit regulations ensured that they were never considered equal or central (literally and figuratively) to the well-being of the Muslim polity.

It is difficult to see the dress and transport regulations as anything other than marginalizing and subordinating. For instance, after recounting various *dhimmī* rules on clothing requirements, al-Kāsānī stated outright that their purpose was to render the *dhimmī* subservient and humbled (*athār al-dhill*) in society.[115] Furthermore, jurists emphasized this feature of these rules, and even stated that the required modes of dress for *dhimmīs* may need to differ from region to region in order to effectuate the underlying purpose of the rules given changing cultural practices.[116]

Given the purpose of these rules, it is not surprising that they feature in contemporary debates about whether Islam is a tolerant or an intolerant faith tradition. When read in isolation, it seems quite reasonable to think that Islam and Islamic law counsel intolerance of the religious Other. In fact, many who uphold the myth of persecution make reference to these rules to illustrate the inherently intolerant nature of Islam, Islamic law, and Muslims generally. Those who uphold the myth of harmony may adopt a historicist approach and suggest that the rules were never applied in actual fact. Between these two poles lie a multitude of approaches, not all of which can be outlined here.

Considering these clothing and transport rules alongside the others addressed herein, though, we can appreciate how these dress and transport rules, through their marginalizing and subordinating effect, contributed to the preservation of an enterprise of governance defined in terms of both an Islamic universalist ethos and an imperial model of rule.[117] The juristic debate on transport and dress requirements reflected certain themes about the public presence of *dhimmīs*. Those themes reveal

114 Al-Ghazālī, *al-Wasīṭ*, 4:207; al-Nawawī, *Rawḍa*, 10:325; al-Shīrāzī, *al-Muhadhdhab*, 3:313; al-ʿAynī, *al-Bināya*, 7:259; Ibn Nujaym, *al-Baḥr al-Rāʾiq*, 5:192; al-Ḥaṭṭāb, *Mawāhib al-Jalīl*, 4:601; al-Qarāfī, *al-Dhakhīra*, 3:459, who states this rules comes from a *ḥadīth* in the collections of Muslim (*bāb al-salām*) and Abū Dāwūd (*adab*), via the companion Abū Hurayra.

115 Al-Kāsānī, *Badāʾiʿ al-Ṣanāʾiʿ*, 9:448. The Ḥanafīs Badr al-Dīn al-ʿAynī and al-Marghīnānī wrote that the purpose of distinguishing *dhimmīs* from Muslims was to manifest the *dhimmīs'* subordination (*al-ṣighār ʿalayhim*) and to prevent any threat to the faith of Muslims who might otherwise consider the *dhimmīs* as possible companions and associates. Al-ʿAynī, *al-Bināya*, 7:259; al-Marghīnānī, *al-Hidāya*, 1:455. See also Ibn Nujaym, *al-Baḥr al-Rāʾiq*, 5:192.

116 Ibn Nujaym, *al-Baḥr al-Rāʾiq*, 5:192.

117 Al-Māwardī, *al-Ḥāwī*, 14:325; al-Nawawī, *Rawḍa*, 10:327. See also al-Muzanī, *Mukhtaṣar al-Muzanī*, 5:385; al-Shīrāzī, *al-Muhadhdhab*, 3:312; al-Qarāfī, *al-Dhakhīra*, 3:459; Abū ʿAbd Allāh b. Mufliḥ, *al-Furūʿ* 6:245; al-Bahūtī, *Kashshāf al-Qināʿ*, 3:144.

how the rules were both constitutive of and constituted by an imperial enterprise of governance that championed an Islamic universalism while countenancing the fact of diversity. The analysis of these and other *dhimmī* rules shows that any imperative to accommodate the Other was counterbalanced by a commitment to an Islamic universalism that was given particular priority in the *public sphere.* Consequently, while jurists made accommodations to include and respect the *dhimmī* in some areas of law, they developed other rules that memorialized the *dhimmīs*' otherness in a Muslim polity. For example, the *dhimmī* could consume alcohol, but could not be *publicly* drunk. The *dhimmī* could own and consume alcohol and pork, but could not use the criminal law powers of the enterprise of governance—which had a deterrent effect on the *general public*—to punish the thief who stole such goods. The *dhimmī* could engage in his or her religious rituals, but not in *public*, where such rituals might be confused as sharing equal status and value with the Islamic ones. Of course, all of these restrictions were subject to variation, depending on the demographics of the town. In a town or village where *dhimmīs* were a majority, some jurists granted *dhimmīs* greater freedom in the public sphere, since concern for the effect of the *dhimmīs*' public presence upon Muslims was limited. At the heart of the *dhimmī* rules, therefore, was a concern with regulating the *dhimmī* in public. But that *public* was not just any public. It was a particular—though nebulous and variable—one where Muslims may or may not have predominated, but in which the Islamic commitments of the enterprise of governance gave content to a public good that jurists took upon themselves to manifest through the law.

3.8 CONSTRUING THE CHARACTER OF JUSTICE: WITNESSING IN THE COURTROOM

In legal disputes, individuals are often asked to be witnesses on behalf of parties to a conflict. A court official must be able to rely on the witness to determine the truth of the matter asserted. Therefore, to be a witness is to participate as an actor in a legal system, as opposed to being merely subjected to it. As an actor in a legal system, a witness affirmatively contributes to the operation of the system. In light of this active and affirmative role that witnesses play, it is perhaps no surprise that Muslim jurists were wary of granting *dhimmīs* the capacity to participate as witnesses in the claim space of Sharīʿa. To allow *dhimmīs* to participate as witnesses alongside Muslims was to view both as equally capable and trustworthy. The implication of such equality, though, ran contrary to the way the *dhimmī* was both included and othered in an Islamic milieu. To avoid such implications, jurists generally denied the *dhimmī* the capacity to be a witness in court while allowing certain exceptions, to be addressed below. *Dhimmīs* could bring their own suits to court, could have Muslims act on their behalf as witnesses, and would have a fair chance at success, all of which has been attested to by Najwa al-Qattan in her important study addressed in Chapter 1. Yet, to permit the *dhimmī* to be a witness in court was to allow the *dhimmī* to contribute to and constitute the boundaries of the claim space of Sharīʿa. For various reasons, as noted below, Muslim jurists were wary of such a possibility.

One way in which jurists denied *dhimmīs* the ability to testify was by repudiating their integrity. Whether a witness's testimony is persuasive or compelling will depend on the probity of the witness, or in other words the witness's trustworthiness. According to Muslim jurists, *dhimmīs* could not be witnesses in court on behalf of another party because they were not trustworthy. They were not trustworthy because, given their disbelief in the Islamic message, they did not and could not have a just character. The relationship between testifying, being just, and being Muslim is inferred from the Qur'ān, which states: "O you who believe, [utilize] witnesses among yourselves when one of you approaches death and issues a bequest, two of just character (*dhawū ʿadl*) from among yourselves, or, if you are traveling the earth, two others from [among people] other than your own..."[118] The verse seems to be addressed to believers who, nearing death, had to ensure their estates were distributed pursuant to the law. To ensure an authoritative will or bequeathing instrument, two witnesses were required, both of whom had to be "from among yourselves" and be just.

But how did jurists understand what it meant to be "just," and how did courts determine the just character of a witness? Furthermore, what did jurists understand by the phrase "traveling the earth"? Who did they include in the phrase "from among yourselves" and under what conditions did they allow those who were from "other than yourselves" to serve as witnesses? Even more, were there people that fell into neither of those two groups, and if so, who were they and how did jurists identify them? Muslim jurists reading the verse above could not and did not ignore the host of questions just noted as they reflected on the capacity of *dhimmīs* to testify in court.

[118] Qur'ān, 5:106. Some held that the reference to the "others" in this verse referred to the People of the Book. Al-Māwardī, *al-Ḥāwī*, 17:61. For more on the importance of this verse on legal debate, see Ibn Qudāma, *al-Mughnī*, 9:182.

Shāfiʿī, Ḥanbalī, Mālikī, and Jaʿfarī jurists generally held that being Muslim is a condition for being a witness in court.[119] For instance, al-Māwardī explicitly stated: "[The unbeliever's] testimony is not accepted either for or against a Muslim regarding bequests or any other matter, whether present in an urban setting or traveling afar."[120] He noted, however, that others held differently in the case of testamentary matters. For instance, some jurists allowed unbelievers, in particular the People of the Book, to be witnesses on testamentary matters in regions where no Muslims were available, but not in urbanized centers where Muslims presumably resided.[121] This exceptional ruling reflected the jurists' adherence to a narrow and strict reading of the Qur'ānic verse noted above, as well as an assumption about the relationship between Muslim demographics and urban development.

Beyond the general rule requiring witnesses to be Muslim,[122] some jurists went further and held that a non-Muslim could not testify as a witness where the testimony was for or against another non-Muslim.[123] This view was based, according to al-Māwardī, on an analysis of Qur'ān 65:2, a verse concerning divorce, which required the use of "two just people from among yourselves" (*dhaway ʿadl minkum*).[124] For Shāfiʿī and Ḥanbalī jurists, *dhimmīs* were not just (*ʿudūl*) since they were not

[119] Khalīl b. Isḥāq, *Mukhtaṣar Khalīl*, 262; al-Ghazālī, *al-Wajīz fī Fiqh al-Imām al-Shāfiʿī*, 2:248; idem, *al-Wasīṭ*, 4:325; al-Muzanī, *Mukhtaṣar al-Muzanī*, 5:413–14; al-Nawawī, *Rawḍa*, 11:222; al-Shīrāzī, *al-Muhadhdhab*, 3:437, who related a *ḥadīth* in which the Prophet said that people of different faiths cannot testify as witnesses for or against each other, except for Muslims who alone can be just, even if their testimony is against their own interests. See also Ibn Qudāma, *al-Mughnī*, 9:185–6, who held that Muslims can testify as witnesses against *kāfirs* despite their religious enmity (*ʿadāwa*) since the Muslims would not abandon the religious requirement of being truthful; al-Bahūtī, *Kashshāf al-Qināʿ*, 6:521, who relied on Qur'ān 65:2 to justify requiring one to be Muslim in order to give testimony; Saḥnūn, *al-Mudawwana al-Kubrā*, 5:156–7, who not only denied the *kāfir* the ability to testify as a witness against those of another religious community, but also held that Muslims can be witnesses against all *kāfirs;* al-Qarāfī, *al-Dhakhīra*, 10:224–5.

[120] Al-Māwardī, *al-Ḥāwī*, 17:61.

[121] Al-Māwardī, *al-Ḥāwī*, 17:61; Abū ʿAbd Allāh b. Mufliḥ, *al-Furūʿ*, 6:483, 497, who recognized the dispute on this issue, but nonetheless required one's Islamic faith as a condition to be a witness; al-Bahūtī, *Kashshāf al-Qināʿ*, 6:521; al-Muḥaqqiq al-Ḥillī, *Sharā'iʿ al-Islām*, 2:371; al-Ḥurr al-ʿĀmilī, *Wasā'il al-Shīʿa*, 13:390. Saḥnūn, *al-Mudawwana al-Kubrā*, 5:157, said that Mālik would not allow this exception; al-Qarāfī, *al-Dhakhīra*, 10:224–5.

[122] Although the verse (Qur'ān, 5:106) narrowly concerned bequests upon impending death, it was (re)presented as raising the question of what counts as just character for witnessing generally, and whether religious identity answers that question.

[123] Al-Māwardī, *al-Ḥāwī*, 17:61. Ibn Qudāma, *al-Mughnī*, 9:184, indicates there are some who allow all *dhimmīs* to be witnesses against other *dhimmīs;* al-Bahūtī, *Kashshāf al-Qināʿ*, 6:521; Saḥnūn, *al-Mudawwana al-Kubrā*, 5:157.

[124] Although this Qur'ānic verse concerns a case of divorce, Muslim jurists relied on the reference to the just witnesses as a basis for developing a legal regime on the requirements to be a witness in court.

members of the Muslim community.[125] In other words, the reference to "two just people from among yourselves" was read to mean witnesses from the Muslim "Us." Unbelievers could not be trusted in their testimony because their difference in faith rendered them not only "Other," but also corrupt in character (*fāsiq*), which would taint their testimony.[126] Muslims, on the other hand, suffered no similar disability. In fact, Shāfiʿī jurists went so far as to suggest hypothetically that a corrupt Muslim (*al-fāsiq al-muslim*) would be more competent (*akmal*) to give testimony than a just unbeliever (*al-kāfir al-ʿadl*) because of the effect the Muslim's commitment to Islam had on ensuring the veracity of even the corrupt Muslim's testimony.[127] Even though the Muslim may be corrupt (*fisq*), jurists presumed that corruption would not rise to the level of corruption that emanates from disbelief. The unbeliever suffered an even greater corruption by virtue of his disbelief, which constituted grounds for exclusion as a witness.[128] For the Mālikīs, *dhimmīs* certainly had the capacity to know the facts; but witnessing was not simply about what one can and cannot know. To be admissible as a witness, one had to be just, free, rationally capable, mature, and Muslim.[129] A *dhimmī* was free, mature, and had the ability to understand and comprehend the facts of a case. However, the *dhimmī* did not meet the requirement of being just, because the character of being just was not separable from being Muslim. Rather, for the Mālikīs, just character was linked to belief in Islam.

Importantly, though, some jurists permitted *dhimmīs* a limited capacity to testify as long as they were testifying against each other. For instance, the Shāfiʿī al-Māwardī allowed a *dhimmī* to testify for or against another *dhimmī* since their shared state of unbelief constituted a ground of affinity between them. That affinity ensured that any witness would act in the other's best interest.[130]

The Ḥanafīs generally permitted *dhimmīs* to testify for or against other *dhimmīs,* even if they did not share the same faith. Ḥanafī jurists

[125] Al-Māwardī, *al-Ḥāwī*, 17:62; Ibn Qudāma, *al-Mughnī*, 9:184–5. Notably, al-Bahūtī, *Kashshāf al-Qināʿ*, 6:529, held that those Muslims who believe in the createdness of the Qurʾān (i.e., the Muʿtazila) lacked a just character.

[126] Al-Māwardī, *al-Ḥāwī*, 17:62.

[127] Al-Māwardī, *al-Ḥāwī*, 17:62.

[128] Al-Māwardī, *al-Ḥāwī*, 17:62; al-Muzanī, *Mukhtaṣar al-Muzanī*, 5:413–14, who argued that the testimony of a *kāfir* cannot be accepted because of his disbelief, for his disbelief is the greatest lie of all, namely against God.

[129] Ibn Rushd al-Jadd, *al-Muqaddimāt*, 2:283–5; al-Qarāfī, *al-Dhakhīra*, 10:153.

[130] Al-Māwardī, *al-Ḥāwī*, 17:62. In fact al-Māwardī related how others held that if the unbeliever is considered just among his people, he can provide witness testimony against other unbelievers. See also al-Muḥaqqiq al-Ḥillī, *Sharāʾiʿ al-Islām*, 2:371, who noted that some allowed any *dhimmī* to testify against another, others allowed only co-religionists to testify against each other, and yet others denied non-Muslims any capacity to testify as witnesses.

argued that in such cases, the *dhimmī* had no substantial incentive to lie. In other words, the reason *dhimmīs* could not testify against Muslims was because *dhimmīs* presumably so resented the fact of Muslim political dominance and sovereignty that they would transfer that enmity to the Muslim party in the court and thereby unfairly act against the individual Muslim's interest.

This Ḥanafī exception is interesting because of how it linked the exceptional rule allowing *dhimmīs* to witness in court to the overall well-being and security of the Islamic enterprise of governance. The exception relies on certain presumptions that reveal how the presumed enterprise of governance contributed to the rule's intelligibility. The first presumption was that the *dhimmī* resided in an Islamically defined enterprise of governance ruled in accordance with a Sharīʿa-based legal system. The second is that *dhimmīs* were in a weak political position, which they resented and would seek to overcome. The third is that *dhimmīs* would transfer their resentment against the Muslim enterprise of governance to individual Muslims, and thereby, for political reasons, would subvert the justice to be meted out in a Sharīʿa-based legal proceeding. The fourth is that while *dhimmīs* could not be witnesses either for or against Muslims, they could participate as witnesses in cases involving other *dhimmīs,* because while they did not share the same faith tradition, they shared a similar subordinated socio-political status. Their shared subordination countered any threat that a *dhimmī* witness would alter or adjust his testimony out of resentment against the reigning political order. Because *dhimmīs,* whether Christian or Jew, lacked political power, they could testify for or against each other without any worry that their testimony might be prejudicial against a party to the case because of the witness's resentment about his subordinated status. Jurists assumed that *dhimmīs* had a natural resentment against the Muslim government, and consequently might target Muslim parties in court with false testimony as a way to target indirectly the Muslim sovereign.[131] Consequently, to allow a *dhimmī* to testify against a Muslim potentially threatened the well-being of the Muslim polity and its sovereign interests, albeit indirectly so. In contrast, to allow a *dhimmī* to testify against another *dhimmī* posed no threat against the enterprise of governance,

The analysis above suggests that the incapacity of *dhimmīs* to be witnesses in court is intimately related to the way the law orders and stratifies society and thereby contributes to the operation of the

[131] Al-Marghīnānī, *al-Hidāya*, 2:122–3; al-ʿAynī, *al-Bināya*, 9:152–4. Notably, both authors denied *mustaʾmins* the right to be witnesses since they have no residency in the Muslim polity and cannot be trusted to act in others' best interests.

enterprise of governance in a diverse setting. *Dhimmīs* who wanted to go to court could file their complaints and have the courts decide their cases pursuant to Sharīʿa-based rules. However, if *dhimmīs* were witnesses in the court, they would be contributing to the operation of law in the claim space of Sharīʿa. They would help officers of the legal system direct how the enterprise of governance would use its institutional force and coercive power on the bodies of others, including Muslims. In this capacity, the *dhimmī* would help constitute the boundaries of the Sharīʿa claim space, and thereby influence the operation of the enterprise of governance. As the discussion of the various legal issues above has already suggested, Muslim jurists included the *dhimmī* in the Muslim polity only to the extent that the *dhimmīs*' inclusion did not undermine a commitment to a particular notion of the *public* defined in terms of Islamic values. As residents in the Islamic polity, *dhimmīs* could not be excluded entirely; unsurprisingly, therefore, different exceptions were proffered to allow them to testify in limited cases. But as outsiders, they also had to be managed and regulated so as not to be potentially subversive agents of an Islamically defined enterprise of governance. To allow *dhimmīs* to witness in court generally and without restriction, for the jurists above, was viewed as permitting them to participate in and potentially to undermine the very processes and institutions that gave content to the values that informed the enterprise of governance and the *public* realm that the jurists wished to insulate from the presence of *dhimmīs*.

3.9 CONCLUSION

This chapter has analyzed various legal doctrines regulating *dhimmīs*. The analysis shows that a fundamental principle animating the *dhimmī* rules was to recognize *and* manage diversity in a Muslim polity in terms of both empire and an Islamic universalism. As indicated above, these two imperatives did not always neatly coincide with one another, and indeed even worked at cross purposes. The *dhimmī* rules, thereby, were legal symptoms of the more general challenge jurists faced when they developed legal regimes for the purpose of governing amidst diversity.

All too often, scholars of Islamic law have researched the *dhimmī* rules in order to answer questions that arise in today's political climate: are Islam, Islamic Law, and Muslims tolerant or intolerant of non-Muslims? While it may be tempting to view these rules as indicative of either the tolerance or intolerance of Islamic law, this chapter illustrates that such an analytic frame is far too limiting. Indeed, the "tolerance/intolerance" dichotomy poses a question that, no matter how it is answered, over-determines the meaning and significance of the *dhimmī* rules for reasons that, far too often, have to do with present debates and polemics as opposed to historically sensitive understandings of Islamic jurisprudence.

Furthermore, the "tolerance" frame more often than not makes the content of the *dhimmī* rules the object of inquiry. The focus of this study is not on making plain the content and arguments underlying the *dhimmī* rules found in premodern *fiqh* collections. Others have laid that groundwork already, and to them a great intellectual debt is owed: Yohanan Friedmann has done an impressive service in presenting the *dhimmī* rules to an English-speaking audience; so too has ʿAbd al-Karīm Zaydān for an Arabic-speaking audience.[132] Building on the work of others, this study is less interested in what the *dhimmī* rules say, and instead is interested in why the *dhimmī* rules existed at all, for what purpose, and to what end. To answer the questions *Why?* and *To what end?* requires, however, an appreciation of the way in which the *dhimmī* rules related to each other and anticipated the fact of diversity in an enterprise of governance.

Premodern jurists did not simply recognize, but rather seemed to take for granted the fact of diversity in a Muslim polity. The issue for them was not whether non-Muslims should or should not reside under the Muslim imperium. Rather, the issue was how best to regulate their presence in a public sphere defined in Islamic terms, whatever those terms might be. Jurists developed the *dhimmī* rules out of a concern that the public presence of the *dhimmīs'* difference might adversely affect the dominance and priority of Islamic core values in an enterprise of governance that at the same time relied on the *dhimmīs* for important fiscal and administrative reasons. For instance, *dhimmīs* living in a Muslim polity were permitted to drink alcohol, but were not permitted to become drunk in public. They could walk along the streets, but had to walk along the sides when Muslims were around. They could bequeath their property, but some jurists limited their freedom to bequeath when such bequests were for charitable endowments that might work against the core values of an Islamic enterprise of governance. The legal debates on the *dhimmī* rules reveal how the jurists at the same time both sought to uphold Islamically defined core values, and endeavored to create space for the *dhimmīs* to live and participate in a polity that jurists framed in terms of the at times competing ethics of empire and Islamic universalism.

The jurists did not always state expressly what they viewed as the public good or the polity's core values. However, analyzing different

[132] Friedman, *Tolerance and Coercion in Islam*; Zaydān, *Aḥkām al-Dhimmiyyīn*.

rules together lays bare considerable insight into how "public good" was itself an area of ongoing contestation and negotiation among jurists using the instruments of law and legal argument. For instance, while we found that *dhimmīs* were exempted from punishment for alcohol consumption, they could not at the same time expect Muslim jurists to protect their property interests in these items as they would other items. This legal limit on the *dhimmīs'* expectation interests illustrates how the general ban on alcohol consumption, though not applied to the *dhimmī,* nonetheless contributed to a "core value" that jurists relied upon to determine subsidiary rules in the areas of criminal and property law. In this case, the ban on alcohol consumption became a juridified public policy principle that gave specific content to the conception of the public good, which in turn informed the jurists as they considered whether the *dhimmī* could petition the government to punish one who steals the *dhimmī*'s stock of alcohol.

In this example, the notion of the public good had a specific doctrinal source (i.e., the source-text on alcohol consumption) that gave it content. In other cases, the core value might be based on assumptions about the enterprise of governance and the implication of diversity within the polity. For instance, *dhimmīs* had the right to own homes and to bequeath property. However, the question of whether *dhimmīs* could create charitable endowments was not a clear matter. As noted above, the answer depended on how the particular charitable endowment might have contributed to and influenced the public sphere. If the *dhimmī*'s charitable endowment was designed to feed the poor, jurists would not object. But if the charitable endowment created and supported a Torah or Bible reading school, the jurists were less than enthusiastic. On the one hand, such charitable endowments would allow *dhimmīs* to ensure the continuity of their communities, allowing the *dhimmīs* to pass on their tradition to their children. But for some jurists, the existence of such schools was counter to the imperatives of an Islamic universalism that gave content and legitimating force to the enterprise of governance. Many jurists (especially Shāfiʿī jurists) prohibited such endowments, since they would perpetuate disbelief in Islamic lands. For others, such endowments posed a security threat to the enterprise of governance. Indeed, al-Shīrāzī was notable in this regard when he equated supporting a charitable endowment for a Torah or Bible reading school to an endowment that armed the Muslim polity's enemies. Notably, the justification of this legal limitation is premised upon a particular political commitment to an Islamic universalist ethos as definitive of the public sphere and thereby the enterprise of governance, which jurists understood would (or should) enforce the *dhimmī* rules through its governing institutions.

The examples in this chapter, in the aggregate, demonstrate the insight that can be gained by viewing the *dhimmī* rules through the frame of Sharīʿa as Rule of Law. If Rule of Law represents a claim space from which arguments of justice are made, that space (to be intelligible as a distinctively legal space) must be bounded lest we find arguments drawing upon the work of Shakespeare or the poetry of Ḥāfiẓ to determine legal outcomes. Certainly such sources may find their way into judicial decision making, but that does not give them authority in the law. Rather, the conditions of authority in law, which will be discussed more extensively in Chapter 5, in the aggregate constitute the boundaries that define and delineate the claim of space of Rule of Law. As suggested throughout this chapter, one significant constitutive feature of the premodern Sharīʿa claim space was the enterprise of governance that premodern jurists had in mind when developing legal doctrines regarding the *dhimmīs.* Chapter 1 showed that the enterprise of governance that animated premodern jurists was an imperial one that was legitimated by a commitment to an Islamic universalism. Together, empire and Islamic univeralism contributed to the intelligibility of the *dhimmī* rules for premodern jurists facing the challenge of governing amidst diversity.

4

The Rationale of Empire and the Hegemony of Law

By viewing Sharīʿa as Rule of Law, this study has thus far aimed to demonstrate how the intelligibility of the *dhimmī* rules reflects the mutually constitutive relationship between law and an enterprise of governance that was characterized in terms of conquest, empire, and Islamic universalism. That background factor of imperial aspiration and organization, animated and justified by the universalist message of Islam, contributed to categorizations and sub-categorizations of different people—Muslim and non-Muslim, permanent resident (*dhimmī*) and temporary resident (*mustaʾmin*). Rules of law were then developed to give the individuals within each category different degrees of liberty and protection within the Muslim polity. The categories had the effect of defining who constituted the "Us" and the "Them." Some people, such as the *dhimmīs,* fell somewhere in between and thereby fueled considerable legal debate about their status, liberty, and expectation interests when living in a Muslim polity; hence the oftentimes confusing and contradictory legal doctrines on the *dhimmī.*

The actual black letter doctrines are less central to this study than the justificatory arguments used to reach them, and the presumed contextual features that made them both possible and intelligible. Those contextual features were the subject of Chapter 1 and gave content to the boundaries of the claim space of Sharīʿa. As suggested thus far, "Sharīʿa as Rule of Law" provides a conceptual frame that allows us to appreciate how the law and enterprise of governance are constitutive features of each other. Sharīʿa as Rule of Law accounts for how a governing model (whether real or imagined) influenced the development of doctrines concerning the status and place of the Other in a Muslim polity. Indeed, as suggested in Chapter 1, the early history of military conquest and expansion contributed to the jurists' political pre-commitments, which in turn influenced their arguments for and against certain legal doctrines concerning the non-Muslim living under Muslim imperium.

While the focus thus far has been on the constitutive role of the imperial model upon the content of the law, this chapter offers a different approach to the study of Sharīʿa as Rule of Law. This chapter seeks to appreciate the way in which jurists contributed to a legal system that itself acted hegemonically upon those who were subjected to it, specifically minorities. The design and operation of institutions of adjudication and the modes of legal argument quite often operated hegemonically upon the interests of minorities who came into the claim space of Sharīʿa to seek justice. This chapter addresses two legal doctrines to showcase the hegemonic nature of law when confronted with a minority claimant. The two legal doctrines concern whether and why a *dhimmī* was subjected to stoning to death as a punishment of adultery, and whether or not the *dhimmī* could seek redress against someone who falsely accused him of illicit sexual intercourse (*qadhf*, hereinafter sexual slander).

4.1 SEX, SHAME, AND THE DIGNITY *(IḤṢĀN)* OF THE OTHER

Under premodern Islamic legal doctrine, adulterers could be stoned to death.[1] The term of art that designated the adulterer (as opposed to the unmarried fornicator) was *muḥṣan*. That term was again central in cases of sexual slander. For instance, Qur'ān 24:45 reads: "And [concerning] those who level a charge against chaste women (*muḥṣanāt*) and do not bring four witnesses, whip them eighty lashes and do not accept their testimony ever, for they are corrupt; except for those who repent thereafter and act righteously. Indeed God is forgiving and merciful."[2]

[1] The stoning punishment for adulterers in Islamic law is based on traditions indicating that the Prophet stoned *muḥṣan* individuals who committed *zinā*. See *ḥadīths* 6812, 6813, and 6814 in *Ṣaḥīḥ al-Bukhārī*, which not only serve as a foundation for stoning as a punishment, but also limit it to those who are *muḥṣan*. A discussion of these *ḥadīths* can be found in Ibn Ḥajr al-ʿAsqalānī, *Fatḥ al-Bārī*, 12:117–27, who defines *muḥṣan* as one who is chaste (*ʿiffa*), has contracted and consummated a marriage, free (*ḥurra*), and Muslim. Likewise, Muslim b. al-Ḥajjāj includes similar traditions, including one in which ʿUmar b. al-Khaṭṭāb argued that the Qur'ān included a verse on stoning, despite such a verse not existing in the text compiled after Muḥammad's death. ʿUmar held that "[s]toning, in the book of God, is imposed on the one committing illicit sex if he is chaste (*idhā aḥṣan*)." Al-Nawawī, *al-Minhāj Sharḥ Ṣaḥīḥ Muslim b. al-Ḥajjāj*, ed. Khalīl Ma'mūn Shīḥā, 3rd ed. (Beirut: Dār al-Maʿrifa, 1996), 11:191–2, commenting on *ḥadīth* 4394. For a general account of the word's meaning, see J. Burton, *EI2*, s.v. "Muḥṣan." Unmarried fornicators are subjected to 100 lashes. See Qur'ān 24:2.

[2] Muslim exegetes do not all agree on the occasion of revelation for this verse, but most hold that it had to do with Muḥammad's wife, ʿĀ'isha. Muḥammad once led an

Jurists argued that the victim of such slander could only seek redress against the slanderer if the former was *muḥṣan.*

Lexicographically, *muḥṣan* and its feminine form (*muḥṣana*) invoke notions of chastity and purity (*ʿafīf*). According to Ibn Manẓūr (d. 711/1311), "every chaste woman is *muḥṣana* ... and every married woman is *muḥṣana*."[3] Furthermore, he wrote "a *muḥṣan* man is [one who is] married, where marriage renders him chaste (*qad aḥṣanahu al-tazawwuj*)."[4] Accordingly, the term *muḥṣan* has been understood to reflect marital status and chastity.

If we consider *muḥṣan* in its literal meaning, then a married *dhimmī* should be *muḥṣan*, thus being liable to stoning for adultery *and* entitled to seek redress for sexual slander. But Muslim jurists denied that *dhimmīs* are *muḥṣan*. Hence, they refused to permit *dhimmīs* to seek redress for sexual slander (*qadhf*). Interestingly, though, they held *dhimmīs* liable to stoning for committing adultery. If *dhimmīs* were not *muḥṣan* for purposes of sexual slander, how could they be stoned for adultery, which required them to be *muḥṣan*?

The inconsistency in these legal rulings is attributable to a source-text that was at the heart of premodern debates about the *dhimmī*'s redress for sexual slander. A tradition from Ibn ʿUmar (d. 73/693), a companion of the Prophet and the son of the second caliph ʿUmar b. al-Khaṭṭāb, reads as follows: "Whoever disbelieves in God is not *muḥṣan*."[5] Another

expedition, accompanied by his wife ʿĀʾisha, who, while the forces were encamped, misplaced her necklace. She went out looking for it, and upon her return to the camp site she discovered that everyone was gone. She stayed in that spot until the arrival of Ṣafwān b. Muʿaṭṭal, who had fallen behind the army and was attempting to catch up with it. He noticed ʿĀʾisha and escorted her to the location of the expedition force's next camp. When the expedition returned to Medina, ʿĀʾisha fell ill and remained indoors. While she was recuperating, the people of Medina began to spread rumors about an affair between her and Ṣafwān. Exegetical sources report that Qurʾān 24:4–5 was revealed to exculpate ʿĀʾisha. Al-Qurṭubī, *al-Jāmiʿ li Aḥkām al-Qurʾān*, 12:115; Abū al-Faḍl Maḥmūd al-Ālūsī, *Rūḥ al-Maʿānī fī Tafsīr al-Qurʾān al-ʿAẓīm wa al-Sabʿ al-Mathānī* (Beirut: Dār al-Fikr, 1997), 10:131–2; Muhammad Husayn Haykal, *The Life of Muhammad*, trans. Ismaʾil Ragi A. al-Faruqi (n.p.: North American Trust Publications, 1976), 331–9; M.A. Salahi, *Muhammad: Man and Prophet* (Shaftesbury: Element, 1995); 383–93; Martin Lings, *Muhammad: His Life Based on the Earliest Sources* (Rocherster, Vermont: Inner Traditions International, 1983), 240–6. Some commentators argued that a different verse (Qurʾān 24:11) arose to prove ʿĀʾisha's innocence, which specifically refers to people who bring forth a false allegation (*ifk*). Al-Ṭabarī, *Tafsīr al-Ṭabarī*, 5:406; al-Qurṭubī, *al-Jāmiʿ*, 12:131. Still others suggested that there is no specific historical context that the *qadhf* verse addresses. Al-Qurṭubī, *al-Jāmiʿ*, 12:115.

[3] Ibn Manẓūr, *Lisān al-ʿArab*, 13:120–1. See also al-Zabīdī, *Tāj al-ʿUrūs*, ed. ʿAlī Shīrī (Beirut: Dār al-Fikr, 1994), 18:149.

[4] Ibn Manẓūr, *Lisān al-ʿArab*, 13:120–1.

[5] Al-Dār Quṭnī, *Sunan al-Dār Quṭnī*, 3:107. This version is complemented by others with similar meanings but different wording. Abū Bakr al-Bayhaqī (d. 458/1066), when relating different versions of this tradition indicated how it is *mawqūf*, which means that the narration of the tradition stops at the Companion and does not reflect the words of the

version states: "The people disbelieving anything about God are not [*muḥṣan*]."[6] In yet another tradition, Kaʿb b. Mālik wanted to marry a Jewish or Christian woman. He asked the Prophet, who advised him against doing so and responded: "She will not make you [*muḥṣan*]."[7] In other words, a Muslim man who marries a non-Muslim woman would not be *muḥṣan,* given his wife's religious difference.[8] The different traditions were subjected to critiques of authenticity; nonetheless substantively they represent variations on a similar theme—namely that non-Muslims were not *muḥṣan* according to premodern Muslim jurists. Furthermore, despite critiques of authenticity, these traditions influenced legal debate in no uncertain terms.[9] In particular, jurists often cited Ibn ʿUmar's version to deny *dhimmīs* the right to redress for sexual slander.

By denying that any non-Muslim could be *muḥṣan,* Ibn ʿUmar's statement created a problem for jurists, who considered adultery to be so harmful to society and the public good that they were unwilling to create exceptions to the general ban for *dhimmīs.* Muslim jurists generally considered adultery to violate a "right of God" (*ḥaqq Allāh*),[10] which was a technical term that often referred to the social implications arising from a particular offense. Such acts were considered corrupt,

Prophet. Al-Bayhaqī, *al-Sunan al-Kubrā*, 8:376. See also Ibn al-Jawzī, *al-Taḥqīq fī Aḥādīth al-Khilāf,* ed. Muḥammad Fāris (Beirut: Dār al-Kutub al-ʿIlmiyya, n.d.), 2:324–5. G.H.A. Juynboll, "*Mursal,*" *Encyclopaedia of Islam, Second Edition.* Eds P. Bearman et al.; Ṣubḥī Ṣāliḥ, *ʿUlūm al-Ḥadīth wa Muṣṭalaḥatuhu* (1959; reprint, Beirut: Dār al-ʿIlm li al-Malāyīn, 1996), 208.

[6] Al-Bayhaqī, *al-Sunan al-Kubrā*, 8:376. This tradition involves a chain of transmission linking Sufyān al-Thawrī and Mūsā b. ʿUqba. According to al-Bayhaqī, this link in any chain of transmission is rejected (*munkar*).

[7] Al-Bayhaqī, *al-Sunan al-Kubrā*, 8:376.

[8] Al-Bayhaqī, *al-Sunan al-Kubrā*, 8:376–7; Ibn al-Jawzī, *al-Taḥqīq*, 2:324–25. This tradition is problematic because one of the narrators in the chain of transmission (Abū Bakr b. Abī Maryam) is considered a weak link (*ḍaʿīf*) and because two of the narrators in the chain never knew each other.

[9] The authenticity of these traditions is not at issue here. Debates on the authenticity of *aḥādīth* (sing. *ḥadīth*) are well known, but are not central to my discussion of the way Muslim jurists internalized a certain logic of the law and used reasoning and tradition to justify a legal decision. For the scholarly debate on *ḥadīth* authenticity, see Joseph Schacht, *The Origins of Muhammadan Jurisprudence* (Oxford: Clarendon Press, 1950); M. Mustafa al-Azami, *On Schacht's Origins of Muhammadan Jurisprudence* (New York: John Wiley & Sons, 1985); Harald Motzki, *The Origins of Islamic Jurisprudence: Meccan Fiqh Before the Classical Schools*, trans. Marion H. Katz (Leiden: Brill Publications, 2001). In fact, while Muslim jurists debated whether *mawqūf* traditions can be used as legal authority, they nonetheless were comfortable relying on Ibn ʿUmar's statement to justify a regime of criminal liability that distributed entitlements and liabilities on the basis of religious belief, as illustrated below. Ṣāliḥ, *ʿUlūm al-Ḥadīth*, 208.

[10] The fact that the term of art invokes God does not necessarily suggest such wrongs are the most contemptible. Rather, an implication of labeling an act as violating a "right of God" is, among other things, to empower the governing authorities to act on behalf of the public to deter and ultimately punish such conduct.

and thus punishing them was deemed a way of "ridding the world of corruption" (*ikhlāʾ al-ʿālam ʿan al-fasād*).[11] Since adultery was deemed to pose a public harm, it would be inconsistent for the ruling authorities to punish only some adulterers and not others. Consequently, given the social impact jurists imputed to adultery, they were unwilling to exclude *dhimmīs* from punitive liability for adultery. However, a precondition for stoning someone for adultery is that the adulterer be *muḥṣan;* but the doctrine on sexual slander holds specifically that *dhimmīs* are not *muḥṣan*. Consequently, the logical implication is that *dhimmīs* should not be stoned for adultery under Islamic law.

To subject *dhimmīs* to stoning for adultery, Muslim jurists read and interpreted competing source-texts in light of the accommodative spirit of the contract of protection, and the ethic of Islamic universalism. Jurists argued that holding *dhimmīs* liable for adultery could be justified on an alternative ground, namely the contract of protection. They said that if the *dhimmīs'* tradition prohibited adultery, then they shared the same belief as Muslims about its evil and corrupt nature. Hence, punishing them for the crime did not violate their tradition or the contract of protection. Consequently, *dhimmīs* were prohibited from committing adultery on the authority of the *dhimmī*'s tradition as introduced into the legal analysis via the contract of protection.

Yet if that was the case, it also raised concerns for jurists that alternative legal doctrines (i.e., the *dhimmīs* tradition) other than Sharīʿa-based ones could have some normative authority in an Islamic polity, though channeled through the contract of protection. This implication, if left unchecked, could have a significant impact on the constitutive features of the claim space of Sharīʿa. Certainly, the contract of protection operated as a Sharīʿa-based frame of analysis within which the *dhimmī* tradition was incorporated; further, it rendered justifiable the punishment of stoning for adultery. Nonetheless jurists worried that doing so would introduce the *dhimmīs'* tradition as an implicit basis for legal justification. As such, this legal approach raised important questions about the priority and superiority of Sharīʿa over and against other possible authorities of law.

[11] Al-ʿAynī, *al-Bināya*, 6:371. For others who held a similar view about the role of the *ḥuqūq Allāh* in generally ridding the world of corruption for the betterment of society, see Ibn Nujaym, *al-Baḥr al-Rāʾiq*, 5:4; al-Khurashī (also, al-Kharāshī), *Ḥāshiyat al-Khurashī ʿalā Mukhtaṣar Sayyid Khalīl*, ed. Zakariyya ʿUmayrāt (Beirut: Dār al-Kutub al-ʿIlmiyya, 1997), 8:329; Marghīnānī, *al-Hidāya*, 1:402; Ṣāliḥ ʿAbd al-Samīʿ al-Ābī al-Azharī, *Jawāhir al-Iklīl*, ed. Muḥammad ʿAbd al-Azīz al-Khālidī (Beirut: Dār al-Kutub al-ʿIlmiyya, 1997), 2:437. The Mālikī jurist Saḥnūn wrote that when a *dhimmī* steals, the punishment for the *ḥadd* crime of theft must be applied and his hand cut off because the harm posed is a general evil (*fasād fi al-arḍ*). But the punishments associated with drinking alcohol and fornication are not to be applied to the *dhimmī*. Saḥnūn, *al-Mudawwana al-Kubrā*, 6:270.

To justify a *dhimmī*'s liability to stoning and to avoid the implication that a *dhimmī*'s legal tradition held normative authority alongside Sharīʿa-based norms, jurists referred to the practice of the Prophet, who reportedly stoned two Jews for committing adultery.[12] They concluded that the Prophet inquired into the *dhimmī*'s tradition to determine, *as a matter of fact*, whether it coincided with the Sharīʿa. If it did, then they argued *dhimmīs* were liable to the Sharīʿa sanction, even if the specific Sharīʿa sanction differed from the sanction in the *dhimmīs*' own tradition. Jurists were not willing to admit that the *dhimmī*'s liability arose by granting legal authority to the *dhimmī*'s legal tradition in the claim space of Sharīʿa. Rather, they maintained that the Sharīʿa provided the only doctrinal rules by which to govern an Islamic polity. The *dhimmī*'s tradition entered only as part of the larger *factual* inquiry that was made to determine the extent of difference and coincidence between the two traditions in the interest of respecting difference and upholding shared value commitments, both of which were aspects of the contract of protection.

In the relevant prophetic tradition, two adulterous Jews were brought to the Prophet for adjudication, but he refrained from doing anything until he could consult Jewish experts on the matter. The Prophet asked them: "What do you [Jews] find in the Torah concerning one who adulterates?" They responded: "We blacken both of their faces, and burden them [with heavy loads], and separate from them [i.e., banish them]...." The Prophet asked them to bring a copy of the Torah in order to verify their testimony about their legal tradition (*in kuntum ṣādiqīn*). They brought a copy, and a Jewish youth read the relevant passages. But when he came to its verse on stoning, he put his hand over the verse and read what followed thereafter. A companion of the Prophet, ʿAbd Allāh b. Salām, told the young man to remove his hand and read the hidden verses, at which point the Prophet learned of the Torah's stoning requirement.[13] The Prophet thereby ordered the two Jewish adulterers to be stoned to death.[14]

[12] From the text of the tradition, it is not clear whether the Jews fornicated or adulterated given the ambiguity in the term *zinā*. However, according to Biblical scholarship, adultery was subject to punishment, not fornication. Freedman, *The Nine Commandments*, 119–26.

[13] A reference to stoning as punishment for adultery in the Torah is found in Leviticus, 20:2, 10. Rabbinic tradition relies on these verses to punish certain adulterers by stoning them to death. Rosenberg and Rosenberg, "Of God's Mercy and the Four Biblical Methods of Capital Punishment," 1169–211, 1183, 1184. However, there seems to be some dispute about the punishment for adulterers. The Talmudic tradition requires strangulation of both parties if two witnesses saw the illicit act. Fram, "Two Cases of Adultery and the Halakhic Decision-Making Process," 277–300, 279.

[14] This narrative is reported in various sources of *ḥadīth*. See for instance al-Nawawī, *Sharḥ Ṣaḥīḥ Muslim*, 11:206–7.

This tradition provided jurists the requisite authoritative source-text to justify stoning non-Muslims for committing adultery. The jurists read the Torah source-text as justifying Sharīʿa-based liability for adultery under the contract of protection, while also avoiding any conflict with the rules on sexual slander. The jurists held that married *dhimmīs* could be stoned for adultery, but not because they were *muḥṣan.* Their liability arose from the fact that their own tradition prohibited adultery. Generally, under the contract of protection, the *dhimmīs'* traditions were to be respected; consequently, to punish the *dhimmīs* for adultery was not an imposition of Sharīʿa-based liability contrary to the *dhimmīs'* tradition, but rather reflected the *dhimmīs'* own traditions against adultery. Given that their tradition included a similar norm against adultery, then subjecting them to stoning was not an undue imposition on their autonomy or values, as protected by the contract of protection. Importantly, though, the jurists inquired into the *dhimmīs'* tradition in order to justify and legitimate the imposition of Sharīʿa-based liability and punishment (i.e., stoning for adultery); the adulterous *dhimmīs* were legitimately subjected to Sharīʿa-based norms against adultery because they implicitly consented to Sharīʿa liability to the extent their own traditions shared similar values and imperatives. In other words, where the *dhimmīs'* normative tradition overlapped with Sharīʿa-based norms, it was consistent with the contract of protection to hold *dhimmīs* liable to those Sharīʿa-based norms. Consequently, the contract of protection made possible and intelligible the inquiry into the *dhimmīs'* tradition, without at the same time rendering the *dhimmīs'* tradition an authoritative source of legal argument. For jurists, the relevant inquiry was a factual one that either supported or rejected the application of Sharīʿa-based liability on the basis of the contract of protection. Ultimately, Sharīʿa-based doctrines were the ones being applied to the exclusion of all others. Hence, Sharīʿa-based doctrines retained their superiority and priority (indeed, hegemony) over all other traditions. Any conflict between competing doctrinal sources was harmonized, the contract of protection was ultimately upheld and respected, and the *dhimmī* was subjected to the imposition and thereby hegemony of the Sharīʿa legal system.

The contract was meant to respect the *dhimmī*'s difference. But viewing Sharīʿa as Rule of Law reveals how the contract both offered a basis for determining shared value commitments, and legitimated the application of Sharīʿa-based obligations upon *dhimmīs* in furtherance of the dominance and legitimacy of the enterprise of governance. This is evidenced by the fact that the *dhimmīs'* punishment for adultery was articulated in terms of the Sharīʿa-based punishment and not their own traditions. The contract provided the politico-legal mechanism for Muslim jurists to hold *dhimmīs* liable given the overlap between their faith commitments and their commitment to abide by the Sharīʿa under the contract of protection. To stone them for adultery undermined neither the primacy of Sharīʿa nor the public interest in punishing adulterers.

4.2 SEXUAL SLANDER AND THE *DHIMMĪ*: RECOGNITION AND REDRESS

Sexual slander posed an evil that was not merely a matter of public concern (*ḥaqq Allāh*), but also a private one (*ḥaqq al-ʿabd*).[15] Noting the private interests implicated in a case of sexual slander, al-Māwardī remarked that dignity was something integral to each person, like his physical well-being and property. He wrote: "What is invoked in the case of [injuries to our] physical well-being and property are the rights of people, and so too in the case of [injuries to our] dignity."[16] However, even though Muslims and *dhimmīs* shared a similar interest in not suffering sexual slander, many jurists held that *dhimmīs* could not seek redress under the Qur'ānic punishment for sexual slander (*qadhf*). This is not to suggest, though, that Muslim jurists were not troubled by the failure to protect the *dhimmī*'s integrity to the same extent as Muslims. Because the injury to the individual would be the same, regardless of the identity of the victim, some Muslim jurists believed the *dhimmī* should have some legal recourse in the event he or she was sexually slandered. Deciding what that recourse would be, though, was a different matter. Of particular interest here is to understand how jurists justified the difference in legal recourse Muslims and *dhimmīs* could pursue in cases of sexual slander. As will become evident, the justifications drew on different interpretive negotiations between the sometimes-competing ethics of accommodation through contract, Islamic universalism, and its corollary of an Islamic superiority.

The legal debate on *dhimmī* recourse as victims of sexual slander was not only about conflicting sources and legal integrity; it also concerned

[15] Al-ʿAynī, *al-Bināya*, 6:371; al-Māwardī, *al-Ḥāwī*, 11:10; al-Qurṭubī, *al-Jāmiʿ*, 12:116; Marghinānī, *al-Hidāya*, 1:400, 402. In fact, the Mālikī jurist Abū Bakr b. al-ʿArabī (d. 543/1148) argued that God considers upholding one's honor and dignity so important that nearly one-third of all prohibitions protect one's dignity (*aʿrāḍ*). Abū Bakr b. al-ʿArabī, *Kitāb al-Qabas*, ed. Muḥammad ʿAbd Allāh Walad Karīm (Beirut: Dār al-Gharb al-Islāmī, 1992), 3:1018. See also, Emon, "*Ḥuqūq Allāh*," 338–9.

[16] Al-Māwardī, *al-Ḥāwī*, 11:10.

whether and to what extent the ethic of Islamic superiority was or should be a constitutive factor of the intelligibility of Sharīʿa-based norms on the *dhimmī*, and whether other counteracting values could also contribute to their intelligibility. For instance, jurists relied on Ibn ʿUmar's tradition that an unbeliever is not *muḥṣan* to permit only Muslims to seek the Qur'ānic form of redress for sexual slander.[17] To explain the underlying logic of this ruling, jurists resorted to the theme of an Islamic and Muslim superiority and, by implication, *dhimmī* subordination. Al-Māwardī, for example, scoffed at the idea that a *dhimmī* might seek redress against a Muslim for sexual slander. For him, a Muslim could not suffer on account of a non-Muslim's dignity.[18] The Mālikī Ibn Rushd al-Ḥafīd (a.k.a. Averroes, d. 595/1198) explained that *iḥṣān* invokes notions of virtue and moral excellence (*faḍīla*), which are absent when Islamic commitment is lacking.[19]

Yet the superiority/subordination thematic dynamic could not hide the fact that the sexually slandered *dhimmī* suffered an actual injury. Indeed, jurists recognized that to disallow completely any redress for the slandered *dhimmī* would be unjust. In other words, an ethic of Islamic superiority and, thereby, of *dhimmī* subordination, may be used to diminish the standing of the *dhimmī* in the Muslim polity; but it could not completely erase the fact that the *dhimmī* suffered an injury from sexual slander. Difference in religious conviction did not change the fact that sexual slander harmed all people across society, regardless of how they might otherwise be stratified.

Consequently, while jurists did not grant the *dhimmī* redress on *Qur'ānic grounds,* they empowered the ruler to provide redress to the *dhimmī* on alternative legal grounds. They held that the ruler, as leader of the enterprise of governance, could use the authority vested in his office to enact and enforce his own ordinances to provide an alternative legal ground by which the *dhimmī* could seek redress. This discretionary authority of the ruler was known as *taʿzīr*.[20] *Taʿzīr* referred to the power and authority of the ruler to legislate on an *ad hoc* basis. As discussed in Chapter 5, *taʿzīr* fell within the more general framework of *siyāsa sharʿiyya* and was a power that jurists granted to the ruler to fill the lacuna that existed when no source-text addressed

[17] Al-Māwardī, *al-Ḥāwī*, 13:255. See also al-Shīrāzī, *al-Muhadhdhab*, 3:345–6.

[18] Al-Māwardī, *al-Ḥāwī*, 13:256. The corollary of this ruling, though, is that *dhimmīs* who sexually slander Muslims could be punished. The conditions for being a perpetrator of sexual slander did not distinguish between being Muslim and non-Muslim. Al-Māwardī, *al-Ḥāwī*, 13:256; al-Shīrāzī, *al-Muhadhdhab*, 3:345.

[19] Ibn Rushd al-Ḥafīd, *Bidāyat al-Mujtahid*, 2:637.

[20] Al-Shīrāzī, *al-Muhadhdhab*, 3:346.

an injury that the legal system, in the interest of justice, could not ignore.[21] On the basis of the authority of his office, the ruler could create rules by which the *dhimmī* could seek redress for sexual slander. These grounds would give the *dhimmī* a form of legal redress, but on grounds and with sanctions separate and distinct from the Qur'ānic crime.[22]

If Islamic law were purely intolerant toward the non-Muslim, it makes little sense to grant *dhimmīs* a mode of redress in this case. Yet Islamic law was clearly not completely tolerant and egalitarian towards the Other, since the grant of an alternative ground for sexual slander only emphasized the *dhimmī*'s stratified and subordinated position in the Islamic polity. Instead of relying solely on the authority of source-texts to ground the *dhimmī*'s redress (or rather, lack thereof), the jurists invoked a different authority entirely, namely the authority of the enterprise of governance to grant legal relief to sexually slandered *dhimmīs*. This example not only deflates the myths of tolerance or intolerance, but it also discloses the mutually constitutive relationship between law and the enterprise of governance. The development of Sharīʿa-based doctrines in this case was premised upon an appreciation of an enterprise of governance that could give relief when other authorities fell short. By permitting the ruler to enact regulations of his own, jurists gave *dhimmīs* legal relief; in doing so, their arguments reveal the way in which the content of the law was developed in light of background assumptions about the enterprise of governance. Likewise, the authority that the enterprise of governance could lawfully exercise (i.e., *taʿzīr*) was defined and delimited by jurists, thus showcasing how law and legal argument constituted and ordered the polity. Reading these rules on sexual slander together, we can appreciate the denial of relief on Qur'ānic grounds and the grant of an alternate basis of relief as reflecting the fact that the intelligibility of both rules was tied to source-texts and institutions of authority, all of which were factored together as jurists developed doctrines to enable effective governance amidst diversity.

[21] Al-Kasānī, *Badāʾiʿ al-Ṣanāʾiʿ*, 9:270; al-Ghazālī, *al-Wasīṭ*, 4:156–7. See also al-Nawawī, *Rawḍa*, 10:174. For a discussion of *taʿzīr* as an alternative ground of authority, see Emon, "*Ḥuqūq Allāh*," 386–90.

[22] Ibn Nujaym, *al-Baḥr al-Rāʾiq*, 5:71; Ibn Mufliḥ, *al-Furūʿ*, 6:87. Interestingly, the Ḥanbalī Ibn Qudāma would allow a *dhimmī* woman who has a son born to a Muslim father to seek redress on Qur'ānic grounds. Ibn Qudāma, *al-Mughnī*, 8:216. See also, al-Muḥaqqiq al-Ḥillī, *Sharāʾiʿ al-Islām*, 2:409, who empowered the *dhimmī* to seek such alternative bases of redress even if the perpetrator was a Muslim.

4.3 TRADITIONS AND THEIR CONTEXT: IBN ʿUMAR AND ʿABD ALLĀH B. SALĀM

The legal arguments used to define *muḥṣan* and address *dhimmī* liability for adultery and redress for sexual slander invoked various themes in the pursuit of justice, such as accommodation, inclusion, and superiority. These themes informed jurists as they developed the above rules on *dhimmī* liability for adultery and redress for sexual slander. The themes guided how jurists chose to read source-texts and to extend their meanings. This section will illustrate how the various themes addressed throughout this study operate at the level of legal interpretation. In the process, the reader will come to appreciate how the conditions of intelligibility also make possible the hegemonic potential of Sharīʿa-based doctrines. To show this, the remainder of this chapter will focus on the two source-texts noted above concerning *dhimmī* liability for adultery and redress for sexual slander. Muslim jurists relied on these two sources as if their meaning were transparent. However, a critical analysis of both texts and their interpretations will show that their meanings are hardly straightforward. The jurists' readings of the two texts illustrate how the themes of universality and subordination were employed to inform legal argument, and even to define the legal subject to the subject him- or herself.

4.3.1 The constitutive force of empire: The Ibn ʿUmar tradition

The first tradition to consider is the one from Ibn ʿUmar, who said that unbelievers are not *muḥṣan*. Ibn ʿUmar, son of ʿUmar b. al-Khattāb, migrated with his father to Medina, abandoning the pagan faith and community they enjoyed in Mecca. He was a witness to the early battles between the Muslims of Medina and the Quraysh tribe of Mecca, and to the Prophet's conquest of Mecca in 630 CE. In his youth, he asked the Prophet if he could fight in the early battles between the Muslims and the Quraysh: the battles of Badr, Uḥud, and Khandaq. The Prophet refused the first two requests, but granted the third when Ibn ʿUmar was fifteen years old.[23] Ibn ʿUmar fought in subsequent raids led by the Prophet, and in expeditions to Syria, Iraq, Egypt, and Persia.[24] In fact, it is reported that he was a prominent figure (*bāriz*) in the fights against the Iraqis, in which he routinely killed them and took the spoils of war due to him.[25]

[23] Al-Dhahabī, *Siyar Aʿlām al-Nubalāʾ*, 4th ed. (Beirut: Muʾassasat al-Risāla, 1986), 3:204; Yūsuf al-Mizzī, *Tahdhīb al-Kamāl fī Asmāʾ al-Rijāl*, ed. Bashshār ʿAwād Maʿrūf, 3rd ed. (Beirut: Muʾassasat al-Risāla, 1994), 15:333; Ibn Khallikān, *Wafayāt al-Aʿyān*, eds Yūsuf ʿAlī Ṭawīl and Maryam Qāsim Ṭawīl (Beirut: Dār al-Kutub al-ʿIlmiyya, 1998), 3:20.

[24] Al-Dhahabī, *Siyar*, 3:208–9.

[25] Al-Dhahabī, *Siyar*, 3:208.

As the Islamic empire expanded, Ibn ʿUmar was content to remain in the Ḥijāz, close to the land in which the Prophet's mission originated. For instance, after the assassination of the third caliph ʿUthman b. ʿAffān (r. 23–34/644–656), the successor caliph ʿAlī b. Abī Ṭālib asked Ibn ʿUmar to take control over Syria, which was at the time ruled by ʿUthmān's relative, Muʿāwiya. ʿAlī believed that Ibn ʿUmar could effectively and efficiently assume control of the region at a time of political turmoil, and that people would obey and follow him; but Ibn ʿUmar declined.[26] When the forces of ʿAlī and Muʿāwiya later fought each other at the Battle of Ṣiffin (36/657), Ibn ʿUmar refused to take sides or participate in any way. In short, Ibn ʿUmar had little interest in politics, administration, or governance. Rather than playing a political role in the early history of Islam after the Prophet's death, Ibn ʿUmar devoted himself to the study of Islam and was respected as an Islamic legal authority who gave legal advice (*aftā*) to people quite regularly. Indeed, his reputation as a legal authority may very well have contributed to the authority his tradition carried for later jurists debating the significance of his words for legal purposes.

An important point to draw from this biography is that Ibn ʿUmar's principal experience in foreign lands was not as a governor or administrator, but rather as a soldier who richly profited from the spoils of war.[27] After the death of the Prophet, he chose to live in Mecca, whose inhabitants had already converted to Islam. Indeed, his biography suggests that his principal experience with non-Muslims was generally limited to the early conquests and raids he joined during the time of the Prophet, in which any non-Muslim was a potential enemy-combatant, as opposed to a resident within Muslim lands. His biography, thereby, prompts us to ask what he might have meant when he said that disbelievers are not *muḥṣan*. Did he intend his statement to have legal effect on criminal liability? Or was it part of a polemic against an image of the non-Muslim as combatant, rather than the non-Muslim as resident of a Muslim polity? Of course, what he meant and how his words were read and understood are two different matters. His experience of the non-Muslim was principally in a context of conquest and imperial expansion. He had no desire to govern and no experience doing so. He saw the non-Muslim not simply as the Other, but as the Other to be fought and conquered. Consequently, any reader who knows Ibn ʿUmar's biography cannot ignore the possibility, if not probability, that Ibn ʿUmar's statement

[26] Al-Dhahabī, *Siyar*, 3:224.

[27] He is said to have worn a silk shawl (*al-mitraf al-khazz*) valued at 500 *dirhams*, and in one instance paid back a lender not only the principal loan, but also an additional ten per cent. Al-Dhahabī, *Siyar*, 3:212, 215.

about the *muḥṣan* was informed by this background of military expansion and conquest, and not a pluralist imperial enterprise of governance.

Whatever Ibn ʿUmar may have meant, jurists considered his tradition a source-text for the legal definition of *muḥṣan*, without regard to the historical context that may have informed his statement. The possibility that Ibn ʿUmar's words were framed by his narrow context of military conquest posits a serious and significant conceptual distance between what Ibn ʿUmar may have meant, and how jurists contending with a pluralist imperial enterprise of governance gave his words a meaning that was informed by the challenges of governing amidst diversity. To acknowledge this distance is to recognize that the legal content of Ibn ʿUmar's words cannot so easily be divorced from the underlying enterprises of governance (whether in fact or as imagined ideal) that operated in the background for both Ibn ʿUmar and the later jurists who interpreted his words. In other words, to view Sharīʿa as Rule of Law is to recognize the inevitability that the law and the enterprise of governance are mutually constitutive. Muslim jurists, caught between the authority of Ibn ʿUmar's tradition and a pluralist imperial vision of governance more generally, held that to be *muḥṣan,* one had be free and not a slave, had to have consummated a marriage, *and had to be Muslim.*[28]

By limiting the *muḥṣan* to Muslims only, jurists ran up against a dilemma. To be stoned for adultery, one must be *muḥṣan.* But if only Muslims could be *muḥṣan,* then non-Muslims could never be stoned for adultery, even if they were married. But as suggested above, this outcome seemed incoherent to premodern Muslim jurists, given their concern about a public sphere that could be threatened by unchecked illicit sexual activity. Why should the adultery of a non-Muslim be considered any different from the adultery of a Muslim? Yet, to ask this question begs the question, why should the dignity interest of a non-Muslim be different than that of a Muslim? These questions loomed large for Muslim jurists, who relied on the various themes of contract, Islamic universalism, subordination, and the challenge of governance amidst diversity to harmonize competing and at times conflicting source-texts, albeit often at the expense of *dhimmī* entitlements, as already addressed above.

4.3.2 The empire of law: Adulterous Jews and ʿAbd Allāh b. Salām

The second tradition about the two adulterous Jews is fascinating because various implications about justice, authority, and the hegemonic

[28] Burton, "Muḥṣan."

potential of the law flow from its literary style. Indeed, the narrative shows that the *dhimmī* rules are an example of how the law generally, and Islamic law in particular, (re)instantiates its own authority by demarcating between peoples, or in other words between Us and the Other. This hegemonic dynamic is embedded in the very features and fabric of the law, or rather in the conditions of its intelligibility. To illustrate the hegemonic potential of legal argument and reasoning, the tradition of the adulterous Jews will be analyzed, with special attention to the relationships between the various participants in this legal narrative.

Of particular interest is ʿAbd Allāh b. Salām, a Jewish convert to Islam who demanded the Torah be re-read. ʿAbd Allāh b. Salām was a Medinese Jewish convert to Islam who was a revered Companion of the Prophet. Reports suggest that he converted to Islam shortly after the Prophet's migration to Medina. Upon converting, he told the Prophet: "O messenger of God, the Jews are a slanderous people (*qawm buht*). If they learn of my conversion, they shall slander me." To prove his point, ʿAbd Allāh asked the Prophet to invite members of his former Jewish community and ask their opinion of him and his conversion. When the Jews came to Muḥammad, he asked for their opinion of ʿAbd Allāh. They said he was a learned, religious man of their community. The Prophet then asked how they would feel about ʿAbd Allāh if they learned he converted to Islam. They expressed disdainful astonishment, after which ʿAbd Allāh came forward to certify that he had converted. After that, the Jews said he was ignorant, contradicting their earlier position. ʿAbd Allāh turned to the Prophet and said: "O messenger of God, didn't I tell you that they are a slanderous people?"[29]

What it meant for ʿAbd Allāh b. Salām to be a learned Jew is unclear, since the seventh-century Arabian Peninsula not only experienced the continued development of Rabbinic Judaism in the Gaonic period, but also witnessed the rise of Karaitism as a schismatic response. These are two different traditions within Judaism, and both demand of their experts different competencies. Consequently, when ʿAbd Allāh b. Salām was represented as a learned Jew, to what tradition of Jewish thought and law did that refer?

The Rabbinic account of Karaitism places its beginning in the second half of the eighth century under the leadership of Anan b. David. Recent scholarship, however, suggests that the Karaite movement existed during the period of the Muslim conquests in the seventh century. Furthermore, prior to the rise of Karaitism, other schismatic movements existed in the region that shared a similar attitude against Rabbinic Judaism.

[29] Al-Dhahabī, *Siyar*, 2:414–15.

Consequently, whether the Karaites existed in seventh-century CE Arabia or not, there were schismatic Jewish movements in the area that shared basic principles on religious authority, namely that the Bible was the sole source of divinely inspired law. Schismatic Jewish movements, such as the Karaites, rejected the authority of Rabbinic and Talmudic Judaism, which are based on the Oral Tradition and proffer interpretive approaches to the Bible that depart from literal readings of the source-text.[30]

The ambiguity in the identity of the Jews in the above narrative is important if the reader is to appreciate who *these* Jews were, *their* relationship to the Torah, and the way in which *they* would have constructed its meaning for *themselves*. In other words, due attention to the historical context of this group and the presumptions they held about law and legal expertise prompt the reader to reflect upon how these Jews represented their tradition to the Prophet, and how the Prophet applied it to them sitting as adjudicator. If these Jews were Rabbinic Jews who engaged in *midrash* and *halakhic* debates, the literal meaning of the Torah would be less significant than how later Rabbis developed compelling interpretations by which this particular community abided. If this were the case, then their act of hiding the verse may have had more to do with their concern about the Prophet adopting a literal reading of the source-text and not appreciating their interpretive traditions that surrounded the Torah at this time. If they were a schismatic group that upheld the centrality of the Biblical text, it might be reasonable to assume that they would adopt a literal, textualist approach to reading the Torah. But if that were the case, then why hide the verse? Perhaps their act of hiding the verse might have been an act of duplicity before the Prophet's court. But why would they have brought the two adulterous Jews to the Prophet in the first place if they did not trust the Prophet's judgment? The historical account is not sufficient to answer any of these questions. Nonetheless, the analysis above shows that the Jewish youth's act of hiding a verse of the Torah is not an easy matter to understand unless we could be better acquainted with the background beliefs and values of the Jews depicted in this tradition.

Even though we do not know whether these Jews were Rabbinic or schismatic, or whether they had alternative modes of resolution at their

[30] Leon Nemoy and W. Zajaczkowsk, "Early Karaism," *The Jewish Quarterly Review* 40, no. 3 (1950): 307–15; L. Nemoy and W. Zajczkowski, "Karaites," *Encyclopaedia of Islam, Second Edition*, IV: 603; Samuel C. Heilman, "Karaites," *Encyclopedia of the Modern Middle East and North Africa*, eds Philip Mattar et al. (New York: Macmillan Reference, 2004), 2:1269–70; Daniel Lasker, Eli Citonne and Haggai Ben-Shammai, "Karaites," *Encyclopaedia Judaica, Second Edition*, eds Michael Berenbaum and Fred Skolnik (Detroit: MacMillan Reference, 2007), 11:785–97; Daniel Frank and L. Nemoy, "Karaites," *Encyclopedia of Religion, Second Edition*, ed. Lindsay Jones (Detroit: Macmillan Reference, 2005): 8: 5082–8.

disposal, we can presume from the narrative that ʿAbd Allāh b. Salām would have known. This raises a fundamental question of why he was there to begin with, and about his role in the narrative of adjudication. If they were Rabbinic Jews, then his focus on the text of the Torah would have shown considerable bad faith and manipulation.[31] If they were schismatic, then perhaps his focus on the text might have been an attempt to cross-examine others whom he felt were (mis)representing a foreign legal tradition, out of respect for the integrity of the Prophet's adjudicatory role as both fact finder and legal adjudicator. Without any information about the Jews at issue, we cannot determine whether it was the Jews or ʿAbd Allāh b. Salām who was acting in good or bad faith when covering or uncovering the relevant verses of the Torah.

The act of hiding the verse has still more to say about the concept of Sharīʿa as Rule of Law. Hiding the verse was represented as a mark of Jews' disingenuity and dishonesty with respect to the scriptural text. Later jurists viewed it as an attempt to depart from the word of God. If anything, the narrative of condemnation operated as a vindication of the authority of the text, which reflects an important value in Islamic law and legal reasoning. In other words, if the Jews in the narrative were Rabbinic, it might make sense for them to hide the verse if they were concerned that the Prophet would not understand or appreciate their approach to Jewish law. The later reprobation of their act in Islamic sources arguably has less to do with these Jews' conception of the Torah, and more to do with vindicating the Islamic legal approach to the primacy of the scriptural text as an authoritative source of law.[32]

If the story has more to do with the dynamics of Islamic legal authority and interpretation, and less to do with the Jews and their representation of the Torah, then a critical reader should pay heed to the dynamics of the adjudication itself. Between ʿAbd Allāh and the Jews sat the Prophet as the arbitrator. The Prophet sat, observed, inquired, and decided. He was far from being the animating force behind the drama; indeed, his distance from the human and community drama permits the reader to see the Prophet as representing a dispassionate justice.

[31] On the intimate connection between the Torah and Talmud for Rabbic Judaism in the 7th century CE, see Rosenberg and Rosenberg, "Of God's Mercy," 1175. On the role of custom in the Gaonic period see Gideon Libson, *Jewish and Islamic Law: A Comparative Study of Custom During the Gaonic Period* (Cambridge: Harvard Law School, 2003).

[32] In this case, we may wonder why the Jews brought their case to the Prophet at all, if they were worried about how the Prophet would understand their law. There is little in the evidence to answer this question. What we have, though, is a narrative about recourse to an institution of justice, without any awareness of whether alternative modes of resolution existed for this Jewish community.

ʿAbd Allāh, however, had an interest in proving his loyalty to Islam by testifying against his former community. ʿAbd Allāh b. Salām was represented as both knowledgeable of the Jewish tradition, and as a righteous member of the Muslim polity. In the narrative, he was, in other words, one of "Us"; but because of his special knowledge of the Jews, he played the role of the native informant, helping the "Us" understand and regulate the "Other." Why the Jews sought the Prophet's adjudication is not clear from the tradition. But they clearly had an interest in presenting the Torah on their terms, and not on someone else's.

In the end, though, the Prophet had to decide. He consulted all parties involved and even showed judicial restraint and humility by requesting a Jewish law expert to inform him about the demands of Jewish law. As arbiter, the Prophet evoked a respect for the defendants, the Jewish tradition, and the neutrality of the judicial office in the interests of justice. And yet, he did not defer to the Jews' construction of their law. Their representation, effectively, became nullified. Instead he looked to ʿAbd Allāh, operating in the narrative as a native informant, to ensure that the Prophet's justice was done. The Prophet was neither protagonist nor antagonist in the human drama, but he was the legal authority who decided the outcome and the way in which the Other's law was represented and given effect.

Arguably, one implication of this tradition, if viewed through the lens of Sharīʿa as Rule of Law, is that legal systems do not contend with legal pluralism very well. Alternative normative bases of decision may be brought to a court or adjudicator, but no matter how different that alternative basis may be, the court will nonetheless understand it, and thereby (re)present it on its own terms. In this case, at the same time that the Prophet sought to respect the Other by learning his or her tradition, he could not entirely trust the Jews' representation of their tradition. Recall that after the Jews presented their community's treatment of adulterers, the Prophet asked them to bring the Torah to confirm their position and to ensure that they were being truthful (i.e., *in kuntum ṣādiqīn*). To trust the Jews in this case would be akin to granting legal authority to a different normative tradition, and to operationalize it within the prevailing mechanisms of law. The more any foreign law does not conform to the prevailing legal order, the more the adjudicator will reflect and represent that foreign tradition in a manner that most accords with the prevailing legal system,[33] in

[33] Elsewhere, I have shown that this occurred to Muslims and the construction of Islamic law under the colonial period of the 19th and 20th centuries. See Anver M. Emon, "The Limits of Constitutionalism in the Muslim World: History and Identity in Islamic Law," in *Constitutional Design for Divided Societies*, ed. Sujit Choudhry (Oxford: Oxford

this case, a literal textualism premised on respect for the apparent meaning of God's revelation.[34] Hence the conception of justice in this tradition disempowered the minority community from representing its own tradition. Instead, the administration of justice was left to the Prophet, who represented the Jew's legal tradition in terms that were most familiar to the dominant, prevailing system of justice—hence the empire of law—in this case, the justice that the Prophet represented, and which later jurists represented. Jewish law, in the case of the two adulterous Jews, was framed by a particular Islamic legal method of textual interpretation. Furthermore, it was read and represented as the applicable law for the Jewish community that sat before the Prophet, regardless of that community's understanding of its own law. The hegemonic potential of the law is evidenced by the fact that the power to define Jewish law was not fully left to the Jews themselves. Rather, the power to define and therefore achieve justice was invested in the Muslim adjudicator, aided by those who, as native informants, were trusted to represent the Other in terms that preserved the integrity of justice, as framed by the prevailing legal system.

4.4 CONCLUSION

The juxtaposition of Chapters 3 and 4 provides distinct analytic approaches to the *dhimmī* rules while building on the same, fundamental theme that lies at the heart of this study. In Chapter 3, with each examination of a legal rule, the reader was introduced to the ways in which general rules of application coexisted with rules of exception for the express purpose of illustrating the complex challenges of governing amidst the fact of diversity. Chapter 4 has offered a deeper historical and textual analysis of the *dhimmī* rules to show how Sharīʿa as Rule of Law reveals how legal argument and reasoning have their own hegemonic potential. Both chapters, together, show that Muslim jurists made choices in their reasoning processes that had to do with more than just

University Press, 2008), 258–86; idem, "Islamic Law and the Canadian Mosaic: Politics, Jurisprudence, and Multicultural Accommodation," *Canadian Bar Review* 87, no. 2 (2009, forthcoming); idem, "Conceiving Islamic Law in a Pluralist Society," 331–55.

[34] Premodern Islamic legal theory (*uṣūl al-fiqh*) upholds the priority of the apparent meaning (*ḥaqīqī, ẓāhir*) over the literary or metaphorical (*majāz*). Mohammad Hashim Kamali, *Principles of Islamic Jurisprudence*, 3rd ed. (Cambridge: Islamic Texts Society, 2003), 158–62. See also, Hossein Modarressi, "Some Recent Analysis of the Concept of majāz in Islamic Jurisprudence," *Journal of the American Oriental Society* 106, no. 4 (1986): 787–91; Wolfhart Heinrichs, "On the Genesis of the ḥaqîqa-majâz Dichotomy," *Studia Islamica* 59 (1984): 111–40.

source-texts or prior precedent. They developed legal doctrines and offered legal justifications for a system of law that both was constitutive of and constituted by an Islamic enterprise of governance that could not avoid governing amidst diversity.

This chapter has gone one step further and illuminated the hegemonic potential of the law and legal administration. On the one hand, the hegemonic potential is merely a feature of the imperium of the enterprise of governance and its legal order. Indeed, one cannot imagine a state or empire without an exertion of power, control, and coercive authority. On the other hand, when minority groups confront the imperium of the enterprise of governance with a claim or request for accommodation, the imperium of the enterprise of governance can become hegemonic in ways that undermine and under-represent the minorities who seek support, protection, or redress. This section suggests that the hegemonic potential of an enterprise of governance—and thereby the content of the law by which it justifies its hegemony—is particularly identifiable at the intersection of the law, the enterprise of governance, and the presence of minorities who make claims on and against both. That hegemony is perhaps unavoidable; but that should not mean we should be complacent.

By introducing Sharīʿa as Rule of Law, this study has offered a model of critique that is both historically and jurisprudentially attuned to the conditions that rendered the *dhimmī* rules intelligible. Adopting arguments based on an Islamic universalism, the priority of Islam over all other traditions, and contractarian approaches to accommodation, jurists ordered their diverse polity using the language of law. To do so, jurists contended with source texts, countervailing principles, and even policy considerations that often conflicted with one another. Their attempts to harmonize legal conflicts, and even their acceptance of inconsistency in the law, may seem disingenuous to those asking the anachronistic question about whether Islamic law is tolerant or intolerant. Viewed from the perspective of Rule of Law, however, their choices and their reconciliation between conflicting sources reflect the messiness that arises when governing amidst diversity.

This is not to suggest, though, that the conclusions they reached on the issues discussed above should not be subjected to critique. Indeed, there are no shortages of critique on this body of Islamic doctrines. Critique offers an antidote to complacency, but for critique to be effective, it must also be responsive to the terms by which the hegemony operates. An important theoretical point to draw from both Chapters 3 and 4 is that to view the *dhimmī* through the lens of Rule of Law provides a different, and arguably more meaningful, perspective on the *dhimmī* rules. More meaningful in that such an approach to the *dhimmī* rules renders them symptoms of the more general challenge of designing institutions and legal doctrines that respond to minority claimants who seek redress or accommodation from an enterprise of governance. While the historiography on the *dhimmī* rules tends to focus on the content of a given rule or set of rules, this study suggests that the content cannot be fully appreciated without also situating the *dhimmī* rules as, in part, constituted by what premodern jurists understood (or imagined) an Islamic enterprise of governance to be.

Beyond the theoretical contribution, the Rule of Law lens also makes possible a dialogic opportunity at a time when such dialogue is increasingly important. To approach the *dhimmī* rules through the framework of Sharīʿa as Rule of Law indirectly supports an overarching theme of this study, namely that the challenge of governing amidst diversity is not unique to Islamic law but rather is shared. To govern pluralistically presents an opportunity to critically reflect about who is "Us," who is "Them," and the extent to which "We" can and should accommodate the "Other" without sacrificing the character and content of the "polity." Certainly with each legal system or enterprise of governance, the conditions of a particular rule's intelligibility will differ; but that does not change the fact that pluralist commitments to governance will always be a messy business. Regardless of historical period, legal system, or enterprise of governance, the challenge of governing amidst diversity has been and continues to be a matter of considerable interest and debate across peoples and across different and even competing enterprises of governance.

Part II

Pluralism, Rule of Law, and the Modern State

5

Sharīʿa as Rule of Law

Part I focused on the treatment of non-Muslims under premodern Islamic legal doctrines. It analyzed various legal doctrines to accomplish two distinct, but interrelated theoretical interventions. First, the analysis showed that to frame the *dhimmī* rules in terms of tolerance/intolerance overdetermines their meaning and implication. Indeed, that particular frame more often has less to do with the historical jurisprudence of Islamic law, and more to do with contemporary debates (and often polemics) about Islam and Muslims today. Second, the analysis has offered an alternative conceptual frame for analyzing the *dhimmī* rules, namely Sharīʿa as Rule of Law. As noted at the outset of this study, Rule of Law here is used to reflect the claim space within which claims of justice are made. Equally important is that the claim space connoted by Rule of Law is bounded or disciplined in light of considerations that extend beyond the parties to a particular case, and include systemic concerns that make justice (and its enforcement) possible, intelligible, and legitimate. In other words, what allows claims to resonate as legal argument—to be intelligible as a species of legal argument—are the boundaries that delimit the claim space.

The aim of this chapter specifically, and Part II more generally, is to explore in greater detail the nature of those boundaries, and appreciate how their alteration over time shifts the intelligibility of a claim about the law. With respect to the intelligibility of Islamic legal arguments, Part II will reveal that the historical shift in the enterprise of governance, from the imperial to the international state system, has altered the conditions of intelligibility for the *dhimmī* rules today. But beyond focusing on the Islamic context, Part II will also feature an analysis of court decisions from the United States, United Kingdom, and France concerning the covered Muslim woman. The juxtaposition of the legal treatment of the Other in premodern Islamic law, the modern Muslim state, and the modern constitutional democratic state will show that regardless of which legal tradition or enterprise of governance is under consideration, arguments of universalism, accommodation, belonging, and othering continue to animate—and perhaps unavoidably so—legal and political debates about governing amidst the fact of diversity.

To undertake such an analysis, though, requires a more rigorous inquiry into the intelligibility of the law. This chapter will explore the conditions of intelligibility of a legal claim, and the ways in which those conditions constitute the boundaries of the claim space of Sharīʿa. As discussed in Chapter I, the *dhimmī* rules arose out of a historical context in which a universalist Islamic ethos was made manifest through imperial ideals of governance. But the rules themselves were fashioned using the language of law. Imperialism created the fact of diversity and constituted, in part, the content of the law. The law, however, was not reducible to a single feature or political dynamic. The multifaceted features of Islamic law as interpretive process, institutions of justice, doctrines, and so on, are among the conditions that demarcated the claim space of law for premodern jurists, and thereby contributed to the intelligibility of legal claims made therefrom. This chapter, in an inductive fashion, draws upon various features of Islamic legal history in an attempt to sketch the boundary of the premodern claim space of Sharīʿa. The sketch that follows in this chapter inserts a historical dimension to the analytic heft of "Sharīʿa as Rule of Law," in order to employ it herein across time and legal systems, moving from the premodern period to the more recent past. The features demarcating the claim space of Sharīʿa that are addressed below (e.g., educational curriculum, the judicial function, theories of legal interpretation and authority, and discretionary powers) are by no means exhaustive; nonetheless, in the aggregate, they provide richness and depth to our understanding of the claim space of Sharīʿa.

The analytic heft of "Sharīʿa as Rule of Law"

To imagine Sharīʿa as a claim space is to account for various features of Islamic legal history and jurisprudence—from educational institutions to adjudicatory ones—that in the aggregate contributed to the background asssumptions that led premodern jurists to reflect on the nature, place, and aim of law in society as they did.[1] Those

[1] This study does not make a historical claim that Sharīʿa as Rule of Law operated in a particular time or space. Rather, it explores the conditions of legal intelligibility in light of the reality (aspirational or otherwise) that jurists had when developing their doctrines. For others who adopt a similar approach to understanding the intelligibility of Islamic law and legal history, see Hallaq, *Sharīʿa: Theory, Practice, Transformations*.

background assumptions helped define and demarcate the claim space within which arguments about the demands of justice were made and rendered intelligible as a species of legitimate legal argument. Chapter 1 addressed various political assumptions that premodern jurists may have held (e.g., universalism and imperialism). This chapter extends that analysis and links it to different but related background assumptions that contributed to how premodern Muslim jurists understood Sharīʿa as a distinctively legal discipline. By exploring the assumptions that contributed to the legality of Sharīʿa, this chapter will build upon how and the extent to which the legality of Sharīʿa was constitutive of and constituted by the enterprise of governance. In other words, this chapter will give further content to the idea of Sharīʿa as a bounded and delimited claim space.

Undoubtedly, this approach to Sharīʿa is vulnerable to critique. Modern reformists are keen to suggest that "Sharīʿa" as a term of art reflects the law in the mind of God, and thereby has no connection to the way in which law and governance actually existed in the past or arises today in the world of lived experience. For them, Sharīʿa is not fully knowable to humans, but it nonetheless constitutes the end of all juridical interpretive agency.[2] This idealized notion of Sharīʿa must be distinguished, they argue, from both the doctrinal rules that jurists developed over centuries (i.e., *fiqh*), and what is often represented as "Sharīʿa" in various Muslim states where Islamic law has been implemented in the form of legislation or through informal social mechanisms.

These distinctions serve two discrete, but related, purposes. First, the distinction between an idealized Sharīʿa and the doctrinal product of human interpretive activity (*fiqh*) limits the authority and legitimacy that *fiqh* rules can carry across time and space.[3] Second, the effort to distinguish the Sharīʿa as ideal from what is legislated and enforced today as Sharīʿa in Muslim states allows opposition parties to challenge the legitimacy a state claims for itself by reference to its enforcement of Islamic law, while avoiding criticism that their opposition runs contrary to Islam or Sharīʿa. In other words, by idealizing the Sharīʿa, reformists and opposition parties attack the ongoing authority of substantive *fiqh* doctrines inherited from the historical tradition, challenge the authority of those who invoke these doctrines to legitimate their enterprise of

[2] Abou El Fadl, *Speaking in God's Name* 32; Emon, "*To Most Likely Know the Law*," 415–40.

[3] For a discussion on the relevance of the distinction between Sharīʿa and *fiqh*, and its relationship to philosophical themes such as authority and objectivity, see Emon, "*To Most Likely Know the Law*."

governance, and ensure their capacity to interpret and engage the religio-legal tradition.

Certainly, the modern state of affairs of Sharīʿa is distinct from what existed in the premodern period, where the doctrines of the historical tradition are viewed as having developed outside the enterprise of governance, and where the moral authority of the Sharīʿa was principally held, in ideal terms, by jurists working outside the enterprise of governance.[4] In contrast, in the modern world, law-making and legitimized coercion are often considered to be rightfully and legitimately in the hands of a centralized sovereign state government that issues decrees or legislation defining the law for a region that is delineated by geo-political territorial boundaries. Indeed, the centralizing feature of the modern state is perhaps its most notable characteristic for some political theorists.[5] The state operates within an international system in which all states are considered equal sovereigns and entitled to their territorial integrity.[6] These states engage each other as actors on a global stage, whether through trade negotiations, diplomatic relations, or international organizations such as the United Nations.

The rise of the modern state has led some commentators to fear that Sharīʿa is dead, and instead has become a tool of political elites.[7] The death of Sharīʿa, they argue, can be traced to a variety of factors: the nineteenth-century reformist efforts in the Muslim world; the advent of the modern, bureaucratic state; or the degeneration of Muslim civil society institutions that had, in the premodern period, contributed to vibrant intellectual discourse and debate.[8] Those states, whose territory was once under the rule of Islamic empires, often incorporate Islamic

[4] Emon, "Islamic Law and the Canadian Mosaic," 391–425; idem, Conceiving Islamic Law in a Pluralist Society," 331–55.

[5] See for instance, James C. Scott, *Seeing Like a State* (New Haven: Yale University Press, 1998).

[6] See for instance, United Nations, *Charter of the United Nations* (San Francisco, October 24, 1945), Art. 2, Sec. 1, which provides: "The Organization is based on the principle of the sovereign equality of all its Members."

[7] Abou El Fadl, "My Friend," 159–62. See also Wael Hallaq, "Can the Sharīʿa Be Restored?" in *Islamic Law and the Challenges of Modernity*, eds Yvonne Haddad and Barbara Stowasser (New York: Altamira Press, 2004), 21–54, 22. Notably, the idea that Sharīʿa is dead, however, presumes a particular view or ideal type of Sharīʿa, usually by reference to its premodern form. If by the death of Sharīʿa is meant that it has lost its moral authority, that is a different matter, and is addressed more fully in Chapter 6 in terms of the modern Muslim state's post-coloniality and the challenge of legal pluralism.

[8] Lama Abu-Odeh, "Commentary on John Makdisi's 'Survey of AALS Law Schools Teaching Islamic Law'," *Journal of Legal Education* 55, no. 4 (2005): 589–91; idem, "The Politics of (Mis)recognition: Islamic Law Pedagogy in American Academia," *American Journal of Comparative Law* 52 (2004): 789–824, emphasizes the role of European transplants in displacing the jurisdiction of a historically defined Islamic law in the Muslim world.

law in their legal systems, but only in piecemeal fashion. Such states generally adopt only premodern Islamic family law in modern personal status codes, while borrowing or modifying legislative schemes from European and North American states on matters of obligations, procedure, commercial law, finance, and so on.[9] Modern lawyers in Muslim states that apply Islamic law do not often study Islamic law in the fashion once taught in premodern *madrasas* (Islamic law colleges) centuries ago, but instead take a few courses on the topic, while focusing mainly on a "secularized" legal curriculum.[10] In fact, Lama Abu-Odeh has vociferously argued that to understand Islamic law in the modern day, one need not concern oneself with the premodern period at all. Islamic law today is immersed within a complex, bureaucratic state system, in which Islamic law is a partial source, if even that, for legal systems that are primarily based on European models of civil law and governance.[11]

If this captures the modern Sharīʿa today, why should anyone take an interest in considering Sharīʿa as Rule of Law? We cannot ignore that many Muslim majority states espouse in their constitutions that Islam is the religion of the state and that the laws of Islam are "a" or "the" source of law for the state.[12] They incorporate aspects of Islamic law in their legislation. And Islamic law features in contemporary political debates about the nature and future of many regions and countries in the world. Perhaps such states are engaged in a delusion, which indeed some have suggested.[13] Perhaps such states are making an effort to incrementally Islamize over a period of time.[14] Or perhaps such states are using Sharīʿa in a more general contest over political legitimacy.[15] This study is mindful of the competing views on Sharīʿa today, while remaining agnostic on what Muslim states (and their elites) are intending to do by invoking Islamic law. What seems clear for the purposes of this study, though, is that Sharīʿa

[9] Abu-Odeh, "The Politics of (Mis)representation," 789, 791.

[10] Abu-Odeh tells of her own legal education in Jordan, where she took only three courses on Islamic law (marriage, divorce, and inheritance) over a four-year legal curriculum: Abu-Odeh, "The Politics of (Mis)recognition," 791.

[11] Abu-Odeh, "The Politics of (Mis)recognition."

[12] For an analysis of such provisions in state constitutions in the Muslim world, see Clark Lombardi, *State Law as Islamic Law in Modern Egypt* (Leiden: Brill, 2006). See also, Emon, "The Limits of Constitutionalism in the Muslim World," 258–86 (Oxford: Oxford University Press, 2008).

[13] Hallaq, "Can the Sharīʿa be Restored?"

[14] See for example, Muhammad Taqi Usmani, "The Islamization of Laws in Pakistan: The Case of *Hudud* Ordinances," *Muslim World* 96, no. 2 (April 2006): 287–304, who writes about the onerous but important task of Islamizing.

[15] For the political implications of Sharīʿa, see Anver M. Emon, "Techniques and Limits of Legal Reasoning in Sharīʿa Today," *Berkeley Journal of Middle Eastern & Islamic Law* 2, no. 1 (2009): 101–24.

remains a contested concept, is invoked for purposes of legitimacy and authority, and is used for or against the enterprise of governance to make claims about what justice requires. In other words, Sharīʿa remains even today an important feature of claims about the demands of justice. That "Sharīʿa," as a term of art, has this characteristic is not in itself surprising. Rather, the challenge for today is to understand how the modern state has affected and influenced the boundaries that constitute the claim space from which arguments about justice and Sharīʿa arise. By attending to the difference between the premodern claim space of Sharīʿa and the modern claim space of the sovereign state, we can better appreciate how such changes have affected the intelligibility of the ongoing resort to premodern legal answers to modern questions of law and governance. By viewing Sharīʿa as Rule of Law, this study argues that regardless of whether or how Sharīʿa manifests itself in a given historical period or in a particular enterprise of governance, it nonetheless represents an ideal that operates in a multitude of ways (e.g., doctrinal, institutional, and so on), and is an important feature of any debate about the enterprise of governance in an Islamic milieu.

It is on this understanding that this study presents Sharīʿa as Rule of Law, situating debates about law in a mutually constitutive relationship with the enterprise of governance. To situate Sharīʿa in this fashion is to acknowledge that the law is not a separate, distinct, and purely independent discipline, autonomous from the context (political or otherwise) in which jurists (premodern or modern) have found themselves. Rather, as scholars of Islamic law have already held, Islamic law is neither insulated from the world, nor autonomous. However disciplined premodern Islamic legal training was, jurists participated in what some might call a "legal culture," a system, or a discipline of inquiry.[16] The premodern jurists who participated in that discipline utilized the law in a manner that sometimes "expresse[d], promote[d], challenge[d], transmit[ted] and support[ed] certain socio-political demands," and at other times "frustrate[d], dilute[d], and ma[de] it possible to thwart" such demands.[17] This chapter will explore different

[16] For studies that invoke this idea of a juristic culture, see Sherman Jackson, *Islamic Law and the State: The Constitutional Jurisprudence of Shihab al-Din al-Qarafi* (Leiden: Brill, 1996); Khaled Abou El Fadl, *Rebellion and Violence in Islamic Law* (Cambridge: Cambridge University Press, 2001).

[17] Abou El Fadl, *Rebellion & Violence*, 322. Indeed, even as the premodern scholars sought to insulate themselves from the over-reach of the ruling regime, they also aimed to protect it. Tayeb El-Hibri shows how premodern scholars provided a narrative of the caliph Hārūn al-Rashīd that was, in part, designed to protect him and his office from undue critique and challenge. Tayeb El-Hibri, *Reinterpreting Islamic Historiography: Hārūn al-Rashīd and the Narratives of the ʿAbbāsid Caliphate* (Cambridge: Cambridge University Press, 1999), 29–30.

aspects of the boundary that demarcated the claim space of Sharīʿa that premodern Muslim jurists imagined. Reflecting on those aspects will provide a historical comparator for the later discussion in this chapter and Chapter 6 on the intelligibility of the *dhimmī* rules specifically, and Islamic law more generally, in the modern Muslim majority state.

Contemporary scholars suggest that premodern Islamic law is best characterized as decentralized and pluralistic, in the domain of jurists and not state agents.[18] But that does not mean that those who claimed to represent Sharīʿa did not imagine themselves as somehow contributing to the governance of society, whether in terms of either an idealized Islamic polity or holding actual office. Indeed, the political legitimacy of a premodern Muslim regime was often considered, in part, dependent upon the application of Sharīʿa within the polity.[19] Likewise, the development of Sharīʿa-based doctrines cannot be divorced from the social and institutional context in which jurists found themselves. That social context may have included transmitted doctrines, the institutionalization of the scholarly profession, and even the institutions of justice within which jurists participated (either directly or indirectly).

An example will help illustrate the nexus between legal debate and the enterprise of governance in the work of premodern Muslim jurists. The first example concerns whether the crime of *qadhf* or false accusation of illicit sex (sexual slander) presented a public wrong or a private one (*ḥaqq Allāh* or *ḥaqq al-ʿibād*). While most jurists agreed that it was an offense against both the public and the individual, they debated whether it was primarily a public wrong or primarily a private wrong. Their answer to that question made possible a series of procedural rules. For instance, the more they considered the offense a public wrong, the more likely would they expand the standing of those who could petition for redress, or deny the victim the ability to waive any redress whatsoever. The more they considered *qadhf* a private wrong, the more they empowered the individual victim to bring suit or waive any redress, and so on.[20]

[18] Abdullahi Ahmed An-Na'im, *Islam and the Secular State: Negotiating the Future of Sharīʿa* (Cambridge: Harvard University Press, 2008), 9–20; 164; S.D. Goitein, "A Turning Point in the History of the Muslim State," in *Studies in Islamic History and Institutions* (Leiden: Brill, 1968), 149–67, 164; Abou El Fadl, *Speaking in God's Name*, 15–17. For further discussion on this point, see below.

[19] Crone, *God's Rule, Government and Islam*; Ann K.S. Lambton, *State and Government in Medieval Islam: An Introduction to the Study of Islamic Political Theory: The Jurists* (Oxford: Oxford University Press, 1981).

[20] Emon, "*Ḥuqūq Allāh*," 337–58.

However jurists decided the initial question or other questions contingent upon the first one, they nonetheless provided answers that betrayed their assumptions about institutional systems of adjudication that involved filing petitions and taking witness statements. In other words, what might facially seem like a substantive legal issue of Islamic criminal law was deeply embedded in an institutional setting in which procedural questions (and thereby institutional assumptions) could not be so easily divorced from the legal analysis. The example above illustrates that as jurists were considering doctrinal rules about criminal law, they were mindful that such doctrinal rules operated within an institutional setting that, in part, constituted the boundaries of the claim space of Sharīʿa, which in their own way contributed content to legal doctrines. To appreciate the nature of the claim space of Sharīʿa, this chapter maps out various doctrinal and institutional features that shaped and disciplined the content of legal argument examines the role of the enterprise of governance as constitutive of that content, and addresses how changes in the enterprise of governance have modified the claim space of Sharīʿā.

5.1 REASON, AUTHORITY, AND SHARĪʿA AS RULE OF LAW

To analyze the *dhimmī* rules by viewing Sharīʿa as Rule of Law brings both reason and authority to bear upon our analysis: authority in the sense of the constitutive features that demarcate the boundaries of the claim space of Sharīʿa; reason in the sense of how intelligibility can shift as the boundaries of the claim space shift and alter. To suggest that a religious legal system is rational and reasoned, though, might strike some as paradoxical. As Jeremy Waldron entertainingly writes, "[s]ecular theorists often assume that they know what a religious argument is like: they present it as a crude prescription from God, backed up with threat of hellfire, derived from general or particular revelation . . ."[21] The authority of religious argument is supposed to arise from source-texts and divine authority. Religious argument is presumed to require a type of obedience that for some, such as Max Weber, is based on "complete personal devotion" as opposed to "ethical, aesthetic, or other such point of view."[22] To inquire into the

[21] Jeremy Waldron, *God, Locke, and Equality: Christian Foundations in Locke's Political Thought* (Cambridge: Cambridge University Press, 2002), 20.

[22] Max Weber, *Economy and Society: An Outline of Interpretive Sociology*, eds Guenther Roth and Claus Wittich, 2 vols (Berkeley: University of California Press, 1978), 1: 242.

authority of reason in a religious legal system would seem, under this view, inapposite at best. Religion and authority seem more likely bedfellows. Those who see this connection are not without due support and justification. Religious law often justifies its claims upon people by reference to an authority, whether that authority is a deity, a prophet, or a sacred text.

However, coupling religion and authority to the exclusion of reason ignores how religious traditions also anticipate recourse to reasoned deliberation as normalized. Premodern Islamic legal philosophy is replete with debates about both the authority and scope of reason. Jurists of varying theological and legal dispositions adopted natural law theories that could account for issues not addressed by authoritative source-texts. To develop new rules of law in light of what God would want, they theorized about the ontological authority of reason. Although starting from different theological positions, jurists nonetheless argued that God created the world for the purpose of benefitting humanity. The natural world can be observed, therefore, to appreciate how the world should be ordered. In other words, jurists of competing theological positions fused fact and value in nature to grant reason ontological authority in the law.[23]

Beyond the ontological authority of reason, jurists acknowledged the epistemic inevitability and need to interpret sources when the language of a source-text is not clear. For instance, the jurist al-Juwaynī (d. 478/1085) was well aware that the scope of interpretive investigation (*ijtihād*) had to be wide enough to account for novel circumstances not addressed by source-texts. He articulated this position in his discussion on *istidlāl,* in which he addressed the epistemic challenges that arise in cases where no source-text governs a matter. He argued:

> Anyone who probes the circumstances of the Companions of the Prophet (*ṣaḥāba*)—may God be pleased with them, and they are the models and exemplars of analysis—would not see any of them in consultative councils lay out a source-text and a derivative meaning to base [an analysis] of a situation. Rather they delved into various opinions without turning to source-texts, whether they existed or not. When the breadth of *ijtihād* is established, as well as the impossibility of limiting what arises therefrom to source-texts, and likewise [given] that the Companions did not always seek out source-texts, the sum total of all of that gives credence to the argument [supporting] *istidlāl.*[24]

[23] Emon, *Islamic Natural Law Theories*; idem, "Natural Law and Natural Rights in Islamic Law," 351–95.

[24] Al-Juwaynī, *al-Burhān fī Uṣūl al-Fiqh* (Beirut: Dār al-Kutub al-ʿIlmiyya, 1997), 2:162–3.

For al-Juwaynī, *istidlāl* provided a site where jurists could employ extra-textual epistemic methods to arrive at conclusions of law. One such method proffered by Ibn Rushd (Averroes) (d. 595/1198) was the syllogism. In his celebrated essay on the relationship between philosophy and Sharīʿa, *Faṣl al-Maqāl* (*The Decisive Treatise*) he argued that source-texts such as the Qur'ān recognize the importance of reflection and reason in the pursuit and fulfillment of God's will and human salvation. In his essay, he recognized the importance of the syllogism:

> Since it has been determined that the Law makes it obligatory to reflect upon existing things by means of the intellect and to consider them; and consideration is nothing more than inferring and drawing out the unknown from the known; and this is syllogistic reasoning or by means of syllogistic reasoning (*al-qiyās aw bi al-qiyās*), therefore, it is obligatory that we go about reflecting upon the existing things by means of [rational] syllogistic reasoning (*al-qiyās al-ʿaqlī*).[25]

Roger Arnaldez writes of Ibn Rushd's affirmation of the syllogism: "If the Law asks to be studied through *qiyās sharʿī*, one is even more strongly justified in studying it through rational syllogism."[26] Whether we look to the natural law tradition in Islam, to the theories of interpretation (*ijtihād*), or the role of formal logic in legal reasoning, the fact remains that jurists accepted the necessity of reasoning in the law.[27]

Of course, none of this reliance on reasoning excluded argument from authority. Indeed, to suggest otherwise would be to ignore important disciplinary features of Islamic law. When jurists articulated the contours of Islamic law, they relied upon the existence of a deity who legislated, a prophet who legislated, and a revealed text in which legislation exists. As the Qur'ān states: "O you who believe, obey God, obey the Prophet and those of you in authority. If you dispute over an issue, turn the matter over to God and the Prophet if you believe in God and the Hereafter."[28] Jurists justified the obligation to abide by such decrees by reference to the fact that the decrees are in authoritative source-texts—in other words, obedience is justified by reference to the argument of authority. Furthermore, for some jurists, the use of

[25] Ibn Rushd (Averroes), "The Book of the Decisive Treatise Determining the Connection Between the Law and Wisdom," in *Decisive Treatise & Epistle Dedicatory*, trans. Charles Butterworth (Provo, Utah: Brigham Young University Press, 2001), 2 (with facing Arabic and English translation).

[26] Roger Arnaldez, *Averroes: A Rationalist in Islam*, trans. David Streight (Notre Dame: Notre Dame University Press, 2000), 81.

[27] Emon, "*Huquq Allah*"; idem, "Techniques and Limits"; idem, "*To Most Likely Know the Law.*"

[28] Qur'ān 4:59.

reason was only authoritative because the Qur'ān said it is: Ibn Rushd, as noted above, derived the authority of reason from the authority of the Qur'ān.

The significance of approaching Sharīʿa as Rule of Law is that the elements of reason and authority are equally part of the analysis. One is not excluded in favor of the other; rather, both are recognized as mutually contributing to the intelligibility of arguments made from within the claim space of Sharīʿa, in which reasoned deliberation operated within bounds defined by authoritative features that both disciplined the scope of reasoned argument and granted it legitimacy.

5.2 SHARĪʿA AS RULE OF LAW: LEGITIMATING AND ENABLING THE ENTERPRISE OF GOVERNANCE (A)

If Sharīʿa as Rule of Law connotes a claim space about the demands of justice in terms of both reason and authority, a fundamental question to address is what justice connotes. For Muslim jurists, justice was not a purely rational ideal; it was embedded between and among peoples living in community. Sharīʿa as Rule of Law, by emphasizing the mutually constitutive relationship between the law and the enterprise of governance, creates a discursive site about the demands of justice in political society. In this fashion, Sharīʿa as Rule of Law is a reminder that jurists were not merely philosophizing about the law in some rarified academic context. They developed their legal discourses mindful of the constitutive relationship between law and the enterprise of governance.

There were two ways by which Sharīʿa-based discourses were constitutive of an Islamic enterprise of governance. First, when jurists described the conditions of legitimate Islamic rule, they linked the legitimacy of any enterprise of governance to the ruler's application and enforcement of Sharīʿa-based norms throughout the polity. Second, the license and scope of discretion the ruler had to govern (i.e., the zone of legislative authority) was made possible and legitimate because of how jurists created legal doctrines to demarcate the space within which the ruler could exercise his discretion for purposes of managing the affairs of the enterprise of governance. Legal doctrines such as *taʿzīr* and *siyāsa sharʿiyya* were legal terms of art that juridified (and thereby legitimated) the authority and scope of the ruler's discretionary power to govern. Consequently, Sharīʿa as Rule of Law captures how jurists utilized legal arguments and reasoning to provide the grounds of legitimacy to the enterprise of governance, and to authorize rulers to maneuver the institutions of governance as certain but delimited circumstances required. In other words, the ruler's authority (and thereby the enterprise of governance) was legitimated and juridically framed in Sharīʿa terms.

For Muslim jurists, no enterprise of governance could be politically legitimate without a set of core values that guided, governed, and delineated the scope of governance. For instance, the tenth-century jurist al-Māwardī (d. 450/1058) wrote that experience dictated that no kingdom could exist without having at its foundation a faith or ideological tradition (*diyāna min al-diyānāt*). Such core values contributed to a sense of community and thereby to a sense of responsibility to preserve that community. As an example, al-Māwardī held that every faith tradition espouses the virtue of knowing God, thus inculcating a sense of duty in the individual to adhere to God's will. By extension, this duty could be directed toward the ruling authority. The efficacy of a given enterprise of governance and its legal system depended upon one's acceptance of responsibility not only toward others but toward the polity at large. Indeed, al-Māwardī remarked that a tradition of value is the foundation upon which all conditions and rules of governance are built: if any kingdom were to stray from its foundational value system, internal schisms and contestations would arise, and thereby adversely affect the legitimacy and continuity of the sovereign.[29] He reminded his reader that rules and regulations in a legal system arose out of a set of foundational commitments that legitimated both an enterprise of governance and obedience to its law in the first place.

Notably, the relevant legitimating tradition that ought to ground an enterprise of governance need not be Islam, according to al-Māwardī. From the perspective of efficiency and order in the polity, Islam need not be the basis for the polity's core values. Espousing the virtues of the Islamic tradition was not central to the more pragmatic concerns among Muslim jurists for good and right governance, although al-Māwardī did not hesitate to assert that the Islamic tradition offered the best path to obedience to God and thereby to good governance.[30] The later jurist, Abū Ḥāmid al-Ghazālī (d. 505/1111), held that whether a polity was governed Islamically or not, its longevity depended on the quality of justice that it upheld. Referring to a prophetic tradition, al-Ghazālī wrote: "Dominion [will] continue even if there is disbelief (*kufr*) but will not continue where

[29] Abū al-Ḥasan Al-Māwardī, *Naṣīḥat al-Mulūk*, ed. Fu'ad ʿAbd al-Munʿim Aḥmad (Alexandria: Mu'assasat Shabāb al-Jāmiʿa, 1988), 85.

[30] Al-Māwardī, *Naṣīḥat*, 88–9.

there is oppression (*ẓulm*)."[31] Al-Ghazālī's advice to rulers was meant to ensure that they were just; the importance of applying Sharīʿa was either assumed by al-Ghazālī or was deemed separate from the question of good governance.[32]

Both al-Māwardī and al-Ghazālī recognized that effective and legitimate governance required a set of values that all could claim were shared and characteristic of the given polity. Those core values were embedded in the various systems that made governance possible. Among those systems was law. Indeed, by articulating the importance of a shared set of values to enable governance, al-Ghazālī and al-Māwardī made possible, indeed even probable, a role for legal language, doctrines, and argument to construe and legitimate the enterprise of governance. Effective and lasting governance required a shared tradition of justice. That tradition may or may not be Islamic. The tradition will differ from one enterprise of governance to another. But the existence of such tradition was, for them, essential for the legitimacy and coherence of an enterprise of governance.

Law offered a language of justice that could capture and instantiate the core values of a particular tradition. In the context of governance, the law thereby has the potential of constituting the enterprise of governance. But that does not mean the relationship is only one way. Rather, as has been suggested throughout this study, the relationship between law and the enterprise of governance is mutual. The imperatives of the enterprise of governance may require the law to create space for the ruler, on the authority of his office, to direct the institutions of governance as he sees fit. Doing so would give legal cover to a ruler exercising discretion to rule as he sees fit. Such legal cover implies that the ruler is not acting pursuant to some sovereign exception, but rather is fully compliant with the law. Indeed, to view Sharīʿa as Rule of Law allows us to recognize how and to what end Muslim jurists created latitude for those who managed the enterprise of governance to maneuver with considerable, though limited, discretion. Appreciating the scope and limitations of that discretionary power illustrates the mutuality between law and the

[31] Abū Ḥāmid Al-Ghazālī, *al-Tibr al-Masbūk fī Naṣīḥat al-Mulūk*, ed. Muḥammad Damaj (Beirut: Mu'assasat 'Izz al-Dīn, 1996), 148.

[32] Qur'ān 11:117 states that despite God's destruction of peoples in the past, those who are righteous will remain untouched: "for never would your Lord destroy a town for being oppressive, while its people act righteously." In his commentary on this verse, al-Qurṭubī remarks that despite a people's disbelief in God (*shirk*, *kufr*), the people will not suffer God's wrath. Instead, he says, "Sin brings one closer to the punishment of extermination in the world than disbelief [in God]." But he is also careful to remind us that the punishment for disbelief is greater in the afterlife anyway. In other words, both injustice and disbelief in God will lead to punishment. But the latter alone is not a reason for ridding them from the world. Al-Qurṭubī, *al-Jāmiʿ li'l-Aḥkām al-Qur'ān*, 9:75–6.

enterprise of governance, and most notably, its limits. As will be shown below, premodern Muslim jurists enabled and empowered the agents of the enterprise of governance to act legitimately without reference to legal regulations or strictures, but only as long as such extra-legal activity fell within a zone of activity that was itself legally delineated.

For instance, as much as Muslim jurists may have attempted to articulate legal doctrines on as many issues as possible, they recognized that inevitably, the political leader would need to make new rules to govern unanticipated situations. Although such discretionary rules would not be based on the epistemic methods sanctioned in the curriculum of legal study (to be addressed below), such rules nonetheless were recognized as authoritative. Although Muslim jurists were unable to determine the rules for such unanticipated situations, they developed legal doctrines to delineate the arena of such discretionary legislative activity. Specifically, they developed the legal doctrines of *taʿzīr* and *siyāsa sharʿiyya.*

Siyāsa sharʿiyya can be understood as "Governance in accordance with the *sharīʿa*," and calls for "harmonisation between the law and procedures of Islamic jurisprudence (*fiḳh*) and the practical demands of governance (*siyāsa*)."[33] Ibn Taymiyya (d. 728/1328) has often been associated with this jurisprudential topic; his interest was to theorize how rulers could and should abide by Sharīʿa-based norms. In other words, his aim was to make rulers subservient to the law. Yet he also recognized that there were zones of activity where Sharīʿa-based doctrines were silent. In such areas, he argued, the ruler had discretionary authority to punish offenders, as long as he did so within the legally defined bounds of that discretionary authority, or in other words, acted within the bounds that jurists defined under the power of *taʿzīr*.[34]

In premodern Islamic jurisprudence, *taʿzīr* was a term of art meaning "discretionary punishment"; it connoted a discretionary authority vested with the ruler or his agents (such as judges) to punish offenders when punishments for the latters' acts were not otherwise provided for by source-texts.[35] *Taʿzīr* was a type of discretionary punishment that jurists granted to the ruling authorities; not even Ibn Taymiyya could deny such authority given the finitude of source-texts and the infinite possibilities of human activity that could nonetheless be subjected to governance and regulation. This is not to suggest that the discretionary

[33] C.E. Bosworth, I.R Netton, and F.E Vogel, "Siyāsa," *Encyclopaedia of Islam, Second Edition*. Eds P. Bearman et al.

[34] Ibn Taymiyya, *al-Siyāsa al-Sharʿiyya fī Iṣlāḥ al-Rāʿī wa al-Raʿiyya* (Beirut: Dār al-Kutub al-ʿIlmiyya, 1988), 101.

[35] M.Y. Izzi Dien, "Taʿzīr (a.)," *Encyclopaedia of Islam, Second Edition*. Eds P. Bearman et al.

authority was absolute. While granting the ruling authority limited discretionary authority, jurists still sought to limit how and to what extent that authority could be utilized.[36]

The jurists al-Kāsānī and al-Ghazālī, for example, held that *taʿzīr* punishments are applied to matters that are not addressed by specific source-texts (*laysa lahā ḥadd muqaddar fī al-sharʿ*), but which nonetheless invoke social or individual interests (*ḥaqq Allāh* or *ḥaqq al-ʿabd*) that the law and enterprise of governance must provide for and protect.[37] In other words, *taʿzīr* provided the enterprise of governance the power to create new legal doctrines that granted entitlements to people and which were enforced through its institutions.[38]

To illustrate how such discretionary authority could work, the Mālikī al-Ḥaṭṭāb (d. 954/1547) considered the situation in which a thief stole less than the minimum amount required to invoke the amputation punishment for theft specified in the Qur'ān. He argued that the ruling authority could nevertheless establish a punishment for the lesser theft on the grounds that such a punishment supported and vindicated private interests in property.[39] The enterprise of governance, in other words, could use *taʿzīr* to create new legal measures in instances where no source-text captured the specific case, and where the case itself posed significant challenges to individual and social interests that might undermine the efficacy, efficiency, and legitimacy of the enterprise of governance. Conceptions of the individual and social good may change over time and across space, as the Mālikī al-Khurashī held (*yakhtalifu bi-ikhtilāf al-nās wa-aqwālihim wa-afʿālihim*).[40] Consequently, *taʿzīr* was the legal mechanism jurists created to grant the enterprise of governance the power and legitimate authority to redress wrongs not specifically provided for by extant precedent or source-texts.

By developing the doctrine of *taʿzīr*, jurists not only anticipated an enterprise of governance, but recognized the important role it had to play in organizing and managing an Islamic polity. The Shāfiʿī al-Baghawī held

[36] For more on *taʿzīr* as a discretionary authority, see Emon, "*Ḥuqūq Allāh*," 386–90.

[37] Al-Kāsānī, *Badāʾiʿ al-Ṣanāʾiʿ*, 9:270; al-Ghazālī, *al-Wasīṭ*, 4:156–7. See also al-Nawawī, *Rawḍa*, 10:174; al-Shīrāzī, *Muhadhdhab*, 3:374.

[38] In the context of the *dhimmī* rules, one example of a *taʿzīr*-based rule concerned the *dhimmī*'s ability to seek redress as a victim of sexual slander. As addressed earlier, though the *dhimmī* could not seek redress pursuant to the Qur'ānic norm, jurists held that the ruler could create a discretionary rule that granted the *dhimmī* legal relief from a patently obviously wrong.

[39] Al-Ḥaṭṭāb, *Mawāhib al-Jalīl*, 8:436–7. On this example, see also al-Shīrāzī, *Muhadhdhab*, 3:373; Abū Muḥammad al-Ḥusayn b. Masʿūd al-Baghawī, *al-Tahdhīb fī Fiqh al-Imām al-Shāfiʿī*, eds ʿĀdil Aḥmad ʿAbd al-Mawjūd and ʿAlī Muḥammad Muʿawwaḍ (Beirut: Dār al-Kutub al-ʿIlmiyya, 1997) 7:428.

[40] Al-Khurashī, *Hāshiyat*, 8:346.

that such wrongs were penalized based on the discretionary jurisdiction of the *imām* who had to consider (*yarā*) the appropriate punishment.[41] Indeed, jurists accepted the fact that the *taʿzīr*-based rules were the product of the *imām*'s reasoning or *ijtihād*. Al-Khurashī stated that *taʿzīr* rules were based on the ruler's investigation (*ijtihād al-imām*) into the totality of circumstances.[42] Likewise, al-Ghazālī held that the duty to investigate (*ijtihād*) new forms of legal recourse fell upon the "*imām*" or political leader, given that such legal measures may be necessary in light of the dynamic nature of people and their contexts.[43] Because the enterprise of governance was charged with upholding the public good, the enterprise had to have some power to authoritatively and legitimately create and construct new legal doctrines that worked to the benefit of both individuals and society at large.[44]

Although jurists granted the enterprise of governance the power of discretionary rule, that power was neither unlimited nor unchecked. For instance, al-Baghawī and other jurists were adamant that *taʿzīr*-based punishments could not exceed the punishments of the *ḥudūd* penalities.[45] Furthermore, al-Baghawi held that since potential *taʿzīr* punishments were subject to the political ruler's attentive inquiry (*mujtahad fīhī*), as opposed to the jurists', they were of qualified precedential authority.[46] Likewise, the Ḥanbalī jurist Ibn Qudāma did not use the term *ijtihād* to describe the ruler's discretionary legislative activity. Rather, he stated merely that resort to *taʿzīr* rules is obligatory if the *imām* considers them necessary (*al-taʿzīr wājib idhā raʾāhu al-imām*).[47] Instead, he emphasized the bounds within which *taʿzīr* discretion can be used, thereby curtailing the scope of the ruler's discretionary authority.[48]

This analysis of *taʿzīr* suggests that within the Islamic legal tradition is a grant of a highly conditioned and circumspect discretionary power to

[41] Al-Baghawī, *al-Tahdhīb*, 7:428. See also, Ibn Qudāma, *al-Mughnī*, 8:324–6; Ibn Nujaym, *al-Baḥr al-Rāʾiq*, 5:68. Al-Khurashī, *Ḥāshiyya*, 8:348, discusses whether any liability arises if the *imām*'s *taʿzīr* exceeds the extent of a *ḥadd* penalty.

[42] Al-Khurashī, *Ḥāshiyya*, 8:346.

[43] Al-Ghazālī, *al-Wasīṭ*, 4:157.

[44] The Ḥanbalī jurist Abū Isḥāq Ibn Mufliḥ wrote that *taʿzīr* punishments are required for any disobedience (*maʿṣiyya*) for which there is no specified punishment (*ḥadd*) or established form of penitence (*kaffāra*). An act of disobedience requires something to inhibit its performance. If there is no specified punishment to deter one from committing the act, *taʿzīr* punishments must be created to fill the legislative void. Responsibility for establishing such discretionary punishment rests with the political authority or *imām*. Abū Isḥāq Ibn Mufliḥ, *al-Mubdiʿ fī Sharḥ al-Muqniʿ*, ed. Zahīr Shawīsh (Beirut: al-Maktab al-Islāmī, 1974), 9:108.

[45] Al-Baghawī, *al-Tahdhīb*, 7:428; Ibn Qudāma, *al-Mughnī*, 8:324–6; Ibn Nujaym, *al-Baḥr al-Rāʾiq*, 5:68. Al-Khurashī, *Ḥāshiyya*, 8:348, discusses whether any liability arises if the *imām*'s *taʿzīr* exceeds the extent of a *ḥadd* penalty.

[46] Al-Baghawī, *al-Tahdhīb*, 7:428.

[47] Ibn Qudāma, *al-Mughnī*, 8:326.

[48] Ibn Qudāma, *al-Mughnī*, 8:324–6.

the enterprise of governance. *Taʿzīr and siyāsa sharʿiyya* were legal terms of art that jurists used to juridify the zone within which the political leader could legitimately delineate new rules in light of new situations without recourse to substantive Sharīʿa-based doctrines. Jurists recognized their own limitations in delineating legal doctrines or *fiqh*, yet used the law to give limited authority to those entrusted with the enterprise of governance to govern as they saw fit. The jurists were not able to determine the content of such discretionary regulations; but they nonetheless sought to define the zone within which such regulations could legitimately arise. By juridifying this zone of discretionary authority, jurists used legal doctrine both to constitute and to delimit the enterprise of governance.

This section has juxtaposed two seemingly distinct areas of discourse in which premodern Muslim jurists both articulated how traditions of value conditioned the legitimacy an enterprise of governance's sovereign can enjoy, and created zones of authority within which the ruling authority could exercise administrative discretion. At one and the same time, jurists conditioned and defined the terms by which an enterprise of governance could claim legitimacy, and granted that same enterprise the authority to act pursuant to its own discretion. The ruler could decide how to regulate matters pursuant to metrics having little or no basis in arguments of legality. Such regulations, though, were authoritative and legitimate because they fell within the area of discretion granted to the ruler by the law. The juxtaposition of these two lines of inquiry show that conceptualizing Sharīʿa as Rule of Law allows us to appreciate the mutually constitutive relation between the law and the enterprise of governance. Far from checking the excesses of the enterprise of governance, the law legitimated the ruler's discretionary decision-making power. Indeed, Sharīʿa as Rule of Law offers a frame for us to recognize and understand the dual role jurists played when developing the law: establishing the conditions of legitimacy of an enterprise of governance, while enabling its operation pursuant to a zone of discretionary power that was not necessarily subjected to legal review.

5.3 SHARĪʿA AS RULE OF LAW: LEGITIMATING AND ENABLING THE ENTERPRISE OF GOVERNANCE (B)

A well-known feature of Islamic legal historiography is the view that the jurists alone claimed authority to define Sharīʿa-based norms, to the exclusion of the ruling regime. As such, jurists could at one and the same time claim that Sharīʿa was independent of the enterprise of governance and nonetheless assert that only by implementing the Sharīʿa could rulers claim legitimacy for their enterprise of governance. This claim of legal independence, often referenced in terms of autonomy or decentralization, is urged by some scholars as a defining feature of the premodern Islamic legal tradition. For instance, Jonathan Brockopp states:

> It seems that the very methods of collecting hadith from many individual sources promoted the view of legal authority which enshrined decentralization. This diffusion of authority among a broad base of individual jurists [*fuqahā'*] made the work of the Umayyad and 'Abbasid caliphs difficult, as they tried to establish a codified form of the law. Their attempts at political control, through appointments and inquisitions, ultimately failed and only served to demonstrate the power of the legal community in resisting centralization of authority.[49]

According to the decentralization thesis, Islamic law and legal doctrines were developed outside the ambit of government.

Those adopting this thesis should not be understood as insulating the jurist from his or her context, political or otherwise. Jurists may have debated the law in light of an ideal or normative vision of a universal empire, but that did not mean they were unmindful of the impact the institutions of governance could and did have on the intelligibility of their legal doctrines and disputes. Islamic legal historians such as Kristen Stilt have shown that jurists were fully aware of the imperatives of governance, and that government officials could have an effect on the application or experience of the law.[50] Abou El Fadl's study on rebellion shows that jurists participated in a corporate culture that was not immune from socio-political demands and realities.[51] In other words, when jurists developed their legal doctrines, they were mindful

[49] Jonathan E. Brockopp, "The Essential Sharīʿah: Teaching Islamic Law in the Religious Studies Classroom," in *Teaching Islam*, ed. Brannon M. Wheeler (New York: Oxford University Press, 2003), 77–93, 81. See also, David Waines, *An Introduction to Islam*, 2nd ed. (Cambridge: Cambridge University Press, 2003), 100, who writes that jurists saw themselves as the "expositors of the prophetic message and the will of Allah to which even the Caliph lke very ordinary believer, was ultimately subject." Furthermore, he writes, while the caliph may provide various regulations in his capacity as ruler, such regulations are separate and distinct from Sharīʿa "pure and simple." Likewise, Abou El Fadl distinguishes between Sharīʿa as the law articulated by jurists, and the administrative practices of the state. He writes: "By the fourth/tenth century, Muslim jurists had estaliblished themselves as the only legitmate authority empowered to expound the law of God." Abou El Fadl, *Islam and the Challenge of Democracy* (Princeton Princeton University Press, 2004), 14.

[50] Kristen Stilt, "The muḥtasib, law, and society in early Mamluk Cairo and Fustat (648–802/1250–1400) (PhD dissertation, Harvard University, 2004); idem, *Islamic Law in Action*.

[51] Abou El Fadl, *Rebellion & Violence*.

of the existence, organization, and demands of political society. Their awareness of the background factors of the enterprise of governance contributed to and helped constitute the boundaries of the claim space of Sharīʿa. Sharīʿa as Rule of Law offers a conceptual approach to the legal tradition that cautions against over-estimating the hard distinction often made in Islamic legal history between the jurists and the ruling authorities. While jurists certainly were scholar-authors of legal treatises and legal exponents of the law,[52] their authority to articulate the law, in contrast to the ruling elite, should not lead to the presumption that their legal doctrines did not also anticipate the existence of government administration, or were not influenced by the demands of an imperial enterprise of governance. Consequently, the intelligibility of their legal discourses cannot be fully appreciated without also accounting for the background factors associated with the enterprise of governance, whether real or imagined. Certainly informal dispute resolution mechanisms existed in early Islamic history, as well as various jurists who offered non-binding legal responses to those who presented questions (e.g., *muftīs*).[53] But those jurists existed alongside the institutional, and at times coercive, power of an enterprise of governance that both relied upon and helped constitute the law.

One example illustrating how the enterprise of governance constituted the boundaries of intelligibility for Sharīʿa-based discourses concerns the issue of whether or not jurists should accept appointments to government offices, such as the position of judge (*qāḍī*). Historians situate the beginnings of the *qāḍī*'s office in the late Umayyad (r. 41–132/661–750 CE) or early ʿAbbāsid periods (r. 132–656/750–1258) of Islamic history. The *qāḍī* started out as an appointee by the executive (e.g., caliph, *ṣulṭān*, etc.) tasked with responsibilities, which in the position's nascency included tax-collecting and government administration, or in other words, responsibilities associated with the furtherance of governance. Only over time did the scope of the office focus on judicial decision-making. As judge, the *qāḍī*'s rulings were backed by the coercive force of the ruling regime.[54]

[52] For more on the jurist as scholar-author, see Wael Hallaq, *Authority, Continuity and Change in Islamic Law* (Cambridge: Cambridge University Press, 2005).

[53] The *muftī* or jurisconsult would issue responsa to those who made inquiries about the law. The *mufti*'s response, or *fatwā*, was deemed non-binding, in contrast to the decision of a *qāḍī*, who exercised the coercive force of the government. For studies on the *muftī*, and the relationship between the *qāḍī*, see Powers, *Law, Society and Culture in the Maghreb, 1300–1500*. See also Masud, Messick, and Powers, eds, *Islamic Legal Interpretation*.

[54] Wael B. Hallaq, *The Origins and Evolution of Islamic Law* (Cambridge: Cambridge University Press, 2005), 57–101.

Because the office of *qāḍī* was embedded within the prevailing enterprise of governance, some jurists were wary of, if not absolutely opposed to, assuming such an office.[55] For them, the independence of the law was at stake. They feared that an unprincipled executive could use his power of appointment to ensure that judges would resolve cases and articulate Sharīʿa-based doctrines in a manner favorable to the ruler. Indeed, they feared for the independence and integrity of the Sharīʿa as a claim space within which arguments of justice could be made even against the ruling authority. Consequently, stories abound about premodern jurists avoiding any and all entanglements with the government.[56] Yet we also find a jurist such as the famous Shāfiʿī al-Māwardī (d. 450/1058), who was highly respected as a scholar and who assumed the office of *qāḍī*.[57]

The inconsistency in historical practice parallels an inconsistency in traditions that counseled both options—to reject or accept judicial appointments. For instance, the Prophet is reported to have said "No man judges except that God most high appoints for him two angels to direct, guide, and ensure his success. If he is unjust, [the angels] abandon him and ascend to heaven."[58] Judging is not an easy matter, and it should not be taken lightly. Jurists interpreted the above prophetic statement to argue that those who judged justly did so with the benefit of angels, and by implication received a divine blessing that could not be ignored or undervalued. The blessings that these jurists believed came with performing the judicial function were further extolled by the companion of the Prophet, Ibn Masʿūd, who said: "Sitting to judge [a dispute] between people pursuant to the demands of truth is more pleasing to me than engaging in worship for seventy years."[59]

In other traditions, though, the Prophet warned against the harm that could arise by assuming the office of *qāḍī*: "He who is made a judge shall be slaughtered without a knife."[60] Such a tradition did not bode well for

[55] Benjamin Jokisch, *Islamic Imperial Law: Harun al-Rashid's Codification Project* (Berlin: Water de Gruyter, 2007), 285.

[56] See for instance, the biography of Sufyān al-Thawrī, who refused to serve as judge in Kūfa. Ibn ʿImād, *Shadharāt al-Dhahb fī Akhbār man Dhahab* (Beirut: Dār al-Kutub al-ʿIlmiyya, n.d.), 1:250. Likewise, Mālik b. Anas refused attempts by rulers to render his *Muwaṭṭāʾ* as a uniform law for the Islamic territories. Jalāl al-Dīn al-Suyūṭī, *Ikhtilāf al-Madhāhib*, ed. ʿAbd al-Qayyūm Muḥammad Shāfīʿ al-Basṭawī (Cairo: Dār al-Iʿtiṣām, 1404 AH), 22–3; Abou El Fadl, *Speaking in God's Name*, 10.

[57] C. Brockelmann, "al-Māwardī Abu ʾl-Ḥasan ʿAlī b. Muḥammad b. Ḥabīb," *Encyclopaedia of Islam, Second Edition*. Eds P. Bearman et al.

[58] Ibn Abī al-Damm, *Kitāb Adab al-Qadāʾ*, ed. Muḥammad al-Qādir ʿAtā (Beirut: Dār al-Kutub al-ʿIlmiyya, 1987), 23.

[59] Ibn Abī al-Damm, *Kitāb Adab al-Qadāʾ*, 23.

[60] Ibn Abī al-Damm, *Kitāb Adab al-Qadāʾ*, 23.

those who considered accepting a judicial appointment.[61] Yet Ibn Abī al-Damm, a premodern jurist writing on the office of the *qāḍī*, recognized that traditions antagonistic to holding office could be interpreted to mean different things. In fact, he said that "slaughter," as used in the above tradition, should be understood metaphorically to mean that the judge must put aside his own desires, or in other words, "slaughter" his own perspective to ensure that he judges justly.[62]

In an effort to account for the conflicting traditions, Ibn Abī al-Damm offered a particular insight into the contentious issue of assuming judicial office:

> The *ḥadīths*[63] supporting [holding office] are based on the benefit (*al-ṣāliḥ*) of adjudication, [one's] ability to bear its burden and uphold the obligation [to adjudicate]. The [*ḥadīths*] against [holding office] are based on [one's] inability to do so. Based on that, *'ulamā'* will enter [the profession] or not. After [the Prophet's death] . . . the first four caliphs continued [to adjudicate] . . . and adjudicated among the people in truth. Their entry into [the office] is principal evidence for the magnitude of its inescapability and the abundance of its reward. Those after [the four caliphs] followed their [practice], and thereafter the Muslim *imāms* of the [next generations] upheld [the practice too].
>
> Those who disliked entering [the profession] included *imāms* of great merit, competence, and righteousness. [Their view] is based on an exaggerated [concern] for preserving their souls and for the ways to reach a state of blamelessness. Indeed the command to [adjudicate] is a significant matter, and perhaps they considered themselves weak or slack. Or [maybe] they feared a diminution in night time worship or study if they were to occupy themselves with [adjudication].

To further illustrate how Sharīʿa as Rule of Law cuts against the decentralization thesis, recall the hypothetical noted in the introduction provided by the Shāfiʿī jurist Abū al-Maʿālā al-Juwaynī (d. 478/1085). As already noted, al-Juwaynī related a hypothetical about a Ḥanafī husband and a Shāfiʿī wife, both of whom are legal scholars or *mujtahids*. The husband declares to his wife in a fit of anger that he divorces her. The question that arose for al-Juwaynī was whether they are in fact divorced: the Ḥanafīs did not recognize a divorce pronounced in a fit of anger, whereas the Shāfiʿīs did. Since the husband and wife, in the hypothetical, are *mujtahids*, there is no reason

[61] Indeed, this was one way to read this tradition. Jokisch, *Islamic Imperial Law*, 285 n. 23.

[62] Ibn Abī al-Damm, *Kitāb Adab al-Qaḍā'*, 23.

[63] Technically, the appropriate Arabic plural of *ḥadīth* is *aḥādīth*. However, I will depart from the technical Arabic grammar rules in order to reduce the burden on readers unfamiliar with Arabic terminology.

why one of them should yield to the opinion of the other. According to al-Juwaynī, the parties had to submit their conflict to a judge to resolve the dispute. According to al-Juwaynī, the judge would decide the matter as he or she saw fit. Importantly, though, the authority of the judge's determination did not rest on the substantive rule of law relied upon to resolve the dispute. Rather the judge's determination was authoritative, for al-Juwaynī because of the *imperium* tied to his institutional position.[64]

In this example, al-Juwaynī implicitly revealed how the background factor of the enterprise of governance informed his analysis of this particular hypothetical. The significance of this assumption can be determined by asking a corollary question about al-Juwaynī's analysis. Reasoning counter-factually, suppose al-Juwaynī made no assumptions at all about an enterprise of governance, or even more, suppose he assumed there was no enterprise of governance at all. In such a case, he arguably would not have referred to the *qāḍī*, since the *qāḍī* would not have been a factor to incorporate into his analysis. He would have had to decide the conflict between the parties on other grounds, not making recourse to this particular procedural approach. What those alternative grounds might have been are hard to speculate on al-Juwaynī's behalf. Nonetheless, the counterfactual illustrates how presumptions about the enterprise of governance not only contributed to, but also made certain legal outcomes intelligible.

This section suggests that any neat bifurcation between the jurists and the ruling elite becomes blurry once Sharīʿa is viewed as Rule of Law. The respective arenas of law and governance necessarily overlapped. Not only did jurists accept appointments to government offices, but they also took into account the facticity of those governmental offices as they developed their jurisprudence and legal doctrines. This is not to suggest that Sharīʿa as Rule of Law collapses law into the realm of politics, or that law bears no autonomy whatsoever. Indeed, as Sherman Jackson's work on al-Qarāfī suggests, the corporate identity of the *madhhab* could hold back an enterprise of governance that sought to exert authority, if not dominance, in the realm of law.[65] But it would be far too simplistic, if not naïve, to think that the law and the enterprise of governance ever were or could be separable in anything but some form of ideal theory.

[64] Al-Juwaynī, *Kitāb al-Ijtihād*, 36–8. For a discussion of al-Juwaynī's hypothetical, see Abou El Fadl, *Speaking in God's Name*, 149–50.

[65] Jackson, *Islamic Law and the State*.

5.4 *MADRASAS* AND CURRICULUM: INSTITUTIONAL SITE AND PEDAGOGIC DISCIPLINE

This chapter thus far has shown that reason, authority, and background assumptions about an enterprise of governance constituted for premodern jurists the boundaries of the claim space of Sharīʿa, and thereby contributed to the intelligibility of a Sharīʿa-based normative claim. This section further elaborates on the boundaries of that claim space by focusing on educational institutions and legal curriculum. Like the other constitutive features addressed so far, these two factors contributed to the conditions of intelligibility of Sharīʿa-based norms. Premodern Sharīʿa education constituted the initial step to entering the Sharīʿa profession. That step brought students into the world of educational institutions (*madrasa*) and legal curricula. These institutions and curricula provided both form and content in a manner that defined and delimited the claim space of Sharīʿa. Indeed, educational curricula provided the touchstone that designated a given argument as distinctively legal and thereby appropriate for asserting from within the claim space of Sharīʿa. To substantiate how the premodern educational system contributed to the boundaries that gave a distinctively legal intelligibility to claims of justice, this section will focus on two features of Sharīʿa education, namely the institutional arrangements of Sharīʿa education and the curriculum of study.

Scholars of the premodern *madrasa* or Islamic law college have shown that it proliferated in part due to the efforts of wealthy individuals who created charitable trusts or *awqāf* (sing. *waqf*) to found educational institutions. The fact that these *madrasas* were privately endowed is often invoked to characterize Islamic law and legal education as outside the purview and control of the government.[66] This independence of the *madrasa* contributed to the development of a scholarly ethic of disciplinary integrity that cut against ruling regimes seeking to co-opt the learned elite to legitimate the regime's actions. Nonetheless, the efforts by the Seljuq vizier Niẓām al-Mulk to endow some of the most wealthy and illustrious law colleges of his day indicate how government officials attempted to qualify the extent to which jurists could claim their discipline to be fully autonomous.

George Makdisi suggests that the *madrasa* was the end result of an institutional development process that aimed to organize and

[66] Abou El Fadl, *Speaking in God's Name*, 16–17; idem, *The Great Theft: Wrestling Islam from the Extremists* (New York: HarperOne, 2007), 35; N.J. Coulson, *A History of Islamic Law* (1964; reprint, Edinburgh: Edinburgh University Press, 1997). This view of the *madrasa* supports the decentralization thesis noted above.

administer the transfer of knowledge. The first institution in which knowledge was transmitted was the mosque (*masjid*). Principally considered a religious place of worship, the mosque became the center of learning in early Islamic history. Even after the birth of the *madrasa* in the eleventh and twelfth centuries,[67] the "mosque preserved its primacy as the ideal institution of learning, and law, its primacy as the ideal religious science."[68] While there were different types of mosques with varying terminology, there is significant agreement that early in Islamic history, most education took place in mosques where scholars would sit in teaching circles (*halqas*) with their students.[69]

As students began to visit mosques for educational purposes in increasing numbers, the need for residential facilities arose, thus contributing to the development of the second institution: the *masjid-khān,* or mosque-residence. The *khān* or college was a residential complex associated with a mosque. "Since the *masdjid* could not serve as a lodging place for teaching staff and students . . . *khans* were founded next to the *masdjids* to serve as lodging for students from out-of-town."[70] The next institutional development was the *madrasa.* It combined the facilities for teaching, thus far characteristic of the *masjid,* with the residential complex introduced by the *masjid-khans.* The *madrasa,* therefore, was where students could both reside and study in a facility that catered to the specific needs of students.

Founders of *madrasas* often used trust law (*waqf*) to formalize their financial commitment and to arrange for the administration of institutional and curricular activities. The desire to create a charitable trust in the form of a *madrasa* as opposed to a mosque may have had much to do with the tax implications associated with such trust arrangements. To avoid paying taxes on accumulated wealth, a donor could create a charitable trust. Because the endowment consumed the capital, the donor was not subject to taxation. But by endowing a *madrasa,* for instance,

[67] J. Pedersen and G. Makdisi, "Madrasa," in *Encyclopedia of Islam,* Rev. Ed. Eds H.A.R. Gibb et al. (Leiden: Brill, 1960–2009), 1125–8.

[68] George Makdisi, *The Rise of Colleges: Institutions of Learning in Islam and the West* (Edinburgh: Edinburgh University Press, 1981), 12. Many other authors stress that the subject matter taught in the *masjids* was the law, and that it is this early concern for the law that eventually gave the *madrasa* its character as a college of law. Jonathan Berkey, *Transmission of knowledge in Medieval Cairo: A Social History of Islamic Education* (Princeton: Princeton University Press, 1992), 47; Pedersen and Makdisi, "Madrasa," 1124. Notably, there is some disagreement on this point. See A.L. Tibawi, "Origin and Character of *Al-Madrasah,*" *Bulletin of the School of Oriental and African Studies 25,* no. 2 (1962): 225–38. More on the curriculum will be discussed below.

[69] See for example, Berkey, *Transmission of Knowledge,* 7; Pedersen and Makdisi, "Madrasa," 1123; Makdisi, *Rise of Colleges,* 10–23.

[70] Pedersen and Makdisi, "Madrasa," 1124.

the donor could nonetheless arrange to receive personal income from the endowment by appointing himself as a salaried administrator.[71] Additionally, he could appoint his heirs as future administrators of the trust. Effectively, the donor generated an income-producing investment for himself and his heirs in perpetuity and at the same time created a tax shelter.

Importantly, under the doctrine of trust law, *masjids* and *madrasas* were treated differently. If a donor endowed a *masjid*, he lost all rights to the property, including the power to appoint himself and his heirs to administrative posts. "[T]he *masdjid*, once the [trust] deed was signed, became a *wakf tahrir*; that is to say, a foundation whose legal status is assimilated to the manumission of a slave. As the master, once he freed his slave, had no further rights over him, the founder, once the deed of his *masdjid* was signed, had no further rights over it."[72] In the case of endowing *masjids*, the grantor could not thereby create for himself and his heirs an income stream for future support and maintenance, as that would impinge on the freedom of the trust. Trust doctrine, therefore, provided an incentive for some to endow *madrasas*, and thus contribute to the development of private endowments for institutions of legal learning.[73]

Those who are considered to represent the Sharīʿa authoritatively have historically been called the *ʿulamāʾ*, or jurists.[74] The tradition the jurists represented was made tangible through the curriculum of legal study, and often within institutional frameworks that created a sense of organization and professionalism (i.e., the *madrasa*). Pedersen and Makdisi note that the starting point of any education in the pre-*madrasa* period was learning the Qurʾān and the *ḥadīth* (traditions from the Prophet Muḥammad). From the study of the Qurʾān and *ḥadīth* arose the science of jurisprudence.[75] In the pre-*madrasa* period, well into the third/ninth century, "the *masdjid* continued to be used for the teaching of one or more of the Islamic sciences, or their ancillaries among the literary

[71] Makdisi indicates, though, that under the Mālikī school, such a possibility does not exist. The Mālikīs do not permit a donor to appoint himself or herself as the administrator of a *waqf*-based institution he or she endowed. Makdisi, *Rise of Colleges*, 238.

[72] Pedersen and Makdisi, "Madrasa," 1128.

[73] Writing in 1980, Ulrich Haarmann noted that no comprehensive study of the beginnings of *waqf* was available. Ulrich Haarmann, "Mamluk Endowment Deeds as a Source for the History of Education in Late Medieval Egypt," *Al-Abhath* 28 (1980): 31–47, 31.

[74] For studies on the *ʿulamāʾ*, see Cl. Gilliot, R.C. Repp, K.A. Nizami, M.B. Hooker, Chang-Kuan Lin, and J.O. Hunwick, "ʿUlamāʾ," *Encyclopaedia of Islam, Second Edition* Eds P. Bearman et al.; Muhammad Qasim Zaman, *The Ulama in Contemporary Islam: Custodians of Change* (Princeton: Princeton University Press, 2007).

[75] Pedersen and Makdisi, "Madrasa," 1123.

arts."[76] It was this early history of the pre-*madrasa* period that defined what would be taught in the *madrasa*, thus constituting a curriculum of education that gave content, and thereby shape, to the claim space of Sharīʿa.

The course of study to become a jurist generally included four years of training in religious law and "ten or more graduate years, leading to a 'license to teach'. The graduate students were trained in the scholastic method,"[77] and studied various topics in the course of becoming a jurist, such as the following:

- Qur'ān: including interpretive sciences, exegesis, and the various readings of the text;
- Ḥadīth: including the interpretive tradition, biographies of transmitters;
- Principles of Religion (*uṣūl al-dīn*);
- Principles of Law (*uṣūl al-fiqh*), i.e., the sources and methodologies of law;
- the legal doctrine of the school of law to which one belongs;
- the divergent doctrines within one school and across legal schools.[78]

This curriculum required the student to engage foundational sources of authority whose provenance was understood according to Islamic jurisprudence to originate with God (e.g., Qur'ān) and the normative practice of the Prophet. Given the foundational role these and other sources played in the curriculum of Sharīʿa-based education, the curriculum gave disciplinary content to the claim space of Sharīʿa, and thereby helped define and delimit it.

The fulfillment and satisfaction of curriculuar requirements would culminate in an *ijāza* or diploma of successful completion of a course of study, thus "guarantee[ing] the transmission of authoritative religious knowledge."[79] An *ijāza* could be issued upon completing a single book or mastering an entire subject area. These diplomas could also authorize the recipient to teach and issue legal responsa (*ijāza al-tadrīs wa al-iftā'*). The conclusion of a course of study in the Islamic educational process was marked by the student receiving such certification. Hence the *ijāza* assumed a central place within the system of education; it was a measure

[76] Pedersen and Makdisi, "Madrasa," 1124.

[77] George Makdisi, "Baghdad, Bologna, and Scholasticism," in *Centres of Learning: Learning and Location in Pre-Modern Europe and the Near East*. Eds Jan Willem Drijvers and A.A. MacDonald (Leiden: Brill, 1995), 141–57.

[78] Makdisi, *Rise of Colleges*, 80.

[79] Makdisi, *Rise of Colleges*, 140.

of accomplishment, training and capacity. It provided an index of a jurist's authority when making claims about the demands of justice.[80]

As much as the *madrasa* was subject to private trust law, and the curriculum provided formalized, if not idealized, prerequisites of instruction and certification, the system of Islamic legal education was not immune from the efforts of government officials to tap into the authority that a legal education offered to those who became arbiters of the moral and legal order. In fact, government officials also endowed *madrasas* that, according to some historians, reflected a government interest in harnessing the authority associated with the study of Sharīʿa to bolster the legitimacy of the enterprise of governance.[81] The political implications of endowing *madrasas* have often been addressed with respect to the endowments of Niẓām al-Mulk (d. 485/1092), the vizier to the Seljuq ṣulṭans Alp Arslan (r. 455–465/1063–1073) and Mālik Shah (r. 465–485/1072–1092). Some suggest that Niẓām al-Mulk founded the first *madrasa* in the Islamic world, the *Niẓāmiyya madrasa* in Baghdad in 459/1067. Other historians, though, suggest that *madrasas* existed much earlier.[82] Nevertheless, an important inference drawn from Niẓām al-Mulk's *Niẓāmiyya* colleges (located in Baghdad, Nishapur, Balkh, Mosul, Herat, and Marv) is that those in political power could and did leverage their wealth to gain control over the religious elite by endowing the most illustrious colleges and the most impressive professorships. For instance, Makdisi states that Niẓām al-Mulk "founded his network of *madrasas* to implement his political policies throughout the vast lands of the empire under his sway."[83] Tibawi goes further and argues that Niẓām al-Mulk could not have founded his *Niẓāmiyyas* as a private individual given the likelihood that he did not have the wealth to do so. Instead, he argues that Niẓām al-Mulk built the *madrasas* in his capacity as a government official, thus tapping government coffers.[84]

Whether government-funded *madrasas* could exert influence on the juristic profession and legal curriculum is not clear, though. Makdisi suggests that at least in premodern Baghdad, with its large number of *madrasas*, a single *madrasa* like the *Niẓāmiyya* could not exercise the kind of power that might be required to implement government-sponsored policies. In Baghdad, there was a variety of *madrasas* with different

[80] Although the scholars write about *ijāzas* extensively, most of their information about the *ijāza* comes from biographical dictionaries. See Makdisi, *Rise of Colleges*, 140–52.

[81] Waines, *An Introduction to Islam*, 85.

[82] Pedersen and Makdisi, "Madrasa," 1126.

[83] George Makdisi, "Muslim Institutions of Learning in Eleventh-century Baghdad," *BSOAS* 24 (1961), reprinted in George Makdisi, *Religion, Law and Learning in Classical Islam* (Surry: Variorum, 1991), 1–56, 51.

[84] Tibawi, *"al-Madrasah,"* 232.

law school affiliations. Each had their own teachers and institutions for appointing faculty. While Makdisi would agree that the jurists constituted a significant political force, he shows that any attempts to control the *'ulamā',* or jurists, via the *Niẓāmiyya* were doomed to failure because of the diversity of schools, with their attendant diversity of opinions, in the vicinity.[85]

Furthermore, Jonathan Berkey suggests that the institutional setting of the *madrasa* was less significant to the education of a jurist than the informal relationship a student had with his teacher. Berkey argues that the informality of teacher–student relationships, rather than the formality of *madrasa* institutions, characterized the premodern Islamic educational system, thereby making the political contest over the *madrasa* less significant for Berkey. "[T]he institutions themselves played no actual role in Islamic education ... Islamic education remained fundamentally informal, flexible, and tied to persons rather than institutions."[86] Berkey bases his argument, though, on negative evidence. He argues that many deeds of trust for *madrasas* do not mention salaries to teachers or stipends for students. Furthermore, he notes that biographical dictionaries generally do not mention the specific schools where scholars taught or studied. Berkey recognizes that none of this evidence suggests that teaching did not occur in such institutions. Rather, he argues that premodern contemporaries "considered the venue of instruction and education to be of secondary importance: what was critical was the character and knowledge of the individuals with whom one had studied."[87]

Between Tibawi, Makdisi, and Berkey, we find competing views about the significance of the *madrasa,* as both a site of legal education and a site of political contest. Often this difference plays into arguments about the autonomy of legal learning from government manipulation or centralization. The more one emphasizes the personal relationship between the teacher and student, the more one implicitly supports the thesis of decentralization between the jurists and the ruling elite. This historical debate has the potential to fuel contemporary debates about the nature of Sharīʿa, and whether modern state efforts to codify Islamic law are legitimate, true, or authentic. This study remains agnostic on the different positions noted above about the site of legal education in the premodern period. Furthermore, even if Berkey is correct in asserting the priority of the teacher–student relationship, nothing denigrates the institutional role of the *madrasa* in organizing and ensuring a system

[85] Makdisi, "Muslim Institutions."
[86] Berkey, *Transmission,* 17–18.
[87] Berkey, *Transmission,* 18.

of licensing.[88] There is no prerequisite that one adopt either the thesis of informality or the thesis of institutional formality to accept that the jurists represented a tradition that conferred upon them an authority about which government officials were wary, or alternatively covetous.[89] The *madrasa* as privately endowed, the scholar as a licensed authority, and the curriculum as a disciplinary feature, helped to constitute the boundaries of the claim space of Sharīʿa, and thereby the intelligibility of claims that issued therefrom. The curriculum of Sharīʿa education disciplined those who studied and attended to the law. In that capacity, it defined what constituted appropriate subjects of study and provided the language of legality by which claims of justice resonated as specifically legal claims emanating from the claim space of Sharīʿa. In this sense, the curriculum and the sources it rendered foundational contributed to the distinctiveness of Sharīʿa as a discipline of inquiry. Additionally, the fact that the *madrasa* became a site of contest between the juristic class and government officials, and continues to be an ongoing site of debate among scholars, reminds us of the sometimes uneasy, but nonetheless mutually constitutive relationship between law and the enterprise of governance.

5.5 *IJTIHĀD* AND EPISTEMIC AUTHORITY: STAYING WITHIN THE BOUNDS

Ijtihād was an important term of art for premodern jurists, and remains so for contemporary Muslims debating the application of Sharīʿa today.[90] *Ijtihād,* as a term of art, directly had to do with the

[88] See also Richard Bulliet, *Patricians of Nishapur. A Study in Medieval Islamic Social History* (Cambridge: Harvard University Press, 1972), 50.

[89] The definition of the *ʿulamāʾ* and whether there is a strict correlation between scholars and legal education in the *madrasa* is a separate debate that is beyond the scope of this study. For scholarly accounts on this issue, see Bulliet, *Patricians of Nishapur;* Roy Mottahedeh, *Loyalty and Leadership in an Early Islamic Society* (Princeton: Princeton University Press, 1980).

[90] From the late 19th century onward, debates on *ijtihād* concerned whether the "door of *ijtihād*" or the license to interpret in the law had been closed in the 10th century when jurists somehow declared that all issues had been decided and there was no need for *de novo* legal analysis. On the debates, see Shaista P. Ali-Karamali and F. Dunne, "The Ijtihad Controversy," *Arab Law Quarterly* 9, no. 3 (1994): 238–57. The historical validity of this alleged closure has been substantially questioned and critiqued in the scholarly literature. Wael B. Hallaq, "Was the Gate of Ijtihād Closed?" *International Journal of Middle East Studies* 16, no. 1 (1984): 3–41. However, modern self-proclaimed reformers nonetheless consider their calls for a new *ijtihād* to be novel and perhaps even edgy. See for example, Irshad Manji, *The Trouble With Islam Today: A Muslim's Call for Reform in Her Faith* (New York: St. Martin's Press, 2003).

license to interpret, derive, and even change the law. Implicitly, it also concerned the extent to which legal interpretations were authoritative for purposes of an enterprise of governance (whether formal or informal) that gave them coercive effect. In their debates about the scope of juristic independent interpretation (*ijtihād*), jurists had to contend with the authority of source-texts, the scope of legal reasoning, and the limits of the authority of any legal outcome given the epistemic limits of the jurist. The debate on *ijtihād,* as will be suggested, is less about whether the law is subject to interpretation, but rather about the authority that can be attached to a particular legal interpretation. Put differently, *ijtihād* is about the legitimacy and authority of a legal argument made within the claim space of Sharīʿa. As suggested below, the authority of a legal claim was theoretically addressed in terms of epistemic capacities and limits. As a technical term of art that encompassed competing theories about the epistemic authority of the law, *ijtihād* helped constitute the boundaries of the claim space of Sharīʿa, beyond which an argument would suffer from a lack of authority as a species of legal argument.

The authority of doctrinal rules of law (*fiqh*), for many premodern jurists, depended on the degree to which they were linked to a particular source-text, such as the Qur'ān or *hadīth* of the Prophet. Consequently, before addressing the various theories of *ijtihād,* it is important to situate it within the larger context of legal authorties in which *ijtihād* was theoretically embedded. One such authority for law is the Qur'ān. Premodern Muslim jurists considered the Qur'ān to be the literal word of God revealed to the Prophet Muḥammad by the angel Gabriel over a period of twenty-two years. The Qur'ān is comprised of 114 chapters with over 6,000 verses, but is hardly a legal treatise of law. Only a fraction of its verses have content that can be classified as "legal," thereby putting jurists in a position to interpret the law by extrapolating new rulings from existing Qur'ānic verse that were not necessarily on point.[91] It is not surprising that jurists used different interpretive techniques to understand the possible import of a Qur'ānic verse. For instance, where two verses contradict one another, exegetes argued that the later

[91] Various commentators suggest that there are anywhere from 80 to 600 verses of the Qur'ān which have content that can be called legal. For instance, Kamali states that the Qur'ān contains 350 legal verses; Kamali, *Principles*, 26. Abdullahi Ahmad An-Na'im, *Toward an Islamic Reformation: Civil Liberties, Human Rights, and International Law* (Syracuse: Syracuse University Press, 1990), 20, notes that some scholars consider 500 or 600 of the over 6,000 verses in the Qur'ān to be legally oriented. However, of those verses, most deal with worship rituals, leaving about eighty (80) verses that deal with legal matters in a strict sense.

revealed verse abrogated the earlier one.[92] Muslim exegetes were also interested in whether a particular verse was revealed before or after Muḥammad's migration from Mecca to Medina in 622 CE. They noted that the verses prior to the migration (i.e., the Meccan verses) reflected universal values that applied to all of humanity. The ones arising after the migration were called Medinan verses; these reflected the role of the Prophet as a political and military leader, as well as chief arbitrator of disputes in Medina. It is therefore not surprising that most of what might be called "legal" in the Qur'ān are Medinan verses.[93] Finally, exegetes often referenced narrative accounts of the context in which a particular verse was revealed to Muḥammad. Those narrative accounts (i.e., *asbāb al-nuzūl*) contributed to the scope of meaning derivable from a given verse.

Given the epistemic role of history in Qur'ānic analysis, it should also not be surprising that the Prophet's history became an important reference for jurists. There are varying accounts of when, why, and how the Prophetic biography and practice became an authoritative source for the law. Some suggest that it was a theoretical development associated with the work of the jurist Muḥammad b. Idrīs al-Shāfiʿī (d. 204/820);[94] while others suggest that his resort to Muḥammad's practice was an attempt to offset the scope of individual reasoning being exercised by early jurists in Iraq.[95] Whatever the reason(s) may have been, the fact remains that by the fourth/tenth century, the practice of the Prophet (Sunna) had assumed a primary position of authority alongside the Qur'ān as a source for legal analysis.[96] Indeed, by that time, narrative accounts of the Prophet's words, actions, and deeds (*ḥadīth*) were

[92] For a general introduction to the Qur'ān and Qur'ānic interpretation, see Michael Cook, *The Koran: A Very Short Introduction* (Oxford: Oxford University Press, 2000); Ahmed von Denffer, *'Ulūm al-Qur'ān: An Introduction to the Sciences of the Qur'ān* (Leicestershire: The Islamic Foundation, 1994). On the doctrine of abrogation, see John Burton, *The Sources of Islamic Law: Islamic Theories of Abrogation* (Edinburgh: Edinburgh University Press, 1990).

[93] The shift in tenor between Meccan and Medinan verses is so distinct that some modern Muslim reformers have suggested that there are two messages in the Qur'ān, and that the Medinan message is so historically bounded as to have limited, if any, salience for Muslims living thereafter. Mahmoud Mohamed Taha, *The Second Message of Islam*, trans. Abdullahi Ahmed An-Na'im (Syracuse: Syracuse University Press, 1996).

[94] On the presumed centrality of al-Shāfiʿī to the development of Islamic legal theory, see Wael Hallaq, "Was al-Shafi'i the Master Architect of Islamic Jurisprudence?," *International Journal of Middle East Studies* 25 (1993): 587–605.

[95] On the early history of *ḥadīth* and its contribution to legal analysis, see Coulson, *A History of Islamic Law*, 149–81; Ignaz Goldziher, *Introduction to Islamic Theology and Law*, trans. Andras and Ruth Hamori (Princeton: Princeton University Press, 1981); Bernard Weiss, *The Spirit of Islamic Law* (Athens, Georgia: The University of Georgia Press, 1998).

[96] On the authority and canonization of *ḥadīth*, see Jonathan Brown, *The Canonization of al-Bukhārī and Muslim* (Leiden: Brill, 2007).

collected and incorporated into various reference works that achieved canonical status in the Muslim world.[97]

The Qurʾān and the *hadīth* cannot and do not address every possible situation that might require legal resolution. To govern such cases, jurists developed different but limited techniques by which they could extend the ruling of a source-text to new and unprecedented circumstances.[98] Jurists wrote that rules based on precedential reasoning (*qiyās*) or consensus (*ijmāʿ*) were sufficiently authoritative for purposes of falling within the claim space of Sharīʿa. What each technique implies about the scope of application or the conditions of their validity is the subject of considerable debate and discussion among both premodern and modern scholars of Islamic law. Historians of Islamic law are often skeptical about the feasibility of identifying a consensus.[99] Likewise, scholars dispute whether *qiyās* is a source or a method of legal deduction.[100] Both approaches raise fundamental questions about how one decides whether a consensus exists, or what constitutes a guiding precedent on a *de novo* issue. Importantly, both the centrality of source-texts and the resort to specific (but limited) techniques of extrapolation contribute to defining the boundaries of the claim space of Sharīʿa, and the conditions of authority and intelligibility of a given claim made from within that claim space.

The rules derived from the Qurʾān or *ḥadīth*, or developed by consensus or analogical reasoning are called *fiqh*. The Islamic doctrinal tradition consists, in part, of numerous encyclopedic collections of *fiqh* on issues such as purification rituals, prayer, alms giving, fasting, pilgrimage, contract, personal injury, bailments, criminal law and procedure, and so on. These collections range from short handbooks to multi-volume encyclopedias that provide the rationales and justifications for a given rule. Some of the larger collections illustrate how and why the various legal schools differ on a particular matter. These differences may have to do with competing assessments of source-texts, or alternatively, competing policies that underlie a given legal conclusion.

For example, premodern Sunnī jurists differed on whether a victim of theft could seek financial compensation for his stolen property in the event the thief no longer possessed the property. The Qurʾānic injunction against theft reads as follows: "Regarding the male and female thieves, cut

[97] On the *ḥadīth* in the law, see Kamali, *Principles*, 58–117. On the canonization of Sunnī *ḥadīth* collections, see Brown, *Canonization*.

[98] For a general discussion of Islamic jurisprudence, including the role of source-texts in the law, see Kamali, *Principles*.

[99] See generally, Kamali, *Principles*, 228–63.

[100] See generally Kamali, *Principles*, 264–305.

their hands as punishment for what they did as a warning from God."[101] This verse provides for corporal punishment but makes no mention of compensatory damages. In a *ḥadīth,* however, Muḥammad is reported to have denied compensation if the thief was subjected to amputation.[102] Jurists of the four Sunnī schools debated the authenticity of this *ḥadīth.* For instance, the Mālikī Ibn Rushd al-Ḥafīd and the Ḥanbalī Ibn Qudāma were skeptical of its authenticity.[103] The Shāfiʿī al-Māwardī stated that in the time of the biblical Jacob, thieves simply compensated their victims for their crimes. He argued that the Qur'ān abrogated that earlier law, and the *ḥadīth* merely corroborated that fact.[104] The Ḥanafīs, however, relied on this tradition to deny compensation to the victim if the thief already suffered amputation. Ḥanafī jurists asserted that the Qur'ān required only one punishment. For them, to impose liability for compensation in addition to the amputation not only contravened the Qur'ānic stipulation of a single punishment, but also the *ḥadīth* denying compensation from a thief who has suffered amputation.[105]

The other schools of law did not rely on that *ḥadīth.* By rejecting that *ḥadīth* as dispositive, they faced a legal issue on which there were no acceptable authoritative texts to guide their decision. Consequently, they had to reason to a legal outcome and justify it. For jurists of the Shāfiʿī, Ḥanbalī, and Mālikī schools, the thief committed a public wrong, and thereby deserved the corporal punishment for retributive purposes. That did not mean, however, that the private party victim suffered no injury. The lost property was not something that jurists could ignore. Consequently, Shāfiʿī and Ḥanbalī jurists concluded that the victim could seek compensatory damage even if the thief had suffered corporal punishment. The Mālikīs, while attentive to the victim's plight, worried that the thief might suffer unduly if he both lost his hand and was

[101] Qur'ān 5:38.

[102] Jalāl al-Dīn al-Suyūṭī, *Sharḥ Sunan al-Nisā'ī* (Beirut: Dār al-Kutub al-ʿArabī, n.d.), 8:93; Ibn Rushd al-Ḥafīd, *Bidāyat al-Mujtahid,* 2:662. See also al-Māwardī, *al-Ḥāwī,* 13:184, who cited a different version of the *ḥadīth* in which the Prophet is reported to have said, "If the thief is amputated, there is no liability for compensation" (*idhā quṭiʿa al-sāriq fa-lā ghurm*). For this version, see also al-Kāsānī, *Badā'iʿ al-Ṣanā'iʿ,* 9:341. Al-ʿAynī, *al-Bināya,* 7:71 cited yet a third version of the *ḥadīth,* which states: "There is no liability for compensation on the thief after his right hand has been amputated" (*lā ghurm 'alā al-sāriq baʿda mā quṭiʿat yamīnuhu*). For other versions of this tradition, see also al-Dār Quṭnī, *Sunan al-Dār Quṭnī,* 3:129–30. Notably, al-ʿAynī said that this tradition occurs in the collections of both al-Nisā'ī and al-Dār Quṭnī: Al-ʿAynī, *al-Bināya,* 7:71.

[103] Ibn Rushd al-Ḥafīd, *Bidāyat al-Mujtahid,* 2:662–3; Ibn Qudāma, *Mughnī,* 8:271.

[104] Al-Māwardī, *al-Ḥāwī,* 13:184. For the Ḥanbalī Abū Isḥāq Ibn Mufliḥ (d. 804/1401), the *ḥadīth* means that no one should be compensated for amputating a thief's hand (i.e., *ujrat al-qāṭiʿ*). Abū Isḥāq Ibn Mufliḥ, *Mubdiʿ,* 9:144.

[105] See, for example, Abū Bakr al-Sarakhsī, *Kitāb al-Mabsūṭ* (Beirut: Dār al-Kutub al-ʿIlmiyya, 1993), 9:157; Kāsānī, *Badā'iʿ al-Ṣanā'iʿ,* 9:340–1.

indebted financially. Indeed, if the thief were poor, the debt might be so burdensome as to be tantamount to a second punishment. Therefore, the Mālikīs concluded that if the thief was sufficiently wealthy from the moment he stole to the moment his hand was amputated, he had to pay compensation. But if he was poor in that period, he owed no compensation. For the Mālikīs, the prospect that such a financial debt might be punitive seemed unduly retributive.[106]

What we see in this brief *fiqh* analysis is the role of the jurist as interpreter of the laws. As interpreter, the jurist was presumed to bring a wealth of training about the Qur'ān and prophetic traditions, methods of interpretation, and knowledge of the vast body of rulings of his own legal school and others. Bringing them all to bear in his legal analysis required an awareness of the authority of source-texts, where they were dispositive, where they were ambiguous, and the lacuna in the source-texts that needed to be supplemented with reasoned legal analysis. Between the source-texts and the *fiqh* rules lay the jurist as interpreter who, as a product of a curriculum of training, derived rules of law.

The different legal opinions and rationales illuminate why "*fiqh*" is a particulary appropriate term for these rulings, given that they represent a human attempt to understand God's will. The Arabic triliteral root *f-q-h* linguistically refers to the capacity and effort to understand, all the while implicitly recognizing, in the context of law, the epistemic vulnerability of any legal determination.[107] Premodern jurists were well aware of the need to interpret; but they also recognized that the inescapability of interpretation introduced a degree of indeterminacy and fallibility into the law. Too much indeterminacy and fallibility could undermine the authority of the law and thereby the confidence in an enterprise of governance whose legitimacy was in part dependent on enforcing that law.

To embrace the imperative of interpretation and to limit its adverse implications on the authority of the law and the enterprise of governance, jurists debated about the appropriate qualifications for and scope of legal interpretation. Their concern about authority and its limits, in large part, animated their debates about *ijtihād* and feeds the present study's interest in the boundaries of Sharīʿa as a claim space. Furthermore, given that jurists were the ones engaging in *ijtihād,* the theoretical debates on the conditions for engaging in *ijtihād* beg further questions about the authority of legal doctrines proffered by an interpretive agent who was

[106] For a fuller discussion of this issue, see Emon, "*Ḥuqūq Allāh,*" 358–72.
[107] See Emon, "*To Most Likely Know the Law.*"

himself conditioned by the constitutive features of the claim space of Sharīʿa, given his presumed education and qualifications.

To expound upon the authority of *ijtihādic* legal arguments, jurists asked whether every jurist was correct in his opinion (*hal kullu al-mujtahid muṣīb*?). Where juristic disagreement (*ikhtilāf*) existed (as illustrated by the above example on theft and compensation), was one view right and the others wrong? What did it mean to be right or wrong? The question of right and wrong assumes an objective, true answer, which is separate and distinct from whether a legal ruling carries authority. For instance, to use the United States as an example, suppose different US Federal Appeals Courts reach different conclusions on a single point of law, and there is no Supreme Court to resolve the conflict. To ask which court is right or wrong is distinct from asking whether and to what extent each decision is authoritative. Of course, even if people accept the authority of different rulings, they will still be tempted to ask which court "got it right."

Premodern Muslim jurists were divided between emphasizing the authority of different rulings and focusing on which legal opinion "got it right."[108] One school, called the *mukhaṭṭiʾa,* focused on the substantive content of the legal conclusion, namely its "rightness" and "wrongness"; they argued that not all jurists were correct. Instead, there was only one right answer to a substantive legal question. The other school, called the *muṣawwiba,* changed the import of the debate by suggesting implicitly that the focus on rightness and wrongness overlooked and ignored the issues of authority and epistemology. Instead, they held that all juristic interpretations were authoritative. For them, there was no single right answer; rather, they based the authority of the legal conclusion, in large part, on the epistemic excellence of the interpreter.[109]

The dispute was intimately related to a more metaphysical (if not deterministic) question, namely whether God has a specific rule of law (*ḥukm muʿayyan*) in mind? To suggest that God has a specific rule of law in mind at all times assumes a theology in which God is intimately and directly involved in the regulation of human conduct. Hence, the purpose of juristic analysis would thereby be to discover what God has already decreed. Alternatively, to argue that God has no specific rule in mind for any potential situation suggests a different theology about God,

[108] See Abou El Fadl, *Speaking in God's Name*, 147–50.

[109] While the *muṣawwiba* were focused on the theory of authority, they were also embedded in a social and institutional context of legal learning and institutions. Hence, while they may hold that jurists who exert epistemic excellence will issue authoritative opinions, other factors that contribute to authority are external to the issue of interpretive excellence, such as law school affiliation.

and thereby implies that law is a much more creative and constructive enterprise. Legal analysis, given this latter theological view, would be less about finding or discovering the immanent law and more about constructing a legal rule that is mindful of God but nonetheless responsive to the highly contingent realities of everyday life.

Those who believed there was only one right answer justified their position by reference to two *ḥadīths*. In the first one, Muḥammad stated: "There are three types of judgments: one leads to heaven and two lead to hell. The one leading to heaven [concerns] one who knows the truth and decides in accordance with it. One who knows the truth but deviates from ruling [according to it] goes to hell, and one who ignorantly adjudicates for the people goes to hell."[110] This tradition sets up the importance of epistemic excellence in adjudication. Even if one adjudicates but is ignorant, the adjudicator is condemned for lacking the appropriate expertise to undertake the task he ultimately did anyway. Whether the ignorant adjudicator gets the "right" answer does not seem to matter. As Ibn Qayyim al-Jawziyya wrote, "whoever adjudicates in a state of ignorance will go to hell, even if his judgment is right."[111] Of course, this should not render the substantive judgment irredeemable. Its provenance may raise doubts about its authority, but presumably that could be rectified by a later jurist who fulfills the necessary due diligence.

The second *ḥadīth* was critically important to the right answer thesis. In it, Muḥammad said: "When a judge interprets to adjudicate and gets the right answer, he receives two rewards. If he adjudicates and gets the wrong answer, he gets one reward."[112] This *ḥadīth*'s meaning, however, draws upon an implicit intertextuality between it and the first *ḥadīth* noted above. In other words, the reference to the judge in the second *ḥadīth* should be read as invoking someone with the requisite training and expertise to engage in *ijtihād*. When reading the two traditions together, the second *ḥadīth* assumes that those who are rewarded for their *ijtihād*—whether right or wrong—performed their due diligence

[110] Ibn Qayyim al-Jawziyya, *ʿAwn al-Maʿbūd: Sharḥ Sunan Abī Dāwūd* (Beirut: Dār al-Kutub al-ʿIlmiyya, 1998), 9:353; Ibn Mājah, *al-Sunan*, eds Muḥammad Nāṣir al-Dīn al-Albānī and ʿAlī al-Ḥalabī al-Atharī (Riyadh: Maktabat al-Maʿārif, 1998), 2:522. For reference to this tradition, see also al-Nawawī, *Sharḥ Ṣaḥīḥ Muslim*, 11/12: 240; Ibn Ḥajar al-ʿAsqalānī, *Fatḥ al-Bārī*, 13:319.

[111] Ibn Qayyim al-Jawziyya, *ʿAwn al-Maʿbūd*, 9:353.

[112] For various accounts of this tradition, see Ibn Mājah, *al-Sunan*, 2:522; Abū Bakr b. al-ʿArabī, *Āriḍat al-Aḥwadhī bī Sharḥ Ṣaḥīḥ al-Tirmidhī* (Beirut: Dār al-Kutub al-ʿIlmiyya, 1997), 6:56–7; al-Mubārak Fūrī, *Tuḥfat al-Aḥwadhī bi Sharḥ Jāmiʿ al-Tirmidhī* (Beirut: Dār al-Kutub al-ʿIlmiyya, n.d.), 4:463; Ibn Qayyim al-Jawziyya, *ʿAwn al-Maʿbūd*,, 9:353–7; al-Nawawī, *Sharḥ Saḥīḥ Muslim*, 12:239–41; al-ʿAynī, *ʿUmdat al-Qārī*, 25:100–1; Ibn Ḥajar al-ʿAsqalānī, *Fatḥ al-Bārī*, 13:318–20.

and ruled in accordance with their investigation and a thorough analysis.[113] If someone is ignorant, he receives no reward whatsoever for his effort and arguably commits a sin by judging at all, given the tradition about the ignorant who adjudicate.[114]

For the *muṣawwiba,* the implications of *ijtihād* had less to do with being right or wrong, but rather with the authority of a legally reasoned conclusion. Summarizing the *muṣawwiba* position, al-Āmidī (d. 631/1233) wrote:

> every *mujtahid* is correct in legal matters. The rule of God (*ḥukm Allāh*) on the matter is not singular, but rather follows the considered opinion of the *mujtahid* (*ẓann al-mujtahid*). Hence the rule of God in the case of each *mujtahid* is the product of his *ijtihād* that leads him to a preponderance of opinion [on the subject].[115]

A legal determination is "correct" (i.e., authoritative) not because it corresponds to a pre-existing truth in the mind of God, but rather because of the quality of the jurist's investigation and his high degree of confidence (*ghalabat al-ẓann*) about his conclusion.[116]

This brief discussion on Islamic interpretation identifies a dichotomy between legal archaeologists (*mukhaṭṭi'a*) and legal constructivists (*muṣawwiba*). The former sought to discover the substantive content of the divine will, which they presumed must exist at all times and for all issues, and can be unearthed by employing the appropriate methods, techniques, and approaches to discover it. The latter did not adopt the same view of God's will.

Yet, the constructivists' rejection of the archaeological position should not lead one to think they disregarded the divine will as part of a legal analysis, or were untroubled by the indeterminacy in the law that their

[113] Ibn Mājah, an early *ḥadīth* collector, read the first tradition as a gloss on the second when he says: "when the judge exerts interpretive analysis, he goes to heaven" (*inna al-qāḍī idhā ijtahada fa-huwa fī al-janna*). One can know the truth or deviate from the truth. But for Ibn Mājah, what determines whether one goes to hell or heaven will be whether he engages in *ijtihād* from a position of knowledge. Ibn Mājah, *al-Sunan,* 2:522.

[114] Al-Nawawī, *Sharḥ Saḥīḥ Muslim,* 11/12:240; al-ʿAynī, *ʿUmdat al-Qārī,* 25:100–1; Ibn Ḥajar al-ʿAsqalānī, *Fatḥ al-Bārī,* 13:318–19; Ibn Qayyim al-Jawziyya, *ʿAwn al-Maʿbūd,* 9:353–4; al-Mubārak Fūrī, *Tuḥfat al-Aḥwadhī,* 4:463. For a list of requisite qualifications that enable one to engage in *ijtihād,* see Ibn Qayyim al-Jawziyya, *ʿAwn al-Maʿbūd,* 9:354.

[115] Al-Āmidī, *al-Iḥkām,* 4:183. See also ʿAbd al-ʿAzīz b. Aḥmad al-Bukhārī, *Kashf al-Asrār ʿan Uṣūl Fakhr al-Islām al-Bazdawī,* ed. Muḥammad al-Muʿtaṣim bi Allāh al-Baghdādī (Beirut: Dār al-Kitāb al-ʿArabī, 1997), 4:33; al-Ghazālī, *al-Mustaṣfā min ʿIlm al-Uṣūl,* 2:363.

[116] Abū al-Ḥusayn al-Baṣrī, *al-Muʿtamad fī Uṣūl al-Fiqh* (Beirut: Dār al-Kutub al-ʿIlmiyya, n.d.), 2:373–4, 381–2. See also al-Ghazālī, *al-Mustaṣfā* (Baghdad), 2:363; al-Juwaynī, *Kitāb al-Ijtihād,* 31; Ibn al-Najjār, *Sharḥ Kawkab al-Munīr: Mukhtaṣar al-Taḥrīr,* eds Muḥammad al-Zuḥaylī and Nazīr Ḥammād (Riyadh: Maktabat al-ʿUbaykān, 1997), 4:492.

position made possible. For many *muṣawwiba* jurists, the authority of a legal conclusion depended in part on whether it posed a close proximity (*al-ashbah*) to what God would want, *had God provided determinate evidence for this issue.* As is often formulaically expressed in the subjunctive tense, the *al-ashbah* rule is what God would have ruled had He legislated on the matter (*lau naṣṣa Allāh ʿalā al-ḥukm, la-naṣṣa ʿalayhi*).[117] By using the subjunctive tense in Arabic, the *muṣawwiba* showed respect for the will of God, empowered jurists to interpret, and granted authority to their *ijtihādic* product in a manner akin to the *mukhaṭṭi'a* jurists. According to the *muṣawwiba,* there is only one *al-ashbah;* all others are wrong.[118] However, by using the subjunctive tense, they were able to argue that although the *al-ashbah* may be singular, it is only a hypothetical rule. It is the rule that would have existed had God actually ruled; but He did not. Hence, there may be only one *ashbah* ruling, but it is not one that anyone can necessarily articulate with determinacy. As much as the *muṣawwiba* endorsed a constructive view of law, they could not ignore the importance of objectivity and determinacy to the law's claim of authority. Their theory of the *al-ashbah,* expressed in the subjunctive tense, allowed them to posit a type of objectivity in the law while also granting their *ijtihādic* product necessary authority.

Despite their apparent differences, the *mukhaṭṭi'a* and *muṣawwiba* jurists did not, nor could they, claim that a jurist could ascertain the true ruling in all its glorious certainty. For instance, assuming the *mukhaṭṭi'a* presumption about a right answer to be true, there is no guarantee on their own theory of *ijtihād* that any particular jurist would or could necessarily find it. In other words, while they believed there is one true answer in a metaphysical sense, they also knew there was no epistemically coherent way to know it with certitude. Consequently, all that remains are juristic opinions (*fiqh*) that, while perhaps not necessarily "right," can still offer authoritative guidance to those living in the world. At most a jurist could develop a legal argument that enjoyed a degree of authority based on the quality of investigation and the jurist's most informed opinion, or in other words *ghalabat al-ẓann.*[119]

With the phrase *ghalabat al-ẓann,* the two schools of thought suddenly elide as their initially distinct jurisprudential starting points coalesce around the issue of authority. *Ghalabat al-ẓann,* which can be translated as "the preponderance of opinion," reflects the authority of a legal argument that, at the same time, preserves one's epistemic humility before an

[117] Al-Baṣrī, *al-Muʿtamad,* 2:371. [118] Al-Baṣrī, *al-Muʿtamad,* 2:371.

[119] Muḥammad al-Asmandī, *Badhl al-Naẓar fī al-Uṣūl,* ed. Muḥammad Zakī ʿAbd al-Barr (Cairo: Maktabat Dār al-Turāth, 1992), 695, 707.

infinite God, grants epistemic authority to the *fiqh* rulings, and links that authority to the legitimacy of an enterprise of governance applying and enforcing *fiqh* rules on the bodies of those subject to its sovereignty. As al-Juwaynī said: "The Lord made the *ghalabat al-ẓann* of each jurist [a sufficient standard of] knowledge for adjudicating by one's considered opinion. No disagreement arises on this [point]."[120] Despite the debate on the metaphysical objectivity of the law, and whether a juristic opinion can be right or wrong, jurists of both theoretical persuasions were left with a particular reality—the imperative to provide a rule of decision given the demands of human existence, the inescapability of conflicts requiring resolution, and an enterprise of governance that was generally tasked with the authority to adjudicate and enforce such resolutions.

The premodern jurist al-Ghazālī offered an example concerning military conquest that illustrates how theoretical concerns about epistemic authority and the authority of legal interpretations directly implicated an enterprise of governance. Suppose a Muslim army faces an enemy who uses Muslims as human shields. The Muslim army is unsure whether, by not firing on the human shields, the enemy will defeat the Muslim army and exterminate the Muslim lands it protects. According to al-Ghazālī, the Muslim soldiers can fire on the enemy, and thereby kill the innocent human shields, only as long as they are so confident as to be nearly certain that the enemy would otherwise over-run Muslim lands. The Muslim army commanders must reach either "certainty or a degree of likelihood that approximates certainty" (*al-qaṭʿ aw ẓann qarīb min al-qaṭʿ*) concerning the threat the enemy poses.[121] The key term of art in this phrase is *ẓann,* which is translated as "degree of likelihood." This is the same term in the phrase *ghalabat al-ẓann,* or preponderance of opinion. In both cases, the term *ẓann* simultaneously connotes an authoritative norm, but one that is not so authoritative as to preclude the possibility of critique. For the purpose of al-Ghazālī's hypothetical, *ẓann* operates as a grant of legitimacy to the military to engage in an act with unfortunate consequences. Whether the Muslim army might owe compensation to the families of the Muslim human shields killed in the process, al-Ghazālī did not say. The point of his hypothetical, though, was to establish a base-level of epistemic analysis that could justify and legitimate a particular act undertaken by or on behalf of the enterprise of governance.

[120] Abū al-Ma'ali Al-Juwaynī, *Kitāb al-Talkhīṣ fī Uṣūl al-Fiqh*, eds ʿAbd Allāh al-Nibalī and Shabbir Aḥmad al-ʿAmrī (Beirut: Dār al-Bashā'ir al-Islāmiyya, 1996), 3:352; See also al-Khaṭīb al-Baghdādi, *Kitāb al-Faqīh wa al-Mutafaqqih* (Cairo: Zakariyya ʿAlī Yūsuf, 1977), 247.

[121] Al-Ghazālī, *al-Mustaṣfā*, 1:644–5.

The debates on *ijtihād* certainly raise important metaphysical questions about truth and knowledge. But regardless of a jurist's metaphysical starting point, none could avoid the imperative to grant authority to a legal interpretation reached with due diligence, despite its unavoidable uncertainty. Granting authority to such legal interpretations had two important implications on the contours and boundaries of the claim space of Sharīʿa. First, the grant of authority allowed the legal interpretation to assume authority over and against others. Or to put it in terms that relate to Sharīʿa as Rule of Law, by granting authority to such legal rulings, jurists enabled and empowered the enterprise of governance to apply and enforce such law justifiably and legitimately through its various institutions and its coercive power. Second, by framing the authority of a given legal interpretation in terms of its epistemic vulnerability, the jurists also ensured that no one, whether jurist or governing official, could overstep the bounds of their capacity and authority. The legitimacy an enterprise of governance could claim by enforcing such rules was, by definition, limited given the epistemic limits in any interpretive endeavor. By building into the authority of a legal ruling an inherent epistemic vulnerability, the legitimacy of any claim about the demands of justice could never be absolute.

5.6 THE MODERN STATE AND THE DISRUPTIONS OF HISTORY ON THE CLAIM SPACE OF SHARĪʿA

Thus far, this chapter has been devoted to exploring various premodern aspects of Islamic legal history that allow us to appreciate the conditions of intelligibility for premodern Islamic legal doctrines, such as the *dhimmī* rules. This chapter has highlighted a selection of those conditions, ranging from educational institutions and curricula; epistemic theories of authority; and the enterprise of governance. In the aggregate, these features or conditions of intelligibility helped to constitute the boundaries of the premodern conception of the claim space of Sharīʿa. As argued above, the intelligibility of premodern rules of *fiqh* is better appreciated by taking into account conditions such as these, which collectively defined, demarcated, and gave shape to the claim space of Sharīʿa, from which arguments about justice were made. If the intelligibility of *fiqh* rules can be revealed by accounting for these constitutive conditions of Sharīʿa, then it necessarily follows that the premodern intelligibility of *fiqh* rules is disrupted when the constitutive features of the claim space of Sharīʿa are changed, altered, or modified.

The boundaries of the Rule of Law claim space can shift for a variety of reasons. In the Islamic context, such shifts arose as a result of colonial domination; the rise of the modern state system; and a diversification (as well as internationalization) of legal education, legal disputes, and legal adjudication. The premodern image of Sharīʿa as Rule of Law today suffers from a discontinuity brought on by European colonialism and the introduction of the modern state in an international system of equally sovereign states. When we speak of Islamic law today, we must recognize that we are subject to a distinctively different enterprise of governance than what animated the premodern juristic imagination. We are also embedded in a context of considerable legal pluralism, wherein the historical tradition of Sharīʿa offers only one among many traditions that can and do constitute the boundaries of the claim spaces of modern states. This last section offers a brief account of the shifts and changes in the way the modern state governs (in contrast to the imperial vision discussed earlier). Those shifts not only redefined the boundaries of the claim space of Sharīʿa, but also the very intelligibility of a Sharīʿa-based argument today.

5.6.1 Colonialism and the narrowing space for Sharīʿa

Since the eighteenth century, the institutional structure that gave real-world significance to Islamic law began to be dismantled or modified by colonial powers. Islamic law posed a challenge for colonial administrators. On the one hand, it offered a local, indigenous tradition of law and order that could not be forcefully removed without engendering massive protest and opposition to colonial administration. On the other hand, the more Islamic law remained part of the socio-legal and political fabric, the more it could be utilized as part of any opposition movement against colonial regimes. In the colonial period, Islam had "played an important role in mobilization against European colonial rule in nearly all Muslim countries," and administrators reasoned that to support the prevailing Islamic legal systems would undermine the colonial venture.[122] Consequently, the colonial period marked a decrease in the degree to which Islamic law was given authority and jurisdiction.

For instance, to protect Europeans living in the Ottoman Empire to conduct and manage trade relations, Western powers negotiated "Capitulation" agreements with the Ottoman sultan, which in part

[122] Allan Christelow, *Muslim Law Courts and the French Colonial State in Algeria* (Princeton: Princeton University Press, 1985), 6–7.

immunized European foreigners from the jurisdiction of the Ottoman courts of law.[123] Their cases were adjudicated by consuls representing the different European countries. Commercial disputes between foreigners and indigenous parties were heard before special tribunals adjudicated by both foreign and Ottoman judges, or were heard before ordinary Ottoman courts generally with the presence of a consular official.[124] As Ottoman leaders looked to Europe for financial investment and deeper economic relations, they were asked to grant foreigners greater immunities from the application of Sharīʿa law, thereby expanding consular jurisdiction in managing the legal affairs of foreigners.

However, granting consular officials jurisdiction to hear such cases contributed to a degree of indeterminacy in legal outcomes. From the chaos of venues that arose with consular jurisdiction, the Mixed Court was established in Egypt to adjudicate cases involving foreign interests, i.e., where one of the parties was a foreigner or where a foreign interest was implicated even if both parties were native Egyptians. Gradually, the Mixed Court acquired greater jurisdiction.[125]

In places like Algeria in the nineteenth century, French colonial officials restructured the prevailing Sharīʿa legal system to create an active commercial market in land with favorable implications for colonial entrepreneurs. Under the prevailing Islamic legal system, much of the land was tied up in family *awqāf* (sing. *waqf*), or trusts, that were held in perpetuity under Islamic law. The Islamic *waqf* structure ensured that property would remain in a family's possession without being dismantled into smaller fragments by the Islamic laws of inheritance. But this Islamic legal arrangement undermined French interests in buying and cultivating land for industrial purposes, and ultimately in creating a land market of freely alienable property. As David Powers writes,

> To exploit the colony's important agricultural and mineral resources, France had settled increasing numbers of its civilians in the Algerian countryside...It was essential that the government facilitate the colonists' acquisition of Muslim land and assure them of their rights...To this end, the French endeavored to elaborate a new system of property law that favored the colonists.[126]

[123] Jasper Y. Brinton, *The Mixed Courts of Egypt*, rev. ed. (New Haven: Yale University Press, 1968), 4.

[124] Brinton, *The Mixed Courts*, 4.

[125] For a history of the Mixed Courts of Egypt, see Brinton, *The Mixed Courts*.

[126] David S. Powers, "Orientalism, Colonialism, and Legal History: The Attack on Muslim Family Endowments in Algeria and India," *Comparative Studies in Society and History* 31, no. 3 (1989): 535–71, 539–40.

To challenge the continuity of these family *awqāf*, two tactics were adopted: marginalize Islamic law by substituting new legal orders, and reinterpret and re-assert Islamic law for Muslims, who were deemed unable to see the truth of their own tradition.[127] However, as Powers explains, the new legal regimes were not sufficient to settle the matter of *waqf* land held in perpetuity. While the government developed new legislative schemes, French jurists began expounding on various features of Islamic law, in particular the family *waqf*. As Powers notes, French orientalist scholars redefined "Islamic law so that it would be in harmony with French legal conceptions."[128]

Importantly, this pattern of limiting or removing the jurisdiction of Sharīʿa-based doctrines and institutions was not perpetuated only by colonial administrators and officials. It was done by Muslim elites themselves, working within the prevailing systems of governance while contending with the increasing plurality of legal regimes with which they came into contact. For instance, in the late nineteenth century, the Ottoman Empire initiated a series of legal reforms that involved adopting and mimicking European legal codes as substitutes for Islamic legal traditions.[129] This imitation of form should not be viewed narrowly as an attempt to modernize by abandoning the Islamic tradition. Frederick F. Anscombe offers an important insight into the logic of this Ottoman reform period, known as the *Tanzimat*. Given domestic contests over power and legitimacy within the Ottoman Empire, the *Tanzimat* were attempts to modernize, but not at the cost of Islam; on the contrary, Anscombe argues that the reforms were meant to bolster the regime's religiously based legitimacy. Although labelled as "westernization," such reforms, when considered alongside prevailing domestic political issues, were "fundamentally shaped by, and for, Muslim interests: healing divisions within the community of believers, reconciling their enduring goals, and concentrating their energies upon defense against external threats."[130] Nevertheless, for the purposes of this study, the *Tanzimat* reforms and others like them were indigenous responses to colonial advancement and legal imposition. In the language of post-colonial theory, they might be understood as subaltern resistance against colonial domination. In offering their own interpretations and codifications of

[127] Powers, "Orientalism, Colonialism, and Legal History."

[128] Powers, "Orientalism, Colonialism, and Legal History," 543.

[129] The reforms emanating from this period are called collectively, the Tanzimat. For a history of the reforms in this period, see Herbert J. Liebesny, *The Law of the Near & Middle East: Readings, Cases and Materials* (Albany: State University of New York Press, 1975), 46–117.

[130] Frederick F. Anscombe, "Islam and the Age of Ottoman Reform," *Past and Present* 208 (August 2010): 159–89, 160.

Islamic law, Muslim elites challenged the occupier's treatment of Islamic law. But they did so by attempting to fit Islamic law into a new legal mold defined in terms of the modern European state as the prevailing enterprise of governance.[131]

Premodern Islamic law was characterized by a multiplicity of opinions, different doctrinal schools, and competing theories of interpretive analysis. In the Ottoman reform period, this complex substantive and theoretical diversity was reduced through a selective process of codification. For instance, when Muslims began to codify Islamic law, such as when the Ottomans drafted the first Islamic code *The Majalla*,[132] they had to decide which rules would dominate. Would they create a Ḥanafī, Mālikī, Ḥanbalī, or Shāfiʿī code for those countries that were mostly Sunnī? And what would they do about their Shīʿa population? Often, these reformers would pick and choose from different doctrinal schools to reach what they felt was the best outcome. This process of selection (*takhayyur*) and harmonization (*talfīq*) of conflicting aspects of premodern opinions allowed reformers to present a version of Islamic law that both drew upon the premodern *fiqh* tradition and paralleled the European model of law in form and structure. In doing so, however, they reduced Islamic law to a set of positivist legal assertions divorced from the historical, institutional, and jurisprudential context that contributed to the intelligibility of the legal docrines.[133] In other words, their reform efforts led to new boundaries for the claim space of law, which thereby impinged upon the premodern content and the intelligibility of Sharīʿa-based doctrines. In other words, the claim space changed, and thereby recast the role Sharīʿa-based doctrines could and would play. The doctrines may have remained the same, but their intelligibility altered with the change in the enterprise of governance. The continuity of premodern Islamic legal doctrines in this new climate begs an important question about the intelligibility of such doctrines in a modified claim space of legal argument.

As another example from an institutional perspective, in 1883 the Egyptian Government adopted the Napoleonic Code as its civil law and created national courts to administer that Code. The result was three

[131] For a brief study of how subaltern communities might fit their indigenous custom or law within models or frameworks that put their respective traditions in at least the same form as the imposed law of the colonialist, see Sally Engle Merry, "Law and Colonialism," *Law and Society Review* 25, no. 4 (1991): 89–122.

[132] For an English translation of the *Majalla*, see C.R. Tyser et al, trans., *The Mejelle: Being an English Translation of Majallah El-Ahkam-I-Adliya and a Complete Code on Islamic Civil Law* (Kuala Lumpur: The Other Press, 2001).

[133] On the process of doctrinal selectivity and its effect on the nature of Sharīʿa, see Hallaq, "Can the Sharīʿa Be Restored?", 210.

Egyptian court systems: the Mixed Courts, the secular National Courts, and the Sharīʿa courts.[134] Then, in 1949 Egypt adopted a uniform civil code borrowed mostly from the French Civil Code, and which also incorporated minimal elements of Islamic law. Subsequently, in 1955 the Sharīʿa courts were disbanded in the country.[135]

These examples illustrate how, under colonial influence, the space for Sharīʿa diminished as legal reforms were implemented, thereby creating a claim space whose boundaries were defined no longer by Sharīʿa-based doctrines or even presuppositions of an imperial enterprise of governance. Rather, in the colonial context, the intelligibility of prior Sharīʿa-based doctrines, to the extent they were even applied, assumed a new meaning and significance. They were embedded in highly pluralist legal contexts in which the Rule of Law claim space was no longer defined in the same way premodern Muslim jurists may have assumed.

5.6.2 Sharīʿa and the modern Muslim state

These alterations of the boundaries of the Sharīʿa claim space do not mean that Sharīʿa has no place or authoritative role in modern Muslim majority states. Rather, it means that the tradition of Sharīʿa has become a constitutive feature of the modern claim space of Rule of Law. That modern claim space is no longer framed by an imperial enterprise of governance, but rather by a sovereign state enterprise of governance. The state coexists and cooperates with other sovereign states in an international arena characterized by bi-lateral and multi-lateral treaty relations, increasing global cooperation (e.g., UN, WTO, G20, EU), and an international legal regime that, in the name of human rights, attempts to penetrate the boundaries of the state, and thereby influence and even constitute a modern state's claim space of justice (e.g., International Criminal Court). In other words, the Rule of Law frame allows us to appreciate how the constitutive features that once defined and delimited the claim space of Sharīʿa have so fundamentally shifted that the intelligibility of contemporary Sharīʿa-based claims that draw upon premodern legal doctrines (*fiqh*) differ radically from how they would be understood if they were utilized in a premodern context and under different conditions of governance.

[134] For a discussion of the gradual demise of Sharīʿa courts in Egypt, see Nathan Brown, *The Rule of Law in the Arab World: Courts in Egypt and the Gulf* (Cambridge: Cambridge University Press, 1997).

[135] For a historical account detailing the move from Islamic to secular law in Egypt, see Brown, *The Rule of Law in the Arab World*, esp. 61–92.

The following four examples will illustrate how modern Rule of Law systems shift the conditions of intelligibility of Sharīʿa-based doctrines. For instance, the modern legal curriculum in law schools across the Muslim world is substantially different from what prevailed in the premodern *madrasa.* The course of study to become a legal specialist in the premodern period involved considerable study of source-texts such as the Qurʾān and *ḥadīth* of the Prophet, theories of interpretation and legal reasoning, theology, and so on. In Muslim states where Islamic law is a feature of the legal system, students of law still take courses in Islamic law and legal methodology. However, as Lama Abu-Odeh recounts her legal eduction in Jordan, law students only take two or three courses on Islamic law during the course of legal study, which often spans a number of years.[136]

A second example concerns the drafting of modern civil codes and the space for Islamic legal content in determining the law of Muslim states. For instance, when ʿAbd al-Razzāq al-Sanhūrī drafted the Egyptian Civil Code of 1949, he relied heavily on the French Civil Code. He was careful, though, to create some space for the potential contribution of Islamic law to the new Egyptian legal order. Reducing the meaning of Sharīʿa to doctrinal premodern rules of law (or *fiqh*), he held that the *fiqh* could fill in any lacuna in the Code or customary law, so long as no *fiqh* ruling contravened a general principle of the Code.[137]

A third example, related to the second one just noted, concerns the limited extent to which Islamic legal doctrines are actually legislated and applied in Muslim countries. The one field of Islamic legal doctrine that is most commonly found in modern state legal systems is Islamic family law (*al-aḥwāl al-shakhṣiya*).[138] Both colonial administrators and Muslim nationalist assemblies preserved Islamic family law in codified form while modernizing other legal areas such as commercial law, contract law, property law, and so on. Indeed, Muslim majority states often implement modified versions of premodern Islamic family law in modern personal status codes,[139] while borrowing or modifying legislative schemes from European and North American states on matters of obligations, procedure, commercial law, finance, and so on.[140] This preservation of family law

[136] Abu-Odeh, "Politics of (Mis)recognition," 791.

[137] ʿAbd al-Razzāq al-Sanhūrī, *al-Wasīṭ fī Sharḥ al-Qānūn al-Madanī al-Jadīd*, ed. Aḥmad al-Marāghī (Cairo: Dar al-Nahda al-ʿArabiyya, 2007), 1:44–50.

[138] For an introduction to the premodern doctrinal tradition of family law and its implementation in modern states in the Muslim world, see Jamal J. Nasir, *The Islamic Law of Personal Status*, 3rd ed. (London: Graham & Trotman, 2002).

[139] For a study on the development of Jordan's Islamic family law regime, see Lynn Welchman, "The Development of Islamic Family Law in the Legal System of Jordan," *International and Comparative Law Quarterly* 37, no. 4 (1988): 868–86.

[140] Abu-Odeh, "The Politics of (Mis)recognition," 789, 791.

arguably placated Islamists who felt threatened by modernization and considered the preservation of traditional Islamic family law to be necessary to maintain an Islamic identity in the face of an encroaching modernity.[141] Yet the preservation of these premodern doctrines in modern statutory format runs contrary to these same states' commitments to human rights treaties, many of which address, for instance, gender equality. The conflict between these two regimes, of law (Islamic family law and human rights law) raises important questions about the intelligibility of these states' family law regimes in large part because modern Muslim states not only legislate premodern Islamic family law, but they also ratify international human rights treaties and appear before treaty bodies to account for and explain their effort (or failure) to improve the conditions of gender equality under their domestic legal regimes.[142]

A fourth and final example involves the resort to constitutionalism as a means of imposing structure and limits on the state and protecting the rights of the state's subjects, such as religious minorities, for example.

[141] Locating an authentic past on the bodies of women within the family has been used to construct modern national identities in post-colonial societies where the past provides an authentic basis for the national identity of new states immersed in a modern world. Traditional family law regimes may be used to bring the values of the past into the present national consciousness to provide a sense of identity in opposition to the norms perceived to emanate from the colonizing world. For an excellent analysis of women, family, and nationalism, see Anne McClintock, "Family Feuds: Gender, Nationalism and the Family," *Feminist Review* 44 (1993): 61–80. For studies on Islamic law, women, and the state, see Denise Kandiyoti, "Women, Islam and the State," *Middle East Report* 173 (1991): 9–14; Mervat F. Hatem, "Modernization, the State, and the Family in Middle East Women's Studies," in *A Social History of Women & Gender in the Modern Middle East*, eds Margaret Meriwether and Judith E. Tucker (Boulder, Colorado: Westview Press, 1999), 63–87. One exception to this colonial-inspired narrative about the narrowing of Sharīʿa is the case of Saudi Arabia. Colonial powers did not seem to exert as much control over Saudi Arabia, and consequently the colonial narrative does not universally apply across the Muslim world. However, I would suggest that the narrative about the reduction of Sharīʿa is not dependent on colonization as its only topos. Rather, the colonial topos is only part of the narrative, which fundamentally involves a relationship between power, law, and the formation of political/nationalist identities. For instance, colonists used a reductive but determinate notion of Islamic law to bolster their legitimacy and ensure administrative efficiency, while also marginalizing the tradition when necessary to attain colonial goals. Likewise, the Saud family's use of Wahhabism as an ideological narrative that trumped tribal loyalties in the Najd, has also allowed the Saudi state to utilize a reductive, often literalist approach to Islamic law to bolster its own political legitimacy and authority.

[142] On the conflict between Islamic family law and international human rights law, see Women Living Under Muslim Laws, *Knowing Our Rights: Women, Family, Laws and Customs in the Muslim World* (New Delhi: Zubaan, 2003); Ann Elizabeth Mayer, *Islam and Human Rights: Tradition and Politics*, 3rd ed. (Boulder: Westview Press, 1998). For an analysis of the dialogue between international treaty bodies and Muslim states regarding gender equality, see Ann Elizabeth Mayer, "Internationalizing the Conversation on Women's Rights: Arab Countries Face the CEDAW Committee," in *Islamic Law and the Challenges of Modernity*, eds Yvonne Yazbeck Yaddad and Barbara Freyer Stowasser (Walnut Creek: AltaMira Press, 2004), 133–60.

The turn to constitutionalism is particularly interesting for the purpose of this study because Muslim majority countries often incorporate Islam or Islamic law into their constitutions, while including express provisions concerning religious freedom and the treatment of religious minorities. In many cases, the reference to Islam or Islamic law is explicit yet undefined. Consequently, these constitutions raise important concerns about the definition and application of Islamic law, and how respect for Islamic law may conflict with provisions protecting religious minorities. In other words, the constitutions, by incorporating both Sharīʿa and protections for religious minorities, beg important questions about the conditions of intelligibility of such constitutions and the jurisprudence that arises therefrom.[143]

Muslim countries may specify in their constitutions that Islam is the state religion,[144] although that is not always the case.[145] Some countries specifically state that the government is secular, keeping religion and state law distinct.[146] Aside from designating a state religion, some Muslim nations also state that Islam is either "a" source or "the" source of law in the country, thereby bringing into sharp focus the constitutional significance of violating a precept of Sharīʿa law.[147]

To protect the interests of religious minorities, Muslim state constitutions may include non-discrimination clauses that protect individuals from religious discrimination. For instance, Article 18 of Bahrain's constitution reads: "People are equal in human dignity, and citizens shall be equal in public rights and duties before the law, without discrimination as to race, origin, language, religion, or belief." Article 14 of Eritrea's constitution provides: "All persons are equal before the law. No person may be discriminated against on account of race, ethnic origin, language, colour, sex, religion, disability, political belief or opinion, or social or economic status or any other factor..." Generally, the equality

[143] For analysis of the historical rules of Sharīʿa as well as critiques of how Muslim states use Sharīʿa to discriminate against non-Muslims, see Zaydan, *Ahkām al-Dhimmiyīn*; An-Na'im, *Toward an Islamic Reformation*; Dallal, "Yemeni Debates on the Status of Non-Muslims in Islamic Law," 181–92; Atabani, "Islamic Sharīʿah and the Status of Non-Muslims," 63–9; Rahman, "Non-Muslim Minorities in an Islamic State," 13–24; Faruqi, "The Rights of Non-Muslims under Islam," 43–66.

[144] See for example, Bahrain (Art. 2), Mauritania (Art. 5), Malaysia (Art. 3); Morocco (Art. 6), Saudi Arabia (Art. 1), Yemen (Art. 2), Tunisia (Art. 1).

[145] See, for example, Albania (Art. 10).

[146] See, for example, Ethiopia (Art. 11), Azerbaijan (Art. 7).

[147] See, for instance, Bahrain (Art. 2), Egypt (Art. 2), Kuwait (Art. 2), Oman (Art. 2), Qatar (Art. 1), Syria (Art. 3). For a sustained review of constitutions in the Arab world, see Nathan J. Brown, *Constitutions in a Non-Constitutional World: Arab Basic Laws and the Prospects for Accountable Government* (SUNY Press, 2001).

clauses are listed among the earliest provisions of "basic rights" and occur without limitation or restriction.

Additionally, Muslim-majority countries may include rights provisions that protect one's religious freedom. Article 29(2) of Indonesia's 1945 constitution provides: "The State guarantees all persons the freedom of worship, each according to his/her own religion or belief." Other countries adopting this unrestrictive approach include: Bosnia-Herzegovina (Art. II, Para. 3), Eritrea (Art. 19),[148] Malaysia (Art. 11), Mali (Art. 4), and Morocco (Art. 6).[149]

But some Muslim countries provide qualifying remarks concerning the scope of one's religious freedom. Article 22 of Bahrain's constitution reads: "Freedom of conscience is absolute. The State shall guarantee the inviolability of places of worship and the freedom to perform religious rites and to hold religious processions and meetings *in accordance with the customs observed in the country*."[150] Article 35 of Kuwait's constitution reads: "Freedom of belief is absolute. The State protects the freedom of practicing religion in accordance with established customs, *provided that it does not conflict with public policy or morals*."[151] Both examples illustrate how a statement of absolute freedom is coupled with ambiguous limiting language about "customs," "public policy," and "morals."

As noted earlier in the case of the *dhimmī* rules, the ambiguity of terms like "public policy" or "public good" raise important questions about who is the relevant public and what is its conception of the good or the moral. The constitutions noted above do not offer any express definition of such terms, and thereby cause concern to some that to preserve public policy, core values, or morals, the rights of individuals (i.e., religious minorities) will be curtailed and limited. As will be shown in the next chapter, this concern is not unfounded.

For the purpose of reflecting on Rule of Law as an analytic lens for understanding Sharīʿa as Rule of Law, the four examples addressed (curriculum, legal pluralism, Islamic family law, and Islamic constitutionalism) reveal how the intelligibility of Islamic legal argument today requires a close analysis of the constitutive features of a given

[148] Article 26 of the Eritrean Constitution allows for limits on the rights enumerated in the constitution on the grounds of national security, public safety, economic well-being of the country, or the public morals and public order of the nation.

[149] However, the substantive protection these provisions provide religious minorities is subject to further speculation. For instance, although Malaysia's Article 11 grants all people the right to profess and practice their religion, the Malaysia case involving Lina Joy suggests that the courts may abdicate their protective role. See Chapter 6 for an extended analysis of that case.

[150] Emphasis added. [151] Emphasis added.

claim space in a modern state context. If one were to define Sharīʿa to include the historical tradition that discriminated on both gender and religious grounds, a conflict would arise between upholding Sharīʿa and protecting certain rights and freedoms that feature prominently in global dialogues on human rights. While the constitutions noted above protect minority rights, the constitutional incorporation of Sharīʿa arguably reflects the priority of values held by the dominant religious group. Indeed, the juxtaposition of these two provisions illustrates the way in which "tolerance" as a conceptual category does not adequately address or reveal the majoritarian dynamics that lie beneath the surface of "tolerance" discourses. The mere resort to theories of accommodation or tolerance, therefore, will not adequately offer insight into the conditions of intelligibility that will allow us to appreciate the constitutive role of Sharīʿa in contemporary legal systems.

The intelligibility of constitutional provisions and family law codes in majority Muslim countries becomes evident once we accept the mutually constitutive relationship between law and the enterprise of governance, the latter being here the post-colonial Muslim-majority state. If modern Muslim state officials tend to view (or represent) Sharīʿa in terms of premodern rules of law,[152] one might wonder why the historical tradition of Islamic law should matter in the twenty-first century. Why not leave it in the past? In the wake of post-colonial nationalist movements in regions such as the Muslim world, some have argued that a "time paradox" has arisen that makes the past substantively relevant for the construction of a legitimate and authoritative modern state and national identity.[153] In the case of Muslim states, that has often meant incorporating premodern Sharīʿa-based rules explicitly into a state's legal framework, in part to bolster the state's legitimacy and authority, and to provide a symbol of post-colonial national identity. Such societies, rising out of the ashes of colonialism, have drawn upon Sharīʿa to constitute features of their legal claim space in order to simultaneously (a) distinguish themselves from their former colonial masters in terms of their national identity; (b) establish their states' legitimate authority; and (c) facilitate their states' participation on a global stage with former colonial powers. The need to be both authentic and authoritative, distinct from prior masters, and participants in a global environment has created a challenge for how a relatively new state formed in the twentieth century can gain domestic

[152] For a historical discussion on the political provenance of this particular conception of Sharīʿa, see Anver M. Emon, "Conceiving Islamic Law in a Pluralist Society"; idem, "Islamic Law and the Canadian Mosaic."
[153] McClintock. "Family Feuds."

legitimacy and distinguish itself internationally without at the same time isolating itself on the global stage.[154]

In looking to the past for a sense of identity, Muslim states certainly had options from the Islamic intellectual tradition. Perhaps Ṣufism, with its mystical tradition, could have been a source of national identity.[155] Likewise, the Islamic philosophical tradition raised considerable questions about religion, politics, and identity that could have been harnessed for creating a sense of the political self. But such substantive modes arguably lack a determinacy that, as already noted above in the case of *ijtihād*, could pose challenges to the legitmacy and authority of an enterprise of governance.

If determinacy was important for purposes of authority and legitimacy in the twentieth century's post-colonial context, it remains important for anchoring a national identity for post-colonial states in the twenty-first century. It is unsurprising that these states turned to historical Islamic legal norms (i.e., *fiqh*), since those doctrines provided an easy and efficient option for newly fashioned Muslim states in the twentieth century. The determinacy of Islamic rules of law can give content to an otherwise nascent modern state, and thereby constitute (in part) the boundaries of newly developed, modernizing legal regimes.[156] Muslim states have incorporated Islamic law in their legal systems to offer determinate content for their legal systems, and thereby contribute to the authority and legitimacy of the new Muslim majority state.[157] From a Rule of Law perspective, we can appreciate how historical doctrines have played two distinct but related roles, namely to give content to the legal regime, and to contribute to the authority and legitimacy of an enterprise of governance arising from the ashes of colonialism.[158]

[154] On how Islamic fundamentalists anchor disputes on political identity by reference to historical tradition, see Roxanne Euben, *Enemy in the Mirror: Islamic Fundamentalism and the Limits of Modern Rationalism: A Work of Comparative Political Theory* (Princeton University Press, 1999).

[155] Historians have noted how Sufi movements have provided an impetus for independence movements against colonial occupation. Itzhak Weismann, *Taste of Modernity: Sufism, Salafiyya, and Arabism in Late Ottoman Damascus* (Leiden: Brill, 2001).

[156] Euben, in her *Enemy in the Mirror*, writes about the communitarian logic underlying Islamic fundamentalism. Her important work is significant for understanding the role of tradition and its perceived continuity into the present as a basis for identity construction.

[157] In fact, the 19th-century Muslim reformer Muḥammad ʿAbduh argued that a nation's laws respond to its prevailing contexts, and thereby suggests that the meaningfulness of law depends on whether it reflects the circumstances, mores, and identity of its people: ʿAbduh, "Ikhtilāf al-Qawānīn bi Ikhtilāf Aḥwāl al-Umam," 309–15.

[158] See Hallaq, "Can the Sharīʿa be Restored?" This is especially true in light of the fact that most Muslim countries do not use Islamic law throughout their legal systems,

What this section suggests is that when examining modern Muslim countries that invoke Sharīʿa, one cannot ignore the fact that the constitutive function of Sharīʿa is both legal and political, and as such can impede attempts to reform its tenets in accordance with human rights values. Consequently, when new constitutions in the Muslim world, such as the Afghan and Iraqi Constitutions, are heralded as steps forward toward democratic government, a question necessarily arises about the extent to which religious minorities are sufficiently protected when Islamic law is also part of the constitutional legal order. This question was most prominently portrayed in 2006 when an Afghan man, Abdul Rahman, was tried in an Afghan court for abandoning the Islamic faith.[159] Likewise, Article 2 of the new Iraqi Constitution provides that no law shall violate the established tenets of Islamic law, the principles of democracy, or the basic freedoms protected under the constitution, among which are included the freedom of conscience (Article 41).[160] This provision of the Iraqi Constitution reveals quite starkly the different constitutive features that operate at both the legal and political level, giving shape to the law while also constituting the enterprise of governance in a post-conflict society.

Islamic law today is immersed within a complex, bureaucratic state system, in which Islamic law is a partial source, if even that, for legal systems that are primarily based on European models of civil law and governance.[161] But that does not mean Sharīʿa plays no role in governing society. Nor does it mean that Sharīʿa should not play a role either: to suggest as much would be to place an artificial (and likely unworkable) limit on what is often a highly dynamic and fraught political process. Indeed, the Arab revolutions of 2011 illustrate how even those who advocated for secular reforms could not and would not necessarily seek to remove or disavow Islam or Islamic movements from the kinds of reforms to pursue. For instance, Dr Rabab El-Mahdi, a professor at the

but only in piecemeal fashion in areas like family law and less often in criminal law.

[159] M. Cherif Bassiouni, "Leaving Islam is not a Capital Crime," *Chicago Tribune* (April 2, 2006), C9; Margaret Wente, "Death to the Apostate," *The Globe and Mail* (March 28, 2006), A19; Wesal Zaman and Henry Chu, "Afghan case dropped but not closed," *Los Angeles Times* (March 27, 2006), A14. For an extended analysis of that case, see Anver M. Emon, "On the Pope, Cartoons and Apostates: Shariʿa 2006," *Journal of Law and Religion* 22, no. 2 (2006–07): 303–21.

[160] For the Iraqi Constitution, see <http://www.uniraq.org/documents/iraqi_constitution.pdf> (accessed March 19, 2012).

[161] Abu-Odeh, "The Politics of (Mis)recognition."

American University of Cairo and an Egyptian political activist, reflected on the role of religion in the evolving reforms in Egypt:

> Let us first agree that "secularism" is a historical and social construct tied to time and place. Hence, both the US and France, for example, are considered secular states, but what this label means and its implications in the two contexts are quite different. So even though I believe in separating religion from politics, I do understand that political Islamism is an important current in Egypt, and that it comes in different forms—some of which are more progressive than others.[162]

The ongoing relevance of Islam and Islamic law in the Muslim world, though, does not change the fact that by taking a reductive, piecemeal, and at times ambiguous approach to Sharīʿa, colonial powers and Muslim elites fundamentally shifted the conditions of intelligibility of Sharīʿa-based normative claims. For many, Sharīʿa is rigid and static: a divine legal system comprised of dogmatic rules and incapable of revision.[163] As this study suggests, this reductive vision of Sharīʿa as rules of law (and not Rule of Law) reflects the way in which modern legal systems in Muslim states constitute a claim space where the boundaries have drastically shifted. Consequently, the modern resort to premodern rules of Sharīʿa arguably reflects less about the premodern tradition of Sharīʿa, and more about the contested conditions of legality, legitimacy, and authority in the modern post-imperial and post-colonial Muslim state.

5.7 CONCLUSION

Defining Sharīʿa is never an easy matter. Some note its lexical meaning—"a way to the watering hole"[164]—thereby emphasizing the sustaining life force that Sharīʿa offers to those who pursue and adhere to it. Others focus on the rules and treatises that reflect the substantive doctrine of the tradition.[165] Yet others concentrate on the theoretical literature of

[162] "Interview with Dr. Rabab El-Mahdi," *Middle East Law and Governance* 3, nos 1 & 2 (2011): 225–9, 227. On the distinct and divergent trends within Islamist groups, such as the Muslim Brotherhood of Egypt, see Carrie Rosefsky Wickham, "The Muslim Brotherhood and Democratic Transition in Egypt," *Middle East Law and Governance* 3, nos 1 & 2 (2011): 204–23.

[163] For a discussion of the impact the reified and static version of Islamic law had on Muslims under colonial occupation, see the excellent study by Scott Alan Kugle, "Framed, Blamed and Renamed: The Recasting of Islamic Jurisprudence in Colonial South Asia," *Modern Asian Studies* 35, no. 2 (2001): 257–313.

[164] Ibn Manẓūr, *Lisān al-ʿArab*, 8:176.

[165] Laleh Bakhtiar and Kevin Reinhart, *Encyclopedia of Islamic Law: A Compendium of the Major Schools* (Chicago: Kazi Publications, 1996).

premodern jurists in which we learn about the authoritative sources of law, methods of legal analysis, and the limits of interpretive agency.[166] Finally, others look to the role of adjudicators, such as *qāḍīs* and *muftīs*, to understand what Sharīʿa has meant in practice, as opposed to theory.[167] Each of these approaches to defining Sharīʿa is, arguably, indicative of the research interest of the particular scholar rather than of Sharīʿa as a whole. For instance, if American law professors are asked "What is American law?" any answer will no doubt be partial. Is it the institutional framework of courts, the federalist system, the casuistic method of the Common Law? Any one of these will no doubt be right, but only in part. Much more to the point, each answer will likely reflect more about the particular research emphasis of a scholar than the overall nature of the legal system.

Premodern Sharīʿa could be studied from a variety of perspectives: educational institutions and curricula; doctrinal sources; methods of adjudication; institutions of dispute resolution; relationship to the executive; and so on. The fact that each of these is a partial answer suggests that together these perspectives reflect something more than the sum of their parts. That "something more" is captured by viewing Sharīʿa as Rule of Law—a bounded claim space within which arguments of justice are made. Given the absence of any definitive definition for Rule of Law, Sharīʿa as Rule of Law reflects less any particular set of institutions or "things" out there in the world, and instead connotes a discursive site about the demands of justice in a society politically organized in terms of certain institutions, ideals, and aspirations. Whether certain institutions or models of governance were historically real or imagined by jurists as they developed their legal arguments is of less relevance than the fact that such institutions and models nonetheless informed jurists as they developed particular doctrines, such as those regulating *dhimmīs*.

The previous chapters explored how premodern *dhimmī* rules were intelligible in light of an ethic of Islamic universalism and an imperial enterprise of governance. This chapter has sought to address other constitutive elements that contributed to the intelligibility of Sharīʿa-based doctrines. As shown above, there were important features, institutional and otherwise, that both informed and disciplined jurists as they articulated legal doctrines. Such features included, but were not limited to, the following:

[166] See for example, Kamali, *Principles*; Hallaq, *A History of Islamic Legal Theories*.
[167] See for example, Powers, *Law, Society and Culture in the Maghrib*; Masud, Messick, and Powers, eds, *Islamic Legal Interpretation*.

- a tradition, professionalization, and institutionalization of learning;
- a jurisprudence that accounted for parallel, complementary, and at times conflicting sources of authority and modes of interpretation; and
- an uneasy relationship with the institutions of the enterprise of governance.

The discussion in Part I about the *dhimmī* rules highlighted how the fact of diversity forced jurists to contend with important questions about authority, identity, and sovereignty. Those questions did not arise only in the case of *dhimmīs,* but as suggested in this chapter, reflected substantive issues that animated jurists as they developed and participated in the premodern Sharīʿa profession that was itself embedded in an Islamically defined imperial enterprise of governance. Consequently, while this study centers on the *dhimmī* rules, expounding those rules is not its point. Rather, this study concentrates on the *dhimmī* rules to illustrate how minorities provide an important focus to appreciate how investigating the intelligibility of legal doctrines reveals the mutually constitutive relationship between the law and the enterprise of governance.

Furthermore, this chapter has attempted to give a historical dimension to the analytic purchase of Rule of Law. With changes in the enterprise of governance—e.g., from an imperial to a nation-state model—and alterations in the boundaries of a Rule of Law claim space, the intelligibility of an old rule developed in a different time and governance context will alter, sometimes quite fundamentally. Legal doctrines (such as the *dhimmī* rules) that had a particular intelligibility in one claim space will have a different one as the claim space changes with alterations to the underlying enterprise of governance. The history of European colonialism and the rise of the modern state in the Muslim world disrupted the premodern imagination of the enterprise of governance that gave shape and content to the claim space of Sharīʿa. Modern reforms in legal doctrines and institutions marginalized one form of legal pluralism (the pluralism of Islamic legal doctrines) to make room for a different legal pluralism, namely the legal regimes of the administrative state, the international order, customary and local norms, as well as Sharīʿa-based rules of law. Embedding Sharīʿa discourses in this modern form of legal pluralism, where Sharīʿa is limited in content and shares authority with other legal orders, has led some commentators to espouse a tragic narrative of Islamic law. That tragic narrative is characterized as a story of subordination, marginalization, and even the death of Islamic law, as new forms of law and order have assumed prominance and priority.[168]

[168] Abou El Fadl, "My Friend." See also Hallaq, "Can the Sharīʿa Be Restored?", 22.

This study avoids adopting any particular narrative about the fate of Sharīʿa. To put it differently, the issue is not about whether Sharīʿa remains alive or is dead, or is a delusion of Islamists. Indeed, even a cursory review of contemporary political science journals suggests that Islam and Islamic law are not disappearing. Far from it. Instead, what has changed is the underlying conditions of intelligibility, in particular the enterprise of governance. This change has dramatic implications on the constitution of the claim space within which Sharīʿa-based claims are made, and thereby on the intelligibility of old rules that are re-implemented in the modern state. In other words, by viewing Sharīʿa as Rule of Law, the intelligibility of legal doctrines can be tracked over time as the mutually constitutive relationship between the law and the enterprise of governance changes as each constituent element changes. This historical dimension to Rule of Law analysis presents an important implication for any methodology of Islamic legal scholarship: any change to the enterprise of governance will change the intellgibility of rules developed under one model of governance but applied in another. As the enterprise changes, so too will the claim space within which Sharīʿa-based claims are made, and thereby the conditions of intelligibility that gave meaning to premodern legal doctrines and discourses. The modern state, immersed in an international system, is beset by a plurality of legal regimes, of which Sharīʿa-based doctrines are one; all of them help define the claim space of modern Rule of Law systems, and all of them claim a degree of authority in conferring legitimacy to the governing process.

To suggest that the alteration to the conditions of intelligibility heralds the death of Sharīʿa or renders Sharīʿa a delusion is effectively to render Sharīʿa into an ideal type insulated from the conditions of goverance in which nonetheless it was and remains embedded. Envisioning Sharīʿa as Rule of Law, however, avoids such essentialization. The history of shifts in the enterprise of governance reveals a fundamental difference between the premodern imagination of the conditions of intelligibility and the modern conditions; yet what the different sets of conditions share is how both the law and the enterprise of governance are mutually constitutive, conferring content, authority, and legitimacy to each other in different and distinct ways. By avoiding the essentialization of Sharīʿa, and instead viewing Sharīʿa as Rule of Law, the reader can appreciate the multitude of ways in which the law, in this case Islamic law, is both constitutive of and constituted by the evolving context of governance, and how the circumstances of that relationship contribute to the intelligibility of a given claim about the demands of justice.

6

The *Dhimmī* Rules in the Post-Colonial Muslim State

In the twenty-first century, debates about Islamic law and the *dhimmī* rules are embedded in a social, cultural, and political context that is not only far removed from what existed centuries ago, but which also gives to the *dhimmī* rules an intelligibility that is quite different from what transpired in the premodern period. For instance, for proponents of the myth of persecution to read the *dhimmī* rules as evidence of the intolerance of Islam, from the time of the Medinan polity till today, is implicitly to ask a *modern* question about "tolerance" concerning rules of law that were answers to premodern questions of considerably different provenance than our own. The implicit question is not wrong so much as misdirected. Likewise, for Islamists to adhere to the *dhimmī* rules as an Islamic model of tolerance and pluralist community is to rely on *premodern* answers to questions that arise from modern dynamics of the international state system and transnational networks of community and exchange.

To understand the meaning and significance of the *dhimmī* rules today requires an appreciation of how the political and legal landscape has shifted since the premodern period. For instance, as suggested in Chapter 5, Muslim jurists developed their legal doctrines in the context of a discipline of legal study and a juristic profession, and were likely cognizant of the ways in which the discipline of their profession contributed to, and was also constituted by, the various features of an enterprise of governance. The jurists' discipline of inquiry rested upon theories of authority, a corpus of foundational source-texts, institutions of adjudication, and a constantly evolving and often tense relationship between them and the ruling authorities. The previous chapters have shown how premodern Muslim jurists developed legal rules pursuant to their interpretive authority, which was itself embedded in a discipline, culture, and institutional setting of education, precedent, principles, and doctrines.[1]

Additionally, though, Part I showed that premodern Muslim jurists developed their legal doctrines, such as those on the *dhimmī,* in light of an imperial image of an Islamically defined enterprise of governance. Premodern jurists were immersed not only in a context of legal education and the juristic profession, but also within an institutional context of governance that they imagined could transform their juristic rulings into enforced legal rules. The governance frameworks for adjudication and enforcement were the means by which Sharīʿa-based doctrines were applied to actual cases in controversy. Whether deciding rules of pleading, sentencing, or litigation, for instance, jurists derived and constructed rules and individual entitlements in light of their assumption that conflicts would be resolved by an institution of adjudication that in part constituted the Islamic enterprise of governance.[2] Indeed, as suggested throughout Part I, jurists' assumptions of an imperial enterprise of governance—with its institutions of administration and enforcement—contributed in part not only to the content of the law, but also to its intelligibility.

As argued toward the end of Chapter 5, though, the conditions of the intelligibility of premodern Sharīʿa-based norms began to drastically shift. Since the eighteenth century, the institutional structure that gave real-world significance to Islamic law began to be dismantled or modified. Pursuant to the Capitulation agreements with the Ottoman Sultan, non-Muslim Europeans were exempted from the jurisdiction of Ottoman courts. In Egypt, the rise of the Mixed Court to hear cases involving non-Muslim parties and interests further eroded the extent to which Sharīʿa defined the claim space of law. When Egypt adopted the Napoleonic Code in the late nineteenth century, and created national courts to adjudicate it, Sharīʿa courts and the law they applied began to lose relevance and institutional efficacy in resolving legal disputes. As discussed in Chapter 5, the intelligibility of premodern Sharīʿa-based norms in the modern international state context suffers from a series of discontinuities between, for instance, the premodern and modern curricula of legal training, the institutions of administration and enforcement, and the premodern imperial mode of governance and the modern sovereign state enterprise. Today, the term "Sharīʿa" more

[1] For a discussion of the curricula that was characteristic of Islamic legal education in the medieval Muslim world, see Makdisi, *Rise of Colleges*.

[2] For examples of how jurists created rules of pleading, litigation, and sentencing in light of presumptions of an efficacious institutional framework, see my discussion of juristic discretion and rights in Emon, "*Ḥuqūq Allāh*."

often than not is made to refer to premodern texts and doctrinal rules that reflect a political, social, and cultural context long gone, and with few if any institutional structures that provide continuity in the process of mediating between text and context. When we speak of Islamic law today, we are not generally referring to Sharīʿa as Rule of Law, but rather to Sharīʿa-based doctrines as one among many constitutive features of a modern Rule of Law claim space. For modern Muslims living as minorities and for Muslim-majority states that consider themselves Islamic, the historical shifts in law and the enterprise of governance present a new context in which old answers lose their relevance.

Old answers are neither right nor wrong, but rather fail to account for what David Scott calls, in his acclaimed critique of post-colonial theory, a history of the present. Scott argues that the present poses a new set of questions that the anti-colonial answers of the early twentieth century no longer answer. The rise of former colonies to the status of independent nation states may have constituted the hoped-for future for anti-colonial theorists of the late nineteenth and early twentieth centuries, but at the beginning of the twenty-first century, Scott poignantly recognizes that the anti-colonialists' hopes, fashioned against the colonial enterprise, have not materialized with the independence of former colonies. He writes painfully and powerfully:

> In many parts of the once-colonized world...the bankruptcy of postcolonial regimes is palpable in the extreme...The acute paralysis of will and sheer vacancy of imagination, the rampant corruption and vicious authoritarianism, the instrumental self-interest and showy self-congratulation are all themselves symptoms of a more profound predicament that has, at least in part, to do with the anxiety of exhaustion. The New Nations project has run out of vital sources of energy for creativity, and what we are left with is an exercise of power bereft of any pretense of the exercise of vision. And consequently, almost everywhere, the anticolonial utopias have gradually withered into postcolonial nightmares.[3]

Scott challenges post-colonial theorists for failing to recognize how the questions that animated anti-colonial writers in the early twentieth century have fundamentally shifted at the beginning of the twenty-first century. The "anxiety of exhaustion" may certainly animate post-colonial theorists as they continue their prodding and analysis. Their critiques, though, are themselves symptoms of a present that has yet to be fully appreciated and understood. The antagonists are no longer solely foreign powers imposing colonial rule on a subject people. Rather,

[3] David Scott, *Conscripts of Modernity: The Tragedy of Colonial Enlightenment* (Durham: Duke University Press, 2004), 2.

with the independence of new nations, the antagonists have changed but the dynamics of power and dominance remain. He argues that post-colonial theorists often critique the responses crafted by early anti-colonial writers against the colonial enterprise, but they fail to account for how the questions that animated early anti-colonialist thinkers have so shifted as to render the post-colonial critique of prior answers irrelevant for the present: "In new historical conditions, old questions may lose their salience, their bite, and so lead the range of old answers that once attached to them to appear lifeless, quaint, not so much wrong as irrelevant."[4] Scott calls for critics to examine the present in order to account for how changes in social, cultural, and political ordering demand attention to how the present poses questions to which old answers are not so much wrong, as much as miss the point. As Scott states: "Significant aspects of the global political landscape have changed, and with these changes have come significant alterations in what we might perhaps call our conditions of worldly expectation and hope."[5]

Scott's critique of post-colonial theorists is relevant for this chapter, particularly as this chapter continues where Chapter 5 left off to perform what Scott would call a history of the present. Chapters 1–4 offered insights into how premodern jurists argued for and justified the *dhimmī* rules in light of an Islamically informed (premodern) imperial enterprise of governance. The intelligibility of the *dhimmī* rules, as was argued in earlier chapters, was ascribed to the rules being symptoms of the more complex challenge of imperial governance amidst diversity. The imperial model created the conditions within which jurists utilized the language of the law to constitute the enterprise of governance in sometimes hegemonic fashion.

As Muslim leaders of Islamic states and/or transnational global networks participate today in the international community, undertake bi-lateral and multi-lateral negotiations, and accede to international conventions, they are confronted with the changed conditions of law and the enterprise of governance. As members of the United Nations, Muslim-majority states ignore to their detriment the principle of the equal sovereignty of separate states, which is enshrined in the UN Charter, and violation of which can result in military action against an aggressor state.[6] This principle, if contrasted with the imperialist mode

[4] Scott, *Conscripts of Modernity*, 5. [5] Scott, *Conscripts of Modernity*, 30.

[6] This study recognizes that despite the ambition to view all states as equally sovereign, the heritage of Western colonialism remains present, whether real or perceived. In the context of international law, Antony Anghie soberingly suggests that the resort to international law may actually reinstantiate historic colonial paradigms. Antony Anghie, *Imperialism, Sovereignty, and the Making of International Law* (Cambridge:

of governance that gave intelligibility to the *dhimmī* rules, immediately raises a fundamental question about whether the premodern *dhimmī* rules can have an intelligible place in modern Muslim polities that are both post-imperial *and* post-colonial. Alternatively, to the extent such rules still find expression today, how do the contemporary conditions of law and governance give a new and different intelligibility to these otherwise old answers? In other words, the premodern *dhimmī* rules, with all their complexities, exceptions, and even inconsistencies, had a particular intelligibility when examined in the context of an *Islamic imperial* enterprise of governance. When the enterprise of governance shifts, whereby a people with a history of imperialism become a people subject to colonialism, the *dhimmī* rules arguably lose their original intelligibility and gain a new one.

For example, Eleonor Doumato addresses whether and to what extent Saudi Arabian school textbooks foster and incite anti-Western sentiment. She is critical of the curriculum, although she has doubts about the extent to which the textbooks contribute to a widespread hatred of the West. Nonetheless, she notes that among the nineth–twelfth grade textbooks she reviewed, some lessons counseled students to show caution concerning the non-Muslim. She writes:

> Without any attempt at historicization, the concept of *ahl al-dhimma* [People of the Covenant] is introduced as if it were an appropriate behavioral model for contemporary social intercourse between Muslims and non-Muslims... Non-Muslims who are *ahl al-kitab* [People of the Book] are given a special status as *ahl al-dhimma*, people in a covenant relationship with Muslim rulers, which secures their property, possessions and religion... With no mediating discussion or attempt to place the restrictions in historical context, the chapter ends with questions posed to the students such as 'What is the judgement about greeting the *ahl al-dhimma* on their holidays?'... leaving the impression that the historical relationship of inferior subject people to superior conquering people is meant as a model with contemporary relevance.[7]

According to Doumato, the textbook's discussion of the *dhimmī* is not meant to incite an aggressive agenda or even speak to an imperial vision in the near or distant future. Rather, Doumato argues that the texts reflect a sense of defensiveness and a people struggling against

Cambridge University Press, 2005). Others critique the rise of globalization as a new form of colonialism in a post-colonial age: Subharbrata Bobby Banerjee and Stephen Linstead, "Globalization, Multiculturalism and Other Fictions: Colonialism for the New Millennium?" *Organization* 8, no. 4 (2001): 683–722.

[7] Eleanor Abdella Doumato, "Manning the Barricades: Islam According to Saudi Arabia's School Texts," *Middle East Journal* 57, no. 2 (Spring 2003): 230–47, 237–8.

a perceived threat to their existence and well-being. Drawing on the work of Martin Marty, Doumato suggests that the Saudi textbooks are designed to inculcate a traditional set of values for people who feel "they have inherited an ancestral past, but then experience a sense of being threatened. The threat may be something vague such as a fear of 'identity diffusion' or secularism, or it might be quite concrete, such as assault by outsiders."[8]

That feeling might explain the irregularity in Nuh H.M. Keller's quasi-translation of *Reliance of the Traveller.* This is an English "translation" of a fourteenth-century Shāfiʿī *fiqh* source entitled *ʿUmdat al-Sālik* by Aḥmad b. al-Naqīb.[9] Originally published in 1991 and then revised in 1994, Keller's text provides both the original Arabic text and a facing English "translation," with commentary and appendices. Interestingly, the book is prefaced with various documents attesting to its authenticity and accuracy in translation.[10] These documents of attestation are akin to the premodern *ijāza,* or diploma. In the premodern period, the *ijāza* was a document that attested to the authority of its holder to teach a certain text or field of knowledge. The modern *ijāza*-like documents in *Reliance* rely on a premodern model of authority and authenticity to assure the modern reader of Keller's authority to translate the text and to teach what he knows to students who seek knowledge of Sunnī orthodox doctrine. By adopting this form of the *ijāza,* the attestation documents invoke premodern features of intelligibility and authority.

Importantly, Keller did not translate the Arabic text fully into English.[11] The effect of this partial translation becomes particularly relevant for the purpose of this study in the section on the *dhimmī* rules. The difference between what the Arabic text provides and how

[8] Doumato, "Manning the Barricades," 233.

[9] Aḥmad b. al-Naqīb al-Miṣrī, *Reliance of the Traveller: A Classic Manual of Islamic Sacred Law,* trans. Nuh H.M. Keller, rev. ed. (Evanston, Illinois: Sunna Books, 1994).

[10] The first attestation is by ʿal-Wakīl al-Durūbī, an Imam in Damascus, Syria, who states that Keller has learned the text from him and understands its contents and its commentaries. The second attestation is by Nūḥ ʿAlī Salmān, the *muftī* of the Jordanian Armed Forces, who stated that he had read the text and considered Keller qualified to translate it into English. Yet another attestation is by Tāha Jābir al-ʿAlwānī, then President of the International Institute of Islamic Thought, based in Herndon, Virginia. Al-ʿAlwānī reported on the English translation of the Arabic text, and stated that his colleague Yūsuf DeLorenzo validated the English translation, and found that it "presents the legal questions in a faithful and precise idiom that clearly delivers the complete legal meaning in a sound English style." And finally, Fatḥ Allāh Ya Sin Jazar, the General Director of Research at al-Azhar University in Cairo, certified that the translation "corresponds to the Arabic original and conforms to the practice and faith of the orthodox Sunni Community." Al-Miṣrī, *Reliance of the Traveller,* xiv, xvi, xviii, xx.

[11] Others have criticized his work for excluding entirely the discussion on slavery that exists in the original premodern text. See Kecia Ali, *Sexual Ethics in Islam: Feminist Reflections on Qur'an, Hadith and Jurisprudence* (Oxford: Oneworld Publications, 2006).

the English is "translated" begs various questions not only about the intelligibility of the *dhimmī* rules in the context of this premodern text, but also (and most importantly) about the significance and intelligibility of *Reliance* as a text of general educational reference for a transnational, post-colonial Muslim readership. For example, the Arabic text provides that *dhimmīs*:

- must abide by Islamic law;
- are punished for illicit sexual relations and theft, but not for being intoxicated;
- must dress differently from Muslims to be distinct and different; and
- may not erect their buildings higher or of equal height as the buildings of Muslims.

The Arabic text also provides that *dhimmīs* are forbidden to build new churches, but it provides an exception to this general ban: if there is a treaty between Muslims and non-Muslims, non-Muslims are not prevented from building religious places of worship if they so choose. Importantly, this exception is in brackets in the Arabic text; Keller did not translate this exception into English. So while he translated the rule demanding that *dhimmīs* wear distinctive dress, he did not translate the exception that permits non-Muslims to build churches in the event of a treaty. This exception is not the only Arabic phrase he failed to translate. He did not translate, for instance, the rule permitting non-Muslims to ride mules and asses but not horses.

Keller's "translation" of *'Umdat al-Sālik,* therefore, is not a full or complete translation of a premodern text. Keller states in his introduction that "[n]ot a single omission has been made from [the Arabic text], though rulings about matters now rare or nonexistent have been left untranslated unless interesting for some other reason. Parts untranslated are enclosed in brackets [in the Arabic]."[12] When he chooses not to translate selections of the Arabic text, Keller encloses the relevant *Arabic passages* in brackets, but does not indicate in the English text when and where he omits his translation. He refuses to include ellipses in the English section since the omitted section is provided fully in Arabic and in brackets, which he writes "was felt to suffice."[13] At most, *Reliance of the Traveller* is a modern (re)presentation of a premodern text. Consequently, its intelligibility and significance cannot be measured in terms of the historical context in which the original text was written.

[12] Al-Miṣrī, *Reliance*, Ix. [13] Al-Miṣrī, *Reliance*, Xi.

Nor can the words on the page, in particular the English words, be read uncritically, as if their meaning is transparent.[14]

Without an express explanation from Keller, any assessment of why certain portions are translated and others are not translated is tentative. But a comparison of Keller's choices with the rationales of the rules as noted in Chapter 3 may reveal how *Reliance* is very much a modern project. As noted in Chapter 3, premodern Muslim jurists debated whether *dhimmīs* could erect new religious buildings or renovate dilapidated ones. As was discussed earlier, whether *dhimmīs* could do so depended on the type of land they occupied, their land tax liability, and whether the Islamic enterprise of governance took control over the land by conquest or treaty. But in the modern context, none of these factors would seem relevant given the absence of an Islamic imperial enterprise of governance. There is no Islamic empire that is conquering new lands with non-Muslims residing therein. The exception in the original Arabic reflects a premodern imagination about the mutually constitutive relationship between law and an imperial enterprise of governance. In the absence of such an enterprise of governance, the exception to the general ban is hardly relevant to the modern Muslim. However, and most tellingly, the same could be said about the general ban itself. In the absence of an imperial enterprise of governance, why the need to preserve the general ban on the construction of churches? Perhaps the general ban is translated without the exception to proffer a romantic image of a Muslim world re-possessed of its former imperial glory. The translation of the ban, without the exception, gives Muslims a telos of redemption, a romantic image of hope, at a time when Muslims live in a post-imperial and post-colonial world where the former glory of Muslim empire has ended. It acts like a balm to the modern pain of subservience Muslims and Muslim majority states suffer in their post-imperial *and* post-colonial condition.[15]

[14] Indeed, some who adopt the myth of persecution read the English text in Keller's *Reliance* as if it were transparently meaningful. They do not problematize the text, nor consider the ideological aim of the translator as equally, if not more, significant to the design and structure of the text. See, for instance, Spencer, *Islam Unveiled*, 143–50. However, as suggested above, such a reading of *Reliance* ignores how the text is doing more than simply conveying the past tradition to a modern audience. It is reshaping it and repackaging it in light of conceptions of identity and community that are not explicitly acknowledged in the text.

[15] Scholars and Muslim reformists have deeply criticized the effect of the West and modernity on the nature and organic integrity of Islam for Muslim today. These criticisms are perhaps so ingrained in and accepted by those such as Keller and the authors of the Saudi textbooks as to animate a framework of analysis that requires no justification. Much has been written on Islam and modernity. For some useful references, see Bassam Tibi, *The Crisis of Modern Islam: A Preindustrial Culture in the Scientific-Technological Age*, trans. Judith von Sivers (Salt Lake City: University of Utah Press, 1988); Fazlur Rahman,

However premodern Muslim jurists may have imagined Sharīʿa as Rule of Law, the contemporary historical moment indicates that much has changed. To the extent the *dhimmī* rules remain part of an ongoing dialogue in Muslim states, they reflect different questions about identity, community, and pluralism than they did in the premodern period. This study's focus on the *dhimmī* rules is not, therefore, a matter of mere historical antiquarianism. Rather, this study suggests that the distance between the premodern vision of Sharīʿa as Rule of Law and the present conditions that influence, affect, and define law and the enterprise of governance in the modern Muslim world demands a reconsideration of the questions to which premodern *dhimmī* rules were offered as answers in the past, and in some cases are still offered as answers today.[16]

A history of the present can proceed in a variety of ways. This chapter does not pretend to offer an exhaustive history of the contemporary moment; no study likely could. Rather, it examines how and why premodern Islamic doctrines, such as the *dhimmī* rules, are invoked in contemporary Muslim debate and state practice in order to reveal the changed conditions of intelligibility surrounding, more generally, the resort to Sharīʿa-based norms in contemporary debates about Islam, Muslims, and the religious Other. Where Sharīʿa as Rule of Law in the premodern period connoted a claim space defined and delimited by various constitutive features, Sharīʿa today is itself a constitutive feature of a given nation-state's claim space, which in turn reflects the changed relationship between law and an enterprise of governance. The question this begs is what constitutive role Sharīʿa plays, how that role changes across different polities, and the distance between its premodern intelligibility and its modern one?

This chapter explores the dynamics of intelligibility and Rule of Law by analyzing the deployment of premodern rules on the *dhimmī* in wrongful death cases in Saudi Arabia. Notably, a case of apostasy

Islam and Modernity: Transformation of an Intellectual Tradition (Chicago: University of Chicago Press, 1982).

[16] For example, few states may attempt to apply Islamic criminal law, but that is both rare and more often carries considerable political symbolism. For instance, the state of Kelantan in Malaysia passed an Islamic criminal law statute, which might raise concerns about Sharīʿa and human rights. But since criminal law is a federal and not a state matter in Malaysia, then the Kelantan legislation becomes a symbol of the politics of Islam in Malaysia, rather than a feature of Malaysia's regulatory powers or even a legal challenge to the international human rights regime. To assume the Kelantan legislation bears the same intelligibility today as it did in the premodern period is to ignore how the shift in the underlying enterprise of governance conditions the meaning and significance of arguments of justice: Vatikiotis, "Malaysia: A political ploy?," 28; "Islam in Asia: For God and Growth in Malysia," *The Economist* 329, no. 7839 (November 27, 1993): 39.

in Malaysia will also be addressed in this chapter. The inclusion of an apostasy case in a study on the *dhimmī* might seem inapposite at first glance. However, as suggested below, the Malaysian apostasy case and the modern invocation of the *dhimmī* rules, when read together, help illuminate modern questions around citizenship and identity (which are features of the modern Rule of Law claim space) that the deployment of premodern apostasy and *dhimmī* rules today are meant to answer.

The analysis below offers insight into the shifting intelligibility of the *dhimmī* rules, along with a deeper understanding of the relationship between law, the enterprise of governance, and the constitutive role of Sharīʿa-based doctrines in defining the claim space for justice in the modern state. As will be shown, the premodern intelligibility of rules such as those governing the *dhimmīs* and apostates relied on certain conceptions of law and the enterprise of governance that no longer prevail. As such, this study suggests that resort to these premodern rules is not so much wrong as it is inapposite, given fundamental alterations to the conditions of intelligibility that inform contemporary questions about how to live and govern amidst diversity.

6.1 FROM EMPIRE TO STATE: RULE OF LAW, SAUDI ARABIA, AND WRONGFUL DEATH DAMAGES

The shifts from an imperial enterprise of governance to the modern state, and from Sharīʿa as Rule of Law to Rule of Law claim spaces that account for plural sources of authority, force a reconsideration of the intelligibility of the *dhimmī* rules as they are applied, in limited circumstances, in modern state systems today. On the one hand, these rules play a very limited role in most Muslim-majority countries. On the other hand, these rules nonetheless continue to contribute to the way in which some Muslims understand their relationship to the religious Other, as illustrated above by reference to Keller's quasi-translation and Doumato's study of Saudi Arabian school books. In limited, but nonetheless significant, cases we find application of some *dhimmī* rules in a contemporary legal regime. One example is Saudi Arabia and its legal doctrine on wrongful death liability.[17]

[17] While other countries may not be explicit about their reliance on the *dhimmī* rules, they nonetheless distinguish between religious groups, thereby perpetuating at the very least the ethos of difference, and at the very most, the ethos of Islamic superiority.

Saudi Arabia has no constitution, but rather has various "Basic Laws." According to Article 26 of the Basic Law of Government (1993), Saudi Arabia "protects human rights in accordance with the Islamic Sharīʿah."[18] Importantly, the scope of human rights protection will significantly depend on how one understands the scope and content of Sharīʿa. In Saudi Arabia, premodern Sharīʿa-based rules govern the majority of cases involving tort, property, and contract.[19] The history of Saudi Arabia's incorporation of Sunnī Islam and Sharīʿa, in particular the Wahhābist strain, as part of its national ethos has been addressed in numerous studies in recent years. Historians have shown that the early resort to Islam and Islamic law as a defining feature of the Saudi state was instrumental in constituting a political identity for the state that transcended regional and tribal networks.[20] The institution of law as an ordering and coercive feature of the government was given an Islamic content that has facilitated the development of a distinctive, Islamically informed nationalism and governing enterprise. Notably, of the four Sunnī Islamic legal schools, the Ḥanbalī school often provides the rule of decision in Saudi Arabia.[21]

The rights conflict arising out of Article 26 of the Basic Law of Governance is illustrated by rules governing the measure of wrongful death damages in Saudi Arabia. According to the Philippine Embassy in Riyadh, Saudi Arabia, the families of Indian expatriates working in the Kingdom can claim wrongful death compensation pursuant to a schedule of fixed amounts, which vary depending on the victim's religious convictions and gender. If the victim is a Muslim male, his family can claim SR100,000. But if the victim is a Christian or Jewish male, the family can only claim half that amount, namely SR50,000. Further, if the victim belongs to another faith group, such as Hindu, Sikh, or Jain, his family can claim approximately SR6,667. The family of a female victim can claim half the amount stipulated for her male co-religionist.[22]

[18] For an English translation of this provision, see Saudi Arabia, *The Basic Law of Governance*, Article 26 (1993): <http://www.servat.unibe.ch/icl/sa00000_.html> (accessed July 28, 2007).

[19] Frank Vogel, *Islamic Law and Legal System: Studies of Saudi Arabia* (Leiden: Brill, 2000), 175, 291.

[20] Madawi al-Rasheed, *A History of Saudi Arabia* (Cambridge: Cambridge University Press, 2002); Abou El Fadl, *The Great Theft*; Ibrahim Karawan, "Monarchs, Mullas and Marshalls: Islamic Regimes?" *Annals of the American Academy of Political and Social Science* (1992): 103–19; Joseph Kechichian, "The Role of the Ulama in the Politics of an Islamic State: The Case of Saudi Arabia," *International Journal of Middle East Studies* (1986): 53–71.

[21] Vogel, *Islamic Law and Legal System*, 10.

[22] <http://www.philembassy-riyadh.org/index.php/component/K2/item/220-qisas-and-diyya-or-blood-money> (accessed May 14, 2012, copy on file with author). See also the document provided on the website of Pakistan's Ministry of Overseas Pakistanis,

Saudi Arabia patterns its wrongful death compensatory regime on early Ḥanbalī rules of tort liability. For example, premodern Muslim jurists held that the *diyya,* or wrongful death compensation, for a free Muslim male was one hundred camels,[23] but if the victim was a Jewish or Christian male, his family could only claim a percentage of that amount. The Shāfiʿīs held that the family was entitled to one-third of what a free Muslim male's family would receive,[24] but the Mālikīs and Ḥanbalīs granted them one-half of what a Muslim's family could obtain.[25] Furthermore, Sunnī and Shīʿa jurists held that if the victim was a Magian (*majūs*), his family was entitled to even less, namely 1/15th of what a free Muslim male is worth.[26] Importantly, 1/15th of SR100,000 is approximately SR6,667, the amount Saudi Arabia grants to the family of non-Muslims who are neither Jewish nor Christian.

which addresses the *diyya* amounts for Muslim men or women killed in Saudi Arabia: <http://www.moops.gov.pk/> with a link to CWA Parep Jeddah (accessed May 14, 2012, copy on file with author).

[23] Al-Ghazālī, *al-Wasīṭ*; al-Shīrāzī, *al-Muhadhdhab.*

[24] al-Shāfiʿī, *Kitāb al-Umm*, 3:113; al-Māwardī, *al-Ḥāwī*, 12:308; al-Ghazālī, *al-Wasīṭ*, 4:64–7; al-Nawawī, *Rawḍa*, 9:258; al-Ramlī, *Nihāyat al-Muḥtāj*, 7:320; al-Shīrāzī, *al-Muhadhdhab*, 3:213.

[25] Mālik b. Anas, *al-Muwaṭṭāʾ* (Beirut: Dār al-Gharb al-Islāmī, 1997), 2:434–5, related that ʿUmar II decided that the *diyya* for a killed Jew or Christian is half the *diyya* for a free Muslim male. See also Ibn Rushd al-Jadd, *al-Muqaddimāt al-Mumahhidāt*, 3:295; Ibn Rushd al-Ḥafīd, *Bidāyat al-Mujtahid*, 2:604–5; al-Qarāfī, *al-Dhakhīra*, 12:356; Ibn Qudāma, *al-Mughnī*, 7:793–5, who said that Aḥmad b. Ḥanbal held the amount was 1/3, but then changed his position to 1/2; Ibn Mufliḥ, *al-Furūʿ*, 6:16, who indicated some would provide the Muslim *diyya* for *dhimmīs* if the latter were killed intentionally. However, Mālikī and Ḥanbalī jurists held that in personal injury cases (*jirāḥāt*), the *diyya* for the injury is whatever a free Muslim male would get. Mālik b. Anas, *al-Muwaṭṭāʾ*, 2:434–5; Saḥnūn, *al-Mudawwana al-Kubrā*, 6:395; al-Bahūtī, *Kashshāf al-Qināʿ*, 6:23–4. There are source-texts in which the Prophet also stipulated that the People of the Book receive only half the wrongful death compensation as compared with a Muslim. See ʿAbd al-Razzāq al-Ṣanʿānī, *Kitāb al-Muṣannaf*, ed. Ayman Naṣr al-Dīn al-Azharī (Beirut: Dār al-Kutub al-ʿIlmiyya, 2000), 9:419 (*ʿaql ahl al-kitāb min al-yahūd wa al-naṣṣārā niṣf ʿaql al-muslim*), where *ʿaql* here refers to blood money.

[26] Al-Shāfiʿī, *Umm*, 3:113; al-Ghazālī, *al-Wasīṭ*, 4:67; al-Māwardī, *al-Ḥāwī*, 12:311; al-Nawawī, *Rawḍa*, 9:258, who said that the *majūs* get *thultha ʿushr* of the *diyya* for a free Muslim male; al-Ramlī, *Nihāyat al-Muḥtāj*, 7:320; al-Shīrāzī, *al-Muhadhdhab*, 3:213; Mālik b. Anas, *al-Muwaṭṭāʾ*, 2:435; Saḥnūn, *al-Mudawwana al-Kubrā*, 6:395; Ibn Rushd al-Jadd, *al-Muqaddimāt al-Mumahhidāt*, 3:296; al-Qarāfī, *al-Dhakhīra*, 12:357; Ibn Qudāma, *al-Mughnī*, 7:796; al-Bahūtī, *Kashshāf al-Qināʿ*, 6:24. Notably, Ibn Qudāma related a minority opinion held by al-Nakhāʾī and others who equated the *diyya* for the *majūs* and free Muslims because both are free and inviolable human beings (*adamī ḥurr maʿṣūm*): Ibn Qudāma, *al-Mughnī*, 7:796. The Jaʿfarī Shīʿa al-Muḥaqqiq al-Ḥillī, *Sharāʾiʿ al-Islām*, 2:489 related three views, namely that Jews, Christians, and Magians are valued at 800 *dirhams*, or all enjoy the same *diyya* as Muslims, or that Christians and Jews are entitled to 4,000 *dirhams*. According to the Jaʿfarī Shīʿa al-Ḥurr al-ʿĀmilī, *Wasāʾil*, 19:141–2, the *diyya* of a free Muslim male is roughly 10,000 *dirhams*, while the *diyya* of a *dhimmī* Jew or Christian is 4,000 *dirhams*, and the *diyya* of the *majūs* is 800 *dirhams*, roughly 40 per cent and 8 per cent, respectively of the *diyya* for a free Muslim male.

An analysis of the premodern wrongful death compensation rules as they would have applied to *dhimmīs* shows that premodern jurists developed these doctrines in light of concerns about the imperial integrity of the early enterprise of governance. Examining the wrongful death rules through the lens of Sharīʿa as Rule of Law reveals that the contemporary intelligibility of these rules in the Saudi Arabian context suffers from a significant discontinuity with the rules' premodern intelligibility. Identifying this discontinuity makes possible important avenues of inquiry about the meaningfulness of these premodern answers to modern questions of governance in the Saudi state.

Doctrinally related to the wrongful death compensation doctrines are the legal rules for *qiṣāṣ*, or retribution, (i.e., *lex talionis*) in cases of negligent homicide. The central questions for premodern Muslim jurists were whether, how, and why legal liability differed depending on the victim's religious commitments. Jurists of the Shāfiʿī, Ḥanbalī, Mālikī, and Shīʿa Jaʿfarī schools maintained generally that if a Muslim killed an unbeliever (*kāfir*), then the Muslim was not to be executed. But if an unbeliever killed a Muslim, then the unbeliever would be executed.[27] Mālikī jurists held that Muslim perpetrators were executed only if they killed their non-Muslim victims while lying in wait (*qatl al-ghīla*).[28] Shīʿa Jaʿfarī jurists would sentence a Muslim to execution if he was a serial murderer of non-Muslims; however, execution was contingent on the victim's family compensating the Muslim perpetrator's family for the difference in wrongful death compensation between the non-Muslim and the Muslim.[29] In other words, if compensatory liability for a Muslim male's wrongful death was one hundred camels, and liability for a Christian or Jewish male victim was fifty camels, the family of the *dhimmī* Jewish or Christian victim had to pay the Muslim serial killer's family fifty camels if the Muslim killer were to be legitimately executed.

The discriminatory application of the death penalty rule is further illustrated by cases where the perpetrator or victim is an apostate from

[27] Al-Shāfiʿī, *al-Umm*, 3:40, who would subject the Muslim killer to prison and *taʿzīr* punishment; al-Ghazālī, *al-Wasīṭ*, 4:36–7; al-Māwardī, *al-Ḥāwī*, 12:10; al-Nawawī, *Rawḍa*, 9:150; al-Shīrāzī, *al-Muhadhdhab*, 3:171; Ibn Qudāma, *al-Mughnī*, 7:652; al-Muḥaqqiq al-Ḥillī, *Sharāʾiʿ al-Islām*, 2:452–3, who also held that the Muslim murderer can be sentenced to discretionary punishment (*taʿzīr*) and monetary compensation (*diyya*); al-Ḥurr al-ʿĀmilī, *Wasāʾil*, 19:127.

[28] In other words, one might argue that lying in wait is an aggravating circumstance that affects sentencing.

[29] Malik b. Anas, *Muwaṭṭāʾ*, 2:434–5; Ibn Rushd al-Ḥafīd, *Bidāyat al-Mujtahid*, 2:582; al-Muḥaqqiq al-Ḥillī, *Sharāʾiʿ al-Islām*, 2:452–3; al-Ḥurr al-ʿĀmilī, *Wasāʾil*, 19:79–80. For others reporting the Mālikī position, see al-ʿAynī, *al-Bināya*, 13:79.

Islam. According to premodern jurists, if a Muslim kills an apostate from Islam, the killer suffers no liability. If an apostate kills a Muslim, however, then the apostate would be executed.[30] Given the theme of universality, and its corollaries of superiority and subordination discussed above, this outcome is perhaps not surprising. Premodern jurists considered a Muslim to be superior to an apostate from Islam, and thereby gave the former preferential treatment under the law. But this particular outcome raises an interesting question about the legal consequences in the event a *dhimmī* kills an apostate from Islam. Juristic views fell into three camps:

- the *dhimmī* is to be executed given his general liability under *qiṣāṣ*;
- the *dhimmī* is not to be executed because the apostate enjoys no legal protection;
- the *dhimmī* is to be executed pursuant to the discretion of the ruler (*siyāsa*), but his estate would not be additionally burdened with compensatory liability since the apostate is not protected under the law.[31]

If an apostate from Islam kills a *dhimmī* living under the protection of the Islamic polity, Muslim jurists generally divided into two camps concerning the apostate's liability:

- the apostate is to be executed;
- the apostate is not to be executed since his prior adherence to Islam gives him a sanctity that transcends his apostasy (at least in relation to a *dhimmī*) and protects him against liability for killing a *dhimmī*.[32]

Whether the premodern *dhimmī* enjoyed superior protection over the Muslim apostate depended on which view a jurist adopted. The multiplicity of views suggests that jurists could not agree on the right balance of interests given that, in both cases, the apostate and the *dhimmī* represented either the failure or limits of an Islamic universalism. Despite the apparent failure or limit of that universalism, all of the different views noted above nonetheless confirmed and upheld the ethic of Islamic universalism and, by implication, an ethic of subordination. An apostate

[30] Al-Ghazālī, *al-Wasīṭ* 4:36–7; al-Bahūtī, *Kashshāf al-Qināʿ*, 5:614; al-Muḥaqqiq al-Ḥillī, *Sharāʾiʿ al-Islām*, 2:455.

[31] Al-Ghazāli, *al-Wasīṭ*, 4:36–7. See also al-Shīrāzī, *al-Muhadhdhab*, 3:172. The Jaʿfarī al-Muḥaqqiq al-Ḥilli, *Sharāʾiʿ al-Islām*, 2:455, would execute the *dhimmī* because the apostate still enjoys, as against the *dhimmī*, the protection that arose with his prior Islamic commitments.

[32] Al-Ghazālī, *al-Wasīṭ*, 4:36–7; al-Shīrāzī, *al-Muhadhdhab*, 3:172.

who was once Muslim and later abandoned Islam, and so became a non-Muslim, could still enjoy the benefit of an Islamic identity over and against someone born, raised, and murdered as a non-Muslim.

Muslim jurists defended this discriminatory application of *qiṣāṣ* liability by reference to a *ḥadīth* in which the Prophet said: "A believer is not killed for an unbeliever." Importantly, the full tradition states: "A believer is not killed for an unbeliever or one without a covenant during his residency."[33] Jurists who constructed discriminatory rules of liability relied on the first half of the *ḥadīth*. Furthermore, they argued that these discriminatory rules reflected the fact that Muslims were of a higher class than their non-Muslim co-residents. For instance, the Shāfiʿī jurist al-Māwardī argued that, as a matter of law, someone from a lower class (*al-adnā*) could be executed to vindicate the interests of someone from a higher class (*al-aʿlā*), but the opposite could not occur.[34] He justified this legal distinction in eschatological terms by citing Qurʾān 59:20, which states: "The companions of the hellfire are not equivalent to the companions of heaven."[35] From this he concluded that just as the Qurʾān denies any equivalence between these groups in eschatological terms, the law should deny any equivalence between them in material terms.[36] Furthermore, using the logical inference of *a minore ad maius*, al-Mawardi held that just as a Muslim bears no liability for sexually slandering a *dhimmī* (see Chapter 4), he cannot be liable for killing one, a much more serious offense.[37]

[33] Al-Māwardī, *al-Ḥāwī*, 12:10; al-Bahūtī, *Kashshāf al-Qināʿ*, 5:616; Ibn Nujaym, *al-Baḥr al-Rāʾiq*, 9:19, who has a variant of this same tradition. For similar traditions and others with common themes, see the discussion in Ibn al-Jawzī, *al-Taḥqīq*, 2:307–9.

[34] Al-Māwardi, *al-Ḥāwī*, 12:11. Al-Nawawī, *Rawḍa*, 9:150, stated that freedom, Islamic faith, and paternity provide exceptions to liability for execution. Where the two parties are of equal status, *qiṣāṣ* liability applies; otherwise, the person of lower status (*al-mafḍūl*) is executed for the higher status victim (*al-fāḍil*), but not the opposite. Al-Shīrāzī, *al-Muhadhdhab*, 3:171, referring to a Qurʾānic verse requiring execution of the free for the free, slave for the slave, and women for women, held that if one is executed for killing someone of an equal social standing, then certainly he should be executed for killing someone who is superior to him (*afḍal minhu*). The Mālikī Ibn Rushd al-Ḥafīd, *Bidāyat al-Mujtahid*, 2:582, said that there is no dispute that the slave is executed for murdering a free male, just as the one of lower status is executed for killing the higher status (*al-anqad bi al-aʿlā*). See also al-Qarāfī, *al-Dhakhīra*, 12:332; al-Bahūtī, *Kashshāf al-Qināʿ*, 5:617.

[35] Al-Māwardī, *al-Ḥāwī*, 12:11–12. The Ḥanbalī al-Bahūtī also relies on the notion of equivalence to justify the differential treatment in sentences for murder: Al-Bahūtī, *Kashshāf al-Qināʿ*, 5:616.

[36] The Mālikī al-Qarāfī, *al-Dhakhīra*, 12:356–7, relied on a similar argument to justify different compensatory payments (*diyya*) for wrongful death, depending on the victim's religious commitments.

[37] Al-Māwardī, *al-Ḥāwī*, 12:13–14. For a discussion of this mode of reasoning in Islamic legal theory, see Hallaq, *History of Islamic Legal Theories*, 96–9.

This is not to suggest that all Muslim schools of law held to this discriminatory application of capital punishment. As explained below, Ḥanafī jurists rejected such discriminatory legal applications, especially when considering the above *ḥadīth* with both halves together. Anticipating a Ḥanafī critique, though, al-Māwardī narrated an incident involving the important premodern Ḥanafī jurist Abū Yūsuf (d. 182/797). According to the story, Abū Yūsuf sentenced a Muslim to death for killing a non-Muslim, which was consistent with Hanafi doctrine. But he subsequently received a disconcerting poem criticizing him for doing so. The poem read as follows:

> O killer of Muslims on behalf of unbelievers!
> You commit an outrage, for the just are not the same as the oppressor.
> O those of Baghdad and its vicinity, jurists and poets!
> Abū Yūsuf [commits] an outrage on the faith when he kills Muslims for unbelievers.
> Make demands, cry for your faith, and be patient, for reward belongs to the patient.[38]

Troubled by the thought of a public outcry, Abū Yūsuf informed the 'Abbāsid caliph Hārūn al-Rashīd (r. 170–193/786–809) about his predicament. Al-Rashīd advised him to use a technical legal loophole to avoid the execution sentence, and thereby dodge any social discord (*fitna*). Specifically, Abū Yūsuf learned that the victim's family could not prove that they paid their poll-tax (*jizya*). Therefore, they could be denied the full protection of and entitlements under the contract of protection. As a result, Abū Yūsuf did not execute the Muslim, and instead held him liable for wrongful death damages. Al-Māwardī, however, glossed the entire story by suggesting that since the original decision led to public dissatisfaction (i.e., *fitna*), it was right and good to avoid that decision generally.[39]

Despite this story and al-Māwardī's gloss on it, Ḥanafī jurists justified executing a Muslim for killing a non-Muslim[40] by reference to a tradition in which the Prophet did so, saying: "I am the most ardent to uphold [one's] security."[41] The Ḥanafī Badr al-Dīn al-'Aynī explained that jurists of other schools discriminated against non-Muslims because they

[38] Al-Māwardī, *al-Ḥāwī*, 12:15–16. [39] Al-Māwardī, *al-Ḥāwī*, 12:15–16.

[40] Muḥammad b. al-Ḥasan al-Shaybānī, *Kitāb al-Aṣl* 4:488 (Wizārat al-Maʿārif li'l-Ḥukūma al-ʿĀliyya al-Hindiyya, 1973), required that the murder be intentional (*ʿamd*); al-ʿAynī, *al-Bināya*, 13:79; al-Marghīnānī, *al-Hidāya*, 2:446.

[41] Al-ʿAynī, *al-Bināya*, 13:79; Ibn Nujaym, *al-Baḥr al-Rāʾiq*, 9:19; Abū Bakr al-Kasānī, *Badāʾiʿ al-Ṣanāʾiʿ*, 10:258. Notably, al-Māwardī, *al-Ḥāwī*, 12:10, held this tradition to be weak.

assumed an inherent inequality between Muslims and non-Muslims. Shafiʿī jurists, he said, considered disbelief (*kufr*) to be a sufficiently material characteristic to deny the equality of a non-Muslim's dignity and inviolability in comparison with a Muslim's.[42]

For Ḥanafī jurists, however, Muslims and non-Muslims were equally inviolable.[43] The Ḥanafīs were certainly aware of the Prophet's tradition rejecting execution of a Muslim for killing a non-Muslim, but they read it as a general rule from which those with a contract of protection were exempted.[44] Given that a contract of protection was in place, they held that one's inviolability (*ʿiṣma*) depended on whether one had the capacity to satisfy his or her legal obligations.[45] Inviolability, in other words, was not contingent on faith commitments, but instead on one's ability to abide by the law, according to the Ḥanafīs. Once the *dhimmī* agreed to be subjected to the laws of a Muslim polity, he became inviolable as a matter of law. Of course, this inviolability did not extend to all non-Muslims, but rather only those living within a Muslim polity under a contract of protection. Non-Muslims living outside Muslim lands, for instance, did not enjoy the same legal protections as non-Muslims within the polity. For the Ḥanafīs, legal arguments invoking territoriality, residence, and contract justified the protection afforded to *dhimmīs*. Disbelief *simpliciter* did not irrevocably undermine the inviolability of a *dhimmī* who lived peacefully in an Islamic polity, according to the Ḥanafīs.[46]

The discussion of the *qiṣāṣ* rules is important in order to appreciate the underlying logic of the rules regulating wrongful death compensation. Indeed, the logic of the former informed the logic of the latter. As noted above, many Sunnī schools of law provided a schedule of compensatory liability for wrongful death that discriminated on religious grounds. However, the Ḥanafīs opposed this discriminatory approach and demanded equal compensation regardless of religious affiliation. They argued that the compensation for a Muslim and a *dhimmī* victim should be the same, since both were equally inviolable and thereby enjoyed

[42] Al-ʿAynī, *al-Bināya*, 13:79.

[43] Ibn Nujaym, *al-Baḥr al-Rāʾiq*, 9:20; al-Kāsānī, *Badāʾiʿ al-Ṣanāʾiʿ*, 10:246, who required the victim to be inviolable (*maʿṣūm al-damm*); Abū al-Fatḥ al-Samarqandī, *Tarīqat al-Khilāf bayna al-Aslāf* (Beirut: Dār al-Kutub al-ʿIlmiyya, 1992), 522–5.

[44] Al-Kāsānī, *Badāʾiʿ al-Ṣanāʾiʿ*, 10:259; al-Marghīnānī, *al-Hidāya*, 2:464.

[45] Al-ʿAynī, *al-Bināya*, 13:80; Ibn Nujaym, *al-Baḥr al-Rāʾiq*, 9:20; al-Marghīnānī, *al-Hidāya*, 2:446. As such, Ḥanafī jurists like al-Kāsānī imposed no *qiṣāṣ* liability for killing a *ḥarbī* or apostate since they are not *maʿṣūm*. Al-Kāsānī, *Badāʾiʿ al-Ṣanāʾiʿ*, 10:246.

[46] Al-ʿAyni, *al-Bināya*, 13:80. Disbelief becomes relevant if the unbeliever threatens the Muslim polity. But since those enjoying a contract of protection (*ʿaqd al-dhimma*) agree to lawfully reside in Muslim lands, they are entitled to legal protection of their lives and property: Al-ʿAyni, *al-Bināya*, 13:81; Ibn Nujaym, *al-Baḥr al-Rāʾiq*, 9:20; al-Kāsānī, *Badāʾiʿ al-Ṣanāʾiʿ*, 10:248, 257–8.

the same protections under the law.[47] Religious commitment was not a relevant factor for them to determine the scope of one's legal entitlements to wrongful death damages.[48] Rather, what mattered for the Ḥanafīs was whether or not the non-Muslim claimants had a contract of protection, thus rendering them *dhimmīs* and bringing them within the polity on equal grounds as Muslims.

To justify their position, the Ḥanafīs looked to Qur'ān 4:92, which addresses the case of a Muslim who has killed another: "and if he [the victim] is from a people with whom you have a treaty (*mithāq*), his people are entitled to a *diyya musallama,* and [the killer] must free a believing slave." The reference to *diyya musallama* is not entirely clear. Literally, it refers to an agreed upon amount. What that amount might be, though, was subject to debate among premodern jurists. For Ḥanafīs, the *diyya* (compensation) owed should not be reduced in the case of *dhimmīs*; for them, Muslims and non-Muslims were entitled to the same *diyya* for wrongful death.[49] As additional support for the Ḥanafī position, Ibn Nujaym referred to the view of the fourth caliph, 'Alī b. Abī Ṭālib (d. 40/661), who held that since *dhimmīs* were obligated in the same way as Muslims, they also enjoyed the same entitlement to damages for personal injury.[50]

The above discussion illustrates how Muslim jurists contended with competing themes of subordination, inclusion, and accommodation to determine the rules of tort liability amidst religious difference in the Muslim polity. The different views indicate that no single position was objectively true or inevitable. Rather, jurists ruled in the light of competing presumptions about identity, community, and political society that constituted the conditions of intelligibility that gave shape to the claim space of Sharīʿa.

Beyond the juristic debates, however, one issue remains to be addressed, namely the initial animus for a premodern rule that halved the *dhimmīs'* wrongful death compensation. The early Muslim historian al-Zuhrī[51] recounted that during the era of the Prophet and his first four successors, non-Muslims would receive the same wrongful

[47] Al-ʿAynī, *al-Bināya*, 13:171; Ibn Nujaym, *al-Baḥr al-Rāʾiq*, 9:75; al-Kāsānī, *Badāʾiʿ al-Ṣanāʾiʿ*, 10:305; al-Marghīnānī, *al-Hidāya*, 2:464; Abū ʿAbd Allāh al-Marwazī, *Ikhtilāf al-Fuqahāʾ* (Riyādh: Maktabat Adwa' al-Salaf, 2000), 429–31.

[48] Al-Kāsānī, *Badāʾiʿ al-Ṣanāʾiʿ*, 10:310.

[49] Al-Kāsānī, *Badāʾiʿ al-Ṣanāʾiʿ*, 10:310–11; al-Qurṭubī, *al-Jāmiʿ li Aḥkām al-Qur'ān*, 3:209–10. Al-Qurṭubī relates competing positions among the legal schools, including a tradition from the Prophet in which Muḥammad decreed for the People of the Book half the *diyya* of a Muslim.

[50] Ibn Nujaym, *al-Baḥr al-Rāʾiq*, 9:75.

[51] For a biography and analysis of al-Zuhrī's historical contributions, see A.A. Duri, *The Rise of Historical Writing Among the Arabs* (Princeton: Princeton University Press, 1983).

death compensation as Muslims. But during the caliphate of Muʿāwiya (r. 41–60/661–680) and thereafter, half the *diyya* originally paid to the family of non-Muslim victims was paid to the public treasury (*bayt al-māl*), thereby supporting the public treasury at the expense of *dhimmīs*. However, the later Umayyad caliph ʿUmar II b. ʿAbd al-ʿAzīz terminated the payments to the public treasury; but, importantly, he did not return that half to the families of non-Muslim victims.[52] His omission in this regard bolstered later legal analysis that limited the *dhimmī*'s wrongful death compensation to one-half of what the family of a Muslim victim could receive under the law. Later sources represent ʿUmar II's decision as a mark of his just rule, as compared to that of Muʿāwiya.[53] The justice at issue concerned the need to restrain the executive from overextending the scope of his power and authority. But ʿUmar II's justice did not extend to ensuring the full and equal compensation of *dhimmīs* for wrongs they suffered.

Why ʿUmar II failed to return the other portion of compensation to the *dhimmīs* is not entirely clear. Blankinship informs us that during ʿUmar II's reign, the Umayyad dynasty experienced financial insecurity as its attempts at expansion suffered military setbacks. Furthermore, and perhaps most importantly, the caliphate needed to enhance its Islamization policy in order to offset the influence of the Christian Byzantine Empire on Christians living in Islamic lands, an issue already addressed with respect to the second caliph's treatment of the Banū Taghlib.[54] Although the legal tradition rarely refers to this narrative from al-Zuhrī, one might surmise that ʿUmar II's failure to grant *dhimmīs* full compensation may reflect an attempt to bolster the regime's commitment to an Islamic universalist ethic at the same time it was struggling against encroachments on its imperial domain.[55] In other words, by halving the *diyya* for *dhimmīs*, premodern Muslim jurists gave legal cover to a practice that arose out of a particular, historical challenge of governance. The legal doctrine on wrongful death compensation may reflect highly contingent political and economic policies that were legitimized by jurists in terms of legal norms that were informed by an Islamic universalism and an imperial ethic that was under attack.

What does this analysis of the *dhimmī* rule on wrongful death compensation offer, given the initial case of Saudi Arabia? First, the

[52] Ibn Rushd al-Ḥafīd, *Bidāyat al-Mujtahid*, 2:605; ʿAbd al-Razzāq al-Ṣanʿānī, *Kitāb al-Muṣannaf*, 9:421 (#18814); Friedmann, *Tolerance and Coercion*, 41.

[53] ʿAbd al-Razzāq al-Ṣanʿānī, *Kitāb al-Muṣannaf*, 9:421.

[54] Blankinship, *The End of the Jihad State*, 93.

[55] In fact, Levy-Rubin remarks that ʿUmar b. ʿAbd al-ʿAzīz adopted a policy toward non-Muslims that reflected an "ideology regarding the ascendancy of Islam over the other religions": Levy-Rubin, *Non-Muslims in the Early Islamic Empire*, 88.

analysis allows us to observe two silences in the premodern and Saudi legal tradition. The first silence is in the premodern legal sources. The doctrinal sources analyzed above do not refer to al-Zuhrī's narrative that explains the conditions under which the *dhimmīs' diyya* was halved. By failing to acknowledge the role of the enterprise of governance in constituting the specific wrongful death damage, jurists gave legal cover to a specifically discretionary act by an agent of the enterprise of governance; in other words, the jurists' silence about the origins of this *diyya* rule reveals the extent to which the enterprise of governance could and did constitute Islamic legal doctrine. The second silence concerns the Saudi state's preference of Ḥanbalī law, thereby silencing the diverse range of opinions on this particular rule throughout Islamic legal history. This second silence shows the power of the modern state to define, constitute, and narrow the claim space for legal argument. In this case, the tensions that animated the differences between schools of legal thought in the premodern period are covered over by the modern state's overdetermination of the law in the interest of governing amidst diversity in a post-imperial, post-colonial context.

Furthermore, the analysis of the *diyya* rule and the Saudi legal context begs an important question about why and to what end the modern Saudi state utilizes a premodern answer to address contemporary questions of tort liability between parties. In other words, by analyzing the *diyya* doctrine through the lens of Sharīʿa as Rule of Law, we may be prompted to inquire into the conditions that give the Saudi wrongful death rule intelligibility in a governance context that is far removed from the one that informed the *diyya* rule, if we are to rely upon al-Zuhrī's account. Certainly Saudi Arabia has the sovereign authority to implement Sharīʿa-based norms. As a modern state (as opposed to a premodern empire), though, Saudi Arabia also participates in an international system composed of legal authorities and norms that contribute to and constitute Saudi Arabia's Rule of Law claim space.[56] Dismissal of international norms can be a precursor to collective international action, ranging from vocal opposition to sanctions to outright invasion within the UN system, for instance.

Those appalled by the discriminatory impact of the wrongful death rules in the Saudi legal system can adopt various strategies of opposition in the international legal arena to redress this situation. They might argue on human rights grounds that this legal outcome is patently discriminatory and violates various human rights documents that

[56] For a general introduction to international law, see Vaughan Lowe, *International Law* (Oxford: Oxford University Press, 2007).

reflect international norms from which Saudi Arabia cannot escape (and thereby define and delimit Saudi Arabia's Rule of Law claim space). For instance, Article 7 of the Universal Declaration of Human Rights pronounces that "[a]ll are equal before the law and are entitled without any discrimination to equal protection of the law." Likewise, Article 19 of the Cairo Declaration of Human Rights in Islam states in part: "All individuals are equal before the law, without distinction between the ruler and the ruled." Neither of these documents requires state ratification. Rather, they enunciate general norms that have arguably become part of customary international law, are *jus cogens*, or at the very least should constitute persuasive authority given that they contribute to the conditions of intelligibility within Saudi Arabia's Rule of Law claim space.

One might even refer to Article 26 of The International Covenant on Civil and Political Rights, which states:

> All persons are equal before the law and are entitled without any discrimination to the equal protection of the law. In this respect, the law shall prohibit any discrimination and guarantee to all persons equal and effective protection against discrimination on any ground such as race, colour, sex, language, religion, political or other opinion, national or social origin, property, birth or other status.

But Saudi Arabia has not ratified this convention, and so recourse to it will yield little by way of persuasive, let alone coercive force.

Certainly these international documents are important references for those committed to international human rights. They may even bolster the efforts of various states to put pressure on a country such as Saudi Arabia to modify its legal system to comport with general human rights principles. However, the problem with the mere resort to human rights documents is that it prioritizes one form of legal authority without adequately accounting for the others that, in the aggregate, contribute to the conditions of intelligibility within a Saudi Arabian Rule of Law claim space. This is underscored by the fact that many Muslim countries ratify international humanitarian conventions with reservations that limit their acceptance of the conventions to the extent that they require violation of the "Sharīʿa."[57] As noted above, Saudi Arabia's Basic Law emphasizes the authority of the most fundamental source-texts of Islamic law, the Qurʾān, and traditions of the Prophet. Saudi Arabia's national

[57] Mayer, *Islam and Human Rights*; idem, "Internationalizing the Conversation on Women's Rights," 133–60; Belinda Clark, "The Vienna Convention Reservations Regime and the Convention on Discrimination Against Women," *The American Journal of International Law* (1991): 281–321.

vision and legitimacy has been built upon its commitment to Islam, albeit a particular approach to Islam associated with the eighteenth-century reformer Muḥammad b. ʿAbd al-Wahhāb.

An alternative approach, premised on the separation of "church and state," might emphasize the need to create a state that treats its citizens equally and opts out of the business of legislating on or about Islam or Islamic law.[58] The separation approach, much like the human rights approach, is committed to improving the status of religious minorities in Saudi Arabia by emphasizing the idea of the "citizen" as the natural category of belonging in the modern state. To proffer this solution, though, is to ignore the history of Saudi Arabia and the way in which Islam and Islamic law have cast the nation, or in other words, have constituted the enterprise of governance. Indeed, such an approach continues to fail because it does not account for the way in which the law and the enterprise of governance are mutually constitutive.

The authority of international legal authorities exists alongside the authority of Islamic legal sources, and both contribute to the boundaries of Saudi Arabia's Rule of Law claim space. They have different provenances, and will have different weights in different states, depending on what legal issue is at stake. A Muslim state such as Tunisia may show an affinity for certain human rights norms over and against a more strict reading of Islamic legal rules on marriage and polygamy.[59] For Saudi Arabia, its Islamic ethos is a cornerstone of its claim to legitimate sovereignty. As such, while it participates in the international system, it will often do so only to the extent that abiding by international norms does not violate principles of Sharīʿa.[60] But importantly, unlike the premodern context, only the government has the power to decide

58 For an example of this argument, see An-Na'im, *Islam and the Secular State.*

59 Tunisia has banned polygamy, despite various Islamic legal sources that permit it. Abdullahi Ahmed An-Na'im, *Islamic Family Law in a Changing World: A Global Resource Book* (London: Zed Books, 2002), 183.

60 For a useful resource of countries and the international treaties (humanitarian and otherwise), see the website maintained by the International Committee of the Red Cross (<http://www.icrc.org/ihl.nsf>) , which includes a list of humanitarian conventions which Saudi Arabia has signed, ratified, or to which it has acceded. To the extent that Saudi Arabia has ratified international humanitarian treaties and conventions, it does so with reservations in favor of Sharīʿa. This practice is common among Muslim states: Michele Brandt and Jeffrey A. Kaplan, "The Tension between Women's Rights and Religious Rights: Reservations to Cedaw by Egypt, Bangladesh and Tunisia," *Journal of Law and Religion* 12, no. 1 (1995–96): 105–42; Andra Nahal Behrouz, "Transforming Islamic Family Law: State Responsibility and the Role of Internal Initiative," *Columbia Law Review* 103, no. 5 (June 2003): 1136–62; Rebecca J. Cook, "Reservations to the Convention on the Elimination of All Forms of Discrimination Against Women," *Virginia Journal of International Law* 30, no. 3 (1989–90): 643–716.

what those principles are and when they will be violated in the interest of abiding by alternative legal authorities.

None of this analysis should suggest that the resort to premodern rules on *diyya* is insulated from critique. Rather, it is to argue for a model of analysis and critique that first understands why premodern answers are being used to address modern questions before offering alternatives.[61] Inadequately accounting for the different constitutive features of a Rule of Law claim space, and failing to recognize the mutually constitutive relationship between law and the enterprise of governance, analysts will miss the larger context that gives intelligibility to a particular legal doctrine. In the present instance, such failure would disregard the way in which the Saudi state, in its formative period, relied on Islam as an organizing principle at a time when much of the Muslim world was under the yoke of European colonialism. Saudi Arabia may have had a different experience with the physical colonialism that its neighbors experienced, but it certainly has endured indirect colonialism. In fact, it continues to endure such indirect hegemony in the form of global trade over natural resources. Consequently, the resort to Islam as an organizing principle of the state and its rules of law arguably functions as a form of anti-colonial resistance. To dismiss the Saudi state's adoption of Islam and Islamic law as unintelligible, antiquated, or even anti-modern, ignores how both are presented as answers to questions about the place and intelligibility of the modern Muslim-majority state in the post-imperial, post-colonial context.

6.2 THE POST-COLONIAL MUSLIM STATE AND THE HEGEMONY OF LAW: SHARĪʿA AND THE *LINA JOY* CASE

The Saudi Arabian case shows how Muslim states use premodern Islamic legal doctrines to respond to the contemporary challenges of governing amidst the diversity of both peoples and legal traditions. One might argue that the contemporary resort to premodern *fiqh* may not seem the most obvious answer to address these issues, and certainly cannot claim to have the same intelligibility as the rules may have had in a premodern Islamic imperial context. Indeed, one might further suggest quite

[61] In the case of countries that apply Islamic law, it will necessarily involve an inquiry into the role of religion in the public sphere—a role that has witnessed a marked increase across different polities and religious communities. José Casanova, *Public Religions in the Modern World* (Chicago: Chicago University Press, 1994); idem, "Public Religions Revisited," in *Religion: Beyond a Concept*, ed. Hent de Vries (New York: Fordham University Press, 2008), 101–19.

reasonably that the institutional setting of governance has changed, that the sources of authority that define (in part) a nation's Rule of Law claim space have multiplied as global cooperation has increased, and that the hegemonic dynamics that gave intelligibility to the premodern *dhimmī* rules are not present in the same way in the modern enterprise of governance.

Despite such critiques, the resort to premodern answers (in the form of *fiqh*) nonetheless remains a constitutive feature of some Muslim-majority state Rule of Law claim spaces. As this section will suggest, the modern resort to premodern answers reflects the fact that to govern amidst diversity is a messy business with no simple answers, particularly for those countries that contend with the predicament of post-coloniality. This section will show, by analyzing a Malaysian apostasy case, that resort to premodern legal doctrines is symptomatic of a much more complicated question than merely governing amidst diversity. The question for modern Muslim-majority states draws upon an inherited Islamic history of empire, and a more recent history of colonialism and their current condition of post-coloniality. For Muslim-majority states, the challenge of governing amidst diversity poses questions about the place, authority, and authenticity of post-colonial Muslim states in the wake of a premodern history of empire (real and/or imagined), and, despite independence, their continued subservience to other states and global institutions that reinstantiate (at least implicitly) the colonial paradigm on a regular basis.[62] Their adherence to Islamic law may offer one means by which they subvert this dynamic. And yet, the way in which they draw upon Islamic law, and fit it together with the other features of their state-based Rule of Law claim spaces, can have the effect of perpetrating a different domination and hegemony over and against the domestic Other.

Antony Anghie compellingly argues in his study on international law that even when the international legal order aspires to global representativeness, it does not provide a level playing field for all nation states. His analysis of certain doctrines in international law, such as the doctrine of sovereignty, suggests that any invocation or application of international law potentially reinstantiates the colonial paradigm of European dominance. According to Anghie, colonialism contributed to and helped constitute the field of international law, which, in the period of colonialism, offered a systemic approach to managing European and

[62] For example, Mark Mazower has ably illustrated the colonial context that gave an initial impetus to the development of the United Nations. Mark Mazower, *No Enchanted Palace: The End of Empire and the Ideological Origins of the United Nations* (Princeton: Princeton University Press, 2009).

non-European relations.[63] Perhaps most significant in Anghie's argument is the claim that the colonial origins of international law are not necessarily separable from the current field or practice of international law. Rather, its colonial origins contributed to a "set of structures that continually repeat themselves at various stages in the history of international law."[64] Far from being peripheral to international law, the colonial paradigm is potentially reinstantiated with each application of international law today.

As noted earlier, international law and international institutions give content to a post-colonial Muslim state's Rule of Law claim space. Yet if Anghie is correct, then the rulers of these states cannot avoid asking "Can the post-colonial world deploy for its own purposes the law which had enabled its suppression in the first place?"[65] This question is not limited merely to the employment of international law. Rather, this question concerns the post-colonial subject in general, whether in the Muslim world or elsewhere. According to David Scott, the post-colonial subject, "inescapably modern as he is obliged by the modern conditions of his life to be. . . must seek his freedom in the very technologies, conceptual languages, and institutional formations in which modernity's rationality" historically sought and justified his prior subservience.[66] As much as the post-colonial Muslim state, for example, constructs its legitimacy by reference to multiple traditions of value (e.g., Islamic law, human rights, international law, constitutionalism), it nonetheless does so using the kinds of technologies of governance that made and continue to make possible subservience and domination over others.

As will be suggested below, the post-colonial Muslim state, despite rising out of anti-colonial resistance, cannot escape the hegemonic paradigm of governance, as will be suggested in the case of *Lina Joy* to be discussed shortly. This hegemonic paradigm is not simply a function of these states' adherence to Islamic law in some fashion. However the modern Muslim state resolves the complex demands made upon it, any solution to governing amidst diversity will be no less hegemonic over the domestic sphere than the European powers were over Muslim lands in the late nineteenth and early twentieth centuries, or than Muslim rulers were in the era of Islamic imperialism. As Anghie remarks: "the post-colonial state, once it emerges from the domination of colonialism,

[63] Anghie, *Imperialism, Sovereignty and the Making of International Law*, 3. For a historical analysis of how international law was deployed to manage the colonial venture, see Martii Koskenniemi, *The Gentle Civilizer of Nations: The Rise and Fall of International Law 1870–1960* (Cambridge: Cambridge University Press, 2004), 98–178.

[64] Anghie, *Imperialism*, 3.

[65] Anghie, *Imperialism*, 8.

[66] Scott, *Conscripts of Modernity*, 168.

immediately asserts itself to be the 'universal' entity that all minorities, for example, must comply with, and it then reproduces the same divisions, between the 'modern' and the 'primitive', that animated the colonial enterprise."[67] Importantly, to go back farther in history, to the extent that the imperial enterprise of governance in the premodern period constituted in part the claim space of Sharīʿa, the reader cannot escape noticing a shared and common feature in both the past and present—namely, the hegemonic character that exists at the intersection of the law and the enterprise of governance. In other words, as much as we have sought to historicize the intelligibility of the *dhimmī* rules in the premodern and modern periods, what remains constant across both periods is how minorities offer an important site to discover the hegemonic potential of law.

In the premodern context, the *dhimmī* rules were the result of a mutually constitutive relationship between the law and an imperial enterprise of governance. In the shift from an imperial model to a post-colonial state model, any invocation of the *dhimmī* rules or other such premodern *fiqh* rules regarding the Other resonates with a different intelligibility. In both contexts, such rules are indices of hegemony, but in the modern context, the hegemonic quality is coupled with a post-colonial anxiety that hides a sense of tragic loss. The use of premodern answers to modern questions reflects a romantic hope for a return to the era of Islamic superiority and imperial dominance, which is idealized in the form of Sharīʿa-based doctrines that become constitutive of modern state Rule of Law claim spaces. In one sense, therefore, the resort to premodern *fiqh* to answer modern questions of governance is an act of anti-colonial defiance. But defiance in the pursuit of what? The quixotic romantic hope for a return to Islamic superiority speaks to the tragedy of loss and dispossession, in both the immediate and distant pasts, that seems to haunt the Muslim world. The modern Muslim state occupies a space in a post-imperial *and* post-colonial era, existing alongside other states that were once its colonial masters. The modern Muslim state is a post-imperial, post-colonial enterprise of governance in which recourse to Islam and a reified version of Sharīʿa operate both as a rejection of the more immediate past and a reclamation of the more distant past, but in a period in which the conditions of both of those pasts no longer prevail.

Notably, the *dhimmī* rules are not the only regime of law in the premodern *fiqh* tradition that manifests these themes in modern Muslim states. As the analysis of a Malaysian case of apostasy will show, rules on apostasy not only help constitute the modern Muslim state enterprise

[67] Anghie, *Imperialism*, 316–17.

of governance, but also reveal the ever present hegemony that arises out of the mutually constitutive relationship between the law and the enterprise of governance generally. The case also illustrates how the hope for a redemptive Islamic state creates more dissonance than deliverance, given the legal and demographic diversity that the modern Muslim state contends with today. The Malaysian case shows that granting primacy to Sharīʿa-based norms creates a dissonance in the trust the state can claim from its subjects, given the plurality of legal authorities that define and delimit Malaysia's Rule of Law claim space.[68] Before turning to a consideration of that case though, a few words about Malaysia's political and legal history are in order.

The Muslim Malays of Malaysia constitute the majority of those who live in the country. Alongside the Muslim Malays live Chinese, Indians, and others, who are distinct on grounds of ethnicity, and often on grounds of religion. Despite their numerical superiority, the Malay Muslims are generally economically marginalized when compared to groups like the ethnic Chinese or the Indians. The economic disparity between the different ethnic groups has contributed to various tensions and conflicts in the country that have often pitted ethnic Malays against ethnic minorities.

Malaysia became a formally independent nation in 1957, comprising eleven states of the Malay Peninsula. In 1963 Singapore and the states of Sabah and Sarawak joined the federation, although Singapore later became an independent nation in 1965. Kuala Lumpur became a federal territory, followed by Lubuan and Putrajaya.[69] The Malaysian nation, therefore, is comprised of different states, federal territories, and a central government, all of which imply different jurisdictions of governance and legislative power. In particular, the division of power between the federal and state governments is significant for understanding the role of Islamic law in the country.

The authority of Islam and Islamic law in Malaysia is enshrined in the country's constitution. Article 3 of the Malaysian Constitution provides that "Islam is the religion of the Federation; but other religions may be practiced in peace and harmony in any part of the Federation."[70] Furthermore, the legislation enacting Islamic legal provisions is

[68] The observations about the nature of Sharīʿa discourses in Malaysia arise in part from my field research conducted while meeting with members of government, the judiciary, and civil society in July of 2007. I want to thank The Asia Foundation for bringing me to the region, and Canada's Department of Foreign Affairs and International Trade, and especially its officers at the High Commission in Malaysia for their programmatic support during my visit.

[69] Abdul Aziz Bari and Farid Shuaib, *Constitution of Malaysia: Text and Commentary*, 2nd ed. (Selangor, Malaysia: Prentice Hall, 2006), 1.

[70] Bari and Shuaib, *Constitution of Malaysia*, 5.

generally focused on family law,[71] and does not apply to non-Muslims.[72] Consequently, between the constitution and prevailing legislation, Islam is given a certain primacy without legally applying to non-Muslims.

The commission charged with drafting the Malaysian Constitution, the Reid Commission, designed it so as not to undermine the rights of non-Muslims to practice their faith freely. Its report stated: "'There was universal agreement that if...[a state religion provision]...were inserted, it must be made clear that it would not in any way affect the civil rights of the non-Muslims.'"[73] Although this may have been part of the initial design of the Malaysian Constitution, the *Lina Joy* case suggests that Sharīʿa-based norms operate in more than just specifically enacted legislation at the state level. Rather, Sharīʿa has become an instrument for defining Malaysian national identity.

6.2.1 The *Lina Joy* case and the anxiety of post-colonial legal pluralism

Lina Joy was born on January 8, 1964 with the given name of Azalina binti Jailani and raised by her Malay Muslim parents to be Malay Muslim. On February 21, 1997 she petitioned the National Registration Department (NRD) to change her name to Lina Lelani because, as she stated, she renounced Islam, became Christian, and wanted to marry a Christian man. She thus desired a new identity card that had her new name, not her old Arabic-sounding name. Importantly, when Lina Joy first sought

[71] While the state of Kelantan legislated an Islamic criminal law statute, it is not enforceable since criminal law falls under federal jurisdiction.

[72] See, for example, the following Malaysian statutes: Islamic Family Law (Federal Territories) Act 1984, section 4; Islamic Family Law (State of Malacca) Enactment 2002, section 4. The conception of Sharīʿa in various enactments in Malaysia can be gleaned from the way the statute defines a Sharīʿa law, or *hukum Syarak*, namely a rule "according to the Mazhab Shafie or any one of the Mazhab Hanafi, Maliki or Hambali" or alternatively according to "any recognized *Mazhab.*" Administration of the Religion of Islam (State of Malacca) Enactment 2002 and Regulations, section 2; Administration of the Religion of Islam (State of Selangor) Enactment 2003, section 2; Syariah Criminal Procedure (Federal Territories) Act 1997, section 2; Islamic Family Law (State of Malacca) Enactment 2002, section 2; Administration of Islamic Law (Federal Territories) Act 1993 (Act 505), section 2; Syariah Criminal Offenses (Federal Territories) Act 1997, section 2; Islamic Family Law (Federal Territories) Act 1984, section 2. The law of Islam, thereby, is understood in terms of the historical schools of Islamic law whose doctrines can be gleaned from treatises centuries old. For instance, section 10 of the Islamic Family Law (State of Malacca) Enactment 2002 states that no Muslim male shall marry a non-Muslim, "except a *Kitabiyah,*" while no Muslim woman shall marry a non-Muslim at all, both of which have Qur'ānic foundations: see Qur'ān 2:221, 5:5. The enactment provides no definition of *Kitabiyah*, but under historical Sharīʿa rules of *fiqh*, Muslim men could marry women from among the People of the Book.

[73] Bari and Shuaib, *Constitution of Malaysia*, 6, quoting The Reid Commission Report, para. 169.

to change her name on her identity card, the cards did not designate whether the card holder was Muslim or not. The NRD rejected her first application to change her name. On March 15, 1999 she submitted a second application to change her name—this time to Lina Joy—stating once again that her conversion to Christianity was her reason for seeking a name change. She received no answer from the NRD. Lina issued a third declaration to the NRD on August 2, 1999, but this time she did not state that her conversion motivated her name change. On October 22, 1999, the NRD granted her application to change her name and advised her to apply for a new identity card. However, at or around this time, a change in regulations required the NRD to print the religious identity of Muslim card holders. Consequently while Lina Joy's new identity card provided her new name, it stated her religious identity as Muslim—the very designation she wanted to avoid by her name change. Had this regulation not come into force, Lina Joy would have received the necessary change to her identity card, allowing her to participate socially and politically in Malaysian society without contending with questions about her religious upbringing given the Arabo-Islamic resonances of her given name. On January 3, 2000, Lina Joy made another application to the NRD to have her religious designation removed from her card. The clerk refused to accept her application because she provided no documentation from the Syariah Court attesting to her renunciation of Islam.

It was at this point that legal proceedings began. Lina Joy claimed at trial that her right to religious freedom, enshrined in Article 11 of the Malaysian Constitution, was violated. She also challenged the authority of the NRD to require more than her own statement of conversion to declare herself non-Muslim. Lina Joy lost her cases at all levels. At the Court of Appeal, the parties agreed to limit their dispute to the administrative law issue of the NRD's authority to require certification of her conversion from the Sharīʿa court. Nonetheless, Article 11 was still raised at the highest court by third-party intervenors to introduce constitutional arguments relevant to the resolution of the case.[74]

While the most significant issue for this section is the debate on Article 11, the case was not ultimately decided on that issue. Nonetheless, a review of the courts' analysis of Article 11 as it pertained to Lina Joy offers an

[74] For the summary of relevant facts pertaining to the *Lina Joy* case, see the dissenting opinion of Federal Court Justice Richard Malanjum, paras 7–26. His opinion can be found on the Malaysian Bar website: "Lina Joy Case: Dissenting Judgment of Justice Richard Malanjum," The Malaysian Bar: <http://www.malaysianbar.org.my/selected_judgements/lina_joy_case_dissenting_judgment_of_justice_richard_malanjum.html> (accessed September 6, 2008). I want to thank Malik Imtiaz, one of the intervening parties at the Federal Court, for sharing his thoughts and reflections on the *Lina Joy* case, and for clarifying the different issues at stake.

important window into the status of Islam in Malaysia; in their analysis of Article 11, the courts articulated a view of the relationship between Islam and the Malaysian nation as reflected in the Constitution.

Article 3 of the Malaysian Constitution, as noted earlier, asserts the primacy of Islam and Islamic law in Malaysia. Article 11, though, enshrines the principle of religious freedom in Malaysia:

> (1) Every person has the right to profess and practice his religion and, subject to Clause (4), to propagate it . . .
>
> (2) No person shall be compelled to pay any tax the proceeds of which are specially allocated in whole or in part for the purposes of a religion other than his own.
>
> (3) Every religious group has the right—
> a. to manage its own religious affairs;
> b. to establish and maintain institutions for religious or charitable purposes; and
> c. to acquire and own property and hold and administer it in accordance with law.
>
> (4) State law and in respect of the Federal Territories of Kuala Lumpur and Lubuan, Federal law may control or restrict the propagation of any religious doctrine or belief among persons professing the religion of Islam.
>
> (5) This article does not authorize any act contrary to any general law relating to public order, public health, or morality.

Certainly the language of Article 11 indicates that one can freely exercise his or her religion in Malaysia. At trial, however, the lower court held that Lina Joy could not use Article 11 to avoid "settling the issue of renunciation of her religion (Islam) with the religious authority which has the right to manage its own religious affairs under Article 11(3)(a) of the Federal Constitution."[75] Likewise, in Lina Joy's appeal to Malaysia's highest court, the Federal Court, the two-person majority stressed the importance of ensuring accuracy, correctness, and administrative accountability. In other words, Lina Joy improperly sought relief in the (secular) courts for an issue that properly belonged to the jurisdiction of the (religious) Sharīʿa courts given the latters' authority to determine whether or not someone is a Muslim.[76]

[75] *Lina Joy v Majlis Agama Islam Wilayah Persekutuan and Anor* [2004] 6 CLJ 242, 249.

[76] The fact that Muslims alone are singled out by the NRD regulations and hence by the High Court's decision was of great concern to Federal Court Justice Malanjum in his dissent at the highest and final level of appeal, where the court decided against Lina Joy: *Lina Joy Case*, paras 44–6.

The judges at all levels of adjudication were fully cognizant of the importance of the secular ideals underlying Article 11, which were embedded in Lina Joy's argument. However, they were unwilling to accept that the Malaysian Constitution enshrined a secular ethos for the state that rendered Islam one among other equally situated religions. Faiza Tamby Chik J., writing for the trial court, stated: "I am of the view by looking at the constitution as a whole, it is the general tenor of the constitution that Islam is given a special position and status, with art. 3 declaring Islam to be the religion of the Federation."[77] The court opinion further stated:

> Article 3(4) does not have the effect of reinforcing the status of the Federation as a secular state as suggested by the plaintiff [Lina Joy] ... Malaysia is not purely a secular state like India or Singapore but is a hybrid between the secular state and the theocratic state. The constitution of this hybrid model accords official or preferential status to Islam but does not create a theocratic state like Saudi Arabia or Iran.[78]

References to Malaysia as a hybrid state and the significance of Islam and Islamic law reveal the court's official prioritization of Islam over and against any other value that might conflict with the Islamic ethos of the state. Indeed, the Federal Court majority opinion stated that the NRD was reasonable in requiring certification of apostasy *from* Islam because the matter of apostasy from Islam is extremely sensitive in the Malaysian context.[79]

Despite the diverse sources of authority that contribute to the claim space of Malaysia's legal system, to prioritize one source over others necessarily contributes to a dissonance in intelligibility, given the normative demands of those other sources upon the very same legal order. Aware of the potential dissonance, the trial court adopted the "principle of harmonious construction" to give effect to all the parts of the Constitution. As such, it sought to reconcile the apparently conflicting provisions. A harmonious reading of the Malaysian Constitution led the trial court to hold that "[t]he declaration in art. 3(1) has the consequence of qualifying a Muslim's absolute right to murtad [apostasize] in art. 11(1) by requiring that compliance to the relevant syariah laws on apostasy is a condition precedent."[80] According to the court, since Lina Joy "is still a Muslim, the finality of her decision to convert out of Islam is within

[77] *Lina Joy* [2004] 6 CLJ 242 at 250. [78] *Lina Joy* [2004] 6 CLJ 242 at 252.

[79] *Lina Joy v Federal Territory Islamic Council, the Government of Malaysia, and Director General of the National Registration Department*, Federal Court of Malaysia, civil appeal no. 01-2-2006 (W), ¶ 10 (hereinafter, *Lina Joy* (FC Maj.)).

[80] *Lina Joy* [2004] CLJ 242 at 253.

the competency of a Syariah Court."[81] In the trial court and again in the Federal Court, Lina Joy's subjective and sincere assertion of her apostasy and conversion to Christianity was of no legal significance. The fact that she stated as part of her pleadings that she did not consider herself Muslim fell on deaf ears. For example, the trial court still considered her a Muslim under the law, and imposed upon her the requirement to seek the necessary certification from a Sharīʿa court to authenticate her apostasy. Furthermore, the Federal Court went so far as to construe the freedom of religion to mean abiding by the dictates of one's faith, even when seeking to exit it.[82] In the Malaysian context, those dictates happen to include for Muslims a separate Sharīʿa legal system. By interpreting the constitution in this way, the court embedded the right of religious freedom in both the language of constitutional rights and institutions of government.

The harmonization of the two constitutional provisions was accomplished in large part by limiting the freedoms of Malaysia's Muslim citizens. Consequently, if one were to assure non-Muslims in Malaysia of their secure position in the state, they might hold that the *Lina Joy* decision actually works to the detriment of Malaysia's Muslims as individual rights holders. But by justifying that limitation by reference to Article 3, the court construed the public good in terms of the integrity, priority, and superiority of Islam as the public ethos of Malaysia, a point emphasized by the Federal Court when it interpreted Article 11.

The prioritization of Islam in Malaysia should recall the various themes of Islamic universalism, Muslim superiority, and (by implication) the subordination of non-Muslims that informed the premodern *dhimmī* rules. By defining Malaysia as a hybrid state and prioritizing Islam in that otherwise hybrid state, the judges involved in the *Lina Joy* case gave legal dressing to a form of Islamic exceptionalism that implicitly subordinated the position of non-Muslims in the Malaysian polity. For instance, because she was born a Muslim, Lina Joy was subjected to Islamic law, unlike people born into other faiths. Not only are non-Muslims in Malaysia not subjected to Islamic law, but they are not even held to their own religious law to the same degree as Muslims are held to theirs. Members of other faiths who convert to Islam are not subject to analogous religious court oversight.[83] Coupled with the various references to the "preferential status" and sensitivities of Islam in the Malaysian Constitution, the limits on Lina Joy's religious freedom reflect how the predominance of an Islamic ethos in Malaysia was read into the constitution (and thereby

[81] *Lina Joy* [2004] CLJ 242 at 254. [82] *Lina Joy* (FC Maj.), ¶ 14.

[83] The Federal Court limited its decision only to Muslims leaving Islam: *Lina Joy* (FC Maj.), ¶ 17.

the Malaysian enterprise of governance) in such a way that should make Malaysia's non-Muslim citizens anxious about their status and standing in the state.[84]

The trial court's language on the content of the public ethos of Malaysia is particularly telling. It stated that the controlling legislation that required Lina Joy to seek redress from the Sharīʿa court "cannot but be said to be in the interest of public order and within the ambit of permissible legislative interference with that fundamental right [of religious freedom]. The provisions strike the correct balance between individual fundamental rights and the interest of public order."[85] In the case of Lina Joy, the trial court's balance operated against the interest of a Malay Muslim citizen seeking to practice her new-found faith freely. No other religious convert had to endure what a Muslim apostate had to endure. By requiring Lina Joy to do so in the interest of the "public good," the court effectively defined the "public good" in the light of an Islamic universalism that, in this case, rendered the Muslim Malay not just an exception to Article 11, but also exceptional (and by implication superior) to non-Muslims in Malaysia who may apostatize from their own minority faith to another tradition, Islam or otherwise.

Lina Joy sought redress under the civil and constitutional law of Malaysia, but instead was told to go to the institutions of religious authority that she sought to escape through her conversion. Despite her efforts to the contrary, she lost her case at all levels of appeal. The highest court in Malaysia, the Federal Court, denied her appeal on May 30, 2007, although with the one non-Muslim justice dissenting. The ultimate and final resolution of the case left Lina Joy without any civil recourse; rather, when the highest court in Malaysia ruled against her, she was required to appear before a Sharīʿa court before the civil authorities could respond to her request to change her identification card.

By requiring Lina Joy to appear before the Sharīʿa court, the secular court forced her to submit herself to a body that would see her as a sinner to be punished and not a right-holder entitled to religious freedom.[86] It also submitted her to a body that she no longer considered authoritative because of her conversion. Nevertheless, the Malaysian courts defined Lina Joy as a Muslim, regardless of her own voice and testimony. In doing so, the court required her to conform to standards that it did not impose on others born to different faiths. The implicit imposition of this "higher

[84] Chow Kum Hor, "Polls role for Churches, Hindu Temples," *The Straights Times*, February 18, 2008; Sholto Byrnes, "Creeping Islamisation," *New Statesman* 19 (September 10, 2007), 136.

[85] *Lina Joy* [2004] CLJ 242 at 259.

[86] "Asia: Lina Joy's Despair; Malaysia," *The Economist* (London), June 2, 2007, 66.

standard" is tantamount to stratifying the Malysian polity, with the Muslims considered superior and all others as subordinate.

The *Lina Joy* case reveals an Islamic universalist ethos that found expression in a modern state, despite a shift in the system of governance. That shift raises important questions about the intelligibility of invoking premodern rules to answer modern questions of governance in a context of multiple legal orders at the domestic and international level. The courts offer a narrative about the hybrid nature of the Malaysian state, the significance of Islam to Malaysia, and the implication of the state's Islamic ethos on the power and authority of its governing institutions. While contending with its post-imperial, post-colonial present, Malaysia's courts attempted to harmonize the multiple legal orders that defined the claim space within which they operated. But the courts could not do so without at the same time adopting a hegemonic position against not only Lina Joy, but all Malaysian citizens, whether Muslim or not. The courts resorted to a type of Islamic universalism that glossed over the discontinuities in the intelligibility of premodern doctrines on apostasy and modern conceptions of the rights-bearing citizen in a constitutional federation. The tragic quality of this case comes from witnessing the inability of the judiciary to recognize that its recourse to premodern answers is simply a different hegemonic model of governance than the colonial one. The judgment does little to quell the anxiety of being post-imperial, post-colonial, and subject to the demands of plural legal orders, not all of which are of the state's own making.

The plurality of legal sources in the modern state is part of the challenge in understanding the place of Islamic law today. "Sharīʿa" in Malaysia is not itself a claim space, but rather is a constitutive component of an entirely different claim space that is defined and delimited by a host of legal authorities. Islamic legal doctrines are surely authoritative in Malaysia, but so too are the constitution, statutes, and various international instruments. They coexist as authoritative sources of law. In the premodern system, diversity was principally a demographic fact. Other religious traditions may have been practiced in the Muslim polity, but they were not considered sources of legal authority alongside the Sharīʿa. Recall that the liability of *dhimmīs* to stoning for adultery was based on a *factual* inquiry into the *dhimmī*'s tradition, but their tradition was not considered an authoritative or legitimate basis for legal decision. In the modern Muslim state, though, Sharīʿa does not hold a monopoly on legal authority. Diversity today refers not only to the diversity of peoples, but also to the multiplicity of legal sources that contribute to the conditions of intelligibility. In a post-colonial context in which the indices of colonialism have not been eradicated (and perhaps never will be),

Sharīʿa (however reified and reduced) can be a calming salve. Its calming effect, though, rests in its contribution to an anti-colonial narrative of political legitimacy for a state that now exercises the technologies of governance in a manner that perpetuates the dominance and hegemony that it once fought against. Indeed, drawing upon the observations of Anghie and David Scott noted above, this study uses Rule of Law to illuminate the hegemonic tendencies that arise when minorities make claims upon the enterprise of governance. At some point, the interests of minority groups may be sacrificed in the interest of a public good that is defined in terms that the minority group may find adversely imposing or even hegemonic. That fact by itself is not unique to the Islamic tradition or the Muslim world. Rather, it traverses both time and space.

6.3 CONCLUSION: THE HEGEMONY OF RULE OF LAW

This chapter has argued that modern recourse to premodern *fiqh* doctrines, specifically the *dhimmī* and apostasy rules, reflects the inescapable challenge of governing amidst diversity, but without duly accounting for how the underlying context of law and governance today fundamentally alters the intelligibility of such *fiqh* doctrines when applied in today's political and legal landscape. Whereas the premodern rules were developed in light of an Islamic imperial enterprise of governance (whether imagined or real), the modern recourse to those premodern answers is made from a position of post-colonial anxiety about the authority of the territorially delimited sovereign state. Muslim elites, whether in majority Muslim countries or in minority contexts, who today invoke *fiqh* doctrines, such as the *dhimmī* rules, do so from a post-imperial and post-colonial perspective, all the while hoping to reinstantiate a past that may have been more imagined than real even for premodern jurists—especially those writing well after the end of the Umayyad dynasty when the imperatives of expansive conquest yielded to the pragmatics of maintaining borders and ensuring political survival.

The attention in this chapter to contemporary trends in the use of the *dhimmī* rules in textbooks and the Saudi legal system shows that their intelligibility is not constant across time and space. The intelligibility of the premodern rules in a premodern imperial context was one thing. But when partially translated by Nuh Keller in his *Reliance of the Traveller*, the intelligibility draws in part upon Keller's transnational, post-colonial Muslim audience in English speaking regions such as North America. Additionally, when premodern *fiqh* rules on wrongful death compensation and apostasy are applied in Saudi Arabia and Malaysia respectively, we cannot ignore how their intelligibility draws upon the post-colonial anxiety of these states, which participate on a global stage and must contend with a plurality of legal traditions (some of foreign and even colonial origin) that constitute, define, or otherwise contribute to their claim space of law. Sharīʿa today is less a claim space of justice, and instead is a set of rules that constitutes, along with other normative traditions, the conditions of intelligibility for a modern state's claim space of justice.[87] With colonialism, colonial resistance, post-colonial nation-building, and Islamization programs as part of the contemporary backdrop, we can appreciate how and why Islamic legal doctrines have been folded into various political ideologies of identity of both the state and the self: the premodern doctrines give content to the dispossessed post-colonial subject and state. As such, to abandon the premodern *fiqh* tradition as a source of answers to modern questions can be viewed by Muslim elites as an attack on the Islamic identity that post-colonial political ideologies seek to construe, whether in Muslim-majority states or even for Muslims living as minorities.[88]

While the post-colonial backdrop may contribute to the intelligibility of contemporary recourse to premodern *fiqh,* that does not change or otherwise alter the hegemonic potential that can arise therefrom. This hegemonic potential is particularly evident when someone makes a claim upon a Muslim-majority state to accommodate a preference that may run contrary to the established public values of the state. To recall the advice of al-Māwardī, some set of core values is necessary to ensure a functioning political order. However, while those core values are necessary for the purpose of governance, they also make possible a hegemonic imperative. Premodern Muslim jurists manifested that imperative in their justifications of various *dhimmī* rules. Saudi Arabia exhibits that imperative in the way it defines and narrows the Islamic content of its legal system. Malaysia's courts demonstrate that imperative in the way they prioritize Islam in their harmonization of apparent conflicts between constitutional provisions. Just like the premodern imperial enterprise of governance and the modern colonial one, the post-colonial Muslim state perpetuates a hegemony of its own, in the name of an Islamic order that exists in an uneasy relationship with the Other who

[87] On the relationship between Sharīʿa and ideological/political developments in the Muslim world, see Chibli Mallat, *The Renewal of Islamic Law: Muhammad Baqer as-Sadr, Najaf and the Shi'i International* (Cambridge: Cambridge University Press, 1993); Hamid Enayat, *Modern Islamic Political Thought* (Austin, Texas: University of Texas Press, 1982); Mansoor Moaddel, *Islamic Modernism, Nationalism, and Fundamentalism: Episode and Discourse* (Chicago: University of Chicago Press, 2005).

[88] Emon, "Techniques of Legal Reasoning."

make claims upon the Muslim state. To recall David Scott's critique of post-colonial theorists, this chapter has argued that the tendency toward hegemony is not simply limited to the era of European colonialism or the modern Muslim state and its technologies of domination. Rather, the hegemonic potential lies in the very relationship between law and the enterprise of governance that this study has sought to highlight by viewing Sharīʿa as Rule of Law.

The sobering point to take away at this stage in the study is that if Rule of Law denotes a claim space defined and delimited in part by the mutually constitutive relationship between the law and the enterprise of governance, then hegemony is an inevitable consequence. While post-colonial theorists may principally locate that hegemony in the European colonial period of the nineteenth and twentieth centuries, this study suggests that by viewing Sharīʿa as Rule of Law, that hegemonic potential can be located no less in the premodern Islamic imperial past, than in the European colonial period, and in the modern post-imperial, post-colonial present as Muslim elites (whether in minority or majority contexts) continue to look to premodern *fiqh* for answers to modern questions about governance amidst the diversity of people and law. As will be further illustrated in the chapter that follows, it need not matter whether the Rule of Law claim space is Islamic or Western, or whether the period under consideration is premodern or modern. Rather, the hegemonic dynamic that is embedded in the mutually constitutive relationship between law and the enterprise of governance seems to make all-too-frequent appearances at the discursive site created by the minority claimant who makes demands upon the enterprise of governance.

7

Religious Minorities and the Empire of Law

This study has predominantly focused on the *dhimmī* rules to demonstrate how they are symptomatic of the challenges that arise when governing amidst diversity. However, as suggested at the end of Chapter 6, this study aspires to extend its paradigm of analysis beyond Islamic legal history to address more generally the challenges that lie at the intersection of law, governance, and pluralism. The *dhimmī,* far from presenting a unique dynamic, actually provides an entry point into the more general challenge of governing amidst diversity. The focus on the *dhimmī* rules and the Muslim world should not suggest, therefore, that the *dhimmī* rules specifically, and Islamic law more generally, are unique in demonstrating the potential, if not inevitability, of such challenges. Whether in the context of premodern Islamic law or modern democratic constitutional states, governing amidst diversity presents an important opportunity to reflect upon the implications of asymmetries in power on the definition of rights, the public good, and the scope of accommodation for minority interests. To illustrate how this challenge is shared across legal systems, this chapter will address the legal arguments used to justify the regulation of religious minorities in what might be considered modern, democratic, constitutional states, in particular the United States, the United Kingdom, and France. Although the chapter addresses different religious minority groups, the focus will be on three legal decisions that regulate the scope and extent to which the covered Muslim woman can cover herself pursuant to her religious beliefs without suffering adverse consequences justified under the law.

7.1 RULE OF LAW AND THE EMPIRE OF THE PUBLIC GOOD

Accommodating the interests of religious minorities can pose concerns about the well-being of the polity at large. When judges resolve such cases, they often do so by employing legal arguments to construe and define the interests of minority claimants, the demands of the public weal, and the appropriate balance to be struck between them. Judges perform such balancing within the claim space of a given Rule of Law system, whose conditions of intelligibility are in part defined by the prevailing enterprise of governance. Consequently, as in the case of *dhimmīs,* legal debates about minority rights and accommodation offer an important site for revealing the boundaries of the Rule of Law claim space of a given polity.

For example, in mid-twentieth century United States, one site of debate involved the religious freedom claims by the Jehovah's Witnesses. In *Minersville School District v Gobitis* (1940), Lillian and William Gobitis were expelled from the public schools of Minersville School District for refusing to salute the US flag as part of a daily school exercise that the local school board required of all students.[1] The Gobitis children, committed Jehovah's Witnesses, were of the age at which school attendance was compulsory under the law. Consequently, when the children were expelled, their parents had to bear the cost of enrolling their children in private school. The father brought suit against the School District, claiming that expelling his children for failing to salute the flag violated his children's due process and religious freedom rights under the First and Fourteenth Amendments of the US Constitution. The trial and appellate courts found for the Gobitis children, but the Supreme Court reversed. In his opinion for the majority, Justice Frankfurter poignantly recognized the task before the Court:

> When does the constitutional guarantee compel exemption from doing what society thinks necessary for the promotion of some *great common end,* or from a penalty for conduct which appears dangerous to the *general good*?... But to affirm that the freedom to follow conscience has itself no limits in the life of a society would deny that very plurality of principles which, as a matter of history, underlies protection of religious toleration ... Our present task then, as so often the case with courts, is to reconcile two rights in order to prevent either from destroying the other.[2]

For Frankfurter J., the school district's requirement to participate in the flag salute exercise was a general rule of application. Its generality spoke to the power of legislative and administrative bodies to compel a particular practice in the interests of a public good, such as national unity.

[1] *Minersville School District v Gobitis,* 310 US 586 (1940). For a discussion of this case, as well as a correction of the family's name (Gobitas), see Martha Nussbaum, *Liberty of Conscience: In Defense of America's Tradition of Religious Equality* (New York: Basic Books, 2008), 199–214.

[2] *Gobitis,* 310 US 586 at 593–4 (emphasis added).

National unity, however, was not more or less important than religious freedom; he recognized both as significant values. Yet he also knew that just because someone happened to have a particular religious belief did not mean that he or she could not be subjected to a general rule that might run against the particular belief in question; rather, in some cases, one value may trump another for reasons that are deemed necessary and justifiable.

Among those reasons that could trump an individual rights claim, according to Frankfurther J., was the preservation of order and tranquility of the polity at large. He noted that in other cases posing a similar conflict of values, "the general laws in question, upheld in their application to those who refused obedience from religious conviction, were manifestations of specific powers of government deemed by the legislature *essential to secure and maintain that orderly, tranquil, and free society without which religious toleration itself is unattainable.*"[3] Order, well-being, and tranquility, according to Frankfurter J., were important features of society and required collective commitment. Without all people participating in ways that contribute to such order, the very framework of society that makes pluralistic coexistence possible would break down. In other words, without a collective commitment to a shared vision of the polity and its well-being, there could be no religious freedom.

The fundamental question, though, was whether the failure to pledge allegiance to the flag in a public school was such a threat to the order, tranquility, and well-being of the polity such that the Gobitis children's religious freedom should be curtailed. For Frankfurter J., the children's actions gravely undermined and threatened the spirit of national unity. He argued as follows:

> The ultimate foundation of a free society is the binding tie of cohesive sentiment. Such a sentiment is fostered by all those agencies of the mind and spirit which may serve to gather up the traditions of a people, transmit them from generation to generation, and thereby create that continuity of a treasured common life which constitutes a civilization. "We live by symbols." The flag is the symbol of our national unity, transcending all internal differences, however large, within the framework of the Constitution. This Court has had occasion to say that " . . . the flag is the symbol of the nation's power—the emblem of freedom in its truest, best sense . . . it signifies government resting on the consent of the governed; liberty regulated by law; the protection of the weak against the strong; security against the exercise

[3] *Gobitis*, 310 US 586 at 595 (emphasis added).

of arbitrary power; and absolute safety for free institutions against foreign aggression."[4]

For Frankfurter J., national unity was an essential condition for order and well-being. He went so far as to say that "[n]ational unity is the basis of national security."[5] As such, he ruled against the Gobitis children. Reframing his holding in terms of this study's Rule of Law framework, Frankfurter J. proffered a legal argument from within a claim space that ultimately constituted and enhanced the enterprise of governance by protecting the actions of the public school board against the challenge posed by a minority claimant.

Writing in dissent, Justice Stone expressed grave concern about permitting an institution within the prevailing enterprise of governance such as the school board to require students to salute the flag in violation of their liberty interests. The effect of the general rule, he suggested, was far too invasive: "For by this law the state seeks to coerce these children to express a sentiment which, as they interpret it, they do not entertain, and which violates their deepest religious convictions."[6] He did not suggest that liberties such as religious freedom must and should always trump claims of national order and well being. He recognized and acknowledged that the government must have the power to ensure the public good, even if at times such efforts run against individual rights guaranteed in the Bill of Rights. Indeed, one might even suggest that this form of hegemony by the enterprise of governance is necessary if a community of people is to be managed in an orderly fashion. He wrote that "the constitutional guaranties of personal liberty are not always absolutes. *Government has a right to survive* and powers conferred upon it are not necessarily set at naught by the express prohibitions of the Bill of Rights."[7] For Justice Stone, though, the *Gobitis* case did not provide an appropriate occasion to override individual freedom in the interest of the state's right to survive. He wrote: "[I]t is a long step, and one which I am unable to take, to the position that government may, as a supposed educational measure and as a means of disciplining the young, compel public affirmations which violate their religious conscience."[8]

[4] *Gobitis*, 310 US 586 at 596.

[5] *Gobitis*, 310 US 586 at 595.Frankfurter J. was aware of the stakes at issue in this case. The claims of a religious minority were weighed against the demands of the polity for national well-being and order. The legislation at issue was neither specific nor particular; it was a general rule of law that was well within the power of the legislature to put into effect. Frankfurter J. seemed especially compelled to respect the power of the legislation in matters such as education, as the Court lacked the competence to advise on education policy.

[6] *Gobitis*, 310 US 586 at 601.

[7] *Gobitis*, 310 US 586 at 602 (emphasis added).

[8] *Gobitis*, 310 US 586 at 602.

Of particular interest to this study is how Justice Stone expressed concern about the unavoidable hegemony suffered by minorities when general rules of application grant the enterprise of governance the authority to uphold and enforce respect for values that are deemed so central that the polity will suffer if exceptions to the general rule are granted. He wrote: "History teaches us that there have been but few infringements of personal liberty by the state which have not been justified, as they are here, *in the name of righteousness and the public good, and few which have not been directed, as they are now, at politically helpless minorities.*"[9] In this one line, Stone J. illustrated what this study holds out as the inescapable hegemony that comes to the fore whenever minorities make claims upon and against the enterprise of governance. The *Gobitis* case exemplifies the analytic contribution that Rule of Law as a claim space gives to our understanding of the dynamics of law and governance.

Importantly, given that a country like the United States is a democratic polity whose legitimacy is premised on its representativeness, some might suggest that a minority group can affect the enterprise of governance by participating in the political system. But this, Justice Stone argued, would place an undue burden on the minority: "This seems to me no more than the surrender of the constitutional protection of the liberty of small minorities to the popular will."[10] He recognized that the political arena operates pursuant to majoritarian norms. To demand the minority to make changes within the political system of a democratic enterprise of governance ignores how the hegemony of the enterprise in the first place is premised on its commitment to values that are shared and common among the majority, and thus create the conditions that require minorities to have recourse to the courts. For Justice Stone, the court must assume the responsibility to provide an institutional site where the minority can be protected from such majoritarianism—a responsibility that he felt the majority in *Gobitis* failed to carry.

Three years later, the Supreme Court overruled *Gobitis* in *West Virginia State Board of Education v Barnette.*[11] *Barnette* involved a state board of education that, acting pursuant to state legislation, required students in its schools to salute the US flag. Refusal to salute the flag was considered an act of insubordination, according to the relevant school board resolution, and would lead to the student's expulsion from school. Furthermore, the expelled student would be considered unlawfully absent from school, thereby imposing criminal liability upon the expelled

[9] *Gobitis,* 310 US 586 at 604 (emphasis added).
[10] *Gobitis,* 310 US 586 at 606.
[11] *West Virginia State Board of Education v Barnette,* 319 US 624 (1943).

student's parents, who were required by law to ensure that their children of school age attended school. No provision was made to exempt Jehovah's Witnesses from the flag salute requirement. The petitioners in *Barnette* were Jehovah's Witnesses, and sought relief from the school board's resolution as it pertained to them.

Delivering the opinion of the Court, Justice Jackson wrote that the issue presented in *Barnette* was not one of conflicting rights, but rather a conflict between the authority of an institution of the enterprise of governance—a state Board of Education—and the right of individuals to freedom of conscience. As he wrote: "The sole conflict is between authority and rights of the individual. The State asserts power to condition access to public education on making a prescribed sign and profession . . . The latter stand on a right of self-determination in matters that touch individual opinion and personal attitude."[12] In other words, the *Barnette* case provides an important example, as does *Gobitis*, of when minority claims upon the state showcase the hegemony that inevitably arises when governing amidst diversity.

Jackson J. recognized that while the symbolism of the flag salute may have its utility in fostering national unity, the power of the state to enforce the flag salute was a wholly different issue. He did not consider the court's function to determine what was an appropriate and effective symbol of national unity; however, it was the court's duty to consider whether the state had the power to require and enforce the provisions in the Board of Education resolution. Jackson J. wrote: "validity of the asserted power to force an American citizen publicly to profess any state of belief, or to engage in any ceremony of assent to one, presents questions of power that must be considered independently of an idea we may have as to the utility of the ceremony in question."[13]

Turning to the *Gobitis* decision, Jackson J. attacked it for assuming the very thing that the Court had to decide, namely whether the state had the power to require the flag salute at the cost of the individual's freedoms. He noted that the *Gobitis* decision presumed that the enterprise of governance had the power and authority to compel children to salute the flag. Jackson J., however, rejected that presumption. He held that while national unity was a noble goal to pursue, courts had to be wary of granting the state the power to instill such unity by compelling a salute to the flag against the freedom and liberty interests of individuals. In other words, far from constituting and enhancing the enterprise of governance, Jackson J. demanded that courts take special care in those cases when individual freedoms are at stake, in particular those of minority groups

[12] *Barnette*, 319 US 624 at 630–1.

[13] *Barnette*, 319 US 624 at 634.

with limited political power, lest the judicial branch, as an instrument of the enterprise of governance, *unduly* constitute, enable, and enhance the enterprise of governance at the expense of the minority claimant. For this reason, he emphasized how the Bill of Rights was designed to remove certain values from the realm of majoritarian politics. He wrote: "The very purpose of the Bill of Rights was to withdraw certain subjects from the vicissitudes of political controversy, to place them beyond the reach of majorities and officials, and to establish them as legal principles to be applied by the courts."[14] For Jackson J., the *Gobitis* case showcased the danger that arises from the mutually constitutive relationship between the law and the enterprise of governance. Jackson J. recognized that in cases featuring a conflict between state authority and the rights of individuals under the Bill of Rights, the judiciary had to stand between the two as a check against the hegemonic power of the state over and against the claims of minority interests; otherwise, the consequences could be dire. Indeed, in a poignant moment he wrote: "Compulsory unification of opinion achieves only the unanimity of the graveyard."[15]

These two US cases offer an initial and relatively contemporary insight into how religious minorities who demand respect and space for their religious practices and beliefs are still viewed as threats to the public good, and thereby to the enterprise of governance. The Gobitis children were not rebels, nor were they espousing hatred of the United States; but they would not participate in an exercise that required them to violate their religious beliefs. The Supreme Court in *Gobitis,* while keen to protect religious freedom, nonetheless saw the case as involving fundamental questions about public good, cohesion, and security—all of which were potentially threatened by a religious minority group seeking exemption from a general rule issued by a competent legislature. The *Gobitis* court resolved the tension between religious freedom and national security by viewing the minority community as a threat from which the state could and had to protect itself. The intelligibility of the *Gobitis* decision rests upon certain presumptions about the public good, the authority of the enterprise of governance, and the perception of the minority claimant as a threat to both. *Barnette,* on the other hand, offers an important reminder that, as much as courts may operate on such presumptions, they need not do so. These competing judicial approaches recall the debate between Muslim jurists about *dhimmī* charitable endowments. While al-Shīrāzī considered a charitable endowment for a Bible or Torah reading school akin to support for arming the polity's enemy, the Ḥanafī school was much more accommodating of *dhimmī* endowments, and less

[14] *Barnette,* 319 US 624 at 638. [15] *Barnette,* 319 US 624 at 641.

willing to prioritize the power and authority of the state over and against the minority group's interests.

The juxtaposition of *Gobitis* and *Barnette* hints at how an appreciation of the hegemonic potential of the law reveals the boundaries that demarcate a Rule of Law claim space, and thereby begs important questions about the content of those boundaries (e.g., public good, individual rights).[16] For instance, *Bruker v Markovitz,* a case from the Supreme Court of Canada, involved a Jewish husband who refused to issue a religious divorce to his wife so that she would be divorced under Jewish law. The couple had signed a consent decree in the province of Quebec in which the husband agreed to appear before a Rabbinical tribunal to issue the divorce, or *Ghet.* He never did. His wife sued thereafter, and the husband retorted that the case involved a religious matter that was outside the purview of the Court. Abella J., writing for the Court, recognized the importance of protecting diversity and religious freedom: Canada's Charter of Rights and Freedoms upholds the fundamental freedom of conscience and religion.[17] That freedom, though, is "subject only to such reasonable limits prescribed by law as can be demonstrably justified in a free and democratic society."[18] By providing for these limits on fundamental freedoms, Section 1 of the Charter effectively contributes to defining the claim space of justice by invoking and incorporating the enterprise of governance as a constitutive feature of the intelligibilty of a legal argument. Abella J. presumed this constitutive feature of the law in her majority opinion when she wrote in various places:

> The right to have differences protected, however, does not mean that those differences are always *hegemonic.* Not all differences are compatible with Canada's *fundamental values* and, accordingly, not all barriers to their expression are arbitrary.[19]
>
> . . .
>
> In my view, an agreement between spouses to take the necessary steps to permit each other to remarry in accordance with *their* own religions constitutes a valid and binding contractual obligation under Quebec law. . . [Such] agreements are consistent with public policy, *our* approach to marriage and divorce, and *our* commitment to eradicating gender discrimination.[20]
>
> . . .

[16] Leslie Green, "On Being Tolerated," in *The Legacy of H.L.A. Hart,* eds M. Kramer et al. (Oxford: Oxford University Press, 2008), 277–98.

[17] *Canadian Charter of Rights and Freedoms,* Part I of the *Constitution Act, 1982,* being Schedule B to the *Canada Act 1982,* Ch. 11 (UK), art. 2(a).

[18] *Canadian Charter of Rights and Freedoms,* art. 1.

[19] *Bruker v Marcovitz,* 2007 SCC 54 at para. 2 (emphasis added).

[20] *Bruker,* 2007 SCC 54 at para. 16 (emphasis added).

> Mediating these highly personal claims to religious rights with the wider public interest is a task that has been assigned to the courts by legislatures across the country. It is a well-accepted function carried out for decades by human rights commissions under federal and provincial statutes and, for 25 years by judges under the *Canadian Charter of Rights and Freedoms,* to ensure that members of the Canadian public are not arbitrarily disadvantaged by their religion.[21]

Members of the minority group are entitled to hold *their* religious views, but at a certain point, if their views do not correspond to *our* values or law, then *our* values can and do trump. For Abella J., minority values cannot be *hegemonic* over Canadian fundamental values. The inviolability of Canadian fundamental values, however defined, presumes their priority against claims of difference that might seek so much accommodation as to undermine those fundamental values. This study does not dispute that for a legal system to operate, certain fundamental values must function as priorities over and against others. Without such values, the integrity of a legal system could come into question. To recall the warning of al-Māwardī, without such foundational values at the core of a legal system, the system will be vulnerable to endless indeterminacy, schisms, and ultimately breakdown.[22]

Importantly for this chapter, though, Abella J. did not consider the priority of these fundamental values to be equally *hegemonic,* even though they are hegemonic from the perspective of the minority group member. Her silence about the hegemony of the law was likely not deliberate; rather, the priority Abella J. gave to these core values (and hence their hegemony) was likely assumed as entirely proper and even taken for granted. They were background factors that contributed to the intelligibility of her legal opinion on behalf of the Court.

The purpose of this section, therefore, is not to critique the US Supreme Court or the Canadian Supreme Court for adhering to a certain conception of the public good or to a set of fundamental values. The fact that such values are fundamental is not at issue,[23] and indeed may be unavoidable for justices sitting on the highest court of review. Instead, this discussion is meant to bring to the surface the ways and extent to which claims about public good and national security are used to do more than deny someone an exception to a general rule of law. The way in which the public good is pitted against the claims of religious minorities reflects powerful ideas about the state. The religious minority that

[21] *Bruker,* 2007 SCC 54 at para. 19.

[22] Al-Māwardī, *Naṣīḥat al-Mulūk,* 85.

[23] However, for Wendy Brown, the fact that these fundamental values trump claims of difference raises concerns about their hegemonic nature. See Brown, *Regulating Aversion.*

makes legal claims on religious freedom grounds becomes a discursive site for debates about the nature and well-being of the enterprise of governance. This chapter and, more generally, this study raises a cautionary flag, as did Jackson J. in *Barnette*, that greater critical vigilance is required at the discursive site created by the mere existence of the minority claimant, given the potentially detrimental hegemonic dynamic revealed by the conceptual framework of Rule of Law as used herein.

7.2 REGULATING THE COVERED MUSLIM WOMAN

That potentially detrimental impact, at least in the case of Jehovah's Witnesses in the United States, may have been obviated by the critical analysis of jurists such as Jackson J. Yet as the enterprise of governance shifts, changes, or encounters new challenges, different minorities will find themselves subjected to the hegemonic imperative of the law. In recent years, in courts in Europe and North America, one minority group that has embodied this discursive site about pluralist governance consists of Muslims and, in particular, the covered Muslim woman. The covered Muslim woman, as depicted in relatively recent legislation and court decisions from Europe and North America, represents something more than an individual who happens to wear a veil. The covered Muslim woman, in the very act of wearing the veil, makes an identity claim that can have political, social, and cultural ramifications. The covered Muslim woman becomes a legal trope in debates about security, the public good, and the justifiable limits on individual rights in the context of governance amidst diversity.

Donning the veil may be a matter of religious commitment, as far as the Muslim woman is concerned. But its physical presence, so obvious and apparent to all around her, renders the veil a speech-act that is "read" and thereby associated with a meaning. That meaning, though, is not necessarily determined by the covered Muslim woman herself. As such, meanings are ascribed and attributed to the veil that may have less to do with what the Muslim woman states or intends, and more with what she is made to represent. In that sense, the meanings provide greater insight into their purveyors, and less insight into the covered Muslim woman herself.[24]

[24] Natasha Bakht unpacks the various arguments often used to justify requiring the covered Muslim woman to uncover, revealing that the arguments have more to do with the value judgments of those who observe and represent the covered Muslim woman, as opposed to reflecting the context in which the covered Muslim woman is observed. Natasha Bakht, "Veiled Objections: Facing Public Opposition to the Niqab," in *Defining*

The covered Muslim woman as a trope is not itself a new idea. In the European imagination before and after the period of European colonialism in the Muslim world, the covered Muslim woman represented all that was novel and mysterious about the lands east of Europe.[25] The covered Muslim woman represented the "exotic," often by bearing it directly on her body. Her hidden face creates for her onlooker a sense of curiosity and enticement that is not lost on marketing agents seeking to increase their market share for consumer goods.[26] For instance, the food company President's Choice uses the image of a covered Muslim woman to market its line of *couscous,* a staple of North African diets.[27] The covered Muslim woman on the box wears a *niqāb* made of luxurious fabric and vibrant color. Her mysterious, smokey eyes beckon the consumer to ingest all she represents. The consumer, captivated by what he sees (and does not see), is beckoned to consume something at once exciting and mysterious.

In recent court decisions, the covered Muslim woman represents a very different trope. Instead of being viewed as exotic, she has become foreign. Far from being an enticement, she is a threat. Her mystery and sensuality have disappeared, leaving courts to view her as a sign of an ominous—though undefined—extremism that can have adverse and unavoidable consequences on other, uncovered Muslim women that the law must thereby protect. In fact, the image of the covered Muslim woman as a threat to the well-being of the national polity was made explicit in the Swiss campaign to constitutionally ban minarets in the country—a campaign that ultimately succeeded.[28] That campaign utilized an image of an ominous looking covered Muslim woman, with missile-like minarets emanating from a Swiss flag.[29] The covered Muslim

Reasonable Accommodation, ed. Lori Beaman (Vancouver: University of British Columbia Press, 2012).

[25] Judy Mabro, *Veiled Half-Truths: Western Traveller's Perceptions of Middle Eastern Women* (London: I.B. Tauris, 1991).

[26] On the constitutive relationship between culture and marketing for consumer goods, see Grant McCracken, "Culture and Consumption: A Theoretical Account of the Structure and Movement of the Cultural Meaning of Consumer Goods," *Journal of Consumer Research* 13 (1986): 461–73.

[27] Specifically, the product is President's Choice "Memories of Marrakech Whole Wheat Couscous," which can be viewed at the following website: <http://reviews.presidentschoice.ca/6584/F16262/reviews.htm> (accessed January 22, 2012).

[28] Christopher Caldwell, "No Minarets, Please," *The Weekly Standard* 15, no. 3 (December 14, 2009); Bandung Nurrohman, "A lesson to draw from the Swiss ban on minarets," *The Jakarta Post*, 15 December 2009, p. 7. See also, Daniel Moeckli, "Of Minarets and Foreign Criminals: Swiss Direct Democracy and Human Rights," *Human Rights Law Review* 11, no. 4 (2011): 774–94, which illustrates the adverse implication of direct democracy on the interests and welfare of minorities in Switzerland.

[29] The image of the campaign posters went viral and can be found on various websites, such as the following: <http://blogs.reuters.com/faithworld/2009/11/30/the-swiss-minaret-ban-and-other-trends-for-islam-in-europe/> (accessed January 22, 2012).

woman in this image is no longer something exotic that is to be craved or desired, but is rather a sign of impending doom and threat.

The image of the covered Muslim woman as threat is not simply fuel for xenophobic political parties that appeal to the lowest common denominator. Rather, in courtrooms in the United States, the United Kingdom, and continental Europe, intelligent judges utilizing respected legal arguments render the Muslim woman a suspect member of the polity because of her insistence upon her right to cover. Like the *dhimmī*, the covered Muslim woman fuels a certain anxious desire to distinguish between "Us" and the "Other." She provokes this anxiety in large part because her insistence on her right to cover is viewed as a challenge to certain norms that are deemed central to the order and well-being of society, such as equality. What those norms mean is not always clear; they are not always defined explicitly, or alternatively they are so presumed and so naturalized as to need no definition. The power of these norms is evident by the fact that, despite their lack of clarity, they are determinative of legal outcomes at the cost of the covered Muslim woman's claim of right.

To illustrate how the covered Muslim woman offers an important site for a critical Rule of Law inquiry, the remainder of this chapter will address three court cases in which the covered Muslim woman provides an occasion to debate about the well-being of the polity, the threat posed to the public good, and the concern for the enterprise of governance over and against the rights of the individual. This chapter will show that the reasoning in each case illustrates similar challenges and dynamics as those witnessed above regarding the *dhimmī* at the intersection of law and the enterprise of governance.

The first case concerns the citizenship application of Ms Faiza Silmi to the French Government. In her case, the Conseil d'Etat upheld the state's rejection of her citizenship application on the ground that her radical religious beliefs made her unsuitable for French citizenship. Just as the *dhimmī* could reside in the Muslim polity and enjoy some benefits, so too could Ms Silmi reside in the French Republic and enjoy some benefits. But the failure to manifest a clear commitment to core French values rendered Ms Silmi excluded from entry as a full participant in French society and politics. Ms Silmi, like the *dhimmī*, was a non-believer so to speak, and so was othered in part to (re)instantiate who "We" are.

The second case involves a woman in the United States who was required to remove her *niqāb* for her driver's license photo, despite the fact that she had previously held a driver's license photo with her face partially covered. Martha Nussbaum briefly reflects on this case and suggests it poses no substantial challenge to America's commitment to religious equality. She writes: "Here is a case where it seems entirely reasonable for the religious interest to lose."[30] However one might regard the outcome of the case, the analysis herein will focus on the reasoning used to justify that outcome. An analysis of the case will show that the Florida court construed the Muslim woman's religious claims in terms of foreign state practice. In doing so, the court effectively construed the plaintiff's constitutional rights as a US citizen by reference to the laws of unspecified states. She was, in other words, construed as a foreigner, despite being a citizen of the United States.

The last case concerns a British Muslim student who wished to wear a *jilbāb* to a school that adopted a mandatory uniform requirement. The school's policy was upheld and the student was told that any limits on her religious beliefs were not significant; and even if the restrictions were significant, the state's interests in imposing the uniform requirement outweighed the student's religious freedom claims. Interestingly, the UK case and the earlier case of the two adulterous Jews discussed in Chapter 4, when juxtaposed, offer important examples for illustrating the hegemonic tendencies of the law when confronted with a minority claimant who makes claims before the institutions of an enterprise of governance.

7.2.1 The covered Muslim woman as unbeliever: Identity, citizenship, and the nation

The covered Muslim woman offers a site of debate about a polity's core values, which in part make the enterprise of governance possible and effective. With the increased diversity in states in Europe and North America resulting from immigration, debates on core values, and thereby the identity of "us" and "them," assume special relevance in the case of Muslims in such countries. Indeed, the 2011 Oslo terrorist attacks committed by Anders Breivik, coupled with the revelation of his 1,500-page manifesto, reveal how such debates can even fuel a sub-culture of hatred and violence.[31] Breivik's manifesto draws upon the work of those adhering to the myth of persecution (e.g., Bat Ye'or, discussed in Chapter 1) to warn against the onset of an Islamization of Europe. As Andreas Malm writes, Breivik relies in his manifesto upon a "staple of mainstream right-of-centre discourse," some of it distinctly fascist, to proclaim his

[30] Nussbaum, *Liberty of Conscience*, 347.

[31] For Anders Breivik's manifesto, *2083: A European Declaration of Independence*, see <http://publicintelligence.net/anders-behring-breiviks-complete-manifesto-2083-a-european-declaration-of-independence/> (accessed March 24, 2012, copy on file with author).

> worries about Muslims establishing no-go areas in cities, sharia courts, swimming pools with Muslim-only sessions, the contradiction between Islam and freedom of speech, the all-Muslim duty to perform jihad and the anti-Semitic inclinations of Muslim communities. And he wants to draw a line.[32]

The debate about core values, identity, and the nation is acute in the case of Muslims in Europe, in particular those Muslims for whom veiling is an important marker of their religious identity and expression. As José Casanova writes,

> The controversies over the Muslim veil in so many European societies and the overwhelming support among the French citizenry, including apparently among the majority of French Muslims, for the restrictive legislation prohibiting the wearing of Muslim veils and other ostensibly religious symbols in public schools, as "a threat to national cohesion," may be an extreme example of illiberal secularism. But in fact one sees similar trends of restrictive legislation directed at immigrant Muslims in liberal Holland, precisely in the name of protecting its liberal, tolerant traditions from the threat of illiberal, fundamentalist, patriarchal customs... Anti-immigrant xenophobic nativism, secularist antireligious prejudices, liberal-feminist critiques of Muslim patriarchal fundamentalism, and the fear of Islamic terrorist networks are being fused indiscriminately throughout Europe into a uniform anti-Muslim discourse ...[33]

European concerns about Muslim immigrants are often expressed in terms of values and ideals that are deemed contrary to Islam are not always specified and often shift across different polities.

According to Casanova, one is not likely to find tolerance in Europe for outright expressions of bigotry or racism against Muslim immigrants. Rather, the concern about Muslims will remain framed in politically correct terms: "we welcome each and all immigrants irrespective of race or religion as long as they are willing to respect and accept our modern, liberal, secular European norms."[34] In other words, the language of tolerance is embedded in a discourse of governance that upholds the priority, if not superiority, of the state's core values. In various instances, the state's core values are not always fully articulated; but such articulation is deemed less relevant than is the presumed dichotomy between Islam as "reactionary, fundamentalist and antimodern" on the

[32] Andreas Malm, "Minaret Myths," *New Statesman* (August 1, 2011), 27.

[33] José Casanova, "Immigration and the New Religious Pluralism: A European Union/ United States Comparison," in *Democracy and the New Religious Pluralism*, ed. Thomas Banchoff (Oxford: Oxford University Press, 2007), 59–84, 64–5.

[34] Casanova, "Immigration and the New Religious Pluralism," 64.

one hand, and the European enterprise of governance as "progressive, liberal, and modern" on the other.[35]

Importantly, the debates about Islam in Europe are not simply debates about religion and the state. They overlap with equally volatile issues surrounding immigration and citizenship. The immigrant who lives among "us" is still an outsider, not yet a full member of the polity. Muslim immigrants, therefore, are Others not only because of their different religious tradition, but also because they are viewed as foreigners who have come to live among Us.

Importantly, the overlap of Islam and immigration in these debates begs questions about the requirements of citizenship, and whether and how those requirements contribute to the tenor, tone, and intensity of the debates that occur about the place, status, and interests of the Muslims who are from elsewhere but live among Us.[36] The literature on citizenship and identity is vast, and this is not the place to offer a full review of the field. However, the literature illustrates how the grant of citizenship and the rights that accrue therefrom are intimately tied to how a state construes and conducts itself in terms of certain core values. For individuals to embrace those core values is to be part of the community. To contest or otherwise challenge those values is to render oneself vulnerable to marginalization, if not outright exclusion, due to a fear for the security and well-being of the nation. As Engin Isin and Bryan S. Turner remark:

> The modern conception of citizenship as merely a status held under the authority of a state has been contested and broadened to include various political and social struggles of recognition and redistribution as instances of claim-making, and hence, by extension, of citizenship. As a result, various struggles based upon identity and difference (whether sexual, "racial", "ethnic", diasporic, ecological, technological, or cosmopolitan) have found new ways of articulating their claims as claims to citizenship understood not merely as a legal status but as political and social recognition and economic redistribution.[37]

[35] Casanova, "Immigration and the New Religious Pluralism," 65.

[36] See for instance, the report from Quebec's Reasonable Accommodation Commission: Bouchard and Taylor, *Building the Future.*

[37] Engin F. Isin and Bryan S. Turner, "Citizenship Studies: An Introduction," in *Handbook of Citizenship Studies*, eds Engin F. Isin and Bryan S. Turner (London: Sage, 2002), 1–10, 2. See also, Engin F. Isin and Bryan S. Turner, "Investigating Citizenship: An Agenda for Citizenship Studies," *Citizenship Studies* 11, no. 1 (2007): 5–17; Audrey Macklin, "Who is the Citizen's Other? Considering the Heft of Citizenship," *Theoretical Inquiries in Law* 8, no. 2 (2007): 333–66, who considers the concept of statelessness as a reference point for appreciating the legal and social aspects of citizenship.

Citizenship, in other words, offers a juridified litmus test to determine who is part of the Us, who is part of the Other, and the entitlements that follow therefrom.

A critical analysis of the legal reasoning in a recent French citizenship case will reveal how a nation's core values are more often assumed than specified. The silence on core values offers an important focal point to consider how the constitutive features of the claim space of law also make possible the hegemonic potential that is revealed through a Rule of Law analysis. This will beg a further question about the extent to which those constitutive elements can be reconsidered without posing a threat to the integrity of the polity.

In 2008, France's Conseil d'Etat rejected a covered Muslim woman's application for citizenship. The fact that she was fluent in French did not matter, as the relevant law permitted the government to deny the grant of citizenship for failure to "assimilate in a manner other than linguistically."[38] The Conseil d'Etat deemed her insufficiently assimilated into French culture because she "adopted radical religious practices that are incompatible with the essential values of French society, and particularly with the principle of gender equality."[39]

In this case, the government's commissioner recited various facts to justify rejecting Ms Faisa Silmi's citizenship application. In particular, the government commissioner emphasized that the claimant

- "attended the prefecture several times for interviews, and each time she appeared wearing clothing in the style of women in the Arab Peninsula: a long dark or khaki one-piece dress down to her feet, a veil covering her hair, forehead and chin and, in combination with the veil, another piece of fabric covering the entire face except for her eyes which showed through a slit, which in this area is called the Niqab;"
- "did not wear the veil when she lived in Morocco and indicated clearly that she only adopted this garment after her arrival in France

[38] For a statement of the case, the relevant legislation, and the conclusions of the government commissioner, see the decision of the Conseil d'Etat, Case 286798, <http://arianeinternet.conseil-etat.fr/arianeinternet/ViewRoot.asp?View=Html&DMode=Html&PushDirectUrl=1&Item=1&fond=DCE&texte=286798&Page=1&querytype=simple&NbEltPerPages=4&Pluriels=True> (accessed March 5, 2012, copy on file with author).

[39] Angelique Chrisafis, "France rejects Muslim woman over radical practice of Islam," *The Guardian*, July 12, 2008, p. 23 (quoting the Conseil d'Etat). See also, Katrin Bennhold, "A Muslim woman too orthodox for France; It bars citizenship over her strict garb," *International Herald Tribune*, July 19, 2008, p. 4; Ronald P. Sokol, "Why France Can't See Past the burqa," *The Christian Science Monitor*, July 21, 2008, p. 9.

at the request of her husband. She says that she wears it more out of habit than conviction;"

- "leads a life that is almost reclusive and removed from French society. She does not have any visitors at her apartment; in the morning she does her housework and goes for a walk with her baby or children, and in the afternoon she goes to visit her father or father-in-law... [S]he is able to go shopping on her own, but admits that usually she goes to the supermarket with her husband."

From these facts, the government commissioner concluded that the claimant had not adopted or otherwise *acquiesced* to the core values of the French Republic, in particular the core value of gender equality. Of particular interest is the way in which the commissioner used the claimant's veiling habit to characterize the quality and content of her values: "She lives in complete submission to the men of her family, which is demonstrated by the clothing that she wears, the organization of her daily life and the statements that she made... showing that she finds this normal."

After reviewing the submissions and evidence, as well as taking into account the European Convention of Human Rights and Fundamental Freedoms, the Conseil d'Etat upheld the government's decision to reject Ms Silmi's application for citizenship. The Conseil d'Etat did not refer to Ms Silmi's veiling in its decision. In fact, it had held in prior cases that wearing the veil is not, by itself, grounds for denying sufficient assimilation into French society.[40] But it nonetheless agreed with the government that despite her French language abilities and her history as a resident in France, her religious values were contrary to the core values of the society and therefore were an obstacle to her application for citizenship.

An analysis of this opinion reveals certain peculiarities about the evidence garnered against the claimant and its interpretation by the government commissioner. For instance, the commissioner noted that while Ms Silmi could go shopping on her own, she usually went with her husband. This particular evidence can be understood in different ways. It may have been that Ms Silmi preferred to shop with her husband because she enjoyed her husband's company, and might otherwise find shopping alone less enjoyable. Maybe he would help carry any merchandise or groceries that she purchased. The government commissioner, on the other hand, represented this piece of evidence with a singularly determinate meaning, namely that Ms Silmi was not an emancipated woman, had not

[40] Conseil d'Etat, Case 286798.

embraced her independence, and therefore had not fully incorporated gender equality as a core value in her life.[41]

Ms Silmi's veiling practice was offered by the government as evidence of her radical beliefs, and therefore a failure to accept French core values. Importantly, according to the commissioner, her decision to wear the *niqāb* was a result of her husband's preference, and did not reflect Ms Silmi's preferences. She did it out of habit rather than out of a particular ideological or theological conviction that pitted her beliefs against the core values of the French Republic.[42] And yet, the commissioner offered this fact as evidence of her failure to adhere to French core values. Habit and conviction, though, are two separate things. But that did not matter for the government commissioner. Arguably, it likely would not matter whether Ms Silmi wore the veil out of habit, had a deep ideological commitment to wearing the veil, or felt she had no choice but to wear the veil. Rather, all that really mattered to the government commissioner was that Ms Silmi wore the veil, period. In other words, by failing to distinguish between habit and conviction, the government commissioner's argument suggests that by the very fact she wore the veil (regardless of the reason), Ms Silmi did not respect her own independence and equal standing in her marriage. Her failure to do so was represented as her failure to embrace French values.[43]

Even if the commissioner were correct in assuming that Ms Silmi did not respect her independence and equality, the commissioner did not seem to consider that Ms Silmi's failure to do so may have reflected concerns that had less to do with French core values and more to do with other factors that, upon further consideration, might paint Ms Silmi's citizenship application in a different light. Supposing, for the sake of argument, that her husband was abusive, either physically or emotionally. Further, suppose he belonged to a conservative value system. In other

[41] In an interview, Ms Silmi rejected the government commissioner's findings of fact, noting that she goes shopping on her own, for instance. Bennhold, "A Muslim woman too orthodox for France," p. 4.

[42] This, of course, assumes that a finding of fact would show her husband to be of such a nature. Without such a finding, the state runs the risk of stereotyping the Muslim male as dangerous, thereby raising questions about who can and should "save" the "endangered" Muslim woman. For a critique of the assumptions, see Sherene Razack, *Casting Out: The Eviction of Muslims from Western Law and Politics* (Toronto: University of Toronto Press, 2008); Lila Abu-Lughod, "Do Muslim Women Really Need Saving?" *American Anthropologist* 104, no. 3 (2002): 783–90.

[43] For an analysis of the complex and dynamic modes of agency that believing Muslim women exercise, contrary to certain liberal presumptions of agency, see Saba Mahmood, *The Politics of Piety: The Islamic Revival and the Feminist Subject* (Princeton: Princeton University Press, 2004).

words, even if Ms Silmi's husband were stereotypically presumed[44] to be a domineering abusive spouse, the government's rejection of her application only imposed on Ms Silmi the cost of not standing up to him.

The Conseil held that Ms Silmi adopted "radical religious practices" (*une practique radicale de sa religion*), which countered the "essential values of French society" (*valeurs essentielles de la communauté française*), with special reference to gender equality. Technically, therefore, the Conseil did not specify the *niqāb* as part of its rationale for rejecting Ms Silmi's application; but neither did it specify the offensive content of Ms Silmi's radical religious practices, nor the offended essential values of French society, with the exception of gender equality—although even gender equality can be a loaded term, as Saba Mahmood and others argue in their critiques of Western feminism.[45] Indeed, the reductive dichotomy between Islam and Europe posited by Casanova substantially animated this decision. For the Conseil to say that Ms Silmi's beliefs were radical was to indulge an implicit dichotomy between Islam as reactionary and fundamentalist, and Europe as liberal and progressive. With that presumption in the background, there was therefore little need to articulate what the values involved were. Indeed, one might suggest that the values were so readily accessible as to require no explication.

The case of Ms Silmi offers an important starting point to reflect on the hegemony that arises at the intersection of law, the enterprise of governance, and the minority claimant. Neither the Conseil d'Etat nor the government commissioner questioned the fundamental nature of French values, in particular gender equality. Nor did they question, let alone articulate specifically, the way in which those fundamental values should and had to take shape in a case such as that of Ms Silmi. The decision rested on a construction of how Ms Silmi should have lived her life if she had adopted core French values. But neither the government commissioner nor the Conseil articulated the filters through which they understood the "facts" of Ms Silmi's life, and by which they decided that she violated core French values. She may have resided in France, have given birth to her children in France, paid taxes, and abided by the laws of the state. Nevertheless, all that seemed to matter for the government commissioner and the Conseil was what she did not do. She did not challenge her husband's conservative traditions. She did not go shopping on her own. She did not socialize frequently or entertain guests at her

[44] On the potential effect of this stereotype of the Muslim male on law and policy, see Razack, *Casting Out*.

[45] Mahmood, *Politics of Piety;* Abu-Lughod, "Do Muslim Women Really Need Saving?"; Ziba Mir-Hosseini, "Muslim Women's Quest for Equality: Between Islamic Law and Feminism," *Critical Inquiry* 32 (2006): 629–45.

home. From this absence or negative, the Conseil created a positive marker of Ms Silmi's identity—she adopted radical religious practices that disqualified her from full entry and membership in the French polity.

The Conseil d'Etat's embrace of an unspecified set of core values was never subjected to critique or self-reflection; rather, the idea and content of such values were simply assumed. This phenomenon is not unusual for the modern constitutional state, whether France or Canada, as instanced in the opinion of Abella J. in *Marcovitz*. Likewise, this phenomenon of silence certainly animated Muslim jurists, who limited the freedom of *dhimmīs* when Islamically defined public values, whatever those might have been, were deemed to be at risk. Recall the concern of jurists about *dhimmīs* creating charitable endowments, building religious buildings, drinking in public, or in some fashion affecting the Islamic character and content of an ambiguous notion of the "public." It is reductive to hold that premodern jurists were purely antagonistic to *dhimmīs*, just as it would be reductive to argue that they were fully welcoming. The contract of protection was designed to include *dhimmīs* in the polity, but only to a certain extent, lest their claims adversely affect the Islamic image of the empire. Ironically, in the seemingly disparate cases of Sharīʿa as Rule of Law and constitutional systems such as France's and even Canada's, the challenge of pluralist governance is not only shared, but appears to be managed in similar fashion. For instance, Abella J. in *Markovits* certainly respected claims of culture and religion, but she stood on guard so that they would not become hegemonic over fundamental Canadian principles whose content did not need to be specified. And here, in the case of Ms Silmi, the Conseil did not need to argue for or justify the priority of French core values. In fact they did not even need to define them. In the case of both the *dhimmī* and Ms Silmi, both lack (or are represented as lacking) a full-fledged commitment to the well-being of the polities in which they lived. They were othered and marginalized, in part out of concern for the well-being of their respective polities. That well-being, though, was rarely identified, and often assumed.

For as long as these assumptions continue unabated, minorities can expect to feel the hegemonic sting that a Rule of Law analysis makes plain. For instance, the contract of protection and the protection of religious freedom offer models by which religious minority groups are protected in their beliefs, in particular those beliefs that run counter to the core values that operate in a polity. This protection of difference, though, does not change the fact that those minorities either can or are presumed to know the core values of their host society. Their presumed ability to know and access those values, coupled with their insistence on their difference, renders them potential threats to the well-being of society. All can and should know the core values; to nonetheless reject them raises fundamental concerns about the minority group's commitment to the polity and the degree to which it can be trusted to work toward the polity's common good. This presumption, coupled all too often with silence about the content of such values, feeds the hegemonic imperative that arises at the discursive site made possible by the minority claimant.

7.2.2 The covered Muslim woman as foreigner: The Rule of (foreign) Law

A covered Muslim woman appeared in a Florida court contesting why she could not wear the *niqāb* when she stood for a driver's license photo. Sultaana Freeman, born in Washington, D.C. in 1967, converted to Islam in 1997, and months later began to wear a veil in accordance with her Islamic beliefs. At this time, she lived in Illinois. When she sought an Illinois driver's license, she was permitted to be veiled for the photo. Later that year, she married her husband and moved to Florida. She did not seek a Florida driver's license until February 2001, months prior to the terrorist attack on the World Trade Center on September 11, 2001.[46]

When Ms Freeman sought a Florida driver's license at her local Department of Motor Vehicles (DMV), she was wearing what the court called "traditional Muslim headdress that included a veil."[47] The DMV clerk was uncertain how to proceed. He asked his supervisor if he could take the picture of Ms Freeman with the headgear remaining. The clerk never mentioned a veil or the *niqāb*. The supervisor, without viewing Ms Freeman independently, permitted the clerk to take the picture of Ms Freeman dressed as she then was. Ms Freeman received her driver's license, which had a picture of her wearing her *niqāb*, and thus covering the lower half of her face. As identification, Ms Freeman presented her Illinois license and social security card, both of which sufficed to establish her identity to the personnel at the Florida DMV.

Ten months after issuing the license, and three months *after* the terrorist attack on the World Trade Center, Ms Freeman received a notice from the DMV requiring her to re-take her driver's license photograph without the *niqāb*, otherwise her license would be revoked. Ms Freeman objected to the new requirement on the ground that her

[46] *Sultaana Lakiana Myke Freeman v State of Florida, Department of Highway Safety and Motor Vehicles* Mp/ 5D03-2296, 2005 Fla Dist Ct App. LEXIS 13904 (Court of Appeal of Florida, Fifth District, September 2, 2005). All references to the facts of the case are drawn from the court of appeals decision.

[47] *Freeman*, 4.

religious beliefs required her to wear the *niqāb.* She was convinced that by asking her to take a full-face photo, the DMV was asking her to choose between sacrificing her religious convictions or her driver's license. As such, she filed a lawsuit alleging a violation of her religious freedom.

The court analyzed Ms Freeman's claims under Florida's Religious Freedom Restoration Act, which requires the state to show a compelling interest in the event that a law, whether of general application or not, substantially burdens an individual's religious freedom. As the court stated: "if Freeman can show a substantial burden on the free exercise of her religion, the state must demonstrate a compelling governmental interest and show that the law is the least restrictive means of furthering its interest."[48] Under this law, the initial legal burden was on the petitioner (here, Ms Freeman) to show that the DMV requirement to reveal her face for the driver's license photograph was a *substantial burden* on the free exercise of her sincere religious beliefs. If Ms Freeman could satisfy her legal burden of proof, the state would be required to show that, despite the substantial burden on her freedom, the legal requirement nonetheless met a compelling state interest and also that the requirement was the least restrictive means of achieving that interest. In other words, the law would impose upon the government a burden of justification only if its requirements substantially burden the petitioner's religious freedom. Put differently, the state could *incidentally* burden one's religious freedom rights, and may impose *slight inconveniences* without having to justify them to the petitioner or to the court. The applicable legal test in the *Freeman* case, therefore, delineated the boundary within which the enterprise of governance could operate without having to justify its actions. In defining the zone of discretionary activity, the legal test helped constitute the enterprise of governance in a manner akin to how premodern Muslim jurists granted the ruler a zone of discretionary authority through the doctrines of *taʿzīr* and *siyāsa sharʿiyya.* As it turned out in the *Freeman* case, Ms Freeman did not satisfy her initial legal burden of proof. The court found that she did not show that the new requirement was a substantial burden on her religious belief. As such, the state did not need to prove its actions were compelling or the least restrictive. Rather, in the confrontation between the state authority and the individual minority claimant, the court not only found against the individual, but it did so in part by freeing the enterprise of governance even from the task of justifying itself.

There was no real question about whether Ms Freeman sincerely believed she must cover herself on religious grounds. The court found her

[48] *Freeman*, 8.

belief sincere. The real question was whether the requirement to unveil for the photograph was a *substantial burden* on her religious freedom. Quoting the Florida Supreme Court's test for substantial burden, the *Freeman* court wrote: "'a substantial burden on the free exercise of religion is one that either compels the religious adherent to engage in conduct that his religion forbids, or forbids him to engage in conduct that his religion requires.'"[49] The debate therefore centered on the debates in Islam concerning the requirement of Muslim women to cover.

The court held that the state's requirement for a full-face photograph did not substantially burden Ms Freeman's religious freedom. Rather, it constituted a "mere interference." To reach its conclusion, the court relied on the testimony of expert witness Khaled Abou El Fadl, a professor of Islamic law at UCLA School of Law:

> Dr. El Fadl testified that in *Islamic countries* there are exceptions to the practice of veiling. Consistent with Islamic law, women are required to unveil for medical needs and for certain photo ID cards. Examples include photo ID cards to be displayed to police, to enter and take professional exams, and for passports. The only qualification is that the taking of the photograph accommodate Freeman's belief. Here, the Department's existing procedure would accommodate Freeman's veiling beliefs by using a female photographer with no other person present.[50]

Ms Freeman, however, was not only concerned about the circumstances under which her picture would be taken. Indeed, she expressly indicated her religious attitude against the depiction of images, sentient and otherwise. Consequently, the existence of her full-face picture on her identity card would be an ongoing imposition on her religious convictions, none of which were doubted as sincerely held.[51] The court did not distinguish between the conditions of taking the picture and the fact that the existence of the full-face photo was, for Ms Freeman, a burden on her religious beliefs. As such, the court seemed to disregard the extent and nature of the injury for which Ms Freeman sought redress.

Most significant for this analysis, though, is the court's reliance on foreign state law and practice to determine the content of Ms Freeman's religious beliefs, and whether Florida's regulation was a substantial

[49] *Freeman*, 10–11, citing Florida's Supreme Court in *Richard Warner et al v City of Boca Raton*, 887 So. 2d 1023.

[50] *Freeman*, 13 (emphasis added).

[51] On the Islamic legal arguments concerning images, pictures, and depictions, see Emon, "On the Pope, Cartoons and Apostates: Sharīʿa 2006," 303–21. Though the legal prohibition against images and depictions can be critiqued, any historical analysis would not be relevant to the court's determination of Ms Freeman's sincerity of belief, given the prevailing legal tests on the matter.

burden on them. Peculiarly, the court made vague references to "Islamic countries" but did not specify which ones. It took notice of laws in "Islamic countries" that allowed women to lift their veils for the purposes of identification photographs, although it did not cite any statute, ministerial decree, or administrative regulation.

This ambiguous reference to unspecified state practices unduly elides religion and the state in a way that raises fundamental questions about the court's understanding of religion, as well as its use of foreign law to interpret a US citizen's rights under the law. The legal doctrines on veiling in Islamic law are not always consistent, given the variety of schools of law and historical developments over time. Most scholars who have written on the issue generally agree that both Muslim men and women must cover those parts of their bodies that are considered private. In Arabic, the term is *ʿawra*. While generally there is agreement on the need to cover one's *ʿawra*, the fundamental question is about how to define the *ʿawra*. A man's *ʿawra* is the area of his body between his navel and knee. He must, at the very least, cover and clothe the area between these two points on his body. For a woman, however, premodern Muslim jurists could not agree. Early in Islamic history, jurists differentiated between the *ʿawra* of a slave woman and a free woman, but by at least the twelfth century, that social status distinction mattered less and less. Instead, jurists suggested that a woman's whole body is *ʿawra*, thus requiring her to cover her face, as well as her hands and feet. Others excluded the face, hands, and feet.[52] The *niqāb*, therefore, reflects a particular view of a woman's body that considers her face part of her *ʿawra*, which thereby must be covered. Ms Freeman's belief that she must cover using a *niqāb*, therefore, has a basis in early Islamic legal history, and subsequently cannot be considered merely idiosyncratic. Even if it were idiosyncratic though, that would not necessarily adversely affect the sincerity of her belief for purposes of legal analysis.

The problem for a modern democratic constitutional court is whether and how to reconcile these various views of Islamic law and veiling with the institutions of a modern regulatory state and technological advancements that allow for different techniques of attesting to and protecting someone's identity. Must premodern doctrines be reconciled with the need to govern effectively in a modern state context, and if so, how? Or in other words, what is the legal significance of Sharīʿa-based requirements to veil within a legal system that is not Sharīʿa-based? This issue raises analogous questions to those noted in Chapter 6 concerning the implications of the modern state on the intelligibility of the *dhimmī*

[52] Abou El Fadl, *Speaking in God's Name*, 233–46, 255–7.

rules in an international state system where the post-colonial Muslim state must contend with the demands of plural legal regimes that make claims upon it. Where the analogue breaks down, though, is that the Florida court was not addressing the veiling requirement in terms of Sharīʿa-based arguments and analysis. In other words, the Sharīʿa-based debate on veiling was not itself at issue in the *Freeman* case. Rather, at issue was how to balance Ms Freeman's religious conviction about veiling, which was relevant because of her religious freedom claim pursuant to state legislation, with administrative requirements such as having one's photo taken for a driver's license, which was also governed by state legislation. The premodern tradition was silent on this issue, not only because of the absence of the regulatory state in the premodern period, but also because premodern jurists did not develop their rules in light of technological advances that are commonplace today. Consequently, the *Freeman* court's recourse to modern state practices in the Muslim world is both unsurprising and in fact quite intelligible. The court arguably viewed such states as offering authoritative answers to contemporary questions of state practice in light of claims of religious identity and freedom.

The Florida court arguably invoked the practices of modern Muslim states as evidence of the content of Islamic law and its doctrines on veiling. But in adopting this approach, the court did not illustrate any interest or awareness of the mutually constitutive relationship between the enterprise of governance and Sharīʿa-based legal doctrines; how the demands of the modern Muslim state contribute to the formulation of Islamic legal practices; and most specifically, how the anxiety of the post-imperial, post-colonial Muslim state bears upon the status of women both politically and legally. To look to Muslim state practice as a proxy for "religious law" is to ignore how a government's Islamic legal practices are at the same time constitutive of and constituted by the post-imperial and post-colonial state. The *Freeman* court relied on an ambiguous set of legal norms that apparently existed in unspecified "Islamic countries" and assumed that those state-based norms provided the necessary standard by which to judge whether Ms Freeman's religious freedom was substantially burdened.

The *Freeman* court's ambiguous references to Islamic countries and their practices raise two important concerns about the court's counter-majoritarianism and the potential democracy deficit that results from its decision. First, by referring to foreign law in the fashion that it did, the Court othered Ms Freeman by deciding her rights under Florida law by reference to the practice of foreign states to which she did not belong. Second, given how the court construed Ms Freeman's religious beliefs, it thereby reasoned that she suffered no substantial impact on her religious freedoms. In doing so, the government was relieved of having to satisfy the legal burden of showing its requirements were both compelling and the least restrictive. The very legal test used to ensure Ms Freeman's rights were not trampled was applied in such a way as to insulate the government from having to justify its conduct. In other words, the court's othering of Ms Freeman allowed it to thereby insulate the government's practice from judicial scrutiny. This result showcases how, at the discursive site created by minority claimants, greater vigilance must be paid to how the institutions that are meant to protect individuals against the state authority can operate as constitutive elements of the state, giving the enterprise legal cover at the cost of minority claimants.

The counter-majoritarianism implicit in the reference to "Islamic state" practices is evident when juxtaposed with ongoing debates about the place of foreign law in US legal decision-making. These debates have contributed to highly animated disputes both inside and outside of the US Supreme Court concerning cases involving the interpretation of constitutional rights. Technically, the *Freeman* case was decided under Florida's Religious Freedom Restoration Act, and so does not fall within the ambit of significant constitutional debates on foreign law and constitutional interpretation. But the debate in the United States on the citation and reliance on foreign law in domestic constitutional cases raises an important set of background questions that offer important entry points for appreciating the way in which the outcome in *Freeman* reveals the mutually constitutive relationship between the law and the enterprise of governance.

The use of foreign law in US jurisprudence is a highly contested issue.[53] In recent cases on the death penalty and anti-sodomy laws, justices of the US Supreme Court have looked to foreign law and practices to interpret the US Constitution in domestic cases.[54] In *Roper v Simmons,* a juvenile death penalty case, Justice Kennedy referred to other countries that prohibit the use of the death penalty for juvenile offenders. Writing for the majority, he stated:

[53] David J. Seipp, "Our Law, Their Law, History, and the Citation of Foreign Law," *Boston University Law Review* 86 (2006): 1417–46; Jeremy Waldron, "Foreign Law and the Modern *Ius Gentium,*" *Harvard Law Review* 119 (2005–06): 129–67.

[54] On the unconstitutionality of sentencing the mentally disabled to the death penalty, see *Atkins v Virginia*, 536 US 304 (2002). On the unconstitutionality of juvenile death penalty, see *Roper v Simmons*, 543 US 551 (2005). On the unconstitutionality of anti-sodomy laws, see *Lawrence v Texas*, 123 S Ct 2472 (2003).

> It is proper that we acknowledge the overwhelming weight of international opinion against the juvenile death penalty... It does not lessen our fidelity to the Constitution or our pride in its origins to acknowledge that the express affirmation of certain fundamental rights by other nations and peoples simply underscores the centrality of those same rights within our own heritage of freedom.[55]

On and off the court, though, Kennedy's stance has suffered significant criticism. In a dissenting opinion in *Roper*, Justice Antonin Scalia retorted: "The basic premise of the Court's argument—that American law should comport with the laws of the rest of the world—ought to be rejected out of hand... What these foreign sources 'affirm'... is the Justices' own notion of how the world ought to be, and their diktat that it shall be so henceforth in America."[56] For Scalia, the use of foreign law to decide domestic constitutional rights issues unduly extends the scope of judicial power and is fundamentally anti-democratic. As Roger P. Alford states, "[u]sing global opinions as a means of constitutional interpretation dramatically undermines sovereignty by utilizing the one vehicle—constitutional supremacy—that can trump the democratic will reflected in state and federal legislative and executive pronouncements."[57] Harold Koh, on the other hand, criticizes the likes of Scalia and Alford by suggesting that the citation to foreign law has been a notable feature of Supreme Court decisions since the beginnings of the country, and contributes to the legitimacy of the state in the global arena.[58]

The *Freeman* court did not specify any particular Islamic country in its opinion. Two states that could reasonably be considered "Islamic countries" are Iran and Saudi Arabia. If the *Freeman* court was referring implicitly to the practices of the Iranian and Saudi Arabian Governments, which may very well allow women to remove their coverings for identification photos, Scalia and Alford are right to worry about the democratic deficit that can arise when citing foreign law indiscriminately. Ms Freeman, a US citizen, was effectively held to rules and regulations to which she neither acceded nor consented. These facts alone are not necessarily dispositive. Indeed, Koh's response cautions against any blanket antagonism against the use of foreign law. Yet given the analysis of the post-colonial Muslim state in Chapter 6, the analysis in *Freeman*

[55] *Roper*, 543 US 551. See also, Jeffrey Toobin, "Swing Shift: How Anthony Kennedy's Passion for Foreign Law Could Change the Supreme Court," *The New Yorker*, September 12, 2005, 42.

[56] *Roper*, 543 US 551 at 624; Toobin, "Swing Shift."

[57] Roger P. Alford, "Misusing International Sources to Interpret the Constitution," *American Journal of International Law* 98, no. 1 (2004): 57–69, 58.

[58] Harold Hongju Koh, "International Law as Part of Our Law," *American Journal of International Law* 98, no. 1 (2004): 43–57, 44.

should give even proponents of foreign law some reason to pause. Ms Freeman sued under Florida's Religious Freedom Restoration Act, but her case was adjudicated by reference to rules that were unstated and unspecified. There was no reference to any legal regulation, let alone a particular country in which such presumed regulations applied. Furthermore, there was no appreciation of the context in which such presumed regulatory measures exist. For instance, in a country such as The Kingdom of Saudi Arabia, women are required to cover themselves lest they suffer the scorn and punishment of the notorious *muṭawwaʿīn* or morality police, who work for the Committee for the Protection of Virtue and Prevention of Vice. The *muṭawwaʿīn* symbolize in this monarchical state "the quid pro quo arrangement of Saudi Arabia—religious sanction in exchange for religious influence. Their special status has protected committee members from criticism and given them virtually unlimited power."[59] While the *muṭawwaʿīn* have come under attack from the public, they continue to do their daily work in the Kingdom.[60] Another country, Iran, has a similar police squad. The Iranian virtue and vice squad have a history of detaining women for showing locks of hair from under their headscarves.[61] The fact that Muslim women in Iran and Saudi Arabia wear the veil in the first place cannot be separated from the state's enforcement of this practice upon them. Consequently, any limited exemptions the state grants Muslim women should be seen in the context of state enforcement of religious conformity, without due respect for the religious freedom of Muslim women in the first place. For the *Freeman* court to rely on general testimony about unspecified Muslim countries that permit women to lift their veils ignores how those exceptions to veiling fall within a larger context of institutional enforcement of religious practice, regardless of belief or choice of women themselves. The lack of transparency and the court's failure to appreciate the democratic deficits it imported into its decision suggests that, despite not being a constitutional case, the *Freeman* case would nonetheless raise the eyebrows of those, like Scalia and Alford, who worry about the democratic deficit that arises by reference to foreign law.

The polarizing debate on foreign law in constitutional decision-making has led some to suggest that the use of foreign law must conform to a rigorous method of analysis that might satisfy the concerns of Scalia and others. Michael D. Ramsey suggests four guidelines for developing a

[59] Dana Moss and Zvika Krieger, "Policing Religion," *New Statesman*, September 3, 2007, 16–17, 17.

[60] Moss and Krieger, "Policing Religion," 17.

[61] "Is This Islam?" *The Economist* 328, no. 7818 (July 3, 1993): 40.

principled method for utilizing foreign and international law in domestic constitutional cases:

> First, there must be a neutral theory as to *which* international materials are relevant and *how* they should be used. Second, we must be willing to "take the bitter with the sweet"—that is to use international materials evenhandedly to constrict domestic rights as well as to expand them. Third, we must get the facts right by engaging in rigorous empirical inquiry about international practices rather than making facile generalizations. And fourth, we must avoid easy shortcuts to international practice that rely on unrepresentative proxies such as United Nations agencies.[62]

These guidelines are meant to make certain that the foreign and international law materials US courts rely upon reflect a democratic commitment. They also ensure international law materials are used consistently, and not so selectively as to nearly predispose the case to certain outcomes over others that might prevail if domestic law alone were considered. Importantly, the imperative to get the facts right requires "a commitment to serious empirical research."[63] Ramsey criticizes the Supreme Court's use of international law to deem unconstitutional the application of the death penalty on the mentally disabled in *Atkins v Virginia*, because the majority relied on advocates' briefs about international law without investigating the law for itself:

> Surely the Court would never state a proposition of U.S. law and cite only an advocate's brief. That it could do so for a matter of international practice displays a lack of commitment to the empirical project, and a lack of respect for international sources. If we (and the Court) cannot bring ourselves to do the empirical project right, that seems further evidence that we are in it only for the results.[64]

The debate about the use of foreign law in domestic rights cases should raise concerns about the implication of the *Freeman* court's decision on future cases that involve covered Muslim women. Although the Florida case was not a constitutional case, it nonetheless subjected Ms Freeman's rights claim to Florida's statutory law. The situation is not strictly analogous to the ones noted above that involve the Supreme Court deciding cases under the Bill of Rights. But that does not change the fact that by relying on foreign practices of unnamed Islamic countries, the *Freeman* decision is vulnerable to similar criticisms of its decision.

[62] Michael D. Ramsey, "International Materials and Domestic Rights: Reflections on *Atkins* and *Lawrence*," *American Journal of International Law* 98, no. 1 (2004): 69–82, 69–70.

[63] Ramsey, "International Materials," 78.

[64] Ramsey, "International Materials," 79.

By relying on unstated foreign state practices, the *Freeman* court ineffectively accounted for its decision. As noted above, the court referenced no particular country. There was no citation of a judicial case, statute, or administrative regulation from one of the unnamed "Islamic countries." There was no indication of whether the alleged regulations of the "Islamic countries" arose out of a representative process that took into account, in some fashion, the will of the people.[65] In the unstated countries where there are exceptions to the veiling requirement, the court failed to determine whether those exceptions reflect a general requirement for women to veil in the first place. For instance, if we assume that the governments of Iran and Saudi Arabia exercise the authority to impose the veiling requirement, it logically follows that they would also permit exceptions where the state deemed such exceptions necessary. Yet at the same time, these countries suffer serious democratic deficits. Saudi Arabia is a monarchy, while Iran's supreme leader and Guardian Council exercise considerable authority, often to the detriment of meaningful representative government.[66] For the *Freeman* court to invoke rules of exception without taking note of the general state of affairs in particular countries was to underestimate the

[65] Had the court found a substantial burden on Ms Freeman's religious freedom, the state would have to show that the requirement for a full-face photo fulfills a compelling state interest, and that the full-face photo is the least restrictive means for achieving the interest. The full-face photo was characterized as pertaining to the importance of identification. Indeed, when the court referred to Muslim state practices, it stated that such countries make exceptions to the veiling requirement for identification purposes, such as passports. Importantly, a passport and driver's license have distinct purposes. Under Florida law, the driver's license is principally a grant of a privilege to drive. It is not primarily or principally designed as an identification document, unlike a passport, which is principally intended to serve as an identification document. Had the court wished to be consistent, it would have compared Florida's full-face photograph requirement with Saudi Arabia's driver's license requirements. However, had it done so, it would have found no guidance on the issue of veiling and driver's licenses, since women are legally prohibited from driving in Saudi Arabia. Other countries have dealt with the issue of religious minorities seeking exemption from full-face photographs for driver's licenses. In *Hutterian Brethren of Wilson County v Alberta*, 2007 ABCA 160, the Alberta Court of Appeals addressed the claims of Hutterites, who wanted a driver's license but without a photo. Hutterite religious beliefs hold that having photographs taken is a sin, and sought for an alternative driver's license format without the photo. The court found that the driver's license is not primarily designed as an identification document. Consequently, there was no significant interest in requiring the full-face photograph. Instead, the court required the province of Alberta to provide a driver's license without a picture, and to indicate that the license does not constitute proof of identity. Notably, in 2009, the Supreme Court of Canada reversed the Court of Appeal's decision: *Alberta v Hutterian Brethren of Wilson County*, 2009 SCC 37.

[66] For a critique of Iran's electoral processes, see Human Rights Watch, "Access Denied: Iran's Exclusionary Elections" (New York: Human Rights Watch, 2005) (<http://www.hrw.org/legacy/backgrounder/mena/iran0605/iran0605.pdf>) (accessed December 3, 2011). On the history of Saudi Arabia and the ruling monarchy, see al-Rasheed, *A History of Saudi Arabia*.

way in which both state-enforced donning and state-enforced removal of the veil are themselves serious burdens upon women's freedom perpetuated by regimes with serious democratic deficits.

Importantly, by viewing exceptions to general requirements of veiling in the Muslim world in isolation, the *Freeman* court defined the scope of Ms Freeman's expectation interests under Florida law in terms of the practices of foreign jurisdictions that are notorious for their violation of human rights norms. To suggest that she suffered no substantial burden to her religious freedom by reference to unnamed Islamic countries was, effectively, to suggest that her expectation interests under Florida law were no more than what she should expect if she were living in a foreign "Islamic country." In other words, the expectation interests of a US citizen were defined by reference to practices in some unstated Muslim country, of which Ms Freeman was not a citizen, and whose laws she had no authority to influence as citizen or democratic participant.

By construing Ms Freeman's faith commitments by haphazard reference to foreign law and thereby finding that she suffered no substantial burden on her religious freedom, the court freed the government from justifying its decision. The definition and application of the legal test, in this case, effectively insulated the government from having to prove a compelling state interest that justified burdening Ms Freeman's religious freedom. Put differently, by othering Ms Freeman, the court upheld and enhanced the enterprise of Florida's regulatory framework for issuing drivers license, as it evolved and developed after the terrorist attacks of September 11, 2001. Indeed, the potential effect of that tragedy on the new DMV regulations cannot be discounted or ignored. The context of security, coupled with a concern about Muslims as threats against the state arguably operated in the background of this case. This feature of the *Freeman* case is analogous to the earlier discussion in Chapter 3 on whether *dhimmīs* could create charitable trusts for Torah or Bible reading schools. Recall how security operated in the background for premodern Muslim jurists such as al-Shīrāzī, who prohibited *dhimmīs* from bequeathing their estates for the purpose of creating such charitable endowments. For al-Shīrāzī, such charities posed a harm to the Islamic polity that was comparable to giving legal validity to trusts that provide the enemies of the state with arms. Certainly, as suggested above, the limit on charitable giving did not adversely affect the *dhimmī*'s ability to bequeath property to other individually named persons. Likewise, the limit on Ms Freeman's religious freedom did not preclude her from believing what she chose or living her life as she chose. But to suggest that the legal limits on the *dhimmī* and Ms Freeman were mere inconveniences unduly ignores the way in which the demands of the enterprise of governance, couched in terms of security, animated the context in which the legal rulings in both of these cases arose.

7.2.3 The hegemony of law and the covered Muslim woman: Rights, security, and democracy

Concerns about the covered Muslim woman as a threat to the public good have arisen in cases involving Muslim girls and women who want to wear certain types of coverings at school or university.[67] In the British case *Begum v The Headteacher and Governors of Denbigh High School*, a Muslim high school student insisted on wearing a form of dress that she believed her religion required of her, but which did not conform to the uniform regulations adopted by the school. The case presents a complex factual narrative that frames the debate about her religious freedom and the school's discretion by reference to the protection of the public good and relatedly the rights of others in a democratic society.[68] A critical analysis of the legal decisions from the different courts involved will highlight how institutions of the law are themselves hegemonic as they re-instantiate not only their own legitimacy but also the legitimacy and authority of the enterprise of governance.

[67] Editorials written about Shabina Begum and her lawsuit reflect the angst over defining what it means to be British, and how the veil is a symbol of what Britain should not become. See, Rodd Liddle, "So Shabina, what's the point of Britain?" *Sunday Times*, March 6, 2005, p. 18, who worried that Denbigh High School's efforts to accommodate Muslims by providing for the *shalwar khameez* was dangerous; Theodore Dalrymple, "Wrong from Head to Toe: A Ridiculous and Ominous Decision in Britain," *Culture Watch* 57, no. 5 (March 28, 2005): 30, who saw the case through the lens of forced marriage, patriarchy, and the oppression of women. For the distance between editorial representations of the *Begum* case, and Ms Begum's own words, see the following interview with Shabina Begum: Jasper Gerard, "Faith, the veil, shopping, and me," *Sunday Times*, March 26, 2006, p. 5.

[68] The factual narrative is taken from the cases themselves, and is reflected in other articles that have also addressed this case. See for instance, Gareth Davies, "Banning the Jilbab: Reflections on Restricting Religious Clothing in the Law of the Court of Appeal in *SB v. Denbigh High School.* Decision of 2 March 2005," *European Constitutional Law Review* 1 (2005): 511–30; idem, "The House of Lords and Religious Clothing in *Begum v. Head Teacher and Governors of Denbigh High School*," *European Public Law* 13, no. 3 (2007): 423–32; Thomas Linden and Tessa Hetherington, "Schools and Human Rights, the *Denbigh High School* Case," *Education Law Journal* 6, no. 4 (2005): 229–48; Thomas Poole, "Of Headscarves and Heresies: The *Denbigh High School Case* and Public Authority Decision-Making Under the Human Rights Act," *Public Law* (2005): 685–95; Mohammad Mazher Idriss, "The Defeat of Shabina Begum in the House of Lords," *Liverpool Law Review* 27 (2006): 417–36; Ian Ward, "Shabina Begum and the Headscarf Girls," *Journal of Gender Studies* 15, no. 2 (2006): 119–31; John Mikhail, "Dilemmas of Cultural Legality: A Comment on Roger Cotterrell's 'The Struggle for Law' and a Criticism of the House of Lords' Opinions in *Begum*," *International Journal of Law in Context* 4, no. 4 (2009): 385–93.

Denbigh High School in central Britain had once been an underperforming school that witnessed tensions along racial lines. The head teacher, Mrs Yasmin Bevan, upon her arrival at the school, worked diligently to transform the school's reputation. Under her leadership, the student body began setting nationwide standards of achievement. In fact, the school started attracting students from outside its official catchment area, in large part because of the school's newly won reputation for providing quality education to its students. Mrs Bevan credited her success, in part, to the recently implemented uniform requirements.

When she developed the requirements, Mrs Bevan took pains to consult a wide array of interested parties, including parents of South Asian and Muslim background, whose children formed a significant percentage of the student body. The uniform requirements attempted to accommodate the diverse cultural traditions at the school. In addition to offering uniforms styled with trousers or skirts, one type for girls was a style of dress common within the South Asian community, known as the *shalwar khameez*. As a school policy, when students would enroll at the school, school officials made every effort to ensure that all parents and students understood the uniform policy.

Ms Begum did not live in the school's catchment, but she nevertheless wanted to attend Denbigh High School. She did so for two years, starting in September 2000, during which time she abided by the uniform requirement without complaint. On September 2, 2002, Ms Begum appeared at school wearing a *jilbāb,* a loose-fitting dress that not only covered her body but also hid her shape. Her brother and another young man accompanied her when she spoke to the Assistant Head Teacher, Mr Stuart Moore. Ms Begum's brother and the other young man informed Mr Moore that Ms Begum wanted to wear the *jilbāb,* invoking her legal and human rights to do so. Mr Moore, struck by the aggressively litigious tone of the two young men,[69] indicated that the uniform policy was not subject to negotiation; he required Ms Begum to go home to change into the appropriate attire before returning to school. Ms Begum, however, would not compromise on the matter; she considered wearing the *jilbāb* a religious requirement. She did not attend Denbigh High School on that day or for years thereafter during which legal proceedings took place.

[69] The High Court of Justice (Admin), the court of first instance, and later the House of Lords expressed disdain for the two young men, who were quick to invoke legal rights and proceedings. Mikhail, however, suggests that to show such disdain is to underappreciate how minority groups embrace the language of the law to assert their equal standing and position in a society not their own. From a critical race perspective, it should not be surprising (indeed it should be encouraging) that minority groups would utilize the language of the law to assert and claim their place within the polity. Mikhail, "Dilemmas of cultural legality," 388–9.

The lawsuit that ensued concerned the scope of both the school's authority to demand compliance with a uniform requirement, and Ms Begum's right to manifest her religious beliefs. Ms Begum claimed that the school had effectively expelled her for her refusal to conform to the uniform requirement. The school argued that it never expelled Ms Begum; it had the discretion to create and enforce a uniform requirement, which is all it did. Ms Begum was free to return to school as long as she adhered to the uniform requirement. After reviewing relevant statutory and regulatory provisions concerning education and school uniform policies, Justice Bennett of the High Court of Justice (Admin) held that the school did not formally expel or exclude Ms Begum from school. She was at all times free to attend her classes, as long as she adhered to the uniform requirement. Certainly, the court recognized that if Ms Begum would not violate her religious requirements, she could not attend classes. But as the initial choice was hers, her restriction from attending classes could not be construed as the school expelling her.

Ms Begum further claimed, however, that the school's actions violated her religious freedom under Article 9 of the European Convention of Human Rights (ECHR). That Article reads as follows:

> 9(1) Everyone has the right to freedom of thought, conscience and religion; this right includes freedom to change his religion or belief and freedom, either alone or in community with others and in public or private, to manifest his religion, or belief, in worship, teaching, practice, and observance.
>
> 9(2) Freedom to manifest one's religion or beliefs shall be subject only to such limitations as are prescribed by law and are necessary in a democratic society in the interests of public safety, for the protection of public order, health or morals, or for the protection of the rights and freedoms of others.

Cognizant of Article 9(2), Bennett J. noted that while Ms Begum was entitled to her beliefs, she could not claim as a matter of right that she could or should be able to manifest her beliefs at any time and in any place she desired. Bennett J. emphasized that Ms Begum had abided by the school requirements for two years without complaint.[70] Also, two neighboring schools offered Ms Begum the opportunity to wear the *jilbāb,* thereby allowing her both to obtain her education and to abide by her religious requirements without having to force Denbigh High School to abandon its uniform policy. Ms Begum was at all times free to pursue

[70] Notably, her earlier compliance seems significant to the High Court of Justice and the House of Lords, despite the fact that the right to religious freedom includes the freedom to change one's beliefs. *Shabina Begum v The Headeacher and Governors of Denbigh High School* [2004] EWHC 1389 (Admin), para. 78; *Begum v The Headteacher and Governors of Denbigh High Scohol* [2006] UKHL 15, para. 25.

her education and to abide by her religious requirements. Consequently, she suffered no violation of her rights under Article 9.

Nonetheless, the court proceeded on the assumption that, were there a violation of Ms Begum's religious freedom, the school's uniform requirements and actions were justified under Article 9(2). Bennett J. found the limitation on religious freedom necessary and justified for two fundamental reasons. First, the court was convinced that the uniform policy contributed to the integrity and cohesion of Denbigh High School's diverse student body—in other words, a public good argument. Bennett J. wrote:

> The evidence . . . clearly establishes that the school uniform policy promotes a positive ethos and a sense of communal identity. Not only does the Shalwar Kameeze satisfy the right of Muslim female pupils to manifest their religion but also it is worn by a number of different faith groups such as Hindus and Sikhs. Thus at the school there is no outward distinction between Muslims, Hindu and Sikh female students. Furthermore there is no outward distinction between Muslim female pupils. Thus any division between those who wear the jilbab and those who wear the Shalwar Kameeze is avoided.[71]

Second, Bennett J. was convinced that to permit Ms Begum to wear the *jilbāb* at Denbigh High School would adversely affect the freedom and liberty of other Muslim girls at the school—a rights-based argument that arguably is conceptually distinct from but overlaps with concerns about the public good. The teachers at Denbigh High School informed the court that other Muslim girls did not want the *jilbāb* to be a uniform option. The students were afraid that by allowing the *jilbāb* as an option, extremist groups would use it to delineate who is a "good" Muslim and who is a "bad" one at school. The worry about such extremism is an important feature of this case. The teachers all spoke about a protest at the school led by extremist Muslims opposed to the secular education of Muslim children. The protest was unrelated to Ms Begum's legal action, but it was nonetheless referenced in relation to Ms Begum's desire to wear the *jilbāb*. The teachers, reflecting the students' concerns, stated that the *jilbāb* was a symbol of extremism. If permitted on school grounds, it would undermine the sense of community that had been hard won, as well as Muslim girls' liberty and freedom. By preserving and upholding the uniform policy, the school could limit the presence of extremism and thereby protect the individual choice of other Muslim girls.

Siding with the school, Bennett J. stated:

[71] *Begum* [2004] EWHC 1389 (Admin), para. 90.

> [I]t is clear from the evidence that there are a not insignificant number of Muslim female pupils at Denbigh High School who do not wish to wear the jilbab and either do, or will, feel pressure on them either from inside or outside the school. The present school uniform policy aims to protect their rights and freedoms. Further, if the choice of two uniforms were permitted for Muslim female pupils, it can be readily understood that other pupils of different or no faiths might well see that as favoring a particular religion.[72]

The court was convinced that the uniform upholds a sense of community that the *jilbāb* would undermine. The *jilbāb* represented the onset of extremism that had to be prevented from entering the school. If the *jilbāb*, and thus extremism, were to be permitted onto the school grounds, the student community in general, and non-*jilbāb*-wearing Muslim girls in particular, would suffer. Consequently, even if Ms Begum's rights had been infringed (which the court found was not the case), the uniform requirement nonetheless would be justified in the interest of promoting community values and protecting the rights of others.

On appeal, Bennett J.'s ruling was overturned. Brooke L.J., writing for the Court of Appeal, found that the uniform requirement infringed Ms Begum's religious freedom under Article 9 and did not satisfy the requirements of Article 9(2) of the ECHR. The school proffered two principal arguments to justify its uniform requirement, namely that it promoted community value and harmony and that it protected the rights of others. Members of the school emphasized the pedagogical importance of instilling in the student body the virtue of civic harmony and responsibility. Brooke L.J. noted that "a major learning objective on the part of the curriculum concerned with citizenship was for pupils to work together positively and cooperatively in a community that fosters respect for all."[73] Commenting on the statement by deputy head teacher Mr Connor, Brooke L.J. wrote:

> It was important in [Mr Connor's] experience to recognise that many adolescents require a lot of support to understand the importance of inclusion, equal opportunities, mutual respect and social cohesion, such as was fostered by the school's uniform policy. He attested to the same concerns among a number of girls at the school as Mr. Moore had mentioned, and he believed that the school had a duty to protect these pupils from inappropriate peer pressures, or pressures from outside extremist groups. There had been an incident in February 2004 when some young men who represented an extremist Muslim group had picketed the school gates and distributed leaflets to the pupils which exhorted Muslims not to send their children to

[72] *Begum* [2004] EWHC 1389 (Admin), para. 90.

[73] *The Queen on the application of Shabina Begum v The Headteacher and Governors of Denbigh High School* [2005] EWCA Civ 199, para. 52.

secular schools. A number of pupils understandably felt harassed by these activities.[74]

In other words, school authorities attested to their perception of the *jilbāb* as a threat to the well-being of the school community, of the school's shared values, and of the well-being of certain members of the community who might fall victim to the machinations of an undefined, but very real fear of extremism.

Brooke L.J. agreed that uniform policies such as the one in question could nonetheless be justified under Article 9(2), theoretically speaking. To survive a challenge on the grounds of Article 9, the school must show that it duly considered the impact of the uniform requirement on Ms Begum's rights. His review of the record revealed to him that the school failed to show it carefully considered and balanced Ms Begum's right to religious freedom with the need for a standard uniform policy for the student body. This was not to suggest, according to Brooks L.J., that the school could not preclude the *jilbāb* from school grounds. Rather, it could do so only upon showing that it engaged in a decision-making process informed by the standards of rights protections provided under the ECHR, which in this case it did not.

The school appealed the decision to the House of Lords, which reversed the appellate court. In its reversal, it criticized Brooke L.J.'s procedure of decision-making as tedious and unduly legalistic for the school board to adopt.[75] Rather, the House of Lords held that a legal resolution of the case must take account of the merits of the school decision, and not just the *way* by which the school made its decisions. On reviewing the merits of the case, three of the five justices at the House of Lords held that Ms Begum suffered no violation of her right to religious freedom; two found that her rights had been infringed, but nonetheless held that the school's uniform policy was justified under Article 9(2) of the Convention.[76] Those who found no infringement also held that, in the alternative, had there been an infringement, the school policy would have been justified under

[74] *Begum* [2005] EWCA Civ 199, para. 54.

[75] The procedural approach adopted by the Court of Appeals has been the subject of considerable debate among commentators on the case. The procedural approach certainly imposes a heavy burden on school officials, which the House of Lords considered unreasonable. Others have suggested, though, that the procedural approach emphasizes the importance of incorporating human rights as part of any administrative decision, and offers administrative agencies such as schools the opportunity to ensure that their discretion does not violate the rights of individuals. For commentary on the procedural issue, see Davies, "The House of Lords," 424–5; Poole, "Of Headscarves and Heresies," 689–94; Linden and Hetherington, "Schools and Human Rights," 236–8.

[76] Baroness Hale and Lord Nicholls considered Ms Begum's right infringed, but considered the school's policy justified. *Begum* [2006] UKHL 15, paras 41, 92–4.

Article 9(2). Among the House of Lords, there were two justifications that were particularly prominent in their decision. One justificatory argument drew upon institutional arguments about court deference to the enterprise of governance: the uniform requirement was justified because of the deference courts owe to government administrators, such as the heads and governors of schools, under doctrines such as the "margin of appreciation," to be discussed below. The second justificatory argument had to do with issues of public good and threats to it, namely that the *jilbāb* was a threat to the well-being of the school community at large, and to the rights of Muslim girls to be free from religious coercion concerning their attire. In other words, the arguments justifying the uniform requirement adopted two tacks. The first approach posited the court in between the government agency (the school board) and the minority claimant, and required the court to adopt a principle of judicial deference to the enterprise of governance (i.e., the doctrine of margin of appreciation). This endorsement of judicial deference illustrates that at the discursive site of the minority claimant, the hegemonic capacity of the law becomes especially apparent, if not poignantly so. The second approach characterized the final outcome as based on concerns for third-party rights and thereby positioned the school board in a more neutral, umpire-like role. Notably, this approach introduced third parties into the equation, but only by reference to the fears of extremism.

The second approach concerning third-party rights will be addressed first, whereas the first approach will be analyzed in the subsequent section. In his lead opinion, Lord Bingham relied on the head teacher, Ms Bevan's, view that the uniform requirement was a significant factor in promoting the public good at the school. He wrote: "The head teacher believes that school uniform plays an integral part in securing high and improving standards, serving the needs of a diverse community, promoting a positive sense of communal identity and avoiding manifest disparities of wealth and style."[77] Prior to Mrs Bevan's arrival, the school had suffered the ill effects of racial tension among the students.[78] The uniform requirement helped overcome those tensions. Now the school was worried that with the *jilbāb* would come "undesirable differentiation between Muslim groups according to the strictness of their views."[79] The head teacher was especially concerned that the *jilbāb* would create ruptures in the school and undermine the purpose of the uniform policy, namely "to promote inclusion and social cohesion," as opposed to fragmentation and difference.

[77] *Begum* [2006] UKHL 15, para. 6.
[78] *Begum* [2006] UKHL 15, para. 18.
[79] *Begum* [2006] UKHL 15, para. 18.

In this case, the *jilbāb* threatened such destructive power because it was viewed as a symbol of extremism. Lord Bingham stated: "Some pupils were resistant to wearing the jilbab as unnecessarily restrictive and associated with an extremist group."[80] Lord Bingham referred to no evidence that linked the *jilbāb* to an extremist ideology or group. Nor was any evidence presented that suggested Ms Begum adhered to extremist ideals. Instead, Lord Bingham noted that "an extreme Muslim group" held a protest outside Denbigh High School in February 2004, protesting against the education of Muslim students in secular schools.[81] All parties recognized that the protest was unconnected to Ms Begum's claim, but it was referenced in large part to rationalize the students' fears of the threat of Islamic extremism, and thereby give content to the argument about protecting third-party rights.

The House of Lords justified the limit on Ms Begum because it protected the rights of third parties, in particular other Muslim girls who were afraid they would be pressured to wear the *jilbāb* as well. Affirming the view of Bennett J., Lord Hoffmann wrote: "The school was entitled to consider that the rules about uniform were necessary for the protection of the rights and freedoms of others."[82] For instance, Baroness Hale stipulated that the veil is part of a larger socio-political phenomenon. Citing scholarship in the field of multiculturalism, Baroness Hale remarked that "strict dress codes may be imposed on women not for their own sake but to serve the ends of others. Hence they may be denied equal freedom to choose for themselves."[83] With this in mind, she then considered how school uniform policies can protect the minds of young *minority* children. She wrote:

> the sight of a woman in full purdah may offend some people, and especially those western feminists who believe that it is a symbol of her oppression, but that could not be a good reason for prohibiting her from wearing it. But schools are different. Their task is to educate the young from all the many and diverse families and communities in this country in accordance with the national curriculum. Their task is to help all of their pupils to achieve their full potential... Fostering a sense of community and cohesion within the school is an important part of that. A uniform dress code can play its role in smoothing over ethnic, religious, and social divisions. But it does more than that. Like it or not, this is a society committed, in principle and in law, to equal freedom for men and women to chose how they will lead their lives within the law. *Young girls from ethnic, cultural or religious minorities*

80 *Begum* [2006] UKHL 15, para. 18.
81 *Begum* [2006] UKHL 15, para. 18.
82 *Begum* [2006] UKHL 15, para. 58.
83 *Begum* [2006] UKHL 15, para. 95.

growing up here face particularly difficult choices: how far to adopt or to distance themselves from the dominant culture.[84]

For Baroness Hale, young members of "ethnic, cultural, or religious minorities" must be given the space and freedom to choose for themselves how they will be in the world. Notably, the third parties being protected are not *all* pupils or even *all* girls. Rather, young girls from minority groups provide a special case for Baroness Hale. Consequently, protecting these young *minority* minds justifies limiting Ms Begum's right to wear the *jilbāb.* In other words, Ms Begum's rights must be construed with the special importance of protecting the space for "ethnic, cultural, or religious minorities growing up here" who must make choices for themselves amidst a presumed context in which their self-fulfillment and full potential are at stake in ways that are, presumably, not present for those who are not part of an ethnic, cultural, or religious minority, who are part of the "here" and the "us" that constitutes the "dominant culture."

For Baroness Hale, protecting the rights of third-party young women from the threats to their self-fulfillment and full potential justified the uniform requirement, and was consistent with recent legal decisions from the European Court of Human Rights—in particular the case of *Leyla Sahin v Turkey.* In *Sahin,* the petitioner alleged that her Article 9 rights had been violated by regulations that prevented her from wearing a headscarf in institutions of higher learning in Turkey. The petitioner, Ms Leyla Sahin, was enrolled at the Faculty of Medicine in Istanbul University. She came from a family of practicing Muslims and considered wearing a headscarf to be her religious duty. Under university regulations, students wearing a headscarf for religious reasons were denied access to university lectures, courses, and tutorials. When Ms Sahin wanted to sit for an oncology examination, she was denied entrance to the examination. She was also denied admission to courses and lectures. Having exhausted domestic means of redress, Ms Sahin petitioned the European Court of Human Rights to hear her case.

The European Court of Human Rights determined that the regulations interfered with Ms Sahin's right to religious freedom under Article 9 of the ECHR, the same provision at issue in the *Begum* case.[85] To address whether the regulations were justified, the Grand Chamber considered the relationship between religious freedom and democracy. Trying to seek a balance between the needs of democracy and the right of religious

[84] *Begum* [2006] UKHL 15, paras 96–7 (emphasis added).

[85] *Leyla Sahin v Turkey,* Application no. 44774/98, ECHR (November 10, 2005), para. 100 *et seq.*

freedom, the Grand Chamber wrote: "In democratic societies, in which several religions coexist within one and the same population, it may be necessary to place restrictions on freedom to manifest one's religion or belief in order to reconcile the interests of the various groups and ensure that everyone's beliefs are respected."[86]

According to the Grand Chamber, the Turkish state's commitment to secularism and democracy must ensure that no individual is unduly pressured by religious groups, extremist or otherwise, to assume a religious attitude without meaningful consent or understanding. The principle of secularism protects "the individual not only against arbitrary interference by the State but from external pressure from extremist groups."[87] Protecting the vulnerable and the easily coerced was in part the justification the Grand Chamber relied upon to uphold Turkey's ban on wearing the religious head scarf. The Grand Chamber recognized that "when examining the question of the Islamic headscarf in the Turkish context, it must be borne in mind the impact which wearing such a symbol, which is presented or perceived as a compulsory religious duty, may have on those who choose not to wear it."[88] Despite the absence of a particular finding of fact about Ms Sahin's extremist ideology, or any actual harm that others would suffer if she wore the veil, the Grand Chamber held that the regulation was justified to protect the rights of others.

Writing in dissent, Judge Tulkens was troubled by the recourse to fear as the basis for legitimating the restriction on Ms Sahin. She wrote: "Only indisputable facts and reasons whose legitimacy is beyond doubt—not mere worries or fears—are capable of satisfying [the requirement of a pressing social need] and justifying interference with a right guaranteed by the Convention."[89] Tulkens' demand for detailed evidence was especially poignant when she asserted that fear of extremism was a central feature of both the Turkish Government's case and the Grand Chamber's decision:

> While everyone agrees on the need to prevent radical Islamism, a serious objection may nevertheless be made to such reasoning. Merely wearing the headscarf cannot be associated with fundamentalism and it is vital to distinguish between those who wear the headscarf and "extremists" who seek to impose the headscarf as they do other religious symbols.[90]

Tulken's objection on this point is significant because of the way in which a fear of extremism in the polity led to the insertion of third-party rights as part of the legal analysis.

[86] *Sahin*, para. 106. [87] *Sahin*, para. 113. [88] *Sahin*, para. 115.
[89] *Sahin* (dissent), para. 5. [90] *Sahin* (dissent) para. 10.

An important aspect of the majority decision in *Sahin,* as well as in *Begum,* was the reference to third-party rights. By invoking concern for third-party *rights* (as opposed to mere public policy), the courts could situate the state (and its institutions) as arbiters between competing rights holders; indeed, the language of rights offered legal cover for what was effectively the courts' use of law to constitute and enhance the enterprise of governance. By invoking the language of rights, the courts could avoid the kind of criticism directed at the *Gobitis* court, which presumed too much of the state's discretionary power and capacity. Tulken's dissent, however, uncovers how the argument about third-party rights was a fiction introduced into the legal analysis to reach a particular result without having to perform a full factual inquiry.

But if the third-party rights argument was a fiction, to what end did it operate? In both *Sahih* and *Begum,* the respective fictions were founded on references to fears of extremism that might take root in the polity, affect third parties, and thereby undermine the public good. Those fears were unproven and unsubstantiated, thus making them fictional. To identify and name the fear, though, reveals what has thus far been hidden from view, namely the interests of the enterprise of governance and its vision for a public that it wants to make manifest. In her dissent, Tulkens revealed how references to fear, security, and extremism—and their effects on third parties—operated as legal covers for the operation of the Turkish enterprise of governance and the vision of the public it desired. The Turkish Government's secularizing agenda, since its inception, is part of a history that is already well known. Its agenda of secularity was posited over and against an Islamist one that is often referenced in various sectors of the public sphere. The secularity of Turkey, in other words, can neither be taken for granted nor considered a foregone conclusion. Consequently, one cannot ignore how the European Court of Human Rights gave legal effect to a fear of extremism by limiting an individual's freedom, presumably in order to protect the rights of third-party individuals, but with the effect of constituting the secular enterprise of governance in Turkey.

In *Begum,* Baroness Hale displayed a sensitivity to Tulken's dissent. However, she considered the context of *Begum* significant enough to warrant limiting Ms Begum's religious freedom rights. For her, the public good of the school and the rights of others were duly upheld by the uniform requirement. She wrote:

> Social cohesion is promoted by the uniform elements of shirt, tie and jumper and the requirement that all outer garments be in the school colour. But cultural and religious diversity is respected by allowing girls to wear either a skirt, trousers, or the shalwar kameez, and by allowing those who

> wished to do so to wear the hijab. This was indeed a thoughtful and proportionate response to reconciling the complexities of the situation. This is demonstrated by the fact that girls have subsequently expressed their concern that if the jilbab were to be allowed they would face pressure to adopt it even though they do not wish to do so. Here is the evidence to support the justification which Judge Tulkens found lacking in the *Sahin* case.[91]

In *Sahin,* the greater good was viewed as coming under threat by an extremism that was haunting in the background, but evidence of that background was never brought forth to be examined. It was assumed, and it thereby uncritically informed the legal reasoning about choice, public good, and the rights of others. Baroness Hale, wanting to avoid that criticism, made reference to the evidence of teenage girls who were worried about the *jilbāb* creating a climate of extremism in their school. Recourse to this evidence, though, raises questions of its sufficiency and suitability in this case. Critical of the House of Lords justification in *Begum,* Gareth Davies writes: "The fact that some pupils or teachers regarded those in the jilbab as extremists or frightening is not a legitimate reason for restriction unless those fears can be objectively justified... Allowing one group of teenagers to assess the threat posed by a religiously different teenager has obvious risks."[92]

The justification of protecting the rights of third parties who might otherwise be denied the choice to wear the veil or not,[93] in both *Sahin* and *Begum,* arguably provided legal cover for the underlying concern about a threat to the public good, and thereby the security of the polity. Indeed, underlying both *Begum* and *Sahin* was a fundamental concern for security in the face of possible extremism. After September 11, 2001 and the bombings in London on July 7, 2005, no one wants to contend with extremism of any sort. Arguably, the justifications provided by the Grand Chamber and the House of Lords were premised on a concern for security, though couched in the language of protecting the public good and the rights of others. The Grand Chamber and the House of Lords were willing to sacrifice the rights of individual women for a greater good that was perceived to be threatened, albeit without evidence showing the basis for such fears as they related to both women's claims.

91 *Begum* [2006] UKHL 15, para. 98.

92 Davies, "The House of Lords and Religious Clothing," 429–30.

93 Notably, the concern about Muslim women's agency in these cases may be criticized on the grounds of inadequately understanding the agency of women who are, at the same time, members of religious communities. See Mahmood, *Politics of Piety.* The concern for female agency in the *Begum* decision is evident by how the judges express concern that Ms Begum speaks only through her brother, and not of her own accord. See Mikhail, "Dilemmas of Cultural Legality," 389.

Begum, *the margin of appreciation, and the hegemony of justice*

Despite its limitations, the *Begum* decision offers a fascinating example of the hegemony that arises at the intersection of law, the enterprise of governance, and the minority claimant. To illuminate how the *Begum* case reveals such hegemonic tendencies, it is useful to revisit an earlier case of such hegemony already addressed concerning the *dhimmī* rules. The juxtaposition of the *Begum* case and the premodern Islamic one is meant to support the general argument of this study, namely that such hegemony is endemic to the plight of minorities across historical periods, legal systems, and political regimes.

Recall the analysis of Prophet Muḥammad's decision to stone two Jews for adultery, as discussed in Chapter 4. In that example, two Jews were brought to the Prophet to be sentenced for committing adultery. Before deciding the appropriate ruling to apply, the Prophet requested the Jewish community at the hearing to explain the Jewish legal rulings and punishment for adultery. A young Jewish man was brought before the Prophet and recited from the Torah, covering his hand over a section of the Torah that required stoning of adulterers. Standing with the Prophet was ʿAbd Allāh b. Salām, a Jewish convert to Islam and companion of the Prophet. Various reports suggest that ʿAbd Allāh was knowledgeable about the Jewish faith and tradition, and that prior to his conversion, the Jewish community considered him a learned man and leader. ʿAbd Allāh asked the young man to remove his hand from the Torah, beneath which was found the passage that requires stoning for adulterers. The Prophet thereupon stoned the two Jews for adultery.

Muslim jurists debated whether this example meant that Jewish law had normative force in an Islamic court, or whether the fact of its correlation with Islamic law simply further legitimated the application of Sharīʿa-based rules on the Jews. That debate has already been addressed in Chapter 4. Of interest here is the role of ʿAbd Allāh b. Salām as a native informant in the Prophet's tribunal, and the way in which the adjudication itself illustrates the hegemonic potential that arises when a minority claimant becomes the focus of the law and the enterprise of governance.

With ʿAbd Allāh b. Salām as the native informant, the Prophet could both ask for and disregard the testimony about Jewish law brought forth by the Jewish community members. In doing so, the Prophet was represented as respecting the true Jewish law, which was viewed as contrary to what the Jewish community itself wanted to espouse as the relevant rule of decision. But what was "true" Jewish law at that time? As discussed earlier, the "truth" of Jewish law may have had less to do with what the Jewish community claimed it to be, and more to do with the methods of Islamic legal analysis and the priority of source-texts and their literal meaning for legal analysis. What the Jewish community wanted as the outcome and why was not explored or addressed in the sources reporting this event. Rather, Sharīʿa as Rule of Law reveals that the claims of minority members are all too often framed in the fashion of the prevailing legal system and the enterprise of governance within which it is embedded.

For instance, suppose counter-factually that the Prophet had asked the Jews why they hid the stoning punishment. Suppose he inquired into the nature of their legal tradition or the interpretive authority of the community and scholar in relationship to the Torah as source-text. These types of questions would involve him showing an appreciation for the interstices of Jewish law and legal theory as constitutive elements of his function as an authoritative adjudicator. To ask and answer these questions could influence and affect both the nature of his judgment, and thereby the nature of Islamic law and legal authority in a pluralist setting. The reports, however, do not indicate that such questions were asked or answered. For later jurists who developed a normative system of order patterned around the Prophet's practice, they looked to this instance to illustrate both the primacy of Sharīʿa-based norms, and the ways in which legal diversity is accounted for as a *matter of fact*, but not necessarily as a *matter of law and legal authority*. In this prophetic case, Jewish law was relevant only to the extent that referencing it respected the diversity of the parties in dispute without undermining the dominance, priority, and jurisdiction of Sharīʿa in terms of its methods of analysis and its dominance as the prevailing legal regime. For this reason, many jurists understood this incident to suggest that sentencing the Jewish adulterers to death by stoning was just and right, given the similar punishments in the Torah. But in no way must that be understood, in their minds, as suggesting that Jewish law had or should have any normative authority alongside Sharīʿa-based doctrines.

In *Begum*, a similar dynamic of hegemony operated, particularly in regard to the courts' respective determinations of what is and is not acceptable under Islamic law. Both parties to the case sought out expert witnesses to attest to the clothing requirements for women in Islamic law. Denbigh High School sought out witnesses from the Muslim community who confidently indicated that the shalwar khameez did not violate Islamic legal requirements. Those same witnesses, however, indicated to Ms Begum's lawyer that the *jilbāb* was the better and more appropriate attire for a Muslim woman who had reached puberty.[94] Both Bennett

[94] *Begum* [2004] EWHC 1389 (Admin), paras 20–2.

J. and the House of Lords noted this conflict but were unconcerned by the contradictions by the expert witnesses. In fact, the internal debates of Muslim scholars were of little consequence to either court's analysis given the prevailing legal standards that looked to the petitioner's sincerity, cogency, and seriousness in belief.[95] As Lord Bingham of the House of Lords wrote: "It is common ground in these proceedings that at all material times the respondent [Begum] sincerely held the religious belief which she professed to hold. It was not the less a religious belief because her belief may have changed... or because it was a belief shared by a small minority of people... [A]ny sincere religious belief must command respect, particularly when derived from an ancient and respected religion."[96]

The subjective approach to religious belief is not an uncommon approach utilized by democratic constitutional courts tasked with exercising judicial review on grounds of religious freedom.[97] On the one hand, the subjective standard has the virtue of respecting a petitioner's conscientious assertion of his or her religious convictions. On the other hand, it disregards the way in which beliefs are themselves embedded in a tradition that gives beliefs and practices a thick or rich meaning.[98]

In the *Begum* cases, Bennett J. and the House of Lords emphasized the individual sincerity of the claimant. In doing so, though, they nonetheless found that Ms Begum suffered no infringement of her religious freedom. They made this finding by invoking the judicial doctrine of "the margin of appreciation." That doctrine requires courts to defer to the decision of local administrative bodies, here represented by their high esteem for the efforts of Mrs Bevan and the governors of the high school. The school, wrote Lord Bingham:

> had taken immense pains to devise a uniform policy which respected Muslim beliefs but did so in an inclusive, unthreatening, and uncompetitive way... It was feared that acceding to [Ms. Begum's] request would or might have significant adverse repercussions. It would in my opinion be irresponsible of any court, lacking the experience, background and detailed knowledge of the head teacher, staff and governors, to overrule their judgment on a matter as sensitive as this. The power of decision has been given to them

[95] *Begum* [2004] EWHC 1389 (Admin), para. 69; *Begum* [2006] UKHL 15, para. 15.
[96] *Begum* [2006] UKHL 15, para. 21.
[97] See for instance, the Canadian Supreme Court decision *Syndicat Northcrest v Amselem*, 2004 SCC 47; [2004] 2 SCR 551.
[98] Benjamin Berger, "Law's Religion: Rendering Culture," *Osgoode Hall Law Journal* 45, no. 2 (2007): 277–314; idem, "The Cultural Limits of Legal Tolerance," in *After Pluralism: Reimagining Religious Engagement*, eds Courtney Benderand Pamela Klassen (New York: Columbia University Press, 2010), 98–123.

> for the compelling reason that they are best placed to exercise it, and I see no reason to disturb their decision.[99]

Likewise, Lord Hoffman held that the House of Lords owed the school a degree of deference as to how it managed its operations. Referring to ECHR jurisprudence on "margin of appreciation," Lord Hoffman wrote: "In my opinion a domestic court should accept the decision of Parliament to allow individual schools to make their own decisions about uniforms... [T]he justification must be sought at the local level and it is there that an area of judgment, comparable to the margin of appreciation, must be allowed to the school."[100] By relying on the margin of appreciation, the court employed legal doctrines that, given concerns about the limits of judicial competence, effectively implied deference to the enterprise of governance, here the governing school board. While courts must be careful not to exceed their competence, this case nonetheless showcases how the court's view of the range of its competence had the effect of enhancing the enterprise of governance.[101]

Deferring to the school's decision was not only legally required of the court, but also very much a testament to the court's trust in the leadership of Mrs Bevan, the head teacher of Denbigh High School. In these cases, Mrs Bevan effectively became the courts' trustworthy resource on the Islamic requirements of veiling, despite also being a party to the case. Consistently, various opinions took note of Mrs Bevan's unique position as a Bengali Muslim woman, her local knowledge of different parts of the Muslim world, her efforts to include the Muslim community in the design of the uniform, and her success in turning Denbigh High School into a high-performing school.

For instance, Bennett J. stated:

> Mrs Bevan, the Headteacher, was born into a Bengali Muslim family and grew up in India, Pakistan and Bangladesh before coming to this country. She has an understanding of the Islamic dress code and the practices adopted by Muslim women.[102]

At the Court of Appeal, Lord Justice Brooke stated:

> The Headteacher, Yasmin Bevan, was born into a Bengali Muslim family. She grew up in India, Pakistan and Bangladesh before coming to this country. She has had a great deal of involvement with Bengali Muslim communities

[99] *Begum* [2006] UKHL 15, para. 34.

[100] *Begum* [2006] UKHL 15, para. 64.

[101] For an analysis and critique of the "margin of appreciation" doctrine in the ECHR jurisprudence on religious freedom, see Gerhard van der Schyff and Adriaan Overbeeke, "Exercising Religious Freedom in the Public Space: A Comparative and European Convention Analysis of General Burqa Bans," *European Constitutional Law Review* 7 (2011): 424–52.

[102] *Begum* [2004] EWHC 1389 (Admin), para. 37.

> in this country and abroad, and she says that she understands the Islamic dress code and the practices adopted by Muslim women. She does not, however, purport to have a detailed knowledge of the theological issues which surfaced in this dispute.[103]

At the House of Lords, we find the following representations of Mrs Bevan:

Lord Bingham:

> The head teacher, Ms. Yasmin Bevan, was born into a Bengali Muslim family and grew up in India, Pakistan and Bangladesh before coming to this country. She has had much involvement with Bengali Muslim communities here and abroad, and is familiar with the codes and practices governing the dress of Muslim women. Since her appointment as head teacher in 1991, when it was not performing well, the school has come to enjoy an outstanding measure of success.[104]

Lord Hoffman:

> Yasmin Bevan, who comes from a Muslim Bengali family, has been head teacher since 1991. Under her leadership, standards of education and behavior at the school have greatly improved. She has consistently been supported by the governors, among whom Muslims are strongly represented.[105]

Lord Scott:

> Moreover the head teacher, Mrs. Yasmin Bevan, who had been appointed in 1991, was born into a Bengali Moslem family and brought up in the subcontinent before moving to this country... The head teacher's background confirms she well understands the Moslem dress code for women.[106]

Combining its doctrinally required deference to school authorities with admiration and respect for Mrs Bevan, the courts in *Begum* effectively construed her as the native informant who, despite being a party to the action, could be relied upon as a source of expertise on what Islamic law required. In the earlier discussion of the stoning of the two Jews, ʿAbd Allāh b. Salām played the role of native informant to the Prophet. Having converted from Judaism, he became an important figure in the narrative, since he represented both knowledge and authority. Also, given his status as a companion of the Prophet, he was considered by later jurists to be a trustworthy source of authority. As sources attest, ʿAbd Allāh b. Salām was lauded as one of the few companions for whom a verse of the Qurʾān was revealed, a testament to his righteous

[103] *Begum* [2005] EWCA Civ 199, para. 2.
[104] *Begum* [2006] UKHL 15, para. 5.
[105] *Begum* [2006] UKHL 15, para. 43.
[106] *Begum* [2006] UKHL 15, paras 74–5.

character.[107] There is little doubt in the Islamic tradition that ʿAbd Allāh b. Salām was venerated, respected, and trusted. He may have once been Jewish, but by the time he appeared in the story of the two adulterous Jews, he was a converted Muslim, native informant. Consequently, when he caught the young Jewish reader covering part of the Torah, ʿAbd Allāh b. Salām effectively excluded the Jewish reader's own representation of the law as unreliable and posited his own as authoritative and trustworthy.

In the *Begum* case, the courts presented Mrs Bevan as assuming a similar role. As an educator and successful school administrator, she manifested commitment to the state's programme of educating young citizens. She utilized a democratically inspired process to develop the uniform requirement, and she made every effort to be inclusive. She was, in other words, one of "Us," both in terms of shared values and commitments to the institutions of the enterprise of governance. She was especially well-positioned to decide on appropriate uniform styles in large part because of her own background as a Bengali Muslim woman who had lived throughout South Asia and was suitably familiar with the Islamic traditions on veiling. In other words, she was also one of "Them." Only Lord Justice Brooke, in the Court of Appeal, was careful to limit the scope of her knowledge and appreciation of the Islamic doctrinal debate when he wrote: "She does not, however, purport to have a detailed knowledge of the theological issues which surfaced in this dispute."[108] At various points in the *Begum* case, Ms Bevan was made to be the native informant who could be trusted to lead the school (and the courts) to a suitable resolution.

By construing Mrs Bevan as a native informant, though, the courts failed to account for a possible intra-Muslim community contest over religious identity, fashion, and authenticity. The shalwar khameez is a style of dress that is common among South Asians. The *jilbāb* on the other hand, is a style of dress more common in the Arab world. Mrs Bevan, of South Asian descent, may very well have been familiar with the requirements for appropriate Muslim attire, and so too may have the Muslim members on Denbigh High School's board of governors. However, they may not have made the court aware of any intra-community tension between South Asian Muslims and Arab Muslims that may have lurked in the backdrop of this particular controversy.[109]

[107] J. Horovitz, "ʿAbd Allāh b. Salām," *Encyclopaedia of Islam, Second Edition*. Eds P. Bearman et al.

[108] *Begum* [2005] EWCA Civ 199, para. 2.

[109] This tension is anecdotally addressed in Manji, *The Trouble With Islam Today*, 134–42; Ed Hussain, *The Islamist* (New York: Penguin Books, 2009), 238.

Just as there was no indication about whether the Jews coming to the Prophet were Rabbinic or schismatic, or whether ʿAbd Allāh b. Salam was of the same or a different Jewish group, there was also no awareness by the *Begum* courts of whether and to what extent any intra-community conflicts informed the views about Islamic dress that the courts heard. Arguably, by finding against Ms Begum, in part because the *jilbāb* is a symbol of extremism, the court may have unwittingly perpetuated stereotypes of Muslim Arabs as extremists.

7.3 CONCLUSION: IS THERE AN ESCAPE FROM HEGEMONY?

This chapter signals a shift in the analysis of the *dhimmī* rules. Throughout this study, appreciating the *intelligibility* of the *dhimmī* rules has been paramount. Intelligibility, though, does not exist in a vacuum, in some pure state of immanent meaning. Rather, as suggested throughout this study, the intelligibility of the *dhimmī* rules has very much depended on how the rules were or are framed. For example, some commentators writing in the decade since September 11, 2001 frame the *dhimmī* rules in terms of security. Viewing the *dhimmī* rules through that frame gives intelligibility not so much to the *dhimmī* rules but rather to the language of "tolerance" and "intolerance," and the stakes that each characterization implies for purposes of state policies of multiculturalism and immigration, and legislative bans on minarets, "Sharīʿa," and Islamic veiling practices.

This study has developed the frame "Rule of Law," instead, to appreciate the intelligibility of the *dhimmī* rules. In doing so, this frame has made possible a historical differentiation between the intelligibility of these rules in a premodern period and the modern period. In the former, jurists imagined these rules as a feature of an imperial enterprise of governance that had a universalist Islamic ethos. In the latter, these rules are embedded in a post-imperial and post-colonial context, where their intelligibility may further differ when the rules are invoked by officials of post-colonial states or leaders of Muslim minority populations subjected to state policies of immigration, assimilation, and multiculturalism.

By traversing both time periods, this study suggests that the *dhimmī* rules are themselves symptomatic of the more general challenge of governing amidst diversity. That challenge is neither unique to the premodern Islamic empire nor the modern Muslim state in which Islam or Islamic law plays a part in the state's legislation or nationalist politics. Rather, as this chapter has suggested, the challenge of governing amidst diversity besets legal systems around the world. For instance, the case of Ms Silmi in France reveals how the legal language of core values and rights constitutes a system of value for a polity and serves as a litmus test about who is "Us" and who is "Them." The legal regimes of immigration and citizenship represent contemporary practices of inclusion and exclusion, which in the case of Ms Silmi, allowed her to reside in France on the one hand, but rendered her unfit for full inclusion on the other. The *Freeman* case reveals how even as courts attempt to incorporate the Other's tradition, they do so in a manner that reinstantiates the domestic legal regime and enterprise of governance. For example, the *Freeman* court elided "law" and "religious law" by focusing on the practices of unnamed Islamic nation-states. Relying on vague references to Islamic state practice, the *Freeman* court framed Ms Freeman's claim by reference to alleged Muslim state practices that ultimately enhanced and enabled the Florida enterprise of governance (i.e., the DMV) at the expense of Ms Freeman's expectation interests as a US citizen. And finally, the House of Lords' reliance on the margin of appreciation to deny Ms Begum legal relief showcases the hegemonic potential that lies at the intersection of law, the enterprise of governance, and the minority claimant who makes claims upon the state. Though the challenges of governing amidst diversity in a premodern Islamic empire, modern Muslim state, and democratic constitutional state are obviously different—both in terms of context and substantive doctrine—juxtaposing the legal treatment of the *dhimmī* and the covered Muslim woman exhibits that the dynamics of governing amidst diversity are eerily similar. The fact that minorities are treated in such fashion is hardly unique to the Islamic tradition. Indeed, the regulation of the covered Muslim woman in courts and legislatures throughout the United States, Canada, the United Kingdom, and Europe shows that the covered Muslim woman today functions as the new *dhimmī* in democratic constitutional states.

At the time this chapter was written, various European and North American polities began introducing (and passing) legislation banning certain types of veiling worn by Muslim women that cover the face. Belgium's and France's lower houses passed such legislation, while other European countries began pursuing similar legislation. In Canada, the province of Quebec tabled for discussion Bill No. 94, which proposed legislation that would prevent Muslim women, whose faces were veiled, from accessing government services. Bill 94, like the French Conseil d'Etat decision on Ms Silmi, made claims about the general good, core values, and how society must operate. In equally stipulative (but unhelpful) fashion, the Bill announced the general, common practice of face-to-face interactions in society. Social interactions should be face-to-face lest they contravene accepted social values—though the Bill is silent on what those values are. Anyone (read: Muslim woman) wanting to defy this general practice must request accommodation. Recalling the security concerns of al-Shīrāzī about *dhimmīs* and their charitable endowments, the Bill states that any accommodation request will be denied if it limits effective communication, identification, *and security* (sec. 6).[110] The term "security" gives subtle but undeniable force to justify the application of the sharp edge of a "general practice" against those who seek accommodation, just as in both *Sahin* and *Begum*. In those two cases, without the security-based fiction of third-party individuals whose rights could be at stake, the cases would have devolved into a contest between state authorities and the individual minority claimant (as is evident in Bill 94), and perhaps all too readily would have revealed the asymmetries in power present in those decisions.

In addition to those adopting a security-based argument, others may find the practice of veiling to violate core fundamental values such as gender equality. The argument that the *burka* and *niqāb* are inherently oppressive to women is an attractive argument. The veil may prompt some to argue that the mere fact a woman veils implies that she lives in a climate of extremism that keeps her from truly speaking her mind and exercising her agency.[111] That implication may be so strong and powerful as to need no further explanation or verification. Indeed, that may explain why and how, despite a weak factual inquiry, the Conseil d'Etat could nonetheless side with the government commissioner on Ms Silmi's application for citizenship.

Ironically, such a presumption has the effect of denying the covered Muslim woman a voice to articulate what veiling means to her and to reasonably expect to be heard. If such implications constitute powerful sources of information and "facts," then it logically follows that given the covered Muslim woman's presumed disempowered status, the rest of "us" must speak up for her.[112] But who are the "us"? In cases involving

[110] For the text of the bill, see the website for Quebec's National Assembly: Bill 94, An Act to Establish Guidelines Governing Accommodation Requests Within the Administration and Certain Institutions, 1st Sess., 39th Legislature, 2010,<http://www.assnat.qc.ca/en/travaux-parlementaires/projets-loi/projet-loi-94-39-1.html> (accessed July 12, 2010).

[111] On the proliferation of such presumptions, see Joan Wallach Scott, *The Politics of the Veil* (Princeton: Princeton University Press, 2007), 4.

[112] As a corrective to this dynamic, see the following collection of essays by American Muslim women: Maria M. Ebrahimji and Zahra T. Suratwala, *I Speak for Myself: American Women on Being Muslim* (Ashland, Oregon: White Cloud Press, 2011).

the presumed disempowered Muslim woman, the "us" often consists of Western feminists and their subaltern allies. However, as shown by Lila Abu-Lughod,[113] Saba Mahmood,[114] and Sherene Razack,[115] well-intentioned Western feminists and their local, native allies have a long history of contributing to the project of empire in the name of women's equality and freedom. In doing so, they deny a voice to the very women they seek to emancipate.

The cases discussed above and the spate of recent legislation on the covered Muslim woman have more in common with the *dhimmī* rules than many may realize or care to admit. Whether in the name of security or equality, the above examples of judicial regulation of the bodies of the Other reveals the mutually constitutive relationship between the law and the enterprise of governance. Whether the tradition is Islamic or democratic constitutional, both share in the very human phenomenon of addressing anxieties about the public good by targeting those who are different and, quite often, powerless to resist.

As much as the *dhimmī* rules and the cases and statutes regulating the covered Muslim woman can be criticized, this study does not seek or otherwise advocate an escape from the hegemonic potential that a Rule of Law analysis reveals. Such an escape is arguably illusory for as long as the law, enterprises of governance, and diversity remain regular features of human experience in the world. There is little doubt that determining the scope of accommodation to be granted to the Other is a difficult task. The more government officials encounter the demands of diverse communities, the more they will need to be mindful not only of what the communities' demands are, but also of the extent to which the prevailing legal order can or cannot accommodate those demands. The more a jurist defers to the foundational values as against claims of difference, the more minority groups may feel unduly oppressed. The more jurists accommodate the demands and values of the Other, the more they may undermine (or be perceived to undermine) the conditions of intelligibility of the prevailing legal order.

As long as people aspire to govern with deference to core values, and as long as those core values reflect majoritarian values, minorities will always suffer, especially at times of crisis—whether defined in terms of imperial decay or global terrorism. It is hard to ignore that the covered Muslim woman is securitized in an increasingly security-conscious world. With the threat of terrorism and the seeming futility of defeating the Hydra-like al-Qaeda, the covered Muslim woman offers an easy target

[113] Abu-Lughod, "Do Muslim Women Really Need Saving?"
[114] Saba Mahmood, *Politics of Piety.* [115] Sherene Razack, *Casting Out.*

for pacifying anxieties about the unseen, undetected, and unexpected terror threat.[116] Whether the language is "security" or "equality," both are postulated as core values without which the polity will not survive. The inability to escape this hegemonic dynamic, though, does not deny the importance of remaining vigilant about the conditions of intelligibility and the hegemonic potential that Rule of Law makes evident.

[116] In Europe, securitization co-mingles with other forces of nationalist anxiety, such as the growing significance of the European Union and the perceived threat it poses to national sovereignty, and the increased flow of formerly colonized regions: Scott, *Politics of the Veil*, 7.

Conclusion

Analyzing the *dhimmī* rules in close detail has allowed us to leave behind the competing tendencies to view these rules through the interpretive lenses of harmony or persecution, tolerance or intolerance. As suggested throughout this study, the language of tolerance and intolerance hides more than it reveals about the intelligibility of the *dhimmī* rules. Such tolerance-talk disregards the ways in which the *dhimmī* rules reflect the challenge of governing amidst diversity, a challenge that is far from unique to the Islamic tradition.

Additionally, framing Sharīʿa as Rule of Law reveals a dynamic that goes beyond the rarified notion of Sharīʿa as a repository of ancient doctrines, and presents a complex image of Sharīʿa that defies neat dichotomies between law and morality, theory and practice, and centralized and decentralized modes of legal ordering. Sharīʿa as Rule of Law recognizes the contested nature of law and legal argument, thereby rendering Sharīʿa as a *claim space* where the *intelligibility* of any claim of justice is dependent upon the constitutive features of the boundaries of that space. Rule of Law permits a consideration of Sharīʿa in general, and the *dhimmī* rules in particular, as embedded within a politico-legal context. It informs and is informed by such factors as the curriculum and institutions of legal education, the institutions of law and adjudication, and of course the presumption of an enterprise of governance.

The analysis of the *dhimmī* rules from a Rule of Law perspective suggests that the specific terms of a given *dhimmī* rule are less interesting than is appreciating how the *dhimmī* rules in the aggregate are symptoms of the more general challenge of governing amidst diversity. As shown throughout Part I, premodern Muslim jurists resolved that challenge in a multitude of ways. For instance, they debated whether the shared capacity to reason to the truth and to the good could justify imposing Sharīʿa-based obligations upon the *dhimmī*. While they disagreed on the normative implications of human reason, they generally recognized that something else was required to justify the imposition of Qurʾānically based general rules upon non-Muslims, as well as the exceptions from general rules of obligation. One particularly powerful legal construct they developed was the contract of protection.

As a juridified political agreement between the Muslim enterprise of governance and the non-Muslims wishing to reside permanently in Muslim-controlled lands, the contract provided the discursive site where jurists debated the extent to which the *dhimmī* was included, excluded, or otherwise marginalized while living in the Muslim polity. Defining that extent was not an easy matter for jurists. Relying on arguments of inclusion, accommodation, and subordination, jurists developed the *dhimmī* rules in a manner that reflected the demands of an imperial enterprise of governance defined by a universalist Islamic ethos.

This analytic approach to the *dhimmī* rules is not a matter of mere historical interest. More than simply being a recounting of premodern rules for those interested in all things antiquarian, this study situates its analysis in light of contemporary debates inside and outside of the Muslim world about the ability of Muslims and non-Muslims to live together, cooperate with one another, and collectively work toward global order and peace. These debates take on increased significance given how reactionary polemics in various countries in Europe and North America are spawning legislative initiatives that limit the scope and extent to which Muslims can manifest their religious identity in the public sphere. More alarmingly, Anders Breivik's terrorist attack in Oslo, Norway in the summer of 2011 and his manifesto reveal how the *dhimmī* rules provide kindling for nativist ideologies of violence in the name of protecting a European identity that some perceive to be under attack. Lastly, at the time of writing, the political successes of Islamist parties in Tunisia and Egypt beg questions about how such political parties will imagine the mutually constitutive relationship between Islamic law and the new states they aim to run amidst their domestic demographic diversity and the legal diversity that is characteristic of the modern state in the international community of states.

The rise of the modern state in the Muslim world signals a fundamental shift in the enterprise of governance, and thereby reshapes the boundaries of the Rule of Law claim space that contribute to the intelligibility of any rule or norm proffered within that claim space. Arguably, the state animates legal thinking today in a similar manner to that in which empire informed premodern Muslim jurists' reflection on the law. The modern sovereign state, defined in part by geo-political boundaries and embedded in an international community of sovereign states, has become over time normalized as the prevailing enterprise of governance. This is not to proffer the state as an ideal form of governance or a telos of human political development. Rather, this is to say that whether the sovereign state is a positive reality or an imagined one,[1] it nonetheless politically and institutionally grounds considerations about what the law is or should be.

With the state as the prevailing enterprise of governance, though, the intelligibility of Sharīʿa-based discourses on law and governance takes on new hues.[2] The post-imperial and post-colonial context of the modern Muslim forces a confrontation with a plurality that is not just demographic, but also normative. Today's Muslim—whether living as a minority or in a Muslim-majority state—exists in an international state system beset by multiple normative orders, all of which constitute a given state's Rule of Law claim space. Consequently, to disregard how this new enterprise of governance conditions the intelligibility of claims of justice is to ignore the way in which the present poses new questions that premodern answers may never have been designed to address. Indeed, the uncritical adoption of premodern doctrines to answer modern questions of governance and politics renders the premodern answers not so much wrong as irrelevant. If cloaked with the garment of redemptive earnestness, adherence to premodern answers runs the risk of becoming a pious stranglehold on the scope of further consideration and reflection on the present.[3]

Analyzing these rules from the perspective of Sharīʿa as Rule of Law permits two important observations about the *dhimmī* rules in particular, and Sharīʿa in general. First, the Rule of Law framework reveals the hegemonic potential that lies at the intersection of the law, the enterprise of governance, and the minority claimant who makes demands for inclusion or accommodation. Secondly, by considering Sharīʿa as Rule of Law in the premodern and modern periods, we can appreciate the

[1] For critiques on the coherence and salience of sovereignty as a fundamental feature of the state and governance, see Anne-Marie Slaughter, *A New World Order* (Princeton: Princeton University Press, 2005); Dmitrios Katsikas, "Non-state Authority and Global Governance," *Review of International Studies* 36 (2010): 113–35; Jacobus Delwaide, "The Return of the State?" *European Review* 19, no. 1 (2010): 69–91; Ian Bremmer, *The End of the Free Market: Who Wins the War Between States and Corporations* (New York: Portfolio, 2010).

[2] Some might otherwise suggest that the modern state should refrain from the establishment of religion entirely. See for instance, An-Na'im, *Islam and the Secular State.* While such arguments have important merits, they do not adequately take into consideration the relationship of law and the enterprise of governance. For instance, commitments to certain political theories, such as democracy, actually make the establishment of Sharīʿa in the legal system meaningful and intelligible for the enterprise of governance.

[3] Arguably this stranglehold is evidenced by the continued prevalence of Islamic marital rules in modern Muslim states. See for instance, in the case of gender reform debates, Fatima Mernissi, *The Veil and the Male Elite: A Feminist Interpretation of Women's Rights in Islam*, trans. Mary Jo Lakeland (New York: Basic Books, 1992); Welchman, "Development of Islamic Family Law"; Hatem, "Modernization, the State and the Family"; Mir-Hosseini, "Construction of Gender."

historical dimension that a Rule of Law analysis necessarily provides. The intelligibility of a given legal rule, as noted throughout this study, is not simply tied to source-texts or the possible interpretive conclusions that can be drawn therefrom. Rather, a rule's intelligibility is dependent on a variety of politico-legal factors that constitute the claim space of Rule of Law. Those factors include not only the disciplinary features of a legal education, but also and most notably the mutually constitutive relationship between the law and the enterprise of governance. That relationship, and its hegemonic potential, is particularly evident when analyzing its operation upon the degree to which religious minorities are free to practice their faith in public and private, as well as participate in society across a range of activities. The importance of history becomes central to a Rule of Law analysis because of the way in which the intelligibility of a given rule is not simply a matter of the literal wording of the rule, but rather reflects the often changing boundaries that define and delimit the claim space from which that rule emanates. As the boundaries change, so too does the intelligibility of any given rule.

* * *

Bringing to the fore how the law normalizes, justifies, and legitimates its hegemony over and against the minority claimant—often out of concern for the integrity and well-being of the enterprise of governance and the majoritarian values it represents—has been a key aim of this study. Part I illustrated the hegemonic potential of the law by reference to premodern rules governing the *dhimmī.* But as Part II showcased, such treatment of minorities is hardly unique to the premodern Islamic legal tradition. The legal regulation of difference,[4] out of concern for the well-being of a given polity, transcends legal and moral traditions, religious and otherwise. For instance, writing about conservative American Christians and their attitude toward pluralism, James Davison Hunter remarks that "difference is always seen as a 'danger,' or at least a potential threat. The 'other' who embodies that difference is a stranger and is construed as either a potential ally (through conversion) or as an enemy."[5] It is not that these Christian communities would not "tolerate" the "Other." Rather,

[4] Difference in this context need not be limited to religious minorities. Arguably, the hegemonic potential made evident by the Rule of Law analysis herein would arise in the case of any class of minority, religious or otherwise. See for instance, Gretchen Ritter, *The Constitution as Social Design: Gender and Civic Membership in the American Constitutional Order* (Stanford: Stanford University Press, 2006), who focuses on the implicit asymmetry in legal contests about the rights of women, and the implication of those contests to women's role and participation in the American polity.

[5] James Davison Hunter, *To Change the World: The Irony, Tragedy, & Possibility of Christianity in the Late Modern World* (Oxford: Oxford University Press, 2010), 219.

as Hunter argues, for many conservative American Christians, "the difference represented by pluralism might be a necessary evil but it would be acceptable only to the extent that the conservatives . . . determined the limits and expressions of that difference."[6] In other words, difference would be tolerable to Hunter's American conservative Christians as long as they also managed the enterprise of governance.

Another example concerns the treatment of gays and lesbians in the United States and Canada in the twentieth century. During the Cold War, lesbians and gay men were targeted by officers of several respective governments as possible threats to the moral and political well-being of the polity. As Kinsman and Gentile show in their recent study, in Cold War national security discourse "homosexuals were construed as suffering from an unreliable and unstable character, which made [them] a threat to national security."[7] They cite various official documents from the 1950s that attest to formal government anti-gay policies in which the gay male or lesbian was transformed from individual citizen into a blight that could spell the doom of democracy and capitalism. For instance, former CIA director Admiral Roscoe Hillenkoetter wrote in the 1950s: "The consistent symptoms of weakness and instability which accompany homosexuality almost always represent danger points of susceptibility from the standpoint of security."[8] Former Canadian Prime Minister John Diefenbaker, addressing the security risk posed by homosexuals, wrote in the 1960s:

> There are many cases in which the loyalty of the individual is not a question. But that individual may still not be reliable as a security risk . . . because of defects of character which subject him to the danger of blackmail . . . It is a fertile field for recruiting by the USSR, where public servants are known to be the companions of homosexuals. Those are the people that are generally chosen by the USSR, in recruiting spies who are otherwise loyal people within their countries.[9]

Diefenbaker's suspicion of homosexuals, who may be loyal but nonetheless security risks, should recall the premodern debates about *dhimmīs* as witnesses and bequeathing charitable trusts for Torah or Bible reading schools. Muslim jurists considered them to be permanent residents in the Muslim polity who were entitled to protection of their

[6] Hunter, *To Change the World*, 219.

[7] Gary Kinsman and Patrizia Gentile, *The Canadian War on Queers: National Security as Sexual Regulation* (Vancouver: University of British Columbia Press, 2010), 7.

[8] Kinsman and Gentile, *Canadian War on Queers*, 8 (quoting from Hillenkoetter's memo).

[9] Kinsman and Gentile, *Canadian War on Queers*, 11 (quoting from Diefenbaker's statement).

lives and property. But some (though not all) of those jurists held that *dhimmīs* could not form charitable trusts that perpetuated values that ran contrary to the polity. Nor could they be trusted to testify truthfully and thereby contribute to the conditions of intelligibility in the claim space of Sharīʿa.

Notably, Diefenbaker's suspicion should also recall the more recent efforts by American security policy experts, led by Lt Gen. William Boykin (ret.) and Lt Gen. Harry Edward Soyster (ret.), to ban Sharīʿa in various states across the United States out of concern for the country's security interests:

> The enemy adheres to an all-encompassing Islamic political-military-legal doctrine known as shariah. Shariah obliges them to engage in jihad to achieve the triumph of Islam worldwide through the establishment of a global Islamic State governed exclusively by shariah, under a restored caliphate.
>
> The good news is that millions of Muslims around the world—including many in America—do not follow the directives of shariah, let alone engage in jihad. The bad news is that this reality reflects the fact that the imposition of strict shariah doctrine is at different stages across Muslim-majority and -minority countries.[10]

Like Diefenbaker, the Boykin–Soyster team recognizes that many Muslims do not necessarily pose a threat to American interests; indeed, such Muslims may even be loyal citizens of the United States. Nonetheless, the Boykin–Soyster team remains ever vigilant against the threat of Sharīʿa lurking in the shadows, ready to transform these loyal Muslims into threats against the well-being of the American polity.

Perhaps the most visible and easily regulated Islamic threat to the well-being of a community or polity is none other than the covered Muslim woman. At the time of writing, the National Assemblies of Belgium and France had passed legislation banning the *niqāb.* The French ban imposes monetary fines on those who violate its terms, and requires attendance at courses on republican values.[11] The French version is especially concerned with protecting a particular, but often unspecified, vision of the public, as were premodern Muslim jurists in regulating the *dhimmī.* Indeed, the French bill's prohibition applies to areas deemed public (*l'espace publique*), a clear signal of the concern about protecting a public space that ought to reflect French values, whatever those may

[10] William G. Boykin, et al., Shariah: *The Threat to America: An Exercise in Competitive Analysis: Report of Team BII* (Washington DC: Center for Security Policy, 2010), 13.

[11] David Gauthier-Villars, "France moves on ban of some Islamic veils," *The Wall Street Journal*, July 14, 2010, A15.

be.[12] Writing about the political controversies surrounding the veil in France, Joan Wallach Scott writes that in these public debates, "the veil denotes both a religious group and a much larger population, a whole 'culture' at odds with French norms and values. The symbolism of the veil reduces differences of ethnicity, geographic origin, and religion to a singular entity, a 'culture,' that stands in opposition to another singular entity, republican France."[13]

As suggested in Chapter 7, the legal treatment of the covered Muslim woman, like the *dhimmī*, reveals the hegemony that can arise when the minority claimant appears at the intersection of the law and the enterprise of governance. A review of recent court decisions in France, the United States, and the United Kingdom shows the courts of these countries marginalize the covered Muslim woman using legal arguments and institutional dynamics that are not entirely different or distinct from those that justified and made possible the premodern *dhimmī* rules. Just as the *dhimmī* was viewed as both insider and outsider, so too are covered Muslim women who insist on their right to manifest a religious practice that raises concerns about their commitment to the core values of the prevailing society, such as gender equality (i.e., the case of Ms Silmi).[14] Just as the *dhimmī*'s freedom and liberty were limited for the sake of an Islamically defined public good, so too is the liberty of the covered Muslim girl who wants to attend school wearing a particular covering that does not conform to uniform requirements that were designed to support, if not constitute, the public good (e.g., *Begum*).[15] The covered Muslim woman may reside in a liberal constitutional state that protects her religious freedom, but the state does so pursuant to legal tests and government interests that affect and influence the way in which her religious commitments are understood, introduced, and rendered intelligible within the legal system (e.g., *Freeman*).[16]

Interestingly, just as the analysis of the *dhimmī* rules exposes how the law constitutes the enterprise of governance, so too does the analysis of the above cases regulating the covered Muslim woman. In

[12] For the language of the Bill and related documents, see the relevant National Assembly website: Bill 2520, Societé: Interdiction de la dissimulation du visage dans l'espace public, 13th legislature (assented to May 10, 2010), <http://www.assemblee-nationale.fr/13/dossiers/dissimulation_visage_espace_public.asp> (accessed, July 14, 2010). As noted earlier, the Quebec version of the ban would make accommodations for covered Muslim women, unless such accommodations pose security risks.

[13] Scott, *The Politics of the Veil*, 17.

[14] See the discussion on Ms Silmi's case in Chapter 7.

[15] See the discussion on the *Shabina Begum* case in Chapter 7.

[16] See the discussion on the *Freeman* case in Chapter 7.

a case such as *Freeman,*[17] the court found no substantial burden on Ms Freeman's religious freedom. As such, the government was not required as a matter of law to show that its limitation of Ms Freeman's religious freedom satisfied a compelling interest and was narrowly tailored. Likewise, in *Begum,*[18] three of the five members of the House of Lords found no infringement of Ms Begum's religious freedom under Article 9 of the European Convention on Human Rights. As such, the school was not legally required to justify its requirement and action against Ms Begum. Finding no infringement in these cases had the effect of enabling and enhancing the relevant enterprise of governance to do as it wished without having to explain or justify its decision. This is not to suggest that doctrines such as the margin of appreciation, which make this effect possible, are inherently suspect as antagonistic to individual rights. But, even if such doctrines serve important jurisprudential purposes, that does not repudiate the observation that in cases such as *Begum,* the application of such doctrines removes the court as a mediating force between the state authority and the individual minority claimant, and instead positions it as enabling and enhancing the governing enterprise to the detriment of the minority member.[19]

While scholars and policy makers may consider the law to be an important check against the enterprise of governance, this study shows

[17] *Sultaana Lakiana Myke Freeman v State of Florida, Department of Highway Safety and Motor Vehicles* Mp/ 5D03-2296, 2005 Fla Dist. Ct. App. LEXIS 13904 (Court of Appeal of Florida, Fifth District, September 2, 2005).

[18] *Shabina Begum (respondent) v The Headteacher and Governors of Denbigh High School* (appellants), [2006] UKHL 15.

[19] One logical extreme of the law's hegemonic potential against minority claimants is reflected in recent writings by respected legal philosopher John Finnis. Finnis upholds as a constitutional principle the state's power to exclude non-enemy aliens residing in countries such as the United Kingdom: "A foreigner's recalcitrant failure to assimilate his conduct, in matters of weight, to the particular conceptions of common and public good that are embodied in our constitution and law can lawfully and appropriately be met by refusing him entry, or requiring his departure." John Finnis, "Nationality, Alienage and Constitutional Principle," *Law Review Quarterly* 123 (July 2007): 417–45, 418. In the abstract, this view may not incite much controversy, but when applied to Muslim immigrants in Britain, Finnis's theoretical arguments reveal the hegemony that the law makes possible against minorities. For instance, after writing about the *Begum* and *Sahin* cases, he argues that if European polities are to believe courts such as the ECHR, then they may need to create incentives for Muslim immigrants to leave Western Europe. He writes: "[C]itizens of countries whose Muslim population is increasing very rapidly by immigration and a relatively high birthrate may ask themselves whether it is prudent . . . to permit any further migratory increase in that population, or even to accept the presence of immigrant non-citizen Muslims without deliberating seriously about a possible reversal—humane and financially compensated for and incentivised—of the inflow." John Finnis, "Endorsing Discrimination between Faiths: A Case of Extreme Speech?" Oxford Legal Studies Research Paper No. 09/2008; Notre Dame Legal Studies Paper No. 08-08; Islamic Law and Law of the Muslim World No. 08-16. Available at SSRN: <http://ssrn.com/abstract=1101522> (accessed December 19, 2011).

that legal arguments and doctrines can and do operate to the contrary, especially in cases where minorities assert claims against the state. Indeed, the mutually constitutive relation between the law and the enterprise of governance is arguably most manifest when members of minority groups—who are already in an asymmetrically disadvantaged position of power—make claims upon the enterprise of governance. This dynamic involving minority groups is not limited to the Islamic legal tradition, but rather is characteristic of the challenges that arise when governing amidst diversity.

Certainly some readers may be uneasy with the conclusions of this study. Those committed to the myth of Islamic persecution may find the parallels drawn to legal traditions elsewhere in the world outrageous. Those compelled to vindicate the myth of an Islamic harmony may find the treatment of the covered Muslim woman not only disgraceful, but also a useful diversion from the often-negative attention paid to the premodern Islamic tradition. At the beginning of the twenty-first century, there is no shortage of finger-pointing by those antagonistic to the Muslim world, or by those who, out of post-colonial angst, are all too happy to point out the hypocrisies and inconsistencies of Western-styled democratic constitutional governance. In both cases, though, the finger-pointing only perpetuates the othering that has been identified in this study as a veritable hallmark of human experience through the ages.

There is no reason to deny that factual differences contribute to boundaries that thereby create the conditions for othering. Such factual differences are part of everyday experience. For instance, to assert a sense of community, family, or even of self often involves asserting a boundary beyond which the Other lies. Communities might internally divide amongst themselves, creating minorities within minorities, or sects within a larger overarching label.[20] The fact of difference is not itself suspect. Rather, the apprehension underlying this study is whether, when, why, and under what circumstances a factual difference should become normatively relevant such as to justify and legitimate differentiation

[20] For instance, S.A. Zaidi recounts the various debates among northern Indian Muslims concerning who is a Muslim. In doing so, he recounts the views of different groupings of Muslims within the larger Muslim community, and shows how even the seemingly fair, but general label of "Muslim" can hide considerable debate, dissent, and fractiousness: S.A. Zaidi, "Who is a Muslim? Identities of Exclusion—North Indian Muslims, c. 1860–1900," *The Indian Economic and Social History Review* 47, no. 2 (2010): 205–29. Likewise, Hunter's account of American Christians illustrates how even an apparently majority religious group is characterized by deep fissures that affect the ways in which Christians view their role in society and the polity: Hunter, *To Change the World*.

between peoples, and as a corollary, when such differentiation is tantamount to illegitimate discrimination.

To take a rather mundane and perhaps indelicate example, we often find separate bathrooms for men and women.[21] Furthermore, in the interest of accommodating the needs of those who are disabled, we may create yet a third bathroom that is specially designated for them and equipped with certain devices designed to aid those who might require assistance. We may even argue (and convincingly so) that differentiation in these cases is right, good, and just. In all these cases, though, we cannot deny that men and women are treated differently, and that the disabled are treated differently from able-bodied people. For some, this example might seem silly; it is so banal that some might think it takes us away from the hard cases of equality that are exemplified by the *dhimmī* rules and the treatment of the covered Muslim woman. This example is only banal, however, because we consider the differences between men, women, and the disabled in this specific situation so obvious, indeed *so very natural*, as to require virtually no argument or rationale to explain why differentiation occurs and is justified. The presumption of naturalness is key to understanding the basis by which differentiation is often justified and legitimated. From a critical perspective, though, that presumption demands our greatest attention and vigilance lest it be used as post-hoc justification to discriminate. As Joan W. Scott reminds us, "maternity was often given as the explanation for the exclusion of women from politics, race as the reason for the enslavement and/or subjugation of blacks, when in fact the causality runs the other way: processes of social differentiation produce the exclusions and enslavements that are then justified in terms of biology or race," or in other words, in terms of presumptions of what we consider obvious, unavoidable, and natural.[22] For example, the banality of the bathroom example above disappears once we consider access to washrooms in the Jim Crow Era in twentieth-century United States, when African Americans had to use separate, and often deficient, facilities.[23] The novel, *The Help,*

[21] While examples in lieu of the loo might be less crude, the example of the bathroom offers an important site for exploring fundamental concerns about equality. See, for instance, Harvey Molotch, "The Rest Room and Equal Opportunity," *Sociological Forum* 3, no. 1 (1988): 128–32.

[22] Joan W. Scott, "The Conundrum of Equality," *Institute for Advanced Studies, Occasional Paper Series* (March 1999) (<http://www.sss.ias.edu/files/papers/papertwo.pdf>) (accessed November 24, 2011). 5.

[23] For more extensive analysis of Jim Crow and racial discrimination, see Charles E. Wynes, "The Evolution of Jim Crow Laws in Twentieth Century Virginia," *Phylon* 24, no. 4 (1967): 416–25; Robert R. Weyeneth, "The Architecture of Racial Segregation: The Challenges of Preserving the Problematical Past," *The Public Historian* 27, no. 4 (Fall

which has become a major motion picture, depicts how presumptions of natural differences could justify what would now be considered highly discriminatory allocations of access to washrooms.[24]

Philosophers since the time of Aristotle have recognized that equality involves *both* treating similarly situated people similarly *and* treating differently situated people differently.[25] The issue, therefore, is not about whether a legal system differentiates or not. The issue, instead, is whether a particular factual difference is so significant as to justify differentiation under the law. In other words, when is it good/right/just to treat people differently? In the above example about washrooms for men, women, and the disabled, we see the paradox of equality at work—sometimes people have to be treated differently in order for justice to be served.[26] They are treated differently because of some characteristic or feature that is deemed so "natural" as to warrant differentiation. Yet, the Jim Crow example illustrates how presumptions of natural, factual difference must be subjected to vigilant scrutiny lest differentiation become unfair or unjust. What such vigilant scrutiny involves is beyond the scope of this study. Instead, the reader is invited to reflect on this matter for himself or herself. Wherever that reflection may lead us to, the Rule of Law framework suggests that such reflection must also account for how any imagined possibility is still limited by the conditions that make the possibility intelligible.

For example, in premodern Islamic theological and legal theory treatises (*kalām, uṣūl al-fiqh*), Muslims jurists asked whether and to what extent a jurist can know the good (*ḥusn*) and the bad (*qubḥ*), and thereby proffer legal rules of obligation or prohibition.[27] This particular debate offered a site where jurists could move from first principles to legal norms. The Ashʿarite al-Bāqillānī argued that one can rationally know the good of an act (*ḥusn al-fiʿl*) or the bad (*qubḥ*) of an act, where such notions are general and abstract. One can make determinations of the bad, for example, on the basis of what one's dispositions find distasteful (*tanfuru ʿanhu al-nufūs*).[28] Significantly, he held that one

2005): 11–44; Elizabeth Abel, "Bathroom Doors and Drinking Fountains: Jim Crow's Racial Symbolic," *Critical Inquiry* 25, no. 3 (Spring 1999), 435–81.

[24] Kathryn Stockett, *The Help: A Novel* (New York: Penguin, 2009).

[25] Aristotle, *Nichomachean Ethics*, 118; al-Fārābī, *Fuṣūl Muntaẓaʿa*, 71; Miskawayh, *The Refinement of Character*, 100–1. For the original Arabic, see Ibn Miskawayh, *Tahdhīb al-Akhlāq*, 123–24.

[26] The banality of this example is also rendered complicated when considering how the neat dichotomy between male and female bathrooms does not account for the transgendered, or those in varying phases of gender-reassignment.

[27] For an extended analysis of this debate and its implications for Islamic natural law jurisprudence, see Emon, *Islamic Natural Law Theories*.

[28] Al-Bāqillānī, *al-Taqrīb wa al-Irshād*, 1:284.

can know without reference to scripture the goodness of the believer striking the unbeliever and the badness of the unbeliever striking the believer.[29]

For al-Bāqillānī, this distinction seemed obvious and apparent, whereas to modern readers it will likely seem abhorrent and unjustifiable. Reflecting on his comment from the perspective of equality, and keeping in mind the paradox of equality, allows us first to inquire into the conditions of intelligibility that allowed al-Bāqillānī to render the factual difference between the believer and non-believer into a basis for what he seemed to consider legitimate differentiation. Arguably, al-Baqillānī's normative claim depended for its intelligibility upon an Islamic universalism and an imperial history, both of which informed how he understood the past and its implications on the relative status of Muslims and non-Muslims in an Islamic enterprise of governance. The conditions that gave his view intelligibility drew upon a historical backdrop of Muslim conquest of lands, reaching from Spain to India by the eighth century CE. Combined with a universal Islamic message and, at the very least, the memory of imperial conquest, this backdrop contributed the conditions of intelligibility for premodern Muslim jurists and theologians such as al-Bāqillānī as they developed Sharīʿa-based norms. Premodern Muslim thinkers such as al-Bāqillānī were embedded in a normative tradition that also contributed to an Islamic imperial enterprise of governance. The mutually constitutive relationship between the normative tradition they developed and the enterprise of governance offered the relevant conditions to allow them to consider the factual difference between the Muslim and the *dhimmī* sufficiently relevant and natural to justify different treatment under the law. That set of conditions defined and delimited the claim space within which Muslim scholars such as al-Bāqillānī operated and articulated norms for ordering the world. In other words, the paradox of equality operated for them in such a way as to make the factual difference between the believer and non-believer so natural and obvious as to render their differentiation between Muslim and non-Muslim right, good, and just.

When the reader of this study turns the final page, it is hoped that he or she will reflect about equality and the normative significance of factual difference. Wherever the reader's imagination takes him or her, though, this study has argued that any imagined possibility will remain embedded in the social, political, and economic dynamics that dominate the given context in which he or she lives. The use of "dominate" is

[29] Al-Bāqillānī, *al-Taqrīb wa al-Irshād*, 1:284.

intentional. Those dynamics can and usually will dominate over and against those who claim and demand space for their difference. When a minority member makes a claim against an enterprise of governance, a discursive site appears that makes plain the hegemonic potential of the law in the interests, quite often, of an enterprise of governance. At that site, as the reader's imagination takes flight, it is hoped the reader might also take account of, if not necessarily work against, the hegemony that can and often does arise.

Bibliography

Note: Entries for the online version of the *Encyclopaedia of Islam, Second Edition*, edited by P. Bearman, Th. Bianquis, C.E. Bosworth, E. van Donzel, and W.E. Heinrichs (Leiden: Brill, 2009; Brill Online, University of Toronto, at <http://www.brillonline.nl/subscriber/entry?entry-islam_SIM> are indicated by the short form "*EI*[2], s.v."

Arabic Sources

'Abd al-Jabbār, Al-Qāḍī. *Sharḥ al-Uṣūl al-Khamsa*. Beirut: Dār Iḥyā' al-Turāth al-'Arabī, 2001.

'Abduh, Muḥammad. "Ikhtilāf al-Qawānīn bi Ikhtilāf Aḥwāl al-Umam." In *al-A'māl al-Kāmila li'l-Imām Muḥammad 'Abduh: al-Kitābāt al-Siyāsiyyā*. Ed. Muḥammad 'Imāra. 309–15. Beirut: al-Mu'assasa al-'Arabiyya, 1972.

Al-Ālūsī, Abū al-Faḍl Maḥmūd. *Rūḥ al-Ma'ānī fī Tafsīr al-Qur'ān al-'Aẓīm wa al-Sab' al-Mathānī*. Beirut: Dār al-Fikr, 1997.

Al-Āmidī, Sayf al-Dīn. *Al-Iḥkām fī Uṣūl al-Aḥkām*. Beirut: Dār al-Fikr, 1997.

Al-Asmandī, Muḥammad. *Badhl al-Naẓar fī al-Uṣūl*. Ed. Muḥammad Zakī 'Abd al-Barr. Cairo: Maktabat Dār al-Turāth, 1992.

Al-'Aynī, Badr al-Dīn. *Al-Bināya Sharḥ al-Hidāya*. Ed. Ayman Ṣāliḥ Sha'bān. Beirut: Dār al-Kutub al-'Ilmiyya, 2000.

——. *'Umdat al-Qārī Sharḥ Ṣaḥīḥ al-Bukhārī*. Ed. 'Abd Allāh Maḥmūd Muḥammad 'Umar. Beirut: Dār al-Kutub al-'Ilmiyya, 2001.

Al-Azharī, Ṣāliḥ 'Abd al-Samī' al-Ābī. *Jawāhir al-Iklīl*. Ed. Muḥammad 'Abd al-Azīz al-Khālidī. Beirut: Dār al-Kutub al-'Ilmiyya, 1997.

Al-Baghawī, Abū Muḥammad al-Ḥusayn b. Mas'ūd. *Al-Tahdhīb fī Fiqh al-Imām al-Shāfi'ī*. Eds 'Ādil Aḥmad 'Abd al-Mawjūd and 'Alī Muḥammad Mu'awwaḍ. Beirut: Dār al-Kutub al-'Ilmiyya, 1997.

Al-Bahūtī. *Kashshāf al-Qinā' 'an Matn al-Iqnā'*. Beirut: Dār al-Kutub al-'Ilmiyya, 1997.

Al-Balādhurī, Aḥmad b. Yaḥyā. *Kitāb Futūḥ al-Buldān*. Ed. M.J. de Goeje. Leiden: Brill, 1966.

Al-Bāqillānī, Abū Bakr. *Al-Taqrīb wa al-Irshād al-Ṣaghīr*. Ed. 'Abd al-Ḥamīd b. 'Alī Abī Zunayd. Beirut: Mu'assasat al-Risāla, 1998.

Al-Baṣrī, Abū al-Ḥusayn. *Al-Mu'tamad fī Uṣūl al-Fiqh*. Beirut: Dār al-Kutub al-'Ilmiyya, n.d.

Al-Bayhaqī, Abū Bakr. *Al-Sunan al-Kubrā*. Ed. Muḥammad 'Abd al-Qādir 'Aṭā. Beirut: Dār al-Kutub al-'Ilmiyya, 1999.

Al-Bukhārī, 'Abd al-'Azīz b. Aḥmad. *Kashf al-Asrār 'an Uṣūl Fakhr al-Islām al-Bazdawī*. Ed. Muḥammad al-Mu'taṣim bi Allāh al-Baghdādī. Beirut: Dār al-Kitāb al-'Arabī, 1997.

Al-Dār Quṭnī. *Sunan al-Dār Quṭnī.* Ed. Magdī al-Shūrā. Beirut: Dār al-Kutub al-ʿIlmiyya, 1996.

Al-Dhahabī. *Siyar Aʿlām al-Nubalāʾ.* 4th ed. Beirut: Muʾassasat al-Risāla, 1986.

Al-Fārābī, Abū Naṣr. *Fuṣūl Muntaẓaʿa.* Ed. Fawzī Najjār. Beirut: Dār al-Mashraq, 1971.

Al-Ghazālī, Abū Ḥāmid. *Al-Mustaṣfā min ʿIlm al-Uṣūl.* Baghdad: Maktabat al-Muthanna, n.d.

——. *Al-Tibr al-Masbūk fī Naṣīḥat al-Mulūk.* Ed. Muḥammad Damaj. Beirut: Muʾassasat ʿIzz al-Dīn, 1996.

——. *Al-Wajīz fī Fiqh al-Imām al-Shāfiʿī.* Eds ʿAlī Muʿawwaḍ and ʿĀdil ʿAbd al-Mawjūd. Beirut: Dār al-Arqam, 1997.

——. *Al-Wasīṭ fī al-Madhhab.* Ed. Abū ʿAmrū al-Ḥusaynī. Beirut: Dār al-Kutub al-ʿIlmiyya, 2001.

Ḥassān, Ḥusayn Ḥāmid. *Naẓariyyat al-Maṣlaḥa fī al-Fiqh al-Islāmī.* Cairo: Dār al-Nahḍa al-ʿArabiyya, 1971.

Al-Ḥaṭṭāb. *Mawāhib al-Jalīl.* Ed. Zakariyyā ʿAmīrāt. Beirut: Dār al-Kutub al-ʿIlmiyya, 1995.

Al-Ḥillī, al-Muḥaqqiq. *Sharāʾīʿ al-Islām fī Masāʾil al-Ḥalāl wa al-Ḥarām.* Ed. Ṣādiq al-Shīrāzī. 10th ed. Beirut: Markaz al-Rasūl al-Aʿẓam, 1998.

Al-Ḥurr al-ʿĀmilī. *Wasāʾil al-Shīʿa.* Beirut: Dār Iḥyāʾ al-Turāth al-ʿArabī, n.d.

Ibn Abī al-Damm. *Kitāb Adab al-Qaḍāʾ.* Ed. Muḥammad al-Qādir ʿAtā. Beirut: Dār al-Kutub al-ʿIlmiyya, 1987.

Ibn al-ʿArabī, Abū Bakr. *Kitāb al-Qabas.* Ed. Muḥammad ʿAbd Allāh Walad Karīm. Beirut: Dār al-Gharb al-Islāmī, 1992.

——. *ʿĀriḍat al-Aḥwadhī bī Sharḥ Ṣaḥīḥ al-Tirmidhī.* Beirut: Dār al-Kutub al-ʿIlmiyya, 1997.

Ibn ʿAsākir,ʿAli b. al-Ḥasan. *Taʾrīkh Madīnat Damashq.* Ed. ʿUmar b. Gharāma al-ʿAmrawī. Beirut: Dār al-Fikr, 1995.

Ibn Ḥajr al-ʿAsqalānī. *Fatḥ al-Bārī: Sharḥ Ṣaḥīḥ al-Bukhārī.* Eds Muḥammad ʿAbd al-Bāqī and Muḥibb al-Dīn al-Khaṭīb. Beirut: Dār al-Maʿrifa, n.d.

Ibn Ḥanbal, Aḥmad. *Musnad al-Imām Aḥmad b. Ḥanbal.* Eds. Samīr Ṭaha al-Majzūb et al. Beirut: al-Maktab al-Islāmī, 1993.

Ibn Ḥazm. *Al-Muḥallā bi'l-Āthār.* Ed. ʿAbd al-Ghaffār Sulaymān al-Bandārī. Beirut: Dār al-Kutub al-ʿIlmiyya, n.d.

Ibn Hishām. *Al-Sīra al-Nabawiyya.* Eds Muṣṭafā al-Saqā, Ibrāhīm al-Abyārī and ʿAbd al-Ḥafīẓ Shalbī. Beirut: Dār al-Maʿrifa, n.d.

Ibn ʿImād. *Shadharāt al-Dhahab fī Akhbār man Dhahab.* Beirut: Dār al-Kutub al-ʿIlmiyya, n.d.

Ibn Isḥāq, Khalīl. *Mukhtaṣar Khalīl.* Ed. Aḥmad ʿAlī Ḥarakāt. Beirut: Dār al-Fikr, 1995.

Ibn al-Jawzī. *al-Taḥqīq fī Aḥādīth al-Khilāf.* Ed. Muḥammad Fāris. Beirut: Dār al-Kutub al-ʿIlmiyya, n.d.

Ibn Khallikān. *Wafayāt al-Aʿyān.* Eds Yūsuf ʿAlī Ṭāwīl and Maryam Qāsim Ṭāwīl. Beirut: Dār al-Kutub al-ʿIlmiyya, 1998.

Ibn Mājah. *Al-Sunan*. Eds Muḥammad Nāṣir al-Dīn al-Albānī and 'Alī al-Ḥalabī al-Atharī. Riyadh: Maktabat al-Ma'ārif, 1998.
Ibn Manẓūr. *Lisān al-'Arab*. 3rd ed. Beirut: Dār Ṣādir, 1994.
Ibn Miskawayh. *Tahdhīb al-Akhlāq wa Taẓhīr al-A'rāf*. Ed. Ibn al-Khaṭīb. N.p.: Maktabat al-Thaqāfa al-Dīniyya, n.d.
Ibn Mufliḥ, Abū 'Abd Allāh. *Al-Furū'*. Ed. Abū al-Zahrā' Ḥāzim al-Qāḍī. Beirut: Dār al-Kutub al-'Ilmiyya, 1997.
Ibn Mufliḥ, Abū Isḥāq. *Al-Mubdi' fī Sharḥ al-Muqni'*. Ed. Zahīr Shawīsh. Beirut: al-Maktab al-Islāmī, 1974.
Ibn al-Najjār. *Sharḥ Kawkab al-Munīr: Mukhtaṣar al-Taḥrīr*. Eds Muḥammad al-Zuḥaylī and Nazīr Ḥammād. Riyadh: Maktabat al-'Ubaykān, 1997.
Ibn Naqīb al-Miṣrī, Ahmad. *Reliance of the Traveller: A Classic Manual of Islamic Sacred Law*. Trans. Nuh H.M. Keller. Rev. ed. Evanston, Illinois: Sunna Books, 1994.
Ibn Nujaym. *Al-Sharḥ al-Baḥr al-Rā'iq*. Beirut: Dār al-Kutub al-'Ilmiyya, 1997.
Ibn Qayyim al-Jawziyya. *'Awn al-Ma'būd: Sharḥ Sunan Abī Dāwūd*. Beirut: Dār al-Kutub al-'Ilmiyya, 1998.
Ibn Qudāma, 'Abd Allāh b. Aḥmad. *Al-Mughnī*. Beirut: Dār Iḥyā' al-Turāth al-'Arabī, n.d.
Ibn Rushd al-Ḥafīd. *Bidāyat al-Mujtahid wa Nihāyat al-Muqtaṣid*. Eds 'Alī Mu'awwaḍ and 'Ādil 'Abd al-Mawjūd. Beirut: Dār al-Kutub al-'Ilmiyya, 1997.
——."The Book of the Decisive Treatise Determining the Connection Between the Law and Wisdom." In *Decisive Treatise & Epistle Dedicatory*. Trans. Charles Butterworth. 1–37. Provo, Utah: Brigham Young University Press, 2001 (with facing Arabic and English translation).
Ibn Rushd al-Jadd. *Al-Bayān wa al-Taḥṣīl*. Beirut: Dār al-Gharb al-Islāmī, 1988.
——. *Al-Muqaddimāt al-Mumahhidāt*. Ed. Muḥammad Ḥajjī. Beirut: Dār al-Gharb al-Islāmī, 1988.
Ibn Taymiyya, Taqī al-Dīn. *Al-Siyāsa al-Shar'iyya fī Iṣlāh al-Rā'ī wa al-Ra'iyya*. Beirut: Dār al-Kutub al-'Ilmiyya, 1988.
Al-Jaṣṣāṣ, Abū Bakr. *Aḥkām al-Qur'ān*. Ed. 'Abd al-Salām Muḥammad 'Alī Shāhīn. Beirut: Dār al-Kutub al-'Ilmiyya, 1994.
——. *Al-Fuṣūl fī al-Uṣūl*. Ed. Muḥammad Muḥammad Tāmir. Beirut: Dār al-Kutub al-'Ilmiyya, 2000.
Al-Juwaynī, Abū al-Ma'ālā. *Kitāb al-Ijtihād min Kitāb al-Talkhīṣ*. Ed. 'Abd al-Ḥamīd Abū Zunayr. Damascus: Dār al-Qalam, 1987.
——. *Kitāb al-Talkhīṣ fī Uṣūl al-Fiqh*. Eds 'Abd Allāh al-Nibalī and Shabbir Aḥmad al-'Amrī. Beirut: Dār al-Bashā'ir al-Islāmiyya, 1996.
——. *Al-Burhān fī Uṣūl al-Fiqh*. Beirut: Dār al-Kutub al-'Ilmiyya, 1997.
Al-Kāsānī, Abū Bakr b. Mas'ūd. *Badā'i' al-Ṣanā'i' fī Tartīb al-Sharā'i'*. Eds 'Alī Muḥammad Mu'awwaḍ and 'Ādil Aḥmad 'Abd al-Mawjūd. Beirut: Dār al-Kutub al-'Ilmiyya, 1997.
Al-Khaṭīb al-Baghdādi. *Kitāb al-Faqīh wa al-Mutafaqqih*. Cairo: Zakariyyā 'Alī Yūsuf, 1977.

Al-Khurashī (also, al-Kharashī). *Ḥāshiyat al-Khurashī ʿalā Mukhtaṣar Sayyid Khalīl.* Ed. Zakariyyā ʿUmayrāt. Beirut: Dār al-Kutub al-ʿIlmiyya, 1997.
Mālik b. Anas. *al-Muwaṭṭāʾ*. Beirut: Dār al-Gharb al-Islāmī, 1997.
Al-Marghīnānī. *Al-Hidāya: Sharḥ Bidāyat al-Mubtadiʾ*. Ed. Muḥammad Darwīsh. Beirut: Dār al-Arqam, n.d.
Al-Marwazī, Abū ʿAbd Allāh. *Ikhtilāf al-Fuqahāʾ*. Maktabat Adwaʾ al-Salaf, 2000.
Al-Māwardī, Abū al-Ḥasan. *Naṣīḥat al-Mulūk*. Ed. Fuʾad ʿAbd al-Munʿim Aḥmad. Alexandria: Muʾassasat Shabāb al-Jāmiʿa, 1988.
——. *Al-Ḥāwī al-Kabīr*. Eds ʿAlī Muḥammad Muʿawwaḍ and ʿĀdil Aḥmad ʿAbd al-Mawjūd. Beirut: Dār al-Kutub al-ʿIlmiyya, 1994.
Al-Mizzī, Yūsuf. *Tahdhīb al-Kamāl fī Asmāʾ al-Rijāl*. Ed. Bashshār ʿAwād Maʿrūf. 3rd ed. Beirut: Muʾassasat al-Risāla, 1994.
Al-Mubārak Fūrī. *Tuḥfat al-Aḥwadhī bi Sharḥ Jāmiʿ al-Tirmidhī*. Beirut: Dār al-Kutub al-ʿIlmiyya, n.d.
Al-Muzanī. *Mukhtaṣar al-Muzanī*. In vol. 5 of al-Shāfiʿī, Muḥammad b. Idrīs al-Shāfiʿī. *Kitāb al-Umm*. Beirut: Dār al-Fikr, 1990.
Al-Nawawī. *Rawḍat al-Ṭālibīn wa ʿUmdat al-Muftīn*. 3rd ed. Beirut: al-Maktab al-Islāmī, 1991.
——. *Al-Minhāj: Sharḥ Ṣaḥīḥ Muslim b. al-Ḥajjāj*. Ed. Khalīl Maʾmūn Shīḥā. 3rd ed. Beirut: Dār al-Maʿrifa, 1996.
Al-Qarāfī, Shihāb al-Dīn. *Al-Dhakhīra*. Ed. Saʿīd Aʿrāb. Beirut: Dār al-Gharb al-Islāmī, 1994.
Al-Qurṭubī. *al-Jāmiʿ li Aḥkām al-Qurʾān*. Beirut: Dār al-Kutub al-ʿIlmiyya, 1993.
Al-Ramlī, Shihāb al-Dīn. *Nihāyat al-Muḥtāj ilā Sharḥ al-Minhāj*. 3rd ed. Beirut: Dār Iḥyāʾ al-Turāth al-ʿArabī, 1992.
Al-Rāzī, Fakhr al-Dīn. *Al-Tafsīr al-Kabīr*. Beirut: Dār Iḥyāʾ al-Turāth al-ʿArabī, 1999.
Saḥnūn b. Saʿīd al-Tanūkhī. *Al-Mudawwana al-Kubrā*. Beirut: Dār Ṣādir, n.d.
Ṣāliḥ, Ṣubḥī. *ʿUlūm al-Ḥadīth wa Muṣṭalaḥatuhu*. 1959. Reprint, Beirut: Dār al-ʿIlm li al-Malāyīn, 1996.
Al-Samʿānī, Abū al-Muẓaffar. *Qawāṭiʿ al-Adilla fī al-Uṣūl*. Ed. Muḥammad Ḥasan Ismāʿīl al-Shāfiʿī. Beirut: Dār al-Kutub al-ʿIlmiyya, 1997.
Al-Samarqandī, Abū al-Fatḥ. *Tarīqat al-Khilāf bayna al-Aslāf*. Beirut: Dār al-Kutub al-ʿIlmiyya, 1992.
Al-Ṣanʿānī, ʿAbd al-Razzāq. *Kitāb al-Muṣannaf*. Ed. Ayman Naṣr al-Dīn al-Azharī. Beirut: Dār al-Kutub al-ʿIlmiyya, 2000.
Al-Sanhūrī, Abd al-Razzāq. *Al-Wasīṭ fī Sharḥ al-Qānūn al-Madanī al-Jadīd*. Ed. Aḥmad al-Marāghī. Cairo: Dar al-Nahda al-ʿArabiyya, 2007.
Al-Sarakhsī, Abū Bakr. *Kitāb al-Mabsūṭ*. Beirut: Dār al-Kutub al-ʿIlmiyya, 1993.
——. *Al-Muḥarrar fī Uṣūl al-Fiqh*. Ed. Abū ʿAbd al-Raḥmān ʿAwīḍa. Beirut: Dār al-Kutub al-ʿIlmiyya, 1996.
Al-Shāfiʿī, Muḥammad b. Idrīs. *Kitāb al-Umm*. Beirut: Dār al-Fikr, 1990.
Al-Shaybānī, Muḥammad b. al-Ḥasan. *Kitāb al-Aṣl*. Wizārat al-Maʿārif liʾl-Ḥukūma al-ʿĀliyya al-Hindiyya, 1973.

Al-Shīrāzī, Abū Isḥāq. *Al-Tabṣira fī Uṣūl al-Fiqh.* Ed. Muḥammad Ḥasan Haytū. 1980. Reprint, Beirut: Dār al-Fikr, 1983.
——. *Al-Muhadhdhab fī Fiqh al-Imām al-Shāfiʿī.* Ed. Zakariyyā ʿAmīrāt. Beirut: Dār al-Kutub al-ʿIlmiyya, 1995.
Al-Subkī, ʿAlī b. ʿAbd al-Kāfī and al-Subkī, Tāj al-Dīn. *Al-Ibhāj fī Sharḥ al-Minhāj.* Beirut: Dār al-Kutub al-ʿIlmiyya, n.d.
Al-Suyūṭī, Jalāl al-Dīn. *Sharḥ Sunan al-Nisāʾī.* Beirut: Dār al-Kutub al-ʿArabī, n.d.
——. *Ikhtilāf al-Madhāhib.* Ed. ʿAbd al-Qayyūm Muḥammad Shāfīʿ al-Basṭawī. Cairo: Dār al-Iʿtiṣām, 1404 AH.
Al-Ṭabarī, Muḥammad b. Jarīr. *Tafsīr al-Ṭabarī min Kitābihi Jāmiʿ al-Bayān ʿan Taʾwīl Āy al-Qurʾān.* Eds Bashshār ʿAwad Maʿrūf and ʿIṣām Fāris al-Ḥarastānī. Beirut: Muʾassasat al-Risāla, 1994.
——. *Taʾrīkh al-Ṭabarī: Taʾrīkh al-Umam wa al-Mulūk.* Beirut: Dār al-Kutub al-ʿIlmiyya, 1995.
Zaydān, ʿAbd al-Karīm. *Aḥkām al-Dhimmiyīn wa al-Mustaʾminīn fī Dār al-Islām.* Beirut: Muʾassasat al-Risāla, 1988.
Al-Ziriklī. *al-Aʿlām.* 12th ed. Beirut: Dār al-ʿIlm li al-Malāyīn, 1997.

English Sources

N.a., "Asia: Lina Joy's Despair; Malaysia." *The Economist (London).* June 2, 2007. p. 66.
N.a., 'Interview with Dr Rabab El-Mahdi," *Middle East Law and Governance* 3, nos 122 (2011). 225–9, 227.
Abel, Elizabeth. "Bathroom Doors and Drinking Fountains: Jim Crow's Racial Symbolic." *Critical Inquiry* 25, no. 3 (Spring 1999): 435–81.
Abou El Fadl, Khaled. "My Friend." In *Conference of the Books: The Search for Beauty in Islam,* 159–62. Lanham: University Press of America, 2001.
——. *Rebellion & Violence in Islamic Law.* Cambridge: Cambridge University Press, 2001.
——. *Speaking in God's Name. Islamic Law, Authority, and Women.* Oxford: Oneworld Publications, 2001.
——. *The Authoritative and Authoritarian in Islamic Discourses: A Contemporary Case Study,* 3rd ed. Alexandria, Virginia: al-Saadawi Publications, 2002.
——. *The Place of Tolerance in Islam.* Boston: Beacon Press, 2002.
——. *Islam and the Challenge of Democracy.* Princeton: Princeton University Press, 2004.
——. *The Great Theft: Wrestling Islam from the Extremists.* New York: HarperOne, 2007.
Abu-Lughod, Lila. "Do Muslim Women Really Need Saving?" *American Anthropologist* 104, no. 3 (2002): 783–90.
Abu-Odeh, Lama. "The Politics of (Mis)recognition: Islamic Law Pedagogy in American Academia." *American Journal of Comparative Law* 52 (2004): 789–824.

——. "Commentary on John Makdisi's 'Survey of AALS Law Schools Teaching Islamic Law'." *Journal of Legal Education* 55, no. 4 (2005): 589–91.
Agamben, Giorgio. *Homo Sacer: Sovereign Power and Bare Life.* Trans. Daniel Heller-Roazen. Palo Alto: Stanford University Press, 1998.
Ahmed, Ziauddin. "The Concept of Jizya in Early Islam." *Islamic Studies* 14, no. 4 (1975): 293–305.
Akasoy, Anna. "*Convivencia* and its Discontents: Interfaith Life in al-Andalus." *International Journal of Middle East Studies* 42 (2010): 489–99.
Alford, Roger P. "Misusing International Sources to Interpret the Constitution." *American Journal of International Law* 98, no. 1 (2004): 57–69, 58.
Ali, Kecia. *Sexual Ethics in Islam: Feminist Reflections on Qur'an, Hadith and Jurisprudence.* Oxford: Oneworld Publications, 2006.
Ali-Karamali, Shaista P. and F. Dunne. "The Ijtihad Controversy." *Arab Law Quarterly* 9, no. 3 (1994): 238–57.
Anderson, Benedict. *Imagined Communities: Reflections on the Origin and Spread of Nationalism.* Rev. Ed. London: Verso, 1991.
Anghie, Antony. *Imperialism, Sovereignty, and the Making of International Law.* Cambridge: Cambridge University Press, 2005.
An-Na'im, Abdullahi Ahmed. "Religious Minorities under Islamic Law and the Limits of Cultural Relativism." *Human Rights Quarterly* 9, no. 1 (1987): 1–18.
——. *Toward an Islamic Reformation: Civil Liberties, Human Rights, and International Law.* Syracuse: Syracuse University Press, 1990.
——. *Islamic Family Law in a Changing World: A Global Resource Book.* London: Zed Books, 2002.
——. *Islam and the Secular State: Negotiating the Future of Sharīʿa.* Cambridge: Harvard University Press, 2008.
Anscombe, Frederick F. "Islam and the Age of Ottoman Reform." *Past and Present* 208 (August 2010): 159–89.
Aristotle. *Nichomachean Ethics.* Trans. Harris Rackham. Hertfordshire: Wordsworth Editions Limited, 1996.
Arnaldez, Roger. *Averroes: A Rationalist in Islam.* Trans. David Streight. Notre Dame: Notre Dame University Press, 2000.
Arneil, Barbara. "John Locke, Natural Law and Colonialism." *History of Political Thought* 13, no. 4 (1992): 587–603.
Asad, Talal. *Formations of the Secular: Christianity, Islam, Modernity.* Palo Alto: Stanford University Press, 2003.
Atabani, Ghazi Salahuddin. "Islamic Sharīʿah and the Status of Non-Muslims." *Religion, Law and Society: A Christian–Muslim Dialogue.* Ed. Tarek Mitri. 63–9. Geneva: WCC Publications, 1995.
Ayoub, Mahmoud. "Dhimmah in Qur'an and Hadith." *Arab Studies Quarterly* 5, no. 2 (1983): 172–82.
——. "The Islamic Context of Muslim–Christian Relations." In *Conversion and Continuity: Indigenous Christian Communities in Islamic Lands, Eighth to Eighteenth Centuries.* Eds Michael Gervers and Ramzi Jibran Bikhazi, 461–77. Toronto: Pontifical Institute of Mediaeval Studies, 1990.

Azami, Muhammad Mustafa. *Studies in Hadith Methodology and Literature.* Burr Ridge, Illinois: American Trust Publications, 1978.

——. *On Schacht's Origins of Muhammadan Jurisprudence.* New York: John Wiley & Sons, 1985.

Bakht, Natasha. "Family Arbitration Using Sharīʿa Law: Examining Ontario's Arbitration Act and its Impact on Women." *Muslim World Journal of Human Rights* 1, no. 1 (2004): Article 7.

——. "Veiled Objections: Facing Public Opposition to the Niqab." In *Defining Reasonable Accommodation.* Ed. Lori Beaman. Vancouver: University of British Columbia Press, 2012.

Bakhtiar, Laleh and Reinhart, Kevin. *Encyclopedia of Islamic Law: A Compendium of the Major Schools.* Chicago: Kazi Publications, 1996.

Bali, Asli. "From Subjects to Citizens? The Shifting Paradigm of Electoral Authoritarianism in Egypt." *Middle East Law and Governance* 1, no. 1 (2009): 38–89.

Balz, Killian. "The Secular Reconstruction of Islamic Law: Egyptian Supreme Constitional Court and the 'Battle Over the Veil' in State-Run Schools." In *Legal Pluralism in the Arab World.* Eds Baudoin Dupret et al., 229–43. The Hague: Kluwer Law International, 1999.

Banerjee, Subharbrata Bobby, and Linstead, Stephen. "Globalization, Multiculturalism and Other Fictions: Colonialism for the New Millennium?" *Organization* 8, no. 4 (2001): 683–722.

Bari, Abdul Aziz and Shuaib, Farid. *Constitution of Malaysia: Text and Commentary.* 2nd ed. Selangor, Malaysia: Prentice Hall, 2006.

Barkey, Karen. *Empire of Difference: The Ottomans in Comparative Perspective.* Cambridge: Cambridge University Press, 2008.

Bassiouni, M. Cherif. "Leaving Islam is not a Capital Crime." *Chicago Tribune,* April 2, 2006, C9.

Behrouz, Andra Nahal. "Transforming Islamic Family Law: State Responsibility and the Role of Internal Initiative." *Columbia Law Review* 103, no. 5 (June 2003): 1136–62.

Ben-Shammai, Haggai. "Jew Hatred in the Islamic Tradition and the Koranic Exegesis." In *Antisemitism Through the Ages.* Ed. Shmuel Almog, 161–9. Oxford: Pergamon Press, 1988.

Benard, Cheryl. *Civil Democratic Islam: Partners, Resources, and Strategies.* Santa Monica: RAND, 2003.

Bennhold, Katrin. "A Muslim woman too orthodox for France; It bars citizenship over her strict garb." *International Herald Tribune.* July 19, 2008. p. 4.

Berger, Benjamin. "Law's Religion: Rendering Culture." *Osgoode Hall Law Journal* 45, no. 2 (2007): 277–314.

——. "The Cultural Limits of Legal Tolerance." In *After Pluralism: Reimagining Religious Engagement.* Eds Courtney Bender and Pamela Klassen, 98–123. New York: Columbia University Press, 2010.

Berkey, Jonathan. *Transmission of Knowledge in Medieval Cairo: A Social History of Islamic Education.* Princeton: Princeton University Press, 1992.

Blankinship, Khalid Yahya. *The End of the Jihad State: The Reign of Hisham Ibn ʿAbd al-Malik and the Collapse of the Umayyads.* Albany: State University of New York Press, 1994.

Bobbitt, Philip. *Constitutional Fate: Theory of the Constitution.* New York: Oxford University Press, 1982.

Bosworth, C.E. "The Concept of *Dhimma* in Early Islam." In *Christian and Jews in the Ottoman Empire: The Functioning of a Plural Society.* Eds Benjamin Braude and Bernard Lewis. 2 vols 1:37–54. New York: Holmes & Meier Publishers, 1982.

Bosworth, C.E., Netton, I.R., and Vogel, F.E. *EI*[2], s.v., "Siyāsa."

Bouchard, Gérard and Taylor, Charles. *Building The Future, A Time for Reconciliation: Report.* Quebec City: Commission de consultation sur le pratiques da'ccomodement reliees aux difference culture 2008.

Boudhiba, Abdelwahab. "The Protection of Minorities." In *The Different Aspects of Islamic Culture: The Individual and Society in Islam.* Ed. A. Boudhiba and M. Maʿruf al-Dawalibi. 331–46. Paris: UNESCO, 1998.

Boykin, William G. et al., *Shariah: The Threat to America: An Exercise in Competitive Analysis: Report of Team BII,* Washington D.C.: Center for Security Policy, 2010. (<http://shariahthethreat.org/wp-content/uploads/2011/04/Shariah-The-Threat-to-America-Team-B-Report-Web-09292010.pdf>) (accessed October 28, 2010).

Brandt, Michele and Kaplan, Jeffrey A. "The Tension between Women's Rights and Religious Rights: Reservations to CEDAW by Egypt, Bangladesh and Tunisia." *Journal of Law and Religion* 12, no. 1 (1995–96): 105–42.

Braude, Benjamin. "Foundation Myths of the *Millet* System." In *Christians and Jews in the Ottoman Empire: The Functioning of a Plural Society.* Eds Benjamin Braude and Bernard Lewis. 2 vols. 1:69–88, 69–72. New York: Holmes & Meier Publishers, 1982.

——. "The Strange History of the Millet System." In *The Great Ottoman–Turkish Civilization.* Ed, Kemal Cicek. 2 vols. 2:409–18. Ankara: Yeni Turkiye, 2000.

——. and Lewis, Bernard, eds. *Christian and Jews in the Ottoman Empire: The Functioning of a Plural Society.* 2 vols. New York: Holmes & Meier Publishers, 1982.

Breiner, Bert F. "*Sharīʿa* and Religious Pluralism." In *Religion, Law and Society: A Christian–Muslim Discussion.* Ed. Tarek Mitri. 51–62. Geneva: WCC Publications, 1995.

Breivik, Anders. *2083: A European Declaration of Independence.* <http://publicintelligence.net/anders-behring-breiviks-complete-manifesto-2083-a-european-declaration-of-independence/> (accessed March 24, 2012).

Bremmer, Ian. *The End of the Free Market: Who Wins the War Between States and Corporations.* New York: Portfolio, 2010.

Brinton, Jasper Y. *The Mixed Courts of Egypt.* Rev. ed. New Haven: Yale University Press, 1968.

Brockelmann, C. *EI*[2], s.v., "al- Māwardī Abu 'l-Ḥasan ʿAlī b. Muḥammad b. Ḥabīb."

Brockopp, Jonathan E. "The Essential Sharīʿah: Teaching Islamic Law in the Religious Studies Classroom." *In Teaching Islam.* Ed. Brannon M. Wheeler. 77–93. New York: Oxford University Press, 2003.

Brown, Jonathan. *The Canonization of al-Bukhārī and Muslim*. Leiden: Brill, 2007.

Brown, Nathan. *The Rule of Law in the Arab World: Courts in Egypt and the Gulf*. Cambridge: Cambridge University Press, 1997.

——. Constitutions in a Non-Constitutional World: Arab Basic Laws and the Prospects for Accountable Government. SUNY Press, 2001.

Brown, Wendy. *Regulating Aversion: Tolerance in the Age of Identity and Empire*. Princeton: Princeton University Press, 2008.

Bulliet, Richard. *Patricians of Nishapur. A Study in Medieval Islamic Social History*. Cambridge: Harvard University Press, 1972.

——. *Conversion to Islam in the Medieval Period: An Essay in Quantitative History*. Cambridge: Harvard University Press, 1979.

Burton, John. *The Sources of Islamic Law: Islamic Theories of Abrogation*. Edinburgh: Edinburgh University Press, 1990.

——. *EI*^{2}, s.v., "Muḥṣan."

Byrnes, Sholto. "Creeping Islamisation." *New Statesman* 19 (September 10, 2007): 136.

Caldwell, Christopher. "No Minarets, Please." *The Weekly Standard* 15, no. 3 (December 14, 2009). Available at <http://www.staging.weeklystandard.com> (accessed May 9, 2012).

Canard, M. "al-Ḥākim Bi-amr Allāh." *Encyclopaedia of Islam*, Ed. P. Bearman, Th. Bianquis, C.E. Bosworth, E. van Donzel and W.P. Heinrichs Leiden: Brill, 2008. (Brill Online, University of Toronto, accessed 05 September 2008 <http://www.brillonline.nl.myaccess.library.utoronto.ca/subscriber/entry?entry=islam_SIM-2637>).

Carothers, Thomas. "The Rule of Law Revival." *Foreign Affairs* 77, no. 2 (Mar–Apr. 1998): 95–106.

Casanova, José. *Public Religions in the Modern World*. Chicago: Chicago University Press, 1994.

——. "Immigration and the New Religious Pluralism: A European Union/United States Comparison." In *Democracy and the New Religious Pluralism*. Ed. Thomas Banchoff. 59–84. Oxford: Oxford University Press, 2007.

——. "Public Religions Revisited." In *Religion: Byond a Concept*. Ed. Hent de Vries, 101–19. New York: Fordham University Press, 2008.

Choudhry, Sujit, ed. *Constitutional Design for Divided Societies: Integration or Accommodation*. Oxford: Oxford University Press, 2007.

Chrisafis, Angelique. "France rejects Muslim woman over radical practice of Islam." *The Guardian*. July 12, 2008. p. 23.

Christelow, Allan. *Muslim Law Courts and the French Colonial State in Algeria*. Princeton: Princeton University Press, 1985.

Cicek, Kemal. "A Quest for Justice in a Mixed Society: The Turks and the Greek Cypriots Before the Sharīʿa Courts of Nicosia." In *The Great Ottoman-Turkish Civilization*. Ed. Kemal Cicek. 2 vols. 2:472–91. Ankara: Yeni Turkiye, 2000.

Clark, Belinda. "The Vienna Convention Reservations Regime and the Convention on Discrimination Against Women." *The American Journal of International Law* (1991): 281–321.

Cogan, Jacob Katz. "The Regulatory Turn in International Law." *Harvard International Law Journal* 52 (2011): 322–72.

Cohen, Mark. "Islam and the Jews: Myth, Counter-Myth, History." In *Jews among Muslims: Communities in the Precolonial Middle East.* Eds Shlomo Deshen and Walter Zenner, 50–63. New York: New York University Press, 1996.

——. "Medieval Jewry in the World of Islam." In *The Oxford Handbook of Jewish Studies.* Ed. Martin Goodman. 193–218. Oxford: Oxford University Press, 2002.

——. *Under Crescent & Cross: The Jews in the Middle Ages.* 1995; Reissue, Princeton: Princeton University Press, 2008.

Cook, Michael. *The Koran: A Very Short Introduction.* Oxford: Oxford University Press, 2000.

Cook, Rebecca J. "Reservations to the Convention on the Elimination of All Forms of Discrimination Against Women." *Virginia Journal of International Law* 30, no. 3 (1989–90): 643–716.

Cosh, Colby. "The Making of a Monster." *Macleans* 124, no. 31 (August 15, 2011): 26.

Coulson, N.J. *A History of Islamic Law.* 1964. Reprint, Edinburgh: Edinburgh University Press, 1997.

Courbage, Youssef and Fargues, Philippe. *Christians and Jews under Islam.* Trans. Judy Mabro. London: I.B. Tauris Publishers, 1997.

Crone, Patricia. *God's Rule, Government and Islam: Six Centuries of Medieval Islamic Political Thought.* New York: Columbia University Press, 2004.

Dallal, Ahmad. "Yemeni Debates on the Status of Non-Muslims in Islamic Law." *Islam and Christian-Muslim Relations* 7 no. 2 (1996): 181–92.

Dalrymple, Theodore. "Wrong from Head to Toe: A Ridiculous and Ominous Decision in Britain." *Culture Watch* 57, no. 5 (March 28, 2005): 30.

Davies, Gareth. "Banning the Jilbab: Reflections on Restricting Religious Clothing in the Law of the Court of Appeal in *SB v. Denbigh High School.* Decision of 2 March 2005." *European Constitutional Law Review* 1 (2005): 511–30.

——. "The House of Lords and Religious Clothing in *Begum v. Head teacher and Governors of Denbigh High School.*" *European Public Law* 13, no. 3 (2007): 423–32.

De Sousa Santos, Boaventura. *Toward a New Legal Common Sense: Law, Globalization, and Emancipation.* 2nd ed. London: Butterworths, 2002.

Delwaide, Jacobus. "The Return of the State?" *European Review* 19, no. 1 (2010): 69–91.

Dennett, Daniel C. *Conversion and the Poll Tax in Early Islam.* Cambridge: Harvard University Press, 1950.

DeSouza, Archie. "Minorities in the Historical Context of Islam." *Al-Mushīr* 40, no. 2 (1998): 72–81.

Dien, M. Izzi. *The Theory and the Practice of Market Law in Medieval Islam: A Study of Kitāb Nisāb al-Iḥtisāb.* Cambridge: E.J.W. Gibb Memorial Trust, 1997.

——. *EI*[2], s.v., "Taʿzīr (a.)."

Donner, Fred McGraw. *The Early Islamic Conquests.* Princeton: Princeton University Press, 1981.

Doumato, Eleanor Abdella. "Manning the Barricades: Islam According to Saudi Arabia's School Texts." *Middle East Journal* 57, no. 2 (Spring 2003): 230–47.

Duri, A.A. *The Rise of Historical Writing Among the Arabs.* Princeton: Princeton University Press, 1983.

Ebrahimji, Maria M. and Suratwala, Zahra T. *I Speak for Myself: American Women on Being Muslim.* Ashland, Oregon: White Cloud Press, 2011.

Ely, John Hart. *Democracy and Distrust: A Theory of Judicial Review.* Cambridge: Harvard University Press, 1980.

Emon, Anver M. "Reflections on the 'Constitution of Medina': An Essay on Methodology and Ideology in Islamic Legal History." *UCLA Journal of Islamic and Near Eastern Law* 1, no. 1 (2001–02): 103–33.

——. "Natural Law and Natural Rights in Islamic Law." *Journal of Law and Religion* 20, no. 2 (2004–05): 351–95.

——. "Conceiving Islamic Law in a Pluralist Society: History, Politics, and Multicultural Jurisprudence." *Singapore Journal of Legal Studies* (December 2006): 331–55.

——. "*Ḥuqūq Allāh* and *Ḥuqūq al-ʿIbād*: A Legal Heuristic for a Natural Rights Regime." *Islamic Law and Society* 13, no. 3 (2006): 325–91.

——. "On the Pope, Cartoons and Apostates: Shariʿa 2006." *Journal of Law and Religion* 22, no. 2 (2006–07): 303–21.

——. "The Limits of Constitutionalism in the Muslim World: History and Identity in Islamic Law." In *Constitutional Design for Divided Societies.* Ed. Sujit Choudhry, 258–86. Oxford: Oxford University Press, 2008.

——. "Islamic Law and the Canadian Mosaic: Politics, Jurisprudence, and Multicultural Accommodation." *Canadian Bar Review* 87, no. 2 (2009): 391–425.

——. Techniques and Limits of Legal Reasoning in Sharīʿa Today," *Berkeley Journal of Middle Eastern & Islamic Law* 2, no. 1 (2009): 101–24.

——. "*To Most Likely Know the Law:* Objectivity, Authority, and Interpretation in Islamic Law." *Hebraic Political Studies* 4, no. 4 (2009): 415–40.

——. *Islamic Natural Law Theories.* Oxford: Oxford University Press, 2010.

——. "Banning Sharīʿa," *The Immanent Frame* (<http://blogs.ssrc.org/tif/2011/09/06/banning-Sharīʿa/>) (accessed October 28, 2011).

——. Lust, Ellen, and Macklin, Audrey. "Interview with Dr. Rabab El-Mahdi." *Middle East Law and Governance* 3. nos 1 & 2 (2011): 225–9.

Enayat, Hamid. *Modern Islamic Political Thought.* Austin, Texas: University of Texas Press, 1982.

Euben, Roxanne. *Enemy in the Mirror: Islamic Fundamentalism and the Limits of Modern Rationalism: A Work of Comparative Political Theory.* Princeton: Princeton University Press, 1999.

Fadel, Mohammad. "The True, the Good, and the Reasonable, The Theological and Ethical Roots of Public Reason in Islamic Law." *Canadian Journal of Law and Jurisprudence* 21, no. 1 (2008): 5–69.

Faruqi, Ismail R. "The Rights of Non-Muslims under Islam: Social and Cultural Aspects." In *Muslim Communities in non-Muslim States*, 43–66. London: Islamic Council of Europe, 1980.

Feldman, Noah. *What We Owe Iraq: War and the Ethics of Nation Building*. Princeton: Princeton University Press, 2006.

Fenton, Paul. "Book Review: Islam and Dhimmitude." *Midstream* 49, no. 2 (2003): 40–1.

Finnis, John. "Nationality, Alienage and Constitutional Principle." *Law Review Quarterly* 123 (July 2007): 417–45.

——. "Endorsing Discrimination between Faiths: A Case of Extreme Speech?" Oxford Legal Studies Research Paper No. 09/2008; Notre Dame Legal Studies Paper No. 08–08; Islamic Law and Law of the Muslim World No. 08–16. Available at SSRN: <http://ssrn.com/abstract=1101522> (accessed December 19, 2011).

Forst, Rainer. "The Limits of Toleration." *Constellations* 11, no. 3 (2004): 312–25.

Fram, Edward. "Two Cases of Adultery and the Halakhic Decision-Making Process." *AJS Review* 26, no. 2 (2002): 277–300.

Frank, Daniel and Leon Nemoy. "Karaites." In *Encyclopedia of Religion, Second Edition*. Ed. Lindsay Jones. 8: 5082–8. Detroit: Macmillan Reference, 2005.

Freedman, David Noel. *The Nine Commandments: Uncovering the Hidden Pattern of Crime and Punishment in the Hebrew Bible*. New York: Doubleday, 2000.

Freidenreich, David M. *Foreigners and Their Food: Constructing Otherness in Jewish, Christian, and Islamic Law*. Berkeley: University of California Press, 2011.

Friedmann, Yohanan. "Classification of Unbelievers in Sunni Muslim Law and Tradition." *Jerusalem Studies in Arabic & Islam* 22, (1998): 163–95.

——. *Tolerance and Coercion in Islam*. Cambridge: Cambridge University Press, 2003.

Frum, David. "What's Right." *National Review* 54, no. 24 (December 23, 2002): 60.

Fukuyama, Francis. *The End of History and the Last Man*. New York: Free Press, 1992.

——. "Reflections on *The End of History:* Five Years Later." *History & Theory* 34, no. 2 (1995): 27–43.

——. "There are No Short Cuts to '*The End of History*'." *New Perspectives Quarterly* 23, no. 2 (2006): 35–8.

Fuller, Lon L. *The Morality of Law*. Rev. ed. New Haven: Yale University Press, 1969.

Gauthier-Villars, David. "France moves on ban of some Islamic veils." *The Wall Street Journal*. July 14, 2010. A15.

Gerard, Jasper. "Faith, the veil, shopping, and me." *Sunday Times* (March 26, 2006): 5.

Gervers, Michael and Ramzi J. Bikhazi, eds. *Conversion and Continuity: Indigenous Christian Communities in Islamic Lands, Eighth to Eighteenth Centuries*. Toronto: Pontifical Institute of Medieval Studies, 1990.

Gibb, H.A.R. *Studies on the Civilization of Islam*. Eds. Stanford Shaw and William Polk. Princeton: Princeton University Press, 1962.

Gilliot, Cl., Repp, R.C., Nizami, K.A., Hooker, M.B., Lin, Chang-Kuan, and Hunwick, J.O. *EI²*, s.v., "Ulamā."

Goddard, Hugh. "Christian-Muslim Relations: A Look Backward and a Look Forwards." *Islam and Christian-Muslim Relations* 11, no. 2 (2000): 195–212.

Goitein, S.D. "A Turning Point in the History of the Muslim State." In *Studies in Islamic History and Institutions,* 149–67. Leiden: Brill, 1968.

Goldziher, Ignaz. *Introduction to Islamic Theology and Law.* Trans. Andras and Ruth Hamori. Princeton: Princeton University Press, 1981.

Goodich, Michael, ed. *Other Middle Ages: Witnesses at the Margins of Medieval Society.* Philadelphia: University of Pennsylvania Press, 1998.

Gottheil, Richard. "Dhimmis and Moslems in Egypt." In *Old Testament and Semitic Studies.* Eds Robert Francis Harber, Francis Brown and George Foot Moore. 2 vols. 1:353–414, 382–4. Chicago: University of Chicago Press, 1908.

——. "A Fetwa on the Appointment of Dhimmis to Office." In *Zeitschrift fur Assyriologie und Verwandte Gebiete.* Ed. Carol Bezold, 203–14. Strassburg: Verlag von Karl J. Trubner, 1912.

——. "An Answer to the Dhimmis." *Journal of the American Oriental Society* 41 (1921): 383–457.

Green, Leslie. *The Authority of the State.* Oxford: Clarendon Press, 1988.

——. "Pluralism, Social Conflict, and Tolerance." In *Pluralism and Law.* Ed. Arend Soeteman, 85–105. London: Kluwer Academic Publishers, 2001.

——. "On Being Tolerated." In *The Legacy of H.L.A. Hart.* 277–298. Ed. M. Kramer et al. Oxford: Oxford University Press, 2008.

Gülen, M. Fethullah. *Toward a Global Civilization of Love and Tolerance.* The Light, Inc., 2004.

Haarmann, Ulrich. "Mamluk Endowment Deeds as a Source for the History of Education in Late Medieval Egypt." *Al-Abhath* 28 (1980): 31–47.

Habermas, Jürgen. "Religion in the Public Sphere." *European Journal of Philosophy* 14, no. 1 (2006): 1–25.

Hacker, Joseph R. "Jewish Autonomy in the Ottoman Empire: Its Scope and Limits. Jewish Courts from the Sixteenth to the Eighteenth Centuries." In *The Jews of the Ottoman Empire.* Ed. Avigdor Levy, 153–202. Princeton: Darwin Press, 1994.

Haddad, Wadi Zaidan. "*Ahl al-Dhimma* in an Islamic State: The Teaching of Abu al-Hasan al-Mawardi's *al-Ahkam al-Sultaniyya.*" *Islam and Christian-Muslim Relations* 7, no. 2 (1996): 169–80.

Hallaq, Wael B. "Was the Gate of Ijtihād Closed?" *International Journal of Middle East Studies* 16, no. 1 (1984): 3–41.

——. "Was al-Shafi'i the Master Architect of Islamic Jurisprudence?" *International Journal of Middle East Studies* 25 (1993): 587–605.

——. *A History of Islamic Legal Theories.* Cambridge: Cambridge University Press, 1997.

——. "Can the Sharīʿa be Restored?" In *Islamic Law and the Challenges of Modernity*. Eds Yvonne Haddad and Barbara Stowasser, 21–54. New York: Altamira Press, 2004.

——. *Authority, Continuity and Change in Islamic Law*. Cambridge: Cambridge University Press, 2005.

——. *The Origins and Evolution of Islamic Law*. Cambridge: Cambridge University Press, 2005.

——. *Sharīʿa: Theory, Practice, and Transformations*. (Cambridge: Cambridge University Press, 2008), 131–2.

Hamidullah, Muhammad. "Status of Non-Muslims in Islam." *Majallat al-Azhar* 45, no. 8 (1973): 6–13.

Hari, Johann. "Amid all this panic, we must remember one simple fact—Muslims are not all the same." *The Independent*. August 21, 2006. P. 25.

Hashemi, Kamran. *Religious Legal Traditions, International Human Rights Law and Muslim States*. Leiden: Martinus Nijhoff Publishers, 2008.

Hatem, Mervat F. "Modernization, the State, and the Family in Middle East Women's Studies." In *A Social History of Women & Gender in the Modern Middle East*. Eds Margaret Meriwether and Judith E. Tucker, 63–87. Boulder, Colorado: Westview Press, 1999.

Haykal, Muhammad Husayn. *The Life of Muhammad*. Trans. Isma'il Ragi A. al-Faruqi. N.p.: North American Trust Publications, 1976.

Hearn, Julie. "The 'Invisible' NGO: US Evangelical Missions in Kenya." *Journal of Religion in Africa* 32, no. 1 (2002): 32–60.

Heilman, Samuel C. "Karaites." In *Encyclopedia of the Modern Middle East and North Africa*. Eds. Philip Mattar et al. 2:1269–70. New York: Macmillan Reference, 2004.

Heinrichs, Wolfhart. "On the Genesis of the ḥaqîqa-majâz Dichotomy." *Studia Islamica* 59 (1984): 111–40.

El-Hibri, Tayeb. *Reinterpreting Islamic Historiography: Hārūn al-Rashīd and the Narratives of the ʿAbbāsid Caliphate*. Cambridge: Cambridge University Press, 1999.

Hodgson, Marshall G.S. *The Expansion of Islam in the Middle Periods*. Vol 2 of *The Venture of Islam*. Chicago: Chicago University Press, 1977.

Hoffman, Murad Wilfried. "The Protection of Religious Minorities in Islam." *Encounters* 4, no. 2 (1998): 137–48.

Hor, Chow Kum. "Polls role for Churches, Hindu Temples." *The Straights Times*. February 18, 2008.

Horovitz, J. *EI*[2], s.v., "ʿAbd Allāh b. Salām."

Human Rights Watch, *"Political Sharīʿa"? Human Rights and Islamic Law in Northern Nigeria*. New York: Human Rights Watch, 2004. (<http://www.hrw.org/reports/2004/nigeria0904/nigeria0904.pdf>) (accessed on August 31, 2008).

——. "Access Denied: Iran's Exclusionary Elections." New York: Human Rights Watch, 2005 (<http://www.hrw.org/legacy/backgrounder/mena/iran0605/iran0605.pdf>) (accessed December 3, 2011).

——. *World Report: 2009.* New York: Human Rights Watch, 2009.

Hunter, James Davison. *To Change the World: The Irony, Tragedy, & Possibility of Christianity in the Late Modern World.* Oxford: Oxford University Press, 2010.

Hunwick, John O. "The Rights of *Dhimmis* to Maintain a Place of Worship: A 15th Century *Fatwā* from Tlemcen." *Al-Qanṭara* 12, no. 1 (1991): 133–56.

Hussain, Ed. *The Islamist.* New York: Penguin Books, 2009.

Hussain, Sheikh Showkat. "Status of Non-Muslims in Islamic State." *Hamdard Islamicus* 16, no. 1 (1993): 67–79.

Ibn Ashur, Muhammad al-Tahir. *Treatise on Maqasid al-Sharīʿah.* Trans. Mohamed el-Tahir el-Mesawi. Herndon, Virginia: International Institute of Islamic Thought, 2006.

Ibn Rushd (Averroes). "The Book of the Decisive Treatise Determining the Connection Between the Law and Wisdom." In *Decisive Treatise & Epistle Dedicatory.* Trans. Charles Butterworth, 1–37. Provo, Utah: Brigham Young University Press, 2001. (with facing Arabic and English translation).

Idriss, Mohammad Mazher. "The Defeat of Shabina Begum in the House of Lords." *Liverpool Law Review* 27 (2006): 417–36.

Irwin, Robert. "Book Reviews: Islam and Dhimmitude: Where Civilizations Collide." *Middle Eastern Studies* 38, no. 4 (2002): 213–15.

——. "Is This Islam." *Economist* 328, no. 7818, (July 3, 1993): 40.

Isin, Engin F. and Turner, Bryan S. "Citizenship Studies: An Introduction." In *Handbook of Citizenship Studies.* Eds Engin F. Isin and Bryan S. Turner, 1–10. London: Sage, 2002.

——. "Investigating Citizenship: An Agenda for Citizenship Studies." *Citizenship Studies* 11, no. 1 (2007): 5–17.

"Islam in Asia: For God and Growth in Malysia." *Economist* 329, no. 7839 (November 27, 1993): 39.

Jackson, Sherman. *Islamic Law and the State: The Constitutional Jurisprudence of Shihab al-Din al-Qarafi.* Leiden: Brill, 1996.

Jennings, Ronald C. *Christians and Muslims in Ottoman Cyprus and the Mediterranean World.* New York: New York University Press, 1992.

——. "Zimmis (Non-Muslims) in Early 17th Century Ottoman Judicial Records: The Sharīʿa Court of Anatolian Kayseri." In *Studies in Ottoman Social History in the Sixteenth and Seventeenth Centuries: Women, Zimmis, and Sharīʿa Courts in Kayseri, Cyprus and Trabzon.* Istanbul: The Isis Press, 1999.

Jokisch, Benjamin. *Islamic Imperial Law: Harun al-Rashid's Codification Project.* Berlin: Water de Gruyter, 2007.

Juynboll, G.H.A. *EI*[2], s.v.,"Mursal."

Kahn, Paul. *Political Theology: Four New Chapters on the Concept of Sovereignty.* New York: Columbia University Press, 2011.

Kamali, Mohammad Hashim. *Principles of Islamic Jurisprudence.* 3rd ed. Cambridge: Islamic Texts Society, 2003.

Kandiyoti, Deniz. "Women, Islam and the State." *Middle East Report* 173 (1991): 9–14.

Karawan, Ibrahim. "Monarchs, Mullas and Marshalls: Islamic Regimes?" *Annals of the American Academy of Political and Social Science* (1992): 103–19.

Kasim, Kasim Abdo. "Religion and Citizenship in Europe and the Arab World." In *The Dhimmis and Political Authority*. Ed. Jorgen S. Nielsen, 31–8. London: Grey Seal, 1992.

Katsikas, Dmitrios. "Non-state Authority and Global Governance." *Review of International Studies* 36 (2010): 113–35.

Kechichian, Joseph. "The Role of the Ulama in the Politics of an Islamic State: The Case of Saudi Arabia." *International Journal of Middle East Studies* (1986): 53–71.

Keller, Nuh H.M. *Port in a Storm: A Fiqh Solution to the Qibla of North America*. Wakeel Books, 2001.

Kennedy, Hugh. *The Prophet and the Age of the Caliphates: The Islamic Near East from the Sixth to the Eleventh Century*. London: Longman, 1986.

Kerman, Joseph. "Thematic Return in Late Bach Fugues." *Music & Letters* 87, no. 4 (2006): 515–22.

Kinsman, Gary and Gentile, Patrizia. *The Canadian War on Queers: National Security as Sexual Regulation*. Vancouver: University of British Columbia Press, 2010.

Koh, Harold Hongju. "International Law as Part of Our Law." *American Journal of International Law* 98, no. 1 (2004): 43–57, 44.

Koskenniemi, Martii. *The Gentle Civilizer of Nations: The Rise and Fall of International Law 1870–1960*. Cambridge: Cambridge University Press, 2004.

Kramer, Gudrun. "Dhimmi ou Citoyen: Réflexions reformists sur le statut de non-musulmans en société Islamique." In *Entre Reforme Sociale et Mouvement National*. Ed. Alain Roussilon, 577–90. Cairo: CEDEJ, 1995.

——. "Dhimmi or Citizen? Muslim–Christian Relations in Egypt." In *The Christian–Muslim Frontier: Chaos, Clash or Dialogue?* Ed. Jorgen S. Nielsen, 35–6. London: I.B. Tauris, 1998.

Kugle, Scott Alan. "Framed, Blamed and Renamed: The Recasting of Islamic Jurisprudence in Colonial South Asia." *Modern Asian Studies* 35, no. 2 (2001): 257–313.

Lafont, Cristina. "Religion in the Public Sphere: Remarks on Habermas's Conception of Public Deliberation in Postsecular Societies." *Constellations* 14, no. 2 (2007): 239–59.

Lambton, Ann K.S. *State and Government in Medieval Islam: An Introduction to the Study of Islamic Political Theory: The Jurists*. Oxford: Oxford University Press, 1981.

Lane, E.W. *Arabic–English Lexicon*. 1863. Reprint, Cambridge: Islamic Texts Society 1984.

Lapidus, Ira. *A History of Islamic Societies*. 1988. Reprint, Cambridge: Cambridge University Press, 1991.

——. "Between Universalism and Particularism: The Historical Bases of Muslim Communal, National, and Global Identities." *Global Networks* 1, no. 1 (2001): 37–55.

Lasker, Daniel, Eli Citonne and Haggai Ben-Shammai. "Karaites." In *Encyclopaedia Judaica, Second Edition*. Eds Michael Berenbaum and Fred Skolnik. 11:785–97. Detroit: MacMillan Reference, 2007.

Lecker, M. "Did Muḥammad Conclude Treaties with the Jewish Tribes Naḍīr, Qurayẓa, and Qaynuqāʿ?" In *Dhimmis and Others: Jews and Christians and the World of Classical Islam*. Eds Uri Rubin and David Wasserstein. 29–36. Tel Aviv: Eisenbrauns, 1997.

——. *EI*², s.v., "al- Ridda (a.)."

Levy, Avigdor. "Introduction." In *The Jews of the Ottoman Empire*. Ed. Avigdor Levy. 1–150. Princeton: Darwin Press, 1994.

Levy-Rubin, Milka. *Non-Muslims in the Early Islamic Empire: From Surrender to Coexistence*. Cambridge: Cambridge University Press, 2011.

Lewis, Bernard. *Semites and Anti-Semites: An Inquiry into Conflict and Prejudice*. New York: W.W. Norton & Co., 1986.

Libesman, Heidi. "Between Modernity and Postmodernity." *Yale Journal of Law and the Humanities* 16 (2004): 413–23.

Libson, Gideon. *Jewish and Islamic Law: A Comparative Study of Custom During the Gaonic Period*. Cambridge: Harvard Law School, 2003.

Lichtenstadter, Ilse. "The Distinctive Dress of Non-Muslims in Islamic Countries." *Historia Judaica* 5, no. 1 (1943): 35–52.

Liddle, Rodd. "So Shabina, what's the point of Britain?" *Sunday Times* (March 6, 2005): 18.

Liebesny, Herbert J. *The Law of the Near & Middle East: Readings, Cases and Materials*. Albany: State University of New York Press, 1975.

Linden, Thomas and Hetherington, Tessa. "Schools and Human Rights, the *Denbigh High School* Case." *Education Law Journal* 6, no. 4 (2005): 229–48.

Lings, Martin. *Muhammad: His Life Based on the Earliest Sources*. Rochester, Vermont: Inner Traditions International, 1983.

Lobe, Jim. "Terror in Oslo." *Washington Report on Middle East Affairs* (September–October 2011): 18.

Lombardi, Clark B. *State Law and Islamic Law in Modern Egypt*. Leiden: Brill, 2006.

Lowe, Vaughan. *International Law*. Oxford: Oxford University Press, 2007.

Ludwig, Frieder. "Christian–Muslim Relations in Northern Nigeria since the Introduction of Sharīʿah in 1999." *Journal of the American Academy of Religion* 76, no. 3 (2008): 602–37.

Lust-Okar, Ellen. "Reinforcing Informal Institutions through Authoritarian Elections: Insights from Jordan." *Middle East Law and Governance* 1, no. 1 (2009): 3–37.

Lydon, Ghislaine. *On Trans-Saharan Trails: Islamic Law, Trade Networks, and Cross-Cultural Exchange in Nineteenth-Century Western Africa*. Cambridge: Cambridge University Press, 2009.

Mabro, Judy. *Veiled Half-Truths: Western Traveller's Perceptions of Middle Eastern Women*. London: I.B. Tauris, 1991.

Macklin, Audrey. "Who is the Citizen's Other? Considering the Heft of Citizenship." *Theoretical Inquiries in Law* 8, no. 2 (2007): 333–66.

Mahmood, Saba. *Politics of Piety: The Islamic Revival and the Feminist Subject*. Princeton: Princeton University Press, 2004.

Makdisi, George. *The Rise of Colleges: Institutions of Learning in Islam and the West*. Edinburgh: Edinburgh University Press, 1981.

——. "Muslim Institutions of Learning in Eleventh-century Baghdad." In *Religion, Law and Learning in Classical Islam*. Surrey: Variorum, 1991.

——. "Baghdad, Botognd, and Scholasticism." In *Centres of Learning: Learning and Location in Pre-Modern Europe and the Near East*. Eds Jan Willem Drijvers and A.A. MacDonald. Leiden: Brill, 1995, 141–57.

Mallat, Chibli. *The Renewal of Islamic Law: Muhammad Baqer as-Sadr, Najaf and the Shi'i International*. Cambridge: Cambridge University Press, 1993.

Malm, Andreas. "Minaret Myths." *New Statesman* (August 1, 2011), 27.

Manji, Irshad. *The Trouble With Islam Today: A Muslim's Call for Reform in Her Faith*. New York: St. Martin's Press, 2004.

March, Andrew. *Islam and Liberal Citizenship: The Search for an Overlapping Consensus*. Oxford: Oxford University Press, 2009.

Marlow, Louise. *Hierarchy and Egalitarianism in Islamic Thought*. Cambridge: Cambridge University Press, 1997.

Masud, Muhammad Khalid, Brinkley Messick and David Powers, eds. *Islamic Legal Interpretation: Muftis and Their Fatwas*. Cambridge: Harvard University Press, 1996.

Mayer, Ann Elizabeth. *Islam and Human Rights: Tradition and Politics*. 3rd ed. Boulder: Westview Press, 1998.

——. "Internationalizing the Conversation on Women's Rights: Arab Countries Face the CEDAW Committee." In *Islamic Law and the Challenges of Modernity*. Eds Yvonne Yazbeck Yaddad and Barbara Freyer Stowasser, 133–60. Walnut Creek: AltaMira Press, 2004.

Mazower, Mark. *No Enchanted Palace: The End of Empire and the Ideological Origins of the United Nations*. Princeton: Princeton University Press, 2009.

McAuliffe, Jane Dammen. "Fakhr al-Dīn al-Rāzī on Ayat al-Jizya and Ayat al-Sayf." In *Conversion and Continuity: Indigenous Christian Communities in Islamic Lands, Eight to Eighteenth Centuries*. Eds Michael Gervers and Ramzi Jibran Bikhazi, 103–19. Toronto: Pontifical Institute of Mediaeval Studies, 1990.

McClintock, Anne. "Family Feuds: Gender, Nationalism and the Family." *Feminist Review* 44 (1993): 61–80.

McCracken, Grant. "Culture and Consumption: A Theoretical Account of the Structure and Movement of the Cultural Meaning of Consumer Goods." *Journal of Consumer Research* 13 (1986): 461–73.

Menocal, Maria Rosa. *The Ornament of the World! How Muslim, Jews, and Christians Created a Culture of Tolerance in Medieval Spain*. Boston: Little, Brown and Company, 2002.

Mernissi, Fatima. *The Veil and the Male Elite: A Feminist Interpretation of Women's Rights in Islam.* Trans. Mary Jo Lakeland. New York: Basic Books, 1992.

Merry, Sally Engle. "Law and Colonialism." *Law and Society Review* 25, no. 4 (1991): 89–122.

Mikhail, John. "Dilemmas of Cultural Legality: A Comment on Roger Cotterrell's 'The Struggle for Law' and a Criticism of the House of Lords' Opinions in *Begum.*" *International Journal of Law in Context* 4, no. 4 (2009): 385–93.

Mir-Hosseini, Ziba. "The Construction of Gender in Islamic Legal Thought and Strategies for Reform." *Hawwa* 1, no. 1 (2003): 1–28.

——. "Muslim Women's Quest for Equality: Between Islamic Law and Feminism." *Critical Inquiry* 32 (2006): 629–45.

Miskawayh, Aḥmad b. Muḥammad. *The Refinement of Character.* Trans. Constantine K. Zurayk. Beirut: American University of Beirut, 1968.

Moad, Edward Omar. "A Path to the Oasis: *Sharīʿah* and Reason in Islamic Moral Epistemology." *International Journal for Philosophy and Religion* 62, no. 3 (2007): 135–48.

Moaddel, Mansoor. *Islamic Modernism, Nationalism, and Fundamentalism: Episode and Discourse.* Chicago: University of Chicago Press, 2005.

Modarressi Tabātabāi, Hussein. *Kharāj in Islamic Law.* London: Anchor Press Ltd, 1983.

——. "Some Recent Analysis of the Concept of majāz in Islamic Jurisprudence." *Journal of the American Oriental Society* 106, no. 4 (1986): 787–91.

Moeckli, Daniel. "Of Minarets and Foreign Criminals: Swiss Direct Democracy and Human Rights." *Human Rights Law Review* 11, no. 4 (2011): 774–94.

Møller, Jørgen and Skaaning, Svend-Erik. "On the Limited Interchangeability of rule of law measures." *European Political Science Review* 3, no. 3 (2011): 371–94.

Molotch, Harvey. "The Rest Room and Equal Opportunity." *Sociological Forum* 3, no. 1 (1988): 128–32.

Morony, Michael G. *Iraq after the Muslim Conquest.* Princeton: Princeton University Press, 1984.

——. "The Age of Conversions: A Reassessment." In *Conversion and Continuity: Indigenous Christian Communities in Islamic Lands, Eighth to Eighteenth Centuries.* Eds Michael Gervers and Ramzi J. Bikhazi, 135–50. Toronto: Pontifical Institute of Medieval Studies, 1990.

Moss, Dana and Krieger, Zvika. "Policing Religion." *New Statesman*, September 3, 2007, 16–17, 17.

Mottahedeh, Roy. *Loyalty and Leadership in an Early Islamic Society.* Princeton: Princeton University Press, 1980.

Motzki, Harald. *The Origins of Islamic Jurisprudence: Meccan Fiqh Before the Classical Schools.* Trans. Marion H. Katz. Leiden: Brill, 2001.

Mumisa, Michael. *Islamic Law: Theory & Interpretation.* Beltsville, Maryland: Amana Publications, 2002.

Murphy, Andrew R. "Toleration and the Liberal Tradition." *Polity* 29, no. 4 (1997): 593–623.

Muztar, A.D. "Dhimmis in an Islamic State." *Islamic Studies* 18, no. 1 (1979): 65–75.

Nasir, Jamal J. *The Islamic Law of Personal Status.* 3rd ed. London: Graham & Trotman, 2002.

Nasr, Vali. *International Relations of an Islamist Movement: The Case of the Jama'at-i Islami of Pakistan.* New York: Council on Foreign Relations, 2000.

Nemoy, L. and Zajaczkowski, W. "Early Karaism." *The Jewish Quarterly Review* 40, no. 3 (1950): 307–15.

——. *EI*², s.v., "Karaites."

Nurrohman, Bandung. "A lesson to draw from the Swiss ban on minarets." *The Jakarta Post.* 15 December 2009. P. 7.

Nussbaum, Martha. *Liberty of Conscience: In Defense of America's Tradition of Religious Equality.* New York: Basic Books, 2008.

Ohnesorge, John K.M. "The Rule of Law." *Annual Review of Law and Social Science* 3 (2007): 99–114.

Pedersen, J., et al. and *EI*², s.v., "Madrasa."

Peerenboom, Randy. "The Future of Rule of Law: Challenges and Prospects for the Field." *Hague Journal of the Rule of Law* 1 (2009): 1–10.

Peirce, Leslie. *Morality Tales: Law and Gender in the Ottoman Court of Aintab.* Berkeley: University of California Press, 2003.

Peri, Oded. "The Muslim waqf and the Collection of jizya in Late Eighteenth-century Jerusalem." In *Ottoman Palestine, 1800–1914: Studies in Economic and Social History.* Ed. Gad G. Gilbar, 287–97. Leiden: Brill, 1990.

Philliou, Christine M. *Biography of an Empire: Governing Ottomans in an Age of Revolution.* Berkeley: University of California Press, 2011.

Polisi, Catherine E. "Universal Rights and Cultural Relativism: Hinduism and Islam Deconstructed." *World Affairs* 167, no. 1 (2004): 41–7.

Poole, Thomas. "Of Headscarves and Heresies: The *Denbigh High School* Case and Public Authority Decision-Making Under the Human Rights Act." *Public Law* (2005): 685–95.

Post, Robert S. "The Social Foundations of Privacy: Community and Self in the Common Law Tort." *California Law Review* 77, no. 5 (1989): 957–1010.

Powers, David S. *Studies in Qur'an and Hadith: The Formation of the Islamic Law of Inheritance.* Berkeley: University of California Press, 1986.

——. "Orientalism, Colonialism, and Legal History: The Attack on Muslim Family Endowments in Algeria and India." *Comparative Studies in Society and History* 31, no. 3 (1989): 535–71.

——. *Law, Society and Culture in the Maghreb, 1300–1500.* Cambridge: Cambridge University Press, 2002.

Prakash, Gyan. "*Orientalism* Now." *History and Theory* 34, no. 3 (1995): 199–212.

Al-Qattan, Najwa. "Dhimmis in the Muslim Court: Legal Automony and Religious. Discrimination." *International Journal of Middle East Studies* 31 (1999): 429–44.

Qureshi, Aijaz Hassan. "The Terms Kharaj and Jizya and Their Implications." *Journal of the Punjab University Historical Society* 12 (1961): 27–38.

Rahman, Fazlur. *Islamic Methodology in History.* Islamabad: Islamic Research Institute, 1964.

——. *Islam and Modernity: Transformation of an Intellectual Tradition*. Chicago: University of Chicago Press, 1982.

——. "Non-Muslim Minorities in an Islamic State." *Journal of the Institute of Muslim Minority Affairs* 7 (1986): 13–24.

Ramadan, Tariq. *Western Muslims and the Future of Islam*. Oxford: Oxford University Press, 2004.

Ramsey, Michael D. "International Materials and Domestic Rights: Reflections on *Atkins and Lawrence*." *American Journal of International Law* 98, no. 1 (2004): 69–82, 69–70.

Raphael, D.D. "The Intolerable." In *Justifying Toleration: Conceptual and Historical Perspectives*, 137–54. Cambridge: Cambridge University Press, 1988.

Al-Rasheed, Madawi. *A History of Saudi Arabia*. Cambridge: Cambridge University Press, 2002.

Al-Raysuni, Ahmad. *Imam al-Shatibi's Theory of the Higher Objectives and Intents of Islamic Law*. Trans. Nancy Roberts. Herndon, Virginia: International Institute of Islamic Thought, 2005.

Raz, Joseph. "The Rule of Law and Its Virtues." *The Law Quarterly Review* 93 (1977): 195–211.

Razack, Sherene. *Casting Out: The Eviction of Muslims from Western Law and Politics*. Toronto: University of Toronto Press, 2008.

Reichert, Elisabeth. "Human Rights: An Examination of Universalism and Cultural Relativism." *Journal of Comparative Social Welfare* 22, no. 1 (2006): 23–36.

Reinhart, Kevin. *Before Revelation: The Boundaries of Muslim Moral Thought*. Albany: SUNY Press, 1995.

Ripstein, Arthur. "Liberty and Equality." In *Ronald Dworkin*. Ed. Arthur Ripstein, 82–108. Cambridge: Cambridge University Press, 2007.

Ritter, Gretchen. *The Constitution as Social Design: Gender and Civic Membership in the American Constitutional Order*. Polo Alto: Stanford University Press, 2006.

Rosenberg, Irene Merker and Rosenberg, Yale L. "Of God's Mercy and the Four Biblical Methods of Capital Punishment." *Tulane Law Review* 78 (2003–04): 1169–211.

Sadan, Joseph. "The 'Latrines Decree' in the Yemen Versus the Dhimma Principle." In *Pluralism and Identity: Studies in Ritual Behavior*. Eds Jan Platvoet and Karel Van Der Toorn. 167–85. Leiden: Brill, 1995.

Said, Edward. *Orientalism*. London: Routledge and Kegan Paul, 1978.

Salahi, M.A. *Muhammad: Man and Prophet*. Shaftesbury: Element, 1995.

Sanneh, Lamin. "Sacred Truth and Secular Agency: Separate Immunity or Double Jeopardy? Sharīʿa, Nigeria, and Interfaith Prospects." *Studies in World Christianity* 8, no. 1 (2002): 31–62.

Sastri, M.L. Roy Choudhury. "The Status of *Dhimmis* in Muslim States, with Special Reference to Mughal India." *The Journal of the Greater India Society* 12, no. 1 (1945): 18–48.

Savory, Roger M. "Relations between the Safavid State and its Non-Muslim Minorities." *Islam and Christian–Muslim Relations* 14, no. 4 (October 2003): 4–58.

Schacht, Joseph. *The Origins of Muhammadan Jurisprudence.* Oxford: Clarendon Press, 1950.

——. *An Introduction to Islamic Law.* 1964. Reprint, Oxford: Oxford University Press, 1993.

——. *EI²*, s.v., "Amān".

Scott, David. *Conscripts of Modernity: The Tragedy of Colonial Enlightenment.* Durham: Duke University Press, 2004.

Scott, James C. *Seeing Like a State.* New Haven: Yale University Press, 1998.

Scott, Joan Wallach. "The Conundrum of Equality." *Institute for Advanced Studies, Occasional Paper* Series (March 1999) (<http://www.sss.ias.edu/files/papers/papertwo.pdf>) (accessed November 24, 2011).

——. *The Politics of the Veil.* Princeton: Princeton University Press, 2007.

Scott, Rachel M. *The Challenge of Political Islam: Non-Muslims and the Egyptian State.* Palo Alto: Stanford University Press, 2010.

Seipp, David J. "Our Law, Their Law, History, and the Citation of Foreign Law." *Boston University Law Review* 86 (2006): 1417–46.

Seligman, Adam B. "Tolerance, Tradition, and Modernity." *Cardozo Law Review* 24, no. 4 (2003): 1645–56.

Shachar, Ayelet. *Multicultural Jurisdictions: Cultural Differences and Women's Rights.* Cambridge: Cambridge University Press, 2001.

Shahîd, Irfan. *EI²*, s.v., "Nadjrān."

Shapiro, Scott. *Legality.* Cambridge: Belknap Press, 2011.

Short, Walter. "The Jizya Tax: Equalty and Dignity under Islamic Law?" In *The Myth of Islamic Tolerance: How Islamic Law Treats Non-Muslims.* Ed. Robert Spencer, 73–90. Amherst, New York: Prometheus Books, 2005.

Shroeder, H.R. "The Fourth Lateran Council of 1215: Canon 68. In *Disciplinary Decrees of the General Councils: Text, Translation, and Commentary.* St Louis: B. Herder, 1937. <http://www.Fordham.edu.halsall/basis/lateran4html> (accessed September 6, 2008).

Sizgorich, Thomas. "Sanctified Violence: Monotheist Militancy as the Tie that Bound Christian Rome and Islam." *Journal of the American Academy of Religion* 77, no. 4 (December 2009): 895–921.

Slaughter, Anne-Marie. *A New World Order.* Princeton: Princeton University Press, 2005.

Sokol, Ronald P. "Why France Can't See Past the burqa." *The Christian Science Monitor.* July 21, 2008. P. 9.

Spencer, Robert. *Islam Unveiled: Disturbing Questions about the World's Fastest-Growing Faith.* San Francisco: Encounter Books, 2002.

——. Ed. *The Myth of Islamic Tolerance: How Islamic Law Treats Non-Muslims.* New York: Prometheus Books, 2005.

——. *The Truth about Muhammad: Founder of the World's Most Intolerant Religion.* Washington D.C.: Regnery Publishing, Inc., 2006.

——. *Religion of Peace? Why Christianity Is and Islam Isn't.* Washington D.C.: Regnery Press, 2007.

Stilt, Kristen. "The muḥtasib, law, and society in early Mamluk Cairo and Fustat (648–802/1250–1400)." PhD dissertation. Harvard University, 2004.

——. *Islamic Law in Action: Authority, Discretion and Everyday Experiences in Mamluk Egypt.* Oxford: Oxford University Press, 2012.

Stockett, Kathryn. *The Help: A Novel.* New York: Penguin, 2009.

Stone, Suzanne Last. "The Intervention of American Law in Jewish Divorce: A Pluralist Analysis." *Israel Law Review,* 34 (Summer 2000): 170–210.

Suberu, Rotimi T. "The Supreme Court and Federalism in Nigeria." *Journal of Modern African Studies* 46, no. 3 (2008): 451–85.

Sunstein, Cass R. and Vermeule, Adrian. "Interpretation and Institutions." *Michigan Law Review* 101, no. 4 (2003): 885–951.

Tabātabā'i, Hossein Modarressi. *Kharāj in Islamic Law.* London: Anchor Press, Ltd., 1983.

Taha, Mahmoud Mohamed. *The Second Message of Islam.* Trans. Abdullahi Ahmed An-Na'im. Syracuse: Syracuse University Press, 1996.

Tamanaha, Brian. *On the Rule of Law: History, Politics, Theory.* Cambridge: Cambridge University Press, 2004.

Taqi Usmani, Muhammad. "The Islamization of Laws in Pakistan: The Case of *Hudud* Ordinances." *Muslim World* 96, no. 2 (April 2006): 287–304.

Taylor, Charles. *Sources of the Self.* Cambridge: Harvard University Press, 1992.

——. *Modern Social Imaginaries.* Durham, North Carolina: Duke University Press, 2004.

Tibawi, A.L. "Origin and Character of *Al-Madrasah.*" *Bulletin of the School of Oriental and African Studies* 25, no. 2 (1962): 225–38.

Tibi, Bassam. *The Crisis of Modern Islam: A Preindustrial Culture in the Scientific-Technological Age.* Trans. Judith von Sivers. Salt Lake City: University of Utah Press, 1988.

Toobin, Jeffrey. "Swing Shift: How Anthony Kennedy's Passion for Foreign Law Could Change the Supreme Court." *The New Yorker,* September 12, 2005, P. 42.

Tritton, A.S. *The Caliphs and their Non-Muslim Subjects: A Critical Study of the Covenant of 'Umar.* London: Frank Cass and Co., Ltd, 1970.

Tucker, Charles E. "Cabbages and Kings: Bridging the Gap for More Effective Capacity-Building." *University of Pennsylvania Journal of International Law* 32 (2011): 101–25.

Tully, James. *Public Philosophy in a New Key.* 2 vols. Cambridge: Cambridge University Press, 2008.

Tyler, Aaron. *Islam, the West and Tolerance: Conceiving Coexistence.* New York: Palgrave MacMillan, 2008.

Tyser, C.R., et al. Trans. *The Mejelle: Being an English Translation of* Majallah El-Ahkam-I-Adliya *and a Complete Code on Islamic Civil Law.* Kuala Lumpur: The Other Press, 2001.

Vajda, G. "Ahl al- Kitāb." *Encyclopaedia of Islam.* Eds P. Bearman, Th. Bianquis, C.E. Bosworth, E. van Donzel and W.P. Heinrichs. Leiden: Brill, 2008. (Brill Online, University of Toronto, accessed 04 September 2008.)

Van der Schyff, Gerhard and Overbeeke, Adriaan. "Exercising Religious Freedom in the Public Space: A Comparative and European Convention Analysis of General Burqa Bans." *European Constitutional Law Review* 7 (2011): 424–52.

Vatikiotis, Michael. "Malaysia: A Political Ploy? Umno dares Islamic Party on Criminal Law." *Far Eastern Economic Review* 155, no. 21 (May 28, 1992): 28.

Vikør, Knut S. *Between God and the Sultan: A History of Islamic Law.* Oxford: Oxford University Press, 2005.

Vogel, Frank. *Islamic Law and Legal System: Studies of Saudi Arabia.* Leiden: Brill, 2000.

Von Denffer, Ahmed. *ʿUlūm al-Qurʾān: An Introduction to the Sciences of the Qurʾān* Leicestershire: The Islamic Foundation, 1994.

Waardenburg, Jacques. "Muslim Studies of Other Religions: The Medieval Period." In *The Middle East and Europe: Encounters and Exchanges.* Eds Geert Jan van Gelder and Ed. de Moor, 10–38. Amsterdam: Rodopi, 1992.

——. ed. *Muslim Perceptions of Other Religions: A Historical Survey.* Oxford: Oxford University Press, 1999.

Waines, David. *An Introduction to Islam.* 2nd ed. Cambridge: Cambridge University Press, 2003.

Waldron, Jeremy. *God, Locke, and Equality: Christian Foundations in Locke's Political Thought.* Cambridge: Cambridge University Press, 2002.

——. "Foreign Law and the Modern *Ius Gentium.*" *Harvard Law Review* 119 (2005–06): 129–57.

Ward, Ian. "Shabina Begum and the Headscarf Girls." *Journal of Gender Studies* 15, no. 2 (2006): 119–31.

Watson, Alan. *Roman Law & Comparative Law.* Athens, Georgia: University of Georgia Press, 1991.

Watt, W. Montgomery. "Musaylima b. Ḥabīb, Abū Thumāma." *Encyclopaedia of Islam.* Eds P. Bearman, Th. Bianquis, C.E. Bosworth, E. van Donzel, and W.P. Heinrichs. Leiden: Brill, 2008. (Brill Online, University of Toronto, accessed 04 September 2008.)

Weber, Max. *Economy and Society: An Outline of Interpretive Sociology.* Eds Guenther Roth and Claus Wittich. 2 vols. Berkeley: University of California Press, 1978.

Weismann, Itzhak. *Taste of Modernity: Sufism, Salafiyya, and Arabism in Late Ottoman Damascus.* Leiden: Brill, 2001.

Weiss, Bernard. *The Spirit of Islamic Law.* Athens, Georgia: The University of Georgia Press, 1998.

Welchman, Lynn. "The Development of Islamic Family Law in the Legal System of Jordan." *International and Comparative Law Quarterly* 37, no. 4 (1988): 868–86.

Wente, Margaret. "Death to the Apostate." *The Globe and Mail*, March 28, 2006, A19.

Weyeneth, Robert R. "The Architecture of Racial Segregation: The Challenges of Preserving the Problematical Past." *The Public Historian* 27, no. 4 (Fall 2005): 11–44.

Wickham, Carrie Rosefsky. "The Muslim Brotherhood and Democratic Transition in Egypt." *Middle East Law and Governance* 3, nos. 1 & 2 (2011): 204–23.

Williams, Bernard. "Tolerating the Intolerable." In *The Politics of Toleration: Tolerance and Intolerance in Modern Life.* Ed. Susan Mendus, 65–75. Edinburgh: Edinburgh University Press, 1999.

Wolfe, Caryn Litt. "Faith-Based Arbitration: Friend or Foe? An Evaluation of Religious Arbitration Systems and Their Interaction with Secular Courts." *Fordham Law Review* 75 (2006): 427–69.

Women Living Under Muslim Laws. *Knowing Our Rights: Women, Family, Laws and Customs in the Muslim World.* New Delhi: Zubaan, 2003.

Wynes, Charles E. "The Evolution of Jim Crow Laws in Twentieth Century Virginia." *Phylon* 24, no. 4 (1967): 416–25.

Ye'or, Bat. *The Dhimmi: Jews and Christians Under Islam.* Cranbury, NJ: Associated University Press, 1985.

——. *Islam and Dhimmitude: Where Civilizations Collide.* Cranbury, NJ: Associated University Press, 2002.

Zaidi, S.A. "Who is a Muslim? Identities of Exclusion—North Indian Muslims, c. 1860–1900." *The Indian Economic and Social History Review* 47, no. 2 (2010): 205–29.

Zakaria, Fareed. "The Rise of Illiberal Democracy." *Foreign Affairs* 76 (1997): 22–43.

Zaman, Muhammad Qasim. *The Ulama in Contemporary Islam: Custodians of Change.* Princeton: Princeton University Press, 2007.

Zaman, Wesal and Chu, Henry. "Afghan case dropped but not closed." *Los Angeles Times*, March 27, 2006, A14.

Zebri, Kate. "Relations Between Muslims and Non-Muslims in the Thought of Western-Educated Muslim Intellectuals." *Islam and Christian–Muslim Relations* 6, no. 2 (1995): 255–77.

Cases, Statutes, Treaties, and Government Documents

Administration of Islamic Law (Malaysian Federal Territories) Act 1993 (Act 505)

Administration of the Religion of Islam (State of Malacca) Enactment 2002 and Regulations

Administration of the Religion of Islam (State of Selangor) Enactment 2003

Afghanistan Rule of Law Project: Field Study of Informal and Customary Justice in Afghanistan. Washington D.C., USAID, 2005.

Alberta v Hutterian Brethren of Wilson County, 2009 SCC 37.

Atkins v Virginia, 536 US 304 (2002).

Begum v The Headteacher and Governors of Denbigh High School [2006] UK HL 15, para. 25.

Bruker v Marcovitz [2007] 3 SCR 607, 2007 SCC 54.

Canadian Charter of Rights and Freedoms, Part I of the Constitution Act, 1982.

Charter of the United Nations.

European Convention of Human Rights.

Hutterian Brethren of Wilson County v Alberta, 2007 ABCA 160.

In re: Mme M (Case '286798). *Le Conseil d'Etat* <http://www.conseil-etat.fr/ce/jurispd/index_ac_1d0820.shtml> (accessed on September 23, 2008).

Iraq Constitution, <http://www.uniraq.org/documents/iraqi_constitution.pdf>.

Islamic Family Law (Malaysian Federal Territories) Act 1984.

Islamic Family Law (State of Malacca) Enactment 2002.

Lawrence v Texas, 123 S Ct 2472 (2003).

Leyla Sahin v Turkey, Application no. 44774/ECHR (November 10, 2005).

Lina Joy v Federal Territory Islamic Council, the Government of Malaysia, and Director General of the National Registration Department, Federal Court of Malaysia, civil appeal no. 01-2-2006 (W).

Lina Joy v Majlis Agama Islam Wilayah Persekutuan & Anor [2004] 6 CLJ 242.

Minersville School District v Gobitis, 310 US 586 (1940).

Ministry of Overseas Pakistanis, see <http://www.moops.gov.pk/>, with a link to CWA Parep Jeddah (accessed May 15, 2012).

Multani v Commission Scolaire Marguerite-Bourgeoys [2006] 1 SCR 256, 2006 SCC 6.

Philippine Embassy, Saudi Arabia, see <http://www.philembassy-rigadh.org.index.php/component/k2/item/220-qisas-and-diyya-or-blood-money> (accessed May 15, 2012).

The Queen on the application of Shabina Begum v Headteacher and Governors of Denbigh High School [2005] EWCA Civ 199.

Richard Warner et al. v City of Boca Raton, 887 So. 2d 1023.

Roper v Simmons, 543 US 551 (2005).

Shabina Begum v The Headteacher and Governors of Denbigh High School [2004] EWHC 1389 (Admin).

Shabina Begum (respondent) *v Headteacher and Governors of Denbigh High School* (appellants), [2006] UKHL 15.

Sultaana Lakiana Myke Freeman v State of Florida, Department of Highway Safety and Motor Vehicles Mp/ 5D03-2296, 2005 Fla Dist Ct App LEXIS 13904 (Court of Appeal of Florida, Fifth District, September 2, 2005).

Syariah Criminal Procedure (Malaysian Federal Territories) Act 1997.

Syndicat Northcrest v Amselem, 2004 SCC 47; [2004] 2 SCR 551.

Taylor, Charles and Bouchard, Gérard. *Building the Future, a Time for Reconciliation: Report*. Quebec City: Commission de consultation sur le pratiques d'accomdement reliées aur differences culturelles, 2008.

United Nations. *Charter of the United Nations*. San Fransico October 24, 1945. Art 2. sec. 1.

United Nations Security Council. *The Rule of Law and Transitional Justice in Conflict and Post-conflict Societies: Report of the Secretary-General*. S/2004/616. August 23, 2004.

US Agency for International Development (USAID). *Afghanistan Rule of Law Project: Field study of Informal and Customary Justice in Afghanistan*. Washinton D.C.: USAID, 2005.

——. *Guide to Rule of Law Analysis: The Rule of Law Strategic Framework; A Guide for USAID Democracy and Governance Officers*. Washington D.C.: USAID, 2010.

West Virginia State Board of Education v Barnette, 319 US 624 (1943).

Index